THIRD EDITION

JavaServer Pages™

Hans Bergsten

PARK LEARNING CENTRE
UNIVERSITY OF GLOUCESTERSHIRE
PO Box 220, The Park
Cheltenham GL50 2RH
Tel: 01242 714333

O'REILLY®

Beijing • Cambridge • Farnham • Köln • Paris • Sebastopol • Taipei • Tokyo

JavaServer Pages™, Third Edition
by Hans Bergsten

Copyright © 2004, 2002, 2001 O'Reilly Media, Inc. All rights reserved.
Printed in the United States of America.

Published by O'Reilly Media, Inc., 1005 Gravenstein Highway North, Sebastopol, CA 95472.

O'Reilly Media, Inc. books may be purchased for educational, business, or sales promotional use. Online editions are also available for most titles (*safari.oreilly.com*). For more information, contact our corporate/institutional sales department: (800) 998-9938 or *corporate@oreilly.com*.

Editor: Brett McLaughlin
Production Editor: Sarah Sherman
Cover Designer: Pam Spremulli
Interior Designer: David Futato

Printing History:

January 2001: First Edition.
August 2002: Second Edition.
December 2003: Third Edition.

Nutshell Handbook, the Nutshell Handbook logo, and the O'Reilly logo are registered trademarks of O'Reilly Media, Inc. The Java Series, *JavaServer Pages*, *Third Edition*, the image of a grey wolf, and related trade dress are trademarks of O'Reilly Media, Inc. Java™ and all Java-based trademarks and logos are trademarks or registered trademarks of Sun Microsystems, Inc., in the United States and other countries. O'Reilly Media, Inc., is independent of Sun Microsystems. Openwave, the Openwave logo, and UP.SDK are trademarks of Openwave Systems Inc. All rights reserved.

Many of the designations used by manufacturers and sellers to distinguish their products are claimed as trademarks. Where those designations appear in this book, and O'Reilly Media, Inc. was aware of a trademark claim, the designations have been printed in caps or initial caps.

While every precaution has been taken in the preparation of this book, the publisher and author assume no responsibility for errors or omissions, or for damages resulting from the use of the information contained herein.

This book uses RepKover™, a durable and flexible lay-flat binding.

ISBN: 0-596-00563-6
[M] [8/05]

3703563643

JavaServer Pages™

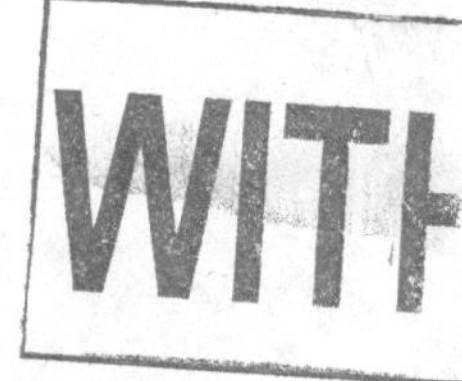
WITH

Other Java™ resources from O'Reilly

Related titles

Enterprise JavaBeans™
Java™ & XML
Java™ Cookbook
Java™ Enterprise in a Nutshell
Java™ I/O
Java™ in a Nutshell
Java™ Performance Tuning
Java™ Programming with Oracle SQLJ
Java™ Security
JavaServer Pages™
Java™ Swing
Learning Java™

Java Books Resource Center

java.oreilly.com is a complete catalog of O'Reilly's books on Java and related technologies, including sample chapters and code examples.

OnJava.com is a one-stop resource for enterprise Java developers, featuring news, code recipes, interviews, weblogs, and more.

Conferences

O'Reilly & Associates brings diverse innovators together to nurture the ideas that spark revolutionary industries. We specialize in documenting the latest tools and systems, translating the innovator's knowledge into useful skills for those in the trenches. Visit *conferences.oreilly.com* for our upcoming events.

Safari Bookshelf (*safari.oreilly.com*) is the premier online reference library for programmers and IT professionals. Conduct searches across more than 1,000 books. Subscribers can zero in on answers to time-critical questions in a matter of seconds. Read the books on your Bookshelf from cover to cover or simply flip to the page you need. Try it today with a free trial.

Table of Contents

Part II. JSP Application Development

Part III. JSP in J2EE and JSP Component Development

Preface

JavaServer Pages™ (JSP) is a technology for web application development that has received a great deal of attention since it was first announced in 1999. Since then, it has gone through three revisions. This book covers the 2.0 version of the specification.

Why is JSP so exciting? One reason is that JSP is Java-based, and Java™ is well suited for enterprise computing. In fact, JSP is a key part of the Java 2™ Enterprise Edition (J2EE) platform and can take advantage of the many Java Enterprise™ libraries, such as JDBC™, JNDI™, and Enterprise JavaBeans™.

Another reason is that JSP supports a powerful model for developing web applications that separates presentation from processing. Understanding why this is so important requires a bit of a history lesson. In the early days of the Web, the only tool for developing dynamic web content was the Common Gateway Interface (CGI). CGI outlined how a web server made user input available to a program, as well as how the program provided the web server with dynamically generated content to send back. CGI scripts were typically written in Perl. (In fact, Perl/CGI scripts still drive numerous dynamic web sites.) However, CGI is not an efficient solution. For every request, the web server has to create a new operating-system process, load a Perl interpreter and the Perl script, execute the script, and then dispose of it when it's done.

To provide a more efficient solution, various alternatives to CGI have been added to programmers' toolboxes over the last few years: FastCGI, for example, runs each CGI program in an external permanent process (or a pool of processes). In addition, mod_perl for Apache, NSAPI for Netscape, and ISAPI for Microsoft's IIS all run server-side programs in the same process as the web server itself. While these solutions offer better performance and scalability, each one is supported only by a subset of the popular web servers.

The Java Servlet API, introduced in early 1997, provides a solution to the portability issue. However, all these technologies suffer from a common problem: HTML code embedded inside programs. If you've ever looked at the code for a servlet, you've probably seen endless calls to `out.println()` that contain scores of HTML tags. For the individual developer working on a simple web site, this approach may work fine, but it makes it difficult for people with different skills to work together to develop a web application.

This embedded HTML code is becoming a significant problem. As web sites become increasingly complex and more critical to an organization's success, the appearance and usability of the web interface becomes paramount. New client technologies, such as client-side scripts and DHTML, are used to develop more responsive and interactive user interfaces, stylesheets can make it easier to globally change fonts and colors, and images make the interface more appealing. At the same time, server-side code is getting more complex, and the demands for reliability, performance, and fault tolerance are increasing. The increasing complexity of web applications requires a development model that allows people with different skills to cooperate efficiently.

JSP provides just such a development model, allowing web page authors with skills in areas such as client-side technologies and usability to work in tandem with programmers who are experienced in server-side technologies, such as multithreading, resource pooling, databases, and caching. While there are other technologies, such as ASP, PHP, and ColdFusion, that support similar development models, none offer all the advantages of JSP.

What's in This Book

This edition of the book covers Version 2.0 of the JSP specification, which was released late 2003. It also covers the related JSP Standard Tag Library (JSTL) specification, Version 1.1, also released late 2003.

You will learn how to use all the JSP standard elements and features, including elements for accessing JavaBeans components; separating the processing over multiple pages to increase reusability and simplify maintenance; and sharing information between pages, requests, and users. You will also learn how to use JSTL for tasks such as conditional processing, integration of database data, internationalization, and XML processing, as well as how to develop your own custom components for tasks not covered by the standard components.

The examples in this book guide you through solutions to common JSP design problems, from basic issues, such as retrieving and validating user input, to more advanced areas, such as developing a database-driven site, authenticating users, providing personalized content, caching data for better performance, and implementing internationalization. The last part of the book describes how you can combine JSP with other Java technologies; in particular, I describe the combination of JSP and servlets using the popular Apache Struts framework, and provide an overview of how JSP fits into the larger scope of J2EE.

Readers of the Second Edition

If you've read the second edition of *JavaServer Pages,* you'll notice that, in this edition, even more of the custom components used in the previous edition have been replaced in favor of the equivalent standard components from JSTL—a specification I've been lucky enough to contribute to and help shape the standard based on many of the ideas explored in the first and second editions. You'll also notice that all the chapters have been modified (some more than others) to cover the new features in the latest versions of the JSP and JSTL specifications. A brand new chapter has been added to describe how to develop custom tag libraries using the new tag file format, and the chapter about custom library development using Java has been substantially expanded to cover the new, simplified tag handler API as well as the new mechanism for including Expression Language functions in a tag library.

All chapters have also been updated to cover the features and clarifications added in the Servlet 2.4 specification on which JSP 2.0 is based. Here's a brief summary of the primary changes in all the specifications covered in this book:

- Incorporation of the Expression Language (EL), first introduced by the JSTL specification in the JSP specification (making it available to all standard and custom components as well as in template text)
- The EL extended with a function call mechanism and a set of common functions added to JST
- Addition of the ability to develop custom tag libraries as tag files (text files with JSP elements) as well as a new, simplified tag handler Java API, and various new tag library features such as support for a dynamic attribute list and executable fragment attributes
- More flexible rules for JSP pages written as XML documents, and support for the JSP directives and scripting elements of XML syntax in regular JSP pages
- New JSP standard elements, primarily to allow more flexible attribute value assignments and to support the new tag file format and XML format enhancements.
- Access to more information in a JSP error page and adjustment of the attribute names to match the Servlet specification
- Stricter container requirements to improve syntax error reporting and debugging support for JSP pages
- XML Schema-based deployment descriptors for all specifications with new configuration options, including automatic include of page segments, page encoding specification, scripting element disabling, and more for JSP
- Addition of a new request listener component type and filters that can be applied to internal requests
- Deprecation of the single thread model for both servlets and JSP
- New JSTL tag library URIs and a few attribute name changes for the XML library

Audience

This book is for anyone who is interested in using JSP technology to develop web applications. In particular, it's written to help those of you who develop JSP-based applications, specifically:

Page authors
: Page authors primarily develop the web interface to an application. This group uses HTML, stylesheets, and client-side code to develop a rich user interface. Page authors also want to learn to use JSP elements in web pages to interact with the other server components, such as servlets, databases, and Enterprise JavaBeans (EJB).

Java programmers
: Java programmers are comfortable with the Java programming language and Java servlets. This group wants to learn how to develop JSP components that page authors can use in the web pages, such as JSP custom actions and JavaBeans, and how to combine JSP with other Java server-side technologies, such as servlets and EJB.

The book is structured into three parts, which I describe shortly, to make it easier to find the material you are most interested in.

What You Need to Know

It's always hard to assume how much you, as the reader, already know. For this book, it was even harder since the material is intended for two types of audiences: page authors and programmers.

I've assumed that anyone reading this book has experience with HTML; consequently, I won't explain the standard HTML elements used in the examples. But even if you're an HTML wiz, this may be your first exposure to dynamic web content and web applications. A thorough introduction to the HTTP protocol that drives all web applications as well as to the concepts and features that are specific to servlet and JSP-based web applications are, therefore, included. If you want to learn more about HTML, I recommend *HTML and XHTML: The Definitive Guide* by Chuck Musciano and Bill Kennedy (O'Reilly).

If you're a page author, I have assumed that you don't know anything about programming, although it doesn't hurt if you have played around with client-side scripting languages, such as VBScript or JavaScript (ECMAScript). Using standard and custom components, you should rarely, if ever, have to deal with Java code. Except for one chapter, which deals specifically with how to embed Java code in a JSP page, none of the examples in Part I and II requires Java programming knowledge.

I have assumed that the programmers reading this book are familiar with Java programming, object-oriented concepts, and Java servlets. If you plan to develop JSP components for page authors and aren't familiar with Java programming, I recommend that you read a Java introduction book, such as *Learning Java* by Patrick Niemeyer and Jonathan Knudsen (O'Reilly). I include a brief introduction to the Servlet API, but I recommend that you also read *Java Servlet Programming* by Jason Hunter and William Crawford (O'Reilly) or another book that covers the servlet technology in detail.

The chapters dealing with database access require some knowledge of SQL and databases in general. I will explain all that you need to know to run the examples, but if you want to develop database-driven applications, you need to know more about databases than what's included in this book.

Organization

This book is structured into three parts. The first part of the book describes the fundamentals of HTTP (the protocol used by all web applications), how servlets and JSP are related, and how to set up a JSP development environment.

The focus of the second part is on developing JSP-based web applications using standard JSP elements, JSTL, and custom components. Through the use of practical examples, you will learn how to handle common tasks, such as validating user input, accessing databases, authenticating users and protecting web pages, localizing your web site, and more. This portion of the book is geared more towards page authors but is also of interest to programmers.

In the third part, you will learn how to develop your own custom actions and JavaBeans, and how to combine JSP with other Java server-side technologies, such as servlets and EJB. This portion of the book is intended for the programming community.

All in all, the book consists of 24 chapters and 6 appendixes as follows.

Part I, JSP Application Basics

Chapter 1, *Introducing JavaServer Pages*
: Explains how JSP fits into the big picture of web applications and how it compares to alternative technologies.

Chapter 2, *HTTP and Servlet Basics*
: Describes the fundamental HTTP and servlet concepts you need to know to use JSP to its full potential.

Chapter 3, *JSP Overview*
: An overview of the JSP features, as well as the similarities and differences between JSP pages and servlets. Also introduces the Model-View-Controller design model and how it applies to JSP.

Chapter 4, *Setting Up the JSP Environment*
: Describes where to get the JSP reference implementation (Apache Tomcat) and how to set it up on your system. Also explains how to install the book examples.

Part II, JSP Application Development

Chapter 5, *Generating Dynamic Content*
: Examines the JSP basics, such as how to create, deploy, and run a JSP page, as well as how to use the JSP elements to generate dynamic content.

Chapter 6, *Using JavaBeans Components in JSP Pages*
: Describes what a JavaBeans component is and how it can be used effectively in a JSP page.

Chapter 7, *Using Custom Tag Libraries and the JSP Standard Tag Library*
: Describes what a custom tag library is and how to deploy and use one, and introduces the JSP Standard Tag Library (JSTL).

Chapter 8, *Processing Input and Output*
: Explains how an HTML form can be used to send data to a web application and how to process the data using JavaBeans and JSTL, as well as what to be aware of when generating dynamic output.

Chapter 9, *Error Handling and Debugging*
: Describes the kinds of errors you may encounter during development of a JSP-based application, and strategies and JSP features that help you deal with them.

Chapter 10, *Sharing Data Between JSP Pages, Requests, and Users*
: Explains the JSP features that let you separate different types of processing in different pages to simplify maintenance and further development. Also describes how sessions can build up information over a sequence of requests from the same user, and how information that applies to all users can be shared using the application scope.

Chapter 11, *Developing Custom Tag Libraries as Tag Files*
: Describes how you can develop actions for a custom tag library as tag files, i.e., regular text files with JSP elements.

Chapter 12, *Accessing a Database*
: Provides a quick overview of relational databases, JDBC, and SQL basics, and introduces the JSTL actions for reading, updating, and deleting database data.

Chapter 13, *Authentication and Personalization*
: Describes how authentication and access control can be implemented using container-provided and application-controlled mechanisms, and how to use the information about who the current user is to personalize the web pages.

Chapter 14, *Internationalization*
: Explains internationalization and localization, the Java features available to implement an internationalized application, and describes the set of JSTL actions that support development of multilingual web sites.

Chapter 15, *Working with XML Data*
: Explains how JSP can generate XML content as well as process XML input using the JSTL XML actions.

Chapter 16, *Using Scripting Elements*
: Describes the JSP elements that let you embed Java code directly in your JSP pages and the type of errors you must be prepared to deal with when you use this feature.

Chapter 17, *Bits and Pieces*
: Covers various areas not discussed in previous chapters, such as using the JSP page XML syntax, combining JSP with client-side code, reusing JSP file segments by including them in JSP pages, precompiling JSP pages, and more.

Part III, JSP in J2EE and JSP Component Development

Chapter 18, *Web Application Models*
: Provides an overview of J2EE and web application architectures using JSP in combination with other Java technologies.

Chapter 19, *Combining JSP and Servlets*
: Describes in detail how JSP can be combined with servlets, as well as the listener and filter component types, using the popular Apache Struts framework.

Chapter 20, *Developing JavaBeans Components for JSP*
: Provides details about JavaBeans components as they relate to JSP, including threading and synchronization concerns for session and application scope beans, as well as how using JavaBeans components can make it easier to migrate to an EJB architecture.

Chapter 21, *Developing Custom Tag Libraries Using Java*
: Describes the JSP Tag Extension mechanism and how to use it to develop custom tag libraries, using many of the custom actions used in the previous chapters as examples.

Chapter 22, *Advanced Custom Tag Library Features*
: Explains the more advanced features that can be leveraged by custom actions, such as developing cooperating actions, syntax and usage validation, attribute value type conversions, and more.

Chapter 23, *Integrating Custom Code with JSTL*
: Describes all the integration hooks provided by the JSTL specification and how to develop custom actions, servlets, listeners, and filters that take advantage of them.

Chapter 24, *Database Access Strategies*
: Provides a brief introduction to JDBC and explains the various strategies available for efficient use of databases in a web application, such as setting up a connection pool and making it available to the application components through the servlet context or JNDI, encapsulating database access code in separate classes or in custom actions, and more.

Part IV, Appendixes

Appendix A, *JSP Elements Reference*
: Contains descriptions of all standard JSP 2.0 elements.

Appendix B, *JSTL Actions and API Reference*
: Contains descriptions of all standard JSTL 1.1 elements, programming interfaces, and support classes.

Appendix C, *JSP Expression Language Reference*
: Contains a description of the JSP EL syntax and rules.

Appendix D, *JSP API Reference*
: Contains descriptions of all implicit objects available in a JSP page as defined by the servlet and JSP APIs, as well as the tag extension mechanism classes and interfaces.

Appendix E, *Book Example Custom Actions and API Reference*
: Contains a description of the custom actions, beans, and utility classes used in the examples.

Appendix F, Web Application Structure and Deployment Descriptor Reference
: Contains a description of the standard web application structure and all elements in the web application deployment descriptor.

If you're a page author, I recommend that you focus on the chapters in Parts I and II. You may want to browse through Part III to get a feel for how things work behind the scene, but don't expect to understand everything if you aren't a Java programmer.

If you're a Java programmer, Part III is where the action is for you. If you're already familiar with HTTP and servlets, you may want to move quickly through Part I. However, this part includes information about the web application concept introduced in the Servlet 2.2 API you may not be familiar with, even if you've worked with servlets for some time. I recommend you read Part II to learn how JSP works, but you may actually want to start with Part III to see how the various components in the examples are implemented before you read Part II to see how they are used.

About the Examples

This book contains a large number of examples that demonstrate useful techniques for input validation, database access, information caching, application-controlled authentication and access control, internationalization, XML processing, and more. The examples include both complete applications, such as an online shopping site, an employee directory, and a personalized project billboard, as well as numerous smaller examples and page fragments. The included example tag library contains 10 or so custom actions you can use directly in your application or as a starting point for your own development. The code for all the examples and most of the custom actions is contained within the text; you can also download all code from the

O'Reilly web site at *http://www.oreilly.com/catalog/jserverpages3/*. In addition, you can see all the examples in action, download the code, ask me questions, find JSP-related products, and more at *http://www.TheJSPBook.com/*.

All examples have been tested with the official JSP 2.0 reference implementation (Apache Tomcat 5) on Windows ME and Linux (Red Hat Linux 7.2) using Sun's Java 2 SDK, Standard Edition (1.4.2). If you would like more information on downloading and installing the Apache Tomcat server for use with the examples, see Chapter 4.

Conventions Used in This Book

Italic is used for:

- Pathnames, filenames, program names, compilers, options, and commands
- New terms where they are defined
- Internet addresses, such as domain names and URLs

Boldface is used for:

- Particular keys on a computer keyboard
- Names of user interface buttons and menus

`Constant width` is used for:

- Anything that appears literally in a JSP page or a Java program, including keywords, data types, constants, method names, variables, class names, and interface names
- Command lines and options that should be typed verbatim on the screen
- All JSP and Java code listings
- HTML documents, tags, and attributes

`Constant width italic` is used for:

- General placeholders that indicate that an item is replaced by some actual value in your own program

`Constant width bold` is used for:

- Text that is typed in code examples by the user

This icon designates a note, which is an important aside to the nearby text.

This icon designates a warning relating to the nearby text.

How to Contact Us

Please address comments and questions concerning this book to the publisher:

O'Reilly & Associates, Inc.
1005 Gravenstein Highway North
Sebastopol, CA 95472
(800) 998-9938 (in the United States or Canada)
(707) 829-0515 (international or local)
(707) 829-0104 (fax)

We have a web page for this book, where we list errata, examples, or any additional information. You can access this page at:

http://www.oreilly.com/catalog/jserverpages3/

To comment or ask technical questions about this book, send email to:

bookquestions@oreilly.com

For more information about our books, conferences, Resource Centers, and the O'Reilly Network, see our web site at:

http://www.oreilly.com/

Acknowledgments for First Edition

I love to write and have always wanted to write a book. After getting a number of articles about Java servlets and a couple of chapters for a server-side Java book published, my confidence was so high that I sent mail to O'Reilly & Associates and asked if they wanted me to write a book about JSP. Much to my surprise (I guess my confidence was not so high after all), they said "Yes!" I knew that it would be more work than I could imagine, and it turned out to be even more than that. But here I am, almost a year later, with 17 chapters and 5 appendixes in a nice stack on my desk, written and rewritten countless times. All that remains is to give thanks to everyone who helped me fulfill this dream.

First, I'd like to thank my editors, Paula Ferguson and Bob Eckstein. Paula was the one who accepted my book proposal in the first place and then helped me through my first stumbling steps of writing the first half of the book. Bob came aboard for the second half and I'm really grateful to him for thoroughly reading everything and giving me helpful advice.

Thanks also to Rob Romano for doing the illustrations, to Christien Shangraw for helping out with the coordination, and to all the production people behind the scenes at O'Reilly who made sure the book got published.

Big thanks also go to the JSP and servlet specification leads, Eduardo Pelegri-Llopart and Danny Coward, for providing feedback, answering all my questions, and clarifying the vague and ambiguous areas of the specifications. You helped me more than I could ask for. I hope my contributions to the specifications repay my debt to some extent.

Thanks also to all of you who helped me improve the book in other ways: Jason Hunter for letting me borrow his connection pool code and Japanese examples; Craig McClanahan, Larry Riedel, Steve Jung (Steve dedicates his effort to the memory of his father, Arthur H. Jung, who passed away March 17, 2000), Sean Rohead, Jerry Croce, Steve Piccolo, and Vikram David for reviewing the book and giving me many suggestions for how to make it better; all the Apache Tomcat developers for making a great JSP reference implementation; and the members of the *jsp-interest* mailing list for all the ideas about what to cover in this book.

Finally, thanks to everyone who encouraged me and kept my spirits high: Mom, Dad, and my sister, for their support and for teaching me to do what I believe in; all my old friends in Sweden, especially Janne Ek and Peter Hellström (and his Dad who helped me with the translation of the German example), Janne Andersson, Roger Bjärevall and Michael Rohdin; Anne Helgren, my writing teacher who convinced me I could do this; and all the guys in and around Vesica Pisces (*http://www.vesicapisces.com/*): Kelly, Brian, Adam, Bill, and James; I really enjoyed getting away from the writing now and then to hang with you and listen to you play.

Acknowledgments for Second Edition

Roughly a year and a half have passed since I finished the first edition of this book, and, man, have things changed! JSP 1.2 has been released, adding new features, big and small, as well as minor adjustments and clarifications. The big news in the JSP space, though, is the JSP Standard Tag Library (JSTL). This library includes actions for most common JSP tasks, making it possible to replace almost all the custom actions I used for the first edition with the corresponding standard version. To cover all the new stuff, I ended up rewriting almost every chapter, and even added a few new ones. At the same time, I clarified a number of things that readers of the first edition have asked me about. It was a lot of fun, and I hope you enjoy the result.

I would like to thank all readers of the first edition for your feedback, especially Ingo Kegel for the refined German text he sent me for the I18N example, and Mike Braden, Lucy Newman, and Masako Onishi for contributing instructions for running the examples with a number of different database engines, posted on the book's web site.

I really appreciate all the help I got from my review team, especially from Steve Bang who picked the book to pieces and gave me many helpful suggestions; and Janne Andersson, Marcus Biervliet, and Pierre Delisle—thanks for spending your precious time reading and sending me feedback.

Many thanks also go to my fellow JSTL and JSP specification group members, especially James Strachan and Shawn Bayern for helping me understand the finer points of XML processing and XPath, and to Pierre Delisle and Eduardo Pelegri-Llopart for running such a smooth process and putting up with my stubbornness in certain areas (you know what I mean) and comments about many picky details.

I would also like to thank Richard Monson-Haefel (author of *Enterprise JavaBeans*, O'Reilly) for explaining the meaning of the J2EE resource declaration details, and George Reese (author of *Database Programming with JDBC and Java*, O'Reilly) for verifying my understanding of how JDBC 2.0 connection pooling is supposed to work and for reviewing Chapter 24.

Thanks also to Bob Eckstein, my editor, for moral support, thoughtful comments, and stacks of hardcopy with scribbled notes, and to all the production people behind the scenes at O'Reilly who made sure the book got published.

Finally, thanks to my parents, my sister and her family, and to all my friends in the real world and in cyberspace, for encouragement and inspiration.

Acknowledgments for Third Edition

Another year has passed, and another version of the JSP specification has made its way through the Java Community Process. The new features added to the new specification so dramatically change how JSP pages are created that we felt that a new major version number was in order, so the latest version is JSP 2.0. Along with JSP 2.0, JSTL Version 1.1 has also been released to align the standard libraries with JSP 2.0. I've added a new chapter, extended others, and revised the rest of the book to cover all the new stuff and to take advantage of the significant improvements in JSP 2.0. I hope you'll enjoy both the book and the new features.

As with the preceding editions of the book, I have many people to thank. First of all, thanks to the people who helped me review the book: Steve Bang, Janne Andersson, Roger Bjärevall, and Mark Roth. I know how busy you all are, so I'm very grateful that you made the time to give me such valuable feedback.

Many thanks also to my new editor, Brett McLaughlin (I wonder why they keep assigning me a new editor for each edition); to the hardworking JSP and JSTL specification leads—Mark Roth, Eduardo Pelegri-Llopart, and Pierre Delisle—and my fellow specification group members; to all readers for your accolades and feedback; and to the O'Reilly staff that turns my writing into a real book.

Finally thanks for all the support from family and friends, for being able to live a life that makes this possible, and for Friday nights with the "sushi gang." Cheers!

—Hans Bergsten

PART I

JSP Application Basics

This part of the book describes the fundamentals of HTTP (the protocol used by all web applications), how servlets and JSP are related, and how to set up a JSP development environment and install the book examples:

CHAPTER 1
Introducing JavaServer Pages

The Java 2 Enterprise Edition (J2EE) has taken the once-chaotic task of building an Internet presence and transformed it to the point where developers can use Java to efficiently create multitier, server-side applications. Today, the Java Enterprise APIs have expanded to encompass a number of areas: RMI and CORBA for remote object handling, JDBC for database interaction, JNDI for accessing naming and directory services, Enterprise JavaBeans for creating reusable business components, Java Messaging Service (JMS) for message-oriented middleware, JAXP for XML processing, JAXR, JAX-RPC and SAAJ for web services, Java Transaction API (JTA) for performing atomic transactions, and much more. In addition, J2EE also supports *servlets*, an extremely popular Java substitute for CGI scripts. The combination of these technologies allows programmers to create distributed business solutions for a variety of tasks.

In late 1999, Sun Microsystems added a new element to the collection of Enterprise Java tools: JavaServer Pages (JSP). JavaServer Pages are built on top of Java servlets and designed to increase the efficiency in which programmers, and even nonprogrammers, can create web content. This book is primarily about JavaServer Pages, covering the latest version of this technology, JSP 2.0, as well as the related JSP Standard Tag Library (JSTL) Version 1.1. It also covers other J2EE technologies, such as servlets and JDBC, with focus on how to combine them with JSP in the most efficient way.

What Is JavaServer Pages?

Put succinctly, JavaServer Pages is a technology for developing web pages that include dynamic content. Unlike a plain HTML page, which contains static content that always remains the same, a JSP page can change its content based on any number of variable items, including the identity of the user, the user's browser type, information provided by the user, and selections made by the user. As you'll see later in the book, this functionality is key to web applications such as online shopping and employee directories, as well as for personalized and internationalized content.

A JSP page contains standard markup language elements, such as HTML tags, just like a regular web page. However, a JSP page also contains special JSP elements that allow the server to insert dynamic content in the page. JSP elements can be used for a variety of purposes, such as retrieving information from a database or registering user preferences. When a user asks for a JSP page, the server executes the JSP elements, merges the results with the static parts of the page, and sends the dynamically composed page back to the browser, as illustrated in Figure 1-1.

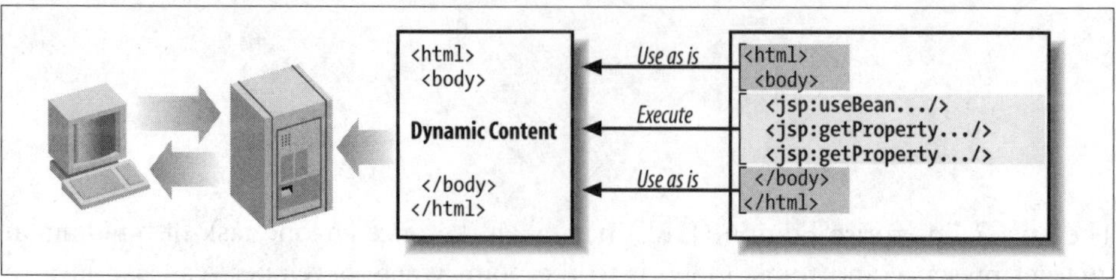

Figure 1-1. Generating dynamic content with JSP elements

JSP defines a number of standard elements that are useful for any web application, such as accessing JavaBeans components, passing control between pages and sharing information between requests, pages, and users. Developers can also extend the JSP syntax by implementing application-specific elements that perform tasks such as accessing databases and Enterprise JavaBeans, sending email, and generating HTML to present application-specific data. One such set of commonly needed custom elements is defined by a specification related to the JSP specification: the JSP Standard Tag Library (JSTL) specification. The combination of standard elements and custom elements allows for the creation of powerful web applications.

Why Use JSP?

In the early days of the Web, the Common Gateway Interface (CGI) was the only tool for developing dynamic web content. However, CGI is not an efficient solution. For every request that comes in, the web server has to create a new operating-system process, load an interpreter and a script, execute the script, and then tear it all down again. This is very taxing for the server and doesn't scale well when the amount of traffic increases.

Numerous CGI alternatives and enhancements, such as FastCGI, mod_perl from Apache, NSAPI from Netscape, ISAPI from Microsoft, and Java servlets from Sun Microsystems, have been created over the years. While these solutions offer better performance and scalability, all these technologies suffer from a common problem: they generate web pages by embedding HTML directly in programming language code. This pushes the creation of dynamic web pages exclusively into the realm of programmers. JavaServer Pages, however, changes all that.

Embedding Dynamic Elements in HTML Pages

JSP tackles the problem from the other direction. Instead of embedding HTML in programming code, JSP lets you embed special active elements into HTML pages. These elements look similar to HTML elements, but behind the scenes they are actually componentized Java programs that the server executes when a user requests the page. Here's a simple JSP page that illustrates this:

```
<%@ taglib prefix="c" uri="http://java.sun.com/jsp/jstl/core" %>
<html>
  <body bgcolor="white">

  <jsp:useBean id="clock" class="java.util.Date" />
  <c:choose>
    <c:when test="${clock.hours < 12}">
      <h1>Good morning!</h1>
    </c:when>
    <c:when test="${clock.hours < 18}">
      <h1>Good day!</h1>
    </c:when>
    <c:otherwise>
      <h1>Good evening!</h1>
    </c:otherwise>
  </c:choose>
  Welcome to our site, open 24 hours a day.
  </body>
</html>
```

This page inserts a different message to the user based on the time of day: "Good morning!" if the local time is before 12 P.M., "Good day!" if between 12 P.M. and 6 P.M., and "Good evening!" otherwise. When a user asks for this page, the JSP-enabled web server executes the logic represented by the highlighted JSP elements and creates an HTML page that is sent back to the user's browser. For example, if the current time is 8:53 P.M., the resulting page sent from the server to the browser looks like this:

```
<html>
  <body bgcolor="white">
  <h1>Good evening!</h1>
    Welcome to our site, open 24 hours a day.
  </body>
</html>
```

A screen shot of this result is shown in Figure 1-2.

In addition to the HTML-like JSP elements, a JSP page can also contain Java code embedded in so-called *scripting elements*. This feature has been part of the JSP specification from the very first version, and it used to be convenient for simple conditional logic. With the introduction of the JSP Expression Language (EL) and the JSP Standard Tag Library (JSTL), however, Java code in a page is rarely needed. In addition, embedding too much code in a web page is no better than using HTML

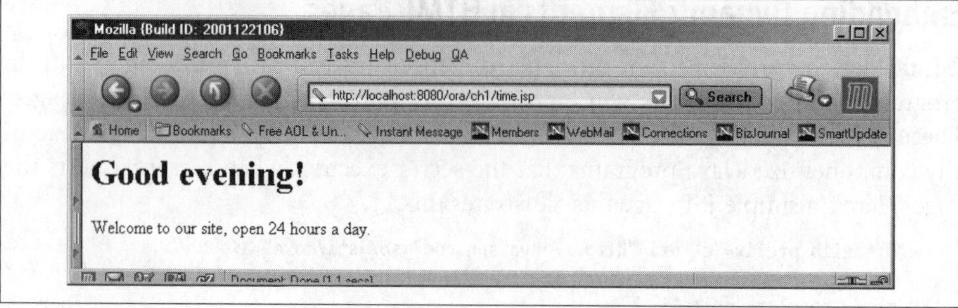

Figure 1-2. The output of a simple JSP page

elements in a server-side program, and often leads to a web application that is hard to maintain and debug. The examples in this book rarely use scripting elements, but they are described in detail in Chapter 16.

Compilation

Another benefit that is important to mention is that a JSP page is always compiled before it's processed by the server. Remember that older technologies such as CGI/Perl require the server to load an interpreter and the target script each time the page is requested. JSP gets around this problem by compiling each JSP page into executable code the first time it's requested (or on demand), and invoking the resulting code directly on all subsequent requests. When coupled with a persistent Java virtual machine on a JSP-enabled web server, this allows the server to handle JSP pages much faster.

Using the Right Person for Each Task

As I alluded to earlier, JSP allows you to separate the markup language code, such as HTML, from the programming language code used to process user input, access databases, and perform other application tasks. One way this separation takes place is through the use of the JSP standard and custom elements; these elements are implemented with programming code and used the same way as page markup elements in regular web pages.

Another way to separate is to combine JSP with other J2EE technologies. For example, Java servlets can handle input processing, Enterprise JavaBeans (EJB) can take care of the application logic, and JSP pages can provide the user interface.

This separation means that with JSP, a typical business can divide its efforts among two groups that excel in their own areas of expertise: a Java web development team with programmers who implement the application logic as servlets, EJBs and custom JSP elements, and page authors who craft the specifics of the interface and use the powerful custom elements without having to do any programming. We'll talk more about this benefit as we move through the book, although I should reiterate that the first half of the book is devoted more to those without programming experience, while the second half is for programmers who wish to combine JSP with other technologies and create their own JSP elements.

Integration with Enterprise Java APIs

Finally, because JavaServer Pages are built on top of the Java Servlets API, JSP has access to all the powerful Enterprise Java APIs, including:

- JDBC
- Remote Method Invocation (RMI) and OMG CORBA support
- JNDI (Java Naming and Directory Interface)
- Enterprise JavaBeans (EJB)
- JMS (Java Message Service)
- JTA (Java Transaction API)
- JAXP (Java API for XML Processing)
- JAXR (Java API for XML Registries), JAX-RPC (Java API for XML-based RPC), and SAAJ (SOAP with Attachments API for Java)
- JavaMail

This means that you can easily integrate JavaServer Pages with your existing Java Enterprise solutions.

Other Solutions

At this point, let's digress and look at some other solutions for dynamic web content. Some of these solutions are similar to JSP, while others are descendants of older technologies. Many don't have the unique combination of features and portability offered by JavaServer Pages.

Active Server Pages (ASP)

Microsoft's Active Server Pages (ASP) is a popular technology for developing dynamic web sites. Just like JSP, ASP lets a page author include logic, such as VBScript and JScript code, in regular web pages to generate the dynamic parts. For complex code, COM (ActiveX) components written in a programming language such as C++ can be invoked by the scripting code. The standard distribution includes components for database access and more, and other components are available from third parties. When an ASP page is requested, the code in the page is executed by the server. The result is inserted into the page, and the combination of the static and dynamic content is sent to the browser.

ASP.NET, the latest version of ASP, adds a number of new features. As an alternative to scripting, dynamic content can be generated by HTML/XML-like elements similar to JSP action elements. For improved performance, ASP.NET pages are compiled as opposed to interpreted, and Common Language Runtime (CLR) languages, such as C#, JScript.NET, and Visual Basic.NET, are used instead of the scripting languages supported in previous ASP versions.

Due to ASP's reliance on native COM code as its component model, it's primarily a solution for the Windows platform. Limited support for other platforms, such as the Apache web server on Unix, is available through third-party products such as Sun Chili!Soft ASP (Sun Microsystems, Inc.) and InstantASP (Halcyon Software). ASP.NET is a part of the complete .NET platform, with the potential for better support on non-Windows platforms. You can read more about ASP and ASP.NET on Microsoft's web site, *http://www.microsoft.com/*.

PHP

PHP* is an open source web scripting language. Like JSP and ASP, PHP allows a page author to include scripting code in regular web pages to generate dynamic content. PHP has a C-like syntax with some features borrowed from Perl, C++, and Java. Complex code can be encapsulated in both functions and classes. A large number of predefined functions are available as part of PHP, such as accessing databases, LDAP directories, and mail servers, creating PDF documents and images, and encrypting and decrypting data. PHP 4, the current version, compiles a page when it's requested, executes it, and merges the result of executing the scripts with the static text in the page, before it's returned to the browser.

PHP is supported on a wide range of platforms, including all major web servers on operating systems like Windows, Mac, and most Unix flavors, and with interfaces to a large number of database engines. More information about PHP is available at *http://www.php.net/*.

ColdFusion

Macromedia's ColdFusion product is another popular alternative for generating dynamic web content. The dynamic parts of a page are generated by inserting HTML/XML-like elements, known as the ColdFusion Markup Language (CFML), into web pages. CFML includes a large set of elements for tasks such as accessing databases, files, mail servers, and other web servers, as well as conditional processing elements such as loops. The latest version of ColdFusion also includes elements for communication with Java servlets and Enterprise JavaBeans. Custom elements can be developed in C++ or Java to encapsulate application-specific functions, and

* The precursor to PHP was a tool called Personal Home Page. Today PHP is not an acronym for anything; it's simply the name for this product.

CFML extensions are available from third parties. ColdFusion didn't initially support scripting languages, but since ColdFusion 4.5, JavaScript-like code can be embedded in the web pages in addition to the CFML tags.

The ColdFusion MX, Enterprise Edition, is supported on Windows, Solaris, HP/UX and Linux, for all major web servers and databases. A special J2EE version of ColdFusion MX extends the ColdFusion features to a number of J2EE application servers. For more information, visit Macromedia's web site at *http://www.macromedia.com/*.

Java servlet template engines

A Java servlet template engine is another technology for separating presentation from processing. When servlets became popular, it didn't take long before developers realized how hard it was to maintain the presentation part when the HTML code was embedded directly in the servlet's Java code. As a result, a number of so-called *template engines* have been developed as open source products to help get HTML out of the servlets.

Template engines are intended to be used with pure code components (servlets) and to use web pages with scripting code only for the presentation part. Requests are sent to a servlet that processes the request, creates objects that represent the result, and calls on a web page template to generate the HTML to be sent to the browser. The template contains scripting code similar to the alternatives described earlier. The scripting languages used by these engines are less powerful, however, since scripting is intended only for reading data objects and generating HTML code to display their values. All the other products and technologies support general-purpose languages, which can (for better or for worse) be used to include business logic in the pages.

Two popular template engines are Velocity (*http://jakarta.apache.org/velocity/*) and FreeMarker (*http://freemarker.org/*).

The JSP Advantage

JSP combines the most important features found in the alternatives:

- JSP supports both scripting- and element-based dynamic content, and allows developers to create custom tag libraries to satisfy application-specific needs.
- JSP pages are compiled for efficient server processing.
- JSP pages can be used in combination with servlets that handle the business logic, the model favored by Java servlet template engines.

In addition, JSP has a couple of unique advantages that make it stand out from the crowd:

- JSP is a specification, not a product. This means vendors can compete with different implementations, leading to better performance and quality. It also leads to a less obvious advantage, namely that when so many companies have invested time and money in the technology, chances are it will be around for a long time, with reasonable assurances that new versions will be backward compatible; with a proprietary technology, this is not always a given.

- JSP is an integral part of J2EE, a complete platform for enterprise class applications. This means that JSP can play a part in the simplest applications to the most complex and demanding.

What You Need to Get Started

Before we begin, let's quickly run through what you need to run the examples and develop your own applications. You really only need three things:

- A PC or workstation, with a connection to the Internet so you can download the software you need
- A Java 2 compatible-Java Software Development Kit (Java 2 SDK)
- A JSP 2.0-enabled web server, such as Apache Tomcat from the Jakarta Project

The Apache Tomcat server is the reference implementation for JSP. All the examples in the book were tested on Tomcat. In Chapter 4, I'll show you how to download, install, and configure the Tomcat server as well as the examples described in this book.

In addition, there are a variety of other tools and servers that support JSP, from both open source projects and commercial companies. Close to 30 different server products support JSP to date, and roughly 10 IDEs and authoring tools with varying degrees of JSP support are listed on Sun's JSP web site (*http://java.sun.com/products/jsp/*). You may want to evaluate some of these products when you're ready to start developing your application, but all you really need to work with the examples in this book is a regular text editor, such as Notepad, vi, or Emacs, and of course the Tomcat server.

So let's get going and take a closer look at what JSP has to offer. You'll need a solid ground to stand on though, so in the next chapter we will start with the foundations on which JSP is built: HTTP and Java servlets.

CHAPTER 2

HTTP and Servlet Basics

Let's start off this chapter by defining the term *web application*. We've all seen regular client-side applications, but what exactly is a web application? Loosely, it can be defined as an application running on a server a user accesses through a thin, general-purpose client. Today, the most common client is a web browser on a PC or workstation, but other kinds of clients are rapidly joining the party, such as wireless PDAs, cell phones, and other specialized devices.

The lofty goal here is to access all the information and services you need from any type of device that happens to be in front of you. This means that the same simple client program must be able to talk to many different server applications, and the applications must be able to work with many different types of clients. To satisfy this need, the protocol of how a client and a server talk to each other must be defined in detail. That's exactly what the HyperText Transport Protocol (HTTP) is for.

The communication model defined by HTTP forms the foundation for all web application design. A basic understanding of HTTP is key to developing applications that fit within the constraints of the protocol, no matter which server-side technology you use. In this chapter, we look at the most important details of HTTP you need to be aware of as a web application developer.

One other item: this book is about using JSP as the server-side technology, so that's what we'll focus on. As you saw in Chapter 1, JSP is based on the Java servlet technology. Both technologies share a lot of terminology and concepts, so knowing a bit about servlets will help you even when you develop pure JSP applications. To really understand and use the full power of JSP, you need to know a fair bit about servlets. Hence, we look at servlet fundamentals in the last section of this chapter.

The HTTP Request/Response Model

HTTP and all extended protocols based on HTTP are based on a very simple communications model. Here's how it works: a client, typically a web browser, sends a *request* for a *resource* to a server, and the server sends back a *response* corresponding to the resource (or a response with an error message if it can't process the request for some reason). A resource can be a number of things, such as a simple HTML file returned verbatim to the browser or a program that generates the response dynamically. This request/response model is illustrated in Figure 2-1.

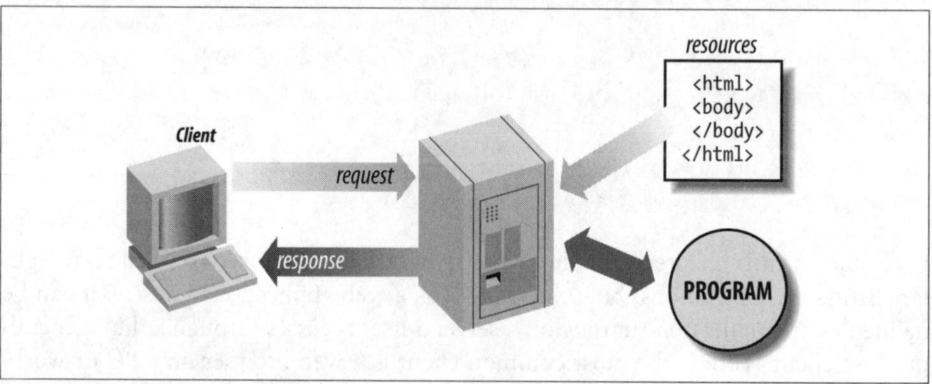

Figure 2-1. HTTP request/response with two resources

This simple model implies three important facts you need to be aware of:

- HTTP is a stateless protocol. This means that the server doesn't keep any information about the client after it sends its response, and therefore it can't recognize that multiple requests from the same client may be related.
- Web applications can't easily provide the kind of immediate feedback typically found in standalone GUI applications such as word processors or traditional client/server applications. Every interaction between the client and the server requires a request/response exchange. Performing a request/response exchange when a user selects an item in a list box or fills out a form element is usually too taxing on the bandwidth available to most Internet users.
- There's nothing in the protocol that tells the server how a request is made; consequently, the server can't distinguish between various methods of triggering the request on the client. For example, HTTP doesn't allow a web server to differentiate between an explicit request caused by clicking a link or submitting a form and an implicit request caused by resizing the browser window or using the browser's **Back** button. In addition, HTTP doesn't contain any means for the server to invoke client specific functions, such as going back in the browser history list or sending the response to a certain frame. Also, the server can't detect when the user closes the browser.

Over the years, people have developed various tricks to overcome the first problem; HTTP's stateless nature. We'll look at them in Chapter 10. The other two problems—no immediate feedback and no details about how the request is made—are harder to deal with, but some amount of interactivity can be achieved by generating a response that includes client-side code (code executed by the browser), such as JavaScript or a Java applet. This approach is discussed briefly in Chapter 17.

Requests in Detail

Let's take a closer look at requests. A user sends a request to the server by clicking a link on a web page, submitting a form, or typing in a web page address in the browser's address field. To send a request, the browser needs to know which server to talk to and which resource to ask for. This information is specified by an HTTP *Uniform Resource Locator* (URL):

```
http://www.gefionsoftware.com/index.html
```

The first part of the URL shown specifies that the request is made using the HTTP protocol. This is followed by the name of the server, in this case *www.gefionsoftware.com*. The web server waits for requests to come in on a specific TCP/IP port. Port number 80 is the standard port for HTTP requests. If the web server uses another port, the URL must specify the port number in addition to the server name. For example:

```
http://www.gefionsoftware.com:8080/index.html
```

This request is sent to a server that uses port 8080 instead of 80. The last part of the URL, */index.html*, identifies the resource that the client is requesting.

A URL is actually a specialization of a *Uniform Resource Identifier* (URI, defined in the RFC-2396* specification). A URL identifies a resource partly by its location, for instance the server that contains the resource. Another type of URI is a *Uniform Resource Name* (URN), which is a globally unique identifier that is valid no matter where the resource is located. HTTP deals only with the URL variety. The terms URI and URL are often used interchangeable, and unfortunately, they have slightly different definitions in different specifications. I'm trying to use the terms as defined by the HTTP/1.1 specification (RFC-2616), which is pretty close to how they are also used in the servlet and JSP specifications. Hence, I use the term URL only when the URI must start with `http` (or `https`, for HTTP over an encrypted connection) followed by a server name and possibly a port number, as in the previous examples. I use URI as a generic term for any string that identifies a resource, where the location can be deduced from the context and isn't necessarily part of the URI. For example, when the request has been delivered to the server, the location is a given, and only the resource identifier is important.

The browser uses the URL information to create the *request message* it sends to the specified server using the specified protocol. An HTTP request message consists of three things: a request line, request headers, and possibly a request body.

* Available at *http://www.ietf.org/rfc/rfc2396.txt*.

The request line starts with the request method name, followed by a resource identifier and the protocol version used by the browser:

```
GET /index.html HTTP/1.1
```

The most commonly used request method is named `GET`. As the name implies, a `GET` request is used to retrieve a resource from the server. It's the default request method, so if you type a URL in the browser's address field, or click on a link, the request is sent as a `GET` request to the server.

The request headers provide additional information the server may use to process the request. The message body is included only in some types of requests, like the `POST` request discussed later.

Here's an example of a valid HTTP request message:

```
GET /index.html HTTP/1.1
Host: www.gefionsoftware.com
User-Agent: Mozilla/5.0 (Windows; U; Win 9x 4.90; en-US; rv: 1.0.2)
Accept: image/gif, image/jpeg, image/pjpeg, image/png, */*
Accept-Language : en
Accept-Charset : iso-8859-1,*,utf-8
```

The request line specifies the `GET` method and asks for the resource named */index.html* to be returned using the HTTP/1.1 protocol version. The various headers provide additional information.

The `Host` header tells the server the hostname used in the URL. A server may have multiple names, so this information is used to distinguish between multiple virtual web servers sharing the same web server process.

The `User-Agent` header contains information about the type of browser making the request. The server can use this to send different types of responses to different types of browsers. For instance, if the server knows whether Internet Explorer or Netscape Navigator is used, it can send a response that takes advantage of each browser's unique features. It can also tell if a client other than an HTML browser is used, such as a Wireless Markup Language (WML) browser on a cell phone or a PDA device, and generate an appropriate response.

The `Accept` headers provide information about the languages and file formats the browser accepts. These headers can be used to adjust the response to the capabilities of the browser and the user's preferences, such as use a supported image format and the preferred language. These are just a few of the headers that can be included in a request message. The HTTP specification, available at *http://www.w3c.org/*, describes all of them.

The resource identifier (URI) doesn't necessarily correspond to a static file on the server. It can identify an executable program, a record in a database, or pretty much anything the web server knows about. That's why the generic term *resource* is used. In fact, there's no way to tell if the */index.html* URI corresponds to a file or something else; it's just a name that means something to the server. The web server is configured to map these unique names to the real resources.

Responses in Detail

When the web server receives the request, it looks at the URI and decides, based on configuration information, how to handle it. It may handle it internally by simply reading an HTML file from the filesystem, or it can forward the request to some component that is responsible for the resource corresponding to the URI. This can be a program that uses database information, for instance, to dynamically generate an appropriate response. To the browser it makes no difference how the request is handled; all it cares about is getting a response.

The response message looks similar to the request message. It consists of three things: a status line, response headers, and an optional response body. Here's an example:

```
HTTP/1.1 200 OK
Last-Modified: Mon, 20 Dec 2002 23:26:42 GMT
Date: Tue, 11 Jan 2003 20:52:40 GMT
Status: 200
Content-Type: text/html
Servlet-Engine: Tomcat Web Server/5.0
Content-Length: 59

<html>
  <body>
    <h1>Hello World!</h1>
  </body>
</html>
```

The status line starts with the name of the protocol, followed by a status code and a short description of the status code. Here the status code is 200, meaning the request was executed successfully. The response message has headers just like the request message. In this example, the `Last-Modified` header gives the date and time for when the resource was last modified. The browser can use this information as a timestamp in a local cache; the next time the user asks for this resource, he can ask the server to send it only if it's been updated since the last time it was requested. The `Content-Type` header tells the browser what type of response data the body contains and the `Content-Length` header how large it is. The other headers are self-explanatory. A blank line separates the headers from the message body. Here the body is a simple HTML page:

```
<html>
  <body>
    <h1>Hello World!</h1>
  </body>
</html>
```

Of course, the body can contain a more complex HTML page or any other type of content. For example, the request may return an HTML page with `<img>` elements. When the browser reads the first response and finds the `<img>` elements, it sends a new request for the resource identified by each element, often in parallel. The server returns one response for each image request, with a `Content-Type` header telling what type of image it is (for instance `image/gif`) and the body containing the bytes that make up the image. The browser then combines all responses to render the complete page. This interaction is illustrated in Figure 2-2.

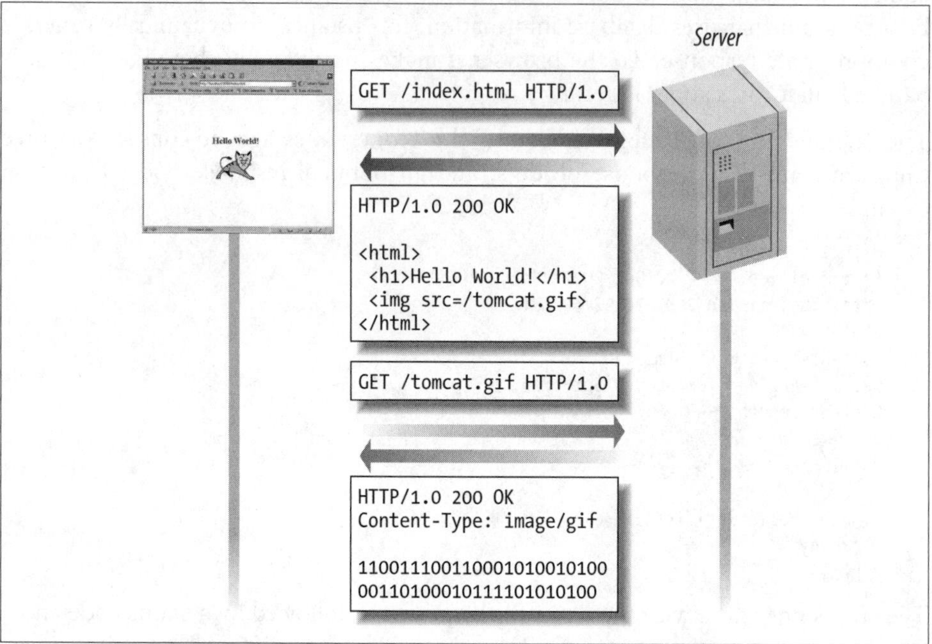

Figure 2-2. Interaction between a web client and a server

Request Parameters

Besides the URI and headers, a request message can contain additional information in the form of parameters. If the URI identifies a server-side program for displaying weather information, for example, request parameters can provide information about the city the user wants to see a forecast for. In an e-commerce application, the URI may identify a program that processes orders, with the user's customer number and the list of items to be purchased transferred as parameters.

Parameters can be sent in one of two ways: tacked on to the URI in the form of a query string or sent as part of the request message body. This is an example of a URL with a query string:

```
http://www.weather.com/forecast?city=Hermosa+Beach&state=CA
```

The query string starts with a question mark (?) and consists of name/value pairs separated by ampersands (&). These names and values must be *URL-encoded*, meaning that special characters, such as whitespace, question marks, ampersands, and all other nonalphanumeric characters are encoded so that they don't get confused with characters used to separate name/value pairs and other parts of the URI. In this example, the space between `Hermosa` and `Beach` is encoded as a plus sign. Other special characters are encoded as their corresponding hexadecimal ASCII value; for instance, a question mark is encoded as `%3F`. When parameters are sent as part of the request body, they follow the same syntax; URL encoded name/value pairs separated by ampersands.

Request Methods

As described earlier, `GET` is the most commonly used request method, intended to retrieve a resource without causing anything else to happen on the server. The `POST` method is almost as common as `GET`; it requests some kind of processing on the server, for instance, updating a database or processing a purchase order.

The way parameters are transferred is one of the most obvious differences between the `GET` and `POST` request methods. A `GET` request always uses a query string to send parameter values, while a `POST` request always sends them as part of the body (additionally, it can send some parameters as a query string, just to make life interesting). If you insert a link in an HTML page using an `<a>` element, clicking on the link results in a `GET` request being sent to the server. Since the `GET` request uses a query string to pass parameters, you can include hardcoded parameter values in the link URI:

```
<a href="/forecast?city=Hermosa+Beach&state=CA">
  Hermosa Beach weather forecast
</a>
```

When you use a form to send user input to the server, you can specify whether to use the `GET` or `POST` method with the `method` attribute, as shown here:

```
<form action="/forecast" method="POST">
  City: <input name="city" type="text">
  State: <input name="state" type="text">
  <p>
  <input type="SUBMIT">
</form>
```

If the user enters "Hermosa Beach" and "CA" in the form fields and clicks on the **Submit** button, the browser sends a request message like this to the server:

```
POST /forecast HTTP/1.1
Host: www.gefionsoftware.com
User-Agent: Mozilla/5.0 (Windows; U; Win 9x 4.90; en-US; rv: 1.0.2)
Accept: image/gif, image/jpeg, image/pjpeg, image/png, */*
Accept-language: en-US
Accept-charset: iso-8859-1,*,utf-8

city=Hermosa+Beach&state=CA
```

Due to the differences in how parameters are sent by GET and POST requests, as well as the differences in their intended purpose, browsers handle the requests in different ways. A GET request, parameters and all, can easily be saved as a bookmark, hard-coded as a link, and the response cached by the browser. Also, the browser knows that no damage is done if it needs to send a GET request again automatically, for instance if the user clicks the **Reload** button.

A POST request, on the other hand, can't be bookmarked as easily; the browser would have to save both the URI and the request message body. Since a POST request is intended to perform some possibly irreversible action on the server, the browser must also ask the user if it's okay to send the request again. You have probably seen this type of confirmation dialog, shown in Figure 2-3, numerous times.

Figure 2-3. Repost confirmation dialog

Besides the GET and POST methods, HTTP specifies the following methods:

OPTIONS
: The OPTIONS method is used to find out what options (e.g., methods) a server or a resource offers.

HEAD
: The HEAD method is used to get a response with all headers generated by a GET request but without the body. It can make sure a link is valid or to see when a resource was last modified.

PUT
: The PUT method is used to store the message body content on the server as a resource identified by the URI.

DELETE
: The DELETE method is used to delete the resource identified by the URI.

TRACE
: The TRACE method is used for testing the communication between the client and the server. The server sends back the request message, exactly as it received it, as the body of the response.

These methods aren't normally used in a web application.

Servlets

The JSP specification is based on the Java servlet specification. In fact, JSP pages are often combined with servlets in the same application. In this section, we take a brief look at what a servlet is, and then discuss the concepts shared by servlets and JSP pages. In Chapter 3, we'll take a closer look at how JSP pages are actually turned into servlets automatically.

If you're already familiar with servlets, this is old news. You can safely skip the rest of this chapter.

Advantages over Other Server-Side Technologies

In simple terms, a servlet is a piece of code that adds new functionality to a server (typically a web server), just like CGI and proprietary server extensions such as NSAPI and ISAPI. But compared to other technologies, servlets have a number of advantages:

Platform and vendor independence
: All the major web servers and application servers support servlets, so a servlet-based solution doesn't tie you to one specific vendor. Also, servlets are written in the Java programming language, so they can be used on any operating system with a Java runtime environment.

Integration
: Servlets are developed in Java and can therefore take advantage of all other Java technologies, such as JDBC for database access, JNDI for directory access, RMI for remote resource access, etc. Starting with Version 2.2, the servlet specification is part of the Java 2 Enterprise Edition (J2EE), making servlets an important ingredient of any large-scale enterprise application, with formalized relationships to other server-side technologies such as Enterprise JavaBeans.

Efficiency
: Servlets execute in a process that is running until the servlet-based application is shut down. Each servlet request is executed as a separate thread in this permanent process. This is far more efficient that the CGI model, where a new process is created for each request. First of all (and most obvious), a servlet doesn't have the overhead of creating the process and loading the CGI script and possibly its interpreter. But another timesaver is that servlets can also access resources that remain loaded in the process memory between requests, such as database connections and persistent state.

Scalability
: By virtue of being written in Java and the broad support for servlets, a servlet-based application is extremely scalable. You can develop and test the application on a Windows PC using the standalone servlet reference implementation, and deploy it on anything from a more powerful server running Linux and

Apache to a cluster of high-end servers with an application server that supports loadbalancing and failover.

Robustness and security
: Java is a strongly typed programming language. This means that you catch a lot of mistakes in the compilation phase that you would only catch during runtime if you used a script language such as Perl. Java's error handling is also much more robust than C/C++, where an error such as division by zero typically brings down the whole server.

  In addition, servlets use specialized interfaces to server resources that aren't vulnerable to the traditional security attacks. For instance, a CGI Perl script typically uses shell command strings composed of data received from the client to ask the server to do things such as send email. People with nothing better to do love to find ways to send data that will cause the server to crash, remove all files on the hard disk, or plant a virus or a backdoor when the server executes the command. While a CGI script programmer must be very careful to screen all input to avoid these threats, such problems are almost nonexistent with a servlet because it doesn't communicate with the server in the same insecure way.*

As you will see in Chapter 3, JSP inherits all these advantages because it's based on the servlet specification.

Servlet Containers

A servlet container is the connection between a web server and the servlets. It provides the runtime environment for all the servlets on the server as defined by the servlet specification, and is responsible for loading and invoking those servlets when the time is right. The container typically loads a servlet class when it receives the first request for the servlet, gives it a chance to initialize itself, and then asks it to process the request. Subsequent requests use the same, initialized servlet until the server is shut down. The container then gives the servlet a chance to release resources and save its state (for instance, information accumulated during its lifetime).

There are many different types of servlet containers. Some containers are called *add-ons*, or *plug-ins*, and are used to add servlet support to web servers without native servlet support (such as Apache and IIS). They can run in the same operating-system process as the web server or in a separate process. Other containers are standalone servers. A *standalone server* includes web server functionality to provide full support for HTTP in addition to the servlet runtime environment. Containers can also be *embedded* in other servers, such as a climate-control system, to offer a web-based interface to the system. A container bundled as part of an application server can

* However, servlet-based web sites are vulnerable to so-called cross site scripting attacks (see *http://www.cert.org/advisories/CA-2000-02.html*) the same way all dynamic web sites are, no matter which technology is used.

distribute the execution of servlets over multiple hosts. The server can balance the load evenly over all containers, and some servers can even provide failover capabilities in case a host crashes.

No matter what type it is, the servlet container is responsible for mapping an incoming request to a servlet registered to handle the resource identified by the URI and passing the request message to that servlet. After the request is processed, it's the container's responsibility to convert the response created by the servlet into an HTTP response message and send it back to the client. This is illustrated in Figure 2-4.

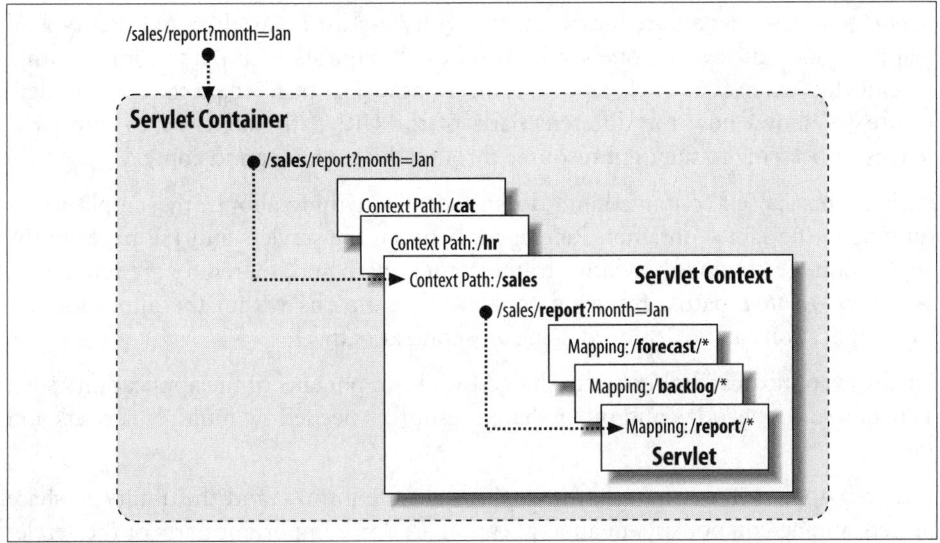

Figure 2-4. Request dispatching

Servlet Contexts and Web Applications

A Java web application is typically made up by a combination of several different types of resources: JSP pages, servlets, applets, static HTML pages, custom tag libraries and other Java class files. Containers compliant with the Servlet 2.2 specification (or later), support a standard, portable way to package all these resources, along with a web application deployment descriptor containing information about how all the resources fit together. The deployment descriptor and all the other web application files are arranged in a well-defined hierarchy within an archive file, called a *web application archive* (WAR). All compliant containers provide tools for installing a WAR file or a special directory where a WAR file is automatically picked up (such as the *webapps* directory in Tomcat). Most containers also support web applications deployed directly in a filesystem using the same file structure as is defined for the WAR file, which can be convenient during development.

Within the container, each web application is represented by a *servlet context*. The servlet context is associated with a unique URI path prefix called the *context path*, as shown in Figure 2-4. For instance, your human resources application can be associated with the context path */hr* and your sales tracking system with the context path */sales*. This allows one servlet container to distinguish between the different applications it serves and dispatch requests like */sales/report?month=Jan* to the sales tracking application and */hr/emplist* to the human resources application.

The remaining URI path is then used within the selected context to decide how to process the request by comparing it to path-mapping rules defined by the application's deployment descriptor. Rules can be defined to send all requests starting with */report* to one servlet and requests starting with */forecast* to another. Another type of mapping rule can say that one servlet handles all requests with paths ending with a specific file extension, such as *.jsp*. This is how JSP page requests are handled. Figure 2-4 shows how the different parts of the URI paths are used to direct the request processing to the right resource through the container and context.

Each context is self-contained and doesn't know anything about other applications running in the same container. References between the servlets and JSP pages in the application are commonly relative to the context path and, therefore, are referred to as *context-relative* paths. By using context-relative paths within the application, a web application can be deployed using any context path.

Finally, a context can hold objects shared by all components of the application,* such as database connections and other shared resources needed by multiple servlets and JSP pages.

The web application structure, the deployment file format, and the ability to share objects among components in an application are three important parts of the servlet specification that also apply to JSP. We will look at all these areas in much greater detail later in this book, starting with the basics in Chapter 5 and adding more advanced features as needed in the following chapters.

* Special considerations must be taken for applications distributed over multiple servers. Chapter 18 describes this in more detail.

CHAPTER 3

JSP Overview

JSP is the latest Java technology for web application development and is based on the servlet technology introduced in the previous chapter. While servlets are great in many ways, they are generally reserved for programmers. In this chapter, we look at the problems that JSP technology solves, the anatomy of a JSP page, the relationship between servlets and JSP, and how the server processes a JSP page.

In any web application, a program on the server processes requests and generates responses. In a simple one-page application, such as an online bulletin board, you don't need to be overly concerned about the design of this piece of code; all logic can be lumped together in a single program. However, when the application grows into something bigger (spanning multiple pages, using external resources such as databases, with more options and support for more types of clients), it's a different story. The way your site is designed is critical to how well it can be adapted to new requirements and continue to evolve. The good news is that JSP technology can be used as an important part in all kinds of web applications, from the simplest to the most complex. Therefore, this chapter also introduces the primary concepts in the design model recommended for web applications and the different roles played by JSP and other Java technologies in this model.

The Problem with Servlets

In many Java servlet-based applications, processing the request and generating the response are both handled by a single servlet class. Example 3-1 shows how a servlet class often looks.

Example 3-1. A typical servlet class

```
public class OrderServlet extends HttpServlet {
    public void doGet((HttpServletRequest request,
        HttpServletResponse response)
        throws ServletException, IOException  {
```

Example 3-1. A typical servlet class (continued)

```
        response.setContentType("text/html");
        PrintWriter out = response.getWriter( );

        if (isOrderInfoValid(request)) {
            saveOrderInfo(request);
            out.println("<html>");
            out.println("  <head>");
            out.println("    <title>Order Confirmation</title>");
            out.println("  </head>");
            out.println("  <body>");
            out.println("    <h1>Order Confirmation</h1>");
            renderOrderInfo(request);
            out.println("  </body>");
            out.println("</html>");
        }
    ...
```

If you're not a programmer, don't worry about all the details in this code. The point is that the servlet contains request processing and business logic (implemented by methods such as `isOrderInfoValid()` and `saveOrderInfo( )`), and also generates the response HTML code, embedded directly in the servlet code using `println( )` calls. A more structured servlet application isolates different pieces of the processing in various reusable utility classes and may also use a separate class library for generating the actual HTML elements in the response. Even so, the pure servlet-based approach still has a few problems:

- Thorough Java programming knowledge is needed to develop and maintain all aspects of the application, since the processing code and the HTML elements are lumped together.
- Changing the look and feel of the application, or adding support for a new type of client (such as a WML client), requires the servlet code to be updated and recompiled.
- It's hard to take advantage of web page development tools when designing the application interface. If such tools are used to develop the web page layout, the generated HTML must then be manually embedded into the servlet code, a process which is time consuming, error prone, and extremely boring.

Adding JSP to the puzzle lets you solve these problems by separating the request processing and business logic code from the presentation, as illustrated in Figure 3-1. Instead of embedding HTML in the code, place all static HTML in a JSP page, just as in a regular web page, and add a few JSP elements to generate the dynamic parts of the page. The request processing can remain the domain of the servlet, and the business logic can be handled by JavaBeans and EJB components.

As I mentioned before, separating the request processing and business logic from presentation makes it possible to divide the development tasks among people with

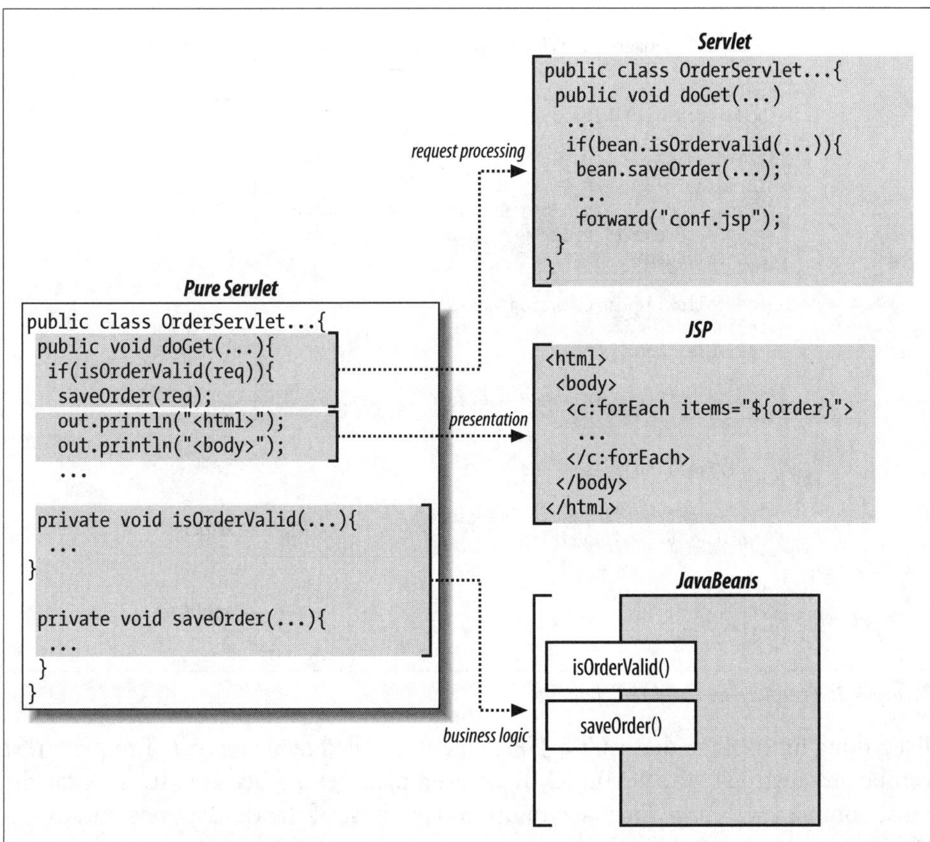

Figure 3-1. Separation of request processing, business logic, and presentation

different skills. Java programmers implement the request processing and business logic pieces, web page authors implement the user interface, and both groups can use best-of-breed development tools for the task at hand. The result is a much more productive development process. It also makes it possible to change different aspects of the application independently, such as changing the business rules without touching the user interface.

This model has clear benefits even for a web page author without programming skills, working alone. A page author can develop web applications with many dynamic features, using the JSP standard actions and the JSTL libraries, as well as Java components provided by open source projects and commercial companies.

The Anatomy of a JSP Page

A JSP page is simply a regular web page with JSP elements for generating the parts that differ for each request, as shown in Figure 3-2.

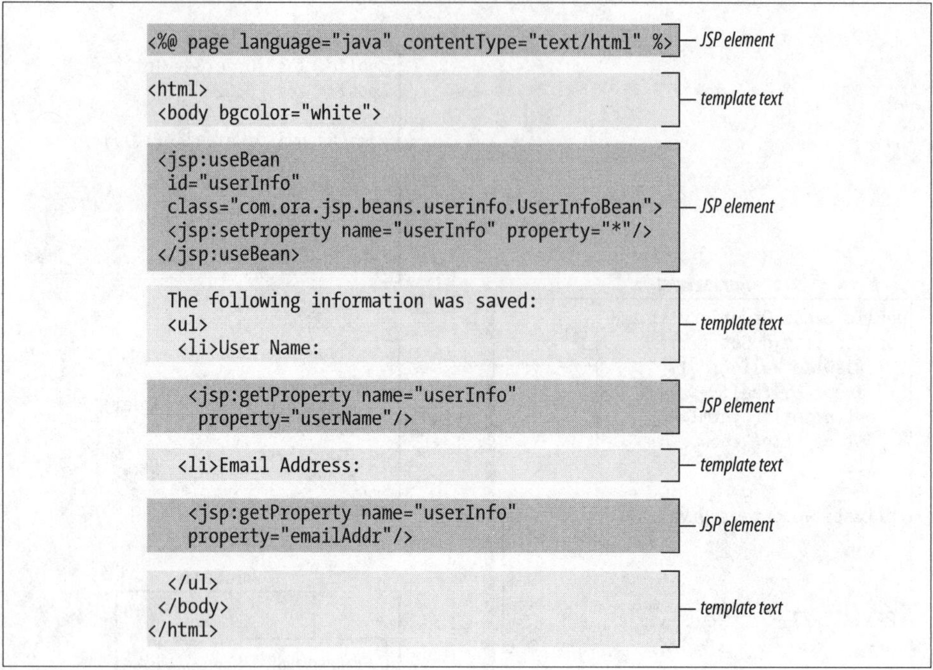

<%@ page language="java" contentType="text/html" %>
JSP element
<html>
<body bgcolor="white">
template text
<jsp:useBean
id="userInfo"
class="com.ora.jsp.beans.userinfo.UserInfoBean">
<jsp:setProperty name="userInfo" property="*"/>
</jsp:useBean>
JSP element
The following information was saved:
<ul>
<li>User Name:
template text
<jsp:getProperty name="userInfo"
property="userName"/>
JSP element
<li>Email Address:
template text
<jsp:getProperty name="userInfo"
property="emailAddr"/>
JSP element
</ul>
</body>
</html>
template text

Figure 3-2. Template text and JSP elements

Everything in the page that isn't a JSP element is called *template text*. Template text can be any text: HTML, WML, XML, or even plain text. Since HTML is by far the most common web page language in use today, most of the descriptions and examples in this book use HTML, but keep in mind that JSP has no dependency on HTML; it can be used with any markup language. Template text is always passed straight through to the browser.

When a JSP page request is processed, the template text and dynamic content generated by the JSP elements are merged, and the result is sent as the response to the browser.

JSP Processing

Just as a web server needs a servlet container to provide an interface to servlets, the server needs a *JSP container* to process JSP pages. The JSP container is responsible for intercepting requests for JSP pages. To process all JSP elements in the page, the container first turns the JSP page into a servlet (known as the *JSP page implementation class*). The conversion is pretty straightforward; all template text is converted to `println()` statements similar to the ones in the handcoded servlet shown in Example 3-1, and all JSP elements are converted to Java code that implements the corresponding dynamic behavior. The container then compiles the servlet class.

Converting the JSP page to a servlet and compiling the servlet form the *translation phase*. The JSP container initiates the translation phase for a page automatically when it receives the first request for the page. Since the translation phase takes a bit of time, the first user to request a JSP page notices a slight delay. The translation phase can also be initiated explicitly; this is referred to as *precompilation* of a JSP page. Precompiling a JSP page is a way to avoid hitting the first user with this delay. It is discussed in more detail in Chapter 17.

The JSP container is also responsible for invoking the JSP page implementation class (the generated servlet) to process each request and generate the response. This is called the *request processing phase*. The two phases are illustrated in Figure 3-3.

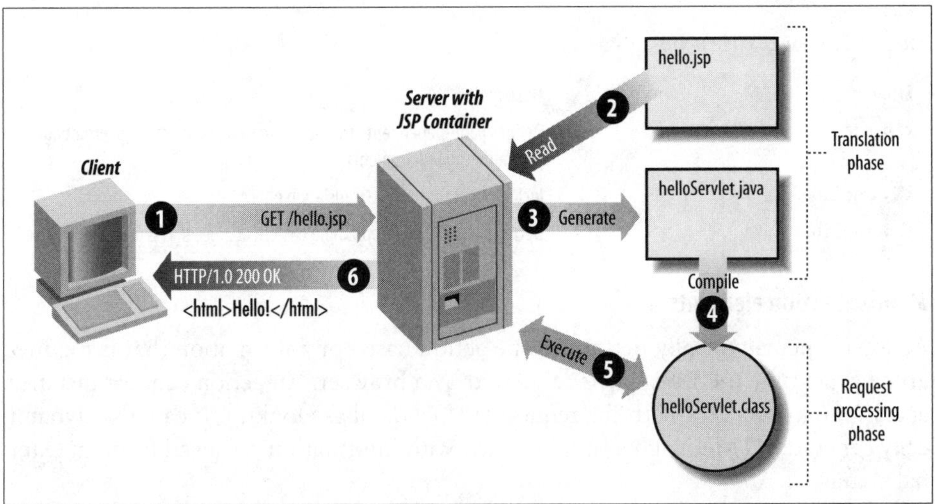

Figure 3-3. JSP page translation and processing phases

As long as the JSP page remains unchanged, any subsequent request goes straight to the request processing phase (i.e., the container simply executes the class file). When the JSP page is modified, it goes through the translation phase again before entering the request processing phase.

The JSP container is often implemented as a servlet configured to handle all requests for JSP pages. In fact, these two containers—a servlet container and a JSP container—are often combined in one package under the name *web container*.

So in a way, a JSP page is really just another way to write a servlet without having to be a Java programming wiz. Except for the translation phase, a JSP page is handled exactly like a regular servlet; it's loaded once and called repeatedly, until the server is shut down. By virtue of being an automatically generated servlet, a JSP page inherits all the advantages of a servlet described in Chapter 2: platform and vendor independence, integration, efficiency, scalability, robustness, and security.

JSP Elements

There are three types of JSP elements you can use: *directive*, *action*, and *scripting*. A new construct added in JSP 2.0 is an Expression Language (EL) expression; let's call this a forth element type, even though it's a bit different than the other three.

Directive elements

The directive elements, shown in Table 3-1, specify information about the page itself that remains the same between requests—for example, if session tracking is required or not, buffering requirements, and the name of a page that should be used to report errors, if any.

Table 3-1. Directive elements

Element	Description
`<%@ page ... %>`	Defines page-dependent attributes, such as session tracking, error page, and buffering requirements
`<%@ include ... %>`	Includes a file during the translation phase
`<%@ taglib ... %>`	Declares a tag library, containing custom actions, that is used in the page

Standard action elements

Action elements typically perform some action based on information that is required at the exact time the JSP page is requested by a browser. An action can, for instance, access parameters sent with the request to do a database lookup. It can also dynamically generate HTML, such as a table filled with information retrieved from an external system.

The JSP specification defines a few standard action elements, most of them listed in Table 3-2.*

Table 3-2. Standard action elements

Action element	Description
`<jsp:useBean>`	Makes a JavaBeans component available in a page
`<jsp:getProperty>`	Gets a property value from a JavaBeans component and adds it to the response
`<jsp:setProperty>`	Sets a JavaBeans component property value
`<jsp:include>`	Includes the response from a servlet or JSP page during the request processing phase
`<jsp:forward>`	Forwards the processing of a request to a servlet or JSP page

* There are a few more action elements, used in combination with these standard actions or custom actions or in very special cases. They are introduced as they are used in the examples later in this book.

Table 3-2. Standard action elements (continued)

Action element	Description
`<jsp:param>`	Adds a parameter value to a request handed off to another servlet or JSP page using `<jsp:include>` or `<jsp:forward>`
`<jsp:plugin>`	Generates HTML that contains the appropriate browser-dependent elements (`OBJECT` or `EMBED`) needed to execute an applet with the Java Plugin software

Custom action elements and the JSP Standard Tag Library

In addition to the standard actions, the JSP specification defines how to develop *custom actions* to extend the JSP language, either as Java classes or as text files with JSP elements. The JSP Standard Tag Library (JSTL) is such an extension, with the special status of being defined by a formal specification from Sun and typically bundled with the JSP container. JSTL contains action elements for the type of processing needed in most JSP applications, such as conditional processing, database access, internationalization, and more. This book covers all the JSTL actions in detail.

If JSTL isn't enough, your team (or a third party) can use these extension mechanisms to develop additional custom actions, maybe to access application-specific resources or simplify application-specific processing. The examples in this book use a few custom actions in addition to the JSTL actions, and one chapter in Part II and three chapters in Part III are dedicated to custom action development.

Scripting elements

Scripting elements, shown in Table 3-3, allow you to add small pieces of code (typically Java code) in a JSP page, such as an if statement to generate different HTML depending on a certain condition. Like actions, they are also executed when the page is requested. You should use scripting elements with extreme care: if you embed too much code in your JSP pages, you will end up with the same kind of maintenance problems as with servlets embedding HTML.

Table 3-3. Scripting elements

Element	Description
`<% ... %>`	Scriptlet, used to embed scripting code
`<%= ... %>`	Expression, used to embed scripting code expressions when the result shall be added to the response; also used as request-time action attribute values
`<%! ... %>`	Declaration, used to declare instance variables and methods in the JSP page implementation class

Expression Language expressions

A new feature in JSP 2.0 is the Expression Language (EL), originally developed as part of the JSTL specification. The EL is a simple language for accessing request data and data made available through application classes. EL expressions can be used directly in template text or to assign values to action element attributes. Its syntax is similar to JavaScript, but much more forgiving; it's constrained in terms of functionality, since it's not intended to be a full-fledged programming language. Rather, it is a glue for tying together action elements and other application components. There are way too many elements of the EL to list here, but they are all introduced in Chapter 5 and described in detail when used in examples.

JavaBeans components

JSP elements, such as action and scripting elements, are often used to work with JavaBeans components. Put succinctly, a JavaBeans component is a Java class that complies with certain coding conventions. JavaBeans components are typically used as containers for information that describes application entities, such as a customer or an order.

JSP Application Design with MVC

JSP technology can play a part in everything from the simplest web application, such as an online phone list or an employee vacation planner, to complex enterprise applications, such as a human resource application or a sophisticated online shopping site. How large a part JSP plays differs in each case, of course. In this section, I introduce a design model called Model-View-Controller (MVC), suitable for both simple and complex applications.

MVC was first described by Xerox in a number of papers published in the late 1980s. The key point of using MVC is to separate logic into three distinct units: the Model, the View, and the Controller. In a server application, we commonly classify the parts of the application as business logic, presentation, and request processing. *Business logic* is the term used for the manipulation of an application's data, such as customer, product, and order information. *Presentation* refers to how the application data is displayed to the user, for example, position, font, and size. And finally, *request processing* is what ties the business logic and presentation parts together. In MVC terms, the Model corresponds to business logic and data, the View to the presentation, and the Controller to the request processing.

Why use this design with JSP? The answer lies primarily in the first two elements. Remember that an application data structure and logic (the Model) is typically the most stable part of an application, while the presentation of that data (the View) changes fairly often. Just look at all the face-lifts many web sites go through to keep up with the latest fashion in web design. Yet, the data they present remains the same.

Another common example of why presentation should be separated from the business logic is that you may want to present the data in different languages or present different subsets of the data to internal and external users. Access to the data through new types of devices, such as cell phones and personal digital assistants (PDAs), is the latest trend. Each client type requires its own presentation format. It should come as no surprise, then, that separating business logic from the presentation makes it easier to evolve an application as the requirements change; new presentation interfaces can be developed without touching the business logic.

This MVC model is used for most of the examples in this book. In Part II, JSP pages are used as both the Controller and the View, and JavaBeans components are used as the Model. The examples in Chapters 5 through 9 use a single JSP page that handles everything, while Chapters 10 through 14 show how you can use separate pages for the Controller and the View to make the application easier to maintain. Many types of real-world applications can be developed this way, but what's more important is that this approach allows you to examine all the JSP features without getting distracted by other technologies. In Part III, we look at other possible role assignments when JSP is combined with servlets and Enterprise JavaBeans.

CHAPTER 4

Setting Up the JSP Environment

This book contains plenty of examples to illustrate all the JSP features. All examples were developed and tested with the JSP reference implementation, known as the Apache Tomcat server, which is developed by the Apache Jakarta project. In this chapter you will learn how to install the Tomcat server and add a web application containing all the examples used in this book. You can, of course, use any web server that supports JSP 2.0, but Tomcat is a good server for development and test purposes. You can learn more about the Jakarta project and Tomcat, as well as how you can participate in the development, at the Jakarta web site: *http://jakarta.apache.org/*.

Installing the Java Software Development Kit

Tomcat 5 is a pure Java web server with support for the Servlet 2.4 and JSP 2.0 specifications. In order to use it, you must first install a Java runtime environment. If you don't already have one, you can download a Java runtime for Windows, Linux, and Solaris at *http://java.sun.com/j2se/*.

I recommend that you download and install the Java 2 SDK (a.k.a. JDK), as opposed to the slimmed-down Runtime Environment (JRE) distribution. The reason is that JSP requires a Java compiler, included in the SDK but not in the JRE.

Another alternative is to use the JRE plus the Jikes compiler from IBM (*http://www10.software.ibm.com/developerworks/opensource/jikes/*). Tomcat can be configured to use Jikes instead of the *javac* compiler available in the Java 2 SDK from Sun; read the Tomcat documentation if you would like to try this. To make things simple, though, I suggest installing the Java 2 SDK from Sun. The examples were developed and tested with Java 2 SDK, Standard Edition, v1.4.2. I suggest that you use the latest version of the SDK available for your platform.

If you need an SDK for a platform other than Windows, Linux, or Solaris, there's a partial list of ports made by other companies at: *http://java.sun.com/cgi-bin/java-ports.cgi*.

Also check your operating-system vendor's web site. Most operating-system vendors have their own SDK implementation available for free.

Installation of the SDK varies per platform but is typically easy to do. Just follow the instructions on the web site where you download the SDK.

Before you install and run Tomcat, make sure that the JAVA_HOME environment variable is set to the installation directory of your Java environment and that the Java *bin* directory is included in the PATH environment variable. On a Windows system, you can see if an environment variable is set by typing the following command in a Command Prompt window:

```
C:\> echo %JAVA_HOME%
C:\jdk1.4.2
```

If JAVA_HOME isn't set, you can set it and include the *bin* directory in the PATH on a Windows system like this (assuming Java is installed in *C:\jdk1.4.2*):

```
C:\> set JAVA_HOME=C:\jdk1.4.2
C:\> set PATH=%JAVA_HOME%\bin;%PATH%
```

On a Windows 95/98/ME system, add these commands to the *C:\AUTOEXEC.BAT* file to set them permanently. Just use a text editor, such as Notepad, and add lines with the set commands. The next time you boot the PC, the environment variables will be set automatically. For Windows NT, you can set them permanently from the **Environment** tab in the **System Properties** tool in the Control Panel, and for Windows 2000 and Windows XP, you can do the same with the Control Panel **System** tool by first selecting the **Advanced** tab and then **Environment Variables**.

If you use Linux, Mac OS X, or some other Unix-based platform, the exact commands depend on the shell you use. With *bash*, which is commonly the default for Linux, use the following commands (assuming Java is installed in */usr/local/jdk1.4.2*):

```
[hans@gefion /] export JAVA_HOME=/usr/local/jdk1.4.2
[hans@gefion /] export PATH=$JAVA_HOME/bin:$PATH
[hans@gefion /] echo $PATH
/usr/local/jdk1.4.2/bin:/usr/local/bin:/bin:/usr/bin
```

Installing the Tomcat Server

Tomcat supports many features and configuration options. In this section, I only describe the basics that you must know to get Tomcat up and running. If you plan to use Tomcat extensively for development or as a production server, refer to *Tomcat: The Definitive Guide* by Jason Brittain and Ian Darwin (O'Reilly).

You can download the Tomcat server in binary format or as source code that you compile yourself. If you're primarily interested in learning about JSP, I recommend that you use the binary download for running the examples in this book and to develop your own applications. If you're a Java programmer and are interested in seeing how Tomcat is implemented, feel free to download the source as well and take a look at the internals.

The binary distribution is available at *http://jakarta.apache.org/site/binindex.cgi*.

On this page you find three types of builds: release builds, milestone builds, and nightly builds. *Release builds* are stable releases that have been tested extensively and verified to comply with the servlet and JSP specifications. *Milestone builds* are created as intermediary steps towards a release build. They often contain new features that aren't yet fully tested but are generally known to work. A *nightly build*, however, may be very unstable. It's actually a snapshot of the latest source code and may have been tested only by the person who made the latest change. You should use a nightly build only if you're involved in the development of Tomcat.

I recommend that you download the latest release build. All examples in this book were developed and tested using the 5.0.12 version, but any release later than 5.0.12 should work fine as well. When you click on the link for the latest release build and select the *bin* directory, you see a list of archive files in different formats, similar to Figure 4-1.

How to continue from here varies a bit depending on your platform.

Windows Platforms

For Windows, select *jakarta-tomcat-5.0.12.zip*[*] and save it to your hard drive, for instance in a directory named *C:\Jakarta*. You can unpack the package either with a ZIP utility program, such as *WinZip*, or by using the *jar* command that's included in the Java distribution. Use the Command Prompt window where you set the JAVA_HOME and PATH environment variables earlier, change to the directory in which you downloaded the ZIP file, and unpack it:

```
C:\> cd Jakarta
C:\Jakarta> jar xvf jakarta-tomcat-5.0.12.zip
```

This creates a directory structure with a top directory named *jakarta-tomcat-5.0.12* with a number of subdirectories. Like most software packages, the top directory contains a file named *README.txt*; do exactly that. Software distributions change and if, for instance, the instructions in this chapter no longer apply when you download the software, the *README.txt* file should contain information about how to get started. Additional details are found in the file named *RUNNING.txt*.

You should also set the `CATALINA_HOME` environment variable to point to the Tomcat installation directory:

```
C:\Jakarta> set CATALINA_HOME=C:\Jakarta\jakarta-tomcat-5.0.12
```

[*] There's also a file with an *.exe* extension in the list of downloads. This is a GUI installer for Windows. While it simplifies the installation, it makes it almost impossible to debug installation problems, and it doesn't work at all for older versions of Windows, e.g., Windows ME. I suggest that you use the command-line installation process described in this chapter, at least until you're familiar enough with Tomcat to handle the GUI installer issues.

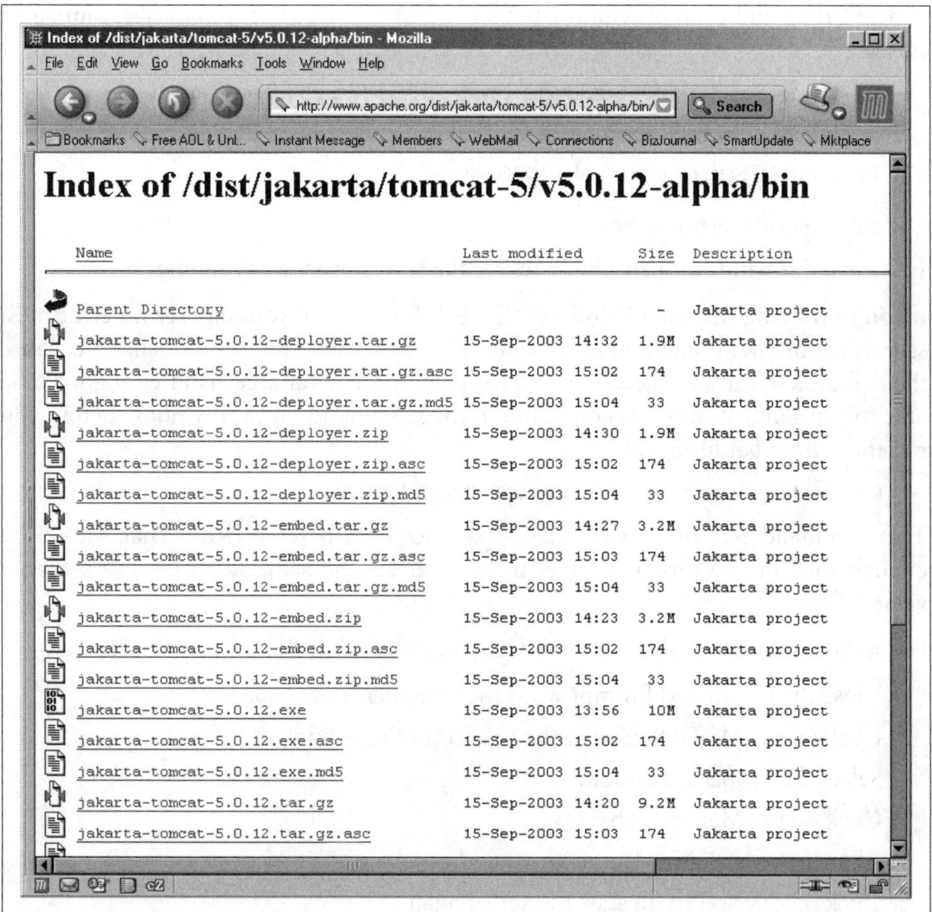

Figure 4-1. Release build packages

If you wonder about the variable name, Catalina is the name of the servlet container, and Jasper is the name of the JSP container; together they are known as the Tomcat server.

The Tomcat installation directory contains a number of subdirectories, described later. The *bin* directory contains Windows batch files for starting and stopping the server. The batch files are named *startup.bat*, *shutdown.bat*, and *catalina.bat*. The *catalina.bat* file is the main script for controlling the server; it's called by the two other scripts: *startup.bat* and *shutdown.bat*. To start the server in a separate window, change to the *bin* directory and run the *startup.bat* file:

```
C:\Jakarta> cd jakarta-tomcat-5.0.12\bin
C:\Jakarta\jakarta-tomcat-5.0.12\bin> startup
```

A new Command Prompt window pops up, and you see startup messages similar to this:

```
Aug 13, 2003 12:53:59 PM org.apache.coyote.http11.Http11Protocol init
INFO: Initializing Coyote HTTP/1.1 on port 8080
Aug 13, 2003 12:53:59 PM org.apache.catalina.startup.Catalina load
INFO: Initialization processed in 2260 ms
...
INFO: Server startup in 7408 ms
```

Just leave this window open; this is where the server process is running.

If you're running this on a Windows 95/98/ME platform, you may see an error message "Out of environment space," when you try to start the server. That's because the default amount of space allocated for environment variables isn't enough. To be able to run Tomcat, run this command in the Command Prompt window before you run the *startup.bat* file again:

```
C:\Jakarta\jakarta-tomcat\bin> COMMAND.COM /E:4096 /P
```

This command sets the environment space to 4096 bytes (4 KB). That should be enough for running this batch file. If you still get the same message, use a higher value.

For some installations, this command may not work. If it doesn't, try this instead:

1. Close the Command Prompt window, and open a new one.
2. Click on the MS-DOS icon at the top left of the window.
3. Select the Properties option.
4. Click on the Memory tab.
5. Change the Initial Environment value from Auto to 4096.
6. Click on OK and try to start the server again.

At this point, the server may not start due to other problems. If so, the extra Command Prompt window may pop up and then disappear before you have a chance to read the error messages. If this happens, you can let the server run in the Command Prompt window with this command instead:

```
C:\Jakarta\jakarta-tomcat-5.0.12\bin> catalina run
```

On Windows NT/2000 and Windows XP, you should first make sure that the Command Prompt window has a large enough screen buffer so that you can scroll back in case the error messages don't fit on one screen. Open the Properties window for the Command Prompt window (right mouse button in the upper left corner), select **Layout** and set the screen buffer size height to a large value (for instance 999). Unfortunately, the Command Prompt screen buffer can't be enlarged for Windows 95/98/ME, so scrolling back isn't an option. If you run into problems on these platforms, double-check that you have installed the Java SDK correctly and that you have set the `JAVA_HOME` and `PATH` environment variables as described earlier.

Unix Platforms (Including Linux and Mac OS X)

For Unix platforms, you can download the *jakarta-tomcat-5.0.12.tar.gz* file, for instance to */usr/local*, and use these commands to unpack it (assuming you have GNU *tar* installed):

```
[hans@gefion /] cd /usr/local
[hans@gefion local] tar xzvf jakarta-tomcat-5.0.12.tar.gz
```

If you don't have GNU *tar* installed on your system, use the following command:

```
[hans@gefion local] gunzip -c jakarta-tomcat-5.0.12.tar.gz | tar xvf -
```

As on Windows, this creates a directory structure with a top directory named *jakarta-tomcat-5.0.12* with a number of subdirectories.

You should also set the `CATALINA_HOME` environment variable to point to the Tomcat installation directory:

```
[hans@gefion local] export CATALINA_HOME=/usr/local/jakarta-tomcat-5.0.12
```

If you wonder about the variable name, Catalina is the name of the servlet container and Jasper is the name of the JSP container; together they are known as the Tomcat server.

The Tomcat installation directory contains a number of subdirectories, described later. The *bin* directory contains Unix scripts for starting and stopping the server. The scripts area named *startup.sh*, *shutdown.sh*, and *catalina.sh*.

Start the server in the background with this command:

```
[hans@gefion jakarta-tomcat-5.0.12] ./startup.sh
```

If you want to have Tomcat start each time you boot the system, you can add the following commands to your */etc/rc.d/rc.local* (or equivalent) startup script:

```
export JAVA_HOME=/usr/local/jdk1.4.2
export CATALINA_HOME=/usr/local/jakarta-tomcat-5.0.12
$CATALINA_HOME/bin/startup.sh
```

Testing Tomcat

The Tomcat installation directory contains a number of subdirectories. All of them are described in the *README.txt* file, but the most important ones are:

bin
: Scripts for starting and stopping the Tomcat server.

conf
: Tomcat configuration files.

webapps
: Default location for web applications served by Tomcat.

Two more subdirectories under the Tomcat home directory are created the first time you start the server:

logs
: Server log files. If something doesn't work as expected, look in the files in this directory for clues as to what's wrong.

work
: A directory for temporary files created by the JSP container and other files. This directory is where the servlets generated from JSP pages are stored.

To test the server, run the startup script as described in the platform-specific sections, and (assuming you're running Tomcat on the same machine as the browser and that you're using the default 8080 port for Tomcat) open a browser and enter this URL in the Location/Address field: *http://localhost:8080/*.

The Tomcat main page is shown in the browser, as in Figure 4-2, and you can now run all servlet and JSP examples bundled with Tomcat to ensure everything works.

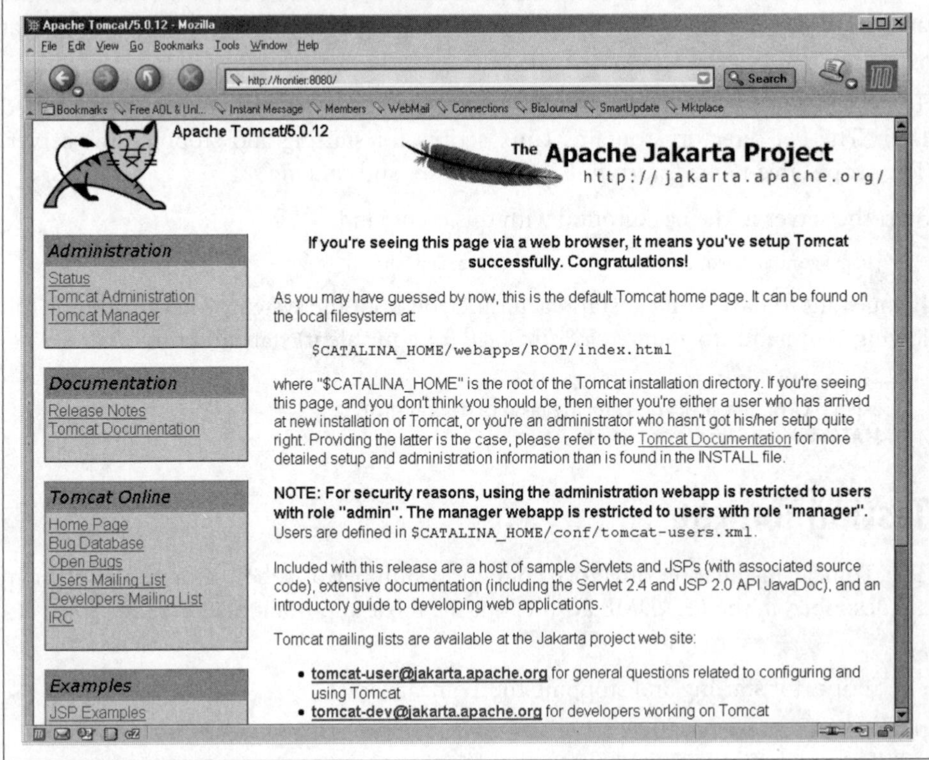

Figure 4-2. The Tomcat main page

If you're trying this on a machine that sits behind a proxy, for instance on a corporate network, and instead of Tomcat's main page you see an error message about not being able to connect to `localhost`, you need to adjust your proxy settings. For Netscape 6 and Mozilla, you find the proxy settings under Edit → Preferences → Advanced → Proxies, and for Internet Explorer 5, you find them under Tools → Internet Options → Connections → LAN Settings. Make sure that the proxy isn't used for local addresses, such as `localhost` and 127.0.0.1.

When you're done testing Tomcat, you stop the server like this:

```
C:\Jakarta\jakarta-tomcat-5.0.12\bin> shutdown
```

Installing the Book Examples

All JSP pages, HTML pages, Java source code, and class files for the examples can be downloaded from the O'Reilly site *http://www.oreilly.com/catalog/jserverpages3/*.

They can also be downloaded from the book web site that I maintain: *http://www.TheJSPBook.com/*.

On this site you find a Download page where you can download the file, called *jspbook3.zip*. Save the file on your hard drive, for instance in *C:\JSPBook* on a Windows platform, and unpack it:

```
C:\JSPBook> jar xvf jspbook3.zip
```

You can use the same command on a Unix platform.

Two new directories are created: *ora* and *src*. The first directory contains all examples described in this book, and the second contains the Java source files for the JavaBeans, custom actions, servlets, and utility classes used in the examples.

The examples directory structure complies with the standard Java web application format described in Chapter 2. You can therefore configure any JSP 2.0-compliant web container to run the examples.

If you like to use a container other than Tomcat, be sure to read the documentation for that container for instructions on how to install a web application.

To install the example application for Tomcat, simply copy the web application directory structure (the *ora* directory) to Tomcat's default directory for applications, called *webapps*. On a Windows platform, you can copy/paste the directory structure with the Windows Explorer tool, or use this command in a Command Prompt window:

```
C:\JSPBook> xcopy /s /i ora %CATALINA_HOME%\webapps\ora
```

On a Unix platform it looks like this:

```
[hans@gefion jspbook] cp -R ora $CATALINA_HOME/webapps
```

Recall from Chapter 2 that each web application in a server is associated with a unique URI prefix (the context path). When you install an application in Tomcat's *webapps* directory, the subdirectory name is assigned automatically as the URI prefix for the application (that is, */ora* in this case).

At this point, you must shut down and restart the Tomcat server. After that, you can point your browser to the *ora* application with the following URL: *http://localhost:8080/ora/*.

You should see a start page, as in Figure 4-3, that contains links for all examples in this book.

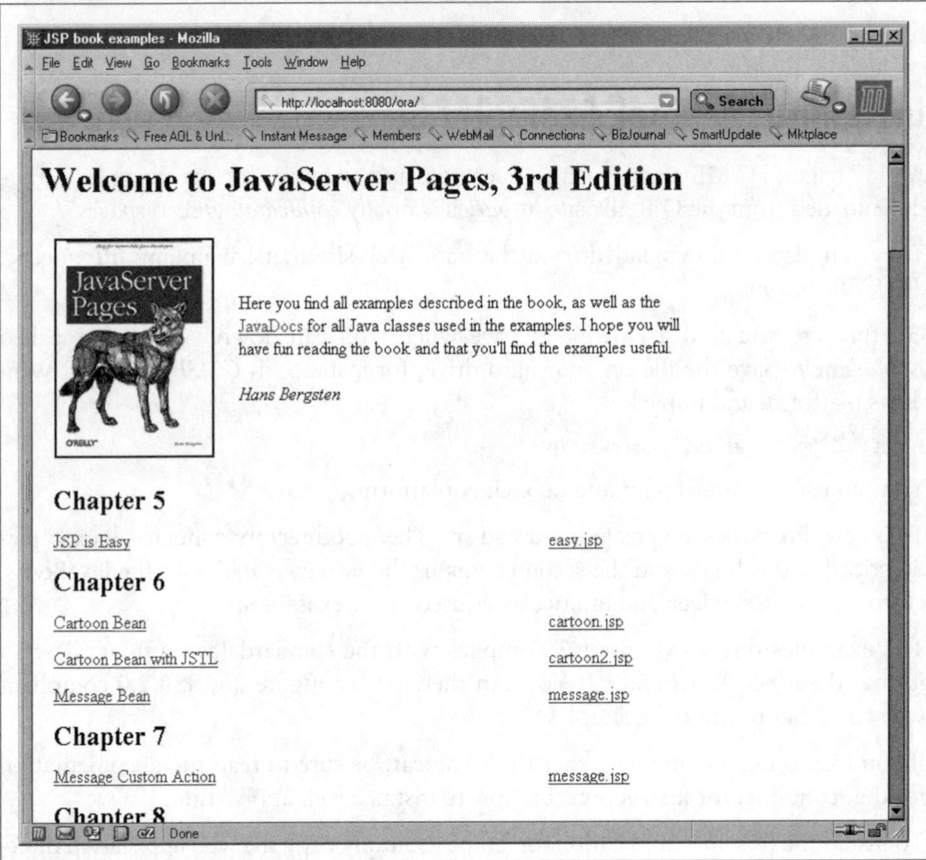

Figure 4-3. JSP book examples start page

Example Web Application Overview

The examples for this book are packaged as a standard Java web application, as described in Chapter 2. All servers compliant with the JSP 2.0 specification support this file structure, so you can use the example application as a guideline when you create your own web applications. How a web application is installed isn't defined by the specification, however, so it varies between servers. With Tomcat, you simply copy the file structure to the special *webapps* directory and restart the server. To modify the configuration information for an application, you need to edit the application's *WEB-INF/web.xml* file using a text editor. Other servers may offer special deployment tools that copy the files where they belong and let you configure the application using a special tool or through web-based forms.

If you look in the *ora* web application directory, you see that it contains an *index.html* file and a number of directories corresponding to chapters in this book. These directories contain all the example JSP and HTML pages.

There's also a *WEB-INF* directory with a *web.xml* file, a *lib* directory, and a *classes* directory. We will look at this in much more detail later, starting in Chapter 5, but here's a quick review:

- The *web.xml* file contains configuration information for the example application in the format defined by the servlet and JSP specifications. It's too early to look at the contents of this file now; we will return to parts of it when needed.
- The *lib* and *classes* directories are standard directories, also defined by the servlet specification. A very common question asked by people new to servlets and JSP (prior to the standard web application format) was, "Where do I store my class files so that the server can find them?" The answer, unfortunately, differed depending on which implementation was used. With the standard web application format, it's easy to answer this question: if the classes are packaged in a JAR file, store the JAR file in the *lib* directory; otherwise use the *classes* directory (with subdirectories mirroring the classes' package structure). The server will always look for Java class files in these two directories.

  The *lib* directory for the example application contains a number of JAR files. The *orataglib_3_0.jar* file contains all the Java class files for the custom actions used in this book, *oraclasses_3_0.jar* contains the class files for beans and servlets used in the examples, *struts.jar* contains the Struts framework classes described in Chapter 19, and *jdom.jar* contains JDOM classes used for a validator example in Chapter 22. The other JAR files contain the JSTL Reference Implementation plus all the packages that the JSTL implementation depends on.

  The *classes* directory contains the class for the JSPSourceServlet that displays the raw source code for the example JSP pages, so you can see what they look like before they are processed by the server. It also contains all *.properties* files with localized text for the example in Chapter 14 and a few test servlets described in Chapter 19.

If you want to try some of your own JSP pages, beans, and custom actions while reading this book, simply add the files to the example application structure: JSP pages in any directory except under *WEB-INF*, and Java class files in either the *classes* or the *lib* directory depending on if the classes are packaged in a JAR file or not. If you want to use the book's custom actions in another application, copy the *orataglib_3_0.jar* file to the *WEB-INF/lib* directory for the other application.

PART II

JSP Application Development

The focus of this part of the book is on developing JSP-based web applications using both standard JSP elements and custom components. Through the use of practical examples, you will learn how to handle common tasks such as validating user input, accessing databases, authenticating users and protecting web pages, localizing your web site, and more:

CHAPTER 5

Generating Dynamic Content

JSP is all about generating dynamic content: content that differs based on user input, time of day, the state of an external system, or any other runtime conditions. JSP provides you with lots of tools for generating this content. In this book, you will learn about them all—standard actions, custom actions, the JSP Standard Tag Library, JavaBeans, the Expression Language and scripting elements. Before going into all of that, however, let's start with a simple example to get a better feel for how the basic JSP elements work.

Creating a JSP Page

Recall from Chapter 3 that a JSP page is just a regular HTML page with a few special elements. A JSP page should have the file extension *.jsp*, which tells the server that the page needs to be processed by the JSP container. Without this clue, the server is unable to distinguish a JSP page from any other type of file and sends it unprocessed to the browser.

When working with JSP pages, you just need a regular text editor such as Notepad on Windows or Emacs on Unix. There are a number of tools that may make it easier for you, such as syntax-aware editors that color-code JSP and HTML elements. Some Interactive Development Environments (IDE) even include a small web container that allows you to easily execute and debug the pages during development. There are also several webpage authoring tools—the type of tools often used when developing regular HTML pages—that support JSP to some degree. You can browse through a fairly extensive list of tools like this at my web site: *http://www.TheJSPBook.com/*. I recommend that you do *not* use them initially, though; it's easier to learn how JSP works if you see the raw page elements before you use tools that hide them.

The first example JSP page, named *easy.jsp*, is shown in Example 5-1.

Example 5-1. JSP page showing a dynamically calculated sum (easy.jsp)

```
<%@ page contentType="text/html" %>
<%@ taglib prefix="c" uri="http://java.sun.com/jsp/jstl/core" %>
<html>
  <head>
    <title>JSP is Easy</title>
  </head>
  <body bgcolor="white">

    <h1>JSP is as easy as ...</h1>

    <%-- Calculate the sum of 1 + 2 + 3 dynamically --%>
    1 + 2 + 3 = <c:out value="${1 + 2 + 3}" />

  </body>
</html>
```

The *easy.jsp* page displays static HTML plus the sum of 1, 2, and 3, calculated at runtime and dynamically added to the response. We'll look at all the different pieces soon, but first you may want to run the example to see how it works.

Installing a JSP Page

A complete web application may consist of several different resources: JSP pages, servlets, applets, static HTML pages, custom tag libraries, and other Java class files. Until very recently, an application with all these components had to be installed and configured in different ways for different servers, making it hard for web application developers to provide easy-to-use installation instructions and tools.

Starting with the Servlet 2.2 specification, there's a standard, portable way to package all web application resources, along with a deployment descriptor. The *deployment descriptor* is a file named *web.xml*, containing information about security requirements, how all the resources fit together, and other facts about the application. The deployment descriptor and all the other web application files are placed in a Web Application Archive (WAR) file, arranged in a well-defined hierarchy. A WAR file has a *.war* file extension and can be created with the Java *jar* command or a ZIP utility program, such as *WinZip* (the same file format is used for both JAR and ZIP files).

Having a standardized web application format lets container vendors develop installation and configuration tools that make it easy to install an application. During installation, the container is free to unpack the contents of the WAR file and store it for runtime use in any way it sees fit, but the application developer needs to deal with only one delivery format.

Even though a container is required to know how to deal only with applications packaged as a WAR file, most (if not all) containers also let you store your application files directly in a filesystem using the same file structure as is defined for the

WAR file. During development, it's more convenient to work with the files in a regular filesystem structure instead of creating an updated WAR file every time you make a change. In Tomcat, for instance, any subdirectory under the *webapps* directory is assumed to be a web application, using the standard web application file structure.

The structure required for both the WAR file and the filesystem is outlined here, using some of the files in the example application for this book:

```
/index.html
/cover.gif
/ch5/easy.jsp
/WEB-INF/web.xml
/WEB-INF/classes/JSPSourceServlet.class
/WEB-INF/lib/orataglib_3_0.jar
...
```

The top level in this structure is the document root for all public web application files, such as HTML pages, JSP pages, and image files—in other words, all the files requested directly by the browser. For instance, the *easy.jsp* file used in this chapter is stored in a subdirectory off the top level called *ch5*. If the application is installed with the context path *ora* (more about this later), you use a URL such as *http://localhost:8080/ora/ch5/easy.jsp* to access the JSP page.

You're probably wondering about the *WEB-INF* directory. This directory contains the application deployment descriptor (*web.xml*), as well as subdirectories for other types of resources, such as Java class files and configuration files. A browser doesn't have access to the files under this directory, so it's a safe place for files you don't want public.

The deployment descriptor file, *web.xml*, is an XML file with configuration information for the application. You will get much more familiar with the contents of this file as you proceed through the book. (Appendix F also contains a complete reference of this file.) In addition, two *WEB-INF* subdirectories have special meaning: *lib* and *classes*. All application class files (such as servlet and custom tag library classes) must be stored in these two directories. The *lib* directory is for Java archive (JAR) files (compressed archives of Java class files). Class files that aren't packaged in JAR files must be stored in the *classes* directory, which can be convenient during development. The files must be stored in subdirectories of the *classes* directory that mirror their package structure, in accordance with the standard Java conventions. For instance, a class in a package named `com.ora.jsp` must be stored in the *WEB-INF/classes/com/ora/jsp* directory.

As with pretty much everything related to JSP, directory and filenames in the web application structure are case-sensitive. If something doesn't work right, the first thing to check is that the *WEB-INF* directory is created with all caps and the case used for a JSP page in the URL matches exactly the case used in the filename. On a Windows platform, you may want to use a Command Prompt window and the *DIR* command to check this, since the Windows Explorer tool adjusts the names and sometimes shows a directory name like *WEB-INF* as *Web-inf*.

Running a JSP Page

Assuming you have installed all book examples as described in Chapter 4, first start the Tomcat server and load the book examples main page by typing the URL *http://localhost:8080/ora/index.html* in the browser address field. Note how the */ora* part of the URL matches the Tomcat *webapps* subdirectory name for the example application. This part of the URL is called the application's *context path*; every web application has a unique context path, assigned one way or another when you install the application. Tomcat uses the subdirectory name as the context path by default, but other containers may prompt you for a path in an installation tool or use other conventions. When you make a request for a web application resource (an HTML or JSP page, or a servlet), the first part of the URL (after the hostname and port number) must be the context path, so the container knows which application should handle the request.

There's one exception to this rule; one application per container may be installed as the default, or root, application. For Tomcat, this application is stored in the *webapps/ROOT* directory, by default. Requests for resources in the default application don't start with a context path (or more accurately, have an empty string as their context path). For instance, the *http://localhost:8080/index.html* URL is used to request a page in the default application.

You can run Example 5-1 by clicking the "JSP is Easy" link from the book examples main page, shown in Figure 5-1. You should see a result like the one shown in Figure 5-2.

The page shown in Example 5-1 contains both regular HTML elements and JSP elements. If you use the View Source function in your browser, you notice that none of the JSP elements are visible in the page source. That's because the server processes the JSP elements when the page is requested, and only the resulting output is sent to the browser. The HTML elements, on the other hand, are sent to the browser as is, defining the layout of the page. To see the unprocessed JSP page in a separate window, you can click on the source link for the *easy.jsp* file in the book example's main page. The source link uses a special servlet to send the unprocessed JSP page directly to the browser instead of letting the server process it. This makes it easier for you to compare the source page and the processed result.

Using JSP Directive Elements

Let's look at each piece of Example 5-1 in detail. The first two lines are JSP *directive elements*. Directive elements specify attributes of the page itself, such as the type of content produced by the page, page-buffering requirements, declaration of other resources used by the page, and how possible runtime errors should be handled. Hence, a directive doesn't directly affect the content of the response sent to the

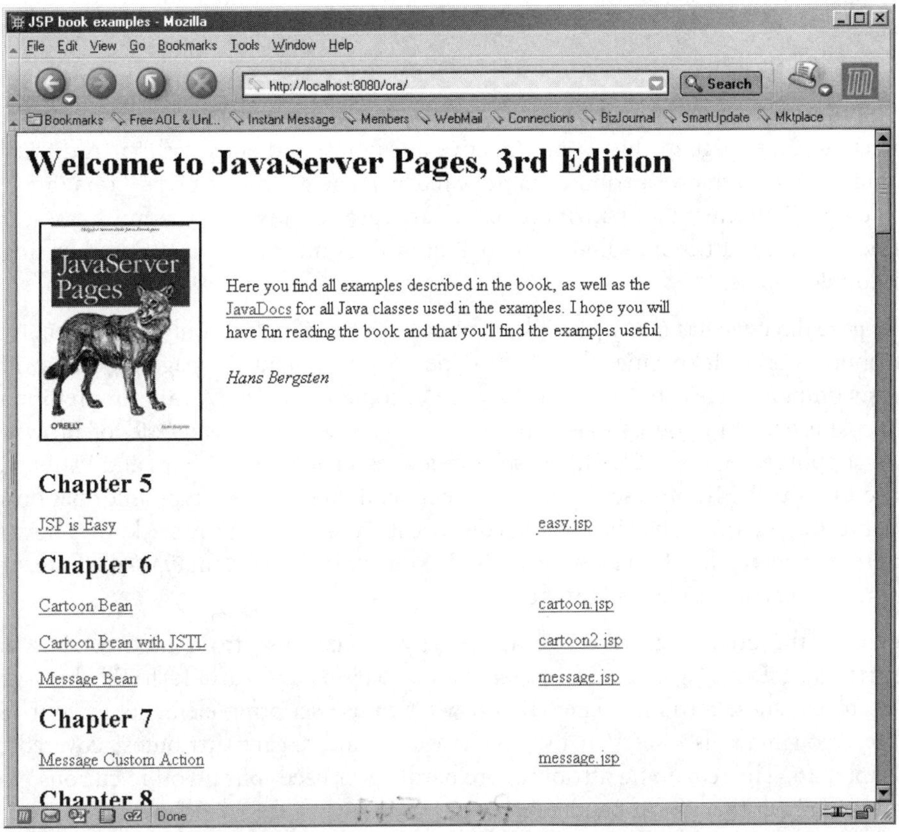

Figure 5-1. JSP book examples main page

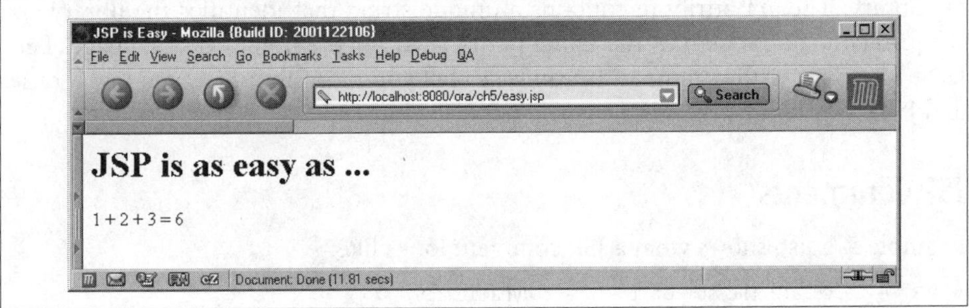

Figure 5-2. The "JSP is Easy" example output

browser, but it tells the container how it should handle the page. There are three different directives that you can use in a JSP page: `page`, `include`, and `taglib`. In this chapter, we're using the `page` and the `taglib` directives. The `include` directive is described in Chapter 17.

JSP pages typically starts with a page directive that specifies the content type for the page:

```
<%@ page contentType="text/html" %>
```

A JSP directive element starts with a directive-start identifier (`<%@`), followed by the directive name (`page` in this case), directive attributes, and ends with `%>`. A directive contains one or more attribute name/value pairs (e.g., `contentType="text/html"`). Note that JSP element and attribute names are case-sensitive, and in most cases, the same is true for attribute values. All attribute values must also be enclosed in single or double quotes.

The `page` directive has many possible attributes. In Example 5-1, only the `contentType` attribute is used. It specifies the MIME-type for the content the page produces. The most common values are `text/html` for HTML content and `text/plain` for preformatted, plain text. But you can also specify other types, such as `text/xml` for browsers that support XML or `text/vnd.wap.wml` for devices such as cell phones and PDAs that have built-in WML browsers. The container sends the content type information to the browser as a response header called `Content-Type`, so the browser knows how to interpret and render the response body. If you omit the `contentType` attribute, the container sets the header to `text/html`.

Some of the other `page` directive attributes you may use from time to time are `errorPage`, `isErrorPage`, `session`, `pageEncoding`, `buffer`, and `autoFlush`. I'll show you how to use these attributes later. If you want to use scripting elements in your JSP pages, you may also need to use the `language` and `import` attributes, covered in Chapter 16. The remaining attributes are hardly ever used, but if you're curious, you can read about them in Appendix A.

The second directive in Example 5-1 is a `taglib` directive. It declares a custom tag library that is used in the page. In Example 5-1, the `taglib` directive declares a JSTL tag library. The `uri` attribute contains a unique string that identifies the library and the `prefix` attribute defines the name prefix used for the library on this page. Let's leave it at that for the moment; I promise to tell you more about custom tag libraries and JSTL later in this chapter.

JSP Comments

Example 5-1 also shows what a JSP comment looks like:

```
<%-- Calculate the sum of 1 + 2 + 3 dynamically --%>
```

Everything between `<%--` and `--%>` is ignored when the JSP page is processed. You can use this type of comment to describe what's going on in the page or to temporarily comment out pieces of the page to test different alternatives. Since a JSP comment is a JSP element, it's never sent to the browser.

Using Template Text

Besides JSP elements, notice that the *easy.jsp* page contains mostly regular HTML, highlighted in Example 5-2.

Example 5-2. JSP page template text

```
<%@ page contentType="text/html" %>
<%@ taglib prefix="c" uri="http://java.sun.com/jsp/jstl/core" %>
<html>
  <head>
    <title>JSP is Easy</title>
  </head>
  <body bgcolor="white">
    <h1>JSP is as easy as ...</h1>
    <%-- Calculate the sum of 1 + 2 + 3 dynamically --%>
    1 + 2 + 3 = <c:out value="${1 + 2 + 3}" />
  </body>
</html>
```

In JSP parlance, this is called *template text*. Everything that's not a JSP element (i.e., not a directive, action or scripting element) is template text. Template text is sent to the browser as is. This means you can use JSP to generate any type of text-based output, such as XML, WML, or even plain text. The JSP container doesn't care what the template text represents.

Using JSP Action Elements

Besides the fixed template text, the *easy.jsp* page also produces dynamic content. It has very simple dynamic content—the sum of 1, 2 and 3 calculated at runtime—but step back a moment and think about the type of dynamic content you see on the Web every day. Common examples might be a list of web sites matching a search criterion on a search engine site, the content of a shopping cart on an e-commerce site, a personalized news page, or messages in a bulletin board. The actual data for the dynamic content can come from many types of sources, for instance from a database, an XML document, or data accumulated in memory based on previous requests. The dynamic data needs to be combined with regular HTML elements into a page with the right layout, navigation bars, the company logo, and so forth, before it's sent to the browser. When using JSP, the regular HTML is the template text described earlier, and the dynamic data is inserted at the appropriate place in the template text using a JSP action element.

A JSP action is executed when a JSP page is requested (this is called the request processing phase, as you may recall from Chapter 3). In other words, JSP *action elements* represent dynamic actions that take place at runtime, as opposed to JSP directives that are used only during the translation phase (when the JSP page is turned into Java servlet code). An action can add text to the response, as in the example used in this chapter, but it can also do other things such as write to a file on the server, send an email, or retrieve data from a database that is later added to the response by other actions. Example 5-3 shows the *easy.jsp* page again, this time with the JSP action element highlighted.

Example 5-3. JSP action elements

```
<%@ page contentType="text/html" %>
<%@ taglib prefix="c" uri="http://java.sun.com/jsp/jstl/core" %>
<html>
  <head>
    <title>JSP is Easy</title>
  </head>
  <body bgcolor="white">

    <h1>JSP is as easy as ...</h1>

    <%-- Calculate the sum of 1 + 2 + 3 dynamically --%>
    1 + 2 + 3 = <c:out value="${1 + 2 + 3}" />

  </body>
</html>
```

An action is represented by an HTML-like element in a JSP page. If the action element has a body, it's represented by an opening tag, possibly with attribute/value pairs, a body, and a closing tag:

```
<prefix:action_name attr1="value1" attr2="value2">
  action_body
</prefix:action_name>
```

This is identical to the HTML element syntax and as with HTML elements, the body of an action element can contain text or other action elements.

If the element doesn't have a body, as in Example 5-3, you can use this shorthand syntax instead:

```
<prefix:action_name attr1="value1" attr2="value2" />
```

Note that the single tag for an element without a body (an empty element) ends with `/>` as opposed to just `>`. If you think this looks like XML syntax, you're absolutely right. The shorthand is equivalent to an opening tag, empty body, and closing tag:

```
<prefix:action_name attr1="value1" attr2="value2"></prefix:action_name>
```

Action elements, or tags as they are often called, are grouped into libraries (known as *tag libraries*). The element name, used in the opening and closing tags, is composed of two parts: a prefix and the action's name, separated by a colon, with no space characters between any parts. Again, if you're familiar with XML syntax, you may recognize that the prefix is used as an XML namespace. You define the namespace prefix you want to use for the library with the `taglib` directive described earlier:

```
<%@ taglib prefix="c" uri="http://java.sun.com/jsp/jstl/core" %>
  ...
  <c:out value="${1 + 2 + 3}" />
```

The prefix serves two purposes: it makes it possible for actions in different libraries to have the same name, and it makes it possible for the container to figure out to which library a specific action belongs. When the container finds an action element, it locates the `taglib` directive that declares the library that corresponds to the action name prefix. The `taglib` directive's `uri` attribute is a unique identifier for the tag library, which the container uses to find the information it needs to process the action.

Actions can be grouped into three categories: standard, custom, and JSP Standard Tag Library.

Standard actions are the actions defined by the JSP specification itself. Table 5-1 lists all standard actions that you can use in a regular JSP page. The JSP standard actions use the prefix `jsp`. Since the prefix is fixed, and the behavior for all standard actions is defined by the specification, you don't declare the standard actions with a `taglib` directive.

Table 5-1. Standard action elements

Action element	Description
`<jsp:useBean>`	Makes a JavaBeans component available in a page
`<jsp:getProperty>`	Gets a property value from a JavaBeans component and adds it to the response
`<jsp:setProperty>`	Set a JavaBeans property value
`<jsp:include>`	Includes the response from a servlet or JSP page during the request processing phase
`<jsp:forward>`	Forwards the processing of a request to a servlet or JSP page
`<jsp:param>`	Adds a parameter value to a request handed off to another servlet or JSP page using `<jsp:include>` or `<jsp:forward>`
`<jsp:plugin>`	Generates HTML that contains the appropriate browser-dependent elements (`OBJECT` or `EMBED`) needed to execute an applet with the Java Plugin software
`<jsp:attribute>`	Sets the value of an action attribute based on the body of this element
`<jsp:body>`	Sets the action element body based on the body of this element. Required when the action element body contains `<jsp:attribute>` action elements
`<jsp:element>`	Dynamically generates an XML element, optionally with attributes and a body defined by nested `<jsp:attribute>` and `<jsp:body>` actions
`<jsp:text>`	Used to encapsulate template text that should be used verbatim; typically only needed in JSP pages written as XML documents

The JSP specification also defines how to develop new actions that can be used in any JSP page. Such actions are called *custom actions*. We'll take a closer look at custom actions in Chapter 7.

JSP Standard Tag Library

The third group is called *JSP Standard Tag Library* (JSTL) actions. Until very recently, programmers had to develop custom actions even for very generic tasks, such as selecting different parts of a page based on a runtime condition or looping through a collection of data; none of the JSP standard actions support these common tasks. The result was, of course, that every Java programmer with some self-respect implemented a set of custom actions for all the generic tasks her JSP team needed. To reduce this programming effort, and avoid the confusion caused by a zillion different implementations of if and loop actions with slightly different features, a group of experienced tag library developers (including yours truly) came together through the Java Community Process to define what's called the JSP Standard Tag Library. Version 1.0 was released in June 2002 and Version 1.1, aligning JSTL with JSP 2.0, was released a year later. While the name of the standard contains the word "library" (singular), it's in fact a set of libraries that group related actions:

Core
: Conditional processing and looping, importing data from external sources, etc.

XML processing
: Processing of XML data, such as transforming and accessing individual elements

Internationalization (I18N) and formatting
: Format and parse localized information, insert localized information in a page

Relational database access (SQL)
: Read and write relational database data

Functions
: A set of generic Expression Language functions

The `<c:out>` action in Example 5-3 is part of the JSTL core library. It adds the result of the expression (written in the Expression Language described in the next section) specified as the `value` attribute to the response. In this case, the evaluation of the expression is the sum of 1, 2, and 3, as shown in Figure 5-2.

The JSP Expression Language

JSTL 1.0 introduced a simple Expression Language (EL) for setting action attribute values based on runtime data from various sources. The specification of this language was later incorporated into the JSP 2.0 specification, so it no longer is just for the JSTL libraries; now it can be used in a portable manner for any tag library, as well as in other contexts than action attributes.

The EL is inspired by JavaScript (or ECMAScript, as it's formally called) and, to some extent, XPath (a language used to access pieces of an XML document), but it is much more forgiving when a variable doesn't contain a value (`null`) and performs more data-type conversions automatically. These features are important for a web application, because the input is mostly in the form of request parameters, which are always text values but often need to be used as numbers or Boolean values (`true` or `false`) by the application. A web application must also handle the absence of a parameter gracefully, and the EL makes provisions for this as well. What you don't find in the EL are statements such as `if/else`, `for`, and `switch`; in JSP, the type of logic implemented by such statements in a general-purpose language are instead implemented as action elements.

To give you a feel for how the EL is used, let's look at the expression used for the JSTL `<c:out>` action in Example 5-1:

```
<c:out value="${1 + 2 + 3}" />
```

An EL expression always starts with the ${ delimiter (a dollar sign plus a left curly brace) and ends with } (a right curly brace). The expression can include literals (like the numeric literals used here), a set of implicit variables that provide access to request data, variables representing application data, and most operators that you're used to from other languages, such as the addition + sign used in this example.

EL expressions can be used to assign values to action attributes marked as accepting a dynamic value (or *request-time attribute value*, as it's formally called). Prior to the introduction of the EL, dynamic attribute values could only be assigned by Java expressions. This has been a common source of confusing syntax errors over the years, so the EL was designed with simple syntax and a forgiving nature to help page authors with this common task. Since the EL is now part of the JSP specification, EL expressions can also be used directly in the page. This snippet can replace the `<c:out>` action in Example 5-1, for instance:

```
1 + 2 + 3 = ${1 + 2 + 3}
```

However, I'll discuss why you may still want to use the `<c:out>` action in Chapter 8.

As in JavaScript, the EL supports literals numbers (e.g., 1 and 0.98), Booleans (`true` and `false`), strings (enclosed by double or single quotes), and the keyword `null` to represent the absence of a value.

You probably recognize the supported operators, shown in Table 5-2, since they are the same as those supported by most languages.

Table 5-2. Expression Language operators

Operator	Operation performed
`.`	Access a bean property or `Map` entry
`[]`	Access an array or `List` element
`()`	Group a subexpression to change the evaluation order
`? :`	Conditional test: *`condition ? ifTrue : ifFalse`*
`+`	Addition
`-`	Subtraction or negation of a value

Table 5-2. Expression Language operators (continued)

Operator	Operation performed
*	Multiplication
/ or div	Division
% or mod	Modulo (remainder)
== or eq	Test for equality
!= or ne	Test for inequality
< or lt	Test for less than
> or gt	Test for greater than
<= or le	Test for less than or equal
>= or ge	Test for greater than or equal
&& or and	Test for logical AND
|| or or	Test for logical OR
! or not	Unary Boolean complement
empty	Test for empty variable values (null, an empty String or an array, Map, or Collection without entries)
func(arg)	A function call, where *func* is the function name and *arg* is a function argument

An EL expression can also contain variables. Variables are named references to data (objects), created by the application or made available implicitly by the EL.

Application-specific variables can be created in many ways—for instance, using the <jsp:useBean> action that we'll use in Chapter 6. They can also be created by custom actions or be passed to the JSP page by a servlet. Every object that is available in one of the JSP scopes, discussed in Chapter 10, can be used as an EL variable.

A set of EL implicit variables, listed in Table 5-3, provides access to all information about a request as well as other generic information.

Table 5-3. Implicit EL variables

Variable name	Description
pageScope	A collection (a java.util.Map) of all page scope variables
requestScope	A collection (a java.util.Map) of all request scope variables
sessionScope	A collection (a java.util.Map) of all session scope variables
applicationScope	A collection (a java.util.Map) of all application scope variables
param	A collection (a java.util.Map) of all request parameter values as a single String value per parameter
paramValues	A collection (a java.util.Map) of all request parameter values as a String array per parameter
header	A collection (a java.util.Map) of all request header values as a single String value per header

Table 5-3. Implicit EL variables (continued)

Variable name	Description
headerValues	A collection (a java.util.Map) of all request header values as a String array per header
cookie	A collection (a java.util.Map) of all request cookie values as a single javax.servlet.http.Cookie value per cookie
initParam	A collection (a java.util.Map) of all application initialization parameter values as a single String value per value
pageContext	An instance of the javax.servlet.jsp.PageContext class, providing access to various request data

Don't worry about how the implicit variables are used right now; the following chapters provide examples that will make all the details clear to you. To give you a taste of how you can use these variables, here's a <c:out> action with an EL expression that uses the implicit param variable to read the value of a request parameter named userName:

```
<c:out value="${param.userName}" />
```

The property accessor operator (a dot) tells the EL to look for the named property (the parameter name in this case) in the specified bean or collection; param is a collection of all request parameters, as shown in Table 5-3. If the property name contains special characters, it has to be quoted, and the array accessor operator must be used instead:

```
<c:out value="${param['user-name']}" />
```

A variable is always of a specific Java data type, and the same is true for action attributes and bean properties. The EL operators also depend on type information. The EL takes care of type conversions in the expected way, however, so you rarely have to worry about it. For instance, if you add a number and a string, the EL tries to convert the string to a number and perform the addition.

The EL is used extensively in this book, illustrating all the different features through numerous examples. A more formal description of the language is also included in Appendix C.

By now should you have a rough idea of what JSP is all about. We have covered how to create and install a JSP page based on the standard web application file structure, and to request a JSP page from a browser. We have also looked at the primary parts of a JSP page—directives, template text, and action elements—and seen how they are processed when the page is requested. Finally, you've got a first glimpse of the JSTL and the JSP EL. In the following chapters, I'll go into detail, and introduce the other JSP and JSTL features you'll need to develop real web applications.

CHAPTER 6

Using JavaBeans Components in JSP Pages

The JavaBeans specification defines a set of programming conventions for Java classes that are used as pluggable components. In layman's terms, tools that have no inside information about a class can use it if it's developed according to these conventions. For instance, a generic GUI builder tool can support any widgets developed as JavaBeans components. A JavaBeans component, or just a *bean* for short, is often used in JSP as the container for the dynamic content to be displayed by a web page. It typically represents something specific, such as a person, a product, or a shopping order. When JSP is combined with servlets, the bean can be created and initialized with data by the servlet and passed to a JSP page that simply adds the bean's data to the response. But even in a pure JSP application, a bean is a useful tool, for instance for capturing and validating user input.

A programmer must develop the bean, but someone who doesn't have any programming experience can then use it in a JSP page. JSP defines a number of standard actions for working with beans, and the JSP Expression Language accepts beans as variables in expressions. In this chapter, we take a closer look at what a bean is and how it can produce dynamic content in a page. We'll return to beans in Chapter 8 to see how they can be used for input validation.

What Is a Bean?

As I said earlier, a bean is simply a Java class that follows certain coding conventions, so it can be used by tools as a component in a larger application. It can be instantiated and made available to the JSP page in a couple of ways. In an application that uses a servlet as a frontend for all business logic, the bean is typically created by the business logic code and sent to the JSP page to include its contents in the response. I describe this approach in detail in Chapter 19 and Chapter 20. The bean can also be created directly by a JSP page. This is the approach used in this chapter.

Data held by a bean is referred to as the bean's *properties*. The property name is case-sensitive and always starts with a lowercase letter. A property is either read-only,

JavaBeans Introduction for Java Programmers

If you need to develop your own beans, here's a brief description of what it takes to be a bean. (You can learn more about bean development for JSP pages in Chapter 20.) Beans are regular Java classes designed according to the set of guidelines defined by the JavaBeans specification. Here's the CartoonBean used in this chapter:

```
package com.ora.jsp.beans.motd;

import java.util.*;
public class CartoonBean implements java.io.Serializable {
    private static int index = -1;
    private List fileNames;

    public CartoonBean( ) {
        initFileList( );
    }

    public String getFileName( ) {
        index++;
        if (index > fileNames.size( ) - 1) {
            index = 0;
        }
        return (String) fileNames.get(index);
    }

    private void initFileList( ) {
        fileNames = new ArrayList( );
        fileNames.add("dilbert2001113293109.gif");
        ...
    }
}
```

You should always use a package name for a bean class to make it easier to use the bean in a JSP page in a portable way. I explain the details in Chapter 20.

A bean class must have a no-argument constructor. This allows a tool to create any bean in a generic fashion knowing just the class name.

The bean properties are accessed through *getter* and *setter* methods. Getter and setter method names are composed of the word *get* or *set*, respectively, plus the property name, with the first character of each word capitalized. Here, `getFileName( )` is the getter method for the property named `fileName`. A getter method has no arguments and returns a value of the property's type, while a setter method takes a single argument of the property's type and has a `void` return type. A readable property has a getter method; a writable property has a setter method. Depending on the combination of getter and setter methods, a property is read-only, write-only, or read/write.

Finally, the bean class should implement the `java.io.Serializable` or the `java.io.Externalizable` interface to allow a tool to save and restore the bean's state.

write-only, or read/write, and has a value corresponding to a specific Java data type (for instance `String`, `java.util.Date`, or `int`). Properties can be read and set through the bean's *accessor* methods, which are regular Java methods named according to the JavaBeans conventions. What you need to know to use a bean in a JSP page is its class name, the property names, the property data types, the property access types, and a description of the data represented by each property. You don't have to worry too much about the data type, since the JSP elements used to get and set properties typically handles the conversion between regular string values and the real Java type transparently. Table 6-1 shows all the required information for the first bean used in this chapter.

Table 6-1. Properties for com.ora.jsp.beans.motd.CartoonBean

Property name	Java type	Access	Description
`fileName`	`String`	Read	The current cartoon image filename

The nice thing about using a bean is that it can encapsulate all information about the item it represents in one simple package. Say you have a bean containing information about a person, such as the person's name, birth date, and email address. You can pass this bean to another component, providing all the information about the user in one shot. Now, if you want to add more information about the user, you just add properties to the bean. Another benefit of using a bean is that the bean can encapsulate all the rules about its properties. Thus, a bean representing a person can make sure the `birthDate` property is set to a valid date.

Declaring a Bean in a JSP Page

Example 6-1 shows a JSP page that uses the bean described in Table 6-1 to display a cartoon strip.

Example 6-1. A page using a bean (cartoon.jsp)

```
<html>
  <head>
    <title>A dose of Dilbert</title>
  </head>
  <body bgcolor="white">
    <h1>A dose of Dilbert</h1>

    <jsp:useBean id="cartoon"
      class="com.ora.jsp.beans.motd.CartoonBean" />
    <img src="images/<jsp:getProperty name="cartoon"
      property="fileName" />">

  </body>
</html>
```

Before you use a bean in a page, you must tell the JSP container the type of bean it is and associate it with a name; in other words, you must declare the bean. The first JSP action in Example 6-1, `<jsp:useBean>`, is used for this purpose:

```
<jsp:useBean id="cartoon" class="com.ora.jsp.beans.motd.CartoonBean" />
```

The `<jsp:useBean>` action is one of the JSP standard actions (identified by the `jsp` prefix). The action creates an instance of the bean class specified by the `class` attribute and associates it with the name specified by the `id` attribute. The name must be unique in the page and be a valid Java variable name; it must start with a letter and can't contain special characters such as dots, plus signs, etc.

Other attributes you can specify for the `<jsp:useBean>` action are `scope`, `type`, and `beanName`. Chapter 10 explores how the `scope` attribute is used. The others are rarely used, but Appendix A contains descriptions of how you can use them if you wish.

Reading Bean Properties

A bean's data is represented by its properties. The `CartoonBean` used in Example 6-1 has only one property, named `fileName`, but other beans may have many different properties. The `fileName` property's value is the name of an image file that contains a cartoon. There are two ways to insert a bean property value in a JSP page. Let's look at them one at a time.

Using the <jsp:getProperty> Action

Once you have created a bean and given it a name using the `<jsp:useBean>` action, you can get the bean's property values with another JSP standard action, named `<jsp:getProperty>`. This action obtains the current value of a bean property and inserts it directly into the response body.

To include the current `fileName` property value in the page, simply use this tag:

```
<jsp:getProperty name="cartoon" property="fileName" />
```

The `name` attribute, set to `cartoon`, refers to the specific bean instance declared by the `<jsp:useBean>` action. The `<jsp:getProperty>` action locates this bean and asks it for the value of the property specified by the `property` attribute. In Example 6-1, the property value is used as the `src` attribute value for an HTML `<img>` element. The result is the page shown in Figure 6-1. The way this bean is implemented, the `fileName` property value changes every time you access the property; when you reload the page, a different cartoon strip is shown.

One thing in Example 6-1 may look a bit strange: an element (`<jsp:getProperty>`) is used as the value of another element's attribute (the `<img>` tag's `src` attribute). While this isn't valid HTML syntax, it *is* valid JSP syntax. Remember that everything that's not recognized as a JSP element is treated as template text. The container doesn't

Figure 6-1. A JSP page with a dynamically inserted image file (Dilbert © UFS. Reprinted by Permission)

even try to interpret what the template text means, so it doesn't recognize it as invalid HTML. As far as the JSP container is concerned, the code in Example 6-1 is as valid as:

```
any old template text <jsp:getProperty name="cartoon"
                              property="fileName" /> more text
```

When the JSP page is processed, the action element is replaced with the value of the bean's property. The resulting HTML that's sent to the browser is therefore valid:

```
<img src="images/dilbert2731150011029.gif">
```

Note that this doesn't mean you can use an action element as the value of another JSP action element attribute. Using it to set an HTML element attribute works only because the HTML element isn't recognized as an element by the container. To set a JSP action attribute to the value produced by another action, you must use the `<jsp:attribute>` standard action instead:

```
<jsp:setProperty name="msg" property="category">
  <jsp:attribute name="value" trim="true">
    <jsp:getProperty name="myBean" property="myProperty" />
  </jsp:attribute>
</jsp:setProperty>
```

Here the `value` attribute of the `<jsp:setProperty>` action (which I'll discuss in a moment) is set using a `<jsp:getProperty>` action nested in a `<jsp:attribute>` action element. The `<jsp:attribute>` action can only be used in the body of a JSP element (not for template data elements). It evaluates its body and sets the attribute named by the mandatory `name` attribute of its parent action element to the output produced by the nested JSP elements. The `trim` attribute is optional, with `true` as the default. If it's set to `true`, leading and trailing whitespace in the body evaluation is removed. Otherwise the result is used as is. If you need to define a body for the action element, in addition to attribute values set with `<jsp:attribute>`, you must define the body with a `<jsp:body>` element. See Appendix A for details about this element.

Using the JSP Expression Language

The JSP Expression Language (EL) also supports access to bean properties. Example 6-2 shows how an EL expression can be used to the same effect as the `<jsp:getProperty>` action used in Example 6-1.

Example 6-2. Reading a bean property with the JSTL EL (cartoon2.jsp)

```
<html>
  <head>
    <title>A dose of Dilbert</title>
  </head>
  <body bgcolor="white">
    <h1>A dose of Dilbert</h1>

    <jsp:useBean id="cartoon"
      class="com.ora.jsp.beans.motd.CartoonBean" />

    <img src="images/${cartoon.fileName}">

  </body>
</html>
```

The bean created by the `<jsp:useBean>` action can be used as a variable in an EL expression. The EL interprets a name of a bean variable followed by a dot and a property name as a request to get the value of the property from the bean. Here the expression is used directly in the template text as part of the HTML `<img>` element's `src` attribute value, retrieving the `fileName` property value from the `carton` bean when the JSP page is requested. Example 6-2 shows this notation in its simplest form, but you can also access properties of properties by adding more elements to the expression:

```
${someBean.aProperty.aPropertyOfTheProperty}
```

In this case, the value of `aProperty` is a bean that has a property named `aPropertyOfTheProperty`. You can add as many property names as needed, without limit. Also note that you can use this bean property syntax for any JSP action attribute that permits EL expression values.

Whether to use `<jsp:getProperty>` or an EL expression to read a bean property value is largely a matter of preference. The `<jsp:getProperty>` action has always been part of the JSP specifications, so you will likely see it used a lot in existing applications. The ability to use an EL expression like this is new in JSP 2.0, and is less verbose and less confusing (no element has to be used as an attribute value). A third alternative that I'll discuss in Chapter 8 is the JSTL `<c:out>` action. For new applications, you may want to use an EL expression or the `<c:out>` action, but if you modify an existing application that must be JSP 1.1-compliant, you must stick to the established conventions and continue to use `<jsp:getProperty>`.

Including Images with JSP

Example 6-1 illustrates an important detail regarding JSP and images. A common question is "How do I use JSP to include a dynamic image in a page?" The short answer is: you don't.

First of all, a response can only contain one type of content* so you can't mix HTML and an image in the same response. You may recall from Chapter 2 that a browser handles an HTML response with `<img>` elements by sending a new request for each image and then merging the HTML and all images. So to include an image in a JSP-generated response, you do the same as you do in a regular HTML page; add an `<img>` element with the URI for the image. The only difference is that the URI may be decided at runtime, as in Examples 6-1 and 6-2.

Secondly, JSP is intended for text responses, not binary responses with image bytes. If you need to generate an image dynamically, you should use a servlet instead. In the JSP page, add the `<img>` element with a URI for the servlet and pass data it may need as request parameters in a query string:

```
<img src="imageGeneratorServlet?width=100&height=100">
```

Setting Bean Properties

If a bean property is writable (write-only or read/write access), there are two actions you can use to set the value: `<jsp:setProperty>` or `<c:set>`.

Using the <jsp:setProperty> Action

One way to set a bean property value is using the standard action: `<jsp:setProperty>`. Table 6-2 shows a bean that is similar to the `CartoonBean` used in the previous example, but it also has a writable property named `category`.

Table 6-2. Properties for com.ora.jsp.beans.motd.MixedMessageBean

Property name	Java type	Access	Description
`category`	`String`	Write	The message category, either `thoughts` or `quotes`
`message`	`String`	Read	The current message in the selected category

* This is true for the general case. An HTTP response can actually contain multiple parts of different types when special headers and delimiters are used, but generating such a response with JSP isn't recommended.

Instead of image files, the MixedMessageBean has a property that contains a funny message (funny to me at least—I hope you agree). The bean maintains messages of different types, and the write-only category property is used to select the type you want. Example 6-3 shows how you can use this feature.

Example 6-3. A page setting a bean property (message.jsp)

```
<html>
  <head>
    <title>Messages of the Day</title>
  </head>
  <body bgcolor="white">
    <h1>Messages of the Day</h1>

    <jsp:useBean id="msg"
      class="com.ora.jsp.beans.motd.MixedMessageBean" />

    <h2>Deep Thoughts - by Jack Handey</h2>

    <jsp:setProperty name="msg" property="category"
      value="thoughts" />

    <i>
      <jsp:getProperty name="msg" property="message" />
    </i>

    <h2>Quotes From the Famous and the Unknown</h2>

    <jsp:setProperty name="msg" property="category"
      value="quotes" />

    <i>
      <jsp:getProperty name="msg" property="message" />
    </i>

  </body>
</html>
```

As in the previous example, the <jsp:useBean> action creates an instance of the MixedMessageBean class. The <jsp:setProperty> action is then used to set the bean's category property value. Like the <jsp:getProperty> action, this action has a name attribute that must match the id attribute of a <jsp:useBean> action and a property attribute that specifies the property to set. The value attribute contains the value to use for the property.

In Example 6-3, the value property is first set to thoughts. This tells the bean to make its read-only message property pick a message from the "Deep Thoughts by Jack Handey" (from the *Saturday Night Live* TV show) collection. A <jsp:getProperty> is used to insert the message in the response. Another <jsp:setProperty> action then sets the category property to quotes, switching to the collection of quotes from various people, and the final <jsp:getProperty> inserts a message from this collection in the page. The result is shown in Figure 6-2.

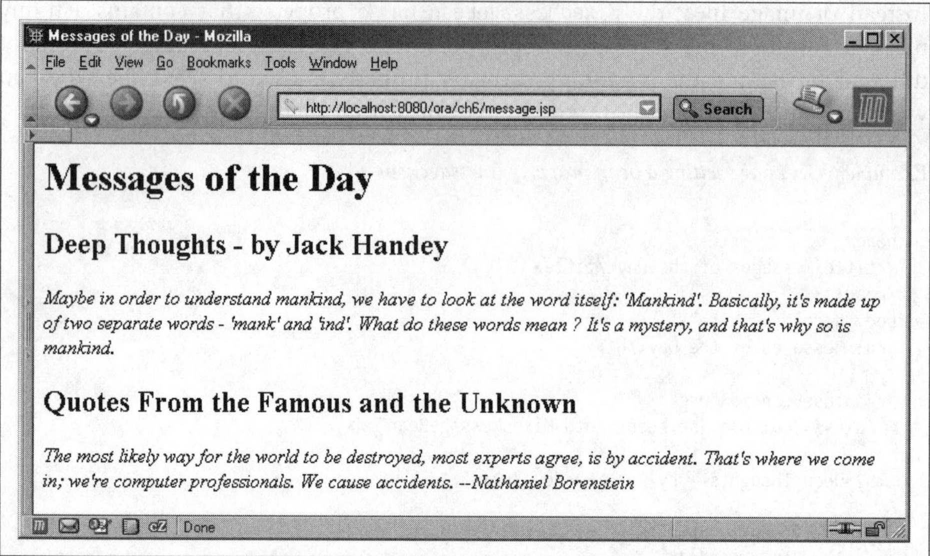

Figure 6-2. Dynamic messages from different categories generated by the same bean

Besides the `property` and `value` attributes, the `<jsp:setProperty>` action supports an attribute named `param`, which is used to set properties to the values submitted as request parameters. We'll look at how you can use this feature in Chapter 8.

Using the JSTL <c:set> Action

An alternative to the `<jsp:setProperty>` standard action is the JSTL `<c:set>` action:

```
...
<c:set target="${msg}" property="category" value="thoughts" />
...
<c:set target="${msg}" property="category" value="quotes" />
...
```

The `target` attribute contains an EL expression that evaluates to the bean, the `property` attribute specifies the property name (as a static string or as an EL expression), and the `value` attribute contains the value (as a static string or as an EL expression).

As with the choice between `<jsp:getProperty>` and an EL expression for reading a property value, using `<jsp:setProperty>` or `<c:set>` is largely a matter of preference. The `<c:set>` action is more flexible as you'll see later, so as long as you don't need to be JSP 1.1 compatible, it should be your first choice.

Automatic Type Conversions

The beans used in this chapter have properties of the Java type `String`, meaning they have plain-text values. But as I mentioned in the beginning of this chapter, a bean property can be of any Java type. As a JSP page author, you typically don't have to worry too much about this, though, since the container can convert text values to other Java types. It handles the most common types all by itself, but for more complex types, it needs a little help from the Java programmer who develops the bean class.

When you use the `<jsp:setProperty>` or the JSTL `<c:set>` action, the container takes care automatically of the conversion from text values to the Java types shown in Table 6-3.

Table 6-3. Conversion of text value to property type

Property type	Conversion method
`boolean` or `Boolean`	`Boolean.valueOf(String)`
`byte` or `Byte`	`Byte.valueOf(String)`
`char` or `Character`	`String.charAt(0)`
`double` or `Double`	`Double.valueOf(String)`
`int` or `Integer`	`Integer.valueOf(String)`
`float` or `Float`	`Float.valueOf(String)`
`long` or `Long`	`Long.valueOf(String)`
`short` or `Short`	`Short.valueOf(String)`
`Object`	`new String(String)`

For other types, such as a `java.util.Date`, the JSP specification defines how a Java programmer can develop a so-called "property editor" to handle the conversion. A property editor associated with a bean can convert a string such as `2002-05-10` to a `Date` object that represents this date. How to do so is described in Chapter 22.

The value returned by `<jsp:getProperty>`, an EL expression directly in template text, or `<c:out>` is always converted to a `String`—no matter what Java type it represents.

CHAPTER 7

Using Custom Tag Libraries and the JSP Standard Tag Library

So far we've covered the JSP basics—the primary parts of a page and installation and execution of a page—and how to use beans to dynamically add content to a page. Before we start working on real applications, let's turn to another fundamental JSP feature: custom tag libraries.

Custom tag libraries are, in my opinion, what make JSP so powerful. They make it possible for page authors to embed pretty much any logic in a page using familiar, HTML-like elements. In this chapter, we take a close look at what a custom tag library is, how to install and use it, and what the JSP Standard Tag Library (JSTL) brings to the table.

What Is a Custom Tag Library?

The JSP standard actions, such as the `<jsp:useBean>` and `<jsp:getProperty>` actions used in Chapter 6, are HTML-like elements for commonly needed functions in a JSP page: creating beans, accessing bean properties, and invoking other JSP pages. But there's a lot more you want to do that isn't covered by the standard actions.

To extend the set of action elements a page author can use in the same familiar way, new actions can be developed, either by a programmer as Java classes or by a page author as *tag files* (a special kind of JSP file). In either case, these actions are called *custom actions*. A custom action can do pretty much anything: it has access to all information about the request, it can add content to the response body as well as set response headers, and it can use any Java API to access external resources such as databases, LDAP servers, or mail servers. The way the JSP container interacts with a custom action also makes it possible for a custom action to conditionally process its body and to abort the processing of the rest of the page. Custom actions can be created for application-specific functions to make it easier for page authors to develop the JSP pages. Some typical examples are shown later in this book.

A custom action is inserted into a page using an HTML-like (actually XML) element. The attribute values, and sometimes the body, you provide tell the action what to do and the data to use. In fact, you have already used a custom action; the `<c:out>` action used in Chapters 5 and 6. It's part of the JSTL core library, and the JSTL libraries are implemented based on the same mechanisms as an application-specific custom tag library.

Behind the scenes, a custom action is implemented either as a Java class or as a tag file. The name of the class or the tag file and other information the container needs to invoke it are specified in a file called a *Tag Library Descriptor* (TLD). A *custom tag library* is simply a collection of the TLD and all files for a related set of custom actions. In most cases, the TLD and all files are packaged in a JAR file to make it easy to install.

So why is it called a custom *tag* library if it's a collection of custom *actions*? Using formal XML terminology, one or more tags (e.g., an opening tag and a closing tag) represent one *element* (the combination of the tags and possibly a body), but the word "tag" is commonly used to refer to both tags and elements because it's easier to say and shorter to type. Hence, the representation of a custom action (the functionality) in a JSP page is really called a *custom action element*. But that's just way too many words for most of us to say over and over again. Replacing "element" with "tag" doesn't help much, so we cut it down to the bare bones and use *custom tag* for both the functional entity and its representation in a page. When the JSP specification was written, no one objected to this sloppy language, so now we're stuck with custom tag libraries containing custom actions. I try to stick to the terms custom action and custom action element in this book, but if I slip, be aware that custom action, custom action element, and custom tag mean the same thing.

Installing a Custom Tag Library

Installing a custom tag library is very easy: just place the JAR file for the library in the *WEB-INF/lib* directory for the web application. If you look in the *WEB-INF/lib* directory for the book examples application, you see a JAR file named *orataglib_3_0.jar*; that's the custom tag library for all custom actions implemented as Java classes used in this book.

Declaring a Custom Tag Library

As you know by now, a JSP page contains a mixture of JSP elements and template text, in which the template text can be HTML or XML elements. The JSP container needs to figure out which is which. It's easy for it to recognize the standard JSP elements (because they all use the `jsp` namespace prefix), but it needs some help to find the elements that represent custom actions. That's where the tag library declaration comes into play.

Brief Custom Action Introduction for Java Programmers

I explain in detail how to develop custom actions as tag files in Chapter 11, and as Java classes in Chapters 21, 22, and 23. But if you're a programmer, I know you're curious, so here's a taste of what goes on behind the scene.

For a custom action implemented in Java, a class called a *tag handler* implements the custom action behavior. The tag handler class implements the `javax.servlet.jsp.tagext.SimpleTag` interface directly or by extending a support class defined by the JSP specification. This is the tag handler for the custom action used in this chapter:

```
package com.ora.jsp.tags.motd;

import java.io.*;
import javax.servlet.jsp.*;
import javax.servlet.jsp.tagext.*;
import com.ora.jsp.beans.motd.*;
public class MixedMessageTag extends SimpleTagSupport {
    private MixedMessageBean mmb =
        new MixedMessageBean( );

    // Attributes
    private String category;

    public void setCategory(String category) {
        this.category = category;
    }

    public void doTag( ) throws IOException {
        mmb.setCategory(category);
        JspWriter out = getJspContext().getOut( );
        out.println(mmb.getMessage( ));
    }
}
```

For each attribute supported by the custom action, the tag handler must implement a bean-style setter method, such as the `setCategory( )` method in this example. The container calls methods defined by the `SimpleTag` interface, such as the `doTag( )` method, to let the tag handler do its thing.

Example 7-1 shows a page that uses a custom action from a custom tag library.

Example 7-1. Custom tag library declaration (message.jsp)

```
<%@ page contentType="text/html" %>
<%@ taglib prefix="ora" uri="orataglib" %>
<html>
  <head>
    <title>Messages of the Day</title>
  </head>
  <body bgcolor="white">
```

Example 7-1. Custom tag library declaration (message.jsp) (continued)

```
    <h1>Messages of the Day</h1>
    <h2>Deep Thoughts - by Jack Handey</h2>
    <i>
      <ora:motd category="thoughts" />
    </i>

    <h2>Quotes From the Famous and the Unknown</h2>
    <i>
      <ora:motd category="quotes" />
    </i>
  </body>
</html>
```

This page displays messages from the same collections as the examples in Chapter 6. The second directive in Example 7-1 is a `taglib` directive, which is used to declare a custom tag library. Now, let's see what this really means. In order for the JSP container to use actions from a tag library, it must be able to do two things: recognize that an element represents a custom action from a specific library, and find the Java class or tag file that implements the custom action logic.

The first requirement—figuring out which library an action belongs to—is satisfied by the `taglib` directive's `prefix` attribute; all elements in the page that use the specified prefix belong to this custom tag library. A custom tag library defines a default prefix, used in the library's documentation and possibly by page-authoring tools that insert custom action elements in a page. You can, however, use any prefix you like except `jsp`, `jspx`, `java`, `javax`, `servlet`, `sun`, or `sunw` (those are reserved by the JSP specification). The prefix I use for all custom actions in this book is `ora`, short for "O'Reilly & Associates, Inc."

The `uri` attribute satisfies the second requirement: finding the class or tag file for each custom action. The attribute contains a string the container uses to locate the TLD for the library, where it finds the Java class or tag file names for all actions in the library. The value can identify the TLD file in a number of ways, but if you use a container that implements the 1.2 (or later) version of the JSP specification, there's really just one way that you need to care about: use the default URI for the library. The default URI is included in the TLD and should also be part of the documentation for the library. It's `orataglib` for the custom tag library described in this book.

When the web application is started, the container scans through the *WEB-INF* directory structure for files with *.tld* extensions (the mandatory extension for a TLD file) and all JAR files containing files with *.tld* extensions in their *META-INF* directory. In other words, the container locates all TLD files. For each TLD, the container gets the library's default URI from the TLD and creates a map from the URI to the TLD that contains it. In your JSP page, you just have to use a `taglib` directive with a `uri` attribute value that matches the default URI.

For this to work in an environment where custom tag libraries can come from multiple vendors as well as from in-house staff, the default URI value must be a globally unique string. A common convention is to use an HTTP URL, such as *http://ora.com/jsptags*. This is one way to be reasonably sure that the value is unique, and it's the choice made for all JSTL tag library URIs. Note that the URL doesn't have to refer to an existing web page; it's just an identifier, and the container doesn't try to access it over the Internet. Others prefer a shorter string, such as `orataglib` or `com.ora.jsptags`. This works equally well as long as the strings are unique in the application.

With the URI and the prefix for the library defined, the container has all it needs to find the custom action implementation. As shown in Figure 7-1, when the container finds an element with a prefix matching a prefix defined by a `taglib` directive, it uses the `uri` attribute value to locate the TLD. In the TLD, it finds a mapping between the action element name and the class or tag file implementation.

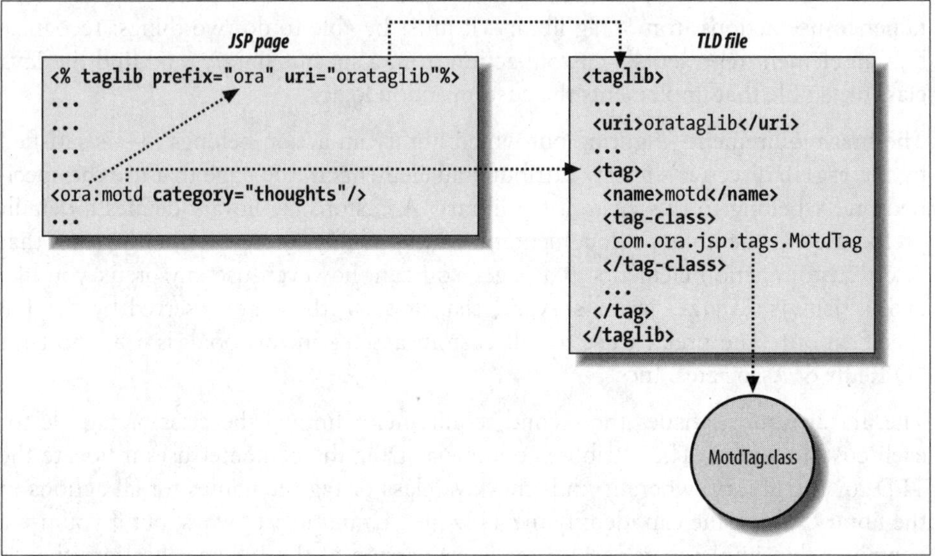

Figure 7-1. Relation between the taglib directive, the TLD, and the implementation (tag handler) for the custom actions

Identifying a Custom Tag Library in a JSP 1.1 Container

Prior to JSP 1.2, the container didn't locate custom tag libraries automatically. If you're stuck with a container that doesn't yet support JSP 1.2, you must tell it exactly where to find the TLD.

The first approach you can use is to specify a symbolic name as the `uri` attribute value, just as in JSP 1.2. But in addition, you must define the mapping from the symbolic name to the location of the library in the deployment descriptor for the application (*WEB-INF/web.xml*):

```
<web-app>
  ...
  <taglib>
    <taglib-uri>
      orataglib
    </taglib-uri>
    <taglib-location>
      /WEB-INF/lib/orataglib_3_0.jar
    </taglib-location>
  </taglib>
  ...
</web-app>
```

The `<taglib-uri>` element contains the symbolic name, and the `<taglib-location>` element contains the path to the tag library JAR file, or to the TLD file itself in case the library isn't packaged in a JAR file.

If the `uri` attribute value doesn't match a symbolic name defined in the *web.xml* file, the container assumes it is a file path:

```
<%@ taglib uri="/WEB-INF/lib/orataglib_3_0.jar" prefix="ora" %>
```

If the path starts with a slash, it's interpreted as a context-relative path (the path to the file from the root of the application installation directory), otherwise as a path relative to the JSP page (known as a *page-relative path*). The file can be either the TLD file itself or a JAR file that includes the TLD file as *META-INF/taglib.tld*.

These two approaches work in JSP 1.2 or 2.0 container as well, but there's rarely a reason to use them because the auto-discovery feature makes life so much easier.

Using Actions from a Tag Library

The custom action described in Table 7-1 does exactly the same thing as the second bean used in Chapter 6: it adds a message from a specified category to a page.

Table 7-1. Attributes for <ora:motd>

Attribute name	Java type	Dynamic value accepted	Description
`category`	`String`	Yes	Mandatory. The message category, either thoughts or quotes.

This custom action has one mandatory attribute named `category`, used to select the type of message you want. Let's get back to the "Java type" and "Dynamic value accepted" columns at the end of this chapter.

Example 7-2 shows the *message.jsp* page again, now with the custom action elements highlighted.

Example 7-2. Custom action elements (message.jsp)

```
<%@ page contentType="text/html" %>
<%@ taglib prefix="ora" uri="orataglib" %>

<html>
  <head>
    <title>Messages of the Day</title>
  </head>
  <body bgcolor="white">
    <h1>Messages of the Day</h1>
    <h2>Deep Thoughts - by Jack Handey</h2>
    <i>
      <ora:motd category="thoughts" />
    </i>

    <h2>Quotes From the Famous and the Unknown</h2>
    <i>
      <ora:motd category="quotes" />
    </i>
  </body>
</html>
```

First note how the `<ora:motd>` element name prefix matches the prefix assigned to the custom tag library by the `taglib` directive. The syntax for a custom action element is the same as for standard actions: an opening tag, possibly with attributes, a body, and a closing tag; or just one tag ending with `/>` if no body is used (as in Example 7-2). Standard actions, JSTL actions and custom actions are all JSP action elements and are used in exactly the same way.

The first occurrence of the custom action sets the `category` attribute to `thoughts` and the second one to `quotes`. The `<ora:motd>` action ("motd" is short for Message Of The Day) adds a message from the specified category to the page, resulting in the response shown in Figure 7-2.

Setting Action Attribute Values

Let's talk about the "Java type" and "Dynamic value accepted" column values in Table 7-1. The category attribute value for the `<ora:motd>` action has the value `String` in the "Java type" column. `String` is the Java type for a text value. Action attributes can be of any Java type, the same as the bean properties discussed in Chapter 6. Say, for instance, that the `<ora:motd>` action had another attribute for setting the number of messages to return. It would make sense for this attribute to be of type `int` (a whole number). The container treats attribute values the same as bean properties and automatically converts text values to numeric and Boolean values, using the same conversion methods, so this attribute could still be set as a text value. The same as for a bean, a Java programmer can also link a property editor to a custom action to convert text values to more complex data structures.

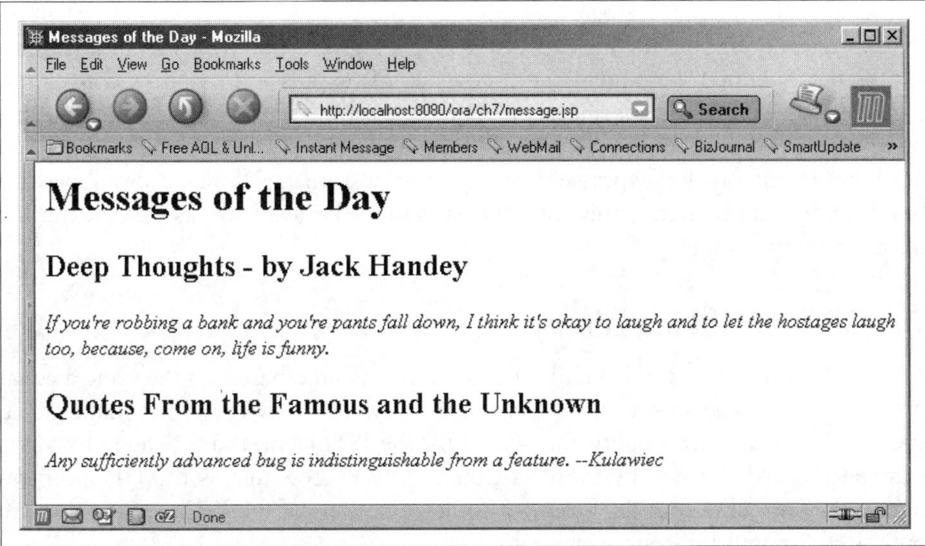

Figure 7-2. Output from the message.jsp page

Editing JSP Pages with an XML Editor

By now it should be clear that all JSP action elements follow the XML notation, so an XML-syntax aware editor seems like a tool that could make your life easier, with features such as automatic indentation, color-coding of elements, and even attribute selection lists for standard HTML and XHTML elements. The only thing that spoils this is that the JSP directive elements don't follow XML syntax, but there's an easy workaround that works for most XML editors.

A JSP container recognizes JSP elements even within XML/HTML comments, while an XML editor typically ignores the comment contents. So the workaround is simply to place the JSP directives within comment delimiters:

```
<!--
<%@ page contentType="text/html" %>
<%@ taglib prefix="ora" uri="orataglib" %>
-->
<html>
  <head>
    <title>Messages of the Day</title>
    ...
```

A custom action attribute may also accept an EL expression as well as a static text value. An EL expression is evaluated for each page request, so it allows you to provide an attribute value that differs between invocations. The value in the "Dynamic Value Accepted" column tells if the attribute can be set by an EL expression. As you can see in Table 7-1, the category attribute for the <ora:motd> action does accept an EL expression. Support for EL expressions isn't a given, but typically all attributes except those named var and scope accept an EL expression value (a convention established by the JSTL specification). For the custom actions in the example tag library used in this book, custom action tables (like Table 7-1) tells you if an attribute accepts an EL expression or not. For custom tag libraries developed in-house or by a third party, this information should be available as part of the tag library documentation.

The JSP Standard Tag Library

As I mentioned earlier, the JSTL libraries are implemented based on the same mechanisms as an application-specific custom tag library. The only thing that makes JSTL special is that the functionality and syntax for the JSTL actions are defined by a formal specification, created by the Java Community Process just as the JSP specification itself. This allows vendors to offer implementations of the JSTL actions that are optimized for their JSP container.

JSTL actually consists of five different tag libraries, which minimizes name collisions among actions in different categories. Table 7-2 shows the default URIs and recommended prefixes for all JSTL libraries.

Table 7-2. URI for the JSTL 1.1 libraries

Library	URI	Prefix
Core	*http://java.sun.com/jsp/jstl/core*	c
XML processing	*http://java.sun.com/jsp/jstl/xml*	x
I18N formatting	*http://java.sun.com/jsp/jstl/fmt*	fmt
Database access	*http://java.sun.com/jsp/jstl/sql*	sql
Functions	*http://java.sun.com/jsp/jstl/functions*	fn

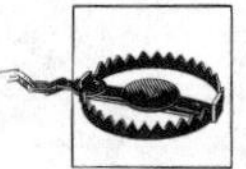

If you've used JSTL 1.0, note that new URIs are used for JSTL 1.1. The change was, unfortunately, needed to preserve backward compatibility for JSTL 1.0 applications deployed in a JSP 2.0 container because the EL expressions are evaluated by the container instead of the tag handlers starting with JSP 2.0.

The first four libraries contain custom actions of the type described in this chapter. We'll take a closer look at all of them in the examples in this book.

The last library in Table 7-2 was added in JSTL 1.1. It contains a set of functions that can be invoked in an EL expression, e.g., ${fn:trim(someVariable)}. Table 7-3 lists all functions in the JSTL function library. They are described in more detail in Appendix C, and you'll see some of them used in the examples in other chapters.

Table 7-3. JSTL functions

Function call syntax	Description
`fn:contains(string, substring)`	Returns `true` if the string contains the substring
`fn:containsIgnoreCase(string, substring)`	Returns `true` if the string contains the substring, ignoring case
`fn:endsWith(string, suffix)`	Returns `true` if the string ends with the suffix
`fn:escapeXml(string)`	Returns the string with all characters that have special meaning in XML converted to their equivalent XML character entity code
`fn:indexOf(string, substring)`	Returns the index for the first occurrence of the substring in the string
`fn:join(array, separator)`	Returns a string composed from the array elements, separated by the separator
`fn:length(item)`	Returns the number of elements in the item if it's a collection or array, or the number of characters in the item if it's a string
`fn:replace(string, before, after)`	Returns a string where all occurrences of the before string have been replaced with the after string
`fn:split(string, separator)`	Returns an array where the elements are the parts of the string that are separated by the separator
`fn:startsWith(string, prefix)`	Returns `true` if the string starts with the prefix
`fn:substring(string, begin, end)`	Returns a part of the string, starting from the begin index up to and including the end index
`fn:substringAfter(string, substring)`	Returns the part of the string that follows the substring
`fn:substringBefore(string, substring)`	Returns the part of the string that precedes the substring
`fn:toLowerCase(string)`	Returns a string with all characters from the input converted to lowercase
`fn:toUpperCase(string)`	Returns a string with all characters from the input string converted to uppercase
`fn:trim(string)`	Returns a string with all leading and trailing whitespace characters in the input string removed

The JSTL specification is still pretty fresh. Over time, I expect all web containers to provide native support for JSTL, but until this happens, you may have to install the JSTL Reference Implementation (RI) developed by the Apache Taglibs open source project as a library named Standard. It's included with the book example application and consists of the JAR files listed in Table 7-4 the *webapps/ora/WEB-INF/lib* directory.

Table 7-4. JSTL Reference Implementation JAR files

File	Description
`dom.jar`	W3C DOM classes, used by the JSTL XML library implementation. Part of JAXP 1.2. It can be removed if you use JDK 1.4.2 or later.

Table 7-4. JSTL Reference Implementation JAR files (continued)

File	Description
`jaxp-api.jar`	Java API for XML Processing (JAXP) 1.2 specification classes, used by the JSTL XML library implementation. It can be removed if you use JDK 1.4.2 or later.
`jdbc2_0-stdext.jar`	JDBC 2.0 Optional Package specification interfaces, used by the JSTL SQL library implementation. Also bundled with Java 2 SDK 1.4 as well as with Tomcat 4, independent of SDK version; it can be removed when using one of these environments.
`jstl.jar`	JSTL specification classes and interfaces.
`sax.jar`	XML.org SAX classes, used by the JSTL XML library implementation. Part of JAXP 1.2. It can be removed if you use JDK 1.4.2 or later.
`standard.jar`	The reference implementation for all JSTL classes and interfaces, developed by the Apache Taglibs project. This is the main JAR file for the JSTL RI.
`xalan.jar`	Apache Xalan XSLT processor, used by the XML JSTL library implementation. It can be removed if you use Sun's JDK 1.4.2 or later, but it may be needed if you use another vendor's JDK 1.4.2.
`xercesImpl.jar`	Apache Xerces XML parser, used by the XML JSTL library implementation. It can be removed if you use JDK 1.4.2 or later.

You can install the JSTL 1.1 RI by copying these JAR files to the *WEB-INF/lib* directory for your web application, but to make sure you get the most up-to-date version, I recommend you get the latest version of the Standard library from the Jakarta Taglibs project instead: *http://jakarta.apache.org/taglibs/*.

To use a JSTL library in your JSP pages, just declare the library you need and use the actions just as any other custom action:

```
<%@ page contentType="text/html" %>
<%@ taglib prefix="c" uri="http://java.sun.com/jsp/jstl/core" %>
<html>
  <head>
    <title>JSP is Easy</title>
  </head>
  <body bgcolor="white">

    <h1>JSP is as easy as ...</h1>

    1 + 2 + 3 = <c:out value="${1 + 2 + 3}" />

  </body>
</html>
```

This book demonstrates the use of all JSTL actions, so you'll see plenty of other examples later.

Using Beans or Custom Actions

The examples used in this chapter show that a custom action can provide the same functionality as a bean. In Chapter 6, we created a `MixedMessageBean`, set its `category` attribute, and retrieved the value of its `message` property to the page:

```
<jsp:useBean id="msg"
  class="com.ora.jsp.beans.motd.MixedMessageBean" />
...
<jsp:setProperty name="msg" property="category"
  value="thoughts" />
...
<jsp:getProperty name="msg" property="message" />
```

In this chapter, we use a custom action to accomplish exactly the same thing:

```
<ora:motd category="thoughts" />
```

This raises the question of when it's better to use one or the other of these two component types. As is often the case in software development, there's no rule applicable to all cases; in other words, we are left with "it depends." My rule of thumb is that a bean is a great carrier of information, and a custom action is great for processing information. Custom actions can use beans as input and output. For instance, an action can save the properties of a bean in a database, or get information from a database and make it available to the page as a bean. In Chapter 8, I will show how a bean can also capture and validate user input in a very powerful way.

Some beans do more than carry information; they encapsulate functionality intended for use in many different environments, such as in applets, servlets, and JSP pages. In a case like this, a custom action can internally use the bean, providing a JSP-specific adapter for the bean to make it easier to use by a page author. This is, in fact, exactly what the `<ora:motd>` action does; internally it uses the bean from Chapter 6 to produce the message.

You now have a lot of knowledge under your belt: how to write and install a JSP page, how to use directive elements, action elements of all kinds (standard, custom, and JSTL actions), what a bean is and how it can be used in JSP, and you have a rough idea of what the JSP EL is all about. We can now move on and see how to use JSP and JSTL to solve some real problems, starting with how to deal with user input in the next chapter.

CHAPTER 8

Processing Input and Output

User input is a necessity in modern web pages. Most dynamic web sites generate pages based on user input submitted through an HTML form. Unfortunately, users seldom enter information in exactly the format you need, so before you can use such input, you need to validate it to make sure it's usable.

And it's not only the input format that's important. Web browsers are also picky about the format of the HTML you send them. For instance, when you generate an HTML form with values taken from a database, a name such as O'Reilly can cause problems. The single quote character after the O can fool the browser into believing it's at the end of the string, so you end up with just an O in your form.

In this chapter, we look at how you can use either JSTL actions or beans to access and validate user input. We also look at how special characters in the output must be treated so they don't confuse the browser.

Reading Request Parameter Values

The HTML specification defines a set of elements for presenting a form with fields in which the user can enter text or select among predefined choices. I'm sure you have encountered these countless times—to tell a vendor about yourself when downloading demo software, to specify what you're looking for on a search engine site, or to select the toppings when you order a pizza online. But you may not be familiar with what's going on behind the scene when you fill out the form and click **Submit**. Example 8-1 shows an HTML page that contains the most commonly used HTML form elements.

Example 8-1. HTML form elements

```
<html>
  <head>
    <title>User Info Entry Form</title>
  </head>
  <body bgcolor="white">
```

Example 8-1. HTML form elements (continued)

```
    <form action="process.jsp" method="post">
      <table>
        <tr>
          <td>Name:</td>
          <td>
            <input type="text" name="userName">
          </td>
        </tr>
        <tr>
          <td>Birth Date:</td>
          <td>
            <input type="text" name="birthDate">
          </td>
          <td>(Use format yyyy-mm-dd)</td>
        </tr>
        <tr>
          <td>Email Address:</td>
          <td>
            <input type="text" name="emailAddr">
          </td>
          <td>(Use format name@company.com)</td>
        </tr>
        <tr>
          <td>Gender:</td>
          <td>
            <input type="radio" name="gender" value="m" checked>Male<br>
            <input type="radio" name="gender" value="f">Female
          </td>
        </tr>
        <tr>
          <td>Lucky number:</td>
          <td>
            <input type="text" name="luckyNumber">
          </td>
          <td>(A number between 1 and 100)</td>
        </tr>
        <tr>
          <td>Favorite Foods:</td>
          <td>
            <input type="checkbox" name="food" value="z">Pizza<br>
            <input type="checkbox" name="food" value="p">Pasta<br>
            <input type="checkbox" name="food" value="c">Chinese
          </td>
        </tr>
        <tr>
          <td colspan=2>
            <input type="submit" value="Send Data">
          </td>
        </tr>
      </table>
    </form>
  </body>
</html>
```

This form could be the frontend to a newsletter subscription site, for instance. In order to send the users information that might interest them, it asks for the birth date, gender, lucky number, and food preferences, along with the full name and email address, for each person that signs up for the service.

The HTML `<form>` element encloses all the other form elements. Its `action` attribute contains the URI for the web server resource (for instance, a JSP page, as in this example) that the form should be submitted to. The method attribute tells the browser which HTTP method to use when submitting the form. Recall from Chapter 2 that the `GET` method is intended for requests that just retrieve information, while the `POST` method is intended for requests that cause irreversible actions, such as saving the form values in a database.

The form in Example 8-1 contains a number of HTML `<input>` elements. Each element has a `type` attribute. The type attribute tells the browser which type of input control to render: `text`, `password`, `checkbox`, `radio`, `hidden`, `file`, `submit`, `reset`, `image`, or `button`. In this example, I use only `text` (a regular text input field), `radio` (a radio button, typically used for mutually exclusive choices), `checkbox` (for multiple optional choices), and `submit` (a button for submitting the form). Some of the other types are used in other examples in this book, but if you need more detailed descriptions you may want read a book specifically about HTML, such as *HTML Pocket Reference* by Jennifer Niederst (O'Reilly) or *HTML & XHTML: The Definitive Guide* by Chuck Musciano and Bill Kennedy (O'Reilly).

When the user clicks the **Submit** button, the browser sends a request to the web-server resource specified by the `<form>` element's `action` attribute, using the method specified by the `method` attribute. All values the user has entered in the text fields and chosen from radio buttons, checkboxes, or select lists, are sent as HTTP request parameters with the request. How the request parameters are sent depends on the request method. For a `GET` request, the parameters are sent as a query string appended to the URL; for a POST request, they are sent in the request body. No matter how they are sent, each parameter is represented by a name/value pair. The name is the name assigned to the form element using the `name` attribute, and the value is either the value entered by the user (for text fields) or the value specified by the element's `value` attribute. Hence, when the form in Example 8-1 is submitted, the request contains parameters named `userName`, `birthDate`, `emailAddr`, and `luckyNumber` containing the text entered by the user (or an empty string if no text was entered) and one parameter named `gender` with the value `m` or `f` depending on which radio button the user selected.

The checkbox controls at the end of Example 8-1 have a slightly more complex behavior. Note that all checkbox `<input>` elements have the same name: `food`. This is how you tell that they belong to the same category. If the user checks off more than one checkbox, the browser sends a request with multiple request parameters named `food`—one for each value. If the user doesn't check off any checkbox (someone on a diet, maybe, or with a more eclectic taste than I), the browser doesn't send a food parameter at all. The HTML <select> element (not shown in this example) works the same way when specified to allow multiple choices.

Now when you've seen how the browser deals with form fields, let's move on to how to access the form data in a JSP page using either JSTL actions or a bean.

Accessing Parameter Values with JSTL Actions

Example 8-2 shows a page with the same form as in Example 8-1, but with the form's action attribute pointing back to the JSP page that contains it and JSTL actions adding the submitted values to the response.

Example 8-2. Accessing parameters with JSTL (input_jstl.jsp)

```
<%@ page contentType="text/html" %>
<%@ taglib prefix="c" uri="http://java.sun.com/jsp/jstl/core" %>

<html>
  <head>
    <title>User Info Entry Form</title>
  </head>
  <body bgcolor="white">
    <form action="input_jstl.jsp" method="post">
      <table>
        <tr>
          <td>Name:</td>
          <td>
            <input type="text" name="userName">
          </td>
        </tr>
        <tr>
          <td>Birth Date:</td>
          <td>
            <input type="text" name="birthDate">
          </td>
          <td>(Use format yyyy-mm-dd)</td>
        </tr>
        <tr>
          <td>Email Address:</td>
          <td>
            <input type="text" name="emailAddr">
          </td>
          <td>(Use format name@company.com)</td>
        </tr>
        <tr>
          <td>Gender:</td>
          <td>
            <input type="radio" name="gender" value="m" checked>Male<br>
            <input type="radio" name="gender" value="f">Female
          </td>
        </tr>
```

Example 8-2. Accessing parameters with JSTL (input_jstl.jsp) (continued)

```
        <tr>
          <td>Lucky number:</td>
          <td>
            <input type="text" name="luckyNumber">
          </td>
          <td>(A number between 1 and 100)</td>
        </tr>
        <tr>
          <td>Favorite Foods:</td>
          <td>
            <input type="checkbox" name="food" value="z">Pizza<br>
            <input type="checkbox" name="food" value="p">Pasta<br>
            <input type="checkbox" name="food" value="c">Chinese
          </td>
        </tr>
        <tr>
          <td colspan=2>
            <input type="submit" value="Send Data">
          </td>
        </tr>
      </table>
    </form>

    You entered:<br>
    Name: <c:out value="${param.userName}" /><br>
    Birth Date: <c:out value="${param.birthDate}" /><br>
    Email Address: <c:out value="${param.emailAddr}" /><br>
    Gender: <c:out value="${param.gender}" /><br>
    Lucky Number: <c:out value="${param.luckyNumber}" /><br>
    Favorite Food:
      <c:forEach items="${paramValues.food}" var="current">
        <c:out value="${current}" /> 
      </c:forEach>
  </body>
</html>
```

If you load the page in a browser, fill out the form and submit it, you end up with a result that looks something like Figure 8-1.

Let's look at how the submitted values end up in the response. All form field values except the Favorite Foods checkbox values are added using a JSTL <c:out> action (Table 8-1) with an EL expression that retrieves the request parameter value, for instance:

```
Name: <c:out value="${param.userName}" /><br>
```

Recall from Chapter 5 that param is an implicit EL variable that represents a collection (a java.util.Map) of all request parameters sent to the page. To get the value of a specific variable, you simply specify the name of the parameter, separated from the collection name with a dot.

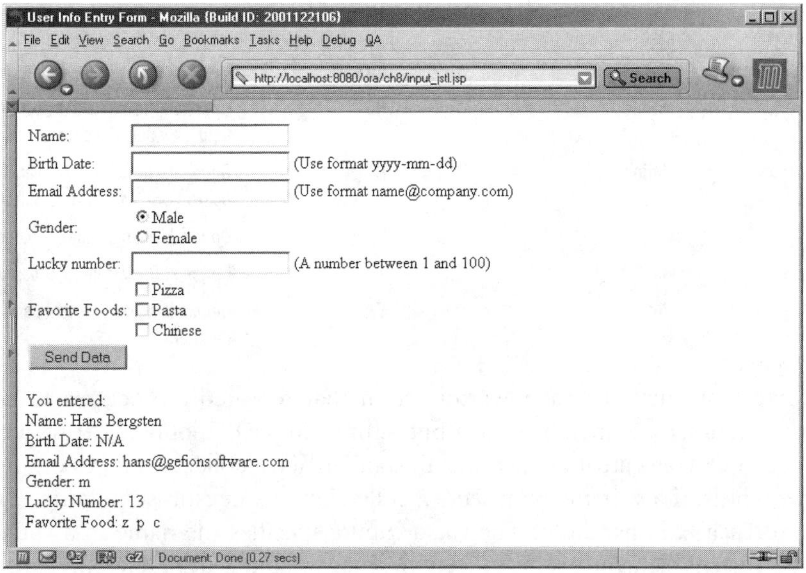

Figure 8-1. Input form

Table 8-1. Attributes for JSTL <c:out>

Attribute name	Java type	Dynamic value accepted	Description
`value`	Any type	Yes	Mandatory. The value to add to the response.
`escapeXml`	boolean	Yes	Optional. `true` if special characters in the value should be converted to character entity codes. Default is `true`.
`default`	Any type	Yes	Optional. The value to use if the value attribute is `null`. Can also be defined by the body.

As described earlier, when a user checks off multiple checkboxes that share the same name, the request contains multiple parameters with the same name. If none is checked, the request doesn't contain the corresponding parameter at all. To display the choices the user made, we need to get all parameter values and a way to deal with them one at a time. The implicit `paramValues` variable and the JSTL `<c:forEach>` (Table 8-2) action satisfy these requirements.

Table 8-2. Attributes for JSTL <c:forEach>

Attribute name	Java type	Dynamic value accepted	Description
`items`	`java.util.Collection`, `java.util.Iterator`, `java.util.Enumeration`, `java.util.Map`, `Object[]` or array of primitive types	Yes	Optional. The collection of values to iterate over. If the value is `null`, no iteration is performed. If not specified, the `begin` and `end` attributes must be specified.

Table 8-2. Attributes for JSTL <c:forEach> (continued)

Attribute name	Java type	Dynamic value accepted	Description
`var`	String	No	Optional. The name of the variable to hold the value of the current element.
`varStatus`	String	No	Optional. The name of the variable to hold a `LoopTagStatus` object.
`begin`	int	Yes	Optional. The first index, 0-based.
`end`	int	Yes	Optional. The last index, 0-based.
`step`	int	Yes	Optional. Index increment per iteration.

The `<c:forEach>` action is a powerful action that repeatedly processes its body a number of times, as defined by its attributes. In Example 8-2, only the `items` attribute is needed. The `items` attribute accepts all standard Java collection types or an array. In other words, if a variable represents a collection of values in some form, chances are `<c:forEach>` can handle it. The `var` attribute specifies the name of a variable to hold the current element of the collection. The variable is available only within the body of the action element.

The implicit `paramValues` variable is a collection of request parameters sent to the page, with each parameter represented by an array of values (rather than the *single* value per parameter held by the `param` variable). Combining the `<c:forEach>` action and the `paramValues` variable makes it easy to loop through all submitted Favorite Food choices and add each one to the response:

```
Favorite Food:
  <c:forEach items="${paramValues.food}" var="current">
    <c:out value="${current}" /> 
  </c:forEach>
```

The `<c:forEach>` action iterates over the array values, and the nested `<c:out>` action adds each value to the response. If no choice was made (the `${paramValues.food}` expression doesn't return anything), the `<c:forEach>` action simply does nothing.

Besides the `items` and `var` attributes used in Example 8-2, `<c:forEach>` also lets you define where in the collection to start and stop the iteration (`begin` and `end`), and if all or just some elements should be processed (`step`). These attributes can also be used without a collection to process the body a fixed number of times:

```
<c:forEach begin="1" end="4">
  ...
</c:forEach>
```

The `varStatus` attribute can be used to name a variable that holds a bean with iteration status details. You can use it when something needs to be done only on the first or last pass through the body, or for even and odd indexes, etc. The iteration status bean (`javax.servlet.jsp.jstl.core.LoopTagStatus`) is described in Appendix B.

Accessing Other Request Data

The param and paramValues variables give you access to request parameters. But there's a lot of information passed with a request besides parameters. Header values can be accessed through the header and headerValues variables, and cookies through the cookie variable. Other request information is available through the EL as properties of the object that represents the request itself, accessed through the implicit pageContext variable's request property. The request property is an instance of a class named javax.servlet.http.HttpServletRequest, and Table 8-3 shows its properties for information that isn't available through the other implicit objects (except a few that aren't appropriate for use in a JSP page).

Table 8-3. Properties for javax.servlet.http.HttpServletRequest

Property name	Java type	Access	Description
authType	String	Read	The name of the authentication scheme protecting the request
characterEncoding	String	Read	The request body character encoding, or null if unknown
contentLength	int	Read	The request body length, or -1 if unknown
contentType	String	Read	The request body MIME type
contextPath	String	Read	The context path for the request
cookies	javax.servlet.http.Cookie[]	Read	The cookies received with the request
locale	java.util.Locale	Read	The client's preferred locale
locales	java.util.Enumeration	Read	A list of all client locales in order of preference
method	String	Read	The request method (e.g., GET, POST)
protocol	String	Read	The protocol name and version, e.g., HTTP/1.1
remoteAddr	String	Read	The client's IP address
remoteHost	String	Read	The client's hostname or IP address if not known
remoteUser	String	Read	The username used to make the request if the page is protected, otherwise null
requestURI	String	Read	The request URI, e.g., */app/page.jsp*
requestURL	StringBuffer	Read	The request URL, e.g., *http://server/app/page.jsp*

Table 8-3. Properties for javax.servlet.http.HttpServletRequest (continued)

Property name	Java type	Access	Description
`scheme`	`String`	Read	The scheme, e.g., `http` or `https`
`servletPath`	`String`	Read	The context-relative path for the request, e.g., */page.jsp*
`serverName`	`String`	Read	The name of the server the request was sent to
`serverPort`	`int`	Read	The port the request was sent to
`secure`	`boolean`	Read	`true` if the request was made over a secure channel (e.g., SSL)
`userPrincipal`	`java.security.Principal`	Read	The `Principal` representing the user making the request if the page is protected, otherwise `null`

Example 8-3 shows a page that displays some of the available information.

Example 8-3. Request information (reqinfo.jsp)

```
<%@ page contentType="text/html" %>
<%@ taglib prefix="c" uri="http://java.sun.com/jsp/jstl/core" %>

<html>
  <head>
    <title>Request Info</title>
  </head>
  <body bgcolor="white">

    The following information was received:
    <ul>
      <li>Request Method:
        <c:out value="${pageContext.request.method}" />
      <li>Request Protocol:
        <c:out value="${pageContext.request.protocol}" />
      <li>Context Path:
        <c:out value="${pageContext.request.contextPath}" />
      <li>Servlet Path:
        <c:out value="${pageContext.request.servletPath}" />
      <li>Request URI:
        <c:out value="${pageContext.request.requestURI}" />
      <li>Request URL:
        <c:out value="${pageContext.request.requestURL}" />
      <li>Server Name:
        <c:out value="${pageContext.request.serverName}" />
      <li>Server Port:
        <c:out value="${pageContext.request.serverPort}" />
      <li>Remote Address:
        <c:out value="${pageContext.request.remoteAddr}" />
```

Example 8-3. Request information (reqinfo.jsp) (continued)

```
      <li>Remote Host:
        <c:out value="${pageContext.request.remoteHost}" />
      <li>Secure:
        <c:out value="${pageContext.request.secure}" />
      <li>Cookies:<br>
        <c:forEach items="${pageContext.request.cookies}" var="c">
            <b><c:out value="${c.name}" /></b>:
          <c:out value="${c.value}" /><br>
        </c:forEach>
      <li>Headers:<br>
        <c:forEach items="${headerValues}" var="h">
            <b><c:out value="${h.key}" /></b>:
          <c:forEach items="${h.value}" var="value">
            <br>
                <c:out value="${value}" />
          </c:forEach>
          <br>
        </c:forEach>
    </ul>
  </body>
</html>
```

The EL expressions used as the `<c:out>` actions' `value` attribute values get various request object properties.

Cookie values can be accessed in two ways: through the implicit `cookie` variable or through the request object's `cookies` property. The first way is the easiest to use when you know the name of the cookie you're looking for; I will show you an example of this in Chapter 13. The second way is used in Example 8-3, since we don't know the cookie names and want to list all of them. A `<c:forEach>` action loops over all cookies received with the request and makes the current cookie available through a variable named `c` within its body. A class named `javax.servlet.http.Cookie`, with the properties `name` and `value`, represents a cookie. The nested `<c:out>` actions add the value of these two properties for each cookie to the response.

Header values can be accessed through the implicit `header` and `headerValues` variables. In Example 8-3, `<c:forEach>` actions loop over all headers and then over all values for each header, adding the names and the values to the response.

Figure 8-2 shows a typical response generated by the JSP page in Example 8-3.

Capturing Parameter Values Using a Bean

As you may remember from Chapter 6, a bean is often used as a container for data, created by some server process and used in a JSP page to display the data. But a bean can also be used to capture user input. The captured data can then be processed by the bean itself or used as input to some other server component (e.g., a component that stores the data in a database or picks an appropriate banner ad to display).

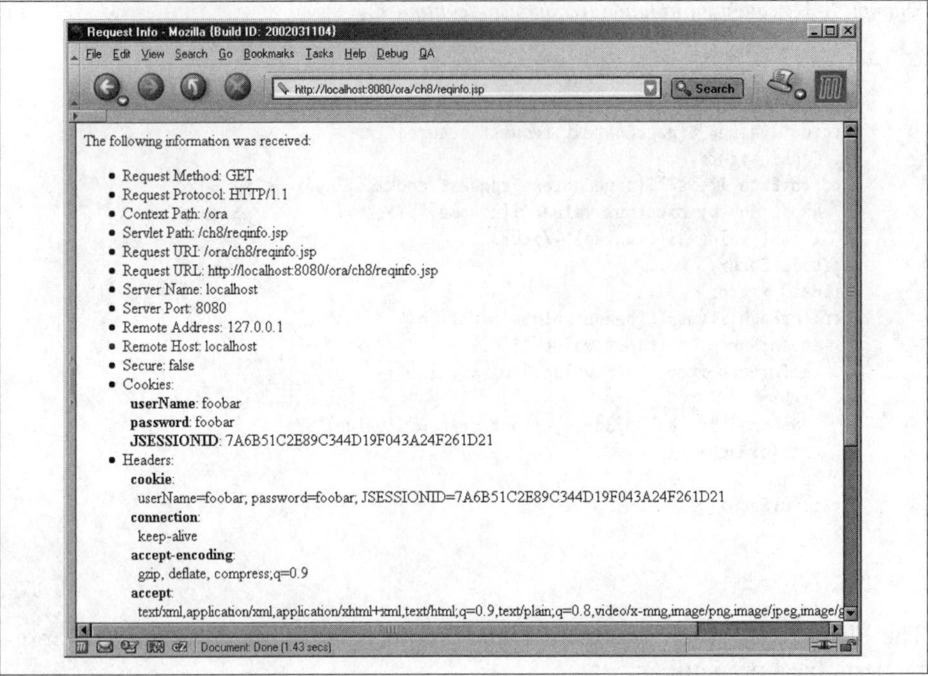

Figure 8-2. Request information displayed with JSTL actions

To capture the user input from the example form, I have implemented a bean named `com.ora.jsp.beans.userinfo.UserInfoBean`, with the properties described in Table 8-4.

Table 8-4. Properties for com.ora.jsp.beans.userinfo.UserInfoBean

Property name	Java type	Access	Description
`userName`	`String`	Read-write	The user's full name
`birthDate`	`String`	Read-write	The user's birth date in the format *yyyy-mm-dd* (e.g., `2002-01-23`)
`emailAddr`	`String`	Read-write	The user's email address in the format *name@company.com*
`gender`	`String`	Read-write	The user's gender (`m` or `f`)
`luckyNumber`	`String`	Read-write	The user's lucky number (between 1 and 100)
`food`	`String[]`	Read/write	The user's favorite food (any combination of `z`, `p`, and `c`)

As shown in the "Access" column in Table 8-4, all properties are read/write, meaning that, in addition to using the bean's properties to generate output, the property values can be set based on user input.

Example 8-4 shows the last part of a JSP page that uses the bean to capture the user input and then displays the values using JSTL actions. The part of the page that contains the form isn't included in Example 8-4 because it's identical to the form part in Example 8-2.

Example 8-4. Capturing parameters with a bean (input_bean.jsp)

```
    ...
    <jsp:useBean id="userInfo"
      class="com.ora.jsp.beans.userinfo.UserInfoBean">
      <jsp:setProperty name="userInfo" property="*" />
    </jsp:useBean>

    You entered:<br>
    Name: <c:out value="${userInfo.userName}" /><br>
    Birth Date: <c:out value="${userInfo.birthDate}" /><br>
    Email Address: <c:out value="${userInfo.emailAddr}" /><br>
    Gender: <c:out value="${userInfo.gender}" /><br>
    Lucky Number: <c:out value="${userInfo.luckyNumber}" /><br>
    Favorite Food:
      <c:forEach items="${userInfo.food}" var="current">
        <c:out value="${current}" /> 
      </c:forEach>
  </body>
</html>
```

At the top of Example 8-4, a `<jsp:useBean>` action element creates the bean and associates it with a name; the `id` attribute specifies a name for the bean and the `class` attribute specifies its fully qualified class name. This is similar to how the action was used to create the beans in Chapter 6, except that here the body contains a nested `<jsp:setProperty>` action element. You must therefore use both an opening tag and a closing tag (`<jsp:useBean ...>` and `</jsp:useBean>`) instead of the empty element shorthand notation (`<jsp:useBean ... />`) used in Chapter 6. The body of a `<jsp:useBean>` action element is processed only when a new bean is created. In this example, that's always the case, but as you'll learn in Chapter 10, there are times when the bean already exists, and the action is needed only to associate the bean with a name.

Now let's take a closer look at the `<jsp:setProperty>` action. In Chapter 6, this action sets a bean property to a static value, such as the message category in the message-producing bean. That's nice, but the real power of this action lies in its ability to set bean properties from request parameter values. This is how it's used in Example 8-4, enabled by the `property` attribute's asterisk (*) value. If you compare the `name` attribute values for all fields in the form with the `UserInfoBean` property names in Table 8-4, you notice that each field name maps to a property name. With `property="*"`, the `<jsp:setProperty>` action sets all bean properties to the value of the corresponding parameters automatically. For this to work, the field name must match the property name exactly, including case. Since bean property names always start with a lowercase letter, so must all the field names. Getting the properties set automatically is great; if you define more properties for your bean, all you have to do to set them is add new matching fields in the form that invokes the JSP page.

Besides the property and value attributes you have seen so far, the <jsp:setProperty> action supports one more attribute: param. If you can't use the same name for the parameters and the property names for some reason, use the param attribute to set a bean property to the value of any request parameter:

```
<jsp:setProperty
  name="userInfo"
  property="userName"
  param="someOtherParam"
/>
```

Here the userName property is set to the value of a request parameter named someOtherParam.

As in Example 8-2, <c:out> actions are used to add the submitted values to the response. The only difference is that in Example 8-4, the EL expressions pick up the values captured by the bean instead of getting the parameter values:

```
Name: <c:out value="${userInfo.userName}" /><br>
```

userInfo is the bean variable created by the <jsp:useBean> action. The property name (userName) is separated from the bean variable name by a dot (the EL property access operator) to tell the EL to get the property value.

The Favorite Food choices are available through a property named food as an array of strings. It's processed with the <c:forEach> action, just as in the JSTL example:

```
Favorite Food:
  <c:forEach items="${userInfo.food}" var="current">
    <c:out value="${current}" /> 
  </c:forEach>
```

Validating User Input

You should never trust your users, at least not when it comes to entering information in the format you need. Often, you need to make sure the input is valid before you continue to process a request. A date, for instance, can be written in many different formats. If you've traveled to the United States, and you're not a U.S. citizen, you probably have had to fill out both an I-94 and a customs declaration form to be admitted by an immigration officer. You may have noticed that on one of the forms you need to write your birth date as *yy/mm/dd* and on the other as *mm/dd/yy*. I always get it wrong.

The entry form used in the examples in this chapter has a number of fields that must be validated: a name must be entered, the birth date must be a valid date, the email address must at least look like a real email address (it's basically impossible to verify that it is in fact real), the gender must be one of m (male) or f (female), the lucky number must be a number between 1 and 100, and if any food favorites are selected, each must be one of z (pizza), p (pasta), or c (Chinese).

Simple input can be validated using the standard JSTL actions, but for more complex validation rules, a bean is a good choice. We will look at both approaches next. If you use JSP combined with servlets, the input validation is typically done by the servlet and the JSP pages are invoked only if the input turns out to be okay. This approach is described in Chapter 19.

Validating User Input Using JSTL Actions

Besides adding validation, let's make the input form example a bit more realistic. Instead of just echoing the entered values at the end of the page, we use them to set the initial values of the form fields. This makes it easier for the user to correct the mistakes. For each invalid value, an error message is also inserted above the incorrect field.

I use a number of JSTL actions that we have not discussed so far and a few tricks to implement these changes. To make all the new stuff easier to digest, we look at the new page in pieces. Example 8-5 shows the top part of the form with the validation and initialization of the Name field.

Example 8-5. Validating the name parameter with JSTL (validate_jstl.jsp)

```
<%@ page contentType="text/html" %>
<%@ taglib prefix="c" uri="http://java.sun.com/jsp/jstl/core" %>

<html>
  <head>
    <title>User Info Entry Form</title>
  </head>
  <body bgcolor="white">

    <form action="validate_jstl.jsp" method="post">
      <input type="hidden" name="submitted" value="true">
      <table>
        <c:if test="${param.submitted && empty param.userName}">
          <tr><td></td>
          <td colspan="2"><font color="red">
            Please enter your Name
          </font></td></tr>
        </c:if>
        <tr>
          <td>Name:</td>
          <td>
            <input type="text" name="userName"
              value="<c:out value="${param.userName}" />">
          </td>
        </tr>
```

The first thing to notice in this example is the HTML field of type "hidden", named submitted with the value true. The browser doesn't display a hidden field, but its value is sent as a regular request parameter when the form is submitted. I use it in this example to avoid displaying error messages when the page is loaded for the first time, before the user has had a chance to enter any data. The `submitted` parameter isn't part of the first request for the page, but when the user submits the form, the `submitted` parameter is sent along with all parameters representing the other HTML fields. Hence, it can be used to test if the parameters should be validated or not.

The validation of the Name field illustrates how it works. The JSTL `<c:if>` action, described in Table 8-5, is used with an EL expression that evaluates to `true` only if the `submitted` parameter has the value `true` and the `userName` parameter is empty. Since the `submitted` parameter isn't part of the initial request to load the page, it doesn't have the value `true`, causing the EL expression to evaluate to `false`. The `<c:if>` action's body is therefore ignored in this case. After submitting the form, however, the `submitted` parameter has the value `true`, so if the `userName` parameter contains an empty string (the user didn't enter a value in the Name field), the body is processed, adding the error message.

Table 8-5. Attributes for JSTL <c:if>

Attribute name	Java type	Dynamic value accepted	Description
`test`	`boolean`	Yes	Mandatory. An expression that evaluates to `true` or `false`.
`var`	`String`	No	Optional. The name of the variable to hold the Boolean result.
`scope`	`String`	No	Optional. The scope for the variable, one of `page`, `request`, `session`, or `application`. `page` is the default.

To make it easy for the user to correct mistakes, the form fields are initialized with the submitted values. The `<c:out>` action with an EL expression that gets the corresponding parameter value takes care of this.

A note about the `empty` operator seems warranted, because this is an operator you don't find in most languages. It's included in the EL to avoid having to deal with the difference between a `null` value (the absence of a value) and the empty string value (`""`) because in a web application, you typically want to treat both cases the same way. Without the `empty` operator, you would have to write all tests like the ones in Example 8-5 like this instead:

```
<c:if test="${param.submitted &&
  (param.userName == null || param.userName == '')}">
```

The `empty` operator is shorthand for the combination of the last two tests. In addition to empty strings and `null`, it also evaluates to `true` for an empty array, `java.util.Collection`, or `java.util.Map`. In other words, you can use it to test for empty collections of all types.

Another fairly unique feature in the EL is that you have a choice with regards to the symbols for the common operators. For instance, instead of using && as the logical AND operator, || for logical OR, and ! for logical NOT, you can use and, or, and not. The relational operators can be written as ==, !=, <, <=, >, and >=, or as eq, ne, lt, le, gt, and ge, respectively. Besides catering to different personal preferences, the motivation for this is to provide a consistent set of operator symbols for use in pure XML documents (as described in Chapter 17) in which some of the most commonly used symbols can cause problems (e.g., < and &&).

Example 8-6 shows the validation and initialization of the Birth Date and Email Address fields.

Example 8-6. Validating the birth date and email parameters with JSTL (validate_jstl.jsp)

```
<c:if test="${param.submitted && empty param.birthDate}">
  <tr><td></td>
  <td colspan="2"><font color="red">
    Please enter your Birth Date
  </font></td></tr>
</c:if>
<tr>
  <td>Birth Date:</td>
  <td>
    <input type="text" name="birthDate"
      value="<c:out value="${param.birthDate}" />">
  </td>
  <td>(Use format yyyy-mm-dd)</td>
</tr>
<c:if test="${param.submitted && empty param.emailAddr}">
  <tr><td></td>
  <td colspan="2"><font color="red">
    Please enter your Email Address
  </font></td></tr>
</c:if>
<tr>
  <td>Email Address:</td>
  <td>
    <input type="text" name="emailAddr"
      value="<c:out value="${param.emailAddr}" />">
  </td>
  <td>(Use format name@company.com)</td>
</tr>
```

As you can see, the processing for these fields is identical to the pattern used for the Name field. A <c:if> action tests if the form is submitted and the parameter corresponding to the field is empty, and if so, adds an error message. The submitted value of the field is added with a <c:out> action.

For the Gender field (radio button), the value must be either m (male) or f (female). This requires a slightly different test condition, as shown in Example 8-7.

Example 8-7. Validating the gender parameter with JSTL (validate_jstl.jsp)

```
<c:if test="${param.submitted &&
  param.gender != 'm' && param.gender != 'f'}">
  <tr><td></td>
  <td colspan="2"><font color="red">
    Please select a valid Gender
  </font></td></tr>
</c:if>
<tr>
  <td>Gender:</td>
  <td>
    <c:choose>
      <c:when test="${param.gender == 'f'}">
        <input type="radio" name="gender" value="m">
          Male<br>
        <input type="radio" name="gender" value="f" checked>
          Female
      </c:when>
      <c:otherwise>
        <input type="radio" name="gender" value="m" checked>
          Male<br>
        <input type="radio" name="gender" value="f">
          Female
      </c:otherwise>
    </c:choose>
  </td>
</tr>
```

In addition to testing if the form is submitted, we must test if the value is `m` or `f`. It's done by simply adding more subexpressions, combined using the `&&` operator. You can combine as many subexpressions as you need in this way.

The Gender field isn't represented by a text field but by a radio button, so another approach is also needed for initializing it with the submitted value. To make a radio button be displayed as selected, the `checked` attribute must be added to the HTML element. The JSTL `<c:choose>` action helps us with this task.

The `<c:choose>` action has no attributes; it just groups and controls any number of nested `<c:when>` actions and optionally one `<c:otherwise>` action. These are the only actions that are accepted as direct child elements of a `<c:choose>` element. A `<c:choose>` block is used to pick one of a set of related, mutually exclusive alternatives. The `<c:choose>` action makes sure that only the first `<c:when>` action (Table 8-6) with a `test` attribute value that evaluates to `true` is processed. If no `<c:when>` action meets its test condition, the `<c:otherwise>` body is processed instead. If you're a programmer, you may recognize this as being similar to a switch statement.

Table 8-6. Attributes for JSTL <c:when>

Attribute name	Java type	Dynamic value accepted	Description
test	boolean	Yes	Mandatory. An expression that evaluates to `true` or `false`.

In Example 8-7, the `<c:choose>` action contains one `<c:when>` action that tests if the gender parameter has the value `f`, and if so, adds both radio button fields with the one representing the `f` choice as selected. The `<c:otherwise>` action adds the radio button fields with the one representing `m` as selected.

The effect is that the `m` choice becomes the default, used if the submitted value is invalid. It may seem redundant to handle invalid values for a parameter representing a radio button, but it isn't. Even though using a group of radio buttons helps the regular user pick a valid value, you must guard against requests submitted through other means than the form. It's easy for someone to submit an HTTP request to your page with any value. For instance, see what happens if you request the page with a query string like this:

```
http://localhost:8080/ora/ch8/validate_jstl.jsp?submitted=true&gender=x
```

Since the page checks for valid values even for the radio buttons, the `x` value for the gender parameter results in an error message.

Next up is the processing of the Lucky Number field, in which the value must be a number between 1 and 100. Example 8-8 shows how you can test for this.

Example 8-8. Validating the lucky number parameter with JSTL (validate_jstl.jsp)

```
<c:if test="${param.submitted &&
  (param.luckyNumber < 1 || param.luckyNumber > 100)}">
  <tr><td></td>
  <td colspan="2"><font color="red">
    Please enter a Lucky Number between 1 and 100
  </font></td></tr>
</c:if>
<tr>
  <td>Lucky number:</td>
  <td>
    <input type="text" name="luckyNumber"
      value="<c:out value="${param.luckyNumber}" />">
  </td>
  <td>(A number between 1 and 100)</td>
</tr>
```

Compared to the test for the Gender field, there's one difference: the subexpressions for less than 1 or greater than 100 are placed within parentheses. Parentheses can be used in an EL expression to override the default rules for in which order subexpressions are evaluated, known as the *operator precedence rules*. The EL operator precedence rules say that the `&&` operator is evaluated before the `||` operator. Without the parentheses around the range check, the expression is evaluated as "if submitted, and the number is less than 1," and only if that is `false`, evaluate "if the number is greater than 100." With the parentheses, it's evaluated as "if submitted" and if that's `true`, evaluate "if the number is less than 1 or greater than 100." In this particular case, the result would be the same, but when you mix `&&` and `||` operators, it's always a good idea to group the subexpressions with parentheses to avoid surprises.

Example 8-9 shows the most complex validation case: the list of food choices. Here the food parameter may have none or many values, and each value must be one of z (pizza), p (pasta), or c (Chinese).

Example 8-9. Validating the food parameter with JSTL (validate_jstl.jsp)

```
        <c:forEach items="${paramValues.food}" var="current">
          <c:choose>
            <c:when test="${current == 'z'}">
              <c:set var="pizzaSelected" value="true" />
            </c:when>
            <c:when test="${current == 'p'}">
              <c:set var="pastaSelected" value="true" />
            </c:when>
            <c:when test="${current == 'c'}">
              <c:set var="chineseSelected" value="true" />
            </c:when>
            <c:otherwise>
              <c:set var="invalidSelection" value="true" />
            </c:otherwise>
          </c:choose>
        </c:forEach>
        <c:if test="${invalidSelection}">
          <tr><td></td>
          <td colspan="2"><font color="red">
            Please select only valid Favorite Foods
          </font></td></tr>
        </c:if>
        <tr>
          <td>Favorite Foods:</td>
          <td>
            <input type="checkbox" name="food" value="z"
              ${pizzaSelected ? 'checked' : ''}>Pizza<br>
            <input type="checkbox" name="food" value="p"
              ${pastaSelected ? 'checked' : ''}>Pasta<br>
            <input type="checkbox" name="food" value="c"
              ${chineseSelected ? 'checked' : ''}>Chinese
          </td>
        </tr>
        <tr>
          <td colspan="3">
            <input type="submit" value="Send Data">
          </td>
        </tr>
      </table>
    </form>
  </body>
</html>
```

The approach I use for this test is to loop through all submitted values (using the paramValues variable) with <c:forEach>, testing each value with the <c:choose> action and nested <c:when> and <c:otherwise> actions, setting a "selected" variable to true for each valid value and an invalidSelection variable to true for an invalid value. To set the variables, I use the JSTL <c:set> action, described in Table 8-7.

Table 8-7. Attributes for JSTL <c:set>

Attribute name	Java type	Dynamic value accepted	Description
value	Any type	Yes	Mandatory, unless the body is used to provide the value. The value to set.
var	String	No	Optional. The name of the variable to hold the value. If not specified, the target and property attributes must be used.
scope	String	No	Optional. The scope for the variable specified by var, one of page, request, session, or application. page is the default.
target	A JavaBeans object or a java.util.Map	Yes	Optional. A Map or a JavaBeans object with a property specified by property.
property	String	Yes	Optional. The property name for the object specified by target that should be set.

Once these test variables are set based on the input, it's easy to decide whether to add an error message; just test if invalidSelection is true.

The test variables also allow us to use the conditional EL operator to decide when to add the checked attribute for checkboxes:

```
<input type="checkbox" name="food" value="z"
${pizzaSelected ? 'checked' : ''}>Pizza<br>
<input type="checkbox" name="food" value="p"
${pastaSelected ? 'checked' : ''}>Pasta<br>
<input type="checkbox" name="food" value="c"
${chineseSelected ? 'checked' : ''}>Chinese
```

The conditional operator works with a Boolean subexpression (an expression that evaluates to true or false), followed by a question mark and two alternative clauses separated by a colon. The first clause is used if the Boolean expression evaluates to true; the second clause is used if it's false. If the test variable for the checkbox is set to true, the text "checked" is added; otherwise an empty string is added.

Validating User Input Using a Bean

If you think using JSTL to validate input looks complicated, you're right. It works fine for simple validation, like making sure a value has a value at all (as for the Name field) or that a parameter has one of a few specific values (as for the Gender choice). But with more complex validation, such as verifying that a parameter holds an email address or a credit-card number, or that a value matches a list of valid values held in a database, we can do a lot better with a bean. In fact, the format of the Birth Date and Email Address fields, and if the Lucky Number is something else than a number, isn't checked at all in the JSTL validation example. Other examples in this book will show how you can use custom actions to do more thorough validation of these types of values, but here we look at how it's done using a bean. Figure 8-3 shows a typical response when some fields have invalid values.

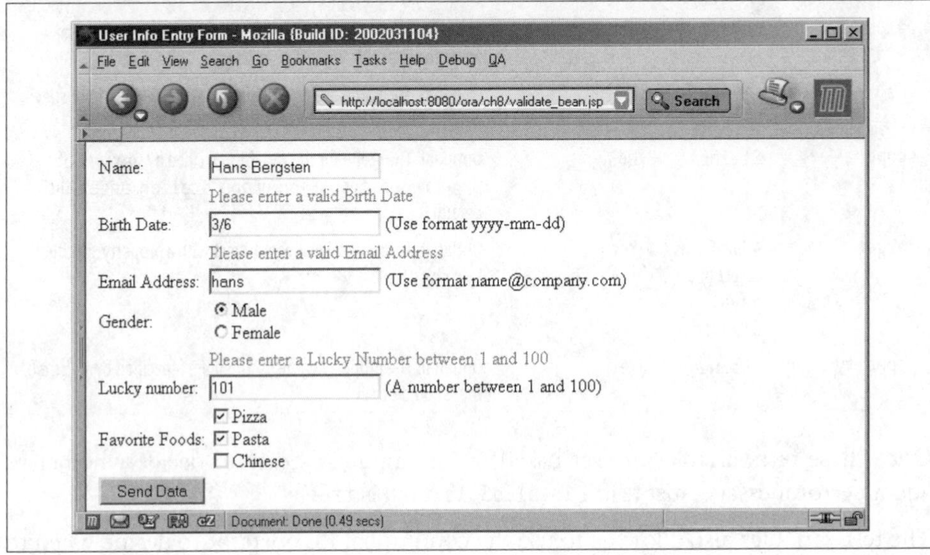

Figure 8-3. Response generated for invalid input

Since a bean is implemented with Java code and has access to all Java APIs, it can do any kind of validation you can dream of. The `UserInfoBean` used in the previous bean example also has a number of validation properties, described in Table 8-8. If you're curious about the bean implementation, it's described in Chapter 20.

Table 8-8. Validation properties for com.ora.jsp.beans.userinfo.UserInfoBean

Property name	Java type	Access	Description
`userNameValid`	`boolean`	Read	Is a user name set?
`birthDateValid`	`boolean`	Read	Is the birth date in the format *yyyy-mm-dd*?
`emailAddrValid`	`boolean`	Read	Is the email address in the format *name@company.com*?
`genderValid`	`boolean`	Read	Is the gender `m` or `f`?
`luckyNumberValid`	`boolean`	Read	Is lucky number between 1 and 100?
`foodValid`	`boolean`	Read	Does the food list only contain `z`, `p`, and `c` elements?
`valid`	`boolean`	Read	Do all properties have valid values?
`pizzaSelected`	`boolean`	Read	Is one of the elements in the food list a `z`?
`pastaSelected`	`boolean`	Read	Is one of the elements in the food list a `p`?
`chineseSelected`	`boolean`	Read	Is one of the elements in the food list a `c`?

All these properties are read-only, because the bean calculates their values based on the properties holding user data. The first six properties correspond one-to-one to the individual user data properties, while the `valid` property provides an easy way to see if all properties have valid values. The last three aren't really validation properties; they tell if a specific food type is part of the list of favorite foods.

These properties make the validation task much easier than in the JSTL example. As before, we look at one piece at the time, starting with the Name field processing in Example 8-10.

Example 8-10. Validating the name with a bean (validate_bean.jsp)

```
<%@ page contentType="text/html" %>
<%@ taglib prefix="c" uri="http://java.sun.com/jsp/jstl/core" %>

<html>
  <head>
    <title>User Info Entry Form</title>
  </head>
  <body bgcolor="white">
    <jsp:useBean id="userInfo"
      class="com.ora.jsp.beans.userinfo.UserInfoBean">
      <jsp:setProperty name="userInfo" property="*" />
    </jsp:useBean>
    <form action="validate_bean.jsp" method="post">
      <input type="hidden" name="submitted" value="true">
      <table>
        <c:if
          test="${param.submitted && userInfo.userNameValid == false}">
          <tr><td></td>
          <td colspan="2"><font color="red">
            Please enter your Name
          </font></td></tr>
        </c:if>
        <tr>
          <td>Name:</td>
          <td>
            <input type="text" name="userName"
              value="<c:out value="${userInfo.userName}" />">
          </td>
        </tr>
```

Like in Example 8-4, the `<jsp:useBean>` and `<jsp:setProperty>` actions capture the user input. The only difference is that these action elements are now at the top of the page. The bean is created and initialized before it tests for valid input and fills out the form with the previously entered values. Using the hidden field to avoid displaying error messages the first time the page is loaded is a trick we used in the JSTL version of the page as well.

The validation and setting the field value is a little bit different than in the JSTL example, but not much. Instead of testing if the `userName` parameter is equal to an empty string, the `userNameValid` bean property is compared to the Boolean value `false`. Even though it doesn't look like we have simplified life much, we have. All logic for deciding what is a valid value is now encapsulated in the bean instead of being coded in the page. If at a future date you decide to develop stricter rules for what a name must look like (maybe scan for profanities), you have to change only the bean; all pages where the bean is used remain the same. The Name field is then set to the value the user submitted, if any, with a `<c:out>` action using the bean's `userName` property value.

Example 8-11 shows how the birth date value is processed.

Example 8-11. Validating the birth date with a bean (validate_bean.jsp)

```
<c:if test="${param.submitted && !userInfo.birthDateValid}">
  <tr><td></td>
  <td colspan="2"><font color="red">
    Please enter a valid Birth Date
  </font></td></tr>
</c:if>
<tr>
  <td>Birth Date:</td>
  <td>
    <input type="text" name="birthDate"
      value="<c:out value="${userInfo.birthDate}" />">
  </td>
  <td>(Use format yyyy-mm-dd)</td>
</tr>
```

Testing the value of the bean's `birthDateValid` property, following the same pattern as for the name, handles the validation. But if you look carefully, you notice that instead of testing for equality with the value `false`, this test uses the `!userInfo.birthDateValid` syntax instead. This is just shorthand for the same kind of test. The `!` operator means "if the value is `true`, treat it as `false`, and vice versa." Formally, this operator is called the *logical complement operator*. I normally use the shorthand syntax because it's easier to type.

What's more interesting in Example 8-6 than the syntax difference is that as with the name parameter test, all validation logic is encapsulated in the bean. Testing if a date is valid can be quite a challenge. For instance, February 29 is a valid date only for a leap year. By delegating the validation to the bean and using only the result in the JSP page, the page author doesn't need to know any of these details. The Birth Date field value is set by, you guessed it, a `<c:out>` action using the bean's `birthDate` property.

The Email Address and the Lucky Number fields are handled the same way as Name and Birth Date.

The Gender field is dealt with pretty much the same as in the JSTL version, as shown in Example 8-12.

Example 8-12. Validating the gender choice with a bean (validate_bean.jsp)

```
<c:if test="${param.submitted && !userInfo.genderValid}">
  <tr><td></td>
  <td colspan="2"><font color="red">
    Please select a valid Gender
  </font></td></tr>
</c:if>
<tr>
  <td>Gender:</td>
  <td>
    <c:choose>
      <c:when test="${userInfo.gender == 'f'}">
        <input type="radio" name="gender" value="m">
          Male<br>
        <input type="radio" name="gender" value="f" checked>
          Female
      </c:when>
      <c:otherwise>
        <input type="radio" name="gender" value="m" checked>
          Male<br>
        <input type="radio" name="gender" value="f">
          Female
      </c:otherwise>
    </c:choose>
  </td>
</tr>
```

The only differences are that the bean's genderValid property is used for the validation test, and the gender property is used to decide which choice to mark as checked, instead of the parameter value used for both these tasks in the JSTL version. Example 8-13 shows that the biggest bang for the buck we get from using a bean instead of just JSTL is the simplified processing of the favorite food choices.

Example 8-13. Validating the food choices with a bean (validate_bean.jsp)

```
<c:if test="${param.submitted && !userInfo.foodValid}">
  <tr><td></td>
  <td colspan="2"><font color="red">
    Please select only valid Favorite Foods
  </font></td></tr>
</c:if>
<tr>
  <td>Favorite Foods:</td>
  <td>
    <input type="checkbox" name="food" value="z"
      ${userInfo.pizzaSelected ? 'checked' : ''}>Pizza<br>
    <input type="checkbox" name="food" value="p"
      ${userInfo.pastaSelected ? 'checked' : ''}>Pasta<br>
    <input type="checkbox" name="food" value="c"
      ${userInfo.chineseSelected ? 'checked' : ''}>Chinese
  </td>
</tr>
```

All the looping and testing of the individual values that is necessary in the JSTL version of the page are now encapsulated in the bean, so all that's needed here is to use the bean's properties to decide whether to add an error message and which checkboxes to check.

Formatting HTML Output

If you enter a value containing double quotes in the Name field in the *validate_jstl.jsp* or the *validate_bean.jsp* page, such as `Prince, "the artist"`, submit the form and look at the HTML code generated by the JSP page using your browser's `View Source` function, you see something like this:

```
<tr>
  <td>Name:</td>
  <td>
    <input type="text" name="userName"
      value="Prince, &#034;the artist&#034;">
  </td>
</tr>
```

Note that the quotes have been replaced with `"`. What's going on here? This is the `<c:out>` action's doing, and it's a very good thing. In the JSP file, double quotes enclose the value of the `<input>` element's `value` attribute. If the value itself includes a double quote, the browser gets confused and interprets the first double quote in the value as the end of the value. To prevent this type of problem, the `<c:out>` action converts all problematic characters to their so-called HTML character-entity equivalents. It converts single quotes, double quotes, less-than signs, greater-than signs, and ampersands to the HTML character entities `'`, `"`, `<`, `>`, and `&`, respectively. The browser handles the converted values without problem.

Besides taking care of the problem with quotes in a dynamic value, this type of character conversion also offers some protection against what's called a *cross site scripting attack*. What this means is that a malicious user submits input that causes problems when it's displayed by the browser. If the special characters aren't converted, entering `<script>window.close()</script>` in the Name field for Example 8-2, for instance, causes the window to disappear. When text like this is added to the response as is, a browser with JavaScript enabled executes the script, with the effect that the browser window is closed. In this example, the malicious user harms only herself, but a more serious scenario is a site where a user can submit text that's then displayed to all other site visitors. A user submitting a partial HTML element can be equally annoying, for instance `<a href=>` turns all text after the entry into an HTML link if the special characters aren't converted. The fact that `<c:out>` converts all special characters solves these particular examples, but unfortunately, I can't guarantee that it solves all clever tricks that someone can come up with. I recommend that you read the CERT information about this vulnerability (*http://www.cert.org/advisories/CA-2000-02.html*) and protect your sites as best you can.

In a few rare cases, converting special characters can in itself cause problems. The `<c:out>` action therefore provides an attribute named `escapeXml` that lets you control the escape behavior. Using `<c:out>` with `escapeXml` set to `false` was the only way to add unescaped EL expression values in JSP 1.2, but with JSP 2.0, a better alternative is to simply put the EL expression directly in the template text. You've already seen examples of this, for instance in Example 8-9 and Example 8-13.

Sometimes, using `<c:out>` results in clumsy and confusing looking HTML code, for instance when used to set the value of an HTML text field element as in examples in this chapter. With JSP 2.0 and JSTL 1.1, you can use the JSTL `fn:escapeXml( )` function to convert special characters instead:

```
<%@ page contentType="text/html" %>
<%@ taglib prefix="c" uri="http://java.sun.com/jsp/jstl/core" %>
<%@ taglib prefix="fn" uri="http://java.sun.com/jsp/jstl/functions" %>
        ...
        <tr>
          <td>Name:</td>
          <td>
            <input type="text" name="userName"
              value="${fn:escapeXml(userInfo.userName)}">
          </td>
        </tr>
        ...
```

EL function support is a new feature in JSP 2.0, and as you may recall, JSTL 1.1 provides a special tag library that contains only functions, declared at the top of this page. The function call syntax is fairly simple. For an EL expression that appears directly in template text, as in this example, you must specify the prefix for the tag library that defines the function (`fn`, in this case) followed by a colon and the name of the function and all arguments within parentheses. For functions defined in a tag library that also contains custom actions, you can omit the function prefix when you use a function in an attribute value for a custom action with the same prefix:

```
<%@ taglib prefix="my" uri="mytaglib" %>
<my:myAction attr="${myFunction(someArg, anotherArg)" />
```

Whether to use `<c:out>` or the `fn:escapeXml( )` function to convert special characters is largely a matter of preference. I tend to use the function for new applications, but I don't bother to replace the `<c:out>` action with the function in old JSP 1.2 applications. A feature provided by the `<c:out>` action that you lose when using the `fn:escapeXml( )` function directly in template text is that you can specify a default value to use if the EL expression evaluates to `null`. This can come in handy in some situations and be a reason for choosing `<c:out>` over the function.

CHAPTER 9

Error Handling and Debugging

When you develop any application that's more than a trivial example, errors are inevitable. A JSP-based application is no exception. There are many types of errors you will deal with. Simple syntax errors in the JSP pages are almost a given during the development phase. And even after you have fixed all the syntax errors, you may still have to figure out why the application doesn't work as you intended because of design mistakes. The application must also be designed to deal with problems that can occur when it's deployed for production use. Users can enter invalid values and try to use the application in ways you never imagined. External systems, such as databases, can fail or become unavailable due to network problems.

Since a web application is the face of the company, making sure it behaves well, even when the users misbehave and the world around it falls apart, is extremely important for a positive customer perception. Proper design and testing is the only way to accomplish this goal.

In this chapter, we look at the types of problems you can expect during development, as well as those common in a production system. You'll see how to track down JSP syntax and design errors, and to deal with runtime problems in a graceful manner.

Dealing with Syntax Errors

The first type of error you will encounter is the one you, or your coworkers, create by simple typos—in other words, syntax errors. The JSP container needs every JSP element to be written exactly as it's defined in the specification in order to process the JSP page. When it finds something that's not right, it tells you. How easy it is to understand what it tells you depends on the type of error, the JSP container implementation, and sometimes, on how fluent you are in computer gibberish.

Element Syntax Errors

All container implementations report syntax errors, but details such as the wording of the messages, how much information the message contains, and where the message is written, differ between them. In this chapter, I show examples only of the messages produced by Tomcat.

Let's first look at how Tomcat reports some typical syntax errors in JSP directives and action elements. Example 9-1 shows a version of the *easy.jsp* page from Chapter 5 with a syntax error.

Example 9-1. Improperly terminated directive (error1.jsp)

```
<%@ page contentType="text/html" >
<%@ taglib prefix="c" uri="http://java.sun.com/jsp/jstl/core" %>
<html>
  <head>
    <title>JSP is Easy</title>
  </head>
  <body bgcolor="white">

    <h1>JSP is as easy as ...</h1>

    1 + 2 + 3 = <c:out value="${1 + 2 + 3}" />

  </body>
</html>
```

The syntax error here is that the page directive on the first line isn't closed properly with `%>`; the percent sign is missing. Figure 9-1 shows what Tomcat has to say about it.

Tomcat reports the error by sending an error message to the browser. This is the default behavior for Tomcat, but it's not mandated by the JSP specification. The specification requires only that a response with the HTTP status code for a severe error (500) is returned, but how a JSP container reports the details is vendor-specific. For instance, the error message can be written to a file instead of the browser. If you use a container other than Tomcat, check the container documentation to see how it reports these types of errors.

The actual error message in Figure 9-1 is what is called an *exception stack trace*. When something goes really wrong in a Java method, it typically throws an exception. An exception is a special Java object, and throwing an exception is the method's way of saying it doesn't know how to handle a problem. Sometimes another part of the program can take care of the problem in a graceful manner, but in many cases, the best that can be done is to tell the user about it and move on. That's what the Tomcat container does when it finds a problem with a JSP page during the translation phase; it sends the exception stack trace to the browser. The stack trace contains a message about what went wrong and where the problem occurred. The message is intended to be informative enough for a user to understand, but the

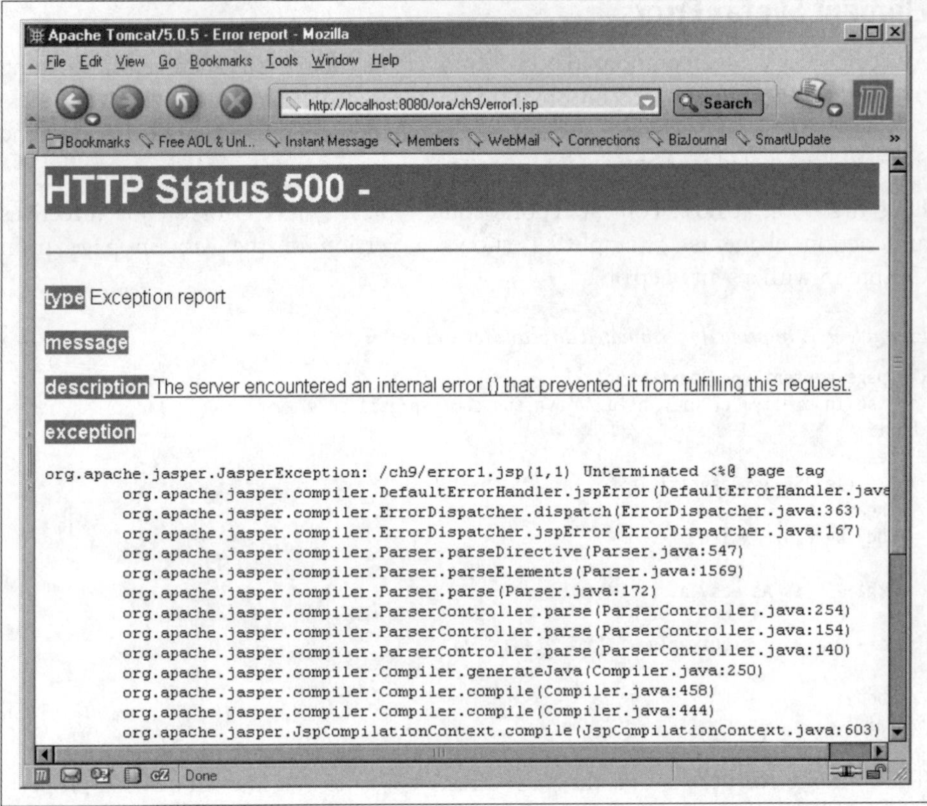

Figure 9-1. Error message about an unterminated JSP directive

actual trace information is of value only to a programmer. As you can see in Figure 9-1, the message is:

```
/ch9/error1.jsp(1,1) Unterminated <%@ page tag
```

The first part of the message is the name of the JSP page. The numbers within parentheses indicate on which line and character position in the file the error was found, and then the message states what the problem is. So this message tells us that a page directive (an element starting with <%@) on the first line isn't terminated as expected. In this case it's both the correct diagnosis and the right location.

Example 9-2 shows another version of *easy.jsp* with a different syntax error.

Example 9-2. Improperly terminated action (error2.jsp)

```
<%@ page contentType="text/html" %>
<%@ taglib prefix="c" uri="http://java.sun.com/jsp/jstl/core" %>
<html>
  <head>
    <title>JSP is Easy</title>
  </head>
```

Example 9-2. Improperly terminated action (error2.jsp) (continued)

```
  <body bgcolor="white">

    <h1>JSP is as easy as ...</h1>

    1 + 2 + 3 = <c:out value="${1 + 2 + 3}" >

  </body>
</html>
```

The syntax error here is almost the same as the "unterminated tag" in Example 9-1, but now it's the `<c:out>` action element that's not terminated properly (it's missing the closing slash required for an empty element). The message reported by Tomcat in this case is:

```
/ch9/error2.jsp(14,0) Unterminated <c:out tag
```

Again, the message gives the line and character position and a brief description of the error. In this case, the position information points to the first character after the syntax error; not perfect but good enough.

Another common error is a typo in an attribute name. The `value` attribute for the `<c:out>` action is misspelled in Example 9-3.

Example 9-3. Mistyped attribute name (error3.jsp)

```
<%@ page contentType="text/html" %>
<%@ taglib prefix="c" uri="http://java.sun.com/jsp/jstl/core" %>
<html>
  <head>
    <title>JSP is Easy</title>
  </head>
  <body bgcolor="white">

    <h1>JSP is as easy as ...</h1>

    1 + 2 + 3 = <c:out valu="${1 + 2 + 3}" />

  </body>
</html>
```

Tomcat reports the problem like this:

```
/ch9/error3.jsp(11,16) According to the TLD attribute value is mandatory
for tag out
```

In this case, the typo is in the name of a mandatory attribute, so Tomcat reports it as missing. If the typo is in the name of an optional attribute, Tomcat reports it as an invalid attribute name.

Example 9-4 shows a type of error that results in a message that is hard to figure out unless you know what's going on.

Example 9-4. Missing end quote in attribute value (error4.jsp)

```
<%@ page contentType="text/html" %>
<%@ taglib prefix="c" uri="http://java.sun.com/jsp/jstl/core" %>
<html>
  <head>
    <title>JSP is Easy</title>
  </head>
  <body bgcolor="white">

    <h1>JSP is as easy as ...</h1>

    1 + 2 + 3 = <c:out value="${1 + 2 + 3} default="Doh!" />

  </body>
</html>
```

If you look carefully at the `<c:out>` element, you see that the closing quote for the `value` attribute is missing. If another attribute is specified for the same element, like the `default` attribute used here, Tomcat reports the problem like this:

```
/ch9/error4.jsp(11,55) equal symbol expected
```

What's happening is that Tomcat includes everything up to the second quote as the value of the `value` attribute. It then assumes that the next word (`Doh!` in this example) is an attribute and complains that the equals sign (and the value) is missing.

Let's close this section with one of the most frustrating scenarios of all, namely forgetting to include a `taglib` directive for the tag library used in the page. This doesn't result in an error message at all, but all custom action elements are treated as template text and just added to the response without being executed. Before pulling all your hair trying to understand why none of your actions are being executed, make sure you have included the `taglib` directive. An easy way to see if this is the problem is to use the browser's `View Source` function: if the source for the response sent to the browser includes action elements, they where not processed by the web container, most likely due to a missing or incorrect `taglib` directive.

The examples here are the most common ones for JSP element syntax errors. Tomcat can give you pretty good information about what's wrong in most of these cases, but this is still an area where improvements are possible. For instance, emerging JSP authoring tools may help by providing GUI-based interfaces that generate the action elements automatically, eliminating this type of syntax problem altogether.

Expression Language Syntax Errors

Prior to JSP 2.0, how well EL syntax errors were reported varied between JSTL implementations and web containers, because the EL wasn't part of the JSP specification. Starting with JSP 2.0, the EL is part of the JSP specification, and all containers are required to analyze the syntax of EL expressions (in attribute values or directly in the template text) during the translation phase and report all syntax errors it finds.

As with the element syntax error messages, the details differ between containers, but let's look at a few EL syntax error examples in this section so you can see what to expect when you use the EL with Tomcat. Other implementations may do better (or worse), but these examples illustrate what to look for.

Example 9-5 shows a page with a subtle syntax error: the curly braces are missing in the EL expression.

Example 9-5. Missing both curly braces (error5.jsp)

```
<%@ page contentType="text/html" %>
<%@ taglib prefix="c" uri="http://java.sun.com/jsp/jstl/core" %>
<html>
  <head>
    <title>JSP is Easy</title>
  </head>
  <body bgcolor="white">

    <h1>JSP is as easy as ...</h1>

    1 + 2 + 3 = <c:out value="$1 + 2 + 3" />

  </body>
</html>
```

This is an easy mistake to make, but it's not recognized as a syntax error at all. To the container, this means that the value is a plain-text value, not an expression. When used with the `<c:out>` action, it's easy to figure out what's wrong because the text value is added to the response as is instead of the being evaluated: `$1 + 2 + 3`. But if you make this mistake with an attribute value that should provide the action with input to process in some way, the problem may not be so easy to spot. For instance, if you forget the curly braces for the `<c:forEach>` `items` attribute, it takes it as a text value and loops once over its body with the text as a single element.

Let's see what happens if you forget only the end curly brace, as shown in Example 9-6.

Example 9-6. Missing end curly brace (error6.jsp)

```
<%@ page contentType="text/html" %>
<%@ taglib prefix="c" uri="http://java.sun.com/jsp/jstl/core" %>
<html>
  <head>
    <title>JSP is Easy</title>
  </head>
  <body bgcolor="white">

    <h1>JSP is as easy as ...</h1>

    1 + 2 + 3 = <c:out value="${1 + 2 + 3" />

  </body>
</html>
```

Tomcat reports this error as shown in Figure 9-2.

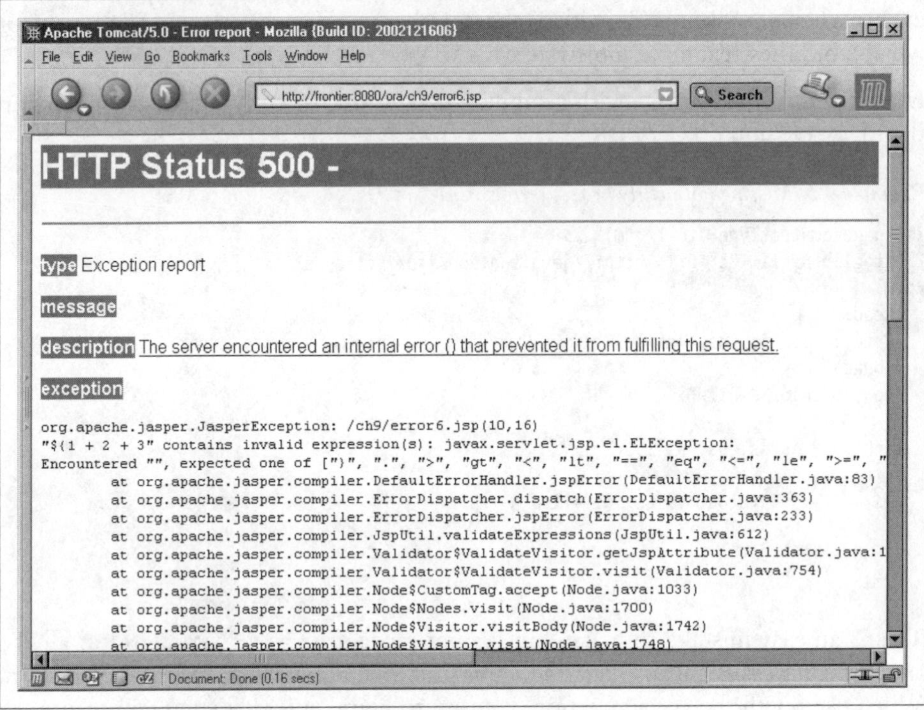

Figure 9-2. EL syntax error message

The error message contains three pieces of information:

- The position:

  ```
  /ch9/error6.jsp(10,16)
  ```

- A generic message that includes the complete EL expression:

  ```
  "${1 + 2 + 3" contains invalid expression(s)
  ```

- A more detailed message about the problem:

  ```
  Encountered "", expected one of ..."
  ```

This isn't so bad. The first two pieces of information make it fairly easy to find the expression that's in error. And the third part makes more and more sense when you've seen messages like this a few times.

Figure 9-2 is a good example of how all true syntax errors are reported by Tomcat (only the detailed messages differ), but some types of errors can't be found until the request-time phase, even though they may be regarded as syntax errors. Example 9-7 illustrates one such case.

Example 9-7. Misspelled property name (error7.jsp)

```
<%@ page contentType="text/html" %>
<%@ taglib prefix="c" uri="http://java.sun.com/jsp/jstl/core" %>
<html>
  <head>
    <title>Looking for information</title>
  </head>
  <body bgcolor="white">

    <h1>Looking for information</h1>

    The Current URI: <c:out value="${pageContext.request.requestUri}" />

  </body>
</html>
```

The problem here is that the property name is misspelled: it should be requestURI ("URI" in all caps) instead of requestUri. In this particular example, the container could actually figure this out at translation time, because pageContext is an implicit variable, so all its properties are known. But the type of an application variable is known only at request time, so it's not possible to notice a misspelled property name for the general case. Tomcat has opted for consistency in how to handle this type of error. The way this error is reported is by throwing an exception with this message:

```
Unable to find a value for "requestUri" in object of class "org.apache.coyote.
tomcat5.CoyoteRequestFacade" using operator "."
```

It contains some details about the error, such as the invalid property name and the object class name, so it's not impossible to match it with its source in the page. But because it's not caught until request time, it's unfortunately impossible to include the line number in a JSP 2.0 container.

Example 9-8 shows an almost identical error, but it results in a completely different result.

Example 9-8. Misspelled parameter name (error8.jsp)

```
<%@ page contentType="text/html" %>
<%@ taglib prefix="c" uri="http://java.sun.com/jsp/jstl/core" %>
<html>
  <head>
    <title>Looking for information</title>
  </head>
  <body bgcolor="white">

    <h1>Looking for information</h1>

    The missing parameter: <c:out value="${param.misspelled}" />

  </body>
</html>
```

Here it's the name of a request parameter that is misspelled, and it's not reported as an error. Instead the expression evaluates to null, which the <c:out> action converts to an empty string. This is by design, and it makes it easier to handle the typical case in which a missing parameter should be handled the same as a parameter with an empty string as the value. If a missing parameter resulted in an exception, you would have to do a lot more testing in all JSP pages, with <c:if> actions and expressions like this all over the place:

```
<c:if test="${!empty param.someParam}">
  <!-- Here it's safe to use the parameter -->
</c:if>
```

The downside is that it makes it harder to find parameter-name spelling errors. The EL handles all types of name/value pair collections, such as the implicit variables representing scopes (pageScope, requestScope, sessionScope, and applicationScope), as well as any application variable of type java.util.Map, the same way.

Debugging a JSP Application

After you have fixed all syntax errors, pat yourself on the back and enjoy the moment. If the application is more than a trivial example, however, this moment will probably be short-lived: you will likely find that one or more things still don't work as you expected. Logic errors, such as not taking care of all possible input combinations, can easily slip into an application during development. Finding and correcting this type of problem is called debugging.

For applications developed in compiled languages such as Java, C, or C++, a tool called a debugger is often used in this phase. It lets you step through the program line by line or run the program until it reaches a break point that you have defined, and lets you inspect the values of all variables in the program. With careful analysis of the program flow in runtime, you can discover why it works the way it does and not the way you want it to. There are debuggers for JSP as well, such as IBM's Visual Age for Java. Such products let you debug a JSP page exactly the same way as a program written in a more traditional programming language.

But a real debugger is often overkill for JSP pages. If your pages are so complex that you feel the need for a debugger, you may want to move code from the pages into JavaBeans or custom actions instead. These components can then be debugged with a standard Java debugger, which can be found in most Java Interactive Development Environments (IDEs). To debug JSP pages, another time tested debugging approach is usually sufficient: simply adding code to print variable values to the screen.

Let's look at how you can use this approach to find an error in an incorrect version of the input validation page from Chapter 8, shown in Example 9-9.

Example 9-9. Logical error (error9.jsp)

```
<%@ page contentType="text/html" %>
<%@ taglib prefix="c" uri="http://java.sun.com/jsp/jstl/core" %>
<%@ taglib prefix="ora" uri="orataglib" %>

<html>
  <head>
    <title>User Info Entry Form</title>
  </head>
  <body bgcolor="white">

    <form action="error9.jsp" method="post">
      <input type="hidden" name="submitted" value="true">
      <table>
        <c:if test="${param.submitted || empty param.userName}">
          <tr><td></td>
          <td colspan="2"><font color="red">
            Please enter your Name
          </font></td></tr>
        </c:if>
        ...
```

No matter what value you enter in the Name field, it still displays the error message. There's clearly something wrong here.

To find out what's going on, you can add a few `<c:out>` actions that include the parameter values and the value of the `<c:if>` test expression in the response:

```
<%@ page contentType="text/html" %>
<%@ taglib prefix="c" uri="http://java.sun.com/jsp/jstl/core" %>
<%@ taglib prefix="ora" uri="orataglib" %>

<html>
  <head>
    <title>User Info Entry Form</title>
  </head>
  <body bgcolor="white">

    \${param.submitted}: <c:out value="${param.submitted}" /><br>
    \${param.userName}:  <c:out value="${param.userName}" /><br>
    \${param.submitted || empty param.userName}:
      <c:out value="${param.submitted || empty param.userName}" />

    <form action="validate_jstl.jsp" method="post">
      <input type="hidden" name="submitted" value="true">
      <table>
        <c:if test="${param.submitted || empty param.userName}">
          <tr><td></td>
          <td colspan="2"><font color="red">
            Please enter your Name
          </font></td></tr>
        </c:if>
        ...
```

The result is shown in Figure 9-3.

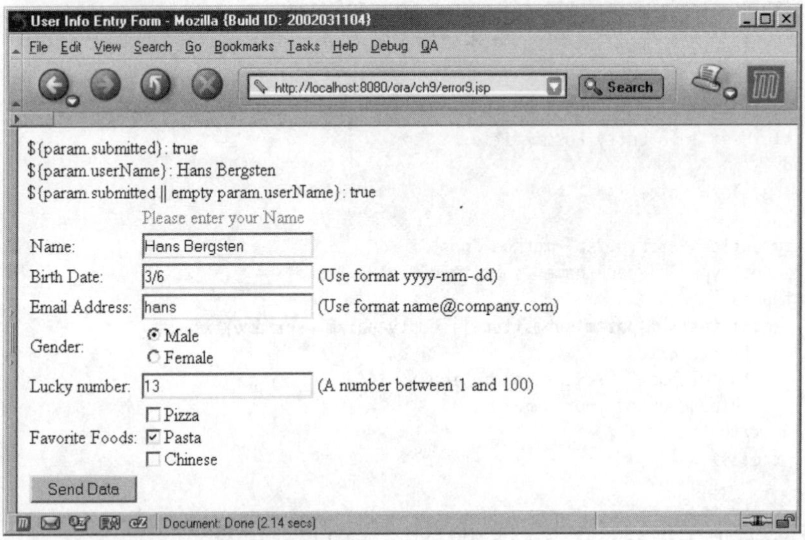

Figure 9-3. Response with debug output

Now it's a bit easier to see why it doesn't work. The parameter values have the expected values, but the EL expression used by `<c:if>` returns `true` even when the `userName` parameter has a value. It's because the `||` operator is used instead of the `&&` operator, so when the `submitted` parameter has the value `true`, the second part of the expression isn't evaluated at all.

A detail illustrated in this example is worth mentioning. See how a backslash (\) precedes each EL expression that is intended to serve as a static text label (followed by the evaluation result) in the debug output? The reason for this is that JSP 2.0 normally evaluates EL expressions found directly in template text. The backslash before the expression acts as an *escape character*, telling the container to output the expression verbatim instead of evaluating it. You rarely need to output expressions (or text that looks like an expression) in a real application, but if you have to, now you know how to do it.

Adding a couple of `<c:out>` actions to see variable values as part of the response in the browser is the easiest way to debug a JSP page. But sometimes multiple pages are involved in the processing of a single request, as you will see in Chapter 10. In this case, it may be better instead to write the debug output to a file or the command window where you started the server. You can use a custom action called `<ora:fileWrite>` (described in Chapter 21) to write to a file instead of the response. To write to the standard log file for the application, place the `<c:out>` action within the custom action like this:

```
<ora:fileWrite fileName="log">
  \${param.submitted}: <c:out value="${param.submitted}" />
  \${param.userName}:  <c:out value="${param.userName}" />
  \${param.submitted || empty param.userName}:
    <c:out value="${param.submitted || empty param.userName}" />
</ora:fileWrite>
```

The name and location of the application log file is container-dependent. Tomcat can be configured to use a separate file for each application, but by default, it writes messages for all applications to files named according to the *logs/<hostname>_log.<date>.txt* pattern, e.g. *logs/localhost_log_2002-03-30.txt*. Instead of log, which is a keyword the <ora:fileWrite> action recognizes as an order to use the application log file, you can specify the absolute file path for any file the container has write access to as the fileName attribute value.

Most containers, including Tomcat,* also let you write messages to the window where it was started. That's where the <ora:fileWrite> action writes when you omit the fileName attribute:

```
<ora:fileWrite>
  \${param.submitted}: <c:out value="${param.submitted}" />
  \${param.userName}:  <c:out value="${param.userName}" />
  \${param.submitted || empty param.userName}:
    <c:out value="${param.submitted || empty param.userName}" />
</ora:fileWrite>
```

Writing to the command window is convenient during development, when you run your own web server started in a command window. Writing to the application log file is useful when you debug an application that is running in a web server you don't have control over or if you need to record the debug messages in a file for further analysis later. But no matter where you tell <ora:fileWrite> to write the info, you typically don't want to use this action in your production code because it always writes.

To make it easy to generate the most common types of debug output only on demand, instead use the <ora:debug> custom action I developed for this book. It's described in Table 9-1.

Table 9-1. Attributes for <ora:debug>

Attribute name	Java type	Dynamic value accepted	Description
type	String	No	Mandatory. One of requestInfo, headers, cookies, params, pageScope, requestScope, sessionScope, or applicationScope.

* Tomcat must be started with the run option for the *catalina* script; otherwise such output is captured in the *catalina.out* log file.

The <ora:debug> action has only one attribute, named type, telling the action the type of debug information to write. To control where the information is written, you send a debug parameter with the request for the page. This request parameter must have one or more of the following values (separated by plus signs):

resp
: Includes the debug information in the response as an HTML table

stdout
: Writes the debug information to System.out

log
: Writes the debug information to the application log file

Let's look at an example. The JSP page shown in Example 9-10 first creates some test data and then uses the debug action to look at various pieces of information.

Example 9-10. Page with the <ora:debug> action (debug.jsp)

```
<%@ page contentType="text/html" %>
<%@ taglib prefix="c" uri="http://java.sun.com/jsp/jstl/core" %>
<%@ taglib prefix="ora" uri="orataglib" %>

<html>
  <head>
    <title>Debug Output</title>
  </head>
  <body bgcolor="white">

    <%-- Add test variables to the request scope --%>
    <c:set var="aString" scope="request" value="Hello World!" />
    <jsp:useBean id="aDate" scope="request" class="java.util.Date" />
    <c:set var="aNumber" scope="request" value="${aDate.minutes}" />

    <h1>Debug Output</h1>

    <ora:debug type="headers" />
    <ora:debug type="cookies" />
    <ora:debug type="params" />
    <ora:debug type="requestScope" />
  </body>
</html>
```

The <c:set> and <jsp:useBean> actions creates three variables in the *request scope* in JSP. Objects placed in the request scope can be accessed by all JSP pages used to process the same request. Don't worry about how this works now; you'll learn more about all the JSP scopes in Chapter 10. Here, it's used only to show you how the <ora:debug> action can display scope information. Next, four <ora:debug> actions display all headers, cookies, request parameters, and request scope variables.

The <ora:debug> action writes information only if the request contains a debug request parameter with a valid value. Therefore, you can keep the action element in your pages all the time and activate it only when you need the debug info. For instance, you can request the page with a URL that includes the debug parameter in the query string like this:

```
http://localhost:8080/ora/ch9/debug.jsp?debug=resp+stdout&a=b
```

You then get a response as shown in Figure 9-4.

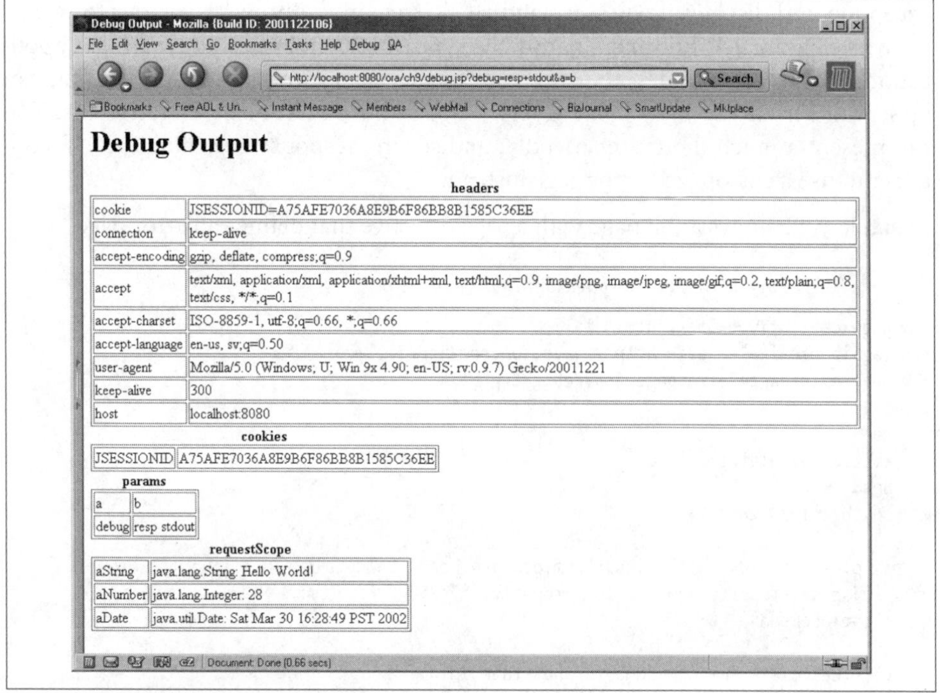

Figure 9-4. Debug output

Because the debug parameter specifies both `resp` and `stdout`, you also get all the debug information in the window in which you started Tomcat.

Dealing with Runtime Errors

Eventually, your application will work the way you want. But things can still go wrong due to problems with external systems your application depends on, such as a database. And even though you have tested and debugged your application, there may be runtime conditions you didn't anticipate.

Well-behaved components, such as beans and JSP actions, deal with expected error conditions in a graceful manner. For instance, the `UserInfo` bean used in Chapter 8 has a `valid` attribute that is `false` unless all properties are set to valid values. Your JSP page can then test the property value and present the user with an appropriate message. The JSTL actions also act gracefully in most situations, for instance the `<c:forEach>` action simply does nothing if the `items` attribute value is `null`.

Some problems are impossible for the component to handle gracefully, however, and the user needs to be told about the problem instead. The standard way Java does this is to throw an exception. Beans, JSP actions, and the EL processor, can throw exceptions when something goes really bad. By default, the JSP container catches the exception and displays its message and stack trace in the browser, similar to what's shown in Figure 9-1. But that's hardly the type of error message you want the application users to see. Besides, the exception messages may reveal information that can be sensitive from a security point of view, such as file paths and SQL statements. You can present a much more user-friendly, and secure, response by telling the JSP container to use a customized error page instead.

Example 9-11 shows a JSP page with a page directive that defines an error page.

Example 9-11. Page with an error page definition (calc.jsp)

```
<%@ page contentType="text/html" %>
<%@ taglib prefix="c" uri="http://java.sun.com/jsp/jstl/core" %>
<%@ page errorPage="errorpage.jsp?debug=log" %>
<html>
  <head>
    <title>Calculator</title>
  </head>
  <body bgcolor="white">

    <jsp:useBean id="calc" class="com.ora.jsp.beans.calc.CalcBean">
      <jsp:setProperty name="calc" property="*" />
    </jsp:useBean>

    <%-- Calculate the new numbers and state info --%>
    <c:set var="currentNumber" value="${calc.currentNumber}" />

    <form action="calc.jsp" method="post">
      <table border=1>
        <tr>
          <td colspan="4" align="right">
            <c:choose>
              <c:when test="${currentNumber == ''}">
                 
              </c:when>
              <c:otherwise>
                <c:out value="${currentNumber}" />
              </c:otherwise>
            </c:choose>
            <input type="hidden" name="currentNumber"
              value="${currentNumber}">
            <input type="hidden" name="previousNumber"
              value="${calc.previousNumber}">
            <input type="hidden" name="currentOperation"
              value="${calc.currentOperation}">
```

Example 9-11. Page with an error page definition (calc.jsp) (continued)

```
          <input type="hidden" name="reset"
            value="${calc.reset}">
        </td>
      </tr>
      <tr>
        <td><input type="submit" name="digit" value=" 7 "></td>
        <td><input type="submit" name="digit" value=" 8 "></td>
        <td><input type="submit" name="digit" value=" 9 "></td>
        <td><input type="submit" name="oper" value="  /  "></td>
      </tr>
      <tr>
        <td><input type="submit" name="digit" value=" 4 "></td>
        <td><input type="submit" name="digit" value=" 5 "></td>
        <td><input type="submit" name="digit" value=" 6 "></td>
        <td><input type="submit" name="oper" value="  *  "></td>
      </tr>
      <tr>
        <td><input type="submit" name="digit" value=" 1 "></td>
        <td><input type="submit" name="digit" value=" 2 "></td>
        <td><input type="submit" name="digit" value=" 3 "></td>
        <td><input type="submit" name="oper" value="  -  "></td>
      </tr>
      <tr>
        <td><input type="submit" name="digit" value=" 0 "></td>
        <td> </td>
        <td><input type="submit" name="dot" value="  .  "></td>
        <td><input type="submit" name="oper" value="  +  "></td>
      </tr>
      <tr>
        <td> </td>
        <td> </td>
        <td><input type="submit" name="clear" value=" C "></td>
        <td><input type="submit" name="oper" value="  =  "></td>
    </table>
  </form>

 </body>
</html>
```

The `errorPage` attribute in the page directive specifies the path for the page to be displayed if an exception is thrown by any JSP element. When the path is specified as in Example 9-11, the error page must be located in the same directory as the page that references it. However, if it starts with a slash (/), it's interpreted as a context-relative path, relative to the application's context path. This means you can define a common error page for all the JSP pages in an application, even if you place them in multiple subdirectories using a path such as `/shared/errorpage.jsp`.

Also note that the error page URI in Example 9-11 includes a query string with the debug parameter:

```
<%@ page errorPage="errorpage.jsp?debug=log" %>
```

The debug parameter lets you use the <ora:debug> action to log information about what went wrong in the error page.

The rest of the page in Example 9-11 implements a simple calculator, shown in Figure 9-5. It's intended only to illustrate how the error page handling works, so I will not describe it in detail. When you're done reading this book, it may be a good exercise to figure it out yourself by looking at the source code.

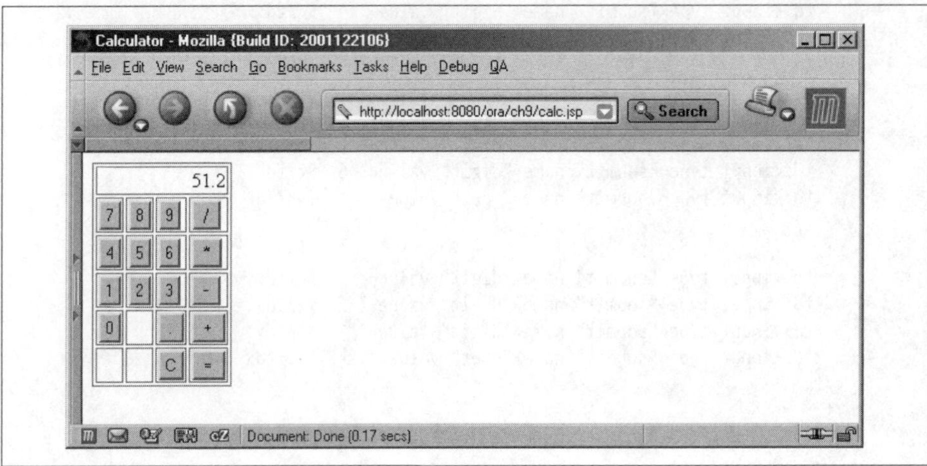

Figure 9-5. Calculator page

If a user tries to divide a number by zero, the CalcBean used in this page throws an exception. This triggers the error page shown in Example 9-12 to be invoked.

Example 9-12. Error page (errorpage.jsp)

```
<%@ page contentType="text/html" %>
<%@ taglib prefix="c" uri="http://java.sun.com/jsp/jstl/core" %>
<%@ taglib prefix="ora" uri="orataglib" %>
<%@ page isErrorPage="true" %>
<html>
  <head>
    <title>Sorry</title>
  </head>
  <body bgcolor="white">
    We're sorry but the request could not be processed.
    Detailed information about the error has been logged so we will
    analyze it and correct whatever is causing it as soon as possible.
    <p>
    Please try again, and
    <a href="mailto:webmaster@mycompany.com">let us know</a> if the
    problem persists.

    <ora:fileWrite fileName="log">
      Error in: ${pageContext.errorData.requestURI}
      Error message: ${pageContext.errorData.throwable.message}
    </ora:fileWrite>
```

Example 9-12. Error page (errorpage.jsp) (continued)

```
    <ora:debug type="params" />
  </body>
</html>
```

At the top of the page is a page directive with the attribute `isErrorPage` set to `true`. This tells the container that the `errorData` property of the implicit `pageContext` variable should be initialized with information about what caused the page to be invoked. The type of the `errorData` property is `javax.servlet.jsp.ErrorData`. This class is a bean with the properties shown in Table 9-2.

Table 9-2. Properties for javax.servlet.jsp.ErrorData

Property name	Java type	Access	Description
`requestURI`	`String`	Read	The context-relative URI for the erroneous request
`servletName`	`String`	Read	The name of the servlet handling the erroneous request
`statusCode`	`int`	Read	The status code for the erroneous request
`throwable`	`Throwable`	Read	The exception thrown by the erroneous request, if any

In Example 9-11, EL expressions access two of these properties: `requestURI`, containing the URI for the page where the error occurred, and `throwable`, containing a reference to the exception thrown by the page. The type of the `throwable` property is `java.lang.Throwable`, which in turn exposes a property named `message` that contains a message about what went wrong.

The EL expressions are nested within the body of the `<ora:fileWrite>` custom action, so their values end up in the application log file instead of in the response. All request parameters are then written to the log file as well, using the `<ora:debug>` custom action. In this way, information about which page caused the problem, the exception that was thrown, and all parameter values that were received with the request causing the problem, is logged in the application log file when something unexpected happens. You can therefore look at the log file from time to time to see what kind of problems occur frequently, and hopefully fine-tune the application to avoid them or at least provide more specific error messages.

The user isn't interested in any of these details, but wants to be assured that the problem is being registered and corrected. The same customized error page that logs all the details also presents an apology and a promise to take care of the problem, as shown in Figure 9-6.

An alternative to specifying an error page with the `errorPage` attribute in a JSP page is to declare an error page in the application deployment descriptor (*web.xml*). Error pages can be declared for specific exception types as well as for response status codes:

```
<error-page>
  <exception-type>java.lang.Throwable</exception-type>
  <location>/errorpage.jsp</location>
```

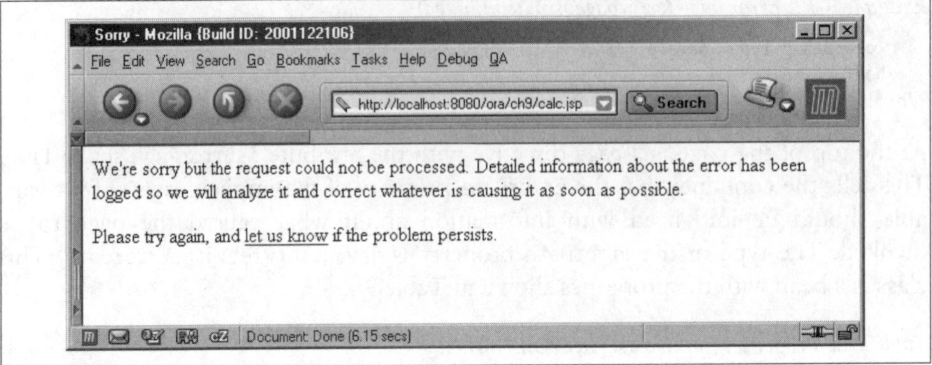

Figure 9-6. Customized error page

```
</error-page>
<error-page>
  <error-code>500</error-code>
  <location>/errorpage.jsp</location>
</error-page>
```

The <error-page> element contains an <exception-type> or an <error-code> element, plus a <location> element with the context-relative path for the servlet, JSP page, or static page to handle the error. The <exception-type> element contains the fully qualified name of the type of exception you want to handle. Similarly, the <error-code> element contains the HTTP response status code to handle. You can include multiple <error-page> elements to use different pages for different exceptions and status codes. For the <exception-type> element, the container picks the one that most closely matches the type of the exception thrown, while it uses an exact match for the <error-code> element.

An error page declaration in the deployment descriptor applies to all resources in the application. If an `errorPage` attribute is also specified in a JSP page, it's used instead of the one declared in the deployment descriptor.

Catching Exceptions

If a particular type of problem frequently shows up in the log files, you may want to fine-tune the error handling and deal more gracefully with the problem. There's a JSTL action named <c:catch>, described in Table 9-3, that can help you with this.

Table 9-3. Attributes for JSTL <c:catch>

Attribute name	Java type	Dynamic value accepted	Description
`var`	`String`	No	Optional. The name of the variable to hold the `java.lang.Throwable` if thrown by elements in the body.

Example 9-13 shows the top part of a modified version of the *calc.jsp* page that uses <c:catch> to catch divide-by-zero exceptions.

Example 9-13. Catching an exception (calc2.jsp)

```
<%@ page contentType="text/html" %>
<%@ taglib prefix="c" uri="http://java.sun.com/jsp/jstl/core" %>
<%@ page errorPage="errorpage.jsp?debug=log" %>

<html>
  <head>
    <title>Calculator</title>
  </head>
  <body bgcolor="white">

    <jsp:useBean id="calc" class="com.ora.jsp.beans.calc.CalcBean">
      <jsp:setProperty name="calc" property="*" />
    </jsp:useBean>

    <%-- Calculate the new numbers and state info --%>
    <c:catch var="error">
      <c:set var="currentNumber" value="${calc.currentNumber}" />
    </c:catch>
    <c:if test="${error != null}">
      <c:set var="currentNumber" value="Error" />
      <jsp:setProperty name="calc" property="reset" value="true" />
    </c:if>
    ...
```

The calc bean's currentNumber property accessor method is the one that performs the calculation. By placing the <c:set> action with the EL expression that reads this property within the body of the <c:catch> action, any exception is caught and saved in a variable named error. The <c:if> block tests if the error variable has a value, and if so, sets the currentNumber variable to "Error" and resets the bean's state by setting its reset property to true. The result is a nicer response than showing an error page; "Error" appears in the calculator's display, and the user can just click C and start over.

Dealing with syntax errors and bugs are part of the application-development process. In this chapter, we have looked at some of the ways you can ease the pain. To minimize the number of syntax errors, you can use the types of JSP development tools listed at the *http://www.TheJSPBook.com* site. The <ora:debug> custom action presented in this chapter helps you to see what's going on at runtime when you debug the application. Finally, you can handle common runtime errors by catching the exceptions with <c:catch> and handle them in the page, and define a customized error page to log information about unexpected errors and say something nice to the user.

CHAPTER 10

Sharing Data Between JSP Pages, Requests, and Users

Any real application consists of more than a single page, and multiple pages often need access to the same information and server-side resources. When multiple pages process the same request (e.g., one page that retrieves the data the user asked for and another that displays it), there must be a way to pass data from one page to another. In an application in which the user is asked to provide information in multiple steps, such as an online shopping application, there must be a way to collect the information received with each request and get access to the complete set when the user is ready. Other information and resources need to be shared among multiple pages, requests, and all users. Examples are information about currently logged-in users, database connection pool objects, and cache objects to avoid frequent database lookups.

In this chapter you will learn how scopes in JSP provide access to this type of shared data. You will also see how using multiple pages to process a request leads to an application that's easier to maintain and expand, and learn about a JSP action that lets you pass control between the different pages.

Passing Control and Data Between Pages

As discussed in Chapter 3, one of the most fundamental features of JSP technology is that it allows for separation of request processing, business logic and presentation, using what's known as the Model-View-Controller (MVC) model. As you may recall, the roles of Model, View, and Controller can be assigned to different types of server-side components. In this part of the book, JSP pages are used for both the Controller and View roles, and the Model role is played by either a bean or a JSP page. This isn't necessarily the best approach, but it lets us focus on JSP features instead of getting into Java programming. If you're a programmer and interested in other role assignments, you may want to take a peek at Chapters 18 and 19. These chapters describe other alternatives and focus on using a servlet as the Controller.

In this section we look at how to separate the different aspects in a pure JSP application, using a modified version of the User Info example from Chapter 8 as a concrete example. In this application, the business logic piece is trivial. However, it sets the stage for a more advanced application example in the next section and the remaining chapters in this part of the book; all of them use the pattern introduced here.

The different aspects of the User Info example can be categorized like this:

- Display the form for user input (presentation)
- Validate the input (request processing and business logic)
- Display the result of the validation (presentation)

A separate JSP page is used for each aspect in the modified version. The restructured application contains the three JSP pages shown in Figure 10-1.

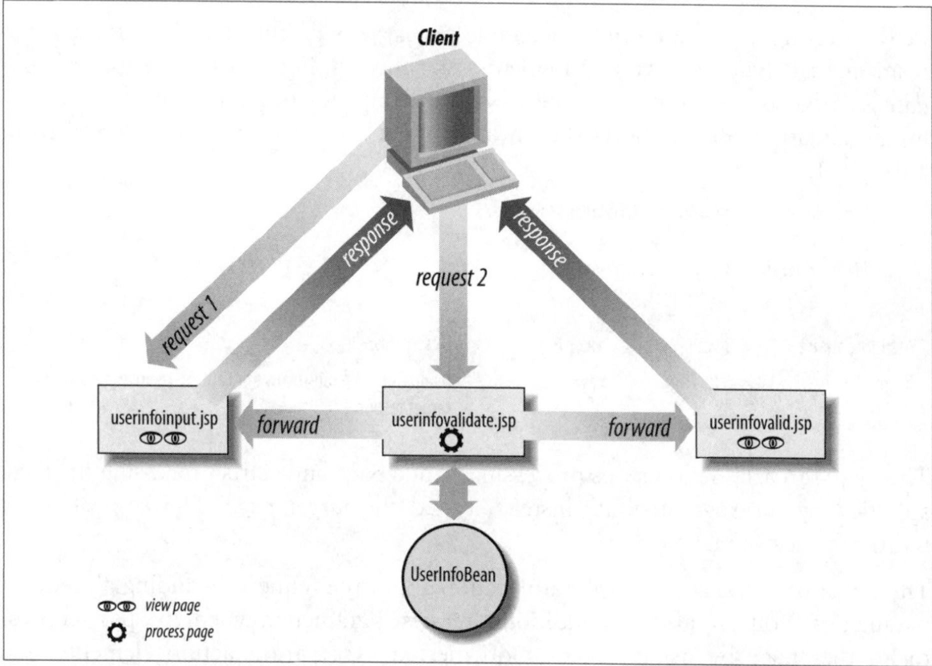

Figure 10-1. User Info application pages

Here's how it works. The *userinfoinput.jsp* page displays an input form. The user submits this form to *userinputvalidate.jsp* to validate the input. This page processes the request using the `UserInfoBean` and passes control to either the *userinfoinput.jsp* page (if the input is invalid) or the *userinfovalid.jsp* page (if the input is valid). If valid, the *userinfovalid.jsp* page displays a "thank you" message. In this example, the `UserInfoBean` represents the Model, the *userinputvalidate.jsp* page the Controller, and *userinfoinput.jsp* and *userinfovalid.jsp* represent the Views.

This gives you the flexibility and maintainability discussed in Chapter 3. If the validation rules change, a Java programmer can change the `UserInfoBean` implementation without touching any other part of the application. If the customer wants a different look, a page author can modify the View JSP pages without touching the request processing or business logic code.

Using different JSP pages as Controller and View means that more than one page is used to process a request. To make this happen, you need to be able to do two things:

- Pass control from one page to another
- Pass data from one page to another

Passing Control from One Page to Another

Before digging into the modified example pages, let's go through the basic mechanisms for satisfying the two requirements. As shown in Figure 10-1, the *userinfovalidate.jsp* page passes control to one of two other pages based on the result of the input validation. JSP supports this through the `<jsp:forward>` action, described in Table 10-1:

```
<jsp:forward page="userinfoinput.jsp" />
```

Table 10-1. Attributes for <jsp:forward>

Attribute name	Java type	Dynamic value accepted	Description
`page`	`String`	Yes	Mandatory. A page-relative or context-relative path for the target resource.

The `<jsp:forward>` action stops processing of one page and starts processing the page specified by the `page` attribute instead, called the *target page*. The control never returns to the original page.

The target page has access to all information about the request, including all request parameters. You can also add additional request parameters when you pass control to another page by using one or more nested `<jsp:param>` action elements (see Table 10-2):

```
<jsp:forward page="userinfoinput.jsp" >
  <jsp:param name="msg" value="Invalid email address" />
</jsp:forward>
```

Table 10-2. Attributes for <jsp:param>

Attribute name	Java type	Dynamic value accepted	Description
`name`	`String`	No	Mandatory. The parameter name.
`value`	`String`	Yes	Mandatory. The parameter value.

Parameters specified with `<jsp:param>` elements are added to the parameters received with the original request. The target page, therefore, has access to both the original parameters and the new ones, and can access both types in the same way. If a parameter is added to the request using a name of a parameter that already exists, the new value is added first in the list of values for the parameter.

The `page` attribute value is interpreted relative to the location of the current page if it doesn't start with a `/`. This called a *page-relative path*. If the source and target page are located in the same directory, just use the name of the target page as the `page` attribute value, as in the previous example. You can also refer to a file in a different directory using notation such as *../foo/bar.jsp* or */foo/bar.jsp*. When the page reference starts with a `/`, it's interpreted relative to the top directory for the application's web page files. This is called a *context-relative path*.

Let's look at some concrete examples to make this clear. If the application's top directory is *C:\Tomcat\webapps\myapp*, page references in a JSP page located in *C:\Tomcat\webapps\myapp\registration\userinfo* are interpreted like this:

page= "bar.jsp"
: *C:\Tomcat\webapps\myapp\registration\userinfo\bar.jsp*

page= "../foo/bar.jsp"
: *C:\Tomcat\webapps\myapp\registration\foo\bar.jsp*

page= "/foo/bar.jsp"
: *C:\Tomcat\webapps\myapp\foo\bar.jsp*

Passing Data from One Page to Another

JSP provides different *scopes* for sharing data objects between pages, requests, and users. The scope defines how long the object is available and whether it's available only to one user or to all application users. The following scopes are defined: *page*, *request*, *session*, and *application*.

Objects placed in the default scope, the *page scope*, are available only within that page. That's the scope used in all examples you have seen so far. The *request scope* is for objects that need to be available to all pages processing the same request, for instance both the page that receives the request initially and the page the first page forwards to. Objects in the *session scope* are available to all requests made from the same browser, and objects in the *application scope* are shared by all users of the application (see Figure 10-2). According to the JSP specification, the name used for an object must be unique within all scopes. This means that if you have an object named `userInfo` in the application scope, for instance, and save another object with the same name in the request scope, the container may remove the first object. Few containers (if any) enforce this rule, but you should ensure you use unique names anyway to avoid portability problems.

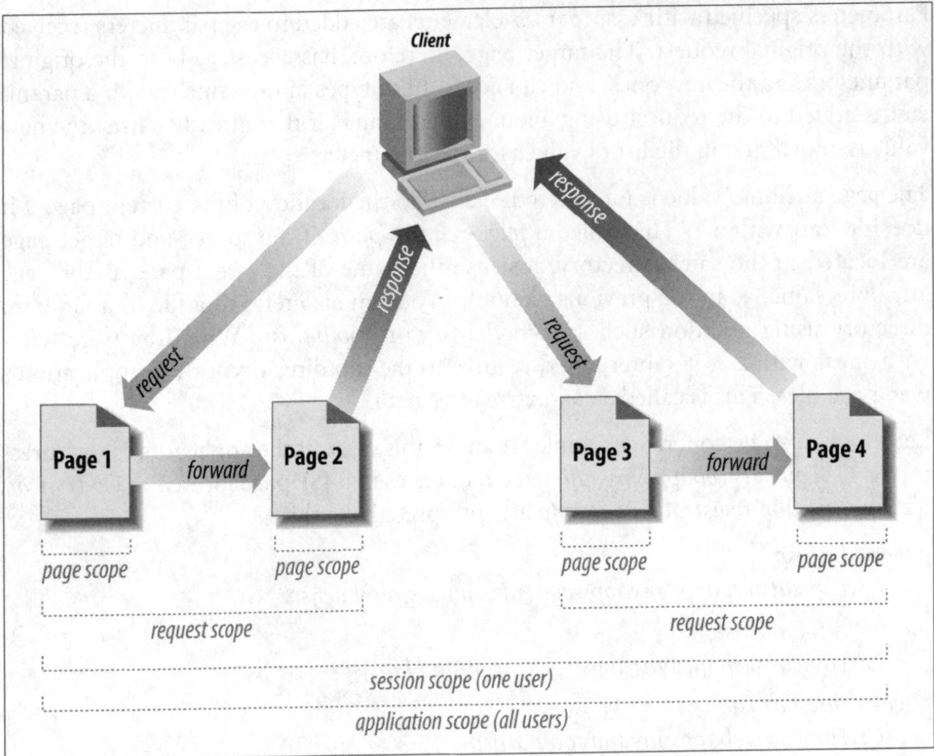

Figure 10-2. Lifetime of objects in different scopes

The <jsp:useBean> action has a scope attribute used to specify the scope for the bean:

```
<jsp:useBean id="userInfo" scope="request"
  class="com.ora.jsp.beans.userinfo.UserInfoBean" />
```

The <jsp:useBean> action ensures that the bean already exists in this scope or that a new one is created and placed in the specified scope. It first looks for a bean with the name specified by the id attribute in the specified scope. If it already exists, for instance created by a previously invoked <jsp:useBean> action or by a servlet, it does nothing.* If it can't find it, it creates a new instance of the class specified by the class attribute and makes it available with the specified name within the specified scope.

If you'd like to perform an action only when the bean is created, place the elements in the body of the <jsp:useBean> action:

```
<jsp:useBean id="userInfo" scope="request"
  class="com.ora.jsp.beans.userinfo.UserInfoBean" >
  <jsp:setProperty name="userInfo" property="*" />
</jsp:useBean>
```

* It actually does one thing when the bean already exists: associates the bean with a scripting variable. This is only of interest if you use JSP scripting elements, so I save a discussion about this until Chapter 16.

In this example, the nested <jsp:setProperty> action sets all properties to the values of the corresponding parameters when the bean is created. If the bean already exists, the <jsp:useBean> action body isn't evaluated. and the <jsp:setProperty> action isn't executed.

The scope attribute can also be used with all JSTL actions that expose variables outside their element bodies to designate where the variable should be created, as you will see later in this chapter.

You can access a bean created by the <jsp:useBean> action as a variable in EL expressions. Typically you just specify the variable name no matter which scope it's saved in, for instance:

```
${userInfo.userName}
```

In this case, the EL looks for the variable in all scopes in the order page, request, session, and application. If it's important to locate a variable in a specific scope, you can use the implicit EL variables representing the different scopes:

```
${pageScope.userInfo.userName}
${requestScope.userInfo.userName}
${sessionScope.userInfo.userName}
${applicationScope.userInfo.userName}
```

Each scope variable represents a collection (a java.util.Map) of all variables in that scope, so with expressions like these, the EL looks for the variable only in the specified scope.

All Together Now

At this point, you have seen the two mechanisms needed to let multiple pages process the same request: passing control and passing data. These mechanisms allow you to employ the MVC design, using one page for request processing and business logic, and another for presentation. The <jsp:forward> action can pass control between the pages, and information placed in the request scope is available to all pages processing the same request.

Let's apply this to the User Info example. In Chapter 8, different output was produced depending on whether or not the user input was valid. If the input was invalid, error messages were added to inform the user of the problem. Even when the input was valid, however, the form—without error messages, of course—was displayed.

No more of that. When we split the different aspects of the application into separate JSP pages as shown in Figure 10-1, we also change the example so that the form is only shown when something needs to be corrected. When all input is valid, a confirmation page is shown instead.

Example 10-1 shows the top part of the *userinfoinput.jsp* page.

Example 10-1. Page for displaying entry form (userinfoinput.jsp)

```
<%@ page contentType="text/html" %>
<%@ taglib prefix="c" uri="http://java.sun.com/jsp/jstl/core" %>

<html>
  <head>
    <title>User Info Entry Form</title>
  </head>
  <body bgcolor="white">
    <jsp:useBean id="userInfo"
      scope="request"
      class="com.ora.jsp.beans.userinfo.UserInfoBean"
    />

    <form action="userinfovalidate.jsp" method="post">
      ...
```

The rest of the page is identical to the one used in Chapter 8. If you compare Example 10-1 with the JSP page used for bean-based validation in Chapter 8, the only differences are that the `userInfo` bean is placed in the request scope (the `scope` attribute is set to `request`), the `<jsp:setProperty>` action for capturing input is gone, and the form's `action` attribute specifies the validation page instead of pointing back to the same page.

The validation page, *userinfovalidate.jsp*, is given in Example 10-2.

Example 10-2. Input validation page (userinfovalidate.jsp)

```
<%@ taglib prefix="c" uri="http://java.sun.com/jsp/jstl/core" %>

<jsp:useBean id="userInfo"
  scope="request"
  class="com.ora.jsp.beans.userinfo.UserInfoBean">
  <jsp:setProperty name="userInfo" property="*" />
</jsp:useBean>

<c:choose>
  <c:when test="${userInfo.valid}">
    <jsp:forward page="userinfovalid.jsp" />
  </c:when>
  <c:otherwise>
    <jsp:forward page="userinfoinput.jsp" />
  </c:otherwise>
</c:choose>
```

This is the request processing page, which uses the bean to perform the business logic. Note that there's no HTML at all in this page, only a `taglib` directive declaring the core JSTL library and action elements. This is typical of a request processing page. It doesn't produce a visible response message, it simply takes care of business and passes control to the appropriate presentation page.

This example is relatively simple. First, a new `userInfo` bean is created in the request scope by the `<jsp:useBean>` action, and its properties are set by the nested `<jsp:setProperty>` action based on the request parameters values submitted from the form, just as in Chapter 8. A `<c:choose>` action element with nested `<c:when>` and `<c:otherwise>` actions test if the input is valid, using the bean's `valid` property. The control is passed to the appropriate View page depending of the result, using the `<jsp:forward>` standard action.

If the input is invalid, the control is passed back to the *userinfoinput.jsp* page. This time the page continues the processing that originated in the *userinfovalidate.jsp* page; the `<jsp:useBean>` action finds the existing `userInfo` bean in the request scope, and its properties are used to fill out the form fields and add error messages where needed.

If all input is valid, the control is instead passed to the *userinfovalid.jsp* page shown in Example 10-3 to present the "thank you" message.

Example 10-3. Valid input message page (userinfovalid.jsp)

```
<html>
  <head>
    <title>User Info Validated</title>
  </head>
  <body bgcolor="white">
    <font color="green" size="+3">
      Thanks for entering valid information!
    </font>
  </body>
</html>
```

This page tells the user all input was correct. It consists only of template text, so this could have been a regular HTML file. Making it a JSP page allows you to add dynamic content later without changing the referring page, however. The result of submitting valid input is shown in Figure 10-3.

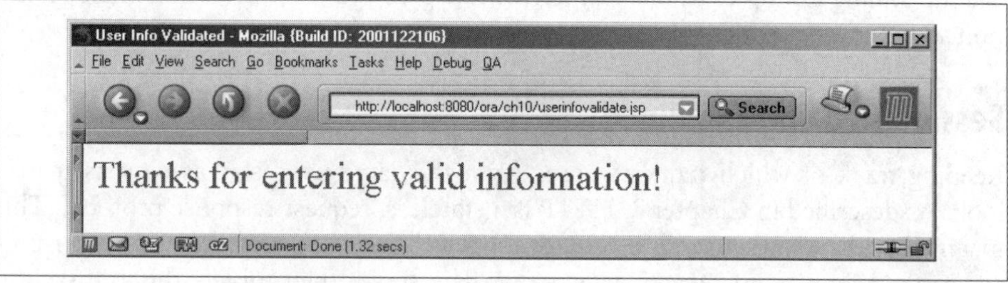

Figure 10-3. The valid input message page

Let's review how placing the bean in the request scope lets you access the same bean in all pages. The user first requests the *userinfoinput.jsp* page (Example 10-1). A new instance of the `userInfo` bean is created in the `request` scope. Because its properties have no values, all form fields are empty at this stage. The user fills out the form and submits it, as a new request, to the *userinfovalidate.jsp* (Example 10-2) page. The previous bean is then out of scope, so this page creates a new `userInfo` bean in the request scope and sets all bean properties based on the form field values. If the input is invalid, the `<jsp:forward>` action passes the control back to the *userinfoinput.jsp* page. Note that we're still processing the same request that initially created the bean and set all the property values. Since the bean is saved in the request scope, the `<jsp:useBean>` action finds it and uses it to generate appropriate error messages and fill out the form with any values already entered.

Sharing Session and Application Data

The request scope makes data available to multiple pages processing the same request. But in many cases, data must be shared over multiple requests.

Imagine a travel agency application. It's important to remember the dates and destination entered to book the flight so that the customer doesn't have to reenter the information when it's time to make hotel and rental car reservations. This type of information, available only to requests from the same user, can be shared through the session scope.

Some information is needed by multiple pages independent of who the current user is. JSP supports access to this type of shared information through the application scope. Information saved in the application scope by one page can later be accessed by another page, even if the two pages were requested by different users. Examples of information typically shared through the application scope are information about currently logged-in users and cache objects that avoid unnecessary database queries for data that is the same for all users.

Figure 10-4 shows how the server provides access to the two scopes for different clients.

The upcoming examples in this chapter will help you to use the session and application scopes.

Session Tracking Explained

Keeping track of which requests come from the same user isn't as easy as it may look. As described in Chapter 2, HTTP is a stateless, request-response protocol. This means that the browser sends a request for a web resource, and the web server processes the request and returns a response. The server then forgets this transaction ever happened. So when the same browser sends a new request; the web server has no idea that this request is related to the previous one. This is fine as long as you're dealing with static files, but it's a problem in an interactive web application.

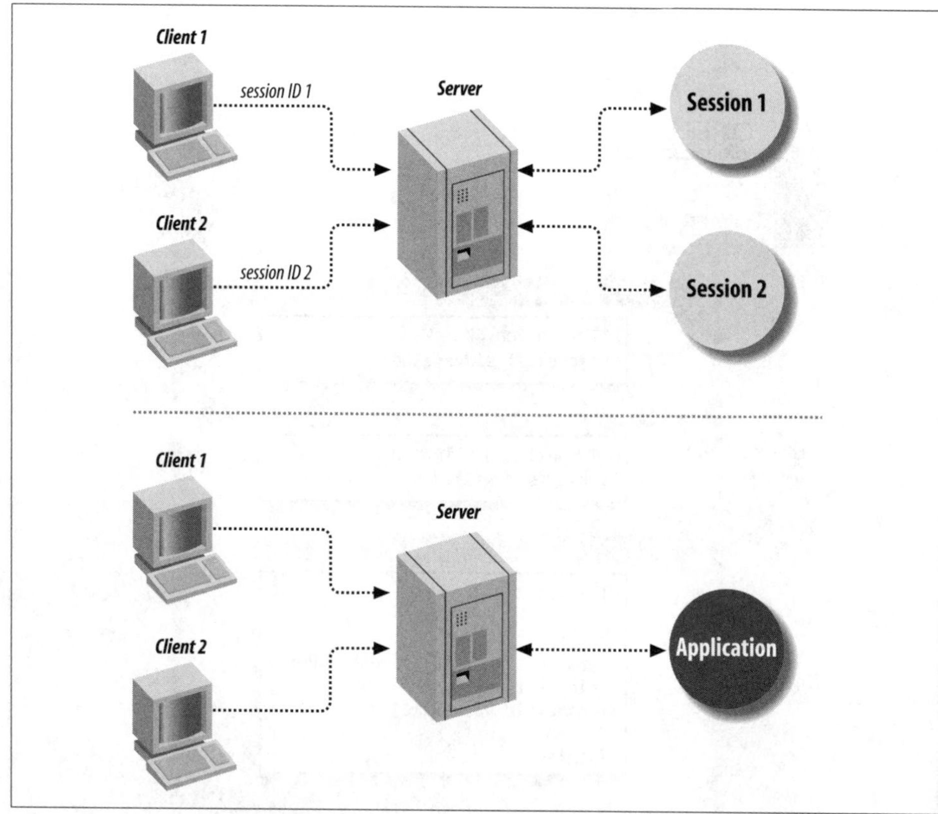

Figure 10-4. Session and application scopes

There are two ways to solve this problem, and they have both been used extensively for web applications with a variety of server-side technologies. The server can either return all information related to the current user (the client state) with each response and let the browser send it back as part of the next request, or it can save the state somewhere on the server and send back only an identifier that the browser returns with the next request. The identifier is then used to locate the state information saved on the server.

In both cases, the information can be sent to the browser in one of three ways (Figure 10-5 outlines these methods):

- As a cookie
- Embedded as hidden fields in an HTML form
- Encoded in the URLs in the response body, typically as links to other application pages (this is known as *URL rewriting*)

A *cookie* is a name/value pair that the server passes to the browser in a response header. The browser stores the cookie for the time specified by the cookie's expira-

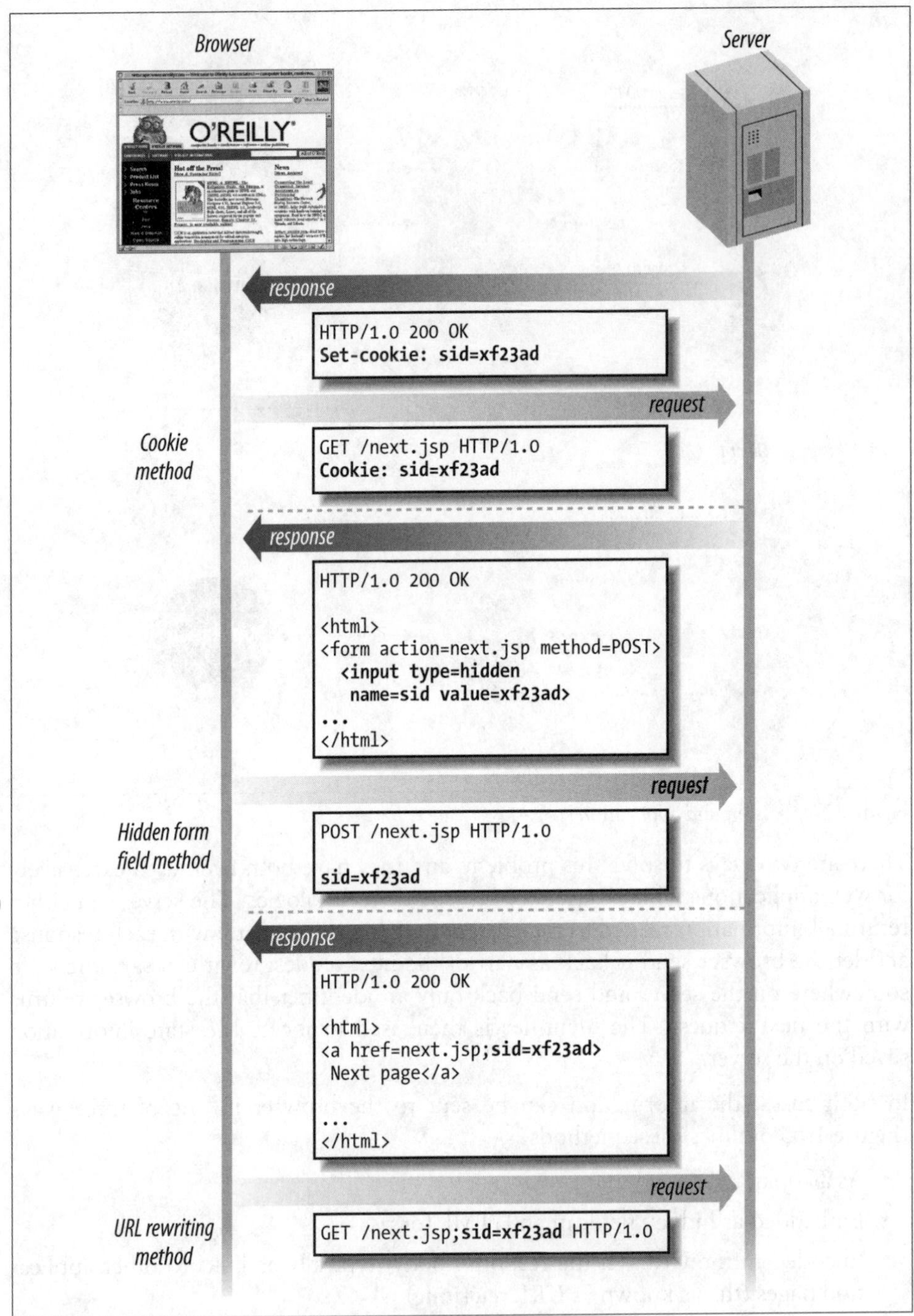

Figure 10-5. Client state information transportation methods

tion time attribute. When the browser sends a request to a server, it checks its "cookie jar" and includes all cookies it has received from the same server (that have not yet expired) in the request headers. Cookies used for state management don't have an explicit expiration time but instead expire as soon as the user closes the browser. Using cookies is the easiest way to deal with the state issue, but some browsers don't support cookies. In addition, a user may disable cookies in a browser that does support them because of privacy concerns. Hence, we can't rely on cookies alone.

If hidden fields in an HTML form are used to send the state information to the browser, the browser returns the information to the server as regular HTTP parameters when the form is submitted. When the state information is encoded in URLs, it's returned to the server as part of the request URL path, for instance when the user clicks on an encoded link.

Sending all state information back and forth between the browser and server isn't efficient, so most modern server-side technologies keep the information on the server and pass only an identifier between the browser and the server. This is called *session tracking*; all requests from a browser that contains the same identifier (session ID) belong to the same session, and the server keeps track of all information associated with the session.

JSP hides all details of cookie-based session tracking and supports the URL rewriting variety with a bit of help from the page author. In addition, the specification allows a container to use the session mechanism built into the Secure Socket Layer (SSL), the encryption technology used by HTTPS. SSL-based session tracking is currently not supported by any of the major servlet containers, but all of them support the cookie and URL rewriting techniques. No matter which mechanism is used, session data is always available to JSP pages through the session scope.* Information saved in the session scope is available to all pages requested by the same browser during the lifetime of a session.

A session starts when the browser makes the first request for a JSP page in a particular application. The application can explicitly end the session (for instance when the user logs out or completes a transaction), or the JSP container can end it after a period of user inactivity (the default value is typically 30 minutes after the last request). Note that there's no way for the server to tell if the user closes the browser, because there's no permanent connection between the browser and the server, and no message is sent to the server when the browser disappears. Still, closing the browser usually means losing the session ID; the cookie expires, or the encoded URLs are no longer available. So when the user opens a browser again, the server can't associate the new request with the previous session, and therefore creates a new session. However, all session data associated with the previous session remains on the server until the session times out.

* Unless the page directive `session` attribute is set to `false`—see Appendix A for details.

Counting Page Hits

A simple page counter can be used to illustrate how the scope affects the lifetime and reach of shared information. The difference between the session and application scopes becomes apparent when you place a counter in each scope. Consider the page shown in Example 10-4.

Example 10-4. A page with counter beans (counter1.jsp)

```
<%@ taglib prefix="c" uri="http://java.sun.com/jsp/jstl/core" %>

<html>
  <head>
    <title>Counter page</title>
  </head>
  <body bgcolor="white">

    <%-- Increment counters --%>
    <c:set var="sessionCounter" scope="session"
      value="${sessionCounter + 1}" />
    <c:set var="applCounter" scope="application"
      value="${applCounter + 1}" />
    <h1>Counter page</h1>

    This page has been visited <b>${sessionCounter}</b> times
    within the current session, and <b>${applCounter}</b> times
    by all users since the application was started.
  </body>
</html>
```

In Example 10-4, JSTL `<c:set>` actions increment counters in the session and application scopes. Note how each counter variable is placed in a specific scope using the scope attribute. The variable placed in the session scope is found every time the same browser requests this page, and therefore counts hits per browser. The application scope variable, on the other hand, is shared by all users, so it counts the total number of hits for this page. If you run this example, you should see a page similar to Figure 10-6.

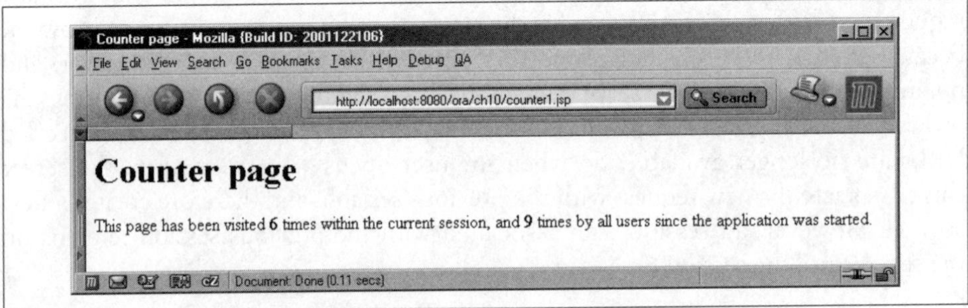

Figure 10-6. A page with session and application page hit counters

Sessions and Multiple Windows

Even though session tracking lets an application recognize related requests, there's still one problem. This problem is related to the server's lack of knowledge of the client, and doesn't become obvious until you start testing an application that depends on session information. Consider what happens if you open two browser windows and start accessing the same web application. Will each window be associated with its own session, or will they share the same session? Unfortunately there's not a clear answer. And it doesn't matter if the server-side logic is implemented as servlets, JSP, ASP, CGI, or any other server-side technology.

The most commonly used browsers, Netscape Navigator and Microsoft Internet Explorer (IE), both let you open multiple windows that are actually controlled by the same operating system process. Older versions of IE (before Version 5) can be configured so that a separate process controls each window instead, and on operating systems other than Windows, you can do this with any browser. When each window runs in its own process, it's easy to answer the question: each window is associated with its own session. It's only when one process controls multiple windows that it gets a bit tricky; in this case, the answer depends on whether URL rewriting or cookies are used for session tracking.

When URL rewriting is used, the first request to the application from one window doesn't include a session ID, because no response with the session ID has been received yet. The server sends back the new session ID encoded in all URLs in the page. If a request is then submitted from the other window, the same thing happens; the server sends back a response with a new session ID. Hence, in this scenario each window is associated with a separate session.

If cookies are used to pass the session ID, the reverse is true. The first request submitted from one window doesn't contain a session ID, so the server generates a new ID and sends it back as a cookie. Cookies are shared by all windows controlled by the same process. When a request is then made from the other window, it contains the session ID cookie received as a result of the first request. The server recognizes the session ID and therefore assumes that the request belongs to the same session as the first request; both windows share the same session.

There's not much you can do about this. If you want each window to have its own session, most servers can be configured to always use the URL rewriting method for session tracking. But this is still not foolproof. The user can open a new window using the mouse pop-up menu for a link (with the session ID encoded in the URI) and ask to see the linked page in a new window. Now there are two windows with the same session ID anyway. The only way to handle this is, unfortunately, to educate your users.

The first time you access the page, none of the counter variables exist, so the `<c:set>` actions create them and set them to 1 (the EL interprets a missing variable as 0 when it's used in an arithmetic operation). As long as you use the same browser, the session and application counters stay in sync. If you exit your browser and restart it, however, a new session is created when you access the first page. The session counter starts from 1 again but the application counter takes off from where it was at the end of the first session.

Note that the counter variables are stored in memory only, so if you restart the server, both counters are reset.

URL Rewriting

As I mentioned earlier, the session ID needed to keep track of requests within the same session can be transferred between the server and the browser in a number of different ways. One way is to encode it in the URLs created by the JSP pages. This is called *URL rewriting*. It's an approach that works even if the browser doesn't support cookies (perhaps because the user has disabled them). A URL with a session ID looks like this:

```
counter2.jsp;jsessionid=be8d691ddb4128be093fdbde4d5be54e00
```

When the user clicks on a link with an encoded URL, the server extracts the session ID from the request URI and associates the request with the correct session. The JSP page can then access the session data in the same way as when cookies keep track of the session ID, so you don't have to worry about how it's handled. What you do need to do, however, is tell the JSP container to encode the URL when needed. To see how it's done, let's add HTML links in the counter page—one link without rewriting and one with. Example 10-5 shows a counter page with this addition.

Example 10-5. A page with links, with and without URL rewriting (counter2.jsp)

```
<%@ taglib prefix="c" uri="http://java.sun.com/jsp/jstl/core" %>

<html>
  <head>
    <title>Counter page</title>
  </head>
  <body bgcolor="white">

    <%-- Increment the counter --%>
    <c:set var="sessionCounter" scope="session"
      value="${sessionCounter + 1}" />

    <h1>Counter page</h1>

    This page has been visited <b>${sessionCounter}</b> times
    within the current session.
    <p>
    Click here to load the page through a
    <a href="counter2.jsp">regular link</a>.
    <p>
    Click here to load the page through an
```

Example 10-5. A page with links, with and without URL rewriting (counter2.jsp) (continued)

```
    <a href="<c:url value="counter2.jsp" />">encoded link</a>.
  </body>
</html>
```

The only differences compared to Example 10-4 are that only the session counter is used and that links back to the same page have been added.

The <a> element's href attribute value for the second link is converted using the JSTL <c:url> action, described in Table 10-3. If the container has received a session ID cookie with the request for the page, the action adds the URL untouched to the response. But for the first request in a session and for requests from a browser that doesn't support cookies or with cookie support disabled, this action adds a rewritten URL, with the session ID added to the URL as shown earlier.

Table 10-3. Attributes for JSTL <c:url>

Attribute name	Java type	Dynamic value accepted	Description
value	String	Yes	Mandatory. An absolute URL, or a context- or page-relative path to encode.
context	String	Yes	Optional. The context path for the application, if the resource isn't part of the current application.
var	String	No	Optional. The name of the variable to hold the encoded URL.
scope	String	No	Optional. The scope for the variable, one of page, request, session, or application. page is the default.

The <c:url> action also encodes query string parameters defined by nested <c:param> actions (see Table 10-4) according to the syntax rules for HTTP parameters:

```
<c:url value="product.jsp">
  <c:param name="id" value="${product.id}" />
  <c:param name="customer" value="Hans Bergsten" />
</c:url>
```

Recall that all special characters, such as space, quote, etc., in a parameter value must be encoded. For instance, all spaces in a parameter value must be replaced with plus signs. When you use the <c:param> action, it takes care of all encoding for the parameters, but in the rare event that the URL specified as the <c:url> value attribute contains special characters, you must replace them yourself. The encoded URL created by the action for this example looks something like this:

```
product.jsp;jsessionid=be8d691ddb4128be0?id=3&customer=Hans+Bergsten
```

Here, the session ID and the request parameters are added, and encoded if needed (the space between "Hans" and "Bergsten" is replaced with a plus sign).

If you're sure that the parameter values never contain special characters that need encoding (or are easy to encode manually in a static value), you can include them as a query string in the <c:url> value instead of using nested <c:param> actions:

```
<c:url value="product.jsp?id=${product.id}&customer=Hans+Bergsten" />
```

Table 10-4. Attributes for JSTL <c:param>

Attribute name	Java type	Dynamic value accepted	Description
name	String	Yes	Mandatory. The parameter name.
value	String	Yes	Mandatory, unless the value is provided as the body instead. The parameter value.

If you want to provide session tracking for browsers that don't support cookies, you must use the <c:url> action to rewrite all URL references in your application: in <a> tags, <form> tags, and <frameset> tags. This means all pages in your application (or at least all pages with references to other pages) must be JSP pages, so that all references can be dynamically encoded. If you miss one single URL, the server will lose track of the session.

I recommend that you spend the time to add <c:url> actions for all references up front, even if you know that all your current users have browsers that support cookies. One day you may want to extend the user base and may lose control over the browsers they use. It's also common that users disable cookies in fear of Big Brother watching. Yet another reason to prepare for URL rewriting from the beginning is to support new types of clients that are becoming more and more common, such as PDAs and cell phones. Cookie support in these small devices isn't a given.

Besides URL encoding, the <c:url> action also converts a context-relative path into a server-relative path, suitable for use in an HTML element. What this means is that all you have to do to refer to a file that's located in a top-level directory for the application from an HTML element is to use <c:url> to convert it to a path the browser interprets correctly. Here's how you can add an image located in the */images* directory for the application from any JSP page, no matter how deep in the directory structure it's located:

```
<img src="<c:url value="/images/logo.gif" />">
```

For an application installed with the context path /example, the result of processing this snippet is:

```
<img src="/example/images/logo.gif">
```

Note how the context path has been prepended to the context-relative path specified as the attribute value. A browser needs this type of server-relative path because it doesn't know anything about contexts or how to handle context-relative paths; these are concepts only the container knows about.

Online Shopping

Now let's look at a more useful example; an online shopping site. Besides showing you examples on how the session and application scopes can be used effectively in a larger application, this example also introduces other useful tools, such as JSTL actions for number formatting and redirection, and EL syntax for getting collection values based on keys determined at runtime.

The application consists of three pages. The main page lists all available products. Each product is linked to a product description page, where the product can be added to the shopping cart. A product is added to the shopping cart by a request processing page. The main page with the product list is then displayed again, but with the current contents of the shopping cart as well, as shown in Figure 10-7.

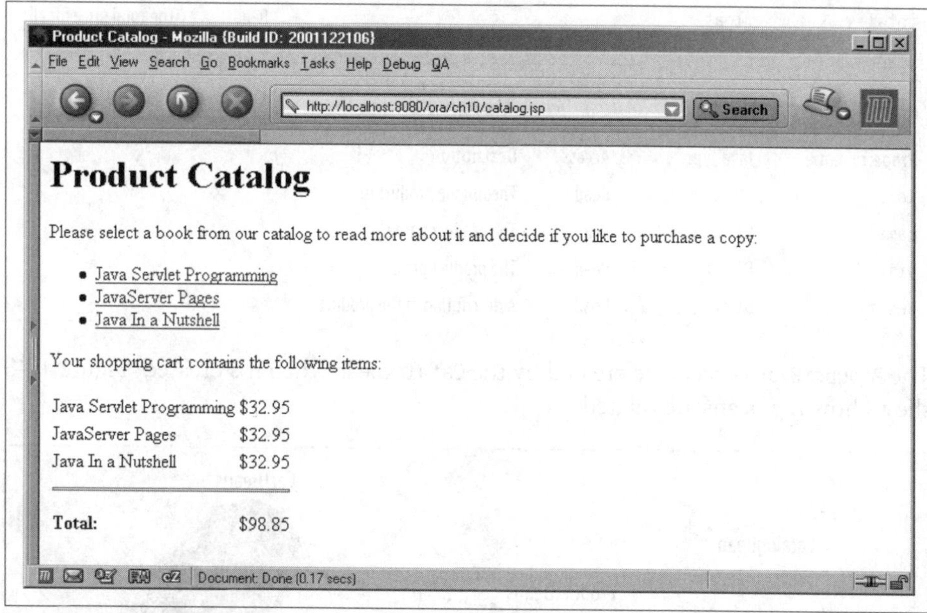

Figure 10-7. The product list and the contents of the shopping cart

Two beans are used to keep track of the products: the `com.ora.jsp.beans.shopping.CatalogBean` contains all available products, and the `com.ora.jsp.beans.shopping.CartBean` represents one user's shopping cart. Each product in the catalog is represented by a `ProductBean`. Table 10-5, Table 10-6, and Table 10-7 show all the properties for the beans.

Table 10-5. Properties for com.ora.jsp.beans.shopping.CatalogBean

Property name	Java type	Access	Description
`productList`	`com.ora.jsp.beans.shopping.ProductBean[]`	Read	A list of all products in the catalog

Table 10-5. Properties for com.ora.jsp.beans.shopping.CatalogBean (continued)

Property name	Java type	Access	Description
productsById	java.util.Map	Read	A Map, keyed on product ID, with all ProductBean instances

Table 10-6. Properties for com.ora.jsp.beans.shopping.CartBean

Property name	Java type	Access	Description
productList	com.ora.jsp.beans.shopping.ProductBean[]	Read	A list of all products in the cart
product	com.ora.jsp.beans.shopping.ProductBean	Write	Adds the product to the cart
total	float	Read	The total price for all products in the cart

Table 10-7. Properties for com.ora.jsp.beans.shopping.ProductBean

Property name	Java type	Access	Description
id	String	Read	The unique product ID
name	String	Read	The product name
price	Float	Read	The product price
descr	String	Read	A description of the product

The ProductBean objects are created by the CatalogBean when it's created. Figure 10-8 shows how the beans are related.

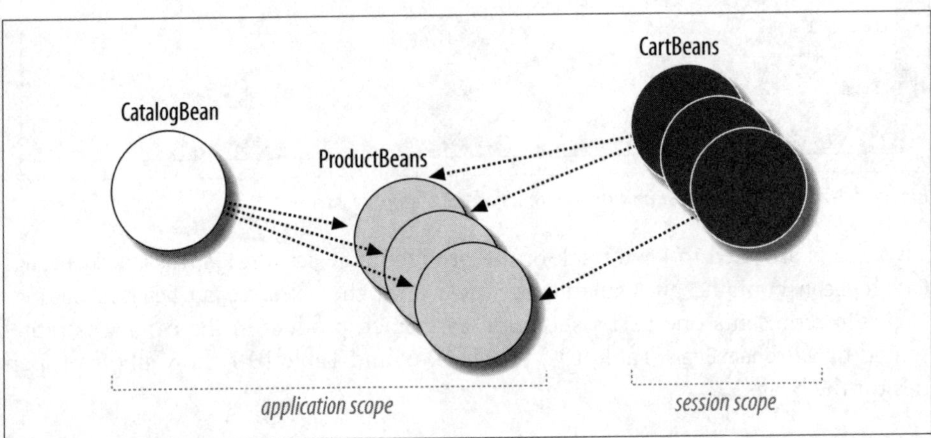

Figure 10-8. Application and session scope beans

The CatalogBean and the ProductBean objects are placed in the application scope, because all users share the same product catalog. To keep track of each user's purchases, separate shopping carts must be used. One CartBean instance per user is therefore placed in the user's unique session scope. When a user picks a product from the catalog, a reference to the corresponding ProductBean is added to the user's CartBean.

The main page for this application is shown in Example 10-6.

Example 10-6. A page with a list of products (catalog.jsp)

```
<%@ page language="java" contentType="text/html" %>
<%@ taglib prefix="c" uri="http://java.sun.com/jsp/jstl/core" %>
<%@ taglib prefix="fmt" uri="http://java.sun.com/jsp/jstl/fmt" %>
<%@ taglib prefix="fn" uri="http://java.sun.com/jsp/jstl/functions" %>

<html>
  <head>
    <title>Product Catalog</title>
  </head>
  <body bgcolor="white">
    <h1>Product Catalog</h1>

    Please select a book from our catalog to read more about it and
    decide if you like to purchase a copy:

    <jsp:useBean id="catalog" scope="application"
      class="com.ora.jsp.beans.shopping.CatalogBean"
    />
    <%--
      Generate a list of all products with links to the product page.
    --%>
    <ul>
      <c:forEach items="${catalog.productList}" var="product">
        <c:url var="productURL" value="product.jsp">
          <c:param name="id" value="${product.id}" />
        </c:url>
        <li>
          <a href="${productURL}">${fn:escapeXml(product.name)}</a>
      </c:forEach>
    </ul>

    <jsp:useBean
      id="cart" scope="session"
      class="com.ora.jsp.beans.shopping.CartBean"
    />
    <%-- Show the contents of the shopping cart, if any --%>
    <c:if test="${!empty cart.productList}">
      Your shopping cart contains the following items:
      <p>
      <table border=0>
        <c:forEach items="${cart.productList}" var="product">
          <tr>
            <td>${fn:escapeXml(product.name)}</td>
            <td>
```

Example 10-6. A page with a list of products (catalog.jsp) (continued)

```
              <fmt:formatNumber value="${product.price}"
                type="currency" />
            </td>
          </tr>
        </c:forEach>
        <tr><td colspan=2><hr></td></tr>
        <tr>
          <td><b>Total:</b></td>
          <td>
            <fmt:formatNumber value="${cart.total}"
              type="currency" />
          </td>
        </tr>
      </table>
    </c:if>
  </body>
</html>
```

The <jsp:useBean> action near the top of Example 10-6 creates an instance of the CatalogBean the first time a user requests the page and saves it under the name catalog. Since the bean is placed in the application scope, all users will then share this single instance.

The <c:forEach> action loops through the list and generates an HTML list item element for each product. The EL expression used as the items attribute value retrieves the catalog bean's property that contains a list of all products in the catalog, named productList (an array of ProductBean objects). The var attribute is set to product, so we can use product as a variable name in the action element body.

The body of the <c:forEach> action is evaluated once per product. The action body contains a mixture of template text, actions and EL expressions to generate an HTML list item element for each product with a link to another page, using the product name as the link text. Let's look at how the link is generated:

```
<c:url var="productURL" value="product.jsp">
  <c:param name="id" value="${product.id}" />
</c:url>
<li>
  <a href="${productURL}">${fn:escapeXml(product.name)}</a>
```

First, the <c:url> action creates the URL for the link by adding the id parameter specified by the nested <c:param> action to the page name and rewriting the resulting URL if cookies aren't supported. Next, an EL expression adds the URL as the HTML link's href attribute value, and another EL expression adds the product name as the link text. Note that the fn:escapeXml( ) function is used to encode possible special characters in the link text, but that the link URL is left unencoded. Leaving the URL variable untouched is important, because otherwise, ampersands used to separate parameters in the URL get corrupted. In this example the URL contains only one parameter, so it works fine even if the value is encoded, but you should leave it unencoded anyway to avoid problems if you need to add another parameter later.

After the code in Example 10-6 for generating the product list, you see almost identical code for generating a list of the current contents of the shopping cart. First, the `<jsp:useBean>` action places the `cart` bean in the session scope, as opposed to the `catalog` bean, which is placed in the application scope. This means that each user gets a unique shopping cart that remains on the server for the duration of the session, while they all share the same catalog. The part of the page that deals with the shopping cart contents is enclosed in a `<c:if>` action, so it's processed only if the `cart` bean's `productList` property contains a nonempty array, in other words, only when there's at least one product in the cart.

Number Formatting

Unless the shopping cart is empty, a second `<c:forEach>` action generates a list of the contents as an HTML table with the name and price of each product. A thing to note here is the use of the `<fmt:formatNumber>` action:

```
<fmt:formatNumber value="${product.price}"
  type="currency" />
```

This is an action from the JSTL I18N formatting library, declared by the second `taglib` directive at the top of the page. It formats the number specified by the `value` attribute as defined by other attributes, such as the `type` attribute used here. The `currency` type tells it to format the number according to default rules for currency values. Other attributes not used here let you define specific rules for the number of decimals to show, where to put number-grouping characters, prefix and suffix, etc. The number is formatted according to the rules for a specific geographical, political, or cultural region, known as a *locale*. A locale defines things such as which characters to use as a decimal separator, thousand grouping, and currency symbol. Locales and all JSTL formatting actions are discussed in detail in Chapter 14, but to give you an idea of how formatting varies between regions, here's an example of the number 10000.00 formatted as currency for USA, Sweden, and Italy:

USA
: $10,000.00

Sweden
: 10 000,00 kr

Italy
: L. 10 000

In Example 10-6, the `<fmt:formatNumber>` action formats the price information for each product and the total for everything in the cart.

Using a Request Parameter as an Index

A link to a description page for each product is generated using the <c:forEach> action in the main page, shown in Example 10-6. The link includes the request parameter id, specifying the product to display information about. When the user clicks on one of the links, the page shown in Example 10-7 is invoked.

Example 10-7. The product description page (product.jsp)

```
<%@ page language="java" contentType="text/html" %>
<%@ taglib prefix="c" uri="http://java.sun.com/jsp/jstl/core" %>
<%@ taglib prefix="fn" uri="http://java.sun.com/jsp/jstl/functions" %>

<html>
  <head>
    <title>Product Description</title>
  </head>
  <body bgcolor="white">

    <jsp:useBean id="catalog" scope="application"
      class="com.ora.jsp.beans.shopping.CatalogBean"
    />
    <%-- Get the specified ProductBean from the catalog --%>
    <c:set var="product" value="${catalog.productsById[param.id]}" />
    <h1>${fn:escapeXml(product.name)}</h1>

    ${fn:escapeXml(product.descr)}
    <p>
    <c:url var="addtocartURL" value="addtocart.jsp">
      <c:param name="id" value="${product.id}" />
    </c:url>

    <a href="${addtocartURL}">
      Add this book to the shopping cart</a>

  </body>
</html>
```

A <jsp:useBean> action at the top of Example 10-7 makes the catalog bean available to the page. Since the same action is used in the *catalog.jsp* page to save the catalog bean in the application scope, it may seem redundant to have it in this page as well. In the normal case, it is. But users may bookmark a page for a specific product and go directly to this page. If the container has been restarted and no one has loaded the *catalog.jsp* page yet, the <jsp:useBean> action makes sure a fresh bean is created in the application scope so the other actions in this page can use it. If the bean already exists, the <jsp:useBean> action uses the existing bean instead, so no harm is done. This is an approach you should consider for all pages that can be bookmarked; make sure all beans used in the page are initialized even in the unusual cases.

Next, a <c:set> JSTL action saves a reference to the ProductBean corresponding to the product ID specified by the id parameter value, to make it easier to access information about the product later in the page. As you may recall from Chapter 8, request parameter values can be accessed as a property of the implicit param variable in an EL expression. What's new in this example is that the parameter value is used to pick a specific element from a collection, using the EL [*element_id*] syntax. In this example, the productsById property of the catalog bean is of type java.util.Map, containing all products in the catalog. A Map is a collection type that provides access to individual elements through an identifier known as a *key*. With the EL, you can specify the key in two ways:

```
${myMap.myKey}
${myMap[myKey]}
```

The first syntax, using a dot to separate the Map variable from the key value, works when you know exactly which key value to use. In other words, the key is a static string. The second syntax must be used when the key value is determined at runtime using another variable, such as the param.id construct used in Example 10-7. You can use the second syntax even when the key is a static string, if you specify it as a string literal, and you *must* use this syntax for static strings if the key name contains dots:

```
${myMap['myKey']}
${myMap['com.thejspbook.myKey']}
```

Note that if you have an object in a scope with a name containing dots, you need to use this syntax with the implicit variable that represents a collection of all variables in the scope:

```
${pageScope['com.thejspbook.myKey']}
```

If you're familiar with JavaScript, you probably recognize the two ways to access data from a collection with key/value pairs. If so, you probably guessed that the [] operator can be used also to access elements of collections of indexed values (such as a java.util.List or a Java array):

```
${myList[0]}
${myList[myVarWithANumericValue]}
```

For an indexed collection, the value within the brackets must be a numeric literal or a subexpresson that represents a numeric value.

The remainder of Example 10-7 uses elements we have already discussed: EL expressions to add the product name and description (represented by properties of the bean referenced by the product variable) to the page, and <c:url> to create the URL rewritten link to the request processing page that adds the product to the shopping cart. The result is shown in Figure 10-9.

The request processing page is shown in Example 10-8.

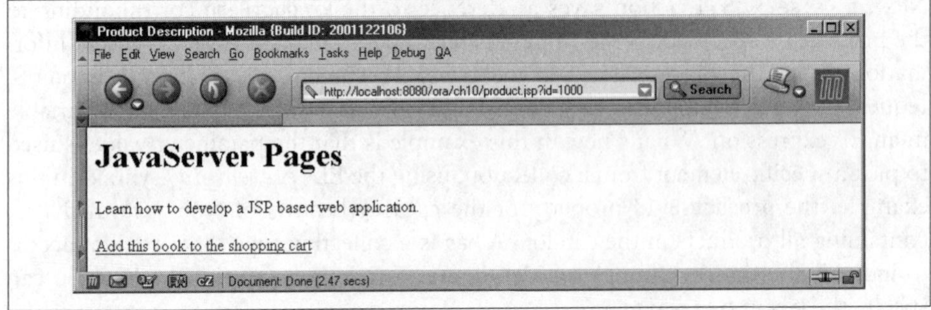

Figure 10-9. The product description page

Example 10-8. Adding a product to the shopping cart (addtocart.jsp)

```
<%@ taglib prefix="c" uri="http://java.sun.com/jsp/jstl/core" %>

<jsp:useBean id="catalog" scope="application"
  class="com.ora.jsp.beans.shopping.CatalogBean"
/>

<%-- Get the specified ProductBean from the catalog --%>
<c:set var="product" value="${catalog.productsById[param.id]}" />

<jsp:useBean
  id="cart"
  scope="session"
  class="com.ora.jsp.beans.shopping.CartBean"
/>

<%-- Add the product to the cart --%>
<c:set target="${cart}" property="product" value="${product}" />

<c:redirect url="catalog.jsp" />
```

This is a request processing page, so it doesn't contain any HTML. The `<jsp:useBean>` actions make sure the `catalog` and `cart` beans are available, for the same reason as in Example 10-7. The first `<c:set>` action saves a reference to the requested product in a variable named `product`, just as in the *product.jsp* page.

A JSTL `<c:set>` action with a couple of attributes I skipped over earlier adds the product to the cart by setting the cart bean's `product` property to the selected product.

The reason the `<c:set>` action is used instead of the standard `<jsp:setProperty>` action described in Chapter 8 is that it's a bit more flexible. The `<c:set>` action lets you set the property specified by the `property` attribute in the bean identified by the `target` attribute to the EL expression specified by the `value` attribute. You can also use these two attributes to add elements to a `Map` object:

```
<c:set target="${myMap}" property="theKey" value="${aValue}" />
```

As you may have noticed by now, as far as the EL is concerned, a `Map` and a bean are just two ways to represent the same concept: a collection of values identified by a name. It's up to the Java programmer who makes objects available for use in a JSP page to pick the most appropriate implementation on a case-by-case basis.

Note that the `target` attribute takes an EL expression that evaluates to the bean and the `property` attribute specifies the name of the property. To some, it may have been more natural to combine these two attributes into one, assigning the value to the evaluation of an EL expression that identifies the property itself. The JSP 2.0 EL, however, doesn't support write operations in the evaluation result, so this isn't possible. It's likely that a future version of the JSP EL will be enhanced to support assignments.

Redirect Versus Forward

Back to the shopping cart example. When *addtocart.jsp* page has added the product to the cart, it needs to invoke the *catalog.jsp* page to show the user the updated cart contents.

There are two ways you can let one page invoke another page: redirecting or forwarding. Forwarding was used in Example 10-2 to display an appropriate page depending on the result of the user input validation. In Example 10-8, redirection is used to display the catalog page after adding a new product to the cart. The `<c:redirect>` JSTL action, described in Table 10-8, sends a redirect response to the browser with the new location defined by the `url` attribute. If URL rewriting is used for session tracking, the URL is encoded with the session ID. If the body of this action contains `<c:param>` actions, described in Table 10-4, each parameter is added to the URL as query string parameters, encoded according to rules in the HTTP specification.

Table 10-8. Attributes for JSTL <c:redirect>

Attribute name	Java type	Dynamic value accepted	Description
`url`	`String`	Yes	Mandatory. An absolute URL, or a context- or page-relative path.
`context`	`String`	Yes	Optional. The context path for the application, if the resource isn't part of the current application.

There's an important difference between a forward and a redirect. When you forward, the target page is invoked through an internal method call by the JSP container; the new page continues to process the same request and the browser isn't aware that more than one page is involved. A redirect, on the other hand, means that the first page tells the browser to make a new request to the target page. The URL shown in the browser is therefore changed to the URL of the new page when you redirect, but stays unchanged when you use forward. A redirect is slower than a forward, since the browser has to make a new request. Also, because it results in a new request, request scope variables are no longer available after a redirect.

So how do you decide if you should use forward or redirect? To a large extent it's a matter of preference. I look at it like this: forwarding is always faster, so that's the first choice. But because the URL in the browser refers to the start page even after the forward, I ask myself what happens if the user decides to reload the start page (or just resize the window: this often reloads the page automatically). In this example, the start page is the page that adds an item to the shopping cart. I don't want it to be invoked again on a reload, so I redirect to the page that displays the catalog and shopping cart content instead. No harm is done if the user reloads this page.

Memory Usage Considerations

You should be aware that all objects you save in the application and session scopes take up memory in the server process. It's easy to calculate how much memory is used for the application scope because you have full control over the number of objects you place there. But the total number of objects in the session scope depends on the number of concurrent sessions, so in addition to the size of each object, you also need to know how many concurrent users you have and how long a session lasts. Let's look at an example.

The `CartBean` used in this chapter is small. It stores only references to `ProductBean` instances, not copies of the beans. An object reference in Java is 8 bytes, so with three products in the cart we need 24 bytes. The `java.util.Vector` object used to hold the references adds some overhead, say 32 bytes. All in all, we need 56 bytes per shopping cart bean with three products.

If this is a site with a modest amount of customers, you may have 10 users shopping per hour. The default timeout for a session is 30 minutes, so let's say that at any given moment, you have 10 active users and another 10 sessions that aren't active but have not timed out yet. This gives a total of 20 sessions times 56 bytes per session, a total of 1,120 bytes. In other words, roughly 1 KB—nothing to worry about.

Now let's say your site becomes extremely popular, with 2,000 customers per hour. Using the same method to calculate the number of concurrent sessions as before, you will have 4,000 sessions at 56 bytes; that's a total of roughly 220 KB—still nothing to worry about. However, if you store larger objects in each session, say the result of a database search with an average size of 10 KB, it corresponds to roughly 40 MB for 4,000 sessions. A lot more but still not extreme, at least not for a site intended to handle this amount of traffic. However, it should become apparent that with that many users, you have to be a bit careful with how you use the session scope.

Here are some things you can do to keep the memory requirements under control:

- Place only objects that really need to be unique for each session in the session scope. In the shopping cart example, each cart contains only references to the product beans (not copies of the beans), and the catalog bean and the product beans are shared by all users.
- Set the timeout period for sessions to a lower value than the default. If you know it's rare that your users leave the site for 30 minutes and then return, use a shorter period. You can change the timeout for all sessions in an application through the application's deployment descriptor (see Appendix F), or by calling `session.setMaxInactiveInterval( )` (see Appendix D) in a custom action, bean, or servlet to change it for an individual session.
- Provide a way to end the session explicitly. A good example is a logout function, or invalidation of the session when something is completed (for instance when an order form is submitted). In a JSP page, you can use the `<ora:invalidate-Session>` custom action described in Chapter 13 to invalidate the session. In a servlet or other custom code, you can use the `HttpSession` `invalidate( )` method (see Appendix D). Invalidating a session makes all objects available for garbage collection (the term used for when the Java runtime removes unused objects to conserve memory).

We have covered a lot of ground in this chapter, so let's recap the key points:

- The scope concept gives you full control over the lifetime and reach of shared information at a convenient abstraction level. However, resist the temptation to keep too much information around in the session scope.
- Action elements for passing control between pages, such as the standard `<jsp:forward>` action and the JSTL `<c:redirect>` action, allow you to allocate different roles to different pages, and the JSTL `<c:url>` action can be used to provide support for cookie-less session tracking.

The scope abstraction and the actions together make it possible to develop JSP-based applications that are easy to maintain and extend.

CHAPTER 11

Developing Custom Tag Libraries as Tag Files

Starting with the 2.0 version of the JSP specification, custom tag library actions can be implemented in two ways: as Java classes or as regular text files containing JSP elements. In prior versions, custom actions could only be implemented as Java classes, putting them out of the reach of nonprogrammers. Another problem with the Java implementation of custom actions is that you're forced to printout HTML code with `println()` calls to produce complex content—the very problem JSP was supposed to solve.

In this chapter I show you how to develop custom actions as plain text files and package them as tag libraries that can be used in JSP pages.

Creating and Using a Tag File

A tag file is a text file that contains JSP elements implementing the functionality of a custom action. You must use a *.tag*[*] filename extension to identify this type of file to the web container. All JSP elements that you can use in a JSP file can also be used in a tag file, with exception to the page directive (a tag file is not a page). There are also a few JSP directives that are only allowed in a tag file, as you will see shortly. Apart from that, creating a tag file is no different than creating a JSP page. Once created and installed, a tag file is used the same as the custom actions implemented in Java that you've seen in previous chapters.

Example 11-1 shows a very simple tag file.

Example 11-1. Simple tag file (copyright.tag)

```
<%@ tag body-content="empty" %>
<%@ taglib prefix="c" uri="http://java.sun.com/jsp/jstl/core" %>
```

* If you write the tag file in XML format, as described in Chapter 17, you must instead use the *.tagx* extension.

Example 11-1. Simple tag file (copyright.tag) (continued)

```
<jsp:useBean id="now" scope="application" class="java.util.Date" />
Copyright &copy; ${now.year + 1900} My Company
```

This tag file inserts a copyright statement with the current year in the calling page. The first line is a tag directive. You may use attributes of this directive to specify a description, icon, or an example that a page-authoring tool can show the designer. Other attributes let you specify whether EL expressions should be processed, as well as various information related to scripting code, i.e., the same type of information as you specify with the page directive in JSP pages. All of these attributes are described in Appendix A.

In most cases, tag file authors only care about the attribute used in Example 11-1: `body-content`. This attribute defines how the custom action element's body should be handled, and that it must have one of these values: `empty`, `scriptless` (the default), or `tagdependent`. If it's `empty` (as in Example 11-1), trying to use a body for the custom action element results in a syntax error. The `scriptless` value means that the body can contain any JSP elements except the type of scripting elements described in Chapter 16. In other words, template text, EL expressions, standard actions, and custom actions are all allowed. As you will see later, the tag file can ask the container to process the actions in a scriptless body when and how often as it wants through the use of standard action named `<jsp:doBody>`. If the `body-content` attribute is set to `tagdependent`, the action element body is treated as pure template text (i.e., action elements and EL expressions in the body are not processed, just handled as plain text).

The rest of the tag file in Example 11-1 looks just like an ordinary JSP page. It declares that it uses the JSTL core library, a `<jsp:useBean>` standard action to create an instance of the `java.util.Date` class representing the current time (if it isn't already available in the application scope), and finally outputs static template text mixed with a dynamic value (the current year) generated by an EL expression: `${now.year + 1900}`.*

Tag files can be placed directly in the web application structure under the *WEB-INF/tags* directory or a subdirectory. Each directory containing tag files represents a separate tag library:

```
WEB-INF/tags/
  mytags/
    copyright.tag
    forEvenAndOdd.tag
    htmlFormat.tag
    motd.tag
  myothertags/
```

* The year property of a `java.util.Date` (represented by the `getYear()` method) contains the current year minus 1900, so here I add 1900 to get the real year.

```
foo.tag
bar.tag
```

Here we have two tag libraries: mytags and myothertags. The mytags library contains the *copyright.tag* file from Example 11-1 plus three other tag files. By default, the name of the custom action implemented by the tag file is the filename minus the *.tag* extension, so the *copyright.tag* file represents a custom action named copyright in the mytags library.

A JSP page must declare that it uses a tag library represented by tag files in the web application structure with a slightly different taglib directive than what we've used in earlier chapters:

```
<%@ page contentType="text/html" %>
<%@ taglib prefix="my" tagdir="/WEB-INF/tags/mytags" %>

<html>
  <body bgcolor="white">
    ...
    <my:copyright/>
  </body>
</html>
```

Note that the tagdir attribute is used instead of the uri attribute. The value of the tagdir attribute is the context-relative path to the directory that contains the tag files for the library. It may seem redundant to have to specify the */WEB-INF/tags* part of the path, since all tag library directories must start with this path. Regardless, the JSP specification group decided to require this to be consistent with other attributes taking path values.

When the JSP container processes this JSP page, it locates the *copyright.tag* file in the *WEB-INF/tags/mytags* directory and turns it into a format that the container can invoke. The conversion details are left open by the JSP specification, allowing container vendors to compete with smart implementations. Tomcat turns the tag file into a Java class and compiles it, but other implementations are possible (e.g., converting it to a proprietary data structure).

Tag files can also be packaged in a JAR file. It requires a bit more work and is primarily of interest for tag files intended to be reused in many applications, so let's defer the details to the end of this chapter. One thing to note at this time, though, is that when the tag files are packaged in a JAR file, the taglib directive is used with the uri attribute exactly as in the previous chapters. This means that tag files packaged in a JAR file are indistinguishable from custom actions implemented as Java classes. You can therefore implement the actions as tag files initially (because it's easier) and convert them to Java classes later (maybe to gain better performance) without having to make any changes in the JSP pages that use them.

Accessing Attribute Values

The tag file in Example 11-1 is too simple to illustrate all that you can do with tag files. For instance, most real-world tag files are controlled through attribute values set by the page author. You may recall from Chapter 7 that the `<ora:motd>` custom action has a `category` attribute for selecting the message category that messages should be picked from. Example 11-2 shows how a tag file implementation of the `<ora:motd>` action declares, accesses, and uses this attribute value.

Example 11-2. Using attributes in a tag file (motd.tag)

```
<%@ tag body-content="empty" %>
<%@ attribute name="category" required="true" %>
<%@ taglib prefix="c" uri="http://java.sun.com/jsp/jstl/core" %>

<jsp:useBean id="mmb" class="com.ora.jsp.beans.motd.MixedMessageBean" />
<c:set target="${mmb}" property="category" value="${category}" />
${mmb.message}
```

Each attribute must be declared with an `attribute` directive in a tag file. In Example 11-2, the `category` attribute is declared using an `attribute` directive with the `name` attribute set to `category`. The `required` attribute is set to `true`, meaning that the page author must specify a value for the `category` attribute; the container complains if the attribute is missing. The default value for `required` is `false`, so you can leave it out for attributes that are optional.

Another attribute of the `attribute` directive, not used in Example 11-2, is `rtexprvalue`. A value of `true` means that the author can specify the value either as a static string or as a *request-time attribute value*, such as an EL expression; `false` means the value must be a static string. The default value is `true`, so you only need to use this attribute if you absolutely require a static value.*

The value the page author assigns to an attribute shows up as a page scope variable in the tag file, with the same name as the attribute. This makes it easy to use it in an EL expression. In Example 11-2, a `<c:set>` action sets the `category` property in a `MixedMessageBean` (which contains the list of messages). The EL expression used as the value gets the `category` page scope variable that represents the `category` attribute.

It's important to note, however, that the page scope seen by the tag file is not the same as the page scope seen by the page that invokes the tag file—I sometimes call the page scope seen by the tag file the *tag scope* to make this distinction. By giving the tag file its own local page scope, there's no chance for confusion between the calling page and the tag file if they use the same names for page scope variables.

* The convention established by JSTL is that only `var` and `scope` attributes should have `rtexprvalue` set to `false`. These attributes may need to be available in the translation phase (hence, have static string values) in a future version of the JSP specification to allow for additional syntax checking and optimizations.

Using Undeclared Attributes

Occasionally, declaring all attributes for a tag file can be a hassle. Say you want to develop a tag file that generates an HTML table, and you want the page author to be able to specify all standard attributes that an HTML table element supports. That's a lot of attributes and the tag file would need to test for the existence of each one. A better approach for this scenario is to use the `tag` directive's `dynamic-attributes` attribute. This attribute declares that the tag file accepts any custom action element attribute. The attribute value is the name of a local page scope variable that holds a collection (a `Map`) with all undeclared attribute names and values. Example 11-3 shows an example of a tag file that uses this approach to generate a table with all request header values.

Example 11-3. Using undeclared attributes in a tag file (headers.tag)

```
<%@ tag body-content="empty" dynamic-attributes="dynattrs" %>
<%@ attribute name="caption" required="true" %>
<%@ taglib prefix="c" uri="http://java.sun.com/jsp/jstl/core" %>

<table
  <c:forEach items="${dynattrs}" var="a">
    ${a.key}="${a.value}"
  </c:forEach>
>
  <caption>${caption}</caption>
  <tr>
    <th>Name</th>
    <th>Value</th>
  </tr>
  <c:forEach items="${header}" var="h">
    <tr>
      <td>${h.key}</td>
      <td>${h.value}</td>
    </tr>
  </c:forEach>
</table>
```

The `dynamic-attributes` attribute declares a variable named `dynattrs` to hold the undeclared attributes, and a JSTL `<c:forEach>` action loops through the collection and adds the name and value for each to the HTML `<table>` element's attribute list. As shown in Example 11-3, you can declare regular attributes in the same tag file. This example declares a mandatory attribute named `caption`, used to add a caption text for the table.

This is how you can use the tag file, shown in Example 11-3, in a JSP page:

```
<%@ page contentType="text/html" %>
<%@ taglib prefix="my" tagdir="/WEB-INF/tags/mytags" %>

<html>
  <head>
```

```
    <title>Headers</title>
  </head>
  <body bgcolor="white">
    <my:headers caption="Request Headers"
      border="1" cellspacing="0" cellpadding="5" />
  </body>
</html>
```

The action element for the tag file defines values for the mandatory `caption` attribute plus three undeclared attributes: `border`, `cellspacing`, and `cellpadding`.

Processing the Action Body

So far, the tag files we've looked at ignore (or actually forbid) the body of the custom action element used to invoke them, but the body is often an important part of the equation. One example is a conditional custom action, such as a variation of the `<c:if>` JSTL action. It needs to process the body if the condition is true. Another example is a custom action that transforms the body in some way or simply uses it as input.

Let's develop a custom action that transforms its body content. It first converts all characters that have special meaning in HTML and XML to the corresponding character entity codes (e.g., < to `<`), and then converts special proprietary codes into HTML elements. A custom action like this can be used to process user input in an online forum to protect it against cross-site scripting attacks while still allowing for limited formatting of the messages. Here's how you can use this custom action in a JSP page:

```
<%@ page contentType="text/html" %>
<%@ taglib prefix="c" uri="http://java.sun.com/jsp/jstl/core" %>
<%@ taglib prefix="my" tagdir="/WEB-INF/tags/mytags" %>

<%-- Create test data --%>
<c:set var="message">
  This is just a lot of text that the browser will format to
  fit the browser window. Attempts to <blink> add HTML elements
  are dealt with by conversion to character entities.
  [code]
  This part I want the browser to leave alone, so that
  all my indentations are left intact:

    public class Foo {
      public String getBar() {
        return bar;
      }
    }
  [/code]
  And then some regular text again.
</c:set>
<html>
```

```
  <head>
    <title>Online Forum</title>
  </head>
  <body bgcolor="white">
    <h1>Online Forum</h1>
    Here's a formatted message:
    <p>
      <my:htmlFormat>
        ${message}
      </my:htmlFormat>
    </p>
  </body>
</html>
```

This page first saves test data containing text, an HTML element, and the proprietary formatting codes in a variable named `message`. In a real application, the text would likely come from a database or some other external source. It then processes the text with the `<my:htmlFormat>` custom action.

The result is shown in Figure 11-1. Note how the `<blink>` HTML element is displayed instead of causing most of the text to blink, and how the formatting is preserved for all text between the proprietary `[code]` and `[/code]` tags.

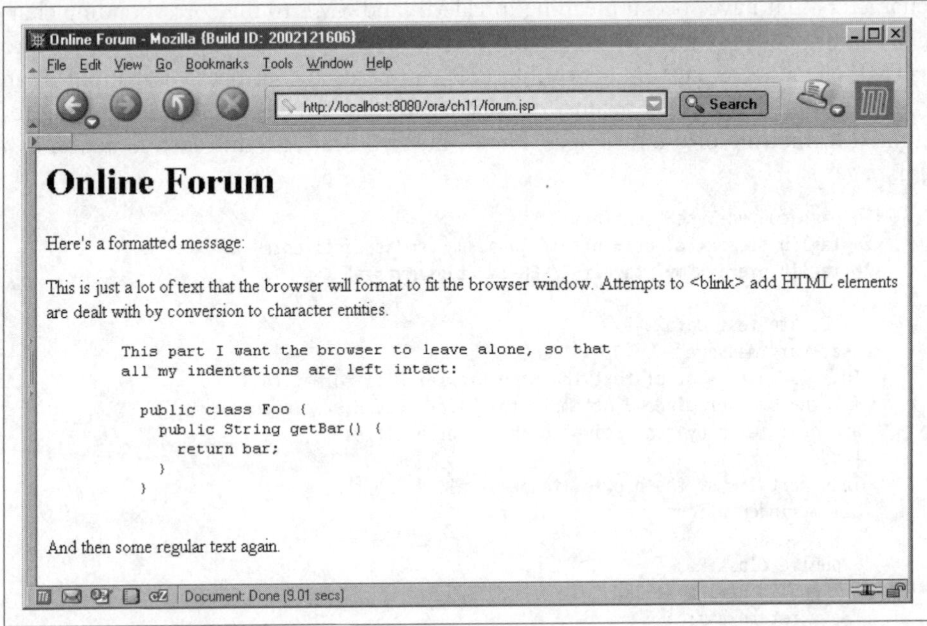

Figure 11-1. Result of text processing with a custom action

Example 11-4 shows the tag file that implements the `<my:htmlFormat>` custom action.

Example 11-4. Processing the body (htmlFormat.tag)

```
<%@ tag body-content="scriptless" %>
<%@ taglib prefix="fn" uri="http://java.sun.com/jsp/jstl/functions" %>
<%@ taglib prefix="c" uri="http://java.sun.com/jsp/jstl/core" %>

<%-- Capture the body evaluation result in a variable --%>
<jsp:doBody var="bodyRes" />

<%-- Convert special characters to character entities --%>
<c:set var="escapedBody" value="${fn:escapeXml(bodyRes)}" />

<%-- Replace "[code]/[/code]" with "<pre>/</pre>" --%>
<c:set var="convBody"
  value="${fn:replace(escapedBody, '[code]', '<pre>')}" />
<c:set var="convBody"
  value="${fn:replace(convBody, '[/code]', '</pre>')}" />

<%-- Output the result --%>
${convBody}
```

Note that the tag directive in Example 11-4 sets the `body-content` attribute to `scriptless`. As I mentioned earlier, this means that the page author is allowed to put template text, standard actions and custom actions, in the body but not scripting elements (i.e., Java code).

It's after the directive elements that this example gets interesting; here's a standard action that we have not discussed before: `<jsp:doBody>`. This action can only be used in tag files. It evaluates the body of the custom action element, meaning that all action elements (if any) in the body are called and the output they produce is mixed with the template text (if any). The result is saved in a variable, using the `var` attribute to name the variable. This attribute is optional, as shown in Table 11-1, and you can use the `varReader` attribute as an alternative. If you don't specify any of these attributes, the result is added to the page invoking the custom action.

Table 11-1. Attributes for <jsp:doBody>

Attribute name	Java type	Dynamic value accepted	Description
`var`	`String`	No	Optional. The name of the variable to hold the body evaluation result as a `String`.
`varReader`	`String`	No	Optional. The name of the variable to hold the body evaluation result as a `java.io.Reader`.
`scope`	`String`	No	Optional. The variable scope; one of `page`, `request`, `session`, or `application`. Default is `page`.

The difference between the var and varReader attributes is the type of Java object used for capturing the result. The var attribute captures it as a String and is sufficient for most cases. When the varReader attribute is used, the result is captured as a java.io.Reader object instead. For large results, this can be slightly more efficient when combined with an action or function for the transformation that reads its input from a Reader. Along with one of var or varReader, you can also specify the scope for the variable with the scope attribute.

The rest of the tag file in Example 11-4 transforms the captured body. First it uses the JSTL fn:escapeXml( ) function to convert all special characters to character entity codes, and then it replaces all occurrences of [code] and [/code] with the HTML <pre> and </pre> tags using the JSTL fn:replace( ) function, to preserve formatting in these sections. Finally, the converted body evaluation result is added to the calling page with a simple EL expression.

Processing Fragment Attributes

Processing the custom action body is easy and powerful as you can see, but wait, there's more! The custom action body is actually just a special case of what's called a *JSP fragment* in the JSP specification. A JSP fragment is an executable representation of a set of dynamic elements (actions and EL expressions), optionally mixed with template text. When the tag file invokes the fragment, all the dynamic elements in the fragment are executed. Since the elements have access to the current values of all scoped variables, the result typically differs from invocation to invocation, and the tag file can invoke it any number of times (e.g., once or none for a conditional action or multiple times for an iteration action).

In Example 11-4, the <jsp:doBody> action invokes the special fragment representing a custom action element body, but named fragments can also be provided as custom action attributes and be invoked by the tag file. Such fragments are invoked with the <jsp:invoke> action, described in Table 11-2.

Table 11-2. Attributes for <jsp:invoke>

Attribute name	Java type	Dynamic value accepted	Description
fragment	String	No	Mandatory. The name of the fragment to invoke.
var	String	No	Optional. The name of the variable to hold the body evaluation result as a String.
varReader	String	No	Optional. The name of the variable to hold the body evaluation result as a java.io.Reader.
scope	String	No	Optional. The variable scope; one of page, request, session, or application. Default is page.

Let's develop a variant of the JSTL <c:forEach> action to illustrate how you can use named fragments. Say you want to loop through all the elements in a collection to generate an HTML table, and you want to render even rows one way and odd rows another. Here's a page that solves this problem by using a custom action with separate fragment attributes for even and odd rows:

```
<%@ page contentType="text/html" %>
<%@ taglib prefix="my" tagdir="/WEB-INF/tags/mytags" %>
<%@ taglib prefix="c" uri="http://java.sun.com/jsp/jstl/core" %>

<html>
  <head>
    <title>Even and Odd Rows</title>
  </head>
  <body bgcolor="white">
    <h1>Even and Odd Rows</h1>
    <table>
      <my:forEvenAndOdd items="a,b,c,d,e">
        <jsp:attribute name="even">
          <c:set var="counter" value="${counter + 1}" />
          <tr bgcolor="red"><td>${counter}: Even Row</td></tr>
        </jsp:attribute>
        <jsp:attribute name="odd">
          <c:set var="counter" value="${counter + 1}" />
          <tr bgcolor="blue"><td>${counter}: Odd Row</td></tr>
        </jsp:attribute>
      </my:forEvenAndOdd>
    </table>
  </body>
</html>
```

A fragment attribute value is defined using the <jsp:attribute> action introduced earlier. The body of this action element makes up the content of the fragment. In the page shown here, each fragment attribute values contain a JSTL <c:set> action for incrementing a counter and HTML table row and cell elements for showing the counter's value plus the static text "Even Row" and "Odd Row", respectively. The fragments also set different row background colors to make the differences clear. The result of processing this page is shown in Figure 11-2.

Note how the current value of the counter page scope variable is used for each new row, and how the rows alternate between the even and odd fragments. Example 11-5 shows the tag file for the <my:forEvenAndOdd> custom action.

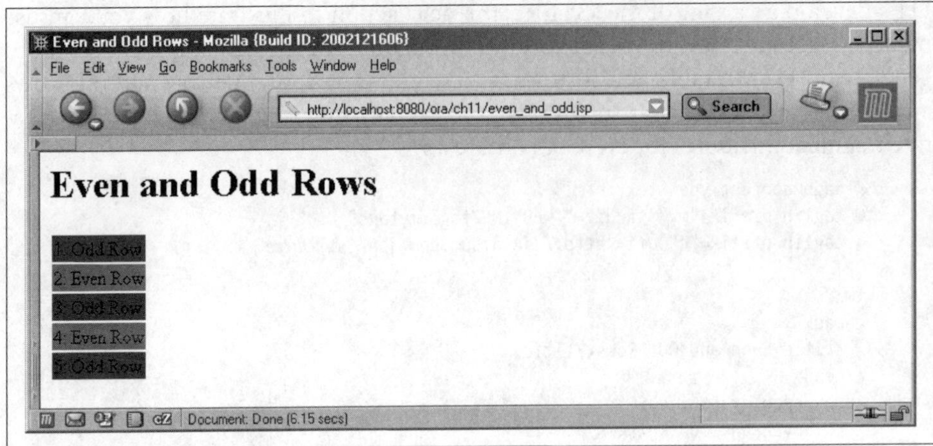

Figure 11-2. Representing even and odd rows as fragments

Example 11-5. Using fragment attributes (forEvenAndOdd.tag)

```
<%@ tag body-content="empty" %>
<%@ attribute name="items" rtexprvalue="true" required="true" %>
<%@ attribute name="even" fragment="true" required="true" %>
<%@ attribute name="odd" fragment="true" required="true" %>
<%@ taglib prefix="c" uri="http://java.sun.com/jsp/jstl/core" %>

<c:forEach items="${items}" varStatus="status">
  <c:choose>
    <c:when test="${status.count % 2 == 0}">
      <jsp:invoke fragment="even" />
    </c:when>
    <c:otherwise>
      <jsp:invoke fragment="odd" />
    </c:otherwise>
  </c:choose>
</c:forEach>
```

The tag directive specifies that the body must be empty; in this example, it must only contain the `<jsp:attribute>` elements (no template text of other elements), and they are considered alternatives to regular element attributes, not body content.

To tell the container to use an executable fragment as the attribute value, the attribute must be declared as such. Note that the `attribute` directive's `fragment` attribute is set to `true` for both the even and odd attributes. Otherwise the container evaluates the `<jsp:attribute>` body once and sets the attribute to the resulting value, as described in Chapter 6.

After the directives in Example 11-5, JSTL actions are used to loop through the list of items, and decide whether it's an even or odd row. The `<jsp:invoke>` action then invokes the appropriate fragment. The result is what you see in Figure 11-2.

Exposing Data to the Calling Page Through Variables

Attributes provide input to a custom action, but sometimes you also need to give the page that contains the custom action access to data produced by the custom action. For instance, the `<my:forEvenAndOdd>` action is not all that useful unless the page can access the current iteration value in the fragments for even and odd rows. To handle this requirement, data can be passed from a custom action to the caller by exposing it through declared variables.

Example 11-6 shows a version of the tag file from Example 11-5 that's been extended to expose the current iteration value as a variable named `current`. All differences between the examples are highlighted.

Example 11-6. Exporting data through variables (forEvenAndOdd2.tag)

```
<%@ tag body-content="empty" %>
<%@ attribute name="items" rtexprvalue="true" required="true" %>
<%@ attribute name="even" fragment="true" required="true" %>
<%@ attribute name="odd" fragment="true" required="true" %>
<%@ variable name-given="current" variable-class="java.lang.Object"
  scope="NESTED" %>
<%@ taglib prefix="c" uri="http://java.sun.com/jsp/jstl/core" %>

<c:forEach items="${items}" varStatus="status" var="current">
  <c:choose>
    <c:when test="${status.count % 2 == 0}">
      <jsp:invoke fragment="even" />
    </c:when>
    <c:otherwise>
      <jsp:invoke fragment="odd" />
    </c:otherwise>
  </c:choose>
</c:forEach>
```

The `variable` directive declares the variable. The `name-given` attribute specifies its name and the `variable-class` attribute its type. (Here I use the most generic class possible, `java.lang.Object`, because the collection to iterate over can contain elements of any type.)

The scope attribute accepts one of three values: `AT_BEGIN`, `AT_END`, or `NESTED`. It controls where the caller sees the variable. Despite its name, it has nothing to do with the scopes we've talked about earlier (page, request, session, and application), so *visibility* would have been a better name for this attribute. If it's set to `AT_BEGIN`, the variable is visible to the caller immediately after the start tag for the custom action element. If the attribute is set to `AT_END`, the variable is visible after the end tag. `NESTED` means it's only visible between the start and end tags.

To make the data visible to the caller, the tag file sets a page scope variable with the name declared by the variable directive. I told you earlier that the tag file has its own page scope, separate from the caller, so the container must do a bit of magic for this to work. For a variable declared as AT_BEGIN or NESTED, it copies the value of the variable in the tag file's page scope to the caller's page scope before invoking a fragment. If the variable is declared as AT_BEGIN or AT_END, it copies the value before exiting the tag file. In the case of a NESTED variable, it also saves and restores the value of the caller's page scoped variable with the same name, if any, before entering and exiting the tag file. Don't worry if this sounds confusing at first; it actually ends up working as you would expect it to.

The tag file in Example 11-6 exposes a variable named current, containing the value of the current iteration value. The local variable is set indirectly with help of the var attribute of the <c:forEach> action. As you may recall, the <c:forEach> action makes the current iteration value available in the page scope variable named by this attribute. By setting the name of the <c:forEach> variable to the name of the declared tag file variable, the variable value set by the <c:forEach> action is also exposed to the caller.

With the new version of the tag file, I can use it to display the current iteration value in each row:

```
<%@ page contentType="text/html" %>
<%@ taglib prefix="my" tagdir="/WEB-INF/tags/mytags" %>
<%@ taglib prefix="c" uri="http://java.sun.com/jsp/jstl/core" %>

<html>
  <head>
    <title>Even and Odd Rows</title>
  </head>
  <body bgcolor="white">
    <h1>Even and Odd Rows</h1>
    <table>
      <my:forEvenAndOdd2 items="a,b,c,d,e">
        <jsp:attribute name="even">
          <c:set var="counter" value="${counter + 1}" />
          <tr bgcolor="red"><td>${counter}: Even Row: ${current}</td></tr>
        </jsp:attribute>
        <jsp:attribute name="odd">
          <c:set var="counter" value="${counter + 1}" />
          <tr bgcolor="blue"><td>${counter}: Odd Row: ${current}</td></tr>
        </jsp:attribute>
      </my:forEvenAndOdd2>
    </table>
  </body>
</html>
```

Note how the exposed variable is used in EL expressions in both fragments.

There's still a problem here: the exposed variable name is hardcoded into the tag file. This may be okay in some cases, but it's better if the variable name can be specified using an attribute, just as you can pick a name with the var attribute for all JSTL actions that expose data. Fortunately, there's a solution, shown in Example 11-7.

Example 11-7. Letting the page author specify the variable name (forEvenAndOdd3.tag)

```
<%@ tag body-content="empty" %>
<%@ attribute name="items" rtexprvalue="true" required="true" %>
<%@ attribute name="var" rtexprvalue="false" required="true" %>
<%@ attribute name="even" fragment="true" required="true" %>
<%@ attribute name="odd" fragment="true" required="true" %>
<%@ variable name-from-attribute="var" alias="current"
  variable-class="java.lang.Object" scope="NESTED" %>
<%@ taglib prefix="c" uri="http://java.sun.com/jsp/jstl/core" %>

<c:forEach items="${items}" varStatus="status" var="current">
  <c:choose>
    <c:when test="${status.count % 2 == 0}">
      <jsp:invoke fragment="even" />
    </c:when>
    <c:otherwise>
      <jsp:invoke fragment="odd" />
    </c:otherwise>
  </c:choose>
</c:forEach>
```

Instead of the name-given attribute used in the previous example, I use the name-from-attribute and alias attributes of the variable directive in Example 11-7. The name-from-attribute attribute value is the name of the custom action attribute used to name the variable. The named attribute (var in this example) must be declared as required and must not accept a request time value. The alias attribute value declares the name of the tag file's local page scope variable, which the JSP container copies to the caller's page scope as described earlier. The aliasing trick is needed because the page author can assign any name for the variable when she uses the custom action, but a fixed name must be used when developing the tag file.

The rest of Example 11-7 is identical to Example 11-6, but I can now specify the variable name in the calling page like this:

```
<%@ page contentType="text/html" %>
<%@ taglib prefix="my" tagdir="/WEB-INF/tags/mytags" %>
<%@ taglib prefix="c" uri="http://java.sun.com/jsp/jstl/core" %>

<html>
  <head>
    <title>Even and Odd Rows</title>
  </head>
  <body bgcolor="white">
    <h1>Even and Odd Rows</h1>
    <table>
      <my:forEvenAndOdd3 items="a,b,c,d,e" var="anyName">
        <jsp:attribute name="even">
          <c:set var="counter" value="${counter + 1}" />
```

```
        <tr bgcolor="red"><td>${counter}: Even Row: ${anyName}</td></tr>
      </jsp:attribute>
      <jsp:attribute name="odd">
        <c:set var="counter" value="${counter + 1}" />
        <tr bgcolor="blue"><td>${counter}: Odd Row: ${anyName}</td></tr>
      </jsp:attribute>
    </my:forEvenAndOdd3>
  </table>
 </body>
</html>
```

Aborting the Page Processing

In Chapter 9, I described how using the `<jsp:forward>` action or the JSTL `<c:redirect>` action shifts processing from the current page to the page specified by the page attribute, effectively aborting processing of the current page. Custom actions implemented as Java classes can cause the same thing to happen.

There's no directive or similar mechanism that a tag file can use to explicitly abort processing, but using `<jsp:forward>`, `<c:redirect>`, or a custom action that aborts page processing in a tag file has the same effect; both the tag file processing and the processing of the page that invokes the tag file stop after it aborts the processing. You can use this feature to, for instance, develop a smart forwarding action that decides which page to forward to based on runtime conditions, such as the time of the day, the current user, or the type of browser accessing the page.

Packaging Tag Files for Easy Reuse

All examples in this chapter use a `taglib` directive with a `tagdir` attribute to specify the directory that contains the tag files. While this is handy for custom actions implemented as tag files in an application you control, it's not as easy as one would want for deployment and use of the tag library in third-party applications. As you may recall from Chapter 7, it's very easy to deploy a tag library packaged as a JAR file; just put the JAR file in the *WEB-INF/lib* directory and use the default URI as the `uri` attribute value in the `taglib` directive.

You can do the same with a tag library developed as tag files, but in this case you must also create a Tag Library Descriptor (TLD) and include it in the JAR file. I described the purpose of the TLD briefly in Chapter 7, but let's take a closer look at it here. Example 11-8 shows the TLD for a tag library with some of the tag files we've developed in this chapter.

Example 11-8. TLD for tag files

```
<?xml version="1.0" encoding="ISO-8859-1" ?>
<taglib xmlns="http://java.sun.com/xml/ns/j2ee"
  xmlns:xsi="http://www.w3.org/2001/XMLSchema-instance"
```

Example 11-8. TLD for tag files (continued)

```
  xsi:schemaLocation="http://java.sun.com/xml/ns/j2ee
    http://java.sun.com/xml/ns/j2ee/web-jsptaglibrary_2_0.xsd"
  version="2.0">

  <tlib-version>1.0</tlib-version>
  <short-name>my</short-name>
  <uri>mytaglib</uri>

  <tag-file>
    <name>copyright</name>
    <path>/META-INF/tags/mytags/copyright.tag</path>
  </tag-file>

  <tag-file>
    <name>forEvenAndOdd</name>
    <path>/META-INF/tags/mytags/forEvenAndOdd.tag</path>
  </tag-file>

  <tag-file>
    <name>htmlFormat</name>
    <path>/META-INF/tags/mytags/htmlFormat.tag</path>
  </tag-file>

</taglib>
```

As you can see, this file is an XML document. Don't worry about the `<taglib>` element attributes; just copy the element exactly as its shown here into your TLD. I describe it in more detail in Chapter 21, along with the TLD elements not covered here.

The first elements provide information about the tag library itself. The `<tlib-version>` element contains the version of this tag library and the `<short-name>` element contains the default namespace prefix for this library. An authoring tool may use the default namespace prefix when it generates the `taglib` directive and action elements, but a page author can pick different prefixes if needed, as described in Chapter 7.

The `<uri>` element is important. This element declares the default URI (identifier) for the library. The value you use for this element is the value that must be used as the `uri` attribute value for the `taglib` directive in the JSP pages to take advantage of the auto-deploy feature, as I described in Chapter 7.

Next comes a `<tag-file>` element for each tag file. The nested `<name>` element gives the name for the custom action. It's typically the same as the filename (minus the *.tag* extension) but you can specify a different name if you want. The `<path>` element holds the path within the JAR file to the tag file. It must start with */META-INF/tags/*. The TLD file itself must also be located in the */META-INF* directory in the JAR file, so you need to create a directory structure like this for the tag files and the TLD:

```
META-INF/
    mytags.tld
```

```
tags/
  mytags/
    copyright.tag
    forEvenAndOdd.tag
    htmlFormat.tag
```

Then create the JAR file with the *jar* command (included with the Java SDK) like this:

```
C:\> jar cvf mytags.jar META-INF
```

This creates a JAR file named *mytags.jar* containing the contents of the *META-INF* directory structure. You can now place this JAR file in the *WEB-INF/lib* directory of any web application that needs the library. When you restart the web container, it will locate the JAR file and its TLD, so that you can identify the tag library in a JSP page with a `taglib` directive like this:

```
<%@ taglib prefix="my" uri="mytags" %>
```

In other words, use the `uri` attribute with the default URI for the library (declared in the TLD), just as for the JSTL libraries we've used in previous chapters, instead of the `tagdir` attribute.

You can also use a TLD to identify tag files placed directly in the filesystem, i.e., not packaged in a JAR file. Doing this allows you to use the `uri` attribute instead of the `tagdir` attribute for the `taglib` directive, potentially saving you from changing the `taglib` directives in a number of JSP pages if you eventually decide to package the tag files in a JAR file for easier reuse in other applications. With this approach, you put the tag files under *WEB-INF/tags* (or a subdirectory) just as in the first examples in this chapter, but you also place a TLD in the *WEB-INF* directory (or a subdirectory, like *tlds*):

```
WEB-INF/
  tlds/
    mytags.tld
  tags/
    mytags/
      copyright.tag
      forEvenAndOdd.tag
      htmlFormat.tag
```

In this case, the `<path>` elements in the TLD must specify the context-relative path to the tag files in the filesystem:

```
<tag-file>
  <name>copyright</name>
  <path>/WEB-INF/tags/mytags/copyright.tag</path>
</tag-file>
```

Other than that, the TLD is the same as in Example 11-7.

CHAPTER 12

Accessing a Database

Almost all the web applications that you see on the Internet access a database. Databases store customer information, order information, product information, even discussion forum messages—in short, all information that needs to survive a server restart and is too complex to handle in plain-text files.

There are many types of databases used in the industry today. However, relational databases are by far the most common. A relational database uses tables to represent the information it handles. A table consists of rows of columns, with each column holding a single value of a predefined data type. Examples of these data types are text data, numeric data, dates, and binary data such as images and sound. A specialized language called Structured Query Language (SQL) is used to access the data. SQL is an ANSI standard and is supported by all major database vendors.

Relational database engines come in all shapes and sizes, from simple one-person databases with limited features, to sophisticated databases capable of handling large numbers of concurrent users with support for transactions distributed over multiple servers and extremely optimized search algorithms. Even though they all use SQL as the data access language, the API used to execute SQL statements is different for each database engine. To help programmers write code that's portable between database engines, the standard Java libraries include an API called the Java Database Connectivity (JDBC) API. JDBC defines a set of classes that can execute SQL statements the same way in any relational database.

The complexity of databases varies extensively. A database for an online discussion forum, for instance, requires only one or two tables, while a database for a human resources system may contain hundreds of related tables. In this chapter, we look at a set of JSTL database actions you can use to build any type of database-driven web application. But if the database is complex, you may want to use another approach: hiding the database behind application-specific beans and custom actions, or moving all database processing to a servlet and using JSP only to show the result. Both these approaches are discussed briefly at the end this chapter and in more detail in Chapters 18, 19, and 24.

Accessing a Database from a JSP Page

JSTL includes a number of actions for database access to make it easy to develop simple database-driven JSP applications. The actions provide the following features:

- Using a connection pool for better performance and scalability
- Supporting queries, updates, and inserts
- Handling the most common data type conversions
- Supporting a combination of database operations in one transaction

Each action is introduced as it's used in the example in this chapter. In addition, you can find a complete description of all the actions in Appendix B.

Application Architecture Example

In this chapter, we build an employee register application. This application contains functions for adding and changing employee information, as well as for looking up employees matching a search criterion. The employee information is stored in a relational database and accessed through the JSTL database access actions.

The employee registration part of the application contains the pages shown in Figure 12-1.

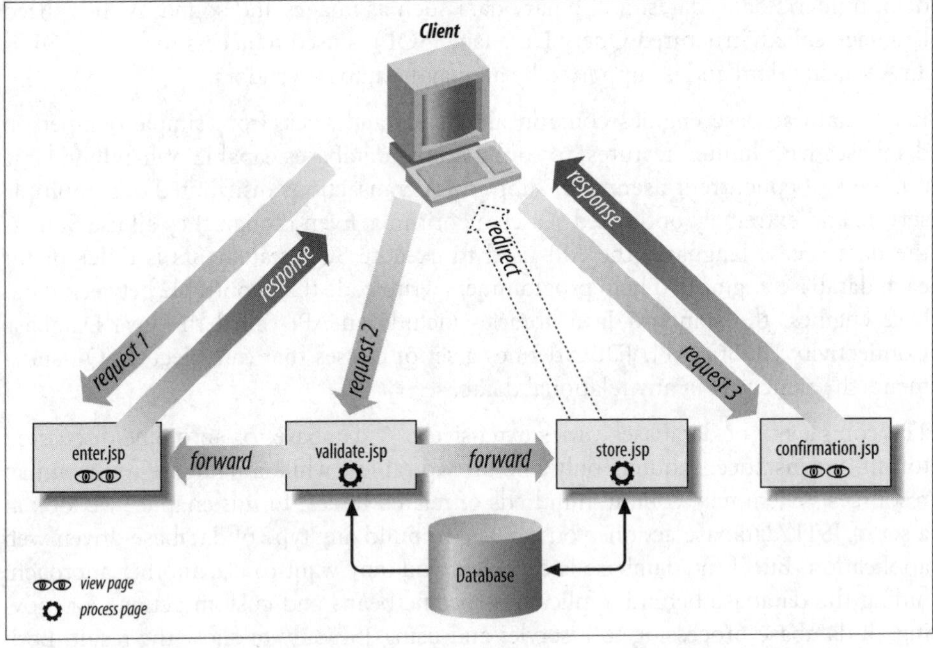

Figure 12-1. Employee registration pages

This example looks similar to the example from Chapter 10. The *enter.jsp* page presents a form in which the user enters information about an employee. When the form is submitted, it invokes the *validate.jsp* page, where all input is validated. If the input is invalid, the request is forwarded back to the *enter.jsp* page to display error messages and the form with all the values the user previously entered. The user can then correct the invalid values and submit the form again. When all input is valid, the *validate.jsp* page forwards the request to the *store.jsp* page where the information is stored in the database. Finally, the *store.jsp* page redirects to the *confirmation.jsp* page, which displays the information actually stored in the database as a confirmation to the user.

Figure 12-2 shows the pages used to implement the employee search function.

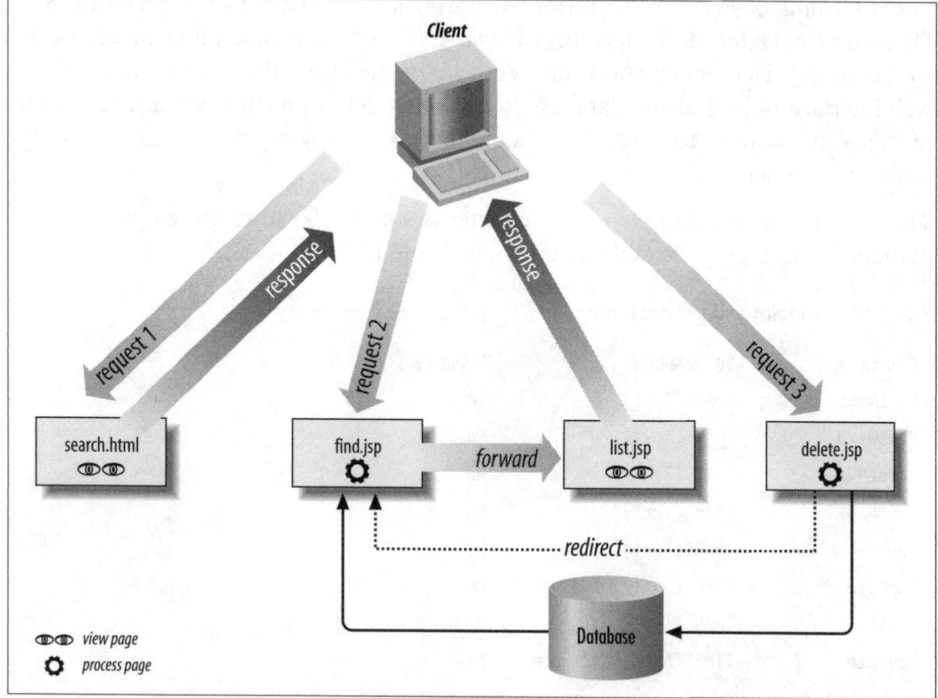

Figure 12-2. Employee search pages

The *search.html* page is a regular HTML page with a form for entering the search criteria. The user can enter a partial first name, last name, and department name. Submitting the form invokes the *find.jsp* page. Here the database is searched for employees matching the criteria specified by the user, and the result is kept in the request scope. The *find.jsp* page forwards to the *list.jsp* page, where the result is displayed. For each employee listed, the *list.jsp* page adds a **Delete** button. Clicking on the **Delete** button invokes the *delete.jsp* page, removing the employee information from the database. The *delete.jsp* then redirects to the *find.jsp* page, to get an updated collection of employees matching the search criteria, and the *find.jsp* forwards to *list.jsp* as before, to show the result after deleting the employee.

Table Example

If you develop a database-driven web application from scratch, you must first develop a database schema. The database schema shows how the persistent information in the application is modeled as a set of related tables. For a large application, this is a great deal of work, and it's extremely important to find the right balance between flexibility and performance of frequent queries. How database schemas are developed is beyond the scope of this book, but there are plenty of other books available on this subject. Examples are C.J. Date's classic and very academic *An Introduction to Database Systems* (Addison Wesley), and a book that's easier to read, *Database Design for Mere Mortals: A Hands-On Guide to Relational Database Design* by Michael J. Hernandez (Addison Wesley). In the event that you're developing a web interface to an existing database, the schema development is already taken care of, but you still need to study the schema to make sure you understand how all the tables fit together.

The schema for the example in this chapter is simple. To store the employee information, we need only the table described in Table 12-1.

Table 12-1. Employee database table

Column name	SQL data type	Primary key?
`UserName`	`CHAR (Text)`	Yes
`Password`	`CHAR (Text)`	No
`FirstName`	`CHAR (Text)`	No
`LastName`	`CHAR (Text)`	No
`Dept`	`CHAR (Text)`	No
`EmpDate`	`DATE (Date/Time)`	No
`EmailAddr`	`CHAR (Text)`	No
`ModDate`	`TIMESTAMP (Date/Time)`	No

In a relational database, one column (or a combination of columns) can be marked as a *primary key*. The primary key uniquely identifies one specific row in the table; no two rows can have the same primary key. Here we use a column named `UserName` as the unique primary key for the table. Each employee must therefore be assigned a unique username, just like the username used to log into an operating system. As you will see in Chapter 13, the username, combined with the password you also find in the Employee table, can be used for application-controlled authentication. Assigning unique usernames can, however, be a problem in a web application available to anyone on the Internet. Therefore, some applications use a numeric code as the unique identifier instead, such as social security number or a generated sequence number. This table is only an example of how to work with databases in JSP, so we'll keep it simple.

The SQL data type name within parentheses in Table 12-1 is the name used in the Microsoft Access product, to help you create the tables in this commonly used database. This is by no means an endorsement of the Access database for a database-driven web site. In fact, I recommend that you *don't* use Access for a real application. It's a product that's intended as a single-user database, and it doesn't work well with the number of accesses typical for a web application. For a real site, you should use a more robust multiuser database such as Oracle, Sybase, DB2, or Microsoft SQL Server. The only reason I use Access in this book when I refer to a specific product is that it's a database you may already have installed. It's also easy to use during development of an application. If you don't have a database installed, and you're not ready to spend big bucks for one of the products just listed, there are plenty of other free or inexpensive databases you can use. One example is MySQL from MySQL AB, a popular database available at *http://www.mysql.com/*. Another is PostgreSQL, an open source database available at *http://postgresql.org/*.

To run the example described in this chapter you must first create the table outlined in Table 12-1 in your database. How to do this varies between database engines, so you need to consult the documentation for the database engine you use.

The DataSource Interface and JDBC Drivers

Before we get started with the examples, let's look at how to identify the database you want to access. The JSTL actions can find this information in many different ways, to make the simple scenario simple and the more complex ones possible. In all cases, though, they get access to the database through an instance of a JDBC interface named `javax.sql.DataSource`.

The `DataSource` interface is part of the Java 2 Standard Edition (J2SE) 1.4, and for prior versions of the J2SE, it's available in the JDBC 2.0 Optional Package. To access a database, a connection to the database must first be established. Opening a database connection is very time-consuming. A nice thing with a `DataSource` is that it can represent something called a *connection pool*. Connection pools are described in more detail in Chapter 24, but it's exactly what it sounds like: a pool of database connections that can be shared by multiple clients. With a connection pool, a connection to the database is opened once and stays open until the application is shut down. When a database action needs a connection, it gets it from the pool through the `DataSource` object and uses it to execute one or more SQL statements. When the action closes the connection, the connection is returned to the pool where it can be picked up by the next action that needs it.

In addition to the DataSource, the JDBC API contains other classes and interfaces that allow a Java application to process SQL statements in a database-independent way. For each specific database engine, an implementation of the interfaces defined by the JDBC API translates the generic calls to a format understood by the engine. This implementation is called a *JDBC driver*. Using different drivers that all provide the same interface allows you to develop your application on one platform (for instance, a PC with an Access database), and then deploy the application on another platform (for instance, a Solaris or Linux server with an Oracle database).

At least in theory it does. SQL is unfortunately one of these standards that leave a few things open, eagerly filled by different vendors' proprietary solutions. Examples include how to handle embedded quotes in a string value, how to deal with the input and output of date and time values, semantics for certain data types, and creation of unique numbers. The JSTL actions take care of some of these, such as string quoting and date/time string format, so if you use these actions and stick to ANSI SQL, you should be able to migrate from one database to another without too much tweaking. However, you should always read your database documentation carefully and try to stay away from proprietary features. Be prepared to spend at least some time in transition when you need to move the application to another database. You can find JDBC drivers for most database engines on the market, both commercial and open source. If you can't get one from your vendor, Sun maintains a list of third-party drivers at *http://industry.java.sun.com/products/jdbc/drivers*.

Okay, so how to create a DataSource instance and make it available to the JSTL actions? If you need to access only one database, you can tell the JSTL actions all they need to know to create a DataSource themselves, using a context parameter in the application's deployment descriptor (the *WEB-INF/web.xml* file):

```
<web-app>
  ...
  <context-param>
    <param-name>
      javax.servlet.jsp.jstl.sql.dataSource
    </param-name>
    <param-value>
      jdbc:odbc:example,sun.jdbc.odbc.JdbcOdbcDriver,scott,tiger
    </param-value>
  </context-param>
  ...
</web-app>
```

The example shows the type of context parameter value you must use for the JDBC-ODBC Bridge driver included in the Java 2 SDK: sun.jdbc.odbc.JdbcOdbcDriver. This driver can access databases that provide an ODBC interface but that have no direct JDBC driver interface, as is the case for Microsoft Access. Sun recommends you not use the JDBC-ODBC driver for a production application, but for development it usually works fine. When you deploy your application, you should use a production-quality driver from your database vendor or a third party.

The context parameter value contains four pieces of information separated by commas: a JDBC URL, a JDBC driver class name, a database account name, and the account password. If any of these parts contains a comma, you must escape it with a backslash.

The first part—the JDBC URL—identifies a specific database. Different JDBC drivers use different URL syntax. All JDBC URLs starts with `jdbc:` followed by a JDBC driver identifier, such as `odbc:` for the JDBC-ODBC bridge driver and `mysql:` for the most commonly used MySQL driver. The rest of the URL identifies the database instance in a driver-dependent way. For the JDBC-ODBC bridge driver, it's an ODBC Data Source Name (DSN). If you use an Access database, you need to create a system DSN for the database using the ODBC control in the Windows Control Panel, as shown in Figure 12-3. Note that you must create a system DSN as opposed to a user DSN. The reason for this is that the web server that executes your JSP pages usually runs as a different user account than the account you use for development. If you specify a user DSN with your development account, the web container will not be able to find it.

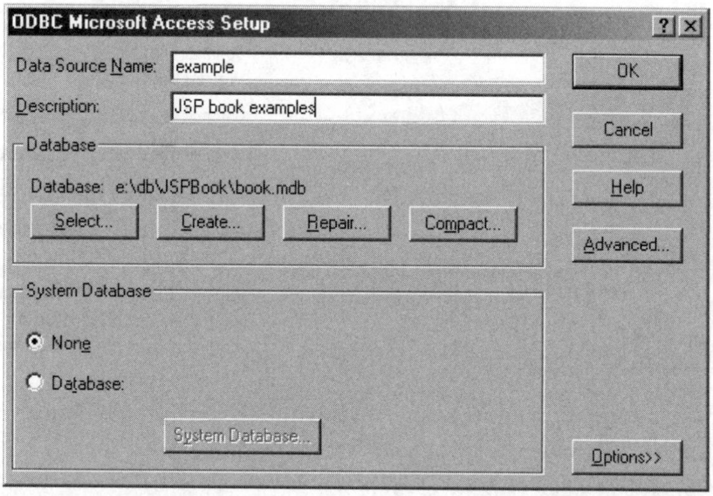

ODBC Microsoft Access Setup

Data Source Name: example

Description: JSP book examples

Database

Database: e:\db\JSPBook\book.mdb

Select... Create... Repair... Compact...

System Database

None

Database:

System Database...

OK

Cancel

Help

Advanced...

Options>>

Figure 12-3. System DSN definition window

The second part—the JDBC driver class name—must be specified as a fully qualified class name—in other words, the class name including the package name. You must install the driver by placing its class files in a place where the web container can find it, typically in the application's *WEB-INF/lib* directory if it's packaged in a JAR file. If the driver is delivered as a ZIP file (as Oracle's JDBC drivers are, for instance), you can still place it in the *WEB-INF/lib* directory if you change the file extension from *.zip* to *.jar*.

The database account name and password define the specific database account to use.

All parts of the context parameter except the JDBC URL are optional. The driver class name can only be left out if the class is loaded by some other part of the application, for instance by a servlet or a listener. For a pure JSP application, you must always specify it. The account name and password can be left out if you use a database that isn't protected by a username and password, for instance an Access database used during development.

If you need to access more than one database, you must work a little bit harder since the context parameter can only define one. During development, or for a simple prototype, you can use the JSTL <sql:setDataSource> action, described in Table 12-2.

Table 12-2. Attributes for JSTL <sql:setDataSource>

Attribute name	Java type	Dynamic value accepted	Description
dataSource	String or javax.sql.DataSource	Yes	Optional. A data source. If specified as a String, it must be a JNDI path or use the same format as the data source context parameter.
driver	String	Yes	Optional. The name of the JDBC driver class used to access the database.
url	String	Yes	Optional. The JDBC URL for the database.
user	String	Yes	Optional. The database account name.
password	String	Yes	Optional. The database account password.
var	String	No	Optional. The name of the variable to hold the data source.
scope	String	No	Optional. The scope for the data source, one of page, request, session, or application. page is the default.

The database information can be specified as the dataSource attribute value in the same form as for the context parameter, or alternatively with the url, driver, user and password attributes. Use the var attribute to specify a name for the data source object and optionally its scope with the scope attribute. Here's an example, using the same database as in the context parameter example:

```
<sql:setDataSource var="example" scope="application"
  driver="sun.jdbc.odbc.JdbcOdbcDriver"
  url="jdbc:odbc:example"
  user="scott"
  password="tiger"
/>
```

You must also tell the database access actions that need the data source which one to use when you're not using the default one:

```
<sql:query
  var="empDbInfo"
  dataSource="${example}"
  sql="SELECT * FROM Employee"
/>
```

The var attribute is actually optional for the <sql:setDataSource> action. If you omit it, the data source is used as the default in the specified scope, in effect hiding the default data source defined by the context parameter or a default set by another <sql:setDataSource> (or a servlet) in a "larger" scope. When a specific data source is not supplied through the dataSource attribute, all JSTL database actions look for a default data source in the order page, request, session and application scope, and finally the context parameter. This setup, with a default that can be defined by both a context parameter and scoped variables is called a *configuration setting* in the JSTL specification.

The DataSource created based on the context parameter information shown earlier or by the <sql:setDataSource> action doesn't represent a connection pool. These two techniques are primarily intended for prototyping, and they are handy when you just want to quickly get a simple example up and running. For the examples in this book, I have used the context parameter to make it easy for you to run them with another driver and JDBC URL; just update the value in the deployment descriptor to match your database and restart the web container.

For a production site, you should use a DataSource that represents a connection pool instead. If you use a web container that supports the Java Naming and Directory Interface (JNDI) API, you can register a DataSource with the container's naming service and specify the JNDI path for the data source as the context parameter value, instead of specifying all the data needed to create a DataSource:

```
<web-app>
  ...
  <context-param>
    <param-name>
      javax.servlet.jsp.jstl.sql.dataSource
    </param-name>
    <param-value>
      jdbc/Example
    </param-value>
  </context-param>
  ...
</web-app>
```

The dataSource attribute supported by all JSTL database actions also accepts a JNDI path. Another alternative is to let a servlet or listener create the DataSource. I describe both the JNDI and servlet or listener alternatives in detail in Chapter 24.

Reading and Storing Information in a Database

The first page the user loads to register an employee in the example application is *enter.jsp*. This page, which contains a form for entering all information about an employee, is shown in Figure 12-4.

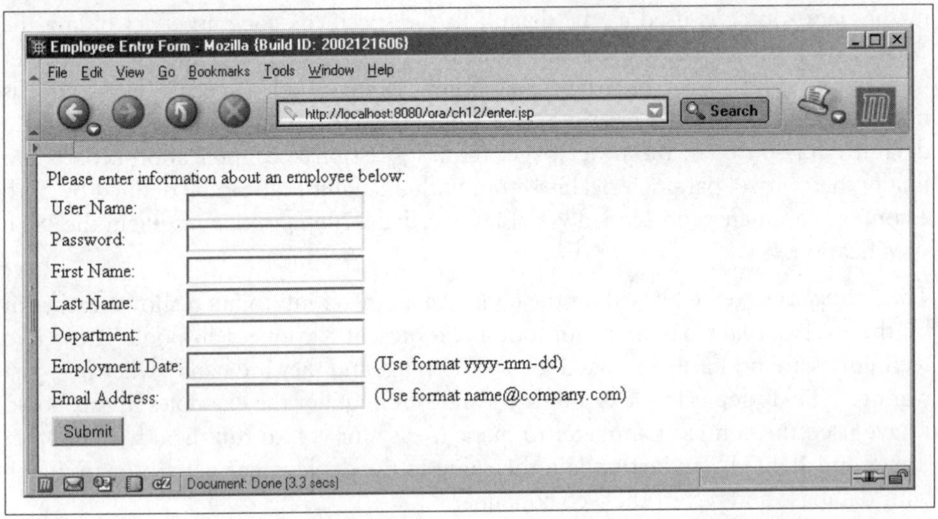

Figure 12-4. Employee information entry form

The input is validated by the *validate.jsp* page when the form is submitted. The *enter.jsp* and *validate.jsp* pages are similar to the pages for input validation discussed in detail in Chapter 10 and don't access the database. Instead of going through these pages now, let's jump directly to the *store.jsp* page where the database access takes place. We'll return to the *enter.jsp* and *validate.jsp* pages at the end of this chapter, to look at some interesting things not related to database access.

Example 12-1 shows the complete *store.jsp* page. This page first searches the database for information about an employee with the specified username. If one is found, the database is updated with all the other employee information the user entered. Otherwise, a new employee entry is stored in the database. All database information about the employee is then collected, and the request is forwarded to the *confirmation.jsp* page. Let's look at the complete page first and then discuss the different pieces in detail.

Example 12-1. Database access page (store.jsp)

```
<%@ taglib prefix="c" uri="http://java.sun.com/jsp/jstl/core" %>
<%@ taglib prefix="sql" uri="http://java.sun.com/jsp/jstl/sql" %>
<%@ taglib prefix="fmt" uri="http://java.sun.com/jsp/jstl/fmt" %>

<%--
  See if the employee is already defined. If not, insert the
```

Example 12-1. Database access page (store.jsp) (continued)

```
  info, else update it.
--%>
<sql:query var="empDbInfo">
  SELECT * FROM Employee
    WHERE UserName = ?
  <sql:param value="${param.userName}" />
</sql:query>
<%--
  Deal with the date values: parse the employment date and create a
  Date object from it, and create a new variable to hold the current
  date.
--%>
<fmt:parseDate value="${param.empDate}" var="parsedEmpDate"
  pattern="yyyy-MM-dd" />
<jsp:useBean id="now" class="java.util.Date" />
<c:choose>
  <c:when test="${empDbInfo.rowCount == 0}">
    <sql:update>
      INSERT INTO Employee
        (UserName, Password, FirstName, LastName, Dept,
          EmpDate, EmailAddr, ModDate)
        VALUES(?, ?, ?, ?, ?, ?, ?, ?)
      <sql:param value="${param.userName}" />
      <sql:param value="${param.password}" />
      <sql:param value="${param.firstName}" />
      <sql:param value="${param.lastName}" />
      <sql:param value="${param.dept}" />
      <sql:dateParam value="${parsedEmpDate}" type="date"/>
      <sql:param value="${param.emailAddr}" />
      <sql:dateParam value="${now}" />
    </sql:update>
  </c:when>
  <c:otherwise>
    <sql:update>
      UPDATE Employee
        SET Password = ?,
            FirstName = ?,
            LastName = ?,
            Dept = ?,
            EmpDate = ?,
            EmailAddr = ?,
            ModDate = ?
        WHERE UserName = ?
      <sql:param value="${param.password}" />
      <sql:param value="${param.firstName}" />
      <sql:param value="${param.lastName}" />
      <sql:param value="${param.dept}" />
      <sql:dateParam value="${parsedEmpDate}" type="date"/>
      <sql:param value="${param.emailAddr}" />
      <sql:dateParam value="${now}" />
      <sql:param value="${param.userName}" />
    </sql:update>
```

Example 12-1. Database access page (store.jsp) (continued)

```
  </c:otherwise>
</c:choose>
<%-- Get the new or updated data from the database --%>
<sql:query var="newEmpDbInfo" scope="session">
  SELECT * FROM Employee
    WHERE UserName = ?
  <sql:param value="${param.userName}" />
</sql:query>
<%-- Redirect to the confirmation page --%>
<c:redirect url="confirmation.jsp" />
```

All JSTL database actions are packaged in their own tag library. At the top of the page in Example 12-1 you'll find the taglib directive for this library that associates it with the sql prefix, similar to the tag libraries used in the previous examples. Most of the JSTL database actions are used in this page. Let's look at them one at a time.

Reading database information

The first JSTL action that accesses the database in Example 12-1 is the <sql:query> action, described in Table 12-3.

Table 12-3. Attributes for JSTL < sql:query>

Attribute name	Java type	Dynamic value accepted	Description
dataSource	javax.sql.DataSource or String	Yes	Optional. The DataSource to use.
sql	String	Yes	Mandatory, unless specified as the body. The SQL statement.
maxRows	int	Yes	Optional. The maximum number of rows to include in the result. Default is all rows.
startRow	int	Yes	Optional. The first row to include in the result, expressed as a 0-based index. Default is 0.
var	String	No	Mandatory. The name of the variable to hold the result.
scope	String	No	Optional. The scope for the variable, one of page, request, session, or application. page is the default.

The <sql:query> action reads information from a database using the SQL SELECT statement, specified in the element's body or as the sql attribute value. A SELECT statement retrieves data from the database by specifying various clauses that identify the table to search in, the columns to return, the search criteria, and other options. If you're not familiar with the SELECT statement, you can read up on it in the documentation for your database. The SELECT statement in Example 12-1 gets all columns in the Employee table for every row in which the UserName column has the value specified in the userName field in the entry form. Since the username is unique in our application, either 0 or 1 row is returned.

The <sql:query> action in this example gets a connection from the default DataSource specified by the context parameter. It then executes the SQL SELECT statement and saves the result in the scope specified by the scope attribute, with the name specified by the var attribute. If no scope is specified, as in this example, the result is saved in the page scope.

Besides the SQL statement, the action element body also contains an <sql:param> action, described in Table 12-4.

Table 12-4. Attributes for JSTL <sql:param>

Attribute name	Java type	Dynamic value accepted	Description
value	Object	Yes	Mandatory, unless specified as the body. The value to use for a placeholder in the enclosing database action.

The <sql:param> action replaces a placeholder, marked with a question mark (?), in the SQL statement with a value. In Example 12-1, the EL expression used for the value attribute gets the userName request parameter value, corresponding to the form field with the same name in the *enter.jsp* page:

```
<sql:query var="empDbInfo">
  SELECT * FROM Employee
    WHERE UserName = ?
  <sql:param value="${param.userName}" />
</sql:query>
```

You *could* use an EL expression in the body instead to insert the userName parameter value directly into the SQL statement, like this:

```
<ora:sqlQuery id="empDbInfo">
  SELECT * FROM Employee
    WHERE UserName = '${params.userName}'
</ora:sqlQuery>
```

But then you run into the problem of string quoting in SQL. Most database engines require a string literal to be enclosed in single quotes in an SQL statement. That's easy to handle by just putting single quotes around the EL expression, like I've done here. What's not so easy is how to handle quotes within the string value. Different database engines employ different rules for how to encode embedded quotes. Most require a single quote in a string literal to be duplicated, while others use a backslash as an escape character or let you enclose the string literal with double quotes if the value includes single quotes. When you use the <sql:param> action, you don't have to worry about this type of formatting at all; the value is set directly in the SQL statement, bypassing all quoting rules.

Another reason for using <sql:param> is that using an EL expression to add a dynamic value to an SQL statement is also a security risk. If a user enters a value such as "foo' OR 1 = 1 --" in the username field, the SQL statement looks like this after the EL expression is processed:

```
SELECT * FROM Employee
    WHERE UserName = 'foo' OR 1 = 1 --'
```

The "OR 1 = 1" part means that this condition is always `true`, making the SQL statements returning all rows instead of only one row matching a specific username. Most databases interpret the "--" part as the start of a comment, so whatever comes after these characters is ignored. Tricks like this can be used to gain access to protected sites or return information that is supposed to be secret. Using <sql:param> prevents this type of attack. Instead of merging the dynamic value and the static text to create an SQL statement that the database then interprets, the <sql:param> action explicitly tells the database to use the provided value in place of the ? when it has interpreted the statement. Hence, there's no way to fool it.

Only one dynamic value is needed in the query in Example 12-1, but an SQL statement can contain as many placeholders as you like, matched by the same number of <sql:param> actions in the <sql:query> element body. The first <sql:param> action replaces the first question mark in the SQL statement with its value, the second replaces the second question mark, and so on. You can include the <sql:param> action elements directly after the corresponding question marks, to make it easier to see which action goes with which question mark:

```
<sql:query var="empDbInfo">
  SELECT * FROM Employee
    WHERE UserName = ?
  <sql:param value="${param.userName}" />
    AND FirstName = ?
  <sql:param value="${param.firstName}" />
</sql:query>
```

The result generated by the <sql:query> action is an instance of the `javax.servlet.jsp.jstl.sql.Result` class. It's a bean with a number of properties for accessing all rows and their column values, as well as properties for the column names and number of rows in the result. We look at most of the `Result` properties later in this chapter, but the only one used in Example 12-1 is the `rowCount` property. It's used to see if the query returned any rows. The `SELECT` statement searches the database for information about the employee entered in the form. If the employee is already registered, the query returns one row—otherwise no rows. This information is used to decide whether to insert or update the employee information:

```
<c:choose>
  <c:when test="${empDbInfo.rowCount == 0}">
    <%-- Insert the employee data --%>
    ...
  </c:when>
```

```
    <c:otherwise>
      <%-- Update the employee data --%>
      ...
    </c:otherwise>
  </c:choose>
```

Inserting database information

An SQL INSERT statement is used to insert new rows in a database table. To execute an INSERT statement, use the <sql:update> action, described in Table 12-5.

Table 12-5. Attributes for JSTL <sql:update>

Attribute name	Java type	Dynamic value accepted	Description
dataSource	javax.sql.DataSource or String	Yes	Optional. The DataSource to use.
sql	String	Yes	Mandatory, unless specified as the body. The SQL statement.
var	String	No	Optional. The name of the variable to hold the result.
scope	String	No	Optional. The scope for the variable, one of page, request, session, or application. page is the default.

The <sql:update> action executes any SQL statement that doesn't return rows: INSERT, UPDATE, and DELETE, and even so-called Data Definition Language (DDL) statements such as CREATE TABLE. These statements do exactly what it sounds like they do: insert, update and delete information, and create a new table, respectively. (Refer to your database documentation for details about the syntax.) For INSERT, UPDATE, and DELETE, the <sql:update> action can optionally save an Integer object, telling how many rows were affected by the statement. The Integer is saved in the scope specified by the scope attribute using the name specified by the var attribute. This feature isn't used in Example 12-1, but in some applications it can be used as feedback to the user or to decide what to do next.

The SQL statement can be specified through the sql attribute or the action's body, and <sql:param> actions can be used to give values to the placeholders in the statement. Multiple <sql:param> actions are used in Example 12-1:

```
<sql:update>
  INSERT INTO Employee
    (UserName, Password, FirstName, LastName, Dept,
      EmpDate, EmailAddr, ModDate)
    VALUES(?, ?, ?, ?, ?, ?, ?, ?)
  <sql:param value="${param.userName}" />
  <sql:param value="${param.password}" />
  <sql:param value="${param.firstName}" />
```

```
    <sql:param value="${param.lastName}" />
    <sql:param value="${param.dept}" />
    <sql:dateParam value="${parsedEmpDate}" type="date"/>
    <sql:param value="${param.emailAddr}" />
    <sql:dateParam value="${now}" />
  </sql:update>
```

Most of the placeholders are replaced with request parameter values, just as for the query. The exceptions are the placeholders for the EmpDate and ModDate columns, which require special attention.

Databases are picky about the format for date and time data types. In Example 12-1 we get the date from the form as a string in the format yyyy-MM-dd (e.g., 2002-03-06), but the EmpDate column is declared as a DATE column, as shown in Table 12-1. Some databases accept a string in the format used for this application as a value for a DATE column, but others don't. To be on the safe side, it's best to convert the string into its native date format, a java.util.Date object, before sending it to the database. It can be done using a JSTL action from the formatting library, assigned the fmt prefix by the taglib directive at the beginning of the page:

```
<fmt:parseDate value="${params.empDate}" var="parsedEmpDate"
  pattern="yyyy-MM-dd" />
```

The <fmt:parseDate> action takes the date or time string specified by the value attribute and interprets it according to the pattern defined by the pattern attribute. The pattern describes the order and format of the year, month, and day parts in the string representation of the date. We'll return to the <fmt:parseDate> action in Chapter 14 to look at all the details, but for now it suffices to say that the pattern description is very flexible. For instance, if you want the user to enter dates in a format such "Tuesday February 19, 2003," you specify the pattern EEEE MMMM dd, yyyy instead of the yyyy-MM-dd pattern used in this example to tell the action how to interpret the date string. If the string value can be interpreted as a date according to the pattern, the action saves a java.util.Date object representing the date as a variable with the name specified by the var attribute. This variable can then replace the placeholder in the SQL statement.

Besides dates, you should also convert numeric values you receive as strings when they are declared as INT, REAL, etc., in the database, using the JSTL <fmt:parseNumber> action. In this example, there are no columns of this type. The JSTL formatting actions are very powerful, but let's save the details for Chapter 14.

The Employee table also has a column named ModDate, to hold the date and time the information was last modified. It is declared as a TIMESTAMP column. To set its value, we need a java.util.Date object that represents the current date and time. It's easy to create one with the <jsp:useBean> action:

```
<jsp:useBean id="now" class="java.util.Date" />
```

The <jsp:useBean> action can create an instance of any class that has a no-arguments constructor, like the java.util.Date class. The instance is saved in the variable named by the id attribute.

Finally, we need to use the <sql:dateParam> action, described in Table 12-6, instead of the <sql:param> action to set the date and timestamp values.

Table 12-6. Attributes for JSTL <sql:dateParam>

Attribute name	Java type	Dynamic value accepted	Description
value	java.util.Date	Yes	Mandatory. The value to use for a placeholder in the enclosing database action.
type	String	Yes	Optional. One of date, time, or timestamp. timestamp is the default.

You have to use <sql:dateParam> because of an unfortunate quirk in the JDBC API. JDBC defines its own classes for date and time values: java.sql.Date, java.sql.Time, and java.sql.Timestamp. These are the only types accepted for date and time value placeholders. The <sql:dateParam> takes a java.util.Date object and turns it into one of the JDBC types based on the type attribute value or to a java.sql.Timestamp if no type is specified.

Updating database information

Once you know how to insert information in a database, updating it is a piece of cake. You just use the <sql:update> action with an SQL UPDATE statement instead of an INSERT statement:

```
<sql:update>
  UPDATE Employee
    SET Password = ?,
        FirstName = ?,
        LastName = ?,
        Dept = ?,
        EmpDate = ?,
        EmailAddr = ?,
        ModDate = ?
    WHERE UserName = ?
  <sql:param value="${param.password}" />
  <sql:param value="${param.firstName}" />
  <sql:param value="${param.lastName}" />
  <sql:param value="${param.dept}" />
  <sql:dateParam value="${parsedEmpDate}" type="date" />
  <sql:param value="${param.emailAddr}" />
  <sql:dateParam value="${now}" />
  <sql:param value="${param.userName}" />
</sql:update>
```

No surprises here. The only difference from how you insert information is the SQL statement. The `UPDATE` statement sets all the specified values for rows matching the `WHERE` clause, in this case the single row for the specified employee.

Generating HTML from a Query Result

Just before the page in Example 12-1 redirects to the confirmation page, there's one more `<sql:query>` action that retrieves the employee information that was just stored in the database:

```
<sql:query var="newEmpDbInfo" scope="session">
  SELECT * FROM Employee
    WHERE UserName = ?
  <sql:param value="${param.userName}" />
</sql:query>
```

The intention here is to present the information actually stored in the database to the user on the final page in this application (shown in Figure 12-5) as a confirmation that the operation was successful.

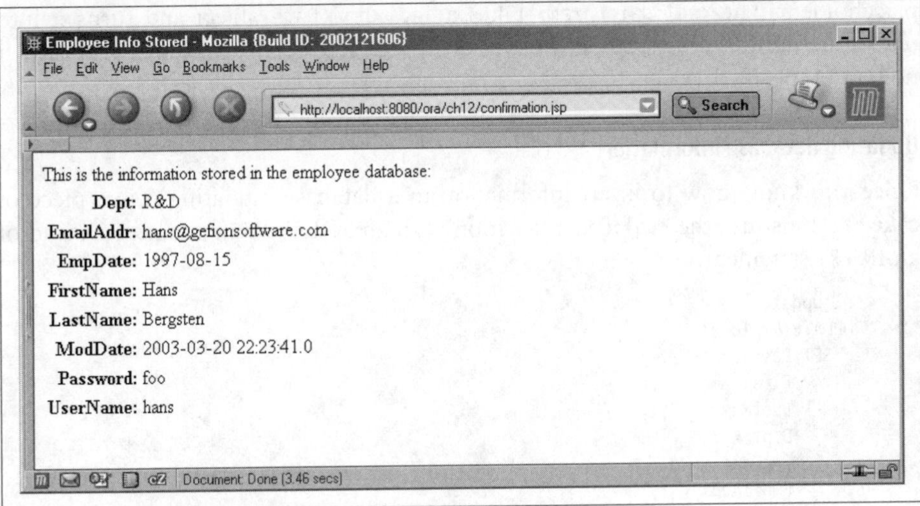

Figure 12-5. Employee registration confirmation page

Since we redirect to the confirmation page, ending the processing of the current request, the result is placed in the session scope. The redirect response tells the browser to automatically make a new request for the confirmation page. Because the new request is part of the same session, it finds the result saved by the previous page. Example 12-2 shows the code for the *confirmation.jsp* page.

Example 12-2. Page displaying query result (confirmation.jsp)

```
<%@ page contentType="text/html" %>
<%@ taglib prefix="c" uri="http://java.sun.com/jsp/jstl/core" %>
```

Example 12-2. Page displaying query result (confirmation.jsp) (continued)

```
<%@ taglib prefix="fn" uri="http://java.sun.com/jsp/jstl/functions" %>

<html>
  <head>
    <title>Employee Info Stored</title>
  </head>
  <body bgcolor="white">
    This is the information stored in the employee database:

    <table>
      <c:forEach items="${newEmpDbInfo.rows}" var="row">
        <c:forEach items="${row}" var="column">
          <tr>
            <td align=right>
              <b>${fn:escapeXml(column.key)}:</b>
            </td>
            <td>
              ${fn:escapeXml(column.value)}
            </td>
          </tr>
        </c:forEach>
      </c:forEach>
    </table>

  </body>
</html>
```

At the top of the page is the same JSP directive for using the JSTL database tag library as in Example 12-1.

An HTML table with cells for all columns in the row retrieved from the `Employee` table is created by two nested `<c:forEach>` actions; the outer one loops over all rows in the result (only one in this case), and the inner one loops over all columns in each row. To understand how it works, we must take a closer look at the `javax.servlet.jsp.jstl.sql.Result` returned by the `<sql:query>` action and saved in a variable named `newEmpDbInfo` in Example 12-1. The `Result` class is a bean with a number of properties that provide read-only access to the query result, described in Table 12-7.

Table 12-7. Properties for javax.servlet.jsp.jstl.sql.Result

Property name	Java type	Access	Description
`rows`	`java.util.SortedMap[]`	Read	The rows returned by the query, as an array of case-insensitive `SortedMap` instances. Each `Map` has one entry per column, using the column name as the key and the column value as the value.
`rowsByIndex`	`Object[][]`	Read	The rows returned by the query, as arrays (rows) of arrays (column values).
`rowCount`	`int`	Read	The number of rows in the result.

Table 12-7. Properties for javax.servlet.jsp.jstl.sql.Result (continued)

Property name	Java type	Access	Description
columnNames	String[]	Read	The column names in the same order as the column values in rowsByIndex.
limitedByMaxRows	boolean	Read	true if the result was truncated due to reaching the limit imposed by the maxRows attribute.

The rows property used as the items attribute value for the outer `<c:forEach>` action contains an array of `java.util.SortedMap` objects. The array contains one `SortedMap` per row. The key is the column name, and the value is the column value. The use of a `SortedMap` instead of a regular `Map` makes it possible to access the values with column names specified with any combination of upper- and lowercase letters. This is an important feature for portability, since some JDBC drivers convert all column names to uppercase in the result, while others keep them as they are defined in the `SELECT` statement.

The inner `<c:forEach>` action loops over the current `SortedMap` entries representing columns. To make it possible to use both the entry's name and value within the action body, the `<c:forEach>` action makes the current entry available as an instance of `java.util.Map.Entry`. This is a simple class with two bean properties, appropriately named `key` and `value`. These properties are used in the inner loop to add table cells with the column name and value. The result is as shown in Figure 12-5.

In most cases, you know the name of the columns you want to use. To generate an HTML table with the values of a set of known columns, you can simply use one `<c:forEach>` action like this:

```
<table>
  <tr>
    <th>First Name</th>
    <th>Last Name</th>
    <th>Department</th>
  </tr>
  <c:forEach items="${newEmpDbInfo.rows}" var="row">
    <tr>
      <td>
        ${fn:escapeXml(row.FirstName)}
      </td>
      <td>
        ${fn:escapeXml(row.LastName)}
      </td>
      <td>
        ${fn:escapeXml(row.Dept)}
      </td>
    </tr>
  </c:forEach>
</table>
```

The <c:forEach> action makes the SortedMap representing the current row available to the actions in the body in a variable named row. EL expressions with column names as keys get the value of the specific columns. The fn:escapeXml() function converts special characters in the column values, if any, as described earlier.

Yet another possibility is to access the column values by their numeric index. To do this, you need to use the rowsByIndex property instead of the rows property to get an array of rows to loop over, and then use the [] operator to specify the (0-based) index for the columns in the EL expressions:

```
<table>
  <tr>
    <th>First Name</th>
    <th>Last Name</th>
    <th>Department</th>
  </tr>
  <c:forEach items="${newEmpDbInfo.rowsByIndex}" var="row">
    <tr>
      <td>
        ${fn:escapeXml(row[2])}
      </td>
      <td>
        ${fn:escapeXml(row[3])}
      </td>
      <td>
        ${fn:escapeXml(row[4])}
      </td>
    </tr>
  </c:forEach>
</table>
```

The Result also gives you access to the column names through the columnNames property. Using this property, you can generate an HTML table with header cells and data cells for all rows in a table without knowing beforehand what columns the result contains:

```
<table>
  <tr>
    <c:forEach items="${empList.columnNames}" var="colName">
      <th>${fn:escapeXml(colName)}</th>
    </c:forEach>
  </tr>
  <c:forEach items="${empList.rowsByIndex}" var="row">
    <tr>
      <c:forEach items="${row}" var="column">
        <td>${fn:escapeXml(column)}</td>
      </c:forEach>
    </tr>
  </c:forEach>
</table>
```

The column names are in the same order as the corresponding values accessed through the rowsByIndex property.

Searching for Rows Based on Partial Information

Let's move to the other part of the application, in which a user can search for an employee based on a partial first name, last name, and department name. The first page, *search.html*, contains a form for entering the search criteria, shown in Figure 12-6.

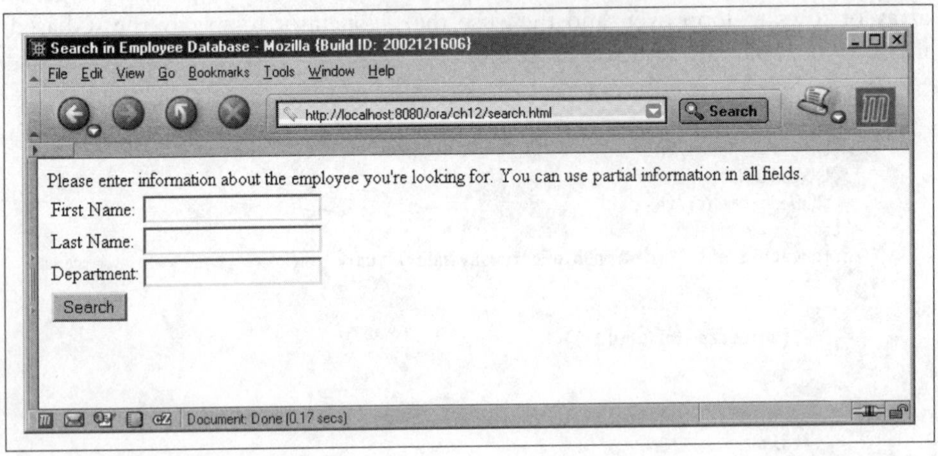

Figure 12-6. Search criteria form

The three fields in the *search.html* page are named `firstName`, `lastName`, and `dept`, and when the user clicks the **Search** button, the *find.jsp* page is invoked with the information the user entered in the corresponding request parameters. Example 12-3 shows the complete *find.jsp* page.

Example 12-3. Search based on partial information (find.jsp)

```
<%@ taglib prefix="sql" uri="http://java.sun.com/jsp/jstl/sql" %>

<%--
  Execute query, with wildcard characters added to the
  parameter values used in the search criteria
--%>
<sql:query var="empList" scope="request">
  SELECT * FROM Employee
    WHERE FirstName LIKE ?
      AND LastName LIKE ?
      AND Dept LIKE ?
    ORDER BY LastName
  <sql:param value="%${param.firstName}%" />
  <sql:param value="%${param.lastName}%" />
  <sql:param value="%${param.dept}%" />
</sql:query>

<jsp:forward page="list.jsp" />
```

As you probably expected, the <sql:query> action searches for the matching employees. But here, the SELECT statement uses the LIKE operator to find rows matching a pattern instead of an exact match. LIKE is a standard SQL operator. It must be followed by a string consisting of fixed text plus wildcard characters. There are two standard wildcard characters you can use: an underscore (_), which matches exactly one character, and a percent sign (%), which matches zero or more characters.

In this example, we want to search for all rows that contain the values specified in the form somewhere in the corresponding column values. The form-field values must therefore be enclosed with percent signs. In Example 12-3, this is accomplished by combining the fixed text (the wildcard characters) with EL expressions for reading the parameter values in the value attribute for the <sql:param> actions that replace the placeholders in the SQL statement. Each <sql:param> action adds a percent sign at the beginning and at the end of the value submitted by the user. If you instead want to find values that start with any sequence of characters but end with the string entered by the user, add a percent sign only at the beginning of the value. If you add the percent sign only at the end of the value, you get the reverse result: values that start with the specified string but end with any characters.

The three LIKE conditions are combined with AND operators in Example 12-3. This means that the SELECT statement finds only rows where all three columns contain the corresponding values entered by the user.

Deleting Database Information

The *find.jsp* page forwards the request to the *list.jsp* page to display the result of the search. It generates an HTML table with one row per employee, as shown in Example 12-4.

Example 12-4. Displaying the search result (list.jsp)

```
<%@ page contentType="text/html" %>
<%@ taglib prefix="c" uri="http://java.sun.com/jsp/jstl/core" %>
<%@ taglib prefix="sql" uri="http://java.sun.com/jsp/jstl/sql" %>
<%@ taglib prefix="fn" uri="http://java.sun.com/jsp/jstl/functions" %>

<html>
  <head>
    <title>Search Result</title>
  </head>
  <body bgcolor="white">

  <c:choose>
    <c:when test="${empList.rowCount == 0}">
      Sorry, no employees were found.
    </c:when>
    <c:otherwise>
      The following employees were found:
      <p>
```

Example 12-4. Displaying the search result (list.jsp) (continued)

```
      <table border="1">
        <th>Last Name</th>
        <th>First Name</th>
        <th>Department</th>
        <th>Email Address</th>
        <th>Modified</th>
        <c:forEach items="${empList.rows}" var="row">
          <tr>
            <td>${fn:escapeXml(row.LastName)}</td>
            <td>${fn:escapeXml(row.FirstName)}</td>
            <td>${fn:escapeXml(row.Dept)}</td>
            <td>${fn:escapeXml(row.EmailAddr)}</td>
            <td>${fn:escapeXml(row.ModDate)}</td>
            <td>
              <form action="delete.jsp" method="post">
                <input type="hidden" name="userName"
                  value="${fn:escapeXml(row.UserName)}">
                <input type="hidden" name="firstName"
                  value="${fn:escapeXml(param.firstName)}">
                <input type="hidden" name="lastName"
                  value="${fn:escapeXml(param.lastName)}">
                <input type="hidden" name="dept"
                  value="${fn:escapeXml(param.dept)}">
                <input type="submit" value="Delete">
              </form>
            </td>
          </tr>
        </c:forEach>
      </table>
    </c:otherwise>
  </c:choose>
  </body>
</html>
```

The result is shown in Figure 12-7.

A <c:forEach> action loops over all rows returned by the query in Example 12-3 to generate an HTML table with some of the column values as described earlier. The last table cell contains a simple HTML form with a **Delete** button that invokes the *delete.jsp* page and a number of hidden fields. The hidden fields hold the value of UserName for the current row, plus all the parameters used to perform the search. Example 12-5 shows how all these parameters are used in the *delete.jsp* page.

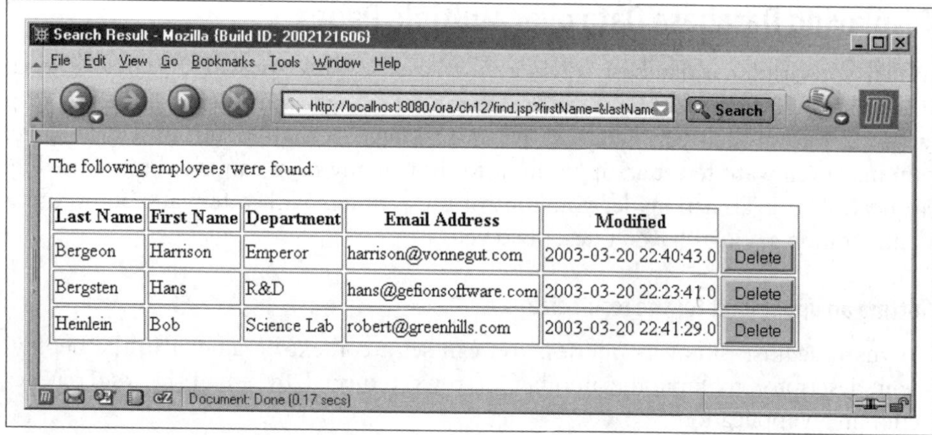

Figure 12-7. Displaying the search result

Example 12-5. Deleting a row (delete.jsp)

```
<%@ taglib prefix="sql" uri="http://java.sun.com/jsp/jstl/sql" %>
<%@ taglib prefix="c" uri="http://java.sun.com/jsp/jstl/core" %>

<sql:update>
  DELETE FROM Employee
    WHERE UserName = ?
  <sql:param value="${param.userName}" />
</sql:update>

<c:redirect url="find.jsp">
  <c:param name="firstName" value="${param.firstName}" />
  <c:param name="lastName" value="${param.lastName}" />
  <c:param name="dept" value="${param.dept}" />
</c:redirect>
```

The `userName` request parameter value uniquely identifies the row to remove. The SQL `DELETE` statement supports the same type of `WHERE` clause condition you have seen used in `SELECT` and `UPDATE` statements previously. Here, the condition is used to make sure only the row for the right employee is deleted. Like the `INSERT` and `UPDATE` statements, a `DELETE` statement is executed with the help of the `<sql:update>` action.

The other parameters passed from the *list.jsp* page are used in the redirect call to the *find.jsp* page. This way, the *find.jsp* page uses the same search criteria as when it was called directly from the *search.html* file, so the new result is consistent with the first. The only difference is that the employee who was just deleted doesn't show up in the list.

Displaying Database Data over Multiple Pages

When you display a database query result based on user-provided search criteria, such as the Employee Search form in Example 12-3, you run the risk of ending up with more rows than you like to show on one page. If the amount of data is large, you may even want to set an upper limit for how many rows can ever be returned by a query. The JSTL actions let you control these things with a few attributes and a configuration setting I haven't described yet.

Setting an upper limit for the result size

To guard against run-away queries, you can set a context parameter in the deployment descriptor to limit the number of rows returned by any JSTL `<sql:query>` action in an application:

```
<web-app>
  ...
  <context-param>
    <param-name>
      javax.servlet.jsp.jstl.sql.maxRows
    </param-name>
    <param-value>
      100
    </param-value>
  </context-param>
  ...
</web-app>
```

The `javax.servlet.jsp.jstl.sql.maxRows` parameter value sets the maximum number of rows any `<sql:query>` action in the application ever adds to the result. You can override this value for an individual action with the `maxRows` attribute. If you want the action to return all matching rows, set it to -1. There's also a `Result` bean property you can use to inform the user that the query returned more rows than permitted by `maxRows`, named `limitedByMaxRows`:

```
<sql:query var="result" maxRows="500""
  sql="SELECT * FROM Employee" />
<c:if test="${result.limitedByMaxRows}">
  Sorry, but we cannot show you all matches. Only the first 500
  are shown below.
</c:if>
```

The `limitedByMaxRows` property is set to `true` whenever the result is truncated, no matter if the maximum number of rows is specified by the context parameter or the attribute.

Getting a limited number of rows at a time

If the potential number of rows is large, you can combine the `<sql:query>` `maxRows` attribute with the `startRow` attribute to get only as many as you like to display on one page at a time. Example 12-6 shows a page with Previous and Next Page links for moving through all rows of a table.

Example 12-6. Using startRow and maxRows to limit result (maxrows.jsp)

```
<%@ taglib prefix="c" uri="http://java.sun.com/jsp/jstl/core" %>
<%@ taglib prefix="sql" uri="http://java.sun.com/jsp/jstl/sql" %>
<%@ taglib prefix="fn" uri="http://java.sun.com/jsp/jstl/functions" %>

<html>
  <head>
    <title>All Employees</title>
  </head>
  <body bgcolor="white">

    <%-- Set number of rows to process --%>
    <c:set var="noOfRows" value="2" />
    <sql:query var="empList"
      sql="SELECT * FROM Employee ORDER BY LastName"
      startRow="${param.start}" maxRows="${noOfRows}"
    />

    <c:choose>
      <c:when test="${empList.rowCount == 0}">
        No one seems to work here any more ...
      </c:when>
      <c:otherwise>
        The following people work here:
        <p>
        <table border="1">
          <th>Last Name</th>
          <th>First Name</th>
          <th>Department</th>
          <th>Email Address</th>
          <c:forEach items="${empList.rows}" var="row">
            <tr>
              <td>${fn:escapeXml(row.LastName)}</td>
              <td>${fn:escapeXml(row.FirstName)}</td>
              <td>${fn:escapeXml(row.Dept)}</td>
              <td>${fn:escapeXml(row.EmailAddr)}</td>
            </tr>
          </c:forEach>
        </table>
      </c:otherwise>
    </c:choose>
    <p>
    <c:choose>
      <c:when test="${param.start > 0}">
        <a href="maxrows.jsp?start=${param.start - noOfRows}">
          Previous Page</a>
      </c:when>
      <c:otherwise>
          Previous Page
```

Example 12-6. Using startRow and maxRows to limit result (maxrows.jsp) (continued)

```
      </c:otherwise>
    </c:choose>
    <c:choose>
      <c:when test="${empList.limitedByMaxRows}">
        <a href="maxrows.jsp?start=${param.start + noOfRows}">
          Next Page</a>
      </c:when>
      <c:otherwise>
          Next Page
      </c:otherwise>
    </c:choose>
  </body>
</html>
```

At the beginning of the page, a `<c:set>` action creates a variable that holds the number of rows to be processed per request. This is just to make it easier to change the number of rows if needed.

The `<sql:query>` action uses the `startRow` attribute to define which row to be the first in the result (the first row has index 0) and the `maxRows` attribute to limit the number of rows. The `startRow` attribute value is specified by a request parameter named `start`. The first time the page is requested, this parameter isn't present so the EL expression evaluates to 0. The `maxRows` attribute value is simply the variable created to hold the number of rows to process. A `<c:forEach>` action generates an HTML table with all rows from the result, as in the previous examples.

Two `<c:choose>` blocks at the end of the page create the Previous and Next Page links. The Previous Page block tests if the `start` parameter has a value greater than 0, and if so, adds a link back to the same page with a `start` parameter with the value of the current `start` parameter minus the number of rows processed per page. If `start` isn't greater than 0, we're already at the first page, so a link placeholder is added instead. The block for the Next Page link follows the same pattern but tests the value of the `limitedByMaxRows` result property instead. If it's `true`, there must be more data available, so you should create a link with the `start` parameter set to the current value plus the number of rows to process.

There are a couple of other things in this example you should be aware of. First, I break my own rule of separating business logic (the database query) from presentation (the HTML table), just to make the processing easier to understand. I hope you see how you can split this over two pages: the one doing the database query forwarding to the one generating the table. The other issue regards the `startRow` attribute. Because there's no database-independent way to ask for only the matching rows starting at a certain index, the `<sql:query>` action simply gets all rows preceding the start index and throws them away. This isn't efficient for a large set of rows. Instead of using `startRow` and `maxRows`, you can use database-specific SQL features or a database column with a sequential value to handle this more efficiently:

```
<sql:query var="empList" dataSource="${example}">
  SELECT * FROM Employee
    WHERE SomeId >= ? AND SomeId < ?
    ORDER BY LastName
  <sql:param value="${param.start}" />
  <sql:param value="${param.start + noOfRows}" />
</sql:query>
```

For a reasonable number of rows, the approach described in Example 12-6 works fine, though.

Run a query once and display the result over multiple pages

If the maximal number of rows that can be returned is small enough to keep in memory as a session or application scope variable, you can use another approach based in the `<c:forEach>` begin and end attributes, as shown in Example 12-7.

Example 12-7. Using begin and end to limit the result (foreach.jsp)

```
<%@ taglib prefix="c" uri="http://java.sun.com/jsp/jstl/core" %>
<%@ taglib prefix="sql" uri="http://java.sun.com/jsp/jstl/sql" %>
<%@ taglib prefix="fn" uri="http://java.sun.com/jsp/jstl/functions" %>

<html>
  <head>
    <title>All Employees</title>
  </head>
  <body bgcolor="white">

    <%-- Set number of rows to process --%>
    <c:set var="noOfRows" value="2" />
    <c:if test="${empList == null}">
      <sql:query var="empList" scope="session"
        sql="SELECT * FROM Employee ORDER BY LastName"
      />
    </c:if>
    <c:choose>
      <c:when test="${empList.rowsCount == 0}">
        No one seems to work here anymore ...
      </c:when>
      <c:otherwise>
        The following people work here:
        <p>
        <table border="1">
          <th>Last Name</th>
          <th>First Name</th>
          <th>Department</th>
          <th>Email Address</th>
          <c:forEach items="${empList.rows}" var="row"
            begin="${param.start}" end="${param.start + noOfRows - 1}">
            <tr>
              <td>${fn:escapeXml(row.LastName)}</td>
              <td>${fn:escapeXml(row.FirstName)}</td>
```

Example 12-7. Using begin and end to limit the result (foreach.jsp) (continued)

```
            <td>${fn:escapeXml(row.Dept)}</td>
            <td>${fn:escapeXml(row.EmailAddr)}</td>
          </tr>
        </c:forEach>
      </table>
    </c:otherwise>
  </c:choose>
  <p>
  <c:choose>
    <c:when test="${param.start > 0}">
      <a href="foreach.jsp?start=${param.start - noOfRows}">
        Previous Page</a>
    </c:when>
    <c:otherwise>
        Previous Page
    </c:otherwise>
  </c:choose>
  <c:choose>
    <c:when test="${param.start + noOfRows < empList.rowsCount}">
      <a href="foreach.jsp?start=${param.start + noOfRows}">
        Next Page</a>
    </c:when>
    <c:otherwise>
        Next Page
    </c:otherwise>
  </c:choose>
  </body>
</html>
```

As in Example 12-6, a noOfRows variable is created at the beginning of the page to hold the number of rows to display per page. A <c:if> action makes sure the database query is executed only if a result doesn't exist in the session scope, where the <sql:query> action places it when it's executed. If the data rarely changes, and the user can't change the query result by providing input used in a WHERE clause, you can cache the result in the application scope instead to minimize the memory needs. If the user can affect the query result, (i.e., user input used in the search criteria), you need to modify the example to compare the input used to generate the result and execute <sql:query> when it's different.

As before, a <c:forEach> action generates an HTML table for the result, but here it only processes some of the rows. The begin attribute is set to the start parameter value, defaulting to 0 if the parameter isn't present. The end attribute is set to the start parameter value plus the number of rows to display, minus one; the end value is the index of the last row to process, so subtracting one means it iterates exactly noOfRows times.

The <c:choose> blocks for the Previous and Next Page links are almost identical to the ones in Example 12-6. The only difference is that the test for the Next Page link now compares the start parameter value plus the number of rows to display to the total number of rows in the result. As long as it's less than the number of rows, there's more to show, and so the link is added.

Validating Complex Input Without a Bean

Before we look at the two remaining database sections, let's go back and take a look at the two application pages we skipped earlier, namely the *enter.jsp* and *validate.jsp* pages used for input to the employee registration.

In Chapter 8, I introduced you to validation of user input using the JSTL `<c:if>` action as well as using an application-specific bean. The bean contains all validation code and can therefore validate the format of complex data, such as date strings, email addresses, and credit-card numbers. This is the approach I recommend, but if you're developing a JSP-based application without access to a Java programmer to develop the beans you need, I'll show you a trick you can use to validate dates and a custom action for email-address validation.

The *validate.jsp* page uses the JSTL `<c:if>` action and the custom action to validate all user input. If an input parameter isn't valid, an error message is saved in a variable, and the request is forwarded back to the *enter.jsp* page. The *enter.jsp* page adds all the error messages to the response, so to the user, the result is identical to the bean-based validation approach you saw in Chapter 8.

Let's look at *validate.jsp* first, shown in Example 12-8.

Example 12-8. Validation with application beans (validate.jsp)

```
<%@ taglib prefix="c" uri="http://java.sun.com/jsp/jstl/core" %>
<%@ taglib prefix="fmt" uri="http://java.sun.com/jsp/jstl/fmt" %>
<%@ taglib prefix="ora" uri="orataglib" %>

<c:set var="isValid" value="true" />
<c:if test="${empty param.userName}">
  <c:set var="userNameError" scope="request"
    value="User Name missing" />
  <c:set var="isValid" value="false" />
</c:if>
<c:if test="${empty param.password}">
  <c:set var="passwordError" scope="request"
    value="Password missing" />
  <c:set var="isValid" value="false" />
</c:if>
<c:if test="${empty param.firstName}">
  <c:set var="firstNameError" scope="request"
    value="First Name missing" />
  <c:set var="isValid" value="false" />
</c:if>
<c:if test="${empty param.lastName}">
  <c:set var="lastNameError" scope="request"
    value="Last Name missing" />
```

Example 12-8. Validation with application beans (validate.jsp) (continued)

```
  <c:set var="isValid" value="false" />
</c:if>
<c:if test="${empty param.dept}">
  <c:set var="deptError" scope="request"
    value="Department missing" />
  <c:set var="isValid" value="false" />
</c:if>

<%-- Validate date by catching a possible exception --%>
<c:catch var="invalidDate">
  <fmt:parseDate value="${param.empDate}" pattern="yyyy-MM-dd"
    var="ignore" />
</c:catch>
<c:choose>
  <c:when test="${empty param.empDate}">
    <c:set var="empDateError" scope="request"
      value="Employment Date missing" />
    <c:set var="isValid" value="false" />
  </c:when>
  <c:when test="${invalidDate != null}">
    <c:set var="empDateError" scope="request"
      value="Invalid Employment Date" />
    <c:set var="isValid" value="false" />
  </c:when>
</c:choose>
<%-- Validate email address format using custom action --%>
<ora:ifValidEmailAddr value="${param.emailAddr}"
  var="isValidEmailAddr" />
<c:choose>
  <c:when test="${empty param.emailAddr}">
    <c:set var="emailAddrError" scope="request"
      value="Email Address missing" />
    <c:set var="isValid" value="false" />
  </c:when>
  <c:when test="${!isValidEmailAddr}">
    <c:set var="emailAddrError" scope="request"
      value="Invalid Email Address" />
    <c:set var="isValid" value="false" />
  </c:when>
</c:choose>
<c:choose>
  <c:when test="${isValid}">
    <jsp:forward page="store.jsp" />
  </c:when>
  <c:otherwise>
    <jsp:forward page="enter.jsp" />
  </c:otherwise>
</c:choose>
```

At the top of Example 12-8, a `<c:set>` action creates a variable named `isValid` with the value `true`. The rest of the page validates each parameter value and sets this variable to `false` if any value is found to be invalid. This makes it easy to decide which page to forward to at the end of the page. In addition, if any value is invalid, another parameter-specific variable is created in the request scope to hold the error message. As you will see later, these error messages are added to the input page to tell the user what's wrong.

For most parameters, a simple `<c:if>` action that tests that some value is submitted is all that's needed. But for the `empDate` and `emailAddr` parameters, any old value isn't enough.

Verifying that a parameter value represents a real date is tricky, since there are so many different ways to write a date. In addition, you need to keep track of leap years and, as you will see in Chapter 14, possibly deal with dates written in different languages as well. Luckily, there's a JSTL action that knows all these rules: the `<fmt:parseDate>` used in Example 12-1. If it's passed a date string that doesn't check out, it throws an exception. Combined with the `<c:catch>` action introduced in Chapter 9, this is all we need to validate a date. The `<fmt:parseDate>` action is placed within a `<c:catch>` action element, catching and saving a possible exception in a variable named `invalidDate`. A `<c:choose>` action then uses one `<c: when>` action to test if a date string is supplied at all and, if it is, tests if the `<fmt:parseDate>` action threw an exception with a second `<c:when>` action. I could have used just a `<c:if>` action to test if an exception was thrown, but the approach used here lets me provide different error messages for no value and an invalid value.

The email address is validated with a custom action named `<ora:ifValidEmailAddr>`, described in Table 12-8.

Table 12-8. Attributes for <ora:ifValidEmailAddr>

Attribute name	Java type	Dynamic value accepted	Description
`value`	`String`	Yes	Mandatory. The value to validate.
`var`	`String`	No	Optional. The name of the variable to hold the result.
`scope`	`String`	No	Optional. The scope for the variable, one of `page`, `request`, `session`, or `application`. `page` is the default.

The action can be used with a body that's evaluated only if the value has a valid email-address format (contains only one at sign and at least one dot, e.g., "hans@gefionsoftware.com"), just like the `<c:if>` action. Here the result is saved in a variable instead and used in a `<c:choose>` block to test for both no value and invalid value, the same as is done for the date value.

If the request is forwarded back to the *enter.jsp* page due to invalid input, the values the user entered are used as the default values for the form fields and the error messages are displayed next to each field. Example 12-9 shows a part of the page for the User Name field.

Example 12-9. Displaying error messages (enter.jsp)

```
...
<tr>
  <td>User Name:</td>
  <td><input type="text" name="userName"
    value="${fn:escapeXml(param.userName)}">
  </td>
  <td>${fn:escapeXml(userNameError)}</td>
</tr>
...
```

The first EL expression sets the value of the input field to the corresponding parameter value. The second EL expression uses the `userNameError` variable created by the *validate.jsp* page if the `userName` parameter value is invalid and adds the message to the page. The results are shown in Figure 12-8.

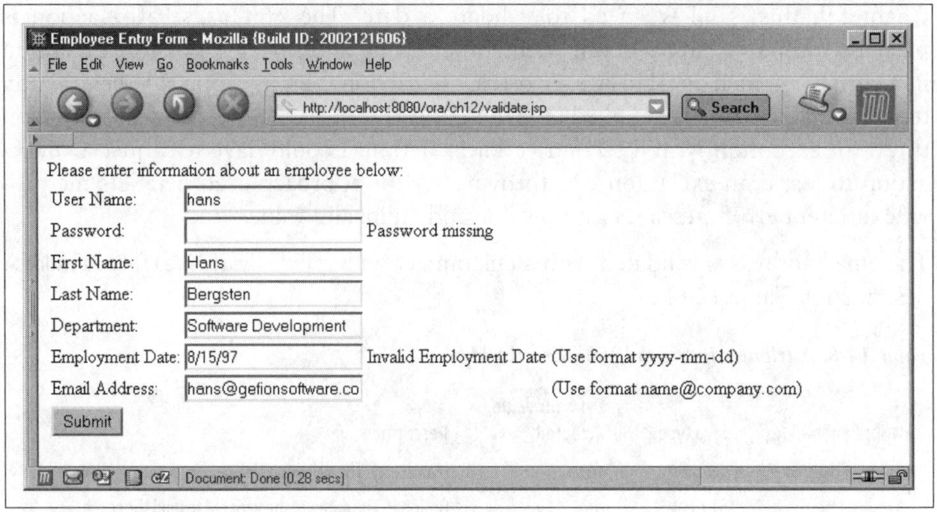

Figure 12-8. The input page with error messages

This is very similar to the examples in Chapter 8. The difference is that a separate page does the validation, creating all error messages as request scope variables that are then used in the input page if they exist, instead of conditionally adding error messages defined in the input page. Which approach is best is a matter of preference.

Using Transactions

There's one important database feature we have not discussed yet. In the examples in this chapter, only one SQL statement is needed to complete all database modifications for each request. This statement either succeeds or fails. However, sometimes you need to execute two or more SQL statements in sequence to update the database. A typical example is transferring money between two accounts; one statement removes some amount from the first account, and another statement adds the same amount to the second account. If the first statement is successful, but the second one fails, you have performed a disappearance act your customers aren't likely to applaud.

The solution to this problem is to group all related SQL statements into what is called a *transaction*. A transaction is an atomic operation, so if one statement fails, they all fail; otherwise, they all succeed. This is referred to as *committing* (if it succeeds) or *rolling back* (if it fails) the transaction. If there's a problem in the middle of a money transfer, for instance, the database makes sure the money is returned to the first account by rolling back the transaction. If no problems are encountered, the transaction is committed, permanently storing the changes in the database.

There's a JSTL database action to handle transactions, described in Table 12-9.

Table 12-9. Attributes for JSTL <sql:transaction>

Attribute name	Java type	Dynamic value accepted	Description
`dataSource`	`javax.sql.DataSource` or `String`	Yes	Optional. The `DataSource` to use.
`isolation`	`String`	Yes	Optional. One of `read_committed`, `read_uncommitted`, `repeatable_read`, or `serializable`.

We will use it for real in Chapter 13, but let's take a quick look at how it could be used in this fictitious example:

```
<sql:transaction>

  <sql:update>
    UPDATE Account SET Balance = Balance - 1000
      WHERE AccountNumber = 1234
  </sql:update>
  <sql:update>
    UPDATE Account SET Balance = Balance + 1000
      WHERE AccountNumber = 5678
  </sql:update>

</sql:transaction>
```

SQL actions that make up a transaction are placed in the body of a `<sql:transaction>` action element. This action tells the nested elements which database to use, so if you need to specify the database with the `dataSource` attribute, you must specify it for the `<sql:transaction>` action.

The `isolation` attribute can specify special transaction features. When the `DataSource` is made available to the application through JNDI or by another application component, it's typically already configured with an appropriate isolation level.

This attribute is therefore rarely used. The details of the different isolation levels are beyond the scope of this book. If you believe you need to specify this value, you can read up on the differences in the JDBC API documents or in the documentation for your database. You should also be aware that some databases and JDBC drivers don't support all transaction isolation levels.

The `<sql:transaction>` action gets a connection from the data source and makes it available to all database actions within its body. If one action fails, the transaction is rolled back; otherwise the transaction is committed at the end of the `<sql:transaction>` body.

Application-Specific Database Actions

You can use the JSTL database actions described in this chapter to develop many types of interesting web applications, such as product catalog interfaces, employee directories, or online billboards, without being a Java programmer. These types of applications account for a high percentage of the web applications developed today. But at some level of complexity, putting SQL statements directly in the web pages can become a maintenance problem. The SQL statements represent business logic, and for more complex applications, business logic is better developed as separate Java classes.

For a complex application, it may be better to use application-specific custom actions instead of the JSTL database actions described in this chapter. For example, all the generic database actions in Example 12-1, to `SELECT` and then `INSERT` or `UPDATE` the database, can be replaced with one application-specific action like this:

```
<myLib:saveEmployeeInfo dataSource="${example}" />
```

Part III, especially Chapter 24, describes how you can develop this type of custom action. Besides making it easier for the page author to deal with, the beauty of using an application-specific custom action is that it lets you evolve the application behind the scene. Initially, this action can be implemented so it uses JDBC to access the database directly, similar to how the JSTL actions work. But at some point it may make sense to migrate the application to an Enterprise JavaBeans architecture, perhaps to support other types of clients than web browsers. The action can then be modified to interact with an Enterprise JavaBeans component instead of accessing the database directly. From the JSP page author's point of view, it doesn't matter; the custom action is still used exactly the same way.

Another approach is to use a servlet for all database processing and only use JSP pages to show the result. You will find an example of this approach in Chapter 19.

CHAPTER 13

Authentication and Personalization

Authentication means establishing that a user really is who he claims to be. Today, it's typically done by asking the user for a username and a matching password, but other options are becoming more and more common. For example, most web servers support client certificates for authentication. Biometrics, which is the use of unique biological patterns such as fingerprints for identification, will likely be another common option in the near future. What's important is that an application should not be concerned with the way a user has been authenticated (since the method may change) but only that he has passed the test.

Access control, or *authorization*, is another security mechanism that's strongly related to authentication. Different users may be allowed different types of access to the content and services a web site offers. When you have established who the user is through an authentication process, access-control mechanisms ensure that the user can only access what he is allowed to access.

In the end, authentication provides information about who the user is, and that's what is needed to provide personalized content and services. For some types of personalization, the procedures we might think of as authentication may be overkill. If the background colors and type of news listed on the front page are the extent of the personalization, a simple cookie can be used to keep track of the user instead. But if personalization means getting access to information about taxes, medical records, or other confidential information, true authentication is definitely needed.

In this chapter we look at different approaches to authentication and access control with JSP, and we use the information about who the user is to provide modest personalization of the application pages. Security, however, is about more than authentication and access control. The last section of this chapter presents a brief summary of other areas that need to be covered for applications dealing with sensitive data.

Container-Provided Authentication

A JSP page is always executing in a runtime environment provided by a container. Consequently, all authentication and access control can be handled by the container, relieving the application developer from the important task of implementing appropriate security controls. Security is hard to get right, so your first choice should always be to use the time-tested mechanisms provided by the container.

Authenticating Users

The servlet specification (starting with Version 2.2), on which JSP is based, describes three authentication mechanisms supported by most web clients and web servers:

- HTTP basic authentication
- HTTP digest authentication
- HTTPS client authentication

In addition, it defines one mechanism that should be implemented by a compliant servlet container:

- Form-based authentication

HTTP basic authentication has been part of the HTTP protocol since the beginning. It's a very simple and not very secure authentication scheme. When a browser requests access to a protected resource, the server sends back a response asking for the user's credentials (username and password). The browser prompts the user for this information and sends the same request again, but this time with the user credentials in one of the request headers so the server can authenticate the user. The username and password are not encrypted, only slightly obfuscated by the well-known base64 encoding. This means it can easily be reversed by anyone who grabs it as it's passed over the network. This problem can be resolved using an encrypted connection between the client and the server, such as the Secure Sockets Layer (SSL) protocol. We talk more about this in the last section of this chapter.

HTTP/1.1 introduced *HTTP digest authentication*. As with basic authentication, the server sends a response back to the browser when it receives a request for a protected resource. But with the response, it also sends a string called a *nonce*. The nonce is a unique string generated by the server, typically composed of a timestamp, information about the requested resource, and a server identifier. The browser creates an MD5 checksum, also known as a *message digest*, of the username, the password, the given nonce value, the HTTP method, and the requested URL, and sends it back to the server in a new request. The use of an MD5 message digest means that the password cannot easily be extracted from information recorded from the network. Additionally, using information such as timestamps and resource information in the nonce minimizes the risk of "replay" attacks. The digest authentication is a great improvement over basic authentication. The only problem is that it's not supported in some of today's web clients and web servers.

HTTPS client authentication is the most secure authentication method supported today. This mechanism requires the user to possess a Public Key Certificate (PKC). The certificate is passed to the server when the connection between the browser and server is established, using a very secure challenge-response handshake process. The certificate is then used by the server to uniquely identify the user. As opposed to the mechanisms previously described, the server keeps the information about the user's identity as long as the connection remains open. When the browser requests a protected resource, the server uses this information to grant or refuse access.

These three mechanisms are defined by Internet standards. They are used for all sorts of web applications, servlet-based or not, and are usually implemented by the web server itself as opposed to the web container. The servlet specification defines only how an application can gain access to information about a user authenticated with one of them, as you will see soon.

The final mechanism, *form-based authentication*, is unique to the servlet specification and is implemented by the web container itself. Form-based authentication is as insecure as basic authentication for the same reason: the user's credentials are sent as clear text over the network. To protect access to sensitive resources, it should be combined with encryption such as SSL.

Unlike basic and digest authentication, form-based authentication lets you control the appearance of the login screen. The login screen is a regular HTML file with a form containing two mandatory input fields—`j_username` and `j_password`—and the action attribute set to the string `j_security_check`:

```
<form method="POST" action="j_security_check">
  <input type="text" name="j_username">
  <input type="password" name="j_password">
</form>
```

From the user's point of view, it works just like basic and digest authentication. When the user requests a protected resource, the login form is shown, prompting the user to enter a username and password. The `j_security_check` action attribute value is a special URI that is recognized by the container. When the user submits the form, the container authenticates the user using the `j_username` and `j_password` parameter values. If the authentication is successful, it redirects the browser to the requested resource; otherwise an error page is returned. We'll get to how you specify the login page and the error page shortly.

Controlling Access to Web Resources

All the authentication mechanisms described so far rely on two pieces of information: user definitions and information about the type of access control needed for the web application resources.

How users, and groups of users, are defined depends on the server you're using. Some web servers, such as Microsoft's Internet Information Server (IIS), can use the operating system's user and group definitions. Others, such as the iPlanet Web Server (formerly Netscape Enterprise Server), let you use their own user directory or an external LDAP server. The security mechanism defined by the servlet specification describes how to specify the access-control constraints for a web application, but access is granted to a *role* instead of directly to a user or a group. Real user and group names for a particular server are mapped to the role names used in the application. How the mapping is done depends on the server, so you need to consult your web server and servlet container documentation if you use a server other than Tomcat.

By default, the Tomcat server uses a simple XML file to define users and assign them roles at the same time. The file is named *tomcat-users.xml* and is located in the *conf* directory. To run the examples in this chapter, you need to define at least two users and assign one of them the role `admin` and the other the role `user`, like this:

```
<tomcat-users>
  <user name="paula" password="boss" roles="admin" />
  <user name="hans" password="secret" roles="user" />
</tomcat-users>
```

Here the user `paula` is assigned the `admin` role, and `hans` is assigned the `user` role. Note that this is not a very secure way to maintain user information (the passwords are in clear text, for instance). This approach is intended to make it easy to get started with container-based security. Tomcat can also be configured to use a database or a JNDI-accessible directory. For a production site, you should use one of these options instead. See the Tomcat documentation for details.

The type of access control that should be enforced for a web application resource, such as a JSP page or all files in a directory, is defined in the web application deployment descriptor (the *WEB-INF/web.xml* file). As you may recall, the deployment descriptor format is defined by the servlet specification, so all compliant servlet containers support this type of security configuration.

Let's look at how you can define the security constraints for the example we developed in Chapter 12. To restrict access to all pages dealing with employee registration, it's best to place them in a separate directory. The directory with all examples for Chapter 13 has a subdirectory named *admin* in which all these pages are stored. The part of the deployment descriptor that protects this directory looks like this:

```
<security-constraint>
  <web-resource-collection>
    <web-resource-name>admin</web-resource-name>
```

```
    <url-pattern>/ch13/admin/*</url-pattern>
  </web-resource-collection>

  <auth-constraint>
    <role-name>admin</role-name>
  </auth-constraint>
</security-constraint>

<login-config>
  <auth-method>BASIC</auth-method>
  <realm-name>ORA Examples</realm-name>
</login-config>

<security-role>
  <role-name>admin</role-name>
</security-role>
```

The <security-constraint> element contains a <web-resource-collection> element that defines the resources to be protected and an <auth-constraint> element that defines who has access to the protected resources. Within the <web-resource-collection> element, the URL pattern for the protected resource is specified with the <url-pattern> element. Here it is set to a pattern for the directory with all the registration pages: /ch13/admin/*. The <role-name> element within the <auth-constraint> element says that only users in the role admin can access the protected resources.

You define the type of authentication to use and a name associated with the protected parts of the application, known as the *realm*, with the <login-config> element. The <auth-method> element accepts the values BASIC, DIGEST, FORM, and CLIENT-CERT, corresponding to the authentication methods described earlier. Any text can be used as the value of the <realm-name> element. The text is shown as part of the message in the dialog the browser displays when it prompts the user for the credentials.

If you use form-based authentication, you must specify the names of your login form and error page in the <login-config> element as well:

```
<login-config>
  <auth-method>FORM</auth-method>
  <form-login-config>
    <form-login-page>/login/login.html</form-login-page>
    <form-error-page>/login/error.html</form-error-page>
  </form-login-config>
</login-config>
```

<security-role> elements are used to declare all role names that must be mapped to users and groups in the container's security domain. This information can be used by an application-deployment tool to help the deployer with this task.

With these security requirement declarations in the deployment descriptor, the web server and servlet container take care of all authentication and access control for you. You may still need to know, however, who the current user is, for instance to personalize the content. If you configure your server to let different types of users access the same pages, you may need to know what type of user is actually accessing a page right now. This information can be accessed using the EL and custom actions, as you will see in a moment.

Let's add another security constraint for the search pages from Chapter 12:

```
<security-constraint>
  <web-resource-collection>
    <web-resource-name>search</web-resource-name>
    <url-pattern>/ch13/search/*</url-pattern>
  </web-resource-collection>

  <auth-constraint>
    <role-name>admin</role-name>
    <role-name>user</role-name>
  </auth-constraint>
</security-constraint>
...

<security-role>
  <role-name>admin</role-name>
</security-role>
<security-role>
  <role-name>user</role-name>
</security-role>
```

With this constraint, the server allows only authenticated users with the roles `admin` and `user` to access the pages in the */ch13/search* directory. Since we add a new role (`user`) for this constraint, we must add the corresponding `<security-role>` element.

You can then use information about who the user is to provide different information. Example 13-1 shows a fragment of a modified version of the *list.jsp* page from Chapter 12.

Example 13-1. Generating the response based on who the current user is (list.jsp)

```
...
        <c:forEach items="${empList.rows}" var="row">
          <tr>
            <td><c:out value="${row.LastName}" /></td>
            <td><c:out value="${row.FirstName}" /></td>
            <td><c:out value="${row.Dept}" /></td>
            <td><c:out value="${row.EmailAddr}" /></td>
            <td><c:out value="${row.ModDate}" /></td>

            <ora:ifUserInRole value="admin" var="isAdmin" />
            <c:choose>
              <c:when test="${isAdmin or
                pageContext.request.remoteUser == row.UserName}">
                <td>${fn:escapeXml(row.UserName)}</td>
                <td>${fn:escapeXml(row.Password)}</td>
              </c:when>
```

Example 13-1. Generating the response based on who the current user is (list.jsp) (continued)

```
          <c:otherwise>
            <td>****</td>
            <td>****</td>
          </c:otherwise>
        </c:choose>
        <c:if test="${isAdmin}">
          <td>
            <form action="delete.jsp" method="post">
              <input type="hidden" name="userName"
                value="${fn:escapeXml(row.UserName)}">
              <input type="hidden" name="firstName"
                value="${fn:escapeXml(param.firstName)}">
              <input type="hidden" name="lastName"
                value="${fn:escapeXml(param.lastName)}">
              <input type="hidden" name="dept"
                value="${fn:escapeXml(param.dept)}">
              <input type="submit" value="Delete">
            </form>
          </td>
        </c:if>
      </tr>
    </c:forEach>
...
```

The amount of information displayed about each employee differs depending on who invokes the page. If the authenticated user is an administrator, the username and password information for all users is displayed, as well as a **Delete** button for removing information about an employee. Otherwise, the username and password fields are filled with asterisks, except for the row with information about the authenticated user herself.

To test if the authenticated user belongs to the `admin` role, a custom action is needed: the `<ora:ifUserInRole>` action (Table 13-1) evaluates its body if the specified role matches a role for the current user. If a variable name is specified by the `var` attribute, it instead saves `true` or `false` in the variable. In Example 13-1, the result of the test is saved in a variable named `isAdmin`.

Table 13-1. Attributes for <ora:ifUserInRole>

Attribute name	Java type	Dynamic value accepted	Description
`value`	`String`	Yes	Mandatory. The role name to test with.
`var`	`String`	No	Optional. The name of the variable to hold the result.
`scope`	`String`	No	Optional. The scope for the variable, one of `page`, `request`, `session`, or `application`. `page` is the default.

The username for the authenticated user can be retrieved with an EL expression, through a property of the `request` object that is accessible through the implicit `pageContext` object: `pageContext.request.remoteUser`. For each row, a `<c:choose>` block conditionally displays the username and password if the authenticated user is an administrator or the user represented by the current row, or just asterisks if it's someone else.

The `isAdmin` variable created by the `<ora:ifUserInRole>` action is used again in the condition for the `<c:if>` action, which conditionally adds the form with the **Delete** button.

Application-Controlled Authentication

Using one of the container-provided mechanisms described in the previous section should be your first choice for authentication. But, by definition, being container-provided means the application cannot dynamically add new users and roles to control who is granted access, at least not through a standard API defined by the servlet and JSP specifications.

For some types of applications, it's critical to have a very dynamic authentication model; one that doesn't require an administrator to define access rules before a new user can join the party. I'm sure you have seen countless sites where you can sign up for access to restricted content simply by filling out a form. One example is a project management site, where registered users can access document archives, discussion groups, calendars, and other tools for distributed cooperation. Another example is a personalized news site that you can customize to show news only about things you care about.

Unless you can define new users programmatically in the database used by an external authentication mechanism, you need to roll your own authentication and access-control system for these types of applications. In this section, we'll look at the principles for how to do this. Note that this approach sends the user's password as clear text, so it has the same security issues as the container-provided basic and form-based authentication methods.

Application-controlled authentication and access control requires the following pieces:

- User registration
- A login page
- The authentication mechanism, invoked by the login page
- Information saved in the session scope as proof of successful authentication
- Validation of the session information in all JSP pages requiring restricted access

We'll reuse the example from Chapter 12 for user registration; this allows us to focus on the parts of an application that require access control. The application is a simple billboard service, where employees can post messages related to different projects they are involved with. An employee can customize the application to show messages only about the projects he is interested in. Figure 13-1 shows all the pages and how they are related.

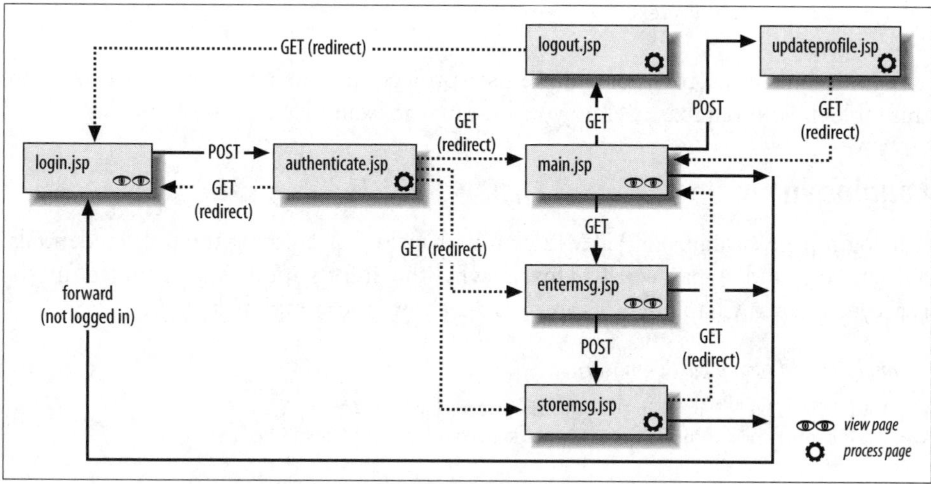

Figure 13-1. Application with authentication and access control

Let's go over it step by step. The *login.jsp* page is our login page. It contains a form that invokes the *authenticate.jsp* page, where the username and password are compared to the information in the employee information database created in Chapter 12. If a matching user is found, the *autheticate.jsp* page creates an `EmployeeBean` object and saves it in the session scope. This bean serves as proof of authentication. It then redirects the client to a true application page. The page the user is redirected to depends on whether the user loaded the *login.jsp* page or tried to directly access an application page, without first logging in. All application pages, specifically *main.jsp*, *entermsg.jsp*, *storemsg.jsp*, and *updateprofile.jsp*, look for the `EmployeeBean` object and forward to the *login.jsp* page if it's not found which forces the user to log in. When the *login.jsp* page is loaded this way, it keeps track of the page the user tried to access so it can be displayed automatically after successful authentication. Finally, there's the *logout.jsp* page. This page can be invoked from a link in the *main.jsp* page. It simply terminates the session and redirects to the *login.jsp* page.

A Table for Personalized Information

Since the sample application in this chapter lets the user personalize the content of the billboard, we need a database table to store information about each employee's choices. The new table is shown in Table 13-2.

Table 13-2. EmployeeProjects database table

Column name	SQL data type	Primary key?
UserName	CHAR (text)	Yes
ProjectName	CHAR (text)	Yes

The table holds one row per unique user-project combination. You need to create this table in your database before you can run the example.

Logging In

The login page contains an HTML form with fields for entering the user credentials: a username and a password. This is why the information was included in the Employee table in Chapter 12. Example 13-2 shows the complete *login.jsp* page.

Example 13-2. Login page (login.jsp)

```
<%@ taglib prefix="c" uri="http://java.sun.com/jsp/jstl/core" %>
<%@ taglib prefix="fn" uri="http://java.sun.com/jsp/jstl/functions" %>

<html>
  <head>
    <title>Project Billboard</title>
  </head>
  <body bgcolor="white">
    <h1>Welcome to the Project Billboard</h1>
    Your personalized project news web site.
    <p>
    <font color="red">
      ${fn:escapeXml(param.errorMsg)}
    </font>

    <form action="authenticate.jsp" method="post">

      <input type="hidden" name="origURL"
        value="${fn:escapeXml(param.origURL)}">

      Please enter your User Name and Password, and click Enter.
      <p>
      Name:
      <input name="userName"
        value="${fn:escapeXml(cookie.userName.value)}"
        size="10">
      Password:
      <input type="password" name="password"
        value="${fn:escapeXml(cookie.password.value)}"
        size="10">
      <input type="submit" value="Enter">
      <p>
      Remember my name and password:
      <input type="checkbox" name="remember"
```

Example 13-2. Login page (login.jsp) (continued)

```
      ${!empty cookie.userName ? 'checked' : ''}>
    <br>
    (This feature requires cookies to be enabled in your browser)
  </form>
 </body>
</html>
```

The form contains the fields for the username and password, and the action attribute is set to the *authenticate.jsp* page as expected. However, it also contains EL expressions that may need an explanation.

The following fragment displays a message that gives a hint as to why the login page is shown after an error:

```
<font color="red">
  ${fn:escapeXml(param.errorMsg)}
</font>
```

The errorMsg request parameter may contain an error message, set by the other pages when they forward to the login page, as you will soon see. If so, the EL expression displays the message. When the user loads the *login.jsp* page directly, the parameter is not available in the request, so nothing is added to the response. Figure 13-2 shows an example of the login page with an error message.

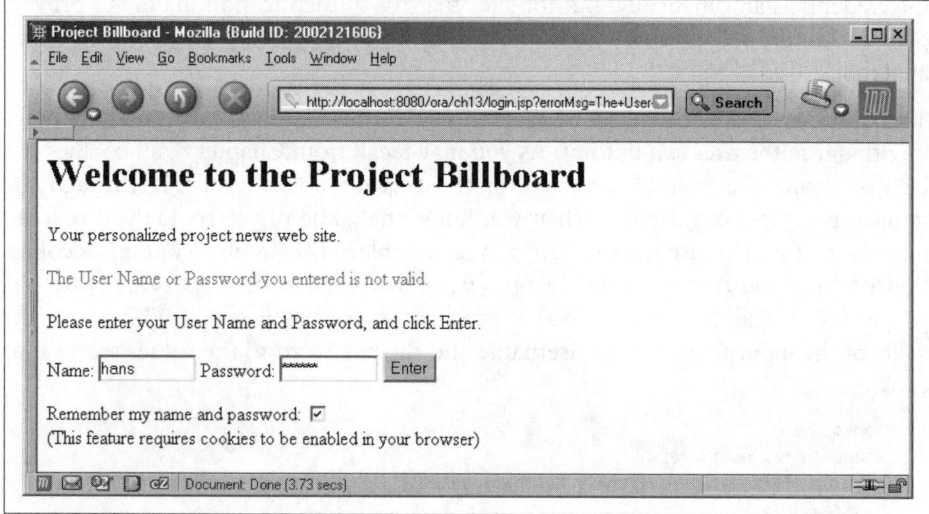

Figure 13-2. Login page with error message

Within the form, you find similar EL expressions:

```
<input type="hidden" name="origURL"
  value="${fn:escapeXml(param.origURL)}">
```

Here, a hidden form field is set to the value of the originally requested URL. The value is passed as a parameter to the login page when another page forwards to it. This is how to keep track of which page the user wasn't allowed access to because he wasn't authenticated yet. Later you'll see how this information is used to load the originally requested page after authentication.

Using cookies to remember the username and password

The more web applications with restricted access a web surfer uses, the more usernames and passwords to remember. After a while, it may be tempting to resort to the greatest security sin of all: writing down all usernames and passwords in a file such as *mypasswords.txt*. This invites anyone with access to the user's computer to roam around in all the secret data.

It can be a big problem keeping track of all accounts. Some sites therefore offer to keep track of the username and password using cookies. Cookies, as you probably remember, are small pieces of text a server sends to the browser. A cookie with an expiration date is saved on the hard disk and is returned to the server every time the user visits the same site until the cookie expires. So is this feature a good thing? Not really, as it amounts to the same security risk as writing down the username and password in a file. Even greater, since anyone with access to the user's computer doesn't even have to find the *mypasswords.txt* file; the browser takes care of sending the credentials automatically. But for sites that use authentication mainly to provide personalization and don't contain sensitive data, using cookies can be an appreciated tool.

This example shows how it can be done. If you decide to use it, make sure you make it optional so the user can opt out. As you may recall from Chapter 8, all cookies can be read using the `cookies` property of the `request` object available through the implicit `pageContext` variable. When you know the name of the cookie you're looking for, it's easier to use the implicit `cookie` variable. This variable contains a collection of `javax.servlet.http.Cookie` objects, which can be used as beans with the properties `name` and `value`. The `value` property is used in Example 13-2 to set the value of the input fields for the username and the password to the values received as cookies:

```
Name:
<input name="userName"
  value="${fn:escapeXml(cookie.userName.value)}"
  size="10">
Password:
<input type="password" name="password"
  value="${fn:escapeXml(cookie.password.value)}"
  size="10">
```

The last part of the form creates a checkbox that lets the user decide if cookies should be used or not. An EL expression with the conditional operator tests if one of the cookies is available and adds the checked attribute for the checkbox if it is:

```
Remember my name and password:
<input type="checkbox" name="remember"
  ${!empty cookie.userName ? 'checked' : ''}>
```

This snippet means that a user who has previously opted for cookie-based tracking gets the checkbox checked but a first time user doesn't. It's a good strategy, because it forces the user to "opt in."

Authentication Using a Database

To authenticate a user, you need access to information about the registered users. For the sample application in this chapter, all user information is kept in a database. There are other options, including flat files and LDAP directories. When a user fills out the login page form and clicks **Enter**, the authentication page shown in Example 13-3 is processed. This is a large page, so each part is discussed in detail after the complete page.

Example 13-3. Authentication page (authenticate.jsp)

```
<%@ taglib prefix="c" uri="http://java.sun.com/jsp/jstl/core" %>
<%@ taglib prefix="sql" uri="http://java.sun.com/jsp/jstl/sql" %>
<%@ taglib prefix="ora" uri="orataglib" %>

<%-- Remove the validUser session bean, if any --%>
<c:remove var="validUser" />

<c:if test="${empty param.userName || empty param.password}">
  <c:redirect url="login.jsp" >
    <c:param name="errorMsg"
      value="You must enter a User Name and Password." />
  </c:redirect>
</c:if>

<%--
  See if the user name and password combination is valid. If not,
  redirect back to the login page with a message.
--%>
<sql:query var="empInfo">
  SELECT * FROM Employee
    WHERE UserName = ? AND Password = ?
  <sql:param value="${param.userName}" />
  <sql:param value="${param.password}" />
</sql:query>

<c:if test="${empInfo.rowCount == 0}">
  <c:redirect url="login.jsp" >
    <c:param name="errorMsg"
```

Example 13-3. Authentication page (authenticate.jsp) (continued)

```
      value="The User Name or Password you entered is not valid." />
  </c:redirect>
</c:if>

<%--
  Create an EmployeeBean and save it in
  the session scope and redirect to the appropriate page.
--%>
<c:set var="dbValues" value="${empInfo.rows[0]}" />
<jsp:useBean id="validUser" scope="session"
  class="com.ora.jsp.beans.emp.EmployeeBean" >
  <c:set target="${validUser}" property="userName"
    value="${dbValues.UserName}" />
  <c:set target="${validUser}" property="firstName"
    value="${dbValues.FirstName}" />
  <c:set target="${validUser}" property="lastName"
    value="${dbValues.LastName}" />
  <c:set target="${validUser}" property="dept"
    value="${dbValues.Dept}" />
  <c:set target="${validUser}" property="empDate"
    value="${dbValues.EmpDate}" />
  <c:set target="${validUser}" property="emailAddr"
    value="${dbValues.EmailAddr}" />
</jsp:useBean>

<%-- Add the projects --%>
<sql:query var="empProjects">
  SELECT * FROM EmployeeProjects
    WHERE UserName = ?
  <sql:param value="${param.userName}" />
</sql:query>

<c:forEach items="${empProjects.rows}" var="project">
  <c:set target="${validUser}" property="project"
     value="${project.ProjectName}" />
</c:forEach>

<c:choose>
  <c:when test="${!empty param.remember}">
    <ora:addCookie name="userName"
      value="${param.userName}"
      maxAge="2592000" />
    <ora:addCookie name="password"
      value="${param.password}"
      maxAge="2592000" />
  </c:when>
  <c:otherwise>
    <ora:addCookie name="userName"
      value="${param.userName}"
      maxAge="0" />
    <ora:addCookie name="password"
      value="${param.password}"
```

Example 13-3. Authentication page (authenticate.jsp) (continued)

```
      maxAge="0" />
  </c:otherwise>
</c:choose>

<%--
  Redirect to the main page or to the original URL, if
  invoked as a result of a access attempt to a protected
  page.
--%>
<c:choose>
  <c:when test="${!empty param.origURL}">
    <c:redirect url="${param.origURL}" />
  </c:when>
  <c:otherwise>
    <c:redirect url="main.jsp" />
  </c:otherwise>
</c:choose>
```

The first thing that happens in Example 13-3 is that the JSTL `<c:remove>` action (Table 13-3) removes a session scope variable named `validUser`, if it exists.

This variable holds an `EmployeeBean` object, and its presence in the session scope indicates that the corresponding user has logged in successfully. If an `EmployeeBean` object is already present in the session scope, it may represent a user that forgot to log out, so it's important to remove it when a new login attempt is made.

Table 13-3. Attributes for JSTL <c:remove>

Attribute name	Java type	Dynamic value accepted	Description
`var`	`String`	No	Mandatory. The name of the variable to remove.
`scope`	`String`	No	Optional. The scope where the variable shall be removed, one of `page`, `request`, `session`, or `application`. Default is to remove the variable from the first scope where it's found.

Next, a `<c:if>` action makes sure that both the username and the password parameters are received. If one or both parameters are missing, the `<c:redirect>` action redirects back to the login page again. Here you see how the `errorMsg` parameter used in the *login.page* gets its value.

If the request contains both parameters, the `<sql:query>` action introduced in Chapter 12 checks for a user with the specified name and password in the database:

```
<sql:query var="empInfo">
  SELECT * FROM Employee
    WHERE UserName = ? AND Password = ?
  <sql:param value="${param.userName}" />
  <sql:param value="${param.password}" />
</sql:query>
```

```
<c:if test="${empInfo.rowCount == 0}">
  <c:redirect url="login.jsp" >
    <c:param name="errorMsg"
      value="The User Name or Password you entered is not valid." />
  </c:redirect>
</c:if>
```

If the query doesn't match a registered user (i.e., `empInfo.rowCount` is 0), the `<c:redirect>` action redirects back to the login page with an appropriate error message. Otherwise, the processing continues.

Creating the validation object

If a match is found, the single row from the query result is extracted, and the column values are used to populate the single value properties of an `EmployeeBean` object. The `EmployeeBean` has the properties shown in Table 13-4.

Table 13-4. Properties for com.ora.jsp.beans.emp.EmployeeBean

Property name	Java type	Access	Description
`username`	`String`	Read/write	The employee's unique username
`firstName`	`String`	Read/write	The employee's first name
`lastName`	`String`	Read/write	The employee's last name
`dept`	`String`	Read/write	The employee's department name
`empDate`	`java.util.Date`	Read/write	The employee's employment date
`emailAddr`	`String`	Read/write	The employee's email address
`projects`	`String[]`	Read/write	A list of all projects the employee is involved in
`project`	`String`	Write	The value is added to the list of projects

The bean is named `validUser` and placed in the session scope using the standard `<jsp:useBean>` action. The first (and only) row in the database result is saved in a variable named `dbValues`, which makes it easier to access the individual column values. All bean properties are then set to the values returned from the database using the JSTL `<c:set>` action:

```
<c:set var="dbValues" value="${empInfo.rows[0]}" />
<jsp:useBean id="validUser" scope="session"
  class="com.ora.jsp.beans.emp.EmployeeBean" >
  <c:set target="${validUser}" property="userName"
    value="${dbValues.UserName}" />
  <c:set target="${validUser}" property="firstName"
    value="${dbValues.FirstName}" />
  <c:set target="${validUser}" property="lastName"
    value="${dbValues.LastName}" />
  <c:set target="${validUser}" property="dept"
    value="${dbValues.Dept}" />
  <c:set target="${validUser}" property="empDate"
    value="${dbValues.EmpDate}" />
```

```
<c:set target="${validUser}" property="emailAddr"
  value="${dbValues.EmailAddr}" />
</jsp:useBean>
```

As I mentioned earlier, this application lets the user select the projects she is interested in, so that only messages related to these projects are shown on the main page. The user's choices are stored in the `EmployeeProjects` database table described in Table 13-2. In the *authenticate.jsp* page, the projects for the current user are retrieved from the `EmployeeProjects` table and used to create the corresponding list in the bean:

```
<sql:query var="empProjects">
  SELECT * FROM EmployeeProjects
    WHERE UserName = ?
  <sql:param value="${param.userName}" />
</sql:query>

<c:forEach items="${empProjects.rows}" var="project">
  <c:set target="${validUser}" property="project"
     value="${project.ProjectName}" />
</c:forEach>
```

To populate the bean, a `<c:set>` action invokes the bean's `project` property setter method once for each row in the query result. The property setter method adds each value to the list of projects held by the bean.

Setting and deleting cookies

If the user asks for the user credentials to be remembered, we need to send the corresponding cookies to the browser. The checkbox value from the login page is sent to the authentication page as a parameter named `remember`:

```
<c:choose>
  <c:when test="${!empty param.remember}">
    <ora:addCookie name="userName"
      value="${param.userName}"
      maxAge="2592000" />
    <ora:addCookie name="password"
      value="${param.password}"
      maxAge="2592000" />
  </c:when>
  <c:otherwise>
    <ora:addCookie name="userName"
      value="${param.userName}"
      maxAge="0" />
    <ora:addCookie name="password"
      value="${param.password}"
      maxAge="0" />
  </c:otherwise>
</c:choose>
```

The `<ora:addCookie>` custom action (Table 13-5) sends cookies to the browser. If the `remember` parameter is received, the cookies are sent with a maximum age value representing 30 days, expressed in seconds (2592000). As long as the user returns to this site within this time frame, the cookies will be sent with the request, and the login page will use the values to automatically fill out the form fields. If the user decides not to use this feature and unchecks the box, the cookies are still sent but with a maximum age of 0. This means that the cookies expire immediately and will never be sent to this server again. If you want to send a cookie to a browser that should be valid only until the user closes the browser, set the maximum age to a negative number (for instance, -1).

Table 13-5. Attributes for <ora:addCookie>

Attribute name	Java type	Dynamic value accepted	Description
`name`	`String`	Yes	Mandatory. The name of the cookie.
`value`	`String`	Yes	Mandatory. The cookie value.
`maxAge`	`int`	Yes	Optional. The number of seconds the cookie shall persist in the browser. Default is -1, causing the cookie to persist until the browser is closed.

Redirect to the application page

The only thing left is to redirect the browser to the appropriate page. If the authentication process is started as a result of the user requesting a protected page without being logged in, the original URL is received from the login page as the value of the `origURL` parameter:

```
<c:choose>
  <c:when test="${!empty param.origURL}">
    <c:redirect url="${param.origURL}" />
  </c:when>
  <c:otherwise>
    <c:redirect url="main.jsp" />
  </c:otherwise>
</c:choose>
```

If this parameter has a value, the browser is redirected to the originally requested page, otherwise to the main entry page for the application.

Checking for a Valid Session

Authentication is only half of the solution. We must also add access control to each page in the application. Example 13-4 shows the *main.jsp* page as an example of a protected page. This page shows all messages for the projects of the user's choice. It also has a form with which the user can change the list of projects of interest and links to a page for posting new messages, and to log out.

Example 13-4. A protected JSP page (main.jsp)

```
<%@ page contentType="text/html" %>
<%@ taglib prefix="c" uri="http://java.sun.com/jsp/jstl/core" %>
<%@ taglib prefix="fn" uri="http://java.sun.com/jsp/jstl/functions" %>

<%-- Verify that the user is logged in --%>
<c:if test="${validUser == null}">
  <jsp:forward page="login.jsp">
    <jsp:param name="origURL" value="${pageContext.request.requestURL}" />
    <jsp:param name="errorMsg" value="Please log in first." />
  </jsp:forward>
</c:if>
<html>
  <head>
    <title>Project Billboard</title>
  </head>
  <body bgcolor="white">

    <h1>Welcome ${fn:escapeXml(validUser.firstName)}</h1>
    Your profile currently shows you like information about the
    following checked-off projects. If you like to update your
    profile, make the appropriate changes below and click
    Update Profile.
    <form action="updateprofile.jsp" method="post">

      <c:forEach items="${validUser.projects}" var="current">
        <c:choose>
          <c:when test="${current == 'JSP'}">
            <c:set var="jspSelected" value="true" />
          </c:when>
          <c:when test="${current == 'Servlet'}">
            <c:set var="servletSelected" value="true" />
          </c:when>
          <c:when test="${current == 'EJB'}">
            <c:set var="ejbSelected" value="true" />
          </c:when>
        </c:choose>
      </c:forEach>
      <input type="checkbox" name="projects" value="JSP"
        ${jspSelected ? 'checked' : ''}>JSP<br>
      <input type="checkbox" name="projects" value="Servlet"
        ${servletSelected ? 'checked' : ''}>Servlet<br>
      <input type="checkbox" name="projects" value="EJB"
        ${ejbSelected} ? 'checked' : ''}>EJB<br>
      <input type="submit" value="Update Profile">
    </form>
    <hr>

    When you're done reading the news, please <a href="logout.jsp">
    log out</a>.

    <hr>
    <a href="entermsg.jsp">Post a new message</a>
```

Example 13-4. A protected JSP page (main.jsp) (continued)

```
    <p>

    <%-- Get all new items --%>
    <jsp:useBean id="news" scope="application"
      class="com.ora.jsp.beans.news.NewsBean" />
    <c:set var="newsItems" value="${news.newsItems}" />

    <%--
      Loop through all user projects and for each, loop through
      all news items and display the ones that match the current
      project.
    --%>
    <table>
      <c:forEach items="${validUser.projects}" var="projectName">
        <tr>
          <td colspan="2">
            <b>Project: ${fn:escapeXml(projectName)}</b>
          </td>
        </tr>
        <c:forEach items="${newsItems}" var="newsItem">
          <c:if test="${newsItem.category == projectName}">
            <tr>
              <td>
                ${fn:escapeXml(newsItem.postedBy)}
              </td>
              <td>
                ${fn:escapeXml(newsItem.postedDate)}
              </td>
            </tr>
            <tr>
              <td colspan="2">
                ${fn:escapeXml(newsItem.msg)}
              </td>
            </tr>
            <tr>
              <td colspan="2"><hr></td>
            </tr>
          </c:if>
        </c:forEach>
      </c:forEach>
    </table>
  </body>
</html>
```

Here's the most interesting piece of Example 13-4, from an access-control point of view:

```
<c:if test="${validUser == null}">
  <jsp:forward page="login.jsp">
    <jsp:param name="origURL" value="${pageContext.request.requestURL}" />
    <jsp:param name="errorMsg" value="Please log in first." />
  </jsp:forward>
</c:if>
```

The proof that a successfully authenticated user requests the page is that there's an `EmployeeBean` available under the name `validUser` in the session scope; the *authenticate.jsp* page places it there only if the username and password are valid. The `<c:if>` action is used to verify this. If the bean is not found, the request is forwarded to the login page, with the `origURL` and `errorMsg` parameters added.

Providing personalized content

The rest of the page shown in Example 13-4 produces a personalized page for the authenticated user. Figure 13-3 shows an example of how it may look for one user.

Figure 13-3. Personalized application page

First, the `validUser` bean properties welcome the user to the site by name. Next comes a form with checkboxes for all projects. The same technique that was used in Chapter 8 is also used here to set the checked attribute for the projects listed in the user's profile. The user can modify the list of projects and click **Update Profile** to invoke the *updateprofile.jsp* page. This page modifies the profile information in the database. We'll take a look at how it's done later.

A NewsBean containing NewsItemBean objects then displays news items for all projects matching the user's profile. The implementations of these beans are intended only as examples. Initially, the NewsBean contains one hardcoded message for each news category, and the news items are kept in memory only. A real implementation would likely store all news items permanently in a database.

Example 13-4 also contains a link to a page where a news item can be posted to the list. If you look at the source for the *entermsg.jsp* file, you'll see that it's just a JSP page with the same access-control test at the top as in Example 13-4 and a regular HTML form that invokes the *storemsg.jsp* file with a POST request. The POST method is appropriate here, since the form fields update information on the server (the in-memory NewsBean database).

The *storemsg.jsp* page is shown in Example 13-5.

Example 13-5. POST page with restricted access (storemsg.jsp)

```
<%@ taglib prefix="c" uri="http://java.sun.com/jsp/jstl/core" %>

<%-- Verify that the user is logged in --%>
<c:if test="${validUser == null}">
  <jsp:forward page="login.jsp">
    <jsp:param name="origURL" value="${pageContext.request.requestURL}" />
    <jsp:param name="errorMsg" value="Please log in first." />
  </jsp:forward>
</c:if>
<%-- Verify that it's a POST method --%>
<c:if test="${pageContext.request.method != 'POST'}">
  <c:redirect url="main.jsp" />
</c:if>
<%-- Create a new news item bean with the submitted info --%>
<jsp:useBean id="newsItem" class="com.ora.jsp.beans.news.NewsItemBean" >
  <jsp:setProperty name="newsItem" property="*" />
  <c:set target="${newsItem}" property="postedBy"
    value="${validUser.firstName} ${validUser.lastName}" />
</jsp:useBean>

<%-- Add the new news item bean to the list --%>
<c:set target="${news}" property="newsItem"
  value="${newsItem}" />

<c:redirect url="main.jsp" />
```

This page creates a new NewsItemBean and sets all properties based on the field parameters passed from the *entermsg.jsp* page, plus the postedBy property using the firstName and lastName properties of the validUser bean. It then adds the new news item to the NewsBean with the <c:set> action and redirects to the main page, where the new item is displayed along with the old ones.

Let's focus on the access-control aspects. At the top of the page, you find the same access-control logic as in all other protected pages. If a user fills out the form in *entermsg.jsp* and walks away from the computer without submitting the form, the session may time out. When the user then returns and clicks **Submit**, the `validUser` bean is not found in the session. The body of the `<c:if>` action is therefore processed, forwarding the request to the login page with the `origURL` parameter set to the URL of the *storemsg.jsp*. After successful authentication, the authentication page redirects to the original URL, the *storemsg.jsp*. However, a redirect is always a `GET` request.* All the parameters sent with the original `POST` request for *storemsg.jsp* are lost; a `POST` request carries the parameter values in the message body, instead of in the URL (as a query string) as a `GET` request does. This mean the original URL saved by the *login.jsp* page doesn't include the parameters. If you don't take care of this special case, an empty `NewsItemBean` is added to the list.

There are at least two ways to deal with this. In Example 13-5, the access-control logic is followed by a `<c:if>` action checking that the request for this page is a `POST` request. If not, it redirects to the main page without processing the request. This is the easiest way to deal with the problem, but it also means that the user will have to retype the message again. The chance that a session times out before a form is submitted is small, so in most cases this is not a big deal; it's therefore the solution I recommend.

If you absolutely must find a way to not lose the `POST` parameters when a session times out, here is a brief outline of a solution:

- Use a `<c:forEach>` action in the login page to loop through all `POST` parameter values and save them as hidden fields in the form, along with a hidden field that tells if the original request was a `GET` or a `POST` request.
- In the authentication page, *forward* to the originally requested URL if the method was a `POST` and *redirect* only if it was a `GET`. The authentication page is always invoked as a `POST` request. A forward is just a way to let another page continue to process the same request, so the originally requested page will be invoked with a `POST` request as it expects, along with all the originally submitted parameters saved as hidden fields in the login page.

Depending on your application, you may also need to save session data as hidden fields in the page that submits the `POST` request, so that the requested page doesn't have to rely on session information. But this leads to another problem. What if someone other than the user who filled out the form comes along and submits it? Information will then be updated on the server with information submitted by a user that's no longer logged in. One way out of this is to also save information about the

* The HTTP specification (RFC 2616) states that a browser is not allowed to change the method for the request when it receives a redirect response (status code 302). But, as acknowledged by HTTP specification, all major browsers available today change a `POST` request to a `GET` anyway.

current user as a hidden field in the form that sends the POST request and let the authentication page compare this information with information about the new user. If they don't match, the client can be redirected to the main application page instead of forwarded to the originally requested URL.

As you can see, there are a number of things to think about. Whether it makes sense to take care of all the issues depends on the application. My general advice is to keep it simple and stick to the first solution unless your application warrants a more complex approach.

Updating the User Profile

The *updateprofile.jsp* page, used if the user makes new project selections in the main page and clicks **Update Profile**, is also invoked through the POST method. It follows the same access-control approach as the *storemsg.jsp* page and is shown in Example 13-6. But what's more interesting with this page is that it shows how to replace multivalue bean and database data, and is an instance of when you need to care about database transactions.

Example 13-6. Updating multiple database rows (updateprofile.jsp)

```
<%@ taglib prefix="c" uri="http://java.sun.com/jsp/jstl/core" %>
<%@ taglib prefix="sql" uri="http://java.sun.com/jsp/jstl/sql" %>

<%-- Verify that the user is logged in --%>
<c:if test="${validUser == null}">
  <jsp:forward page="login.jsp">
    <jsp:param name="origURL" value="${pageContext.request.requestURL}" />
    <jsp:param name="errorMsg" value="Please log in first." />
  </jsp:forward>
</c:if>

<%-- Verify that it's a POST method --%>
<c:if test="${pageContext.request.method != 'POST'}">
  <c:redirect url="main.jsp" />
</c:if>

<%-- Update the project list in the bean --%>
<c:set target="${validUser}" property="projects"
  value="${paramValues.projects}" />

<sql:transaction>
  <%-- Delete the old project (if any) and insert the new ones --%>
  <sql:update>
    DELETE FROM EmployeeProjects
      WHERE UserName = ?
    <sql:param value="${validUser.userName}" />
  </sql:update>
  <c:forEach items="${validUser.projects}" var="project">
    <sql:update>
```

Example 13-6. Updating multiple database rows (updateprofile.jsp) (continued)

```
      INSERT INTO EmployeeProjects
        (UserName, ProjectName) VALUES(?, ?)
      <sql:param value="${validUser.userName}" />
      <sql:param value="${project}" />
    </sql:update>
  </c:forEach>
</sql:transaction>
<%-- Redirect to main page --%>
<c:redirect url="main.jsp" />
```

The list of new projects selected by the user is sent to the *updateprofile.jsp* page as the `projects` request parameter, with one value per checked checkbox. The `projects` bean property is updated using the `<c:set>` action with the value of an EL expression that returns all values of the parameter as an array (note that the `paramValues` implicit variable is used, as opposed to the `param` variable). The data type for the `projects` property is `String[]`, meaning it can be set to an array of strings.

If the user deselects all checkboxes in the *main.jsp* page (Example 13-4), all projects must be removed from the bean as well. Using the `<c:set>` action takes care of this requirement. When no checkbox is selected, the `projects` request parameter is not sent, and the EL expression returns `null`, clearing the project list property value.

The `EmployeeProjects` table (Table 13-1) contains one row per project for a user, with the username in the `UserName` column and the project name in the `ProjectName` column. The easiest way to update the database information is to first delete all existing rows, if any, and then insert rows for the new projects selected by the user. Because this requires execution of multiple SQL statements, and all must either succeed or fail, the `<sql:update>` actions are placed within the body of a `<sql:transaction>` action element. If the first `<sql:update>` action is successful but one of the others fails, the database information deleted by the first is restored so the database correctly reflects the state before the change.

To delete the rows in the database, the `<sql:update>` action is used with an SQL `DELETE` statement. The `WHERE` clause condition restricts the statement so that only the rows for the current user are deleted. The `<c:forEach>` action then loops through all projects registered in the `validUser` bean. The body of the `<c:forEach>` action contains an `<sql:update>` action that executes an `INSERT` statement for each project:

```
<c:forEach items="${validUser.projects}" var="project">
  <sql:update>
    INSERT INTO EmployeeProjects
      (UserName, ProjectName) VALUES(?, ?)
    <sql:param value="${validUser.userName}" />
    <sql:param value="${project}" />
  </sql:update>
</c:forEach>
```

Within the action element's body, the `<sql:param>` action sets the value for the `ProjectName` column to the current iteration value; a new value is used for each pass through the `projects` property array. The `UserName` column has the same value in each row, so the `<sql:param>` action always sets it to the `validUser` bean's `userName` property value.

Logging Out

Because the proof of authentication is kept in the session scope, the user is automatically logged out when the session times out. Even so, an application that requires authentication should always provide a way for the user to explicitly log out. This way a user can be sure that if he leaves the desk, no one else can come by and use the application.

The main page in the example application contains a link to the logout page, shown in Example 13-7.

Example 13-7. Logout page (logout.jsp)

```
<%@ taglib prefix="c" uri="http://java.sun.com/jsp/jstl/core" %>
<%@ taglib prefix="ora" uri="orataglib" %>

<%--
  Terminate the session and redirect to the login page.
--%>
<ora:invalidateSession/>

<c:redirect url="login.jsp" />
```

This page explicitly terminates the session using the `<ora:invalidateSession>` custom action (no attributes supported) and then redirects back to the login page. Invalidating the session means that all session scope variables are removed, and the session is marked as invalid. The next time someone logs in, a new session is created.

The `<ora:invalidateSession>` custom action implementation is very simple and arguable overkill. If you don't mind using JSP scripting elements (described in Chapter 16) in your pages, this scriptlet is an alternative to using the custom action:

```
<% session.invalidate(); %>
```

If you want to test the sample application described in this chapter, you must first create at least one user with the example application developed in Chapter 12. To see how the automatic redirect to the originally requested page works, you can open two browser windows and log in from both. They both share the same session (assuming cookies are enabled), so if you log out using one window and then try to load the "post a new message" page with the other, you are redirected to the login page. After you enter your username and password, you're redirected to the page for posting a message.

Other Security Concerns

In this chapter we have discussed only authentication and access control, but there's a lot more to web application security. You also need to ensure that no one listening on the network can read the data. In addition, you need to consider ways to verify that no one has hijacked the data and modified it before it reaches its final destination. Common terms for these concerns are *confidentiality* and *data privacy* for the first, and *integrity checking* for the second.

On an intranet, users can usually be trusted not to use network listeners to get to data they shouldn't see. But on the Internet, you can make no assumptions. If you provide access to sensitive data, you have to make sure it's protected appropriately. Network security is a huge subject area and clearly not within the scope of this book. Therefore I will touch only on the most common way to take care of both confidentiality and integrity checking, namely the Secure Socket Layer (SSL) protocol.

SSL is a protocol based on public key cryptography; it relies on a public key and a private key pair. Messages sent by someone, or something (like a server), are encoded using the private key and can be decoded by the receiver only by using the corresponding public key. Besides confidentiality and integrity checking, public key cryptography also provides very secure authentication; if a message can be decoded with a certain public key, you know it was encoded with the corresponding private key. The keys are issued, in the form of certificates together with user identity information, by a trusted organization such as VeriSign (*http://www.verisign.com/*).

Both the browser and the server can have certificates. However, the most common scenario today is that only the server has a certificate and can thereby positively identify itself to the browser. The SSL protocol takes care of this server authentication during the handshaking phase of setting up the connection. If the server certificate doesn't match the server's hostname, the user is warned, or the connection is refused. If the browser also has a certificate, it can authenticate the browser to the server in a more secure fashion than basic and digest authentication.

Even if only a server certificate is used, the communication between the browser and the server is still encrypted. This means that the issue of sending passwords as clear text for the basic and form-based authentication, as well as the application-controlled authentication we developed in this chapter, is nullified.

Most web servers today support server certificates and SSL. When you use HTTP over SSL (HTTPS), the URLs start with `https` instead of `http`. Not all applications need the kind of tight security offered by HTTPS, but you should be aware of all security threats and carefully evaluate if the risks of not using SSL are acceptable for your application.

CHAPTER 14

Internationalization

Taking the term World Wide Web literally means that your web site needs to respect the local languages and customs of all visitors, no matter where they come from. More and more, large web sites provide content in several different languages. Just look at sites like Yahoo!, which provide directory services in the local language of more than 20 countries in Europe, Asia Pacific, and North and South America. Other good examples are CNN, with local news for 3 continents in 7 different languages, and Vitaminic (*http://www.vitaminic.com/*), a site with MP3 music and artist information customized for different countries. If the site contains only static content, it's fairly easy to support multiple languages: just make a static version of the site for each language. But this approach is not practical for a site with dynamic content. If you develop a separate site for each language, you will have to duplicate the code that generates the dynamic content as well, leading to maintenance problems when errors are discovered or when it's time to add new features. Luckily, Java and JSP provide a number of tools to make it easier to develop one version of a site that can handle multiple languages.

The process of developing an application that caters to the needs of users from different parts of the world includes two phases: internationalization and localization.

Internationalization means preparing the application by identifying everything that will be different for different geographical regions and providing means to use different versions of all these items instead of hardcoded values. Examples of this are labels and messages, online help texts, graphics, format of dates, times and numbers, currencies, measurements, and sometimes even the page layouts and colors. Instead of spelling out the word internationalization, the abbreviation I18N is often used. It stands for "an I followed by 18 characters and an N."

When an application has been internationalized, it can also be *localized* for different regions. This means providing the application messages, help texts, graphics, and so forth, as well as rules for formatting dates/times and numbers, for one or more regions. Localization is sometimes abbreviated L10N, following the same logic as the

I18N abbreviation. Support for new regions can be added without changing the application itself, simply by installing new localized resources.

In this chapter, we first look at the basic Java classes used for internationalization. If you're not a programmer, you can skim through this section without worrying about the details. (However, you should understand the terminology, and knowing a bit about the inner workings of these classes also makes it easier to understand the rest of the chapter.) We then develop a web application in which visitors can answer a poll question and see statistics about how other visitors have answered, using a set of JSTL actions that hide the Java classes and make internationalization a lot easier. The poll site is localized for three languages. The initial language selection is based on the user's browser configuration, but users can also explicitly select one of the supported languages.

The last part of this chapter discusses the issues related to interpreting localized input and the special considerations needed for dealing with languages containing other characters than those used in Western European languages.

How Java Supports Internationalization and Localization

Java was designed with internationalization in mind and includes a number of classes to make the effort as painless as possible. The primary class used for internationalization represents a specific geographical region. Instances of this class are used by other classes to format dates and numbers, and include localized strings and other objects in an application. There are also classes for dealing with different character encodings, as you will see later in the chapter.

The Locale Class

All Java classes that provide localization support use a class named `java.util.Locale`. An instance of this class represents a particular geographical, political, or cultural region, as specified by a combination of a language code and a country code. Java classes that perform tasks that differ depending on a user's language and local customs—so called locale-sensitive operations—use a `Locale` instance to decide how to operate. Examples of locale-sensitive operations are interpreting date strings and formatting numeric values.

You create a `Locale` instance using a constructor that takes the country code and language code as arguments:

```
java.util.Locale usLocale = new Locale("en", "US");
```

Here, a `Locale` for U.S. English is created. George Bernard Shaw (a famous Irish playwright) once observed that "England and America are two countries divided by a common language," so it's no surprise that both a language code and a country code are needed to describe some locales completely. The language code, a lowercase two-letter combination, is defined by the ISO 639 standard available at *http://www.ics.uci.edu/pub/ietf/http/related/iso639.txt*. The country code, an uppercase two-letter combination, is defined by the ISO 3166 standard, available at *http://www.chemie.fu-berlin.de/diverse/doc/ISO_3166.html*. Tables 14-1 and 14-2 show some of these codes.

Table 14-1. ISO-639 language codes

Language code	Language
`af`	Afrikaans
`da`	Danish
`de`	German
`el`	Greek
`en`	English
`es`	Spanish
`fr`	French
`ja`	Japanese
`pl`	Polish
`ru`	Russian
`sv`	Swedish
`zh`	Chinese

Table 14-2. ISO-3166 country codes

Country	Country code
Denmark	DK
Germany	DE
Greece	GR
Mexico	MX
New Zealand	NZ
South Africa	ZA
United Kingdom	GB
United States	US

As luck would have it, these two standards are also used to define language and country codes in HTTP. As you may remember from Chapter 2, a browser can send an `Accept-Language` header with a request for a web resource such as a JSP page. The value of this header contains one or more codes for languages the user prefers, based on how the browser is configured. If you use a Netscape 6 or Mozilla browser, you can specify your preferred languages in the Edit → Preferences dialog, under the Navigator → Languages tab. In Internet Explorer 5, you find the same thing in Tools →

Internet Options when you click the Languages button under the General tab. If you specify more than one language, they are included in the header as a comma-separated list:

```
Accept-Language: en-US, en, sv
```

The languages are listed in order of preference, with each language represented by just the language code or the language code and country code separated by a dash (-). This example header specifies the first choice as U.S. English, followed by any type of English, and finally Swedish. The HTTP specification allows an alternative to listing the codes in order of preference, namely adding a so-called *q-value* to each code. The q-value is a value between 0.0 and 1.0, indicating the relative preference between the codes. Very few browsers use this alternative today, however.

The `Accept-Language` header helps you localize your application. You could write code that reads this header and creates the corresponding `Locale` instances. The good news is you don't have to do this yourself; the web container takes care of it for you and makes the locale information available through properties of the implicit `pageContext` object:

```
${pageContext.request.locale}
${pageContext.request.locales}
```

The `locale` property contains the `Locale` with the highest preference ranking; the `locales` (plural) property contains a collection of all locales in order of preference. All you have to do is match the preferred locales to the ones your web application supports. The easiest way to do this is to loop through the preferred locales and stop when you find one your application supports. As you will see later, the JSTL I18N actions relieve you of this as well, but now you know how it can be done.

Formatting Numbers and Dates

Let's look at how a locale can be used. One thing we who live on this planet have a hard time agreeing on is how to write dates and numbers. The order of the month, the day, and the year; if the numeric value or the name should be used for the month; what character to use to separate the fractional part of a number; all of these details differ between countries, even between countries that speak the same language. And even though these details may seem picky, using an unfamiliar format can cause a great deal of confusion. For instance, if you ask for something to be done by 5/2, an American thinks you mean May 2 while a Swede believes that it's due by February 5.

Java provides two classes to deal with formatting of numbers and dates for a specific locale, appropriately named `java.text.NumberFormat` and `java.text.DateFormat`, respectively.

The JSTL `<fmt:formatNumber>` action, used in Chapter 10 to format the price information for items in a shopping cart, is based on the `NumberFormat` class. By default, the

NumberFormat class formats numbers based on the locale of the underlying operating system. If used on a server configured to use a U.S. English locale, it formats them according to American customs; on a server configured with an Italian locale, it formats them according to Italian customs, and so forth. But you can also explicitly specify a locale, to format numbers according to the rules for other locales than the one used by the operating system. You will soon see how to tell the JSTL formatting actions to use a specific locale or figure out which one to use based on the Accept-Language header.

The DateFormat class works basically the same way, but how dates are written differs a lot more between locales than numbers do, because the day and month names are sometimes spelled out in the local language. The JSTL <fmt:formatDate> action, used to format date and time values, is based on the DateFormat class.

Using Localized Text

Automatic translation of numbers and dates into the local language is a great help, but until automatic translation software is a lot smarter than it is today, you have to translate all the text used in the application yourself. A set of Java classes can help you pick the right version for a specific locale.

The main class for dealing with localized resources (such as text, images, and sounds) is named java.util.ResourceBundle. This class is actually the abstract superclass for the two subclasses that do the real work, ListResourceBundle and PropertyResourceBundle, but it provides methods that let you get an appropriate subclass instance, hiding the details about which subclass actually provides the resources. Details about the difference between these two subclasses are beyond the scope of this book. Suffice it to say that the JSTL actions can use resources provided through either of them.

For most web applications, an instance of the PropertyResourceBundle is used. A PropertyResourceBundle instance is associated with a named set of localized text resources; a key identifies each resource. The keys and their corresponding text values are stored in a regular text file, known as a *resource bundle file*:

```
site_name=The Big Corporation Inc.
company_logo=/images/logo_en.gif
welcome_msg=Hello!
```

Here three keys, site_name, company_logo, and welcome_msg, have been assigned values. The key is a string, without space or other special characters, and the value is any text. If the value spans more than one line, the line break must be escaped with a backslash character (\):

```
multi_line_msg=This text value\
continues on the next line.
```

The file must use the *.properties* extension, for instance *sitetext.properties*, and be located in the classpath used by the Java Virtual Machine (JVM). In the case of web applications, you can store the file in the application's *WEB-INF/classes* directory, because this directory is always included in the classpath.

To localize an application, you create separate resource bundle files for each locale, all with the same main name (called the *base name*) but with unique suffixes to identify the locale. For instance, a file named *sitetext_es_MX.properties*, where `es` is the language code for Spanish, and `MX` is the country code for Mexico, can contain the text for the Mexican Spanish locale. The JSTL actions that deal with localized text find the resource bundle that most closely matches the selected locale or a default bundle if there is no match. We'll look at an example in detail in the next section.

Besides the `ResourceBundle` class, there's a class named `java.text.MessageFormat` you can use for messages composed of fixed text plus variable values, such as "An earthquake measuring <u>6.7</u> on the Richter scale hit <u>Northridge</u>, <u>CA</u>, on <u>January 17</u>, <u>1994</u>.", where each underline represents a variable value. The JSTL actions support this type of formatted messages as well, as you will see in the next section.

Generating Localized Output

Now that you have an understanding of the type of internationalization support Java provides, let's look at a concrete example. However, instead of using the internationalization classes directly in the pages, we'll use the JSTL I18N actions based on these classes.

The example application, briefly described in the introduction to this chapter, lets visitors voice their opinion by selecting one of the answers to a question, as well as seeing how others have answered. The text, numbers, and dates are available in three different languages. Figure 14-1 shows all the pages used in this application and how they are related.

The first page the user sees is the *poll.jsp* page, shown in Figure 14-2. The language that displays the contents the first time this page is requested is based on the `Accept-Language` request header value. The top part of the page contains radio buttons for the three supported languages and a **Submit** button. If the user wants the application to be presented in another language, he selects the corresponding radio button and clicks **Submit**, causing the page to be requested again, this time with a language parameter included in the request. The value of the language parameter is then used to select the corresponding locale and display the page in the selected locale's language. Information about the selected locale is saved as session data, so it's available to all the other application pages as well.

The *poll.jsp* page also includes the question, linked to a page with background information for the question, and a group of radio buttons representing the different answers, as well as a **Submit** button. Clicking on the **Submit** button invokes the

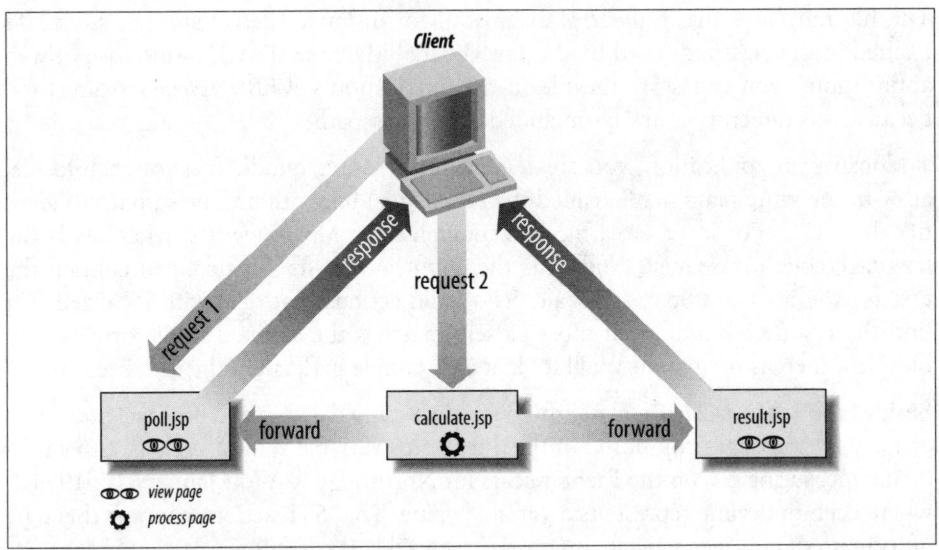

Figure 14-1. Localized poll application pages

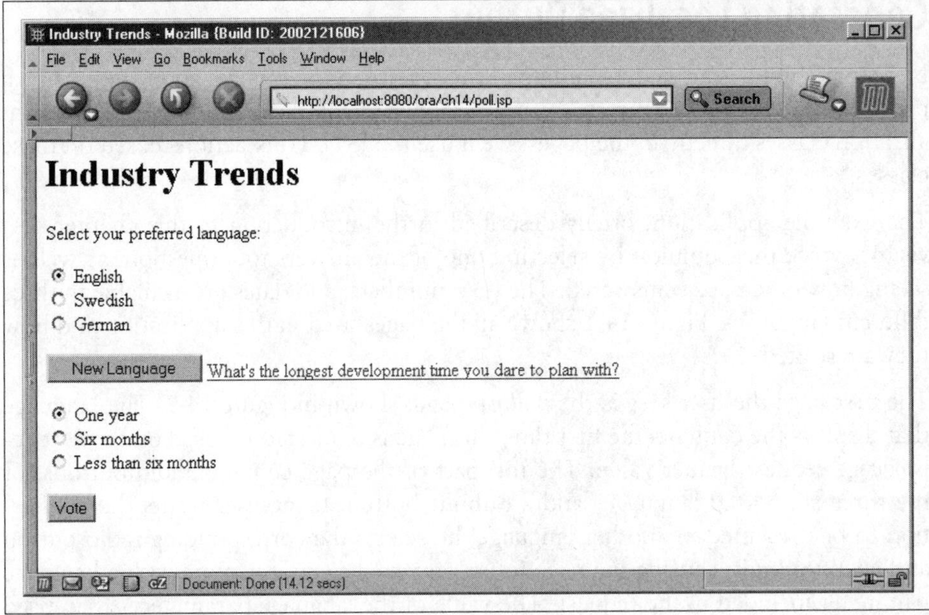

Figure 14-2. The language selection and question page

calculate.jsp page, in which the choice is first validated. If it's valid, it's added to the global poll result. The request is then forwarded to the *result.jsp* page, which displays the poll statistics with all numbers formatted according to the selected locale. If it's not valid, the request is forwarded back to the *poll.jsp* page.

Both the *poll.jsp* page and the *result.jsp* page are designed to show text, numbers, and dates according to the selected locale using the JSTL I18N actions. This approach is perfect when the amount of text is small; only one set of pages has to be maintained. But if a page needs to contain a great deal of text, typing it into a properties file and escaping all line breaks may not be the best approach. Some pages also need to use different layouts, colors, images, and general appearance based on the locale. In this case, it's easier to use a separate page per locale. The pages providing more detailed information about the question in this example illustrate this approach. The link on the *poll.jsp* page leads to different JSP pages depending on the selected language, named according to the same naming convention as `ResourceBundle` properties files: *details_en.jsp*, *details_de.jsp*, and *details_sv.jsp* for the English, German, and Swedish pages, respectively. Let's look at the one-page and the multipage approaches separately.

Using One Page for Multiple Locales

Example 14-1 shows the *poll.jsp* page. That's where the magic of locale selection happens, and the selection is then used to produce text in the corresponding language throughout the page.

Example 14-1. Language selection and vote page (poll.jsp)

```
<%@ page contentType="text/html" %>
<%@ taglib prefix="c" uri="http://java.sun.com/jsp/jstl/core" %>
<%@ taglib prefix="fmt" uri="http://java.sun.com/jsp/jstl/fmt" %>
<%--
  Set the locale to the selected one, if any. Otherwise, let the
  <fmt:setBundle> action pick the best one based on the Accept-Language
  header.
--%>
<c:if test="${param.language == 'en'}">
  <fmt:setLocale value="en" scope="session" />
</c:if>
<c:if test="${param.language == 'sv'}">
  <fmt:setLocale value="sv" scope="session" />
</c:if>
<c:if test="${param.language == 'de'}">
  <fmt:setLocale value="de" scope="session" />
</c:if>
<fmt:setBundle basename="pages" var="pagesBundle" />
<fmt:setBundle basename="labels" scope="session" />
<html>
  <head>
    <title>
      <fmt:message key="title" />
    </title>
  </head>
  <body bgcolor="white">
    <h1>
      <fmt:message key="title" />
    </h1>
```

Example 14-1. Language selection and vote page (poll.jsp) (continued)

```
    <fmt:message key="select_language" />:
    <form action="poll.jsp">
      <p>
      <c:set var="currLang" value="${pagesBundle.locale.language}" />
      <input type="radio" name="language" value="en"
        ${currLang == 'en' ? 'checked' : ''}>
      <fmt:message key="english" /><br>
      <input type="radio" name="language" value="sv"
        ${currLang == 'sv' ? 'checked' : ''}>
      <fmt:message key="swedish" /><br>
      <input type="radio" name="language" value="de"
        ${currLang == 'de' ? 'checked' : ''}>
      <fmt:message key="german" /><br>
      <p>
      <input type="submit"
        value="<fmt:message key="new_language" />">
    </form>

    <a href="<fmt:message key="details_page" bundle="${pagesBundle}" />">
      <fmt:message key="question" />
    </a>

    <form action="calculate.jsp" method="post">
      <input type="radio" name="answerId" value="1" checked>
      <fmt:message key="answer1" />
      <br>
      <input type="radio" name="answerId" value="2">
      <fmt:message key="answer2" />
      <br>
      <input type="radio" name="answerId" value="3">
      <fmt:message key="answer3" />
      <p>
      <input type="submit"
        value="<fmt:message key="submit" />">
    </form>
  </body>
</html>
```

At the top of the page, the `taglib` directives identify the JSTL libraries. Besides the JSTL core library used in previous chapters, this page also declares the JSTL I18N and formatting library with the prefix `fmt`.

After the tag library declarations follows a section that determines if the page is invoked with the `language` parameter, to request a specific language to be used. If it is, and the requested language is one supported by this application, the body of the matching `<c:if>` action element is processed to set the corresponding locale explicitly. This is where we encounter the first I18N action: `<fmt:setLocale>`, described in Table 14-3.

Table 14-3. Attributes for JSTL <fmt:setLocale>

Attribute name	Java type	Dynamic value accepted	Description
`value`	`String`	Yes	Mandatory. A lowercase ISO-639 language code, optionally followed by an uppercase ISO-3166 country code, separated from the language code with a hyphen (-) or an underscore (_).
`variant`	`String`	Yes	Optional. Vendor- or browser-specific variant.
`scope`	`String`	No	Optional. The scope for the locale setting, one of `page`, `request`, `session`, or `application`. `page` is the default.

This action creates an instance of the `Locale` class corresponding to the `value` and `variant` attribute values and saves it in the specified scope. The `value` attribute must include a language code. It may also include a country code, separated from the language code with a hyphen (-) or an underscore (_). The `variant` attribute is rarely used, but the I18N Java classes used behind the scene support it, so the JSTL action supports it as well. It can specify a locale that applies to a specific platform in addition to a language and a country. One example is if you use a locale to select help texts, you may want to provide one set of descriptions for Internet Explorer and another for Netscape browsers. In Example 14-1, only the language code is specified, and the locale setting is saved in the session scope to apply it to all pages requested by the same user.

The variable that the `<fmt:setLocale>` sets is a configuration variable—in other words a variable with an implementation-dependent name used to set the default for a specific scope, as described in Chapter 12. It's backed by a context parameter that can set a global default:

```
<web-app>
  ...
  <context-param>
    <param-name>
      javax.servlet.jsp.jstl.fmt.locale
    </param-name>
    <param-value>
      en-US
    </param-value>
  </context-param>
  ...
</web-app>
```

The first time the page is invoked, no language is specified. Hence, the `language` parameter is not received with the request so none of the `<c:if>` conditions is matched. In this case, the supported locale that is the closest match to the language preferences defined by the user through the browser settings should be used. The `<fmt:setBundle>` action, described in Table 14-4, takes care of this task.

Table 14-4. Attributes for JSTL <fmt:setBundle>

Attribute name	Java type	Dynamic value accepted	Description
`basename`	`String`	Yes	Mandatory. The resource bundle base name.
`var`	`String`	No	Optional. The name of the variable to hold the `LocalizationContext` instance.
`scope`	`String`	No	Optional. The scope for the localization context setting; one of `page`, `request`, `session`, or `application`. `page` is the default.

In Example 14-1, I use this action to load two separate resource bundles: one that contains the names of language-specific pages and one that contains all localized text.

The `basename` attribute is mandatory and identifies a specific resource bundle. Properties files for all locales supported by the sample application, named according to the pattern *basename_locale.properties*, represent each bundle: *labels_en.properties*; *labels_de.properties* and *labels_sv.properties*; and *pages_en.properties*, *pages_de.properties*, and *pages_sv.properties*. All properties files are located in the *WEB-INF/classes* directory for the application, making them part of the classpath the I18N classes use to locate resource bundles. If a default locale has been established using the `<fmt:setLocale>` action or the locale configuration setting, the `<fmt:setBundle>` action simply loads the resource bundle corresponding to the base name for the selected locale. In Example 14-1, this is the case when a `language` parameter with a value matching one of the supported locales is sent with the request.

But what happens if no `language` parameter is sent or when its value doesn't match a supported locale? In this case, the `<fmt:setBundle>` action has to decide which of the supported locales most closely matches the user's preferences. Recall that the user's language preferences are sent with the request in the `Accept-Language` header. The `<fmt:setBundle>` action compares this list to the set of available locale-specific bundles for the base name and picks the best one. For each locale in the list, it first tries to find a locale that matches all parts specified for the preferred locale: language, country, and variant. If it doesn't find a perfect match, it drops the variant and tries again. If it still can't find a match, it drops the country. As soon as it finds a bundle for one of the locales using this algorithm, it uses it and ignores the other locales. This means that with English, German, and Swedish as the available locales and an `Accept-Language` header containing the value "sv, en-US", the Swedish locale is selected (it's listed first, so it has higher priority). With an `Accept-Language` header such as "fr, en-US", the English locale is selected, since the highest priority locale (`fr`) is not available, and the closest match for the `en-US` locale is the `en` locale. If the application has bundles for both the `en` file and the `en-US` locale, the `en-US` locale is used because it's an exact match for the user's preferences.

An interesting case is what happens if none of the locales in the Accept-Language header matches an available locale. The best the <fmt:setBundle> action could do on its own would be to randomly pick one of the available locales, but that's no good. Instead you need to tell it which locale to use in this case. It's called the *fallback locale* in the JSTL specification, and it's defined as a configuration setting. You can set its context parameter like this in the deployment descriptor:

```
<web-app>
  ...
  <context-param>
    <param-name>
      javax.servlet.jsp.jstl.fmt.fallbackLocale
    </param-name>
    <param-value>
      en
    </param-value>
  </context-param>
  ...
</web-app>
```

Here I set the en locale as the fallback, so if none of the preferred locales match, the <fmt:setBundle> action tries to locate a bundle with the en locale. If it still can't find a matching bundle, it falls back to the ultimate backup: the so-called root bundle. The root bundle is represented by a bundle without any locale information, for instance a file named *labels.properties* in the example application.

The <fmt:setBundle> action also supports the var and the scope attributes. They let you specify the name of a variable for the bundle and the scope where it should be stored. The type of the variable is javax.servlet.jsp.jstl.fmt.LocaleContext. It's a simple class that holds an instance of the java.util.ResourceBundle that was selected as well as a java.util.Locale instance for the locale that matched it. This variable can be used as an attribute value for other I18N actions to tell them which bundle to use. That's what I do for the bundle with page names in Example 14-1. If you omit the var attribute, the action saves the localization context in a configuration variable for the scope instead. It is then used as the default for all JSTL I18N actions that use a bundle. I use this approach for the bundle that contains all text, and I specify the session scope so it's available to all pages requested by the same user.

As for all configuration setting, you can also define the base name for a resource bundle to use by default as a context parameter:

```
<web-app>
  ...
  <context-param>
    <param-name>
      javax.servlet.jsp.jstl.fmt.localizationContext
    </param-name>
    <param-value>
      labels
    </param-value>
```

```
    </context-param>
    ...
  </web-app>
```

The context parameter value is used by the I18N actions that need a localization context if it's not established in another way, for instance by a `<fmt:setBundle>` action.

To extract the localized text from a resource bundle and add it to the response, you use the `<fmt:message>` action, described in Table 14-5.

Table 14-5. Attributes for JSTL <fmt:message>

Attribute name	Java type	Dynamic value accepted	Description
key	String	Yes	Mandatory, unless specified as the body. The message key.
bundle	javax.servlet.jsp.jstl. LocalizationContext	Yes	Mandatory, unless a default is established by the localization context configuration setting or by a `<fmt:bundle>` action. A context with a resource bundle that contains the message.
var	String	No	Optional. The name of the variable to hold the message.
scope	String	No	Optional. The scope for the message variable; one of page, `request`, `session`, or `application`. page is the default.

The `<fmt:message>` action looks up the message identified by the key attribute value in the bundle specified by the `bundle` attribute and adds it to the response. If it can't find a message for the key, it adds the key enclosed in question marks instead. The `var` attribute can be used to save the localized message in the named variable instead. The variable is saved in the page scope, unless another scope is specified by the `scope` attribute.

The `bundle` attribute can be omitted if a localization context configuration setting is used to establish a default bundle, as is the case in Example 14-1. It can also be omitted if the `<fmt:message>` action is nested within the body of a `<fmt:bundle>` action element, described in Table 14-6.

Table 14-6. Attributes for JSTL <fmt:bundle>

Attribute name	Java type	Dynamic value accepted	Description
basename	String	Yes	Mandatory. The resource bundle base name.
prefix	String	Yes	Optional. A prefix to use for all key names in the bundle.

When you use the `<fmt:bundle>` action to establish the localization context for the nested actions, you can specify a key prefix as well. The `prefix` attribute is a convenience feature that comes in handy if your resource bundle keys have very long names. For instance, if all keys start with `com.mycompany.labels`, you can specify this as the prefix and use only the last part of the key name for the `<fmt:message>` actions that pull messages from the bundle.

If you look carefully at Example 14-1, you'll notice that the only static content in the page consists of HTML elements; all text is added by the `<fmt:message>` action, using localized messages from the resource bundle matching the selected locale. Here's how the `labels` resource bundle file for the English locale, *labels_en.properties* file looks:

```
title=Industry Trends
select_language=Select your preferred language
new_language=New Language
english=English
swedish=Swedish
german=German
question=What's the longest development time you dare to plan with?
answer1=One year
answer2=Six months
answer3=Less than six months
result1=One year {0, number, integer}% ({1, number, integer})
result2=Six months {0, number, integer}% ({1, number, integer})
result3=Less than six months {0, number, integer}% ({1, number, integer})
submit=Vote
number_of_votes=Total number of votes
result=Poll result
```

The value of the `title` key, used by the first two `<fmt:message>` actions, is set to "Industry Trends"; that's what appears as the title and header of the page when the English locale is selected. If the Swedish locale is selected, the text "Industri Trender" (the value specified for the `title` key in the *lables_sv.properties* file) is used instead.

To let the user pick another language than the one selected based on the `Accept-Language` header, the page contains a form with a set of radio buttons and a **Submit** button. Every time the page is displayed, the radio button group must reflect the currently selected language. The only sure way to find out which language is selected is to ask the `LocalizationContext` created by the `<fmt:setBundle>` action. The `LocalizationContext` class can be used as a bean with properties named `locale` and `resourceBundle`. The `locale` property contains a `Locale` instance that represents the locale used to pick the resource bundle. The `Locale` class can also be used as a bean, with a property named `language`. Armed with this knowledge, it's easy to write an EL expression that gets the current language:

```
...
    <c:set var="currLang" value="${pagesBundle.locale.language}" />
    <input type="radio" name="language" value="en"
      ${currLang == 'en' ? 'checked' : ''}>
...
```

The <c:set> action gets the current language using an EL expression that first gets the Locale from the LocalizationContext stored in the pagesBundle variable and then the language from the Locale. The result is saved in a variable named currLang, which is then used in the EL expressions for each radio button to set the checked attribute for the one that matches the current language.

All radio button elements have the name language, which means that they form a group in which only one can be selected. When the user clicks on the **Submit** button, the same page is requested with the value of the selected radio button included as a request parameter named language. As described earlier, this parameter is then used to switch to the selected language.

Next comes another form with radio buttons representing the three alternative answers to the poll question. All radio buttons are named answerId. The texts for the question, the answers, and the **Submit** button are displayed in the current language using the <fmt:message> action. When the user selects an answer and clicks on the **Submit** button, the *calculate.jsp* page, shown in Example 14-2, is invoked.

Example 14-2. Validation and calculation of votes (calculate.jsp)

```
<%@ taglib prefix="c" uri="http://java.sun.com/jsp/jstl/core" %>

<jsp:useBean id="pollResult" scope="application"
  class="com.ora.jsp.beans.poll.PollBean" />

<jsp:useBean id="answer" class="com.ora.jsp.beans.poll.AnswerBean" >
  <jsp:setProperty name="answer" property="*" />
</jsp:useBean>

<c:choose>
  <c:when test="${answer.valid}" >
    <c:set target="${pollResult}" property="answer"
      value="${answer}" />
    <jsp:forward page="result.jsp" />
  </c:when>
  <c:otherwise>
    <jsp:forward page="poll.jsp" />
  </c:otherwise>
</c:choose>
```

As with all pure logic pages, this page contains only action elements; no response text is generated. A PollBean in the application scope keeps track of the answers from all visitors, and an AnswerBean in the page scope captures and validates a single answer. The AnswerBean has a property named answerId, set to the value of the corresponding request parameter using the <jsp:setProperty> action. It also has a valid property, used in the <c:when> action to test if the answer is valid or not. In this example, it returns true if the answer ID is valid (1, 2, or 3). However, in a real application, you may want to include other validation rules. For instance, if the poll information is stored in a database, you can use cookies or a username to make sure each user answers only once. If the answer is valid, a `<c:set>` action sets the answer property of the PollBean to the valid answer, and the request is forwarded to the *result.jsp* page to display the poll statistics. Figure 14-3 shows a sample of the results page with the Swedish locale.

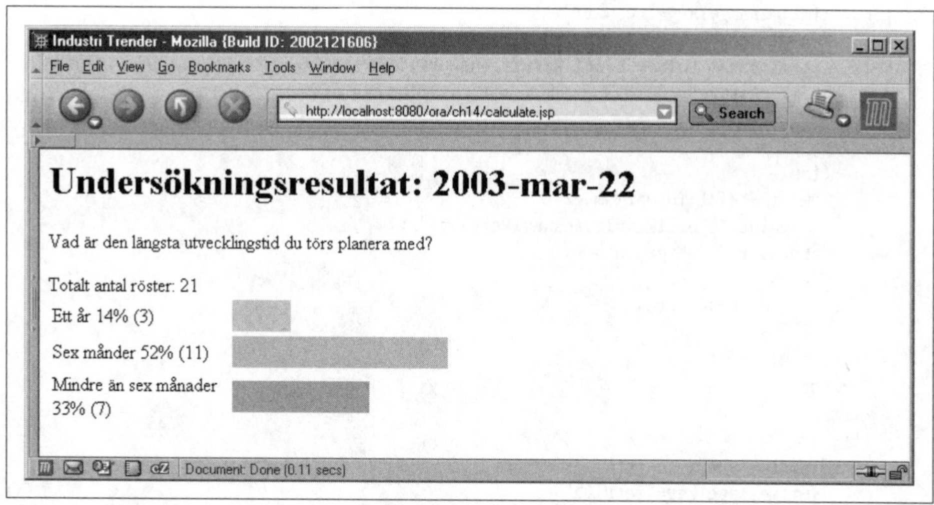

Figure 14-3. The result page using the Swedish locale

The *result.jsp* page, shown in Example 14-3, uses a couple of JSTL I18N actions we haven't talked about so far to display the localized date and numbers.

Example 14-3. Showing the result (result.jsp)

```
<%@ page contentType="text/html" %>
<%@ taglib prefix="c" uri="http://java.sun.com/jsp/jstl/core" %>
<%@ taglib prefix="fmt" uri="http://java.sun.com/jsp/jstl/fmt" %>

<html>
  <head>
    <title>
      <fmt:message key="title" />
    </title>
  </head>
  <body bgcolor="white">
    <jsp:useBean id="pollResult" scope="application"
         class="com.ora.jsp.beans.poll.PollBean" />
    <jsp:useBean id="now" class="java.util.Date" />
    <h1>
      <fmt:message key="result" />:
      <fmt:formatDate value="${now}" />
    </h1>

    <fmt:message key="question" />
    <p>
    <fmt:message key="number_of_votes" />:
```

Example 14-3. Showing the result (result.jsp) (continued)

```
    <fmt:formatNumber value="${pollResult.total}" />
    <table width="70%">
      <tr>
        <td width="30%">
          <fmt:message key="result1">
            <fmt:param value="${pollResult.answer1Percent}" />
            <fmt:param value="${pollResult.answer1}" />
          </fmt:message>
        </td>
        <td>
          <table
            width="<fmt:formatNumber
              value="${pollResult.answer1Percent}"/>%"
            bgcolor="lightgreen">
            <tr>
              <td> </td>
            </tr>
          </table>
        </td>
      </tr>
      <tr>
        <td width="30%">
          <fmt:message key="result2">
            <fmt:param value="${pollResult.answer2Percent}" />
            <fmt:param value="${pollResult.answer2}" />
          </fmt:message>
        </td>
        <td>
          <table
            width="<fmt:formatNumber
              value="${pollResult.answer2Percent}"/>%"
            bgcolor="lightblue">
            <tr>
              <td> </td>
            </tr>
          </table>
        </td>
      </tr>
      <tr>
        <td width="30%">
          <fmt:message key="result3">
            <fmt:param value="${pollResult.answer3Percent}" />
            <fmt:param value="${pollResult.answer3}" />
          </fmt:message>
        </td>
        <td>
          <table
            width="<fmt:formatNumber
              value="${pollResult.answer3Percent}"/>%"
            bgcolor="orange">
            <tr>
              <td> </td>
```

Example 14-3. Showing the result (result.jsp) (continued)

```
          </tr>
        </table>
      </td>
    </tr>
  </table>
</body>
</html>
```

This page uses the `<fmt:message>` action to add the localized text, just like the *poll.jsp* page.

A `<jsp:useBean>` action creates a variable that represents the current date and time, and this value is then added to the response with the `<fmt:formatDate>` action, described in Table 14-7. When you play around with this application, you see how the date format changes depending on the language you select.

Table 14-7. Attributes for JSTL <fmt:formatDate>

Attribute name	Java type	Dynamic value accepted	Description
`value`	`java.util.Date`	Yes	Mandatory. The date to format according to the selected locale.
`pattern`	`String`	Yes	Optional. A custom pattern to use for both the date and time parts.
`type`	`String`	Yes	Optional. Which part to format. One of `time`, `date`, or `both`. Default is `date`.
`dateStyle`	`String`	Yes	Optional. The predefined pattern to use for the date part. One of `default`, `short`, `medium`, `long`, or `full`. The default is `default`.
`timeStyle`	`String`	Yes	Optional. The predefined pattern to use for the time part. One of `default`, `short`, `medium`, `long`, or `full`. The default is `default`.
`timeZone`	`String` or `java.util.TimeZone`	Yes	Optional. Time zone for the date/time.
`var`	`String`	No	Optional. The name of a variable to hold the formatted value.
`scope`	`String`	No	Optional. The scope for the variable, one of `page`, `request`, `session`, or `application`. `page` is the default.

The `<fmt:formatDate>` action supports many attributes, but all except `value` are optional. The `var` and `scope` attributes are used as in all other JSTL actions: to specify the name of a variable to hold the result and optionally in which scope to store it.

All the other attributes deal with how the value should be formatted. The `type` attribute specifies if the result should contain just the date, just the time, or both. The `dateStyle` and `timeStyle` attributes allow you to specify predefined patterns for the date and the time part. The patterns vary between locales. For the English locale, the following chart shows the result of applying the predefined patterns for the date and time parts:

`default`	Feb 22, 2002 1:01:15 PM
`short`	2/22/02 1:01 PM
`medium`	Feb 22, 2002 1:01:15 PM
`long`	February 22, 2002 1:01:15 PM PST
`full`	Friday, February 22, 2002 1:01:15 PM PST

To use a custom pattern instead of one of the predefined patterns, you can use the `pattern` attribute. The pattern uses a number of symbols to define which parts should be included, and in which form (i.e., as a number or a name). A complete description is included in Appendix B, but the following chart shows a few examples using the English locale:

`yyyy-MM-dd HH:mm:ss`	2002-02-22 13:01:15
`yyyy-MM-dd hh:mm a`	2002-02-22 01:01 PM
`MMMM dd, hh:mm a z`	February 22, 01:01 PM PST

Finally, you can use the `timeZone` attribute to adjust the value to a specific time zone. Internally, Java handles date and time values as *coordinated universal time* (UTC), a time zone-neutral format, if you will. But when you create a text representation of a date, it must be displayed based on a specific time zone. If you do not specify a time zone, the value is formatted based on the current time-zone settings (more about this shortly). The value of the `timeZone` attribute can be a standard abbreviation (e.g., "PST," "GMT"), a full name (e.g., "Europe/Stockholm"), or a GMT offset (e.g., "GMT+1"), specified as a static text value or a `String` variable.

Instead of specifying a time zone for each action that needs it, you can use the `<fmt:setTimeZone>` action, described in Table 14-8, to change the default in the same way as for the locale and localization context. It can also be set by a context parameter named `javax.servlet.jsp.jstl.fmt.timeZone`.

Table 14-8. Attributes for JSTL <fmt:setTimeZone>

Attribute name	Java type	Dynamic value accepted	Description
`value`	`String` or `java.util.TimeZone`	Yes	Mandatory. The time zone. A `String` value must be an abbreviation, full name, or GMT offset.
`var`	`String`	No	Optional. The name of a variable to hold the `TimeZone` object.
`scope`	`String`	No	Optional. The scope for the variable, one of `page`, `request`, `session`, or `application`. `page` is the default.

Yet another alternative is the `<fmt:timeZone>` action described in Table 14-9. It establishes the time zone for all actions in its body.

Table 14-9. Attributes for JSTL <fmt:timeZone>

Attribute name	Java type	Dynamic value accepted	Description
`value`	`String` or `java.util.TimeZone`	Yes	Mandatory. The time zone. A `String` value must be an abbreviation, full name, or GMT offset.

Back to Example 14-3. Another new action used in this page is the `<fmt:formatNumber>` action, used to format numbers according to the rules for the selected locale. It's described in Table 14-10.

Table 14-10. Attributes for JSTL <fmt:formatNumber>

Attribute name	Java type	Dynamic value accepted	Description
`value`	`String` or `Number`	Yes	Mandatory, unless specified as the body. The number to format according to the selected locale.
`pattern`	`String`	Yes	Optional. A custom pattern to use for both the date and time parts.
`type`	`String`	Yes	Optional. The number type. One of `number`, `currency`, or `percentage`. Default is `number`.
`currencyCode`	`String`	Yes	Optional. ISO-4217 currency code.
`currencySymbol`	`String`	Yes	Optional. Currency symbol.
`groupingUsed`	`boolean`	Yes	Optional. Should the formatted value use a grouping character? Default is `true`.
`maxIntegerDigits`	`int`	Yes	Optional. Maximum number of digits in the integer portion.
`minIntegerDigits`	`int`	Yes	Optional. Minimum number of digits in the integer portion.
`maxFractionDigits`	`int`	Yes	Optional. Maximum number of digits in the fractional portion.
`minFractionDigits`	`int`	Yes	Optional. Minimum number of digits in the fractional portion.
`var`	`String`	No	Optional. The name of a variable to hold the formatted value.
`scope`	`String`	No	Optional. The scope for the variable, one of `page`, `request`, `session`, or `application`. `page` is the default.

The <fmt:formatNumber> action is the companion to the <fmt:formatDate> action, so it offers similar features. The use of the value, var, and scope attributes should be familiar by now. The value can be specified as static text, a String variable, or a Number variable.

The other attributes let you specify various formatting rules. The type attribute specifies if the number should be formatted as a regular number, as currency or as a percent value. The currencyCode or currencySymbol attribute can specify the currency symbol when type is set to currency, as an ISO-4217 code (e.g., "USD") or as the actual symbol (e.g., "$"), respectively. This can be useful when you need to show prices expressed in a fixed currency, but you want the amount to be formatted according to the selected locale.

You can use the remaining attributes to adjust the default formatting rules defined by the type: groupingUsed, maxIntegerDigits, minIntegerDigits, maxFractionDigits, and minFractionDigits. The attribute names should be self-explanatory.

The pattern attribute specifies a custom pattern, the same as with the <fmt:formatDate> action. Appendix B contains a complete reference of the symbols you can use, but here are some examples for the English locale to give you an idea of what a pattern looks like when it's applied to 10000:

#,###.00	10,000.00	Two decimals, mandatory
#,###.##	10,000	Two decimals, optional
#%	1000000%	Multiplied by 100, with a percent sign

When the pattern attribute is specified, it overrides the type attribute and all the format adjustment attributes.

The first occurrence of the <fmt:formatNumber> action in Example 14-3 is used to display the total number of votes, just before the table that shows the distribution of the votes.

The table with details about the distribution comes next. Here I have used a trick with nested tables to generate a simple bar chart. I also use the <fmt:message> action described earlier in a new way:

```
...
    <table width="70%">
      <tr>
        <td width="30%">
          <fmt:message key="result1">
            <fmt:param value="${pollResult.answer1Percent}" />
            <fmt:param value="${pollResult.answer1}" />
          </fmt:message>
        </td>
        <td>
          <table
            width="<fmt:formatNumber
              value="${pollResult.answer1Percent}"/>%"
```

```
        bgcolor="lightgreen">
        <tr>
          <td> </td>
        </tr>
      </table>
    </td>
  </tr>
  ...
```

The main table contains a row with two cells for each poll answer. The first cell is just a regular cell, with the answer text, the percentage of votes with this answer, and the absolute number of votes with this answer. The value is inserted by a `<fmt:message>` action with nested `<fmt:param>` actions. This is a technique you can use when the localized message contains dynamic values—in this case, the percentage and absolute number of votes. A message of this type looks like this:

```
result1=One year {0, number, integer}% ({1, number, integer})
```

The message contains placeholders for dynamic values within curly braces. A number associates each placeholder with a `<fmt:param>` action, starting with 0 for the first one. Optionally, the value type can be specified with one or more comma-separated keywords, as in this example. Appendix B describes all options.

The next cell is also interesting. It contains a nested table, and the width of the table is set to the same percentage value as the percentage of votes with this answer. By specifying a required space (using the ` ` HTML code) as the value of the single cell and a unique background color, the result is a simple dynamic bar chart. As the percentage values of the answers change, the width of each nested table changes as well, as shown in Figure 14-3. Pretty neat!

Using a Separate Page per Locale

The JSTL I18N actions make it easy to use the same page for all locales. But as described earlier, sometimes it's better to use a separate page per locale. The poll example uses this approach for the detailed description of the question.

As shown in Example 14-1, the *poll.jsp* page uses a resource bundle with the base name `pages` to hold the name of the details page for each locale. Here's how the *pages_sv.properties* looks:

```
details_page=details_sv.jsp
```

This makes it possible to use the `<fmt:message>` action to dynamically generate a link to a separate page for each locale:

```
<a href="<fmt:message key="details_page" bundle="${pagesBundle}" />">
  <fmt:message key="question" />
</a>
```

Here, I specify the bundle for the `<fmt:message>` action explicitly since the pages bundle is not the default bundle.

All that remains is to create a page per supported locale. Example 14-4 shows the Swedish page.

Example 14-4. Swedish details page (details_sv.jsp)

```
<%@ page contentType="text/html" %>
<%@ taglib prefix="fmt" uri="http://java.sun.com/jsp/jstl/fmt" %>

<html>
  <head>
    <title>
      <fmt:message key="title" />
    </title>
  </head>
  <body bgcolor="yellow">
    <h1>
      <font color="blue">
        <fmt:message key="question" />
      </font>
    </h1>
      <font color="blue">
        Idag introduceras nya teknologier och affärsideer mycket
        snabbt. Produkter som såg ut som givna vinstbringare
        igår är idag så vanliga att det inte går att tjäna
        pengar på dem, med flera versioner tillgängliga gratis
        som Open Source. En affärsplan baserad på inkomst från
        annonser på en populär web site, eller att lägga till
        ".com" till företagsnamnet, väcker inte samma intresse
        hos investerare idag som det gjorde för bara några månader
        sedan.
        <p>
        I en industri som rör sig så här snabbt, hur lång tid
        törs du allokera till utveckling av en ny produkt eller
        tjänst, utan att riskera att den är ointressant när den
        väl är färdig?
      </font>
  </body>
</html>
```

As you can see, most of this page consists of Swedish text. The colors of the Swedish flag (yellow and blue) are also used as the background, header, and text colors. The detail pages for the other locales follow the same pattern. When the amount of text is large and other details of the page differ, like the colors in this example, it's often convenient to use a separate page for each locale instead of the one-page approach described earlier.

A Brief History of Bits

Let's shift gears a little and discuss additional issues to consider when dealing with non-Western European languages. Once upon a time, not so long ago, bits were very expensive. Hard disks for storing bits, memory for loading bits, communication equipment for sending bits over the wire; all the resources needed to handle bits were costly. To save on these expensive resources, characters were initially represented by only seven bits. This was enough to represent all letters in the English alphabet, 0 through 9, punctuation characters, and some control characters. That was all that was really needed in the early days of computing, because most computers were kept busy doing number crunching.

But as computers were given new tasks, often dealing with human-readable text, 7 bits didn't cut it. Adding one bit made it possible to represent all letters used in the Western European languages, but there are other languages besides the Western European languages, even though companies based in English-speaking countries often seem to ignore them. Eight bits is not enough to represent all characters used around the world. This problem was partly solved by defining a number of standards for how eight bits should be used to represent different character subsets. Each of the 10 ISO-8859 standards defines what is called a *charset*: a mapping between 8 bits (a byte) and a character. For instance, ISO-8859-1, also known as Latin-1, defines the subset used for Western European languages, such as English, French, Italian, Spanish, German, and Swedish. This is the default charset for HTTP. Other standards in the same series are ISO-8859-2, covering Central and Eastern European languages such as Hungarian, Polish, and Romanian, and ISO-8859-5, with Cyrillic letters used in Russian, Bulgarian, and Macedonian. You can find information about all 10 charsets in the ISO-8859 series at *http://czyborra.com/charsets/iso8859.html*.

Such languages as Chinese and Japanese contain thousands of characters but with 8 bits, you can only represent 256. A number of multibyte charsets have therefore been defined to handle these languages, such as Big5 for Chinese, Shift_JIS for Japanese, and EUC-KR for Korean.

As you can imagine, all these different standards make it hard to exchange information encoded in different ways. To simplify life, the Unicode standard was defined by the Unicode Consortium, which was founded in 1991 by companies such as Apple, IBM, Microsoft, Novell, Sun, and Xerox. Unicode uses 2 bytes (16 bits) to define unique codes for 49,194 characters in Version 3.0, covering most of the world's languages. Java uses Unicode for its internal representation of characters, and Unicode is also supported by many other technologies, such as XML and LDAP. Support for Unicode is included in all modern browsers, such as Netscape and Internet Explorer since Version 4. If you like to learn more about Unicode, visit *http://www.unicode.org/*.

What does all this mean to you as a web application developer? Well, since ISO-8859-1 is the default charset for HTTP, you don't have to worry about this at all when you work with Western European languages. But if you would like to provide content in another language, such as Japanese or Russian, you need to tell the browser which charset you're using so it can interpret and render the characters correctly. In addition, the browser must be configured with a font that can display the characters.

You find information about fonts for Netscape at *http://home.netscape.com/eng/intl/* and for Internet Explorer at *http://www.microsoft.com/ie/intlhome.htm*.

JSP is Java, so the web container uses Unicode internally, but the JSP page is typically stored using another encoding, and the response may need to be sent to the browser with different encoding still. There are two page directive attributes that can specify these charsets. The `pageEncoding` attribute specifies the charset for the bytes in the JSP page itself, so the container can translate them to Unicode when it reads the file. The `contentType` attribute can contain a charset in addition to the MIME type, as shown in Figure 14-4. This charset tells the container to convert the Unicode characters used internally to the specified charset encoding when the response is sent to the browser. It is also used to set the charset attribute in the `Content-Type` header to tell the browser how to interpret the response. If a `pageEncoding` is not specified, the charset specified by the `contentType` attribute is used to interpret the JSP page bytes as well, and vice versa if `pageEncoding` is specified but not a `contentType` charset. If a charset is not specified at all, ISO-8859-1 is used for both the page and the response.[*]

Enough theory. Figure 14-4 shows a simple JSP page that sends the text "Hello World" in Japanese to the browser. The Japanese characters are copied with permission from Jason Hunter's *Java Servlet Programming* (O'Reilly).

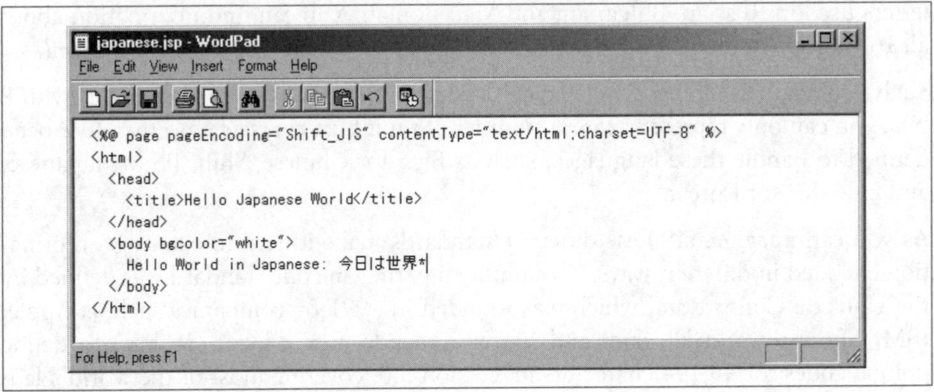
japanese.jsp - WordPad
File Edit View Insert Format Help
<%@ page pageEncoding="Shift_JIS" contentType="text/html;charset=UTF-8" %>
<html>
<head>
<title>Hello Japanese World</title>
</head>
<body bgcolor="white">
Hello World in Japanese: 今日は世界*
</body>
</html>
For Help, press F1

Figure 14-4. Japanese JSP page (japanese.jsp)

To create a file with Japanese or other non-Western European characters, you obviously need a text editor that can handle multibyte characters. The JSP page in Figure 14-4 was created with WordPad on a Windows NT system, using a Japanese font called MS Gothic and saved as a file encoded with the Shift_JIS charset. Shift_JIS is therefore the charset specified by the `pageEncoding` attribute, so the container

* For a JSP Document (a JSP page in XML format, described in Chapter 17), UTF-8 or UTF-16 is the default, as determined by the XML parser.

knows how to read the file. Another charset called UTF-8 is specified for the response by the contentType attribute, using the charset attribute. UTF-8 is an efficient charset that encodes Unicode characters as one, two, or three bytes, as needed, supported by all modern browsers (e.g., Netscape and Internet Explorer, Versions 4 or later). It can be used for any language, assuming the browser has access to a font with the language character symbols.

Note that the page directive that defines the charset for the file must appear as early as possible in the JSP page, before any characters that can only be interpreted when the charset is known. I recommend you insert it as the first line in the file to avoid problems.

Handling Localized Input

So far we have discussed how to generate pages in different languages, but most applications also need to deal with localized input. As long as you're supporting only Western European languages, the only thing you typically need to worry about is how to interpret dates and numbers. The JSTL I18N actions can help you with this as well.

Example 14-5 shows a JSP page with the same form for selecting a language as in Example 14-1, plus a form with one field for a date and another for a number.

Example 14-5. Date and number input form (input.jsp)

```
<%@ page contentType="text/html" %>
<%@ taglib prefix="c" uri="http://java.sun.com/jsp/jstl/core" %>
<%@ taglib prefix="fmt" uri="http://java.sun.com/jsp/jstl/fmt" %>

<%--
  Set the locale to the selected one, if any. Otherwise, let the
  <fmt:bundle> action pick the best one based on the Accept-Language
  header.
--%>
<c:if test="${param.language == 'en'}">
  <fmt:setLocale value="en" scope="session" />
</c:if>
<c:if test="${param.language == 'sv'}">
  <fmt:setLocale value="sv" scope="session" />
</c:if>
<c:if test="${param.language == 'de'}">
  <fmt:setLocale value="de" scope="session" />
</c:if>
<fmt:setBundle basename="input" var="inputBundle" />
<fmt:setBundle basename="input" scope="session" />
<html>
  <head>
    <title>
      <fmt:message key="title" />
    </title>
```

Example 14-5. Date and number input form (input.jsp) (continued)

```
  </head>
  <body bgcolor="white">
    <h1>
      <fmt:message key="title" />
    </h1>

    <fmt:message key="select_language" />
    <form action="input.jsp">
      <c:set var="currLang" value="${inputBundle.locale.language}" />
      <input type="radio" name="language" value="en"
        ${currLang == 'en' ? 'checked' : ''}>
        <fmt:message key="english" /><br>
      <input type="radio" name="language" value="sv"
        ${currLang == 'sv' ? 'checked' : ''}>
        <fmt:message key="swedish" /><br>
      <input type="radio" name="language" value="de"
        ${currLang == 'de' ? 'checked' : ''}>
        <fmt:message key="german" /><br>
      <p>
      <input type="submit"
        value="<fmt:message key="new_language" />">
    </form>

    <form action="process.jsp" method="post">
      <fmt:message key="date" /><br>
      <br>
      <jsp:useBean id="now" class="java.util.Date" />
      <input type="text" name="date">
      (<fmt:formatDate value="${now}" dateStyle="full" />)
      <p>
      <fmt:message key="number" /><br>
      <br>
      <input type="text" name="number">
      (<fmt:formatNumber value="1000.9" pattern="####.00"/>)
      <p>
      <input type="submit"
        value="<fmt:message key="submit" />">
    </form>
  </body>
</html>
```

The language selection part, the use of a bundle, and the `<fmt:message>` action to display localized test are exactly as in Example 14-1; if a specific language is requested, the corresponding locale is set for the session, otherwise the `<fmt:setBundle>` action figures out which one to use based on the `Accept-Language` header.

The second form in the page—with the date and number entry fields—uses the `<fmt:formatDate>` and `<fmt:formatNumber>` actions described earlier to add samples for the date and number, respectively. This helps the user to use the required format for the values. I set the `dateStyle` attribute to `full`, just to make the difference between the languages more visible. The default style is a better choice for a real application.

On to the most interesting part. Example 14-6 shows the JSP page that processes the submitted values.

Example 14-6. Processing localized input (process.jsp)

```
<%@ page contentType="text/html" %>
<%@ taglib prefix="fmt" uri="http://java.sun.com/jsp/jstl/fmt" %>

<html>
  <head>
    <title>Parsed Date and Number</title>
  </head>
  <body bgcolor="white">
    <h1>Parsed Date and Number</h1>

    Date string converted to the internal Java Date type:
    <fmt:parseDate value="${param.date}" dateStyle="full" />
    <p>
    Number string converted to the internal Java Number type:
    <fmt:parseNumber value="${param.number}" pattern="####.00" />
  </body>
</html>
```

This page reads and interprets (parses) the localized text values for the date and number sent as parameters and converts them to the appropriate Java objects that represent dates and numbers, using the `<fmt:parseDate>` and `<fmt:parseNumber>` actions described in Tables 14-11 and 14-12.

Table 14-11. Attributes for JSTL <fmt:parseDate>

Attribute name	Java type	Dynamic value accepted	Description
`value`	`String`	Yes	Mandatory, unless specified as the body. The text value to parse as a date according to the selected locale.
`pattern`	`String`	Yes	Optional. A custom pattern to use for both the date and time parts.
`type`	`String`	Yes	Optional. What the value contains. One of `time`, `date`, or `both`. Default is `date`.
`dateStyle`	`String`	Yes	Optional. The predefined pattern to use for the date part. One of `default`, `short`, `medium`, `long`, or `full`. The default is `default`.
`timeStyle`	`String`	Yes	Optional. The predefined pattern to use for the time part. One of `default`, `short`, `medium`, `long`, or `full`. The default is `default`.
`timeZone`	`String` or `java.util.TimeZone`	Yes	Optional. Time zone for the date/time.
`parseLocale`	`String` or `java.util.Locale`	Yes	Optional. The locale used to parse the value.

Table 14-11. Attributes for JSTL <fmt:parseDate> (continued)

Attribute name	Java type	Dynamic value accepted	Description
var	String	No	Optional. The name of a variable to hold the result, a java.util.Date object.
scope	String	No	Optional. The scope for the variable, one of page, request, session, or application. page is the default.

Table 14-12. Attributes for JSTL <fmt:parseNumber>

Attribute name	Java type	Dynamic value accepted	Description
value	String	Yes	Mandatory, unless specified as the body. The value to parse as a number according to the selected locale.
pattern	String	Yes	Optional. A custom pattern to use for both the date and time parts.
type	String	Yes	Optional. The number type. One of number, currency, or percentage. Default is number.
parseLocale	java.util.Locale	Yes	Optional. The locale used to parse the value.
integerOnly	boolean	Yes	Optional. true if only the integer portion should be parsed.
var	String	No	Optional. The name of a variable to hold the result, a Number.
scope	String	No	Optional. The scope for the variable, one of page, request, session, or application. page is the default.

<fmt:parseDate> and <fmt:parseNumber> complement the <fmt:formatDate> and <fmt:formatNumber> actions, and support most of the same attributes to describe the format of the value to be parsed. Note that the parsing actions in Example 14-6 specify the same text format as the formatting actions that generate the samples in the form: dateStyle is set to full and pattern to ####.00. This allows the parsing actions to handle text values in the prescribed format for the locale selected and saved in the session by the I18N actions in the *input.jsp* page.

In this example, the parsed values are simply added to the response in their default format to prove that the parsing works no matter which language you select. In a real application, the parsed values can be used as input to another action that requires a java.util.Date or Number object instead of a text value representing a date or a number, for instance the database actions:

```
<fmt:parseDate value="${param.date}" dateStyle="full"
  var="parsedDate" />
<fmt:parseNumber value="${param.number}" pattern="####.00"
```

```
    var="parsedNumber" />

  <sql:update>
    INSERT INTO MyTable (DateCol, NumberCol) VALUES(?, ?)
    <sql:dateParam value="${parsedDate}" />
    <sql:param value="${parsedNumber}" />
  </sql:update>
```

Both parsing actions throw exceptions if the specified value cannot be interpreted as a number or a date. You can embed the actions in the body of a `<c:catch>` action element, as shown in Chapter 12, to deal with invalid values.

Dealing with Non-Western European Input

An HTML form can be used for input in languages other than Western European, but the charset discussed earlier comes into play here as well. First of all, when you create a page with a form for entering non-Western European characters, you must tell the browser which charset should be used for the user input. One way to give the browser this information is to hardcode a charset name as part of the `contentType` attribute of the `page` directive, as in Figure 14-4:

```
<%@ page pageEncoding="Shift_JIS"
  contentType="text/html;charset=UTF-8" %>
```

The user can then enter values with the characters of the corresponding language (e.g., Japanese symbols).

But there's something else to be aware of here. When the user submits the form, the browser first converts the form-field values to the corresponding byte values for the specified charset. It then encodes the resulting bytes according to the HTTP standard URL encoding scheme, the same way special characters such as space and semicolon are converted when an ISO-8859-1 encoding is used. The bytes for all characters other than ISO-8859-1 a–z, A–Z, and 0–9, are encoded as the byte value in hexadecimal format, preceded by a percent sign. For instance, the symbols for "Hello World" in Japanese are sent like the following if the charset for the form is set to UTF-8:

```
%E4%BB%8A%E6%97%A5%E3%81%AF%E4%B8%96%E7%95%8C
```

This code represents the URL-encoded UTF-8 byte codes for the five Japanese symbols (three bytes for each symbol). In order to process this information, the container must know which charset the browser used to encode it. The problem is that even though the HTTP specification says that the charset name must be sent in the `Content-Type` request header, most browsers don't. It's therefore up to you to keep track of this and tell the container which charset to use to decode the parameter values. If a fixed charset is used (e.g., always UTF-8, as in this example), you can use the `<fmt:requestEncoding>` (see Table 14-13) like this in the page that processes the input:

```
<fmt:requestEncoding value="UTF-8" />
```

This action tells the container which charset to use, so parameter values accessed after the action element are decoded correctly. Note that you must insert this action before any actions that access request parameters; the container may decode all parameters in one shot, so it must be told which charset to use before the first parameter is used.

Table 14-13. Attributes for JSTL <fmt:requestEncoding>

Attribute name	Java type	Dynamic value accepted	Description
value	String	Yes	Optional. The charset to use when decoding parameters. Default is the charset saved by another JSTL I18N action as a session variable.

As long as you need to deal with only one non-Western European language, this is not so hard. But what if you need to handle input in multiple non-Western European languages, picked at runtime in the same fashion as in the previous examples for Western European languages, with each language using a different charset? Luckily, the JSTL I18N actions make this a lot easier than it sounds. Example 14-7 shows a JSP page with a form for entering a date and a text value in Japanese, Russian, or Greek.

Example 14-7. Non-Western European input page (input_nw.jsp)

```
<%@ page contentType="text/html" %>
<%@ taglib prefix="c" uri="http://java.sun.com/jsp/jstl/core" %>
<%@ taglib prefix="fmt" uri="http://java.sun.com/jsp/jstl/fmt" %>

<c:set var="lang" value="${param.language}" />
<c:choose>
  <c:when test="${lang == 'el'}">
    <fmt:setLocale value="el" scope="session" />
  </c:when>
  <c:when test="${lang == 'ru'}">
    <fmt:setLocale value="ru" scope="session" />
  </c:when>
  <c:otherwise>
    <fmt:setLocale value="ja" scope="session" />
    <c:set var="lang" value="ja" />
  </c:otherwise>
</c:choose>
<fmt:setBundle basename="dummy" scope="session" />
<html>
  <head>
    <title>
      Non-Western European Input Test
    </title>
  </head>
  <body bgcolor="white">
    <h1>
```

Example 14-7. Non-Western European input page (input_nw.jsp) (continued)

```
      Non-Western European Input Test
    </h1>

    <form action="input_nw.jsp">
      <input type="radio" name="language" value="ja"
        ${lang == 'ja' ? 'checked' : ''}>
        Japanese<br>
      <input type="radio" name="language" value="el"
        ${lang == 'el' ? 'checked' : ''}>
        Greek<br>
      <input type="radio" name="language" value="ru"
        ${lang == 'ru' ? 'checked' : ''}>
        Russian<br>
      <p>
      <input type="submit"
        value="New Language">
    </form>

    <form action="process_nw.jsp" method="post">
      Enter a date:<br>
      <jsp:useBean id="now" class="java.util.Date" />
      <input type="text" name="date">
      (<fmt:formatDate value="${now}" dateStyle="full" />)
      <p>
      Enter some text:<br>
      <input type="text" name="text">
      <p>
      <input type="submit" value="Send" >
    </form>
  </body>
</html>
```

This page looks similar to the one used for Western European input in Example 14-5. Besides the set of supported languages, and that English is used for all descriptive text (because I don't know the other languages) the main difference is that Japanese is selected if no language is requested or the requested one is not supported, instead of letting a `<fmt:setBundle>` action pick a language based on the `Accept-Language` header. The reason for this is that you can define only one fallback locale for an application, and I already defined it as the English locale for the previous examples in this chapter. If that was not the case, I could have used exactly the same approach here and defined the Japanese locale as the fallback locale. Even so, I still use a `<fmt:setBundle>` action in this page, with a dummy base name. This is just a hack to overwrite the default localization context. Without it, the JSTL formatting and parsing actions pick up the locale from the default localization context set for the session by the other examples. The final difference is that the data entry form now contains a field for a text value instead of a field for a numeric value, just to show you how to deal with pure text in non-Western European languages. Everything else is the same, and this similarity between the two examples illustrates the beauty of the JSTL I18N actions; they hide a lot of the details you otherwise have to take care of yourself.

One detail you have to deal with when you support input in non-Western European languages is the setting of the charset for the form page. Note that no charset is specified as part of the `contentType` attribute. The charset is instead set automatically by the first JSTL I18N action that sets the locale for the page. In Example 14-7, it's done by the `<fmt:setLocale>` action, but all JSTL I18N actions that select a locale based on the `Accept-Language` header, such as `<fmt:setBundle>`, do the same. In addition to setting the charset for the response generated by the page, these actions also save the selected charset as a session scope variable named `javax.servlet.jsp.jstl.i18n.request.charset`. You'll soon see why this is important.

Example 14-8 shows the *process_nw.jsp* page, the page that processes the input.

Example 14-8. Processing non-Western European input (process_nw.jsp)

```
<%@ page contentType="text/html;charset=UTF-8" %>
<%@ taglib prefix="c" uri="http://java.sun.com/jsp/jstl/core" %>
<%@ taglib prefix="fmt" uri="http://java.sun.com/jsp/jstl/fmt" %>
<%@ taglib prefix="fn" uri="http://java.sun.com/jsp/jstl/functions" %>

<fmt:requestEncoding />
<html>
  <head>
    <title>Processing Non-Western European Input</title>
  </head>
  <body bgcolor="white">
    <h1>Processing Non-Western European Input</h1>

    Text string converted to a Java Unicode string:
    ${fn:escapeXml(param.text)}
    <p>
    Date string converted to the internal Java Date type:
    <fmt:parseDate value="${param.date}" dateStyle="full" />
  </body>
</html>
```

The good news is that the most interesting difference between this page and the one for processing Western language input in Example 14-6 is the `<fmt:requestEncoding>` action at the beginning of the page. This action sets the charset used to read the request parameters, as described earlier. Note that I don't specify a specific charset using the `value` attribute. In this case, the action first looks for a `Content-Type` header (in case browsers one day actually comply with the HTTP specification) and then for the charset saved by a JSTL I18N action in the variable `javax.servlet.jsp.jstl.i18n.request.charset`. After setting the request encoding, all parameter values accessed through the EL expressions are converted to Unicode. The page directive `contentType` for the *process_nw.jsp* page specifies the UTF-8 charset for the response, so that all languages can be displayed correctly.

To recap, the full round-trip goes like this. The charset for the page with the form is set dynamically based on the selected language by the I18N actions. When the form is submitted, the request parameters are passed to the target page, encoded with the charset used for the page with the form. They get decoded to Unicode by the EL expressions based on the encoding set by the `<fmt:requestEncoding>` action, and then encoded as UTF-8 in the response due to the `contentType` attribute value.

That's all there's to it. There are a couple of things you should be aware of, though. First of all, the I18N JSTL actions can set the charset for the response only as long as no part of the response has been sent to the browser (this is true for all response headers). By default, JSP pages are buffered using a large enough buffer for this to be rarely a problem, but if it doesn't work for your own pages, try extending the buffer size as described in Chapter 16. Another issue is that this functionality is based on the assumption that all containers deal with the charset setting in the same way. Unfortunately, the JSP 1.2 and Servlet 2.3 specs were vague about these details, for instance, whether a charset defined by the `contentType` attribute has precedent over a charset defined dynamically by an action. A specification errata (clarification) was issued to correct this, but some JSP 1.2 containers may still not behave as expected. The JSP 2.0 and Servlet 2.4 specifications include clarifications of these details as well, so with a web container compliant with these specification versions, you shouldn't have a problem.

When all goes as planned, the result of processing Greek input looks like Figure 14-5.

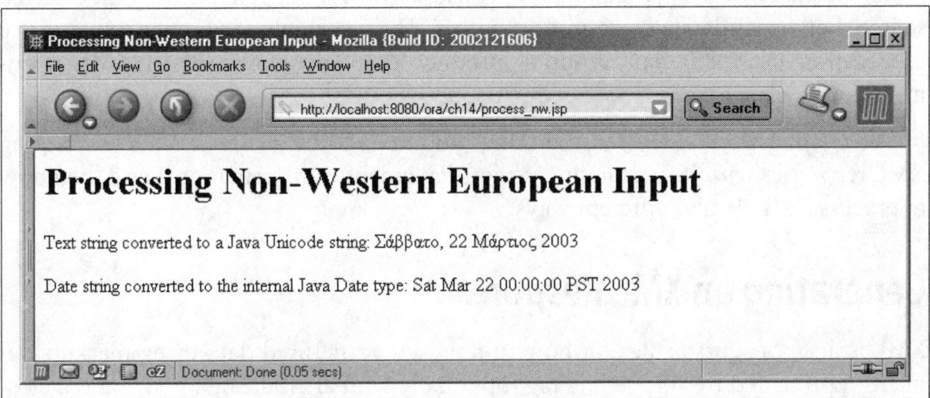

Figure 14-5. Processed Greek input

As with the Western European input example, the decoded request parameter values are just added to the response. In a real-world application you can do anything you like with the values, such as storing them in a database.

CHAPTER 15

Working with XML Data

There's no escape from Extensible Markup Language (XML) these days. It's everywhere: in configuration files, messages between servers, web pages, even databases. Wherever there's structured data, XML is often found close by.

As I mentioned earlier, JSP pages can generate any type of text, including XML. In the simplest case, the JSP page includes static XML elements as template text and a few actions to add the dynamic data, similar to the HTML examples in previous chapters. A more sophisticated page gets raw XML data from somewhere and transforms it to different XML formats depending on the type of browser making the request.

More and more, web applications also consume XML data generated by an external source, perhaps a database or another server. Such an application may extract price information from different vendors' product catalogs, published as XML documents, and create a side-by-side comparison.

In this chapter we first look at the things you need to be aware of when generating XML responses with JSP, including device-dependent transformations, and then how to process XML data in different ways.

Generating an XML Response

XML is a set of syntax rules for how to represent structured data using markup elements represented by an opening tag (optionally with attributes), a body, and a closing tag:

```
<employee id="123">
  <first-name>Hans</first-name>
  <last-name>Bergsten</last-name>
  <telephone>310-555-1212</telephone>
</employee>
```

This XML example contains four elements: `<employee>`, `<first-name>`, `<last-name>`, and `<telephone>`.

By selecting sensible element names, an XML file may be understandable to a human, but to make sense to a program, it must use only a restricted set of elements in which each element has a well-defined meaning. This is known as an *XML application* (the XML syntax applied to a certain application domain). A couple of examples are the Wireless Markup Language (WML) used for browsers in cellular phones and other small devices, and XHTML, which is HTML 4.0 reformulated as an XML application. Another example is the web application deployment descriptor, used to configure various aspects of a standard Java web application, as you have seen in the previous chapters.

As I mentioned in Chapters 3 and 5, everything in a JSP page that is not a JSP element is template text. In all examples so far, I have used HTML as the template text, but it can be any markup, for instance XHTML or WML XML elements. Example 15-1 shows a JSP page that sends a simple phone book to a wireless device, using the XML elements defined by the WML specification as the template text.

Example 15-1. WML phone book JSP page (phone_wml.jsp)

```
<?xml version="1.0"?>
<!DOCTYPE wml PUBLIC "-//WAPFORUM//DTD WML 1.1//EN"
  "http://www.wapforum.org/DTD/wml_1.1.xml">
<%@ page contentType="text/vnd.wap.wml" %>
<wml>
  <card id="list" newcontext="true">
    <p>Phone List</p>
    <p>
      <anchor>Bergsten, Hans
        <go href="#Bergsten_Hans"/>
      </anchor>
      <br/>
      <anchor>Eckstein, Bob
        <go href="#Eckstein_Bob"/>
      </anchor>
      <br/>
      <anchor>Ferguson, Paula
        <go href="#Ferguson_Paula"/>
      </anchor>
    </p>
  </card>

  <card id="Bergsten_Hans">
    <p>Bergsten, Hans</p>
    <p>
      Phone: 310-555-1212
      <do type="prev" label="Back">
        <prev/>
      </do>
    </p>
  </card>
  <card id="Eckstein_Bob">
    <p>Eckstein, Bob</p>
```

Example 15-1. WML phone book JSP page (phone_wml.jsp) (continued)

```
    <p>
      Phone: 800-555-5678
      <do type="prev" label="Back">
        <prev/>
      </do>
    </p>
  </card>
  <card id="Ferguson_Paula">
    <p>Ferguson, Paula</p>
    <p>
      Phone: 213-555-1234
      <do type="prev" label="Back">
        <prev/>
      </do>
    </p>
  </card>
</wml>
```

A discussion of the WML elements is outside the scope of this book, but let's look at some important details of the JSP page. The first line in Example 15-1 is an *XML declaration*, telling which version of XML the document conforms to. Some WML browsers are very picky about this being the first thing in an XML document, and even whitespaces—regular spaces, linefeed characters, and tab characters—before the declaration can throw them off. In all examples you have seen so far, the JSP page directive has been on the first line. Here, I have moved it down so that the linefeed character that ends the directive line doesn't cause any problems.

The second and third lines in Example 15-1 contain an XML *document type declaration*. This identifies the so-called Document Type Definition (DTD) for the document, basically the definition of all XML elements a conforming document of this type can contain. Here, it's the DTD for the WML 1.1 elements.

The JSP page directive on the fourth line is important. The content type for a JSP page is `text/html` by default. For a WML document, you must instead specify the content type `text/vnd.wap.wml`. Otherwise the WML browser doesn't accept the document.

The rest of the page in Example 15-1 is just static WML code. To run this example, you need a WML browser. I've used the WML browser included in the Openwave Systems Inc. SDK 4.1, available at *http://developer.openwave.com/resources/sdk.html*, to test the examples in this chapter. Figure 15-1 shows what the phone-list menu card and one details card look like in this WML browser.

Transforming XML into HTML

You may also have heard about the Extensible Stylesheet Language (XSL). XSL defines one set of XML elements to transform an XML document into some other type of document, and another set of elements to produce a formatted version of an

Figure 15-1. Phone list in WML browser (UP.SDK image courtesy of Openwave Systems Inc.)

XML document suitable for display. Browsers and other programs that need to render an XML document with different styles for different elements, such as a bold large font for a header and a regular font for paragraph text, use the formatting part of XSL. The transformation part of XSL is referred to as XSLT. XSLT can turn a source XML document, such as a document representing an order, into different forms using different stylesheets. This is useful in business-to-business (B2B) applications, where different partners often require the same information in slightly different formats. You can read more about XSL and XSLT at *http://www.w3.org/TR/xsl/*.

In a web application, XSLT can transform structured XML data into HTML. Example 15-2 shows an example of a JSP page in which the same phone book information used in Example 15-1 is transformed into an HTML table.

Example 15-2. Transforming XML to HTML (phone_html.jsp)

```
<%@ page contentType="text/html" %>
<%@ taglib prefix="c" uri="http://java.sun.com/jsp/jstl/core" %>
<%@ taglib prefix="x" uri="http://java.sun.com/jsp/jstl/xml" %>
<html>
  <head>
    <title>Phone List</title>
  </head>
  <body bgcolor="white">

    <c:import url="htmltable.xsl" var="stylesheet" />
    <x:transform xslt="${stylesheet}">
```

Example 15-2. Transforming XML to HTML (phone_html.jsp) (continued)

```
      <?xml version="1.0" encoding="ISO-8859-1"?>
      <employees>
        <employee id="123">
          <first-name>Hans</first-name>
          <last-name>Bergsten</last-name>
          <telephone>310-555-1212</telephone>
        </employee>
        <employee id="456">
          <first-name>Bob</first-name>
          <last-name>Eckstein</last-name>
          <telephone>800-555-5678</telephone>
        </employee>
        <employee id="789">
          <first-name>Paula</first-name>
          <last-name>Ferguson</last-name>
          <telephone>213-555-1234</telephone>
        </employee>
      </employees>
    </x:transform>

  </body>
</html>
```

At the top of the page, the `taglib` directive for the JSTL XML library is included, along with the directive for the JSTL core library used in previous chapters.

To transform the XML data, you first need to get hold of the XSLT stylesheet. The JSTL `<c:import>` action, described in Table 15-1, loads the stylesheet from the file specified by the `url` attribute and saves it in the variable named by the `var` attribute.

Table 15-1. Attributes for JSTL <c:import>

Attribute name	Java type	Dynamic value accepted	Description
`url`	`String`	Yes	Mandatory. A page- or context-relative path, or an absolute URL.
`context`	`String`	Yes	Optional. The context path for another application.
`charEncoding`	`String`	Yes	Optional. The character encoding for the imported content. Default is the encoding specified by the protocol used for the import or ISO-8859-1 if no encoding is found.
`var`	`String`	No	Optional. The name of the variable to hold the result as a `String`.
`scope`	`String`	No	Optional. The scope for the variable, one of `page`, `request`, `session`, or `application`. `page` is the default.
`varReader`	`String`	No	Optional. The name of the variable to expose the result as a `Reader` to the body.

The <c:import> action is very versatile. You can use it to import data from resources in the same application, another application on the same server (identified by the context attribute), and even from an external server by specifying an absolute URL for any protocol supported by the web container, such as HTTP, HTTPS, or FTP. Parameters can be defined either in the URL as a query string or using nested <c:param> actions. The imported data can be saved as a String in any scope, or exposed as a java.io.Reader to actions within the element's body. Using a Reader is slightly more efficient, because the <c:import> action doesn't have to read the input in this case; it just wraps a Reader around the input stream that a nested action then reads directly. I'll show you an example of this later. When you import a resource (such as a JSP page) that belongs to the same application, the target resource has access to all request parameters and variables in the request scope, the same way as when you use the <jsp:forward> action (Chapter 10).

The transformation is performed by a JSTL action named <x:transform>, described in Table 15-2.

Table 15-2. Attributes for JSTL <x:transform>

Attribute name	Java type	Dynamic value accepted	Description
doc	String, java.io.Reader, javax.xml.transform.Source, org.w3c.dom.Document, or the types exposed by <x:parse> and <x:set>	Yes	Mandatory, unless specified as the body. The XML document to transform.
xslt	String, java.io.Reader, javax.xml.transform.Source	Yes	Mandatory. The XSLT stylesheet.
docSystemId	String	Yes	Optional. The system identifier for the XML document.
xsltSystemId	String	Yes	Optional. The system identifier for the XSLT stylesheet.
result	javax.xml.transform.Result	Yes	Optional. A Result object used to capture or process the transformation result.
var	String	No	Optional. The name of the variable to hold the result as a org.w3c.dom.Document.
scope	String	No	Optional. The scope for the variable; one of page, request, session, or application. page is the default.

The XML document to transform can be specified as the body, as in Example 15-2, or as a variable through the doc attribute. The example XML document contains elements representing information about employees. The xsl attribute is set to the XSL stylesheet imported by the <c:import> action. It contains XSLT elements for transforming the XML document into an HTML table. In Example 15-2, both the var and the result attributes are omitted, so the <x:transform> action adds its result to the response. This is the most common use, but the var and result attributes can be used if the transformation result needs to be captured and processed further.

Descriptions of all the XSLT elements would fill a book all by itself, but Example 15-3 shows the stylesheet used here to give you an idea of how XSLT looks.

Example 15-3. XSL stylesheet that generates an HTML table (htmltable.xsl)

```
<?xml version="1.0"?>
<xsl:stylesheet version="1.0"
  xmlns:xsl="http://www.w3.org/1999/XSL/Transform">

  <xsl:template match="employees">
    <table border="1" width="100%">
      <tr>
        <th>ID</th>
        <th>Employee Name</th>
        <th>Phone Number</th>
      </tr>
      <xsl:for-each select="employee">
        <tr>
          <td>
            <xsl:value-of select="@id"/>
          </td>
          <td>
            <xsl:value-of select="last-name"/>,
            <xsl:value-of select="first-name"/>
          </td>
          <td>
            <xsl:value-of select="telephone"/>
          </td>
        </tr>
      </xsl:for-each>
    </table>
  </xsl:template>

</xsl:stylesheet>
```

The XSLT elements are similar to JSP action elements in that they perform some action rather than identify information types. The XSLT elements select and process pieces of the source XML document. Here, the <xsl:template> element selects the top <employees> element in the source XML document, the <xsl:for-each> element loops over all nested <employee> elements, and the <xsl:value-of> elements extract the attribute values and nested elements for each <employee> element. The non-XSLT elements are used as template data, the same way as in JSP. You get the idea.

An XSLT stylesheet can use parameters to represent dynamic data, provided to the XSLT processor when a document is transformed:

```
<?xml version="1.0"?>
<xsl:stylesheet version="1.0"
  xmlns:xsl="http://www.w3.org/1999/XSL/Transform">

  <xsl:param name="empName" />

  <xsl:template match="employees/employee[name = $empName]">
  ...
```

The parameter in this example limits the `<employee>` elements to be processed to those that have a `<name>` element with the value specified by the parameter.

To pass the parameter value to the XSLT stylesheet, you must use a nested `<x:param>` action in the `<x:transform>` body:

```
<x:transform xslt="${stylesheet}">
  <x:param name="empName" value="${param:empName}" />
  <?xml version="1.0" encoding="ISO-8859-1"?>
  <employees>
    <employee id="123">
      <first-name>Hans</first-name>
      <last-name>Bergsten</last-name>
      <telephone>310-555-1212</telephone>
    </employee>
    ...
</x:transform>
```

Here I pass on a request parameter value to the stylesheet, but you can, of course, use any EL expression as the value.

XML documents, including XSLT stylesheets, can contain references to external entities, for instance in the XSL `<xsl:include>` and `<xsl:import>` elements. If these references are written as relative paths in the document, a base URI must be used to establish what they are relative to. You can pass base URIs for the XSLT stylesheet and the XML source to the `<x:transform>` action through the `xsltSystemId` and the `docSystemId` attributes. The value can be any valid URI, such as an absolute file or HTTP URL or a context- or page-relative path.

Transforming XML into a Device-Dependent Format

A web application can use XSLT to respond with different content depending on the type of device making the request. Example 15-4 shows a page that serves both HTML and WML browsers by applying different stylesheets to the same XML document, transforming it to the appropriate markup for the browser that requests it.

Example 15-4. XSL stylesheet that generates HTML or WML (phone.jsp)

```
<%@ taglib prefix="c" uri="http://java.sun.com/jsp/jstl/core"
%><%@ taglib prefix="x" uri="http://java.sun.com/jsp/jstl/xml"
```

Example 15-4. XSL stylesheet that generates HTML or WML (phone.jsp) (continued)

```
%><%@ taglib prefix="fn" uri="http://java.sun.com/jsp/jstl/functions"
%><%@ taglib prefix="ora" uri="orataglib"
%><c:choose><c:when
test="${fn:contains(header.Accept, 'text/vnd.wap.wml')}"
><ora:setHeader name="Content-Type" value="text/vnd.wap.wml"
/><c:import url="wml.xsl" var="stylesheet"
/></c:when><c:otherwise><ora:setHeader name="Content-Type" value="text/html"
/><c:import url="html.xsl" var="stylesheet"
/></c:otherwise></c:choose><x:transform xslt="${stylesheet}">
  <?xml version="1.0" encoding="ISO-8859-1"?>
  <employees>
    <employee id="123">
      <first-name>Hans</first-name>
      <last-name>Bergsten</last-name>
      <telephone>310-555-1212</telephone>
    </employee>
    <employee id="456">
      <first-name>Bob</first-name>
      <last-name>Eckstein</last-name>
      <telephone>800-555-5678</telephone>
    </employee>
    <employee id="789">
      <first-name>Paula</first-name>
      <last-name>Ferguson</last-name>
      <telephone>213-555-1234</telephone>
    </employee>
  </employees>
</x:transform>
```

There are a number of things to note here. First, see how messy the page looks. That's because the start tag for all JSP directives and actions in this page are written on the same line as the end tag for the preceding element, to make sure that no extra linefeeds are added to the response. As described earlier, leading whitespace (such as linefeed characters) in a WML page can cause a WML browser to reject the page.

Because the page can serve both HTML and WML content, the page directive's `contentType` attribute cannot be used to set the content type. Instead, the content type needs to be set dynamically. This page uses a JSTL function and a custom action to handle this. The JSTL `fn:contains( )` function checks if the HTTP `Accept` header contains the content type for WML. This piece of information is used to decide which type of content to return. If the browser accepts WML, the `<ora:setHeader>` custom action sets the `Content-Type` header dynamically to `text/vnd.wap.wml`, otherwise to `text/html`. The `<c:import>` actions import the appropriate stylesheet, *wml.xsl* or *html.xsl*, based on the device type making the request, and the `<x:transform>` action finally transforms the XML document accordingly.

For a simple example like this, letting an XSLT stylesheet transform the XML source into a complete web page works fine. However, on most real web sites, the HTML version of the site differs significantly from the WML version. You want to provide a rich interface for HTML browsers with a nice layout, navigation bars, images, colors, and fonts, and typically as much content as you can fit on each page. A WML browser, on the other hand, has a very small screen with limited layout, font, and graphics capabilities. Developing an efficient interface for this type of device is very different. A more practical approach for combining XML, XSLT, and JSP to serve different types of browsers is to keep the actual content (articles, product information, phone lists, etc.) in a device-independent XML format, but use separate JSP pages for each device type. The JSP pages can then use the `<x:transform>` action to transform the key content and merge it with the device-dependent template text to form a complete page suitable for each specific device type, like in Example 15-1.

Processing XML Data

XSLT is great for transforming an XML source into another format, but sometimes you need to process the XML data in other ways. For instance, you may want to use part of the XML data in a database query to get additional information and compose a response that merges the two data sources, or reformat date and numeric information in the XML source according to the user's preferred locale. To process XML data in this way, the JSTL XML library includes a number of actions for picking out pieces of an XML document, as well as iteration and conditional actions similar to the ones in the core library, but adapted to work specifically with XML data.

In this section, we look at an example that uses most of the JSTL XML actions. The XML data comes from the O'Reilly Meerkat news feed. Meerkat scans a large set of Rich Site Summary (RSS)—an XML application suitable for news, product announcements, and similar content—sources frequently and makes the aggregated data available in a number of formats, including a superset of the RSS format that includes category, source, and date information for each story. You can learn more about Meerkat and how to use it at *http://www.oreillynet.com/pub/a/rss/2000/05/09/meerkat_api.html*. Example 15-5 shows a sample of the XML data that Meerkat can deliver.

Example 15-5. Meerkat XML news feed format

```
<?xml version="1.0"?>
<!DOCTYPE meerkat_xml_flavour
  SYSTEM "http://meerkat.oreillynet.com/dtd/meerkat_xml_flavour.dtd">

<meerkat>

  <title>Meerkat: An Open Wire Service</title>
  <link>http://meerkat.oreillynet.com</link>
  <description>
    Meerkat is a Web-based syndicated content reader providing
    a simple interface to RSS stories.  While maintaining the original
    association of a story with a channel, Meerkat's focus is on
    chronological order -- the latest stories float to the top,
```

Example 15-5. Meerkat XML news feed format (continued)

```
    regardless of their source.
  </description>
  <language>en-us</language>

  <image>
    <title>Meerkat Powered!</title>
    <url>http://meerkat.oreillynet.com/icons/meerkat-powered.jpg</url>
    <link>http://meerkat.oreillynet.com</link>
    <width>88</width>
    <height>31</height>
    <description>
      Visit Meerkat in full splendor at meerkat.oreillynet.com
    </description>
  </image>

  <story id="881051">
    <title>
      Clay Shirky: What Web Services Got Right ... and Wrong
    </title>
    <link>
      http://www.oreillynet.com/pub/a/network/2002/04/22/clay.html
    </link>
    <description>
      Web Services represent not just a new way to build Internet
      applications, says Clay Shirky in this interview, but the second
      stage of peer-to-peer, in which distinctions between clients and
      servers are all but eliminated.
    </description>
    <category>General</category>
    <channel>O'Reilly Network</channel>
    <timestamp>2002-04-23 17:02:50</timestamp>
  </story>
  ...
</meerkat>
```

The example application processes this XML data in a number of ways. First, it extracts some information about the Meerkat service itself and adds it to the page, so the user can see where the data comes from. It then gets all <category> elements and builds a list of unique category names. This list is used to build an HTML select list, from which the user can pick one category to filter the data. The XML data is then filtered accordingly, and an HTML table with matching stories is generated. Just for fun and to illustrate the use of the conditional XML actions, all stories in the General category are displayed against a light green background. The result is shown in Figure 15-2.

Example 15-6 shows the JSP page that does all the processing.

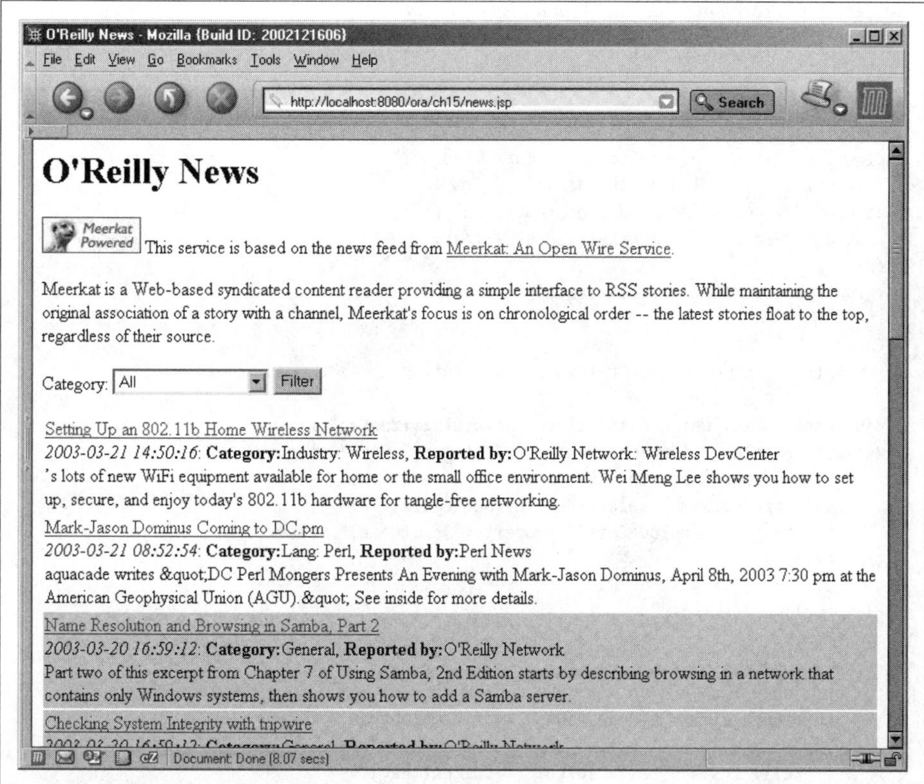

Figure 15-2. The XML-base news service application

Example 15-6. Processing XML data (news.jsp)

```
<%@ page contentType="text/html" %>
<%@ taglib prefix="c" uri="http://java.sun.com/jsp/jstl/core" %>
<%@ taglib prefix="x" uri="http://java.sun.com/jsp/jstl/xml" %>

<%--
  Get new XML data if the cached version is older than
  1 hour.
--%>
<c:set var="cachePeriod" value="${60 * 60 * 1000}" />
<jsp:useBean id="now" class="java.util.Date" />
<c:if test="${(now.time - cacheTime) > cachePeriod}">
  <c:import url="http://meerkat.oreillynet.com/?&p=4999&_fl=xml&t=ALL"
    varReader="xmlSource">
    <x:parse var="doc" doc="${xmlSource}" scope="application" />
  </c:import>
  <c:set var="cacheTime" value="${now.time}" scope="application" />
</c:if>

<html>
  <head>
```

Example 15-6. Processing XML data (news.jsp) (continued)

```
    <title>O'Reilly News</title>
  </head>
  <body bgcolor="white">
    <h1>O'Reilly News</h1>
    <img src="<x:out select="$doc/meerkat/image/url" />">
    This service is based on the news feed from
    <a href="<x:out select="$doc/meerkat/link" />">
      <x:out select="$doc/meerkat/title" /></a>.
    <p>
    <x:out select="$doc/meerkat/description" />

    <%--
      Create a list of unique categories present in the XML feed
    --%>
    <jsp:useBean id="uniqueCats" class="java.util.TreeMap" />
    <x:forEach select="$doc/meerkat/story/category" var="category">
      <%-- Need to convert the XPath node to a Java String --%>
      <x:set var="catName" select="string($category)" />
      <c:set target="${uniqueCats}" property="${catName}" value="" />
    </x:forEach>

    <form action="news.jsp">
      Category:
      <select name="selCat">
        <option value="ALL">All
        <c:forEach items="${uniqueCats}" var="current">
          <option value="<c:out value="${current.key}" />"
            <c:if test="${param.selCat == current.key}">
              selected
            </c:if>>
            <c:out value="${current.key}" />
          </option>
        </c:forEach>
      </select>
      <input type="submit" value="Filter">
    </form>

    <%-- Filter the parsed document based on the selection --%>
    <c:choose>
      <c:when test="${empty param.selCat || param.selCat == 'ALL'}">
        <x:set var="stories" select="$doc//story" />
      </c:when>
      <c:otherwise>
        <x:set var="stories"
          select="$doc//story[category = $param:selCat]" />
      </c:otherwise>
    </c:choose>

    <%-- Generate a table with data for the selection --%>
    <table>
      <x:forEach select="$stories">
        <tr>
```

Example 15-6. Processing XML data (news.jsp) (continued)

```
          <x:choose>
            <x:when select="category[. = 'General']">
              <td bgcolor="lightgreen">
            </x:when>
            <x:otherwise>
              <td>
            </x:otherwise>
          </x:choose>
            <a href="<x:out select="link" />">
              <x:out select="title" /></a>
            <br>
            <i><x:out select="timestamp" /></i>:
            <b>Category:</b><x:out select="category" />,
            <b>Reported by:</b><x:out select="channel" />
            <br><x:out select="description" />
          </td>
        </tr>
      </x:forEach>
    </table>
  </body>
</html>
```

At the top of the page, the XML source is retrieved from the Meerkat server using the same `<c:import>` action used in the previous examples. There are two noteworthy differences, though: the `url` attribute specifies an absolute URL and the imported data is exposed as a `Reader` instead of as a `String`. I mentioned both these features earlier. In this example, using a `Reader` is appropriate because the data may be large, and it's only of interest to the nested `<x:parse>` action.

Caching Data

Before we look at the `<x:parse>` action in detail, I'd like to say a few words about the caching technique used in this example. The Meerkat data is updated only on an hourly basis, so it's pointless to ask for it more frequently. It's also expensive in terms of time and computing resources to import and parse the XML data. By caching the parsed data for an hour, the web application gets more responsive and avoids putting load on the Meerkat server unnecessarily.

The caching technique used here simply creates a timestamp for the data in the form of a `java.util.Date` object and saves it together with the data itself in the application scope, using standard and JSTL core actions. When a new request is received, it's tested to see if the cache is older than the predefined cache period (one hour in this example). If it is, a fresh copy is imported, parsed, and saved in the application scope again, along with the timestamp. Otherwise the cached data is used. You can use this technique for any type of processing that's expensive, for instance retrieving data from a database or performing complex calculations.

Parsing XML Data

Before you can access the XML data with the JSTL XML actions, the imported document must be parsed and converted to a data structure the actions can read. That's what the `<x:parse>` action does (see Table 15-3).

Table 15-3. Attributes for JSTL <x:parse>

Attribute name	Java type	Dynamic value accepted	Description
`doc`	`String` or `java.io.Reader`	Yes	Mandatory, unless specified as the body. The XML document to parse.
`systemId`	`String`	Yes	Optional. The system identifier for the XML document.
`filter`	`org.xml.sax.XMLFilter`	Yes	Optional. An `XMLFilter` to be applied to the XML document.
`var`	`String`	No	Optional. The name of the variable to hold the result as an implementation-dependent type.
`scope`	`String`	No	Optional. The scope for the variable, one of `page`, `request`, `session`, or `application`. `page` is the default.
`varDom`	`String`	No	Optional. The name of the variable to hold the result as a `org.w3c.dom.Document`.
`scopeDom`	`String`	No	Optional. The scope for the DOM variable, one of `page`, `request`, `session`, or `application`. `page` is the default.

The XML document to parse can be specified as the body or as a `String` or `Reader` variable. In Example 15-3, I use the `Reader` exposed by the `<c:import>` action to get the best performance. A base URI for interpretation of relative URIs in the document can be specified by the `systemId` attribute, the same way as for the `<x:transform>` action.

The parse result can be saved either as an implementation-dependent data structure (named by the `var` attribute) or as a standard `org.w3c.dom.Document` object (named by the `varDom` attribute), in any scope. You should use the latter only if you need to process the parse result with a custom action or other custom code because the implementation-dependent type is typically optimized in terms of memory use and ease of access, and it's supported by all the other JSTL XML actions that use a parse result. The implementation-dependent data structure is saved as an application scope variable in Example 15-3, where it's picked up by the other XML actions in the page.

If the XML document is large and you're only interested in a very small part of it, you can provide an implementation of the `org.xml.sax.XMLFilter` interface to the action, typically created and configured by a servlet, a filter, or a listener (the filter and listener component types are described in Chapter 19). As the name implies, an

`XMLFilter` can remove the parts you don't need, making the parsing process more efficient. For more about XML filters, I suggest you look at the documentation of the interface or read a book about Java and XML, such as Brett McLaughlin's *Java and XML* (O'Reilly).

Accessing XML Data Using XPath Expressions

With the parsing out of the way, we can turn to how to access parts of the XML data. The JSTL XML library contains a number of actions for this purpose, similar to the ones you're familiar with from the JSTL core library: `<x:out>`, `<x:set>`, `<x:if>`, `<x:choose>`, `<x:when>`, `<x:otherwise>`, and `<x:forEach>`. The main difference between the XML and the core flavor is that the XML actions use a special language for working with XML data, named XPath, instead of the standard JSP EL. XPath 1.0 is a W3C recommendation that has been around since 1999, and it's used in XSLT stylesheets and other XML applications.* The language details are beyond the scope for this book, but here's a brief summary.

An XPath expression identifies one or more nodes (root, elements, attributes, namespace attributes, comments, text, and processing instructions) in an XML document. The simplest expression type is a plain *location path*, similar to a Unix filesystem path, to a set of nodes in the document. For instance, the path */meerkat/image/url* identifies the `<url>` element in the Meerkat XML document:

```
...
<meerkat>

  <title>Meerkat: An Open Wire Service</title>
  <link>http://meerkat.oreillynet.com</link>
  <description>
    Meerkat is a Web-based syndicated content reader providing
    a simple interface to RSS stories.  While maintaining the original
    association of a story with a channel, Meerkat's focus is on
    chronological order -- the latest stories float to the top,
    regardless of their source.
  </description>
  <language>en-us</language>

  <image>
    <title>Meerkat Powered!</title>
    <url>http://meerkat.oreillynet.com/icons/meerkat-powered.jpg</url>
    ...
```

A location path that starts with double forward slashes identifies all nodes of a certain type, regardless of their position in the document hierarchy. For instance, `//description` identifies all `<description>` elements, so it finds two elements in the sample XML document:

* Available at *http://www.w3.org/TR/xpath*.

```
...
<meerkat>
  ...
  <description>
    Meerkat is a Web-based syndicated content reader providing
    a simple interface to RSS stories.  While maintaining the original
    association of a story with a channel, Meerkat's focus is on
    chronological order -- the latest stories float to the top,
    regardless of their source.
  </description>
  ...
  <image>
    ...
    <description>
      Visit Meerkat in full splendor at meerkat.oreillynet.com
    </description>
    ...
```

A path is always interpreted relative to a specific context, such as the complete document or a subset of its nodes. When you use XPath expressions as JSTL XML action attributes, the context can be represented by a variable and can also be adjusted by actions such as the `<x:forEach>` action. Besides the type of paths described here, an XPath expression can also include function calls, literals, operators, and special syntax for identifying attributes. Some of these features are used in Example 15-3, but I recommend that you learn more about them if you're going to use the JSTL XML actions. Check out the XPath chapter from Elliotte Rusty Harold and W. Scott Means's *XML in a Nutshell* (O'Reilly), available online at *http://www.oreilly.com/catalog/xmlnut/chapter/ch09.html*, and Robert Eckstein's *XML Pocket Reference* (O'Reilly). The XPath tutorial by Miloslav Nic and Jiri Jirat, available at *http://www.zvon.org/xxl/XPathTutorial/General/examples.html*, is another good resource.

Let's look at how XPath expressions are used with the JSTL `<x:out>` action (see Table 15-4) to add the general Meerkat information that appears at the beginning of the page:

```
<img src="<x:out select="$doc/meerkat/image/url" />">
This service is based on the news feed from
<a href="<x:out select="$doc/meerkat/link" />">
  <x:out select="$doc/meerkat/title" /></a>.
<p>
<x:out select="$doc/meerkat/description" />
```

Table 15-4. Attributes for JSTL <x:out>

Attribute name	Java type	Dynamic value accepted	Description
`select`	`String`	No	Mandatory. An XPath expression to be evaluated.
`escapeXml`	`boolean`	Yes	Optional. `true` if special characters in the value should be converted to character entity codes. Default is `true`.

All JSTL actions that accept XPath expressions do so only for their select attribute, to avoid confusion with other attributes that accept JSP EL expressions. For the first <x:out> action, the select attribute contains an XPath expression that starts with the doc variable (containing the parse result) followed by a location path for the <url> element. The <x:out> action converts the XPath evaluation result to a Java String and adds it to the response.

The way the doc variable is used here establishes the context for the XPath expression. Variables can appear anywhere in an XPath expression and always start with a dollar sign, followed by the name of the variable. XPath expressions used with the JSTL actions have access to almost the same type of dynamic data as an EL expression. Any application variable in any JSP scope can be accessed by its name, just as in an EL expression. The doc variable is an example of this. Important differences are that in an XPath expression, all variable names start with a dollar sign, and the EL property and element access operators (. and [ ]) aren't recognized, so you can't use syntax like bean.propertyName in an XPath expression. A workaround is to save the property or element value in a new variable, and use it in the XPath expression:

```
<c:set var="myProperty" value="${myBean.myProperty}" />
<x:out select="$doc/root/myElement[@myAttribute = $myProperty]" />
```

Here the property value finds elements with an attribute that matches a bean property value. Also note that the XPath expression itself is not identified by any special syntax, as opposed to an EL expression that must always be enclosed by ${ and }.

In addition to application data, most of the information represented by EL implicit variables is available to an XPath expression with a slightly different syntax, most noticeable that a colon is used as a separator instead of a dot (see Table 15-5).

Table 15-5. XPath implicit variables

XPath expression	Description
$param:myParam	The myParam request parameter
$header:Accept	The Accept request header
$cookie:password	The password cookie
$initParam:myConfig	The myConfig context parameter
$pageScope:myVariable	The myVariable variable from the page scope
$requestScope:myVariable	The myVariable variable from the request scope
$sessionScope:myVariable	The myVariable variable from the session scope
$applicationScope:myVariable	The myVariable variable from the application scope

The JSTL <x:forEach> action (Table 15-6) lets you loop through the nodes that matches an XPath expression.

Table 15-6. Attributes for JSTL <x:forEach>

Attribute name	Java Type	Dynamic value accepted	Description
select	String	No	Mandatory. An XPath expression to be evaluated.
var	String	No	Optional. The name of the variable to hold the value of the current element.
varStatus	String	No	Optional. The name of the variable to hold a LoopTagStatus object.
begin	int	Yes	Optional. The first index, 0-based.
end	int	Yes	Optional. The last index, 0-based.
step	int	Yes	Optional. Index increment per iteration.

This action is used in Example 15-3 to extract the text from all <category> elements and build a sorted list of unique category names, that is then used to generate an HTML selection list:

```
<jsp:useBean id="uniqueCats" class="java.util.TreeMap" />
<x:forEach select="$doc/meerkat/story/category" var="category">
  <%-- Need to convert the XPath node to a Java String --%>
  <x:set var="catName" select="string($category)" />
  <c:set target="${uniqueCats}" property="${catName}" value="" />
</x:forEach>
```

A <jsp:useBean> action creates a java.util.TreeMap to hold the list. By using a map, the list of category names is automatically trimmed to unique names, since the keys in a map must be unique.* The TreeMap is a map type that sorts its keys, taking care of the sorting requirement. The XPath expression used for the <x:forEach> action matches all <category> elements. The action then evaluates its body once per element node, where the <c:set> action adds a map entry with the text value as the key and an empty string as the value.

An important detail here is that the value of the loop variable (category) contains an instance of an XPath node object, not the string needed for the Map. One way to convert an XPath node to a string is to use the XPath string( ) function. That's what I do here. The <x:set> action (Table 15-7) converts the current node to a Java String and saves it as a variable that is then used by <c:set> to set the Map entry. Tricks like this are unfortunately needed to bridge the XPath and Java domains in some cases.

* A java.util.TreeSet would actually be more appropriate, but there is no JSTL action that can add elements to a set.

Table 15-7. Attributes for JSTL <x:set>

Attribute name	Java type	Dynamic value accepted	Description
select	String	No	Mandatory. An XPath expression to be evaluated.
var	String	No	Mandatory. The name of the variable to hold the value of the current element.
scope	String	No	Optional. The scope for the variable; one of page, request, session, or application. page is the default.

You can look at Example 15-3 to see how a <c:forEach> action is then used to loop over all map entries and use the key values to build the HTML select list.

Next we need to decide which stories to display. This is also accomplished with the help from the <x:set> action:

```
<c:choose>
  <c:when test="${empty param.selCat || param.selCat == 'ALL'}">
    <x:set var="stories" select="$doc//story" />
  </c:when>
  <c:otherwise>
    <x:set var="stories"
      select="$doc//story[category = $param:selCat]" />
  </c:otherwise>
</c:choose>
```

The JSTL core <c:choose> action with nested <c:when> and <c:otherwise> actions tests the value of the selCat request parameter. The first time the page is requested, this parameter is not present. In this case, as well as when it has the value ALL, an <x:set> action with an XPath expression that matches all <story> elements (and their subnodes) extracts the data to be displayed and saves it in a variable named stories.

If the user selects a specific category and clicks the **Filter** button, however, the selCat parameter is received with the request. In this case, another <x:set> action extracts only the <story> elements that match the selected category. It does this by using an XPath expression that contains a predicate with a Boolean expression:

```
$doc//story[category = $param:selCat]
```

XPath processes this expression by first collecting all nodes matching //story in the context represented by the doc variable, and then removing all nodes where the Boolean expression evaluates to false. In the Boolean expression, the text for the <category> element of each selected node is compared to the value represented by the $param:selCat variable: the selCat request parameter value.

The final part of the sample application loops over the selected nodes and generates an HTML table, with a light green background for the cells that contains stories in the General category:

```
<table>
  <x:forEach select="$stories">
```

```
      <tr>
        <x:choose>
          <x:when select="category[. = 'General']">
            <td bgcolor="lightgreen">
          </x:when>
          <x:otherwise>
            <td>
          </x:otherwise>
        </x:choose>
          <a href="<x:out select="link" />">
            <x:out select="title" /></a>
          <br>
          <i><x:out select="timestamp" /></i>:
          <b>Category:</b><x:out select="category" />,
          <b>Reported by:</b><x:out select="channel" />
          <br><x:out select="description" />
        </td>
      </tr>
    </x:forEach>
  </table>
```

The `<x:forEach>` action is again used to loop through the set of nodes, but as opposed to when it was used to create the category name list, the current element is not exposed to the body as a variable. This illustrates another `<x:forEach>` feature, namely that the action adjusts the current XPath context seen by nested JSTL XML actions. When the body is evaluated, the current context for XPath expressions is the current node. An expression such as `category[. = 'General']` used by the nested `<x:when>` action, is therefore evaluated in the context of the current story node, checking the value of its `<category>` element. The expression evaluates to `true` if the text in the `<category>` element equals the string "General". The `<x:out>` actions use similar XPath expressions to extract data from the current `<story>` element.

The last part of Example 15-3 also illustrates the use of most of the conditional JSTL XML actions: `<x:choose>`, `<x:when>`, and `<x:otherwise>`. They have the same function as the corresponding JSTL core elements; `<x:choose>` groups a number of `<x:when>` actions and optionally one `<x:otherwise>` action, where the body of the first `<x:when>` action with a `select` attribute that evaluates to `true`, or the `<x:otherwise>` body if none of them do, is processed. Only the `<x:when>` action has attributes, described in Table 15-8.

Table 15-8. Attributes for JSTL <x:when>

Attribute name	Java type	Dynamic value accepted	Description
`select`	`String`	No	Mandatory. An XPath expression to be evaluated as a Boolean.

The result of the XPath expression in the `select` attribute is converted to a Boolean using the XPath `boolean()` function; any valid number except 0, a nonempty string, and an expression that matches at least one node is converted to `true`. All other values are converted to false. Note that this means that the string "false" evaluates to true.

The only JSTL XML action I don't use in this example is <x:if>, described in Table 15-9.

Table 15-9. Attributes for JSTL <x:if>

Attribute name	Java type	Dynamic value accepted	Description
select	String	No	Mandatory. An XPath expression to be evaluated as a Boolean value.
var	String	No	Optional. The name of the variable to hold the Boolean result.
scope	String	No	Optional. The scope for the variable; one of page, request, session, or application. page is the default.

It works exactly like the corresponding action in the JSTL core library, except that the select attribute is evaluated as XPath boolean( ) the same way as for <x:when>.

The examples in this chapter show how the JSTL XML actions let you process XML documents pretty much any way you can think of. You can transform a document using a stylesheet, parse and access parts of the document in many ways, save a part as a variable, or add it to the response. As illustrated by the examples in this chapter, you can mix the JSTL XML actions with the other JSTL actions (or custom actions) and use application variables and request data in XPath expressions to select parts based on runtime conditions.

CHAPTER 16

Using Scripting Elements

Before reading this book, you may have heard that JSP is all about including Java code in web pages. If so, you may wonder why you haven't seen any Java code in the examples so far. That's because there's really no reason to embed raw Java code in JSP pages anymore. With JSP 1.0, it was the only way to do anything interesting. JSP 1.1 removed most reasons by introducing custom actions, but many developers figured developing custom actions for simple conditionals and loops was not worth the trouble and continued to embed Java code snippets for these things. Even with JSP 1.2, you still had to use Java code to assign dynamic values to JSP action element attributes, but JSTL 1.0 (and the EL it introduced) removed these excuses for most cases. With JSP 2.0, where the EL is part of the JSP specification so it can be used for all attributes and the greatly simplified mechanisms for developing custom actions, there are really no good reasons for embedding Java in your JSP pages.

JSP continues to support the scripting elements for putting code in JSP pages—even though their use is now discouraged—because all Java specifications go to great lengths to be backward compatible. There are three types of scripting elements: *scriptlets* for a block of code to be executed, *expressions* for a single statement to be evaluated with its result added to the response, and *declarations* for declaring variables and methods. In this chapter we look at how to use all of them, and the type of problems you should be prepared to encounter if you do.

Because using scripting elements means writing Java code, you should know how to program in Java before you read this chapter. If you don't know Java programming, my advice is that you steer clear from the scripting elements altogether and use the EL, JSTL and other custom actions exclusively.

Using page Directive Scripting Attributes

The page directive has two attributes that may be used when you use scripting elements: `language` and `import`:

```
<%@ page language="java" import="java.util.*" %>
```

The language attribute specifies the scripting language used in the page. All containers are required to support Java.[*] java is also the default value for the language attribute, but, for clarity, you may still want to specify it. Some JSP implementations support other languages besides Java and, hence, allow other values for the language attribute. For instance, both JRun (*http://www.macromedia.com/*) and Resin (*http://www.caucho.com/*) support JavaScript in addition to Java.

The JSP specification requires that the classes in the java.lang, javax.servlet, javax.servlet.jsp, and the javax.servlet.http packages are available by default to scripting elements when Java is used as the scripting language. If you use classes from packages other than these, they can be imported with the import attribute, to make it possible to use the short class names in the scripting elements.

If you need to import more than one package, you can use multiple page directives with import attributes in the same page or use one with a comma-separated list of import declarations. In other words, this directive:

```
<%@ page import="java.util.*, com.ora.jsp.util.*" %>
```

has the same effect as these two directives:

```
<%@ page import="java.util.* " %>
<%@ page import="com.ora.jsp.util.*" %>
```

Starting with JSP 2.0, classes without a package declaration (i.e., that are part of the *unnamed package*) are no longer supported. This is because the servlet the container creates from the JSP page (the page implementation class) may use a vendor-dependent package name. Java does not allow the use of classes from the unnamed package to be used in a class that belongs to a named package, and Sun's Java compiler (starting with the J2SE 1.4 version) enforces this rule.

Implicit JSP Scripting Objects

Scripting elements can use predefined variables that the container assigns as references to *implicit objects* (Table 16-1) to access request and application data. These objects are instances of classes defined by the servlet and JSP specifications. Appendix D contains complete descriptions of all methods for each class, and they are briefly introduced here and used in a number of examples in this chapter.

Table 16-1. Implicit JSP objects

Variable name	Java type
application	javax.servlet.ServletContext
config	javax.servlet.ServletConfig

[*] In fact, Java is the only scripting language formally supported in the JSP specification, but the specification leaves room for other languages to be supported.

Table 16-1. Implicit JSP objects (continued)

Variable name	Java type
exception	java.lang.Throwable
out	javax.servlet.jsp.JspWriter
page	java.lang.Object
pageContext	javax.servlet.jsp.PageContext
request	javax.servlet.http.HttpServletRequest
response	javax.servlet.http.HttpServletResponse
session	javax.servlet.http.HttpSession

These objects provide access to the same information (and more) as the implicit variables you can use in EL expressions, but it's not a one-to-one match:

`pageContext`
: The `pageContext` variable contains a reference to an instance of the class named `javax.servlet.jsp.PageContext`. It provides methods for accessing references to all the other objects and attributes for holding data that is shared between components in the same page. It's the same object that you can access with the `${pageContext}` EL expression. Attribute values for this object represent the page scope; they are the same objects as are available to the EL world as a `Map` represented by the `${pageScope}` expression.

`request`
: The request variable contains a reference to an instance of a class that implements an interface named `javax.servlet.http.HttpServletRequest`. It provides methods for accessing all the information that's available about the current request, such as request parameters, attributes, headers, and cookies. It's the same object that you can access with the `${pageContext.request}` EL expression. Attribute values for this object represent the request scope; they are the same objects as are available to the EL world as a `Map` represented by the `${requestScope}` expression.

`response`
: The `response` variable contains a reference to an object representing the current response message. It's an instance of a class that implements the `javax.servlet.http.HttpServletResponse` interface, with methods for setting headers and the status code, and adding cookies. It also provides methods related to session tracking. These methods are the `response` methods you're most likely to use. The same object can be accessed with the `${pageContext.response}` EL expression.

`session`
: The `session` variable allows you to access the client's session data, managed by the server. It's assigned a reference to an instance of a class that implements the `javax.servlet.http.HttpSession` interface, which provides access to session data as well as information about the session, such as when it was created and when a

request for the session was last received. It's the same object that you can access with the ${pageContext.session} EL expression. Attribute values for this object represent the session scope; they are the same objects as are available to the EL world as a Map represented by the ${sessionScope} expression.

application
: The application variable contains a reference to the instance of a class that implements the javax.servlet.ServletContext interface that represents the application. This object holds references to other objects that more than one user may require access to, such as a database connection pool shared by all application users. It also contains log( ) methods you can use to write messages to the container's log file. It's the same object that you can access with the ${pageContext.servletContext} EL expression. Attribute values for this object represent the application scope; they are the same objects as are available to the EL world as a Map represented by the ${applicationScope} expression.

out
: The out object is an instance of javax.servlet.jsp.JspWriter. You can use the print( ) and println( ) methods provided by this object to add text to the response message body. In most cases, however, you will just use template text and JSP action elements instead of explicitly printing to the out object.

exception
: The exception object is available only in error pages and contains information about a runtime error. It's the same object that you can access with the ${pageContext.exception} EL expression.

The remaining two implicit objects (config and page) are so rarely used in scripting elements that I don't discuss them here. If you're interested, you can read about them in Appendix D.

All variable names listed in Table 16-1 are reserved for the implicit object references. If you declare your own variables in a JSP page, you must not use these reserved variable names.

Using Scriptlets

The scriptlet element can be used to add a whole block of code to a page, including variable declarations. The code block must be enclosed by a scriptlet start-identifier, <%, and an end-identifier, %>. Example 16-1 shows a scriptlet that creates test data for action elements.

Example 16-1. Scriptlet creating test data (scriptlet.jsp)

```
<%@ page language="java" contentType="text/html" %>
<%@ page import="java.util.*" %>
<%@ taglib prefix="c" uri="http://java.sun.com/jsp/jstl/core" %>
<%@ taglib prefix="fn" uri="http://java.sun.com/jsp/jstl/functions" %>
```

Example 16-1. Scriptlet creating test data (scriptlet.jsp) (continued)

```
<%
  // Create an ArrayList with test data
  ArrayList list = new ArrayList( );
  Map author1 = new HashMap( );
  author1.put("name", "John Irving");
  author1.put("id", new Integer(1));
  list.add(author1);
  Map author2 = new HashMap( );
  author2.put("name", "William Gibson");
  author2.put("id", new Integer(2));
  list.add(author2);
  Map author3 = new HashMap( );
  author3.put("name", "Douglas Adams");
  author3.put("id", new Integer(3));
  list.add(author3);
  pageContext.setAttribute("authors", list);
%>
<html>
  <head>
    <title>Search result: Authors</title>
  </head>
  <body bgcolor="white">
    Here are all authors matching your search critera:
    <table>
      <th>Name</th>
      <th>Id</th>
      <c:forEach items="${authors}" var="current">
        <tr>
          <td>${fn:escapeXml(current.name)}<td>
          <td>${fn:escapeXml(current.id)}<td>
        </tr>
      </c:forEach>
    </table>
  </body>
</html>
```

The scriptlet element contains Java code that creates a `java.util.ArrayList` with `java.util.HashMap` elements and saves the list as a page scope attribute named `authors` by calling the `setAttribute( )` method on the implicit pageScope object. The `ArrayList` is then used as the `items` attribute value in a `<c:forEach>` action. You can use a scriptlet like this to test the main page functionality before the real data source is available. In the final version, the scriptlet can be removed, and the data passed to the page from another page or a servlet.

Let's look at another example, in which the implicit `request` object is inquired about the current client type to display different messages depending on whether the Internet Explorer or Netscape Navigator browser is used. Example 16-2 shows the complete page.

Example 16-2. Browser dependent page (fragment.jsp)

```
<%@ page language="java" contentType="text/html" %>
<html>
  <head>
    <title>Browser Check</title>
  </head>
  <body bgcolor="white">

    <%
       String userAgent = request.getHeader("User-Agent");
       if (userAgent.indexOf("MSIE") != -1) {
    %>
         You're using Internet Explorer.
    <% } else if (userAgent.indexOf("Mozilla") != -1) { %>
         You're probably using Netscape.
    <% } else { %>
         You're using a browser I don't know about.
    <% } %>
  </body>
</html>
```

The first scriptlet uses the `getHeader()` method of the `request` object to get the value of the `User-Agent` header. This header contains a string with clues about the browser making the request. The header value is then used in a number of `if` statements to make an educated guess about the browser type and tell the user the result.

What's most interesting here is that a number of scriptlets are used, each one containing only a fragment of a Java statement:

`<% if (userAgent.indexOf("MSIE") != -1) { %>`
: An `if` statement, testing if the header contains "MSIE", with a block start brace.

`<% } else if (userAgent.indexOf("Mozilla") != -1) { %>`
: The `if` block end brace and an `else-if` statement, testing if the header contains "Mozilla", with its block start brace.

`<% } else { %>`
: The `else-if` block end brace, and a final `else` block start brace, handling the case when none of the strings are found.

`<% } %>`
: The final `else` block end brace.

While none of the scriptlets by itself is a valid Java statement, the JSP container combines the fragments in the four scriptlets with code for writing the template text to the response body to form a valid statement. The end result is that when the first `if` statement is `true`, "You're using Internet Explorer" is displayed; when the second `if` statement is `true`, "You're probably using Netscape" is displayed. If none of the `if` statements are `true`, the final `else` block is used, displaying "You're using a browser I don't know about."

The tricky part when using scriptlets like this is making sure that all the start and end braces are in place. If you miss just one of the braces, the code that the JSP container generates isn't syntactically correct. And, unfortunately, the error message that you get isn't easy to interpret.

Using Expressions

A JSP *expression* element is used to insert the result of a scripting code expression into the response. It's the Java scripting equivalent to an EL expression directly in template text. An expression starts with <%= and ends with %>. Note that the only syntax difference compared to a scriptlet is the equal sign (=) in the start identifier. Examples are:

```
<%= userInfo.getUserName( ) %>
<%= 1 + 1 %>
<%= new java.util.Date( ) %>
```

The result of the expression is written to the response body, converted to a `String` if needed. One thing is important to note: as opposed to statements in a scriptlet, the code in an expression must not end with a semicolon. This is because the JSP container combines the expression code with code for writing the result to the response body. If the expression ends with a semicolon, the combined code will not be syntactically correct.

As with EL expressions, a Java expression can also be used to assign a dynamic value to an action element attribute, but with a few restrictions as described later in this chapter.

Using Declarations

I have described two of the three JSP scripting elements in this chapter so far: scriptlets and expressions. There's one more called a *declaration* element, which is used to declare Java variables and methods in a JSP page. My advice is this: don't use it. Let me explain why.

In general, Java variables can be declared either within a method or outside the body of all methods in a class, like this:

```
public class SomeClass {
  // Instance variable
  private String anInstanceVariable;

  // Method
  public void doSomething( ) {
    String aLocalVariable;
  }
}
```

A variable declared outside the body of all methods is called an *instance variable*. Its value can be accessed from any method in the class, and it keeps its value even when the method that sets it returns. A variable declared within the body of a method is called a *local variable*; it can be accessed only within the method where it's declared. When the method returns, the local variable disappears.

Recall from Chapter 3 that a JSP page is turned into a servlet class when it's first requested, and the JSP container creates one instance of this class. If more than one user requests the same page at the same time, the single instance is used for all requests. Each user is assigned what is called a *thread* in the server, and each thread executes the same method in the JSP implementation class instance. When more than one thread executes the same code, you have to make sure the code is *thread safe*. This means that the code must behave the same when many threads are executing as when just one thread executes the code.

Multithreading and thread-safe code strategies are best left to experienced programmers. However, using a JSP declaration element to declare variables exposes your page to multithreading problems. That's because a variable that's declared using a JSP declaration element ends up as an instance variable in the generated servlet, not as a local variable in a method. All threads share the instance variable, so if one thread changes its value, the new value is seen by all threads. To put this in JSP terms, if the instance variable is changed because one user accesses the page, all users accessing the same page will use the new value.

When you declare a variable within a scriptlet element instead of in a JSP declaration block, the variable ends up as a local variable in the generated servlet's request processing method. Each thread has its own copy of a local variable, so a local variable doesn't cause any problems even when more than one thread executes the same code. If the value of a local variable is changed, it will not affect the other threads.

That being said, let's look at a simple example. We use two `int` variables; one declared as an instance variable using a JSP declaration, and the other declared as a local variable with a scriptlet. We increment them both by one and display the new values. Example 16-3 shows the test page.

Example 16-3. Using a declaration element (counter.jsp)

```
<%@ page language="java" contentType="text/html" %>
<%!
  int globalCounter = 0;
%>
<html>
  <head>
    <title>A page with a counter</title>
  </head>
  <body bgcolor="white">
    This page has been visited: <%= ++globalCounter %> times.
    <p>
```

Example 16-3. Using a declaration element (counter.jsp) (continued)

```
    <%
      int localCounter = 0;
    %>
    This counter never increases its value: <%= ++localCounter %>
  </body>
</html>
```

The JSP declaration element is right at the beginning of the page in Example 16-3, starting with `<%!` and ending with `%>`. Note the exclamation point (!) in the start identifier; that's what makes it a declaration as opposed to a scriptlet. The declaration element declares an instance variable named `globalCounter`, shared by all requests for the page. In the page body, a JSP expression increments the variable's value and adds it to the page. Next comes a scriptlet, enclosed by `<%` and `%>`, that declares a local variable named `localCounter`. It is then incremented and added to the page by the last expression element.

When you run this example, the `globalCounter` value increases every time you load the page, but `localCounter` stays the same. Again, this is because `globalCounter` is an instance variable, while `localCounter` is a local variable.

In this example, nothing terribly bad happens if more than one user hit the page at the same time. The worst that could happen is that you skip a number or show the same `globalCounter` value twice. This can happen if two requests come in at the same time, and both requests increment the value before it's inserted in the response. You can imagine the consequences, however, if you use an instance variable to save something more important, such as a customer's credit-card number or other sensitive information. So even though it may be tempting to create an instance variable (using a JSP declaration) to keep a value such as a counter between requests, I recommend that you stay away from this technique. Using objects in the session and application scopes, as described in Chapter 10, is a far better approach.

A JSP declaration element can also be used to declare a method that can then be used in scriptlets in the same page. The only harm this can cause is that your JSP pages end up containing too much code, making it hard to maintain the application. I recommend that you use beans, custom actions, or EL functions instead, but to be complete, Example 16-4 shows an example of how it can be done.

Example 16-4. Method declaration and use (color.jsp)

```
<%@ page language="java" contentType="text/html" %>
<%!
  String randomColor( ) {
    java.util.Random random = new java.util.Random( );
    int red = (int) (random.nextFloat( ) * 255);
    int green = (int) (random.nextFloat( ) * 255);
    int blue = (int) (random.nextFloat( ) * 255);
    return "#" +
      Integer.toString(red, 16) +
```

Example 16-4. Method declaration and use (color.jsp) (continued)

```
        Integer.toString(green, 16) +
        Integer.toString(blue, 16);
    }
%>
<html>
  <head>
    <title>Random Color</title>
  </head>
  <body bgcolor="white">

    <h1>Random Color</h1>

    <table bgcolor="<%= randomColor( ) %>" >
      <tr><td width="100" height="100"> </td></tr>
    </table>

  </body>
</html>
```

The method named `randomColor( )`, declared between `<%!` and `%>`, returns a randomly generated `String` in a format that can be used as an HTML color value. This method is then called from an expression element to set the background color for a table. Every time you reload this page, you see a single table cell with a randomly selected color.

jspInit() and jspDestroy( )

If you know a bit about servlets, you know that a servlet has two methods the container calls when the servlet is loaded and shut down, respectively. These methods are called `init( )` and `destroy( )`, and they allow the servlet to initialize instance variables when it's loaded and clean up when it's shut down. As you already know, a JSP page is turned into a servlet, so it has the same capability. However, with JSP, the methods are called `jspInit( )` and `jspDestroy( )` instead.

Again, I recommend that you don't declare any instance variables for your JSP pages. If you follow this advice, there's also no reason to declare the `jspInit( )` and `jspDestroy( )` methods. But I know you're curious, so here's an example of how they can be used.

Expanding on Example 16-3, the `jspInit( )` method can set an instance variable to a `java.util.Date( )` object, which represents the date and time when the page was initialized. This variable can then be used in the page to show when the counter was started:

```
<%@ page language="java" contentType="text/html" %>
<%@ page import="java.util.Date" %>
<%!
  int globalCounter = 0;
```

```
  java.util.Date startDate;

  public void jspInit( ) {
    startDate = new java.util.Date( );
  }

  public void jspDestroy( ) {
    ServletContext context = getServletConfig().getServletContext( );
    context.log("test.jsp was visited " + globalCounter +
      " times between " + startDate + " and " + (new Date( )));
  }
%>
<html>
  <head>
    <title>A page with a counter</title>
  </head>
  <body bgcolor="white">
    This page has been visited: <%= ++globalCounter %> times
    since <%= startDate %>.
  </body>
</html>
```

The `jspDestroy( )` method retrieves a reference to the `ServletContext` for the page and writes a message to the container's log file. As you may recall, the implicit `application` variable contains a reference to the `ServletContext`, so you may wonder why it's not used here. The reason is that the implicit variables are local variables in the method that the JSP container generates to process the page requests; hence, they aren't available to the methods you declare yourself.

Mixing Action Elements and Scripting Elements

Even when you use custom actions and the JSTL, you may want occasionally to use small amounts of scripting code., e.g., as a quick fix or for prototyping, when creating a custom action, or an EL function seems like overkill. You can also use Java code to set an action attribute value.

Using an Expression Element to Set an Attribute

In all examples so far, dynamic action attribute values are set using EL expressions, but an alternative is using a Java expression. In either case, the custom action attribute must accept what's formally called a *request-time attribute value*.

Here is an example of how a Java expression can be used to set the `value` attribute of the standard `<jsp:param>` action:

```
<jsp:forward page="prodInfo.jsp">
  <jsp:param name="id" value='<%= request.getParameter("prodId") %>' />
</jsp:forward>
```

The value attribute is set to the value of a request parameter. The container evaluates the request-time attribute value when the page is requested, and the corresponding attribute is set to the result of the expression. The Java type for the result of the expression must match the type of the attribute you set this way. In the <jsp:param> value attribute case, the expression must be of type String, but other action attributes may be of any type, including custom classes. This is in contrast to when an EL expression used; the container always tries to convert the EL expression evaluation result type to the attribute type, but with Java expressions it's up to you to make sure they match.

Another difference between using Java and EL expressions when assigning an attribute value is that with a Java expression, you can't combine expressions and static text as you can with EL expressions. For instance, this is illegal:

```
<jsp:param name="ranking"
  value='Ranking: <%= request.getParameter("ranking") %>' />
```

Instead, you have to combine the static text and the dynamic value within the expression:

```
<jsp:param name="ranking"
  value='<%= "Ranking: " + request.getParameter("ranking") %>' />
```

One subtle detail in this example is that the attribute value is enclosed with single quotes instead of the usual double quotes. That's because the expression itself must use double quotes around the getParameter( ) argument. An alternative to enclosing the expression in single quotes is to escape the double quotes with backslashes in the expression:

```
<jsp:forward page="prodInfo.jsp">
  <jsp:param name="id" value="<%= request.getParameter(\"prodId\") %>"/>
</jsp:forward>
```

Request-time attribute values are supported for most of the standard action attributes and can be supported by custom action attributes as well, but it's not a given. In the tables describing action elements that you see throughout this book as well as in Appendix A, B, and E, all attributes that accept a request-time attribute value has a "Yes" in the "Dynamic value accepted" column.

One reason for not supporting a request-time attribute value is that some attribute values must be known when the page is converted into a servlet. For instance, the class attribute value in the <jsp:useBean> action must be known in the translation phase so that the JSP container can generate valid Java code for the servlet. Request-time attribute values also require a bit more processing than static string values, so it's up to the action developer to decide if request-time attribute values are supported or not. Whether or not an attribute accepts a request-time attribute value is declared in the Tag Library Descriptor (TLD). I discuss implementation of custom actions and the TLD in Chapter 21, so let's defer the details until then.

Accessing Scoped Variables in Scripting Code

The term variable is generally used for any dynamic data an application manipulates, but when we talk about JSP and scripting elements, it's important to be more specific.

JSP custom actions, including the JSTL actions, can expose data through what is called scoped variables, typically named by a var and an optional scope attribute. A *scoped variable* is an object that lives in one of the JSP scopes: page, request, session, or application. As mentioned earlier, the scopes are actually collections of named object references that correspond to the attributes that the implicit pageContext, request, session, and application objects provide access to.

Another type of variable is a scripting variable. A *scripting variable* is a variable declared in a JSP scriptlet or declaration, using the language defined for the page (typically Java). To read or manipulate data with scripting code, you need a scripting variable that holds a reference to the object that contains the data.

The distinction between the variable types becomes apparent when you mix actions that expose data only as scoped variables with scripting elements. To use the data exposed by the action in a scripting element, you must first tell the container to create a scripting variable for it and assign it the value of the scoped variable. The easiest way to do this is to use the standard <jsp:useBean> action:

```
<%@ taglib prefix="fmt" uri="http://java.sun.com/jsp/jstl/fmt" %>
<%@ page import="java.util.Date" %>

<fmt:parseDate value="${param.birthDate}"
  pattern="yyyy-MM-dd"
  var="birthDate"
/>
<jsp:useBean id="birthDate" class="java.util.Date" />
<%
  String ageCategory = null;
  int thisYear = new Date().getYear( );
  int age = thisYear - birthDate.getYear( );
  if (age < 10) {
    ageCategory = "kid";
  }
  else if (age < 20) {
    ageCategory = "teenager";
  }
  else if (age < 65) {
    ageCategory = "adult";
  }
  else {
    ageCategory = "retired";
  }
%>
```

In this example, <fmt:parseDate> parses a date submitted as a request parameter and saves the result as a java.util.Date in a page scope variable named birthDate. The <jsp:useBean> action finds the scoped variable and creates a scripting variable of the type java.util.Date with the same name as the scoped variable and assigns it the value of the scoped variable. The scriptlet can then use the scripting variable created by the <jsp:useBean> action.

Alternatively, you can declare and assign the scripting variable with scripting code:

```
<%@ taglib prefix="fmt" uri="http://java.sun.com/jsp/jstl/fmt" %>
<%@ page import="java.util.Date" %>

<fmt:parseDate value="${param.birthDate}"
  pattern="yyyy-MM-dd"
  var="birthDate"
/>
<%
  Date birthDate = (Date) pageContext.getAttribute("birthDate");
  String ageCategory = null;
  int thisYear = new Date().getYear( );
  int age = thisYear - birthDate.getYear( );
```

Compared to using the <jsp:useBean> action, you must first know which implicit object represents the scope the scoped variable is placed in and call its getAttribute( ) method. All implicit objects that represent a JSP scope provide the getAttribute( ) method. As shown here, you must also cast the return value to the correct type, because the getAttribute( ) returns an Object.

You can save or replace an object in any scope with the setAttribute( ) method:

```
public void setAttribute(String name, Object value)
```

To remove an object, use the removeAttribute( ) method:

```
public void removeAttribute(String name)
```

One thing to watch for when you use scripting variables and scoped variables to access the same object is illustrated by this page:

```
<%@ page language="java" contentType="text/html" %>
<%@ taglib prefix="c" uri="http://java.sun.com/jsp/jstl/core" %>
<%@ taglib prefix="fn" uri="http://java.sun.com/jsp/jstl/functions" %>

<html>
  <head>
    <title>Not *NSYNC</title>
  </head>
  <body bgcolor="white">

    <jsp:useBean id="artistName"
      scope="request" class="java.lang.String" />
    <% artistName = "U2"; %>
    And the winner is ... ${fn:escapeXml(artistName)}
  </body>
</html>
```

The <jsp:useBean> action makes a request scope object (perhaps placed there by a servlet) available through a scripting variable named artistName, a scriptlet assigns a new value to the scripting variable, and finally the value of artistName is added to the response with an EL expression. The question is, does the response contain the original value assigned to the request scope object or the value assigned by the scriptlet code? The answer is: the original value. This is because the EL doesn't have access to scripting variables, only to objects in one of the JSP scopes and the implicit EL variables. To make an object available to the EL from a scriptlet, you need to explicitly save it in the appropriate scope. If you add this line of code in the scriptlet block to replace the scoped variable, the new value is added to the response instead of the original value:

```
<%
  artistName = "U2";
  request.setAttribute("artistName", artistName);
%>
```

This is true also for actions that access scoped variables directly, not only for the EL. If you replace the object a scripting variable references, you must also replace the object the scoped variable references by calling setAttribute( ) if you want actions and the EL to reference the new object.

For custom actions you can tell the container to automatically declare a scripting variable and assign it a reference to the scoped variable the action exposes; I'll show you how in Chapter 22. In this case, scripting code can access the exposed data directly through the scripting value. JSTL actions, on the other hand, do not use this feature so you must always use <jsp:useBean> or the getAttribute( ) method in a scriptlet to bridge the gap between the two types of variables.

Dealing with Scripting Syntax Errors

When you use scripting elements you must be prepared to deal with a new class of syntax errors. The scripting code is inserted into the servlet code, generated based on the JSP page in the translation-phase, more or less as is. A syntax error in a scripting element may therefore result in an error the JSP container can't report in a sensible way.

Directives and action elements don't have this problem. The container reads the JSP page and generates servlet code by replacing all JSP directives and action elements with code that produces the appropriate result. To do this, it needs to analyze these types of elements in detail. If there's a syntax error in a directive or action element, it can easily tell which element is incorrect (as you saw in Chapter 9). A syntax error in a scripting element, on the other hand, isn't discovered when the JSP page is read, but instead when the generated servlet is compiled with a Java compiler. The compiler reports an error in terms of its location in the generated servlet code (as opposed to the location in the JSP page), with messages that don't always make sense to a JSP page author.

Before we look at some real error examples, let's briefly look at how the scripting code is embedded in the generated servlet to really understand the problem. Example 16-5 shows a simple JSP page that uses all three scripting element types.

Example 16-5. JSP page with all scripting element types (allinone.jsp)

```
<%@ page language="java" contentType="text/html" %>
<%@ page import="java.util.Date" %>
<%!
  private String getGreeting( ) {
    Date now = new Date( );
    String greeting = null;
    if (now.getHours( ) < 12) {
      greeting = "Good morning";
    }
    else if (now.getHours( ) < 18) {
      greeting = "Good day";
    }
    else {
      greeting = "Good evening";
    }
    return greeting;
  }
%>
<html>
  <head>
    <title>All Scripting Elements</title>
  </head>
  <body bgcolor="white">
    <%= getGreeting( ) %>
    <% if (request.getParameter("name") == null) { %>
      stranger!
    <% } else { %>
      partner!
    <% } %>
    How are you?
  </body>
</html>
```

In this page, an `import` attribute imports the `java.util.Date` class. This class is used in a declaration element that defines a method named `getGreeting( )`. The method returns a `String` with an appropriate greeting depending on the time of day. An expression element invokes the method and adds the result to the response. Finally, scriptlet elements add either "stranger!" or "partner!" depending on if a request parameter is received or not. This may not make much sense, but it demonstrates the use of all scripting types.

Example 16-6 shows the servlet code the container may create based on this page.

Example 16-6. Servlet generated from JSP page

```
package org.apache.jsp;

import java.util.Date;
import javax.servlet.*;
import javax.servlet.http.*;
import javax.servlet.jsp.*;
import org.apache.jasper.runtime.*;

public class allinone$jsp extends HttpJspBase {

          private String getGreeting( ) {
            Date now = new Date( );
            String greeting = null;
            if (now.getHours( ) < 12) {
              greeting = "Good morning";
            }
            else if (now.getHours( ) < 18) {
              greeting = "Good day";
            }
            else {
              greeting = "Good evening";
            }
            return greeting;
          }
    public void _jspService(HttpServletRequest request,
        HttpServletResponse  response)
        throws java.io.IOException, ServletException {

        JspFactory _jspxFactory = null;
        PageContext pageContext = null;
        HttpSession session = null;
        ServletContext application = null;
        ServletConfig config = null;
        JspWriter out = null;
        Object page = this;
        String  _value = null;
        try {
            _jspxFactory = JspFactory.getDefaultFactory( );
            response.setContentType("text/html");
            pageContext =
                _jspxFactory.getPageContext(this, request, response,
                    "", true, 8192, true);

            application = pageContext.getServletContext( );
            config = pageContext.getServletConfig( );
            session = pageContext.getSession( );
            out = pageContext.getOut( );

                out.write("\r\n");
                out.write("\r\n");
                out.write("\r\n<html>\r\n  <head>\r\n);
                out.write("  <title>All Scripting Elements</title>\r\n);
```

Example 16-6. Servlet generated from JSP page (continued)

```
                out.write("</head>\r\n  <body bgcolor=\"white\">\r\n");
                out.print( getGreeting( ) );
                out.write("\r\n    ");
                 if (request.getParameter("name") == null) {
                out.write("\r\n      stranger!\r\n    ");
                 } else {
                out.write("\r\n      partner!\r\n    ");
                 }
                out.write("\r\n    How are you?\r\n);
                out.write("  </body>\r\n</html>\r\n");
        } catch (Throwable t) {
            if (out != null && out.getBufferSize( ) != 0)
                out.clearBuffer( );
            if (pageContext != null) pageContext.handlePageException(t);
        } finally {
            if (_jspxFactory != null)
                _jspxFactory.releasePageContext(pageContext);
        }
    }
}
```

The generated servlet in Example 16-6 looks a lot more complex than a hand-coded version would. That's because all implicit objects and a number of internal support objects must always be initialized (a hand-coded version doesn't need this generic initialization). The method for processing the request is named `_jspService( )`, invoked by the `service( )` method in the base class. These details aren't important, so let's instead see what happens to the `import` attribute and all scripting elements.

The `import` attribute results in a Java import statement, as expected. The declaration element is inserted as is, at the top level of the class, outside the `_jspService( )` method. This means that all variables declared in a JSP declaration element end up as instance variables, as opposed to local variables, and that methods in a declaration element don't have access to the JSP implicit variables. If a method needs an implicit variable value, it must be passed as an argument to the method.

The expression element is also inserted as is but wrapped in an `out.write( )` call. This is why you mustn't use a semicolon at the end of a JSP expression; it would cause a syntax error when the expression is used as an `out.write( )` argument.

Finally, the scripting elements: because they are mixed with other code in the generated servlet, they have the highest potential to cause problems. We will look at some specific examples later, but note how `out.write( )` calls are inserted for all template text in between the scriptlet code. In a more complex page, such as one that has an action element enclosed by scriptlet code fragments, the code gets a lot more complex, and the chance for strange side effects increases.

Scripting Syntax Error Examples

Let's look at some examples of problems you need to deal with if you use scripting elements.

Example 16-7 shows a modified version of the page used earlier to illustrate how scripting elements end up in the generated servlet. It has two errors: a semicolon is incorrectly used in the expression, and the closing bracket for the else block in the last scriptlet is missing.

Example 16-7. Invalid semicolon use and missing end bracket (error1.jsp)

```
<%@ page language="java" contentType="text/html" %>
<%@ page import="java.util.Date" %>
<%!
  private String getGreeting( ) {
    Date now = new Date( );
    String greeting = null;
    if (now.getHours( ) < 12) {
      greeting = "Good morning";
    }
    else if (now.getHours( ) < 18) {
      greeting = "Good day";
    }
    else {
      greeting = "Good evening";
    }
    return greeting;
  }
%>
<html>
  <head>
    <title>Invalid semicolon use and missing end bracket</title>
  </head>
  <body bgcolor="white">
    <%= getGreeting( ); %>
    <% if (request.getParameter("name") == null) { %>
      stranger!
    <% } else { %>
      partner!

    How are you?
  </body>
</html>
```

This is the error description Tomcat sends to the browser (with some line breaks added to make it fit the page):

```
org.apache.jasper.JasperException: Unable to compile class for JSP

An error occurred at line: 24 in the jsp file: /ch16/error1.jsp

Generated servlet error:
```

```
D:\jakarta-tomcat-5.0\work\localhost\ora\ch16\error1_jsp.java:67: ')' expected.
                out.write(String.valueOf(getGreeting( ); ));
                                                        ^

An error occurred at line: 24 in the jsp file: /ch16/error1.jsp

Generated servlet error:
D:\jakarta-tomcat-5.0\work\localhost\ora\ch16\error1_jsp.java:67: Illegal start
Of expression
                out.write(String.valueOf(getGreeting( ); ));
                                                          ^

An error occurred at line: -1 in the jsp file: null

Generated servlet error:
D:\jakarta-tomcat-5.0\work\localhost\ora\ch16\error1_jsp.java:75:
'catch' without 'try'.
        } catch (Throwable t) {
          ^

D:\jakarta-tomcat-5.0\work\localhost\ora\ch16\error1_jsp.java:47:
'try' without 'catch' or 'finally'.
}
^

D:\jakarta-tomcat-5.0\work\localhost\ora\ch16\error1_jsp.java:86:
'}' expected.
}
 ^
5 errors
```

The first two error messages are for the invalid semicolon in the expression. Because it includes the expression code, it's fairly easy to understand. At the beginning of the error report, there's a reference to the JSP page file and the line in the page where the first error occurred, but all the other line numbers refer to the servlet code, not the JSP page.

The messages for the missing brace probably don't make much sense to you. The error messages refer to invalid use of `catch` and `try`, which doesn't seem to match any code in the JSP page scriptlets. That's because the code with the missing brace is inserted into the block of code generated to output template text, invoke actions, and so forth, as discussed earlier, so the compiler gets confused about what the real problem is.

How can you find the real problem when you get this type of message? If you're a Java programmer, you can look at the generated servlet source file and try to figure out what's really wrong. Most JSP containers can be configured so that the generated source code is saved for you to look at. For Tomcat it's the default, and the name of the file is shown in the error message.

But if you're not a programmer, the only thing you can do is to study all scriptlets in your JSP page carefully and try to figure out what's wrong. That's not always easy, and it's a good reason to avoid scripting elements in your JSP pages. When you have to use scripting, use only extremely simple code and be very careful with the syntax.

Let's look at some other common syntax errors so you at least know the types of messages to expect. Example 16-8 illustrates a typical mistake.

Example 16-8. Scriptlet instead of expression (error2.jsp)

```
<%@ page language="java" contentType="text/html" %>
<%@ page import="java.util.Date" %>
<html>
  <head>
    <title>Scriptlet instead of expression</title>
  </head>
  <body bgcolor="white">
    Howdy
    <% if (request.getParameter("name") == null) { %>
      stranger!
    <% } else { %>
      partner!
    <% } %>
    It's <% new Date().toString( ) %> and all is well.
  </body>
</html>
```

This is simply a case where the opening tag for a JSP expression (<%=) has mistakenly been written as the opening tag for a JSP scriptlet (<%). It looks like an innocent error, but the error message isn't giving you much help to find it:

```
org.apache.jasper.JasperException: Unable to compile class for JSP

An error occurred at line: 14 in the jsp file: /ch16/error2.jsp

Generated servlet error:
D:\jakarta-tomcat-5.0\work\localhost\ora\ch16\error2_jsp.java:56: ';' expected
                new Date().toString( )
                                      ^

1 error
```

Again, the scripting code and the generated code clash, resulting in a message that's hard to understand. But at least you can recognize the code from the JSP page and try to see what's really wrong.

Another common mistake has to do with how the Java compiler deals with classes in the unnamed package. Consider the page in Example 16-9 that uses a class named `GreetingBean` that doesn't belong to a specific package.

Example 16-9. Using a class from the unnamed package (error3.jsp)

```
<%@ page language="java" contentType="text/html" %>
<html>
  <head>
    <title>Using a class from the unnamed package</title>
  </head>
  <body bgcolor="white">
    <jsp:useBean id="greeting" class="GreetingBean" />
    <%= greeting.getGreeting( ) %>
  </body>
</html>
```

This results in an error report like this, even if the class file for the bean is located where it should (either in *WEB-INF/classes* or in a JAR file in *WEB-INF/lib*):

```
org.apache.jasper.JasperException: Unable to compile class for JSP

An error occurred at line: 7 in the jsp file: /ch16/error3.jsp

Generated servlet error:
D:\jakarta-tomcat-5.0\work\localhost\ora\ch16\error3_jsp.java:48:
cannot resolve symbol
symbol: class GreetingBean
location: class org.apache.jsp.error3_jsp
                GreetingBean greeting = null;
                ^

An error occurred at line: 7 in the jsp file: /ch16/error3.jsp

Generated servlet error:
D:\jakarta-tomcat-5.0\work\localhost\ora\ch16\error3_jsp.java:50:
cannot resolve symbol
symbol: class GreetingBean
location: class org.apache.jsp.error3_jsp
                greeting = (GreetingBean) pageContext.getAttribute(...)
                            ^

An error occurred at line: 7 in the jsp file: /ch16/error3.jsp

Generated servlet error:
D:\jakarta-tomcat-5.0\work\localhost\ora\ch16\error3_jsp.java:53:
cannot resolve symbol
symbol: class GreetingBean
location: class org.apache.jsp.error3_jsp
               greeting = (GreetingBean) java.beans.Beans.instantiate(...);
                           ^
3 errors
```

This is a problem I touched on earlier. Note that the error messages say that the symbol `GreetingBean` can not be found in the class `org.apache.jsp.error3_jsp`. The package prefix happens to be the package name Tomcat uses for the generated servlets, and other containers use different names. The important thing is that the Java compiler assumes that an unqualified class name refers to a class in the same package as the class it compiles, unless it's been imported with an import statement. Since classes from the unnamed package cannot be imported into a class that belongs to a package, the only recourse is to place the `GreetingBean` class in a package and use the fully qualified class name in the `class` attribute of the `<jsp:useBean>` action. If you need to refer to the class in scripting code, you may also want to add a page directive with an `import` attribute to the JSP page:

```
<%@ page language="java" contentType="text/html" %>
<%@ page import="com.mycompany.GreetingBean" %>
<html>
  <head>
    <title>Using a class from the unnamed package</title>
  </head>
  <body bgcolor="white">
    <jsp:useBean id="greeting" class="com.mycompany.GreetingBean" />
    <%= greeting.getGreeting( ) %>
  </body>
</html>
```

The misleading and confusing error messages reported for scripting syntax errors are, in my opinion, a big problem and one that's hard to solve completely, even with better JSP container implementations and tools. It can be minimized, but it's always hard for a container to pinpoint the real problem when scripting code is mixed with other generated code. My only advice at this point is (again) to avoid scripting code as much as possible.

CHAPTER 17
Bits and Pieces

In the previous chapters, I have demonstrated the standard JSP features as well as the JSTL actions and a few custom actions through practical, complete examples. But some features are hard to fit nicely into these examples without losing focus, so I describe them separately in this chapter instead. Topics covered here include buffering of the response body, ways to include shared page segments, global configuration settings, using client-side code to provide a more interactive interface, preventing JSP pages from being cached, writing JSP pages as well-formed XML documents, and a discussion about the different types of URIs used in JSP pages.

Buffering

There's one important thing about how a JSP page is processed that has not been covered in any example so far: buffering of the response body. As you may recall from Chapter 2, an HTTP response message contains both headers and a body. The headers tell the browser such things as what type of data the body contains (HTML text, an image), the size of the body, if the body can be cached, and so forth. Headers are also used to set cookies and to tell the browser to automatically get another page (a redirect). All response headers must be sent to the browser before the body is sent.

As soon as a JSP page writes something to the body of the message, the JSP container may start sending the response to the browser. It's then too late to set headers, since they have to be sent first. In a servlet, you have full control over when something is written to the response body, so you can make sure that you set all headers you need before you generate the body. In a JSP page, however, it's not that easy. Everything you put in a JSP page that is not a JSP element is written to the response body automatically by the JSP container. Here's the top part of the *autheticate.jsp* page from Chapter 13:

```
<%@ taglib prefix="c" uri="http://java.sun.com/jsp/jstl/core" %>
<%@ taglib prefix="sql" uri="http://java.sun.com/jsp/jstl/sql" %>
```

```
<%@ taglib prefix="ora" uri="orataglib" %>

<%-- Remove the validUser session bean, if any --%>
<c:remove var="validUser" />
...
```

It doesn't contain any HTML, so you may think that this doesn't add anything to the response body. But it does. This page snippet contains six lines: five lines with JSP elements and one blank line. The JSP elements themselves are evaluated by the JSP container and never show up in the response, but the linefeed character at the end of each line is not a JSP element, so it's added to the response body.

Later in the same page, custom actions are used to set cookies, or in other words, set response headers:

```
<c:choose>
  <c:when test="${!empty param.remember}">
    <ora:addCookie name="userName"
      value="${param.userName}"
      maxAge="2592000" />
    <ora:addCookie name="password"
      value="${param.password}"
      maxAge="2592000" />
  </c:when>
  <c:otherwise>
    <ora:addCookie name="userName"
      value="${param.userName}"
      maxAge="0" />
    <ora:addCookie name="password"
      value="$param.password}"
      maxAge="0" />
  </c:otherwise>
</c:choose>
```

This doesn't work if the linefeed characters added to the body have caused the response to be sent to the browser (the response has been *committed*, as it's called in the servlet specification). Besides not being able to set headers after the response has been committed, the servlet specification also prohibits a request being forwarded when data has already been written to the response body. This is because when you forward to another JSP page or servlet, the forwarding target should have full control over the request. If the originating page has already started to generate the response body, the target is no longer in charge.

Buffering solves this problem. Instead of sending the response to the browser as soon as something is written to the response body, the JSP container writes everything that's not a JSP element and all dynamic content generated by JSP elements to a buffer. At some point, such as when the buffer is full or the end of the page is reached, the container sends all headers that have been set, followed by the buffered body content. So in this example, all linefeed characters end up in the buffer, and the cookie headers are set. When the whole page has been processed, the JSP container sends all headers first and then the contents of the buffer. Works like a charm.

You can control the size of the buffer and what to do when the buffer is full with two page directive attributes:

```
<%@ page buffer="12kb" autoFlush="false" %>
```

The `buffer` attribute accepts a value that specifies the minimum size of the buffer; the container may choose to use a bigger buffer than specified. The value must be the number of kilobytes followed by `kb`. A buffer that holds at least 8 KB is used by default. The keyword `none` is also accepted. If you use this keyword, the JSP container will not perform any buffering of the response body.

The `autoFlush` attribute can be set to `true` or `false`, with `true` being the default. It specifies what to do when the buffer is full. If the value is `true`, the buffered content is sent (flushed) to the browser when the buffer is full, and the rest of the page gets buffered until the buffer is full again. If you specify the value `false`, the JSP container throws an exception when the buffer is full, ending the processing of the page.

In most cases, you want to use the default values. If you have an extremely large page in which you set headers at the end of the page, you may need to increase the buffer size. Eight kilobytes, however, is enough for most pages. Disabling buffering may make sense if you have a page that generates the result slowly, and you want to send what's ready to the browser as soon as possible. But even if you disable the JSP buffering, the servlet container may still do some buffering of the result, so there's no guarantee that it will be sent immediately. No matter what value you use for the `buffer` attribute, however, you can force the buffer to be flushed with a scriptlet like this:

```
<% out.flush(); %>
```

Setting the `autoFlush` attribute to `false` is rare. A possible use for this is if you have no control over the size of the dynamic content you generate, and you want to make sure the processing is aborted if you reach a certain limit.

Including Page Segments

You can use either a JSP directive or a standard action to include content in a JSP page. This is a useful technique when parts of all pages in an application are the same, such as headers, footers, and navigation bars.

The JSP `include` directive reads the content of the specified page in the translation phase (when the JSP page is converted into a servlet) and merges it with the original page:

```
<%@ include file="header.htmlf" %>
```

The `file` attribute is a relative path. If it starts with a slash, it's a context-relative path, interpreted relative to the context path assigned for the application. If it doesn't start with a slash, it's a page-relative path, interpreted relative to the path for the page that includes the file.

The included file can contain either only static content (such as HTML) or it can be a file with JSP elements. Its content is merged with the page that includes it, and the resulting page is converted into a servlet as described in Chapter 3. This means that the main page and all included pages share all page scope data. Scripting variables declared in JSP declarations, scriptlets, or actions, such as `<jsp:useBean>` or custom actions that introduce scripting variables, are also shared. Consequently, if the main page declares a variable, and the same name is used for another variable in an included page, it results in a translation phase error, because the combined page can't be compiled.

The JSP specification recommends you use a different file extension than *.jsp* for partial JSP pages that you include using the `include` directive, because they typically aren't complete, valid JSP pages. An alternative extension you can use is *.jspf* ("f" as in fragment, the term used for partial pages before JSP 2.0 started to use the same term for executable attribute values; the term *segment* is now used for partial pages, but the recommended file extensions remain). I follow this recommendation for HTML files as well and use *.htmlf* as the extension for static files that aren't complete HTML pages.

What happens when the file specified by the `include` directive changes isn't specified by the JSP specification. With some containers, you must change the modification date for the main page, for example using the *touch* command on a Unix system, before the changes take effect. An alternative is to delete the class file (the compiled version of the page) for the page. Other JSP containers may detect changes in included files automatically and go through the translation phase just like when you modify the main JSP page.

Another thing to be aware of is that the size of the compiled Java code (bytecode) for a method is limited to 64 KB by the Java Virtual Machine specification. This is normally not a problem, but if you use the `include` directive to include large files, you may run into this restriction in some JSP implementations. A workaround is to use the `<jsp:include>` action instead.

The `<jsp:include>` standard action is an alternative to the `include` directive; it includes another resource at runtime:

```
<jsp:include page="navigation.jsp" />
```

The action is executed in the request-processing phase instead of the translation phase. The `page` attribute value is interpreted as a relative URI, the same way as the `include` directive's `file` attribute. The `<jsp:include>` action doesn't include the actual contents of the specified page; it includes the response produced by executing the page. This means you can specify any type of web resource (e.g., a servlet, a JSP page, or a static HTML page) that produces a text response. The JSP container invokes the specified resource by an internal function call. Hence, the included resource is helping to process the original request and therefore has access to all objects in the request scope as well as all original request parameters.

Note, though, that it doesn't have access to any page-scope attributes or scripting variables declared in the main page.

<c:import> Versus <jsp:include>

As you may recall from Chapter 15, there's also a JSTL action named `<c:import>`. It can include the response produced by another application resource, just like the `<jsp: include>` action, but it can also include data from external resources, such as a different web application or an FTP server.

With the introduction of `<c:import>`, there are few reasons to use the less powerful `<jsp:include>`. Theoretically, it may be slightly faster because its implementation is simpler, but it's probably not a noticeable difference.

Since the page is not included until the main page is requested, you can use a request time attribute value for the page attribute to decide which page to include depending on a runtime condition, and add request parameters that can be read by the included page:

```
<jsp:include page="${pageSelectedAtRuntime}" >
  <jsp:param name="aNewParamer" value="aStaticValue" />
  <jsp:param name="anotherParameter" value="${aDynamicValue}" />
</jsp:include>
```

If you change the included JSP page, the new version is used immediately. This is because the included page is treated the same way as a JSP page invoked directly by a browser; the container detects that the page has been modified and goes through the translation phase before it invokes it.

Besides the page attribute, the `<jsp:include>` action also supports a `flush` attribute. It specifies whether the response body should be flushed before the page is included. If you have used a JSP 1.1 container, you've probably learned to always specify this attribute with the value `true`. This was a requirement in JSP 1.1 due to limitations in the Servlet 2.2 API, with the serious drawback that the main page couldn't set headers or forward to another page after the `<jsp:include>` action element. I'm happy to tell you that this limitation was removed in JSP 1.2. The `flush` attribute is now optional, and `false` is the default value.

Table 17-1 outlines the differences between the `include` directive and the `<jsp: include>` action.

Table 17-1. Differences between the include directive and the <jsp:include> action

Syntax	When	What
`<%@ include file="relativeURI" %>`	Translation phase	Static text (HTML, JSP) merged with the JSP page before it's converted to a servlet.

Table 17-1. Differences between the include directive and the <jsp:include> action (continued)

Syntax	When	What
`<jsp:include page="relativeURI" flush="true|false" />`	Request processing phase	The response text generated by executing the page or servlet.

Let's look at a concrete example of how you can use the two methods for including pages. Example 17-1 shows a page that includes three other pages.

Example 17-1. Including pages (page1.jsp)

```
<%@ page contentType="text/html" %>
<%@ include file="header.htmlf" %>
<table width="90%">
  <tr>
    <td valign="top" align="center" bgcolor="lightblue">
      <jsp:include page="navigation.jsp" />
    </td>
    <td valign="middle" align="center" width="80%">
      This is page 1
    </td>
  </tr>
</table>
<%@ include file="footer.htmlf" %>
```

The example application contains two more main pages, *page2.jsp* and *page3.jsp*, that differ from *page1.jsp* only in the text they contain (i.e., "This is page 2," "This is page 3"). The common header and footer for all pages in the example application consist of static HTML, shown in Examples 17-2 and 17-3. The `include` directive is used to include the header and footer files in each main page.

Example 17-2. Header (header.htmlf)

```
<html>
  <head>
    <title>Welcome to My Site</title>
  </head>
  <body bgcolor="white">
    <h1>My Site</h1>
```

Note that the *header.htmlf* file is not a complete HTML page. It contains only the start tags for the `<html>` and `<body>` elements.

Example 17-3. Footer (footer.htmlf)

```
<hr>
  Copyright &copy; 2003 My Company
  </body>
</html>
```

The end tags for the <body> and <html> tags are included in the *footer.htmlf* file. Merging the *header.htmlf*, one of the main pages, and the *footer.htmlf* files results in a complete HTML page.

Each page in the example application also has a navigation bar, with labels for all pages in the application. The labels are links to the corresponding pages, except for the current page, which is just written as plain text as shown in Figure 17-1.

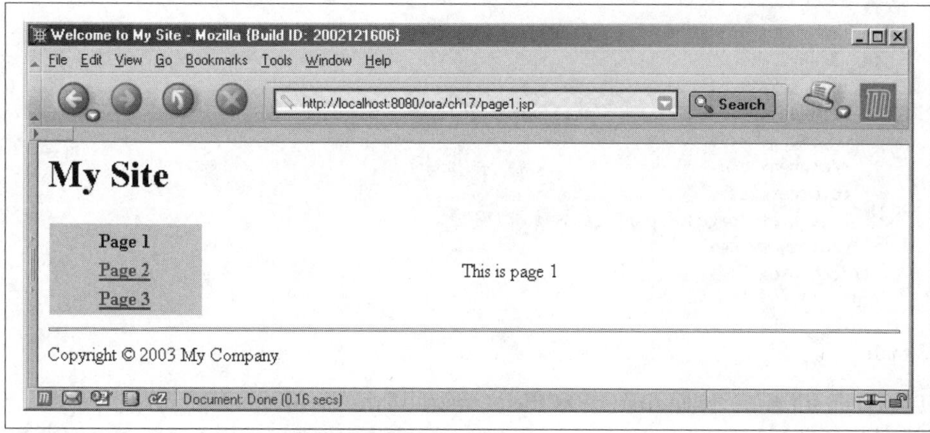

Figure 17-1. A page composed by including other pages

The JSP code for the navigation bar is separated out into its own file, shown in Example 17-4, and included in each page with the <jsp:include> action as shown earlier in Example 17-1.

Example 17-4. Navigation bar with JSTL actions (navigation_jstl.jsp)

```
<%@ taglib prefix="c" uri="http://java.sun.com/jsp/jstl/core" %>

<c:set var="uri" value="${pageContext.request.servletPath}" />
<table bgcolor="lightblue">
  <tr>
    <td>
      <c:choose>
        <c:when test="${uri == '/ch17/page1.jsp'}">
          <b>Page 1</b>
        </c:when>
        <c:otherwise>
          <a href="page1.jsp">Page 1</a>
        </c:otherwise>
      </c:choose>
    </td>
  </tr>
  <tr>
    <td>
      <c:choose>
        <c:when test="${uri == '/ch17/page2.jsp'}">
```

Example 17-4. Navigation bar with JSTL actions (navigation_jstl.jsp) (continued)

```
          <b>Page 2</b>
        </c:when>
        <c:otherwise>
          <a href="page2.jsp">Page 2</a>
        </c:otherwise>
      </c:choose>
    </td>
  </tr>
  <tr>
    <td>
      <c:choose>
        <c:when test="${uri == '/ch17/page3.jsp'}">
          <b>Page 3</b>
        </c:when>
        <c:otherwise>
          <a href="page3.jsp">Page 3</a>
        </c:otherwise>
      </c:choose>
    </td>
  </tr>
</table>
```

The navigation bar page first saves the context-relative path for the current page in a variable named uri with a <c:set> action and an EL expression that gets the path by reading the servletPath property from the request object accessed through the implicit pageContext variable. This works because the request object reflects the information about the page that includes the navigation bar page, not about the included page. An HTML table is then built with one cell for each main page in the application. In each cell, a <c:choose> block tests whether the cell represents the current page. If it does, the page name is written as bold text; otherwise, it's written as an HTML link.

Example 17-4 can be simplified with a custom action that does all the testing and generates the appropriate HTML instead, as shown in Example 17-5.

Example 17-5. Navigation bar with custom action (navigation.jsp)

```
<%@ page contentType="text/html" %>
<%@ taglib prefix="ora" uri="orataglib" %>
<table bgcolor="lightblue">
  <tr>
    <td>
      <ora:menuItem page="page1.jsp">
        <b>Page 1</b>
      </ora:menuItem>
    </td>
  </tr>
  <tr>
    <td>
      <ora:menuItem page="page2.jsp">
```

Example 17-5. Navigation bar with custom action (navigation.jsp) (continued)

```
        <b>Page 2</b>
      </ora:menuItem>
    </td>
  </tr>
  <tr>
    <td>
      <ora:menuItem page="page3.jsp">
        <b>Page 3</b>
      </ora:menuItem>
    </td>
  </tr>
</table>
```

The `<ora:menuItem>` action inserts the HTML found in its body into the page. If the page specified by the page attribute is the current page, the HTML is inserted as is. Otherwise, it's embedded in an HTML link element, as the `<c:choose>` block in Example 17-4. But unlike the JSTL version of this page, the `<ora:menuItem>` action also performs URL rewriting on the HTML link URL if needed (this includes the session ID in the URL).

You may wonder why I use the `include` directive for the header and footer and the `<jsp:include>` action for the navigation bar. Either one will do for all files in this example, but I chose the action for the navigation bar because this page needs to be updated as new pages are added to the application. Using the action guarantees that the new version of the file is used immediately. I picked the directive for the header and footer pages because there's a slight performance penalty with using the action (the container must make a function call at request time). In this example, I assumed that both the header and footer contain stable information. In the rare event that they change, I'm willing to force the JSP container to go through the translation phase by deleting the class files corresponding to each main page or changing the modification date for each page as described earlier.

Global Configuration Options

You can use the application deployment descriptor (*web.xml*) to define configuration options that apply to a group of JSP pages. These options are defined as subelements of the `<jsp-property-group>` element, which in turn is a subelement of the `<jsp-config>` element. More than one `<jsp-property-group>` element can be used, each with one or more nested `<url-pattern>` elements that associate the properties with all JSP pages that match the specified URL patterns:

```
<web-app>
  ...
  <jsp-config>
    <jsp-property-group>
      <url-pattern>*.jsp</url-pattern>
```

```
    ...
  </jsp-property-grop>
  <jsp-property-group>
    <url-pattern>/jsp12/*</url-pattern>
    ...
  </jsp-property-grop>
</jsp-config>
...
</web-app>
```

With exception for automatic include properties (described later), the JSP container applies the properties only from the `<jsp-property-group>` with the URL pattern that most closely matches the requested page. The specified properties apply to an entire translation unit, i.e., both the main JSP page and all files it includes using the `include` directive (with the exception for the file encoding property, which applies to individual files).

The URL pattern format and interpretation are the same as for servlet and filter mappings, described in Chapter 19. That is, one of the following types of patterns can be used:

Exact match rule
: A complete context-relative path, e.g., `/admin/authenticate.jsp`. This rule matches only the specific path.

Longest path prefix rule
: A context-relative path with a wildcard character (*), e.g., `/admin/*`. This rule matches all request with the same path before the wildcard character, and if there's more than one pattern that matches, the one with the longest matching path applies.

Extension rule
: A wildcard character (*) followed by a dot and a file extension, e.g., `*.jsp`. This rule matches all requests that end with the specified extension.

The container compares each request URL to the defined mapping rules, looking for matches in the order exact match, longest path-prefix and extension, and applies the properties mapped to the first pattern that matches.

Declaring a File as a JSP Page

If a request matches a URL pattern defined within any `<jsp-property-group>` element, it's implicitly defined to be a JSP page, i.e., a file the JSP container must process. A potential use for this feature is to define additional extensions that should be treated as JSP pages:

```
<web-app ...>
  ...
  <jsp-config>
    <jsp-property-group>
```

```
        <url-pattern>*.html</url-pattern>
      </jsp-property-group>
    </jsp-config>
    ...
  </web-app>
```

A deployment descriptor like this tells the container to process all requests with an *.html* extension as JSP pages; this might be used to add a piece of dynamic content to a previously static web site without having to rename all files.

Controlling the Interpretation of EL Expressions

Starting with JSP 2.0, EL expressions can directly be used in template text and in attribute values for any action element. A JSP application written for a prior version of the JSP specification, however, may use constructs that look like EL expressions and expect them to be used as literal strings instead of being evaluated.

To deal with this potential problem, the JSP 2.0 specification defines two ways to disable EL expression evaluation. First, EL expression evaluation is *disabled* by default for a web application with a deployment descriptor that is not Servlet 2.4 conformant (i.e., an application developed for a previous version of the Servlet and JSP specifications), and it's *enabled* by default for a web application with a Servlet 2.4 deployment descriptor. This guarantees that an old JSP application can be deployed in a JSP 2.0 container with full backwards compatibility, while a sensible default is provided for new applications. Second, the EL expression evaluation can be explicitly disabled in a JSP 2.0 application—for a single page with the `elIgnored` page attribute, or for a set of JSP pages with an `<el-ignored>` element in a JSP group:

```
  <web-app ...>
    ...
    <jsp-config>
      <jsp-property-group>
        <url-pattern>*.jsp</url-pattern>
        <el-ignored>true</el-ignored>
      </jsp-property-group>
    </jsp-config>
    ...
  </web-app>
```

The ability to disable EL evaluation in a JSP 2.0 application allows you to migrate an old application to the new JSP 2.0 features a few pages at a time, ensuring that the pages that have not yet been migrated behave as they did with JSP 1.2. If you define the EL evaluation mode with an `<el-ignored>` element in the deployment descriptor, you can override this setting with the `elIgnored` page attribute in individual pages. For instance, you can disable EL evaluation for all JSP pages with the deployment descriptor snippet shown here, and selectively enable it with the `elIgnored` attribute in each JSP page that's reviewed and migrated to JSP 2.0:

```
  <%@ page elIgnored="false" %>
```

Controlling the Use of Scripting Elements

With all the new features available through the JSP EL, JSTL, and custom actions, scripting elements are rarely needed. A company may decide to implement a policy of forbidding scripting elements altogether, avoiding all the potential problems that scripting introduces. A policy like this can be enforced with the `<scripting-invalid>` element, for all or selected parts of the application:

```
<web-app ...>
  ...
  <jsp-config>
    <jsp-property-group>
      <url-pattern>*.jsp</url-pattern>
      <scripting-invalid>true</scripting-invalid>
    </jsp-property-grop>
  </jsp-config>
  ...
</web-app>
```

With this configuration, the container refuses to process a JSP page that contains any scripting element (i.e., a scripting declaration, expression, or scriptlet). Since this represents a policy decision, there's no way to override this value in an individual JSP page.

Specifying the File Encoding

As you may recall from Chapter 14, the character encoding used for a JSP file can be defined within the file by the `pageEncoding` page attribute. This is all fine and dandy, as long as the file is in an encoding that uses the ASCII mapping for bytes 0 through 127; if not, the encoding cannot be read from the file. Some character encodings, such as UTF-16 and EBCDIC, don't share these byte-value mappings, so another approach is needed. The `<page-encoding>` element offers this alternative for classic JSP pages:

```
<web-app ...>
  ...
  <jsp-config>
    <jsp-property-group>
      <url-pattern>/ja/*</url-pattern>
      <page-encoding>Shift_JIS</page-encoding>
    </jsp-property-grop>
  </jsp-config>
  ...
</web-app>
```

This example tells the container to use the `Shift_JIS` encoding when reading a file in the */ja* directory. As opposed to all other property settings, this setting applies to individual files rather than to the entire translation unit. This means that in addition to files requested directly, the specified file encoding is used for all files under */ja* (in this example) added with an include directive in any JSP page, no matter what path is used to request that JSP page.

For JSP pages in XML syntax (so-called JSP Documents, described later), the file encoding is always determined based on the XML prolog in the file as described in the XML specification, so neither the `pageEncoding` attribute nor the `<page-encoding>` element should be used. If they are still used, and they specify a different encoding than the one determined according to the XML rules, the container doesn't accept the file and reports it as a translation error.

Specifying Automatically Included Files

If a lot of tag libraries are used for an application, or a set of pages need the same page attribute values to be set, it's easier to maintain the application if all the common declarations are placed in one file that is then included in all JSP pages. You can do so with the `include` directive, but then you run the risk of forgetting to include the file in a page. JSP 2.0 introduces a better solution: automatic includes.

You can use one or more `<include-prelude>` elements to include files at the beginning of all JSP pages that match the JSP property group URL pattern, and one or more `<include-coda>` elements to include files at the end of the JSP files. As opposed to all other configuration properties, you can even use multiple JSP property groups to define these two elements; the include elements from all groups that match the request URL are applied:

```
<web-app ...>
  ...
  <jsp-config>
    <jsp-property-group>
      <url-pattern>*.jsp</url-pattern>
      <include-prelude>/WEB-INF/segments/taglibDecl.jspf</include-prelude>
      <include-prelude>/WEB-INF/segments/errorPageDecl.jspf</include-prelude>
      <include-coda>/WEB-INF/segments/copyright.jspf</include-coda>
    </jsp-property-grop>
    <jsp-property-group>
      <url-pattern>/main/*</url-pattern>
      <include-prelude>/WEB-INF/segments/noSessionDecl.jspf</include-prelude>
    </jsp-property-group>
  </jsp-config>
  ...
</web-app>
```

In this example, I use one group for the `*.jsp` pattern that include files with common tag library and error page declarations at the beginning of each file, plus a copyright notice at the end of each file. I also define a group for the `/main/*` pattern, including a file with a page attribute that disables sessions. A request like */mycontext/main/index.jsp* matches the patterns for both groups, so the files defined in both groups are included. For a request like */mycontext/shopping/cart.jsp*, only the first group's URL pattern matches, so only the files defined in this group are included.

Declaring Files as JSP Documents

As I will show you later in this chapter, JSP pages can be written as well-formed XML documents, using a slightly different syntax for things like tag library declarations and other directives than what you've seen so far. The default extension for a JSP page in the XML format is *.jspx*, starting with the JSP 2.0 specification. To make it possible to use other extensions, and to allow applications that use this extension for regular JSP files, the `<is-xml>` element can be used to control whether a file should be processed as a JSP page in XML format:

```
<web-app ...>
  ...
  <jsp-config>
    <jsp-property-group>
      <url-pattern>*.jspx</url-pattern>
      <is-xml>false</is-xml>
    </jsp-property-grop>
    <jsp-property-group>
      <url-pattern>*.svg</url-pattern>
      <is-xml>true</is-xml>
    </jsp-property-grop>
  </jsp-config>
  ...
</web-app>
```

As with EL evaluations, the default for this property depends on which version of the servlet specification the application's deployment descriptor adheres to, in order to guarantee backward compatibility. If the application has a pre-2.4 deployment descriptor, the *.jspx* extension means nothing special; files with this extension are not considered to be JSP pages at all. For an application with a 2.4 deployment descriptor, files with a *.jspx* extension are processed as JSP XML pages by default.

The deployment descriptor snippet shown here defines two JSP groups. The first one disables the *.jspx* default extension, so that files with this extension are instead handled as regular JSP pages. The second one declares that files with an *.svg* extension must be handled as JSP pages in XML syntax.

Mixing Client-Side and Server-Side Code

I touched on the difference between server-side code and client-side code in Chapter 3. JSP is a server-side technology, so all JSP elements, such as actions and scriptlets, execute on the server before the resulting page is sent to the browser. A page can also contain client-side code, such as JavaScript code or Java applets, to provide a more interactive user interface. This code is executed by the browser itself.

A JSP page can generate JavaScript code dynamically the same way it generates HTML, WML, or any other type of text contents. Therefore, you can add client-side scripting code to your JSP pages. The important thing to keep in mind here is that even though you can include JavaScript code in your JSP page, the container doesn't see it as code at all. It treats it as template text and just sends it to the browser together with the rest of the response. Also remember that the only way a browser can invoke a JSP page is to send an HTTP request; there is no way that a JavaScript event handler such as `onClick` or `onChange` can directly invoke a JSP element such as an action, a scriptlet, or a Java method declared with a JSP declaration in a JSP page. A client-side script can ask the browser to make a request for a complete page, but there is no way that the script can process the response and use it to do something such as populate a selection list with the data.

Applets can make your pages more interesting and provide an easier-to-use interface than what's possible with pure HTML. As you will see, JSP includes a standard action for generating the HTML needed for embedding applets in a page in a browser-independent way.

Generating JavaScript Code

Example 17-6 shows a modified version of the User Info page used in the examples in Chapter 10.

Example 17-6. Input form with client-side validation code (clientscript.jsp)

```
<%@ page contentType="text/html" %>
<%@ taglib prefix="c" uri="http://java.sun.com/jsp/jstl/core" %>
<%@ taglib prefix="fn" uri="http://java.sun.com/jsp/jstl/core" %>

<html>
  <head>
    <title>User Info Entry Form</title>
    <script language="JavaScript">
      <!-- Hide from browsers without JavaScript support
      function isValidForm(theForm) {
        if (isEmpty(theForm.userName.value)) {
          theForm.userName.focus( );
          return false;
        }
        if (!isValidDate(theForm.birthDate.value)) {
          theForm.birthDate.focus( );
          return false;
        }
        if (!isValidEmailAddr(theForm.emailAddr.value)) {
          theForm.emailAddr.focus( );
          return false;
        }
        if (!isValidNumber(theForm.luckyNumber.value, 1, 100)) {
          theForm.luckyNumber.focus( );
          return false;
        }
        return true;
      }
```

Example 17-6. Input form with client-side validation code (clientscript.jsp) (continued)

```
      function isEmpty(aStr) {
        if (aStr.length == 0) {
          alert("Mandatory field is empty");
          return true;
        }
        return false;
      }
      function isValidDate(dateStr) {
        var matchArray = dateStr.match(/^[0-9]+-[0-1][0-9]-[0-3][0-9]$/)
        if (matchArray == null) {
          alert("Invalid date: " + dateStr);
          return false;
        }
        return true;
      }
      function isValidEmailAddr(emailStr) {
        var matchArray = emailStr.match(/^(.+)@(.+)\.(.+)$/)
        if (matchArray == null) {
          alert("Invalid email address: " + emailStr);
          return false;
        }
        return true;
      }
      function isValidNumber(numbStr, start, stop) {
        var matchArray = numbStr.match(/^[0-9]+$/)
        if (matchArray == null) {
          alert("Invalid number: " + numbStr);
          return false;
        }
        if (numbStr < start || numbStr > stop) {
          alert("Number not within range (" + start + "-" +
            stop + "): " + numbStr);
          return false;
        }
        return true;
      }
      -->
    </script>
  </head>
  <body bgcolor="white">
    <jsp:useBean id="userInfo"
      scope="request"
      class="com.ora.jsp.beans.userinfo.UserInfoBean"
    />

    <form action="userinfovalidate.jsp" method="post"
      onSubmit="return isValidForm(this)">
      <input type="hidden" name="submitted" value="true">
      <table>
        <c:if
          test="${param.submitted and userInfo.userNameValid == false}">
          <tr><td></td>
```

Example 17-6. Input form with client-side validation code (clientscript.jsp) (continued)

```
      <td colspan="2"><font color="red">
        Please enter your Name
      </font></td></tr>
    </c:if>
    <tr>
      <td>Name:</td>
      <td>
        <input type="text" name="userName"
          value="${fn:escapeXml(userInfo.userName)}">
      </td>
    </tr>
    <c:if test="${param.submitted and not userInfo.birthDateValid}">
      <tr><td></td>
      <td colspan="2"><font color="red">
        Please enter a valid Birth Date
      </font></td></tr>
    </c:if>
    <tr>
      <td>Birth Date:</td>
      <td>
        <input type="text" name="birthDate"
          value="${fn:escapeXml(userInfo.birthDate)}">
      </td>
      <td>(Use format yyyy-mm-dd)</td>
    </tr>
    <c:if test="${param.submitted and not userInfo.emailAddrValid}">
      <tr><td></td>
      <td colspan="2"><font color="red">
        Please enter a valid Email Address
      </font></td></tr>
    </c:if>
    <tr>
      <td>Email Address:</td>
      <td>
        <input type="text" name="emailAddr"
          value="${fn:escapeXml(userInfo.emailAddr)}">
      </td>
      <td>(Use format name@company.com)</td>
    </tr>
    <c:if test="${param.submitted and not userInfo.genderValid}">
      <tr><td></td>
      <td colspan="2"><font color="red">
        Please select a valid Gender
      </font></td></tr>
    </c:if>
    <tr>
      <td>Gender:</td>
      <td>
        <c:choose>
          <c:when test="${userInfo.gender == 'f'}">
            <input type="radio" name="gender" value="m">
              Male<br>
```

Example 17-6. Input form with client-side validation code (clientscript.jsp) (continued)

```
              <input type="radio" name="gender" value="f" checked>
                Female
            </c:when>
            <c:otherwise>
              <input type="radio" name="gender" value="m" checked>
                Male<br>
              <input type="radio" name="gender" value="f">
                Female
            </c:otherwise>
          </c:choose>
        </td>
      </tr>
      <c:if test="${param.submitted and not userInfo.luckyNumberValid}">
        <tr><td></td>
        <td colspan="2"><font color="red">
          Please enter a Lucky Number between 1 and 100
        </font></td></tr>
      </c:if>
      <tr>
        <td>Lucky number:</td>
        <td>
          <input type="text" name="luckyNumber"
            value="${fn:escapeXml(userInfo.luckyNumber)}">
        </td>
        <td>(A number between 1 and 100)</td>
      </tr>
      <c:if test="${param.submitted and not userInfo.foodValid}">
        <tr><td></td>
        <td colspan="2"><font color="red">
          Please select only valid Favorite Foods
        </font></td></tr>
      </c:if>
      <tr>
        <td>Favorite Foods:</td>
        <td>
          <input type="checkbox" name="food" value="z"
            ${userInfo.pizzaSelected ? 'checked' : ''}>Pizza<br>
          <input type="checkbox" name="food" value="p"
            ${userInfo.pastaSelected ? 'checked' : ''}>Pasta<br>
          <input type="checkbox" name="food" value="c"
            ${fn:escapeXml(userInfo.chineseSelected}) ? 'checked' : ''}>Chinese
        </td>
      </tr>
      <tr>
        <td colspan=2>
          <input type="submit" value="Send Data">
        </td>
      </tr>
    </table>
  </form>
 </body>
</html>
```

The only differences are that a client-side validation function is defined in a `<script>` element and that the method is invoked by the `onSubmit` JavaScript event handler added to the `<form>` element. When the user submits the form, the browser first executes the `isValidForm( )` JavaScript function to validate all input field values. Only if all values pass the test is the form actually submitted to the *userinfovalidate.jsp* page specified as the form's action URL. This means that the user is alerted to mistakes much faster, and the server is relieved from processing invalid requests.

However, the server also performs the validation when the form is finally submitted, in exactly the same way as described in Chapter 8. This is important, because you don't know if the user's browser supports JavaScript or if scripting has been disabled in the browser.

Please note that the JavaScript validation code shown in Example 17-6 is far from perfect. It's really intended only as an example. You can find much better validation code on sites such as the JavaScript Source (*http://javascript.internet.com/*). You may also want to put large amounts of JavaScript code such as this in a separate file to make the JSP page easier to read and maintain. Most browsers that support scripting allow you to specify an external source for the scripting code with the `src` attribute:

```
<html>
  <head>
    <title>User Info Entry Form</title>
    <script language="JavaScript" src="validate.js"></script>
  </head>
  <body bgcolor="white">
  ...
```

Using server-side data in JavaScript code

In Example 17-6, all JavaScript code is written as static template text. However, nothing prevents you from generating parts of the JavaScript code dynamically, for instance a JavaScript array with values retrieved from a database by the JSP page. Example 17-7 shows a page that uses JavaScript code for setting the value of a selection list based on the selection made in another list. To run this example, you need a database with two tables named `Sizes` and `Toppings`, each with two columns named `Name` (of type `CHAR`) and `Id` (of type `INT`).

Example 17-7. Dynamic selection setting (selections.jsp)

```
<%@ page contentType="text/html" %>
<%@ taglib prefix="c" uri="http://java.sun.com/jsp/jstl/core" %>

<html>
  <head>
    <title>Online Pizza</title>
    <script language="JavaScript" src="dynamicscript.jsp"></script>
  </head>
  <body bgcolor="white"
```

Example 17-7. Dynamic selection setting (selections.jsp) (continued)

```
  onLoad="setList(document.pizza.sels, values[0]);">
  <form name="pizza">
    Please make your pizza order selections below:
    <br>
    <select name="categories"
      onChange="setList(this.form.sels, values[this.selectedIndex]);">
      <option value="0">Size
      <option value="1">Toppings
    </select>
    <br>
    <select name="sels" size="6">
      <option>
        <c:forEach begin="1" end="25"> </c:forEach>
      </option>
    </select>
  </form>
 </body>
</html>
```

The form in Example 17-7 contains two selections lists named `categories` and `sels`. When the user selects a category from the first list, the JavaScript `onChange` handler calls a JavaScript function named `setList( )` to set the options in the second list. The `setList( )` function takes two arguments: a reference to the selection list that should be updated and an array with the choice values. The JavaScript `values` array contains nested arrays: one array for each selection category, containing another set of arrays for the choices within each category. Each choice array contains two elements: the name of the choice (e.g., "Pepperoni") and the value to use for the `<option>` element's value attribute (i.e., a unique ID for each choice). To set the initial values, the `onLoad` event handler for the `<body>` element calls the `setList( )` function with the subarray that contains the choices for the first category.

The *dynamicscript.jsp* file specified as the source for the `<script>` element generates the JavaScript `setList( )` function and `values` array. Example 17-8 shows how this JSP page fills the `values` array with values retrieved from two database tables.

Example 17-8. Dynamically generated JavaScript code (dynamicscript.jsp)

```
<%@ page contentType="application/x-javascript"%>
<%@ taglib prefix="c" uri="http://java.sun.com/jsp/jstl/core" %>
<%@ taglib prefix="sql" uri="http://java.sun.com/jsp/jstl/sql" %>
<%@ taglib prefix="fn" uri="http://java.sun.com/jsp/jstl/functions" %>

<sql:setDataSource var="pizza"
  driver="org.gjt.mm.mysql.Driver"
  url="jdbc:mysql:///test"
/>

<sql:query var="sizes" dataSource="${pizza}">
  SELECT * FROM Sizes
</sql:query>
```

Example 17-8. Dynamically generated JavaScript code (dynamicscript.jsp) (continued)

```
<sql:query var="toppings" dataSource="${pizza}">
  SELECT * FROM Toppings
</sql:query>

values = new Array(
  new Array(
    <c:forEach items="${sizes.rows}" var="size" varStatus="s">
      new Array("${fn:escapeXml(size.Name)}", "${size.Id}")
      <c:if test="${not s.last}">,</c:if>
    </c:forEach>
  ),
  new Array(
    <c:forEach items="${toppings.rows}" var="topping" varStatus="s">
      new Array("${fn:escapeXml(topping.Name)}", "${topping.Id}")
      <c:if test="${not s.last}">,</c:if>
    </c:forEach>
  )
);
function setList(selectCtrl, itemArray) {
  // Remove current items
  for (i = selectCtrl.options.length; i >= 0; i--) {
    selectCtrl.options[i] = null;
  }
  for (i = 0; i < itemArray.length; i++) {
    selectCtrl.options[i] = new Option(itemArray[i][0]);
    selectCtrl.options[i].value = itemArray[i][1];
  }
}
```

When the browser requests a JavaScript file it expects the response to be of type `application/x-javascript`. The page directive's `contentType` attribute in Example 17-8 takes care of that. The JSTL database actions described in Chapter 12 are used to get the data from the two tables. In this example, I use the `<sql:setDataSource>` action to create a `DataSource` instead of using the default (configured in the deployment descriptor) I used in Chapters 12 and 13. I tell the `<sql:query>` to use this `DataSource` by specifying the `dataSource` attribute. This way I can test this page with a different database from the one used for the other examples. In a production environment, I'd remove the `<sql:setDataSource>` action and make a real `DataSource` available in one of the ways described in Chapter 24.

The rest of the page consists of static JavaScript code (highlighted) and JSTL actions that generate JavaScript array creation code. For each category ("Sizes" and "Toppings"), a `<c:forEach>` action loops through the corresponding database query result and generates a JavaScript subarray with strings for the choice name and value. Here's a sample of the resulting JavaScript code sent to the browser:

```
values = new Array(
  new Array(
    new Array("Small",
```

```
            "0")
        ,
        new Array("Large",
            "1")
        ,
        new Array("X-Large",
            "2")
    ),
    ...
```

To decide whether to add a comma after the JavaScript subarray, I use the status bean optionally exposed by the `<c:forEach>` action. The name of the variable to hold the bean is specified by the `varStatus` attribute. Within the loop, I test the value of its `last` property. It's set to `true` by `<c:forEach>` when it processes the last element in the collection, so I add a comma as long as it's `false`.

When you mix code for the client and server like this, just remember which code executes where and when. To the code in the JSP page executing on the server, the JavaScript code it generates is just plain text; it doesn't even try to understand it. It's only when the page that contains the dynamically generated JavaScript code reaches the browser that it becomes meaningful and can be executed. The browser, on the other hand, couldn't care less that the JavaScript code was created by a JSP page; it has no idea how the code was created. It should be clear then, that JavaScript code can't call Java code in the JSP page and vice versa.

Using Java Applets

A Java applet is a Java class that is identified by a special element in an HTML page. The browser loads the class and executes it. An applet can provide a nice user interface on a web page. The problem is that the browsers don't keep up with the Java release cycles for the native Java support. Many users still have browsers that support only JDK 1.0, and more current browsers have so many limitations and bugs in their implementations that you're still limited to JDK 1.0 features to make the applet work.

To address this issue, Sun provides a Java runtime environment that can be integrated in a browser using the browser's native plug-in API. The product is appropriately named the Java Plugin, and as of this writing the JDK 1.4 version is available for Netscape Navigator and Internet Explorer on Windows, Linux, and Solaris. For an up-to-date list of supported platforms, visit Sun's Java Plugin page at *http://java.sun.com/products/plugin/*.

With the Java Plugin, you can use the latest Java features in your applets, such as the Swing GUI classes, collection classes, enhanced security, and more. But there's one more hurdle you have to jump. The HTML element you need in a page to get the Java Plugin (or any plug-in component) installed and loaded by the browser differs between Internet Explorer and Netscape Navigator. For Netscape, you need to use the <embed> element, while Internet Explorer requires the <object> element. Fortunately, JSP provides an easy solution to this problem, namely the <jsp:plugin> action.

The <jsp:plugin> action looks at the User-Agent request header to figure out which type of browser is requesting the page and inserts the appropriate HTML element for using the Java Plugin to run the applet. Example 17-9 shows an example borrowed from the Tomcat JSP examples.

Example 17-9. Embedding an applet in a JSP page (applet.jsp)

```
<%@ page contentType="text/html" %>
<html>
  <head>
    <title>Embedding an applet</title>
  </head>
  <body bgcolor="white">
    <h1>Embedding an applet</h1>
    <jsp:plugin type="applet" code="Clock2.class"
      codebase="applet"
      jreversion="1.2" width="160" height="150" >
      <jsp:params>
        <jsp:param name="bgcolor" value="ccddff" />
      </jsp:params>
      <jsp:fallback>
        Plugin tag OBJECT or EMBED not supported by browser.
      </jsp:fallback>
    </jsp:plugin>
  </body>
</html>
```

The <jsp:plugin> action has three mandatory attributes: type, code, and codebase. The type attribute must be set to either applet or bean (to include a JavaBeans object), code is used to specify the class name, and codebase is the absolute or relative URL for the directory or archive file that contains the class. Note that the applet class must be stored in a directory that can be accessed by the web browser, that is, part of the public web page structure for the application (such as in *webapps/myapp/myapplet.class*). While class files for beans and custom actions are typically stored in the *webapps/myapp/WEB-INF lib* and *classes* subdirectories, you can't store applet classes in these directories, because they are accessible only to the container. The different locations makes sense when you think about where the code is executed: the applet is loaded and executed by the browser; beans and custom action classes are loaded and executed by the container. In Example 17-9, the applet class file is stored in an *applet* subdirectory of the directory that holds the JSP page.

The <jsp:plugin> action also has a number of optional attributes, such as the width, height, and jreversion attributes used here. Appendix A contains a description of all attributes.

The body of the action element can contain nested elements. The `<jsp:params>` element, which in turn contains one or more `<jsp:param>` elements, provides parameter values to the applet. In Example 17-9, the applet's `bgcolor` parameter is set to the hexadecimal RGB value for light blue. The `<jsp:fallback>` element can optionally specify text that should be displayed instead of the applet in a browser that doesn't support the HTML `<object>` or `<embed>` element.

Figure 17-2 shows what the page in Example 17-9 looks like in a browser.

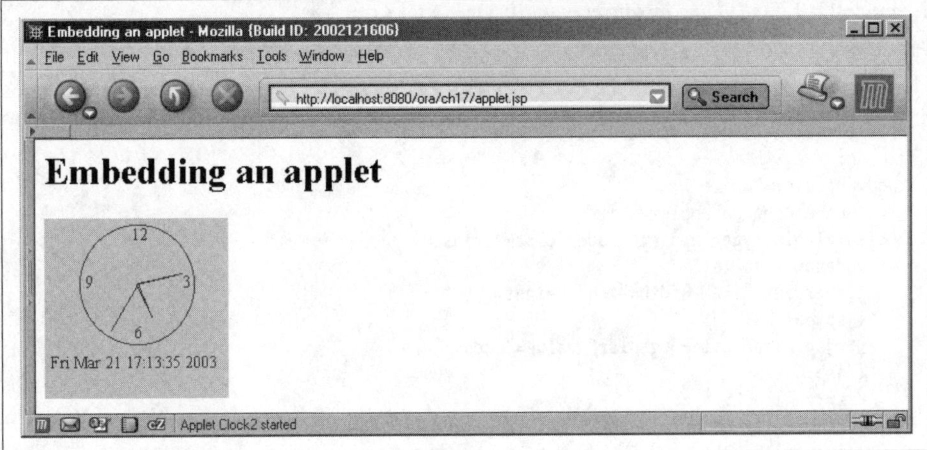

Figure 17-2. A page with an applet using the Java Plugin

An applet can communicate with the server in many different ways, but how it's done is off-topic for this book. If you would like to learn how to develop applets that communicate with a server, I suggest that you read Jason Hunter and William Crawford's *Java Servlet Programming* (O'Reilly). It includes a chapter about different applet-server communication options.

Precompiling JSP Pages

To avoid hitting your site visitors with the delay caused by the conversion of a JSP page into a servlet on the first access, you can precompile all pages in the application. Another use of precompilation is if you don't want anyone to change the pages in a JSP-based application after the application has been deployed. In this case, you can precompile all pages, define URL mappings for all JSP pages in the application deployment descriptor, and install just the Java class files for the compiled pages. We look at both these scenarios in this section.

One way of precompiling all pages in an application is to simply run through the application in a development environment and make sure you hit all pages. You can then copy the class files together with all the rest of the application to the production server when you deploy the application. Where the class files are stored varies between containers. Tomcat stores all JSP page implementation classes in its *work* directory by default, in a subdirectory per web application. As long as the modification dates of the class files are more recent than the corresponding JSP pages, the production server uses the copied class files.

The JSP specification also defines a special request parameter that can give the JSP container a hint that the page should be compiled without letting the page process the request. An advantage of using this method is that you can automatically invoke each page, perhaps using a simple load-testing tool, without having to provide all the regular request parameters the pages use. Because the pages aren't executed, application logic that requires pages to be invoked in a certain order or enforces similar rules can't interfere with the compilation. The request parameter name is `jsp_precompile`, and valid values are `true` and `false`, or no value at all. In other words, the following URLs are all valid:

/ora/ch17/applet.jsp?jsp_precompile
/ora/ch17/applet.jsp?jsp_precompile=true
/ora/ch17/applet.jsp?jsp_precompile=false

The third example is not very useful, because if the parameter value is `false`, the request is simply ignored. A JSP container that receives a request like the ones in the first and second example should compile the JSP page (go through the translation phase) but not let the page process the request. Most JSP containers support this feature, even though the specification doesn't require it. A compliant JSP container is allowed to ignore the compilation request, as long as it doesn't let a JSP page process a request that includes a `jsp_precompile` parameter with the value `true` or no value at all.

When you have compiled the JSP pages, you can package your application without the JSP pages themselves, using only the generated servlet class files. You do this by adding URL mapping definitions in the application deployment descriptor, so that a request for a certain JSP page is served directly by the corresponding servlet instead:

```
<web-app>
  ...
  <servlet>
    <servlet-name>easy</servlet-name>
    <servlet-class>org.apache.jsp.ch5.easy_jsp</servlet-class>
  </servlet>
  ...
  <servlet-mapping>
    <servlet-name>easy</servlet-name>
    <url-pattern>/ch5/easy.jsp</url-pattern>
  </servet-mapping>
  ...
</web-app>
```

The <servlet> element maps the servlet class name to a symbolic name. The class name for a JSP page implementation class (the generated servlet) is container-dependent; this example uses the type of class name Tomcat creates. The <servlet-mapping> element then tells the container to invoke the class when it receives a request matching the defined pattern, which is the context-relative path for the JSP page.

There are two reasons why you might want to precompile the JSP pages and define URL mappings for them. One reason is that using the servlet class directly is slightly faster, since the container doesn't have to go through the JSP container code to figure out which servlet class to use. The other reason is that if you don't include the JSP pages in the application packet, no one can change the application. This can be an advantage if you resell prepackaged JSP-based applications.

Doing all this by hand is a lot of work. Fortunately, the Apache *Ant* Java-based build tool (available at *http://ant.apache.org/*) combined with the *JspC* tool that's part of Tomcat can do all this for you. *Ant* uses an XML file that defines the tasks needed to build an application from source files. *JspC* (JSP Compiler) is a Java class that uses Tomcat's JSP container to generate servlet classes for all JSP pages in an application and creates the URL mapping declarations automatically.

After you have installed *Ant*, create an *Ant* build file, named *build.xml*, with this content (you find a file like this in the root directory for the examples application):

```
<project name="Precompile" default="all" basedir=".">

  <target name="jspc">
    <taskdef classname="org.apache.jasper.JspC" name="jasper2" >
      <classpath id="jspc.classpath">
        <pathelement location="${java.home}/../lib/tools.jar"/>
        <fileset dir="${tomcat.home}/server/lib">
          <include name="*.jar"/>
        </fileset>
        <fileset dir="${tomcat.home}/common/lib">
          <include name="*.jar"/>
        </fileset>
      </classpath>
    </taskdef>

    <jasper2
             validateXml="false"
             uriroot="${webapp.path}"
             webXmlFragment="${webapp.path}/WEB-INF/generated_web.xml"
             outputDir="${webapp.path}/WEB-INF/src" />
  </target>

  <target name="compile">
    <mkdir dir="${webapp.path}/WEB-INF/classes"/>
    <mkdir dir="${webapp.path}/WEB-INF/lib"/>

    <javac destdir="${webapp.path}/WEB-INF/classes"
```

```
            optimize="off"
            debug="on" failonerror="false"
            srcdir="${webapp.path}/WEB-INF/src"
          excludes="**/*.smap">
        <classpath>
          <pathelement location="${webapp.path}/WEB-INF/classes"/>
          <fileset dir="${webapp.path}/WEB-INF/lib">
            <include name="*.jar"/>
          </fileset>
          <pathelement location="${tomcat.home}/common/classes"/>
          <fileset dir="${tomcat.home}/common/lib">
            <include name="*.jar"/>
          </fileset>
          <pathelement location="${tomcat.home}/shared/classes"/>
          <fileset dir="${tomcat.home}/shared/lib">
            <include name="*.jar"/>
          </fileset>
        </classpath>
        <include name="**" />
        <exclude name="tags/**" />
      </javac>
    </target>

    <target name="all" depends="jspc,compile">
    </target>
  </project>
```

The build file first defines a target (build step) named `jspc` that uses the *JspC* tool to generate Java source files for all JSP pages in a web application. The source files are created in the *WEB-INF/src* directory. *JspC* also generates `<servlet>` and `<servlet-mapping>` elements for each JSP page and places them in *WEB-INF/generated_web.xml*. The second target, named `compile`, creates the *WEB-INF/classes* and *WEB-INF/lib* directories if they don't exist, and then compiles all the generated Java source files for the JSP pages with the class files ending up in the *WEB-INF/classes* directory.

To process this build file, use a command shell and change directory to where the *build.xml* file is located. For the examples application, this is *webapps/ora*, if you have installed the examples as described in Chapter 4. Then run this command:

```
C:\> ant -Dtomcat.home=%CATALINA_HOME% -Dwebapp.path=.
```

If the *build.xml* file is located in some other directory than the application root directory, specify the real path for the `-Dwebapp.path` argument. Running this command creates compiled versions of all JSP pages and places the class files under *WEB-INF/classes* and the mapping elements in the *WEB-INF/generated_web.xml* file. If you have a *web.xml* file with other configuration setting, just copy the contents of the *generated_web.xml* file into the real *web.xml* file; if you don't have any other setting, just rename the file to *web.xml* and add an XML declaration and the root element, as shown in Appendix F. You can now remove the JSP pages, because the mappings tells the container to invoke the precompiled class files directly.

There is one more thing you need to be aware of. *JspC* is not part of the JSP specification; it's a tool that is available only for Tomcat. Other containers may contain similar tools, though. Using *JspC* or a similar tool works fine as long as you compile and deploy the generated servlet classes using the same web container product. But a web container uses its own internal classes in the generated servlets, which means that if you generate the servlets with one web container (such as Tomcat) and deploy them in another (such as New Atlanta's ServletExec), you must also deliver the internal classes. For Tomcat, these classes are packaged in the *common/lib/jasper-runtime.jar* file, and you're free to deliver this JAR file with your application. If you use a precompilation tool that belongs to some other container, you need to read the documentation and see where the internal classes it needs are stored. Also make sure the tool has a license that allows you to redistribute those classes before you bundle them with your application.

Preventing Caching of JSP Pages

A browser can cache web pages so that it doesn't have to get them from the server every time the user asks for them. Proxy servers can also cache pages that are frequently requested by all users going through the proxy. Caching helps cut down the network traffic and server load, and provides the user with faster responses. But caching can also cause problems in a web application in which you really want the user to see the latest version of a dynamically generated page.

Both browsers and proxy servers can be told not to cache a page by setting response headers. You can use a scriptlet like this in your JSP pages to set these headers:

```
<%
  response.addHeader("Pragma", "no-cache");
  response.setHeader("Cache-Control", "no-cache, no-store, must-revalidate");
  response.addHeader("Cache-Control", "pre-check=0, post-check=0");
  response.setDateHeader("Expires", 0);
%>
```

An alternative is to use a custom action that's included with the book examples:

```
<%@ taglib uri="orataglib" prefix="ora" %>
<ora:noCache/>
```

The `<ora:noCache>` action sets the exact same headers as the scriptlet example, but it's cleaner.

The reason so many headers are needed is that different browsers and proxies respect different headers. The `Pragma` header is intended for old HTTP/1.0 clients. According to the HTTP/1. 0 specification, this header is really a request header but proxies and some browsers are known to respect it even when it's used as a response header. The `Cache-Control` header is an HTTP/1.1 header, so older browsers may not recognize it. The `no-cache` and `no-store` values mean that the client is not allowed to save a local copy of the page, and the must-revalidate that it must always ask the server if a new version is available. The second set of Cache-Control values are "extensions" supported by Internet Explorer, with basically the same meaning as the standard values used in the first set. The Expires header, finally, is defined by the HTTP/1.0 specification, so all browsers should recognize it. The value is the date and time when the response is no longer valid. The setDateHeader( ) method converts the value 0 to Thu, 1 Dec 1970 00:00:00 GMT; in other words, a date way in the past to ensure that the client gets a new copy every time this page is requested.

There's a subtle difference between telling the browser that the response has already expired and telling it not to cache the response. According to the HTTP/1.1 specification, if you say only that the response has expired, the browser is supposed to show a cached copy when the user uses the **Back** button or selects the page from the history list. It should ask the server for a new version only when the user makes an explicit request for the page by clicking a link, submitting a form, or typing the URL in the address field. However, if you tell the browser not to cache the response, it's not allowed to ever use a cached copy, not even for a **Back** button or history list selection. This is the safest model for responses that include sensitive information intended only for an authorized user, but it may not be the right choice for all responses.

By including or excluding the Pragma and Cache-Control headers, you can get the behavior that is appropriate for your specific application. In theory, that is. Unfortunately, browsers don't always behave as they should. Most (if not all) versions of Netscape and Mozilla, for instance, don't cache a response that has expired so excluding the cache headers makes no difference. Some versions of Internet Explorer are infamous for ignoring the cache headers, forcing you to use <http-equiv> elements in the page instead of (or in addition to) setting the headers to avoid a response to be cached. For more on the Internet Explorer problems, see *http://support.microsoft.com/default.aspx?scid=kb;EN-US;q222064*. Finally, some proxy and caching servers ignore all of this. An ugly but effective workaround in this case is to generate unique URLs for all application pages by including a query string parameter with a new value for each request, for instance using a counter like this:

```
<c:set var="${counter + 1}" scope="application" />
<a href="mypage.jsp?nocache=${counter}">
  This page is never cached</a>
```

As you can see, in the real world it can be hard to get this right. I recommend that you set the appropriate headers for the behavior you want first, assuming that the browsers and proxies used by the web application users are specification-compliant. Then test with the set of browser versions you want to support, using all the caching options each browser supports. Revert to <http-equiv> elements or the unique query string solution only if nothing else works.

Writing JSP Pages as XML Documents

An important part of JSP 2.0 is the added flexibility for writing JSP pages as well-formed, namespace-aware XML documents. Such JSP pages are referred to as *JSP Documents*, to distinguish them from the type of plain JSP pages described in the rest of this book. Tag files, described in Chapter 11, can also be written as XML documents. While all examples in this section show JSP Documents, you should be aware that everything said about JSP Documents also applies to tag files in XML format.

The main differences between a plain JSP page and a JSP Document are:

- Template data and JSP elements, taken together, must form a well-formed XML document, which optionally can be validated. This means, among other things, that XML element equivalents must be used instead of the regular JSP directive and scripting elements.
- A JSP Document is initially processed as a namespace aware XML document, meaning that standard XML entity resolution applies, page encoding determination is performed as defined by the XML specification, namespace declarations are honored and apply to both JSP elements and template data elements, XML quoting rules apply (special characters in attribute values and text nodes must be encoded), etc.
- Whitespace is processed in the same manner as when XSLT is used to process an XML document. That is, text nodes that contain only whitespace are dropped, except for text nodes in the body of a `<jsp:text>` element (where whitespace is preserved).
- An XML declaration may be generated for the response.

Prior to JSP 2.0, a JSP Document had to use `<jsp:root>` as its root element, making this syntax of interest primarily for validation and authoring tools. The more flexible rules introduced in JSP 2.0 extend the use of the XML syntax to other areas, such as pages used to generate any well-formed XML document and pages created with XML-aware editors.

Apart from the differences listed here, a JSP Document is processed as a regular JSP page after it's been successfully processed (and validated, if necessary) as an XML document, so you can use all standard and custom actions, as well as EL expressions in the document.

Identifying a JSP Document

The container needs help to recognize a JSP page as a page using the XML syntax. A JSP 2.0 container follows these rules, in this order:

- The requested page has an extension matching the URL pattern of a JSP group declaration in the *web.xml* file with `<is-xml>` set to `true`, as described earlier.

- The requested page has the *.jspx* extension, unless this extension has been disabled by a JSP group with `<is-xml>` set to `false`. For a tag file in XML syntax, the *.tagx* extension must be used.
- The requested page is identified as a JSP page (through the default *.jsp* extension or an extension defined by a JSP group declaration) and its root element is `<jsp:root>`.

The third rule was the only one supported by JSP 1.2, as I mentioned earlier, and it's primarily kept for backward compatibility. For new applications, you probably want to rely on one of the first two rules instead.

Let's use a simple JSP Document to discuss the syntax requirements in more detail. Example 17-10 shows a JSP Document that illustrates most of the things you need to consider, as well as the main features available for this format.

Example 17-10. A JSP Document (jspdocument.jspx)

```
<html
  xmlns="http://www.w3c.org/1999/xhtml"
  xmlns:jsp="http://java.sun.com/JSP/Page"
  xml:lang="en" lang="en">

  <jsp:output doctype-root-element="html"
    doctype-public="-//W3C//DTD XHTML 1.0 Transitional//EN"
    doctype-system="http://www.w3c.org/TR/xhtml1/DTD/xhtml1-transitional.dtd"/>

  <jsp:directive.page contentType="text/html" />

  <head>
    <title>A JSP Document</title>
  </head>
  <body bgcolor="white">
    <h1>All Request Parameters</h1>

    <ul>
      <c:forEach xmlns:c="http://java.sun.com/jsp/jstl/core"
        items="${paramValues}" var="current">
        <li>
          ${current.key}:
          <c:forEach items="${current.value}" var="parValue">
            <br/>${parValue}
          </c:forEach>
        </li>
      </c:forEach>
    </ul>

    <jsp:element name="${param.element}">
      <jsp:attribute name="style">${param.style}</jsp:attribute>
      <jsp:body>${param.body}</jsp:body>
    </jsp:element>
```

Example 17-10. A JSP Document (jspdocument.jspx) (continued)

```
  </body>
</html>
```

The JSP Document in Example 17-10 generates a list of all parameters received with the request and an element based on the parameter data.

The `<html>` element contains two `xmlns` attributes. These attributes are used to declare namespaces in an XML document. The first one declares the XHTML namespace as the default namespace for the document. The second one declares that elements with the prefix `jsp` belong to the JSP namespace, identified by the *http://java.sun.com/JSP/Page* URI. You must use this declaration in a JSP Document where you use JSP standard actions. You can actually declare a prefix other than `jsp` for the standard actions in a JSP Document. I suggest, however, that you stick to the default prefix unless you absolutely have to use another (e.g., because you need to use the `jsp` prefix for another namespace in the generated response); using a different prefix is likely to just cause confusion.

Custom Tag Library Declarations

Custom tag libraries are declared and associated with a prefix through namespace declarations in a JSP Document. In Example 17-10, you see that the JSTL core tag library is declared with an `xmlns` prefixed attribute in the `<c:forEach>` element. As in XML, you can declare all namespaces you need either in the root element or in nested elements (where it applies only to that element and its children). The custom tag library prefix is the part of the attribute name following `xmlns:`, and the attribute value is usually the URI for the library (as defined either in the *web.xml* file or in the TLD file for the library). That's how the JSTL core library is declared in Example 17-10. If you want to use the TLD or JAR file path instead of a URI value, you must use a value starting with `urn:jsptld:` followed by the path, for instance:

```
<html xmlns:ora="urn:jsptld:/WEB-INF/lib/orataglib_3_0.jar"
  ...>
```

If the custom tag library consists of a set of tag files directly in the web application structure (i.e., a library that you would identify with the `tagdir` attribute of a `taglib` directive in a regular JSP page), the value must start with `urn:jsptagdir:`, followed by the path to the directory:

```
<html xmlns:my="urn:jsptagdir:/WEB-INF/tags/mytags"
  ...>
```

Generating a DOCTYPE Declaration

Because the page in Example 17-10 generates an XHTML response, the response body should start with a DOCTYPE declaration for XHTML. This is not a JSP specification requirement, but for XML documents defined by a DTD or an XML Schema, it's always a good idea. The `<jsp-output>` action with the `doctype-root-element`, `doctype-public`, and `doctype-system` attributes adds a DOCTYPE declaration based on the attribute values at the top of the response body. With the attribute values used in Example 17-10, the generated declaration looks like this:

```
<!DOCTYPE html PUBLIC "-//W3C//DTD XHTML 1.0 Transitional//EN"
  "http://www.w3c.org/TR/xhtml1/DTD/xhtml1-transitional.dtd">
```

The `doctype-public` attribute is optional. If you omit it, the action generates a declaration without a public identifier.

Note that if you include a DOCTYPE declaration that specifies a DTD in the JSP Document itself, it applies to the JSP Document, not to the generated response. In this case, the container validates the JSP Document against the specified DTD.

XML Syntax for JSP Directives and Scripting Elements

The syntax used for JSP directives and scripting elements in a regular JSP page won't fly in a JSP Document; this syntax is not well-formed XML. You must use these XML elements with equivalent meaning instead:

`<jsp:directive.page` *`attribute_list`* `/>`
: Corresponds to `<%@ page` *`attribute_list`* `%>`, in which the attribute list contains all the attributes supported by the page directive, as described in Appendix A.

`<jsp:directive.include file="`*`file_path`*`" />`
: Corresponds to `<%@ include file="`*`file_path`*`" %>`.

`<jsp:declaration> ... </jsp:declaration>`
: Corresponds to `<%! ...%>`.

`<jsp:expression> ... </jsp:expression>`
: Corresponds to `<%= ... %>`.

`<jsp:scriptlet> ... </jsp:scriptlet>`
: Corresponds to `<% ... %>`.

The `<jsp:directive.page>` element with the `contentType` attribute in Example 17-10 shows you a concrete example of this syntax.

Generating Elements Dynamically

Example 17-10 contains a JSP standard action that you have not seen in previous examples, combined with a couple of actions that are more familiar:

```
<jsp:element name="${param.element}">
  <jsp:attribute name="style">${param.style}</jsp:attribute>
  <jsp:body>${param.body}</jsp:body>
</jsp:element>
```

The `<jsp:element>` action generates a new XML element in the response with the name specified by the `name` attribute. The `<jsp:attribute>` and `<jsp:body>` elements perform the same function as in previous chapters—adding an attribute and a body to the element, respectively. Together, these standard actions allow you to create any XML element, with any number of attributes and a body based on the evaluation result of their bodies, while still keeping the JSP Document as a well-formed XML document. For instance, if the page in Example 17-10 receives the parameters `element` with the value `p`, `style` with the value `font-weight:bold`, and `body` with the value `Hello+World`, this element is generated:

```
<p style="font-weight:bold">Hello World</p>
```

Encoding Non-XML Data and Special Characters

Since a JSP Document is a formal XML document, all template data must be well-formed XML. Example 17-10 is well-formed because it contains XHTML elements, such as the `<ul>` and `<li>` elements, represented by opening and closing tags, and an empty `<br/>` tag.

If you use a JSP Document to generate a response in a format that is not XML-based, you can embed the template data that is not well-formed in XML CDATA sections. For instance, if the response must be accessible to older browsers that only understand HTML 3.2, you can't use the XHTML `<br/>` empty tag syntax, but using HTML 3.2 syntax with a single opening `<br>` tag violates the well-formedness requirement. Embedding the HTML 3.2 single opening `<br>` tag in a `CDATA section` solves the problem; it satisfies the container's well-formed XML requirement and feeds the browser the HTML 3.2 tag it understands:

```
<ul>
  <c:forEach items="${paramValues}" var="current">
    <li>
      ${current.key}:
      <c:forEach items="${current.value}" var="parValue">
        <![CDATA[<br>]]>${parValue}
      </c:forEach>
    </li>
  </c:forEach>
```

In an XML document, special characters such as greater-than and less-than in an element body (or attribute) must be replaced with character entity codes, for example, the < character must be replaced with `<` and > must be replaced with `>`. These characters are common in Java code, so if you need to use scripting elements in a JSP Document, you can use a CDATA section to work around this issue as well:

```
<jsp:scriptlet>
  <![CDATA[
    if (someNumber > 0) {
      isValid = true;
    }
  ]]>
</jsp:scriptlet>
```

Another case where special characters must be dealt with is in request-time attribute values. For EL expressions, you must use the XML-safe operators—and, lt, gt, le, and ge instead of &&, <, >, <=, and >=—or use character entity codes in the expression: &&, <, >, <=, and >=. For a scripting request-time attribute value, you must also use a slightly different syntax than in a regular JSP page:

```
<jsp:setProperty name="emp" property="hireDate"
  value="%= new java.util.Date( ) %" />
```

The difference, as shown here, is that the troublesome less-than and greater-than signs are removed.

Using the <jsp:root> Element

Most JSP Documents developed for JSP 2.0 don't use the <jsp:root> element, but it's still supported. Potential reasons for using it in JSP 2.0 are if you need to generate a sequence of XML documents (i.e., the result has more than one root element) or if you want to generate content that is not XML at all but you prefer to use XML syntax in the JSP page (e.g., because you're using an XML-aware editor).

The <jsp:root> element has a mandatory version attribute, and it can be used to declare the JSP namespace and custom tag libraries used in the page with xmlns attributes:

```
<jsp:root
  xmlns:jsp="http://java.sun.com/JSP/Page"
  xmlns:c="http://java.sun.com/jsp/jstl/core"
  version="2.0">

  ...

</jsp:root>
```

The version attribute value is the JSP specification version the document complies with, and it must be 1.2 or 2.0. Other than that, a JSP Document with <jsp:root> as its root element looks just the same as the JSP Documents described earlier. The element only serves to identify the page as a JSP Document, and it's not included in the response produced by the page.

XML Declaration Generation

When the container processes a JSP Document, it adds an XML declaration like this to the response in most cases:

```
<? xml version="1.0" encoding="encodingValue" ?>
```

The encoding attribute value is the response character encoding defined by a page directive with a contentType attribute containing a character encoding, as described in Chapter 14, or UTF-8 if it's not defined in the JSP Document.

The XML declaration is generated by default for a JSP Document, unless `<jsp:root>` is used as the root element. You can use the `<jsp:output>` standard action to suppress the generation of the declaration, or to force it to be generated for a `<jsp:root>` document:

```
<jsp:output omit-xml-declaration="true" />
```

The `omit-xml-declaration` attribute accepts one of four values: with the value `true` or `yes`, the declaration is not generated; if set to `false` or `no`, it is. A reason to omit the declaration is when the generated response is included into another document, for instance using the `<jsp:include>` action in another JSP Document.

For tag files written in XML syntax, no XML declaration is generated by default, since their output typically gets mixed with the content of the page that invokes them. In the rare event you need one, you can use the `<jsp:output>` action in the tag file with `omit-xml-declaration` set to `false` or `no`.

How URIs Are Interpreted

One thing that can be confusing in a JSP-based application is the different type of URIs used in the HTML and JSP elements. The confusion stems from a combination of conflicting terms used to describe URIs in the HTTP, servlet, and JSP specifications, and the fact that some types of URIs are interpreted differently in the HTML and servlet worlds.

In HTML, URIs are used as attribute values in elements such as `<a>`, `<img>`, and `<form>`. JSP elements that use URI attribute values are the `page`, `include`, and `taglib` directives and the `<jsp:forward>` and `<jsp:include>` actions. JSTL and custom actions can also define attributes that take URI values.

The HTTP/1.1 specification (RFC 2616, with more details in RFC 2396) defines a URI as a string, following certain rules, that uniquely identifies a resource of some kind. A URL is just a special kind of URI that includes a location (such as the server name in an HTTP URL). An absolute URI is a URL that starts with the name of a so-called scheme, such as `http` or `https`, followed by a colon and then the rest of the resource identifier. An example of an absolute URI for a resource accessed through the HTTP protocol is:

```
http://localhost:8080/ora/ch12/login.jsp
```

Here `http` is the scheme, `localhost:8080` is the location (a server name and a port number), and `/ora/ch12/login.jsp` is the path.

The URIs in HTML elements are interpreted by the browser. A browser needs the absolute URI to figure out how to send the requests for the resources referenced by the HTML elements. It uses the scheme to select the correct protocol and the location to know where to send the request. The path is sent as part of the request to the server, so the server can figure out which resource is requested. But when you write a URI in an HTML document, such as the `action` attribute of a form element or the src attribute of an image element, you don't have to specify an absolute URI if the resource is located on the same server. Instead you can use just the URI path:

```
<img src="/images/hello.gif">
```

This type of URI is called an *absolute path*, meaning it contains the complete path for the resource within a server; the only difference compared to an absolute URI is that the scheme and location is not specified. The browser interprets an absolute path URI as a reference to a resource on the server that produced the response, so it adds the scheme and location it used to make the request. It then has the absolute URI it needs to make a request for the referenced resource.

Another type of URI is called a *relative path*, because it's interpreted relative to the path of the current page. A relative path doesn't start with a slash:

```
<form action="authenticate.jsp">
<img src="../images/hello.gif"
```

Here the action attribute references a JSP file at the same level in the path structure as the page that contains the reference. The src attribute value uses the ../ notation to refer to a resource one level up in the structure. The browser interprets a relative path URI as relative to the path for the request that produced the page. If the two relative paths in this example are used in a page generated by a request for *http://localhost:8080/ora/ch13/login.jsp*, the browser interprets them as the following absolute URIs:

```
http://localhost:8080/ora/ch13/authenticate.jsp
http://localhost:8080/ora/images/hello.gif
```

Relative URI paths offer a lot of flexibility. If all references between the web resources in an application are relative, you can move the application to a different part of the path structure without changing any URIs. For instance, if you move the pages from */ora/ch13* to */billboard*, the relative paths still reference the same resources.

So far, so good. Now let's see what happens in a Java web container when it receives a request. The first part of a URI for a servlet or JSP page has a special meaning. It's called the *context path*; one example is the */ora* path used for all examples in this book. As described in Chapter 2, a servlet container can contain multiple web applications, handled by a corresponding servlet context. Each web application is associated with a unique context path, assigned when the web application is installed. When the web container receives a request, it uses the context path to select the servlet context that's responsible for handling the request. The container hands over the request to the selected context, which then uses the URI path minus the context path to locate the requested resource (a servlet or a JSP page) within the context. For instance, an absolute URI such as *http://localhost:8080/ora/ch13/login.jsp* is interpreted by the container as a request for a JSP page named */ch13/login.jsp* within the context with the context path */ora*.

Because a web application can be assigned any context path when the application is installed, the context path must not be part of the URIs used in JSP elements (and servlet methods) to refer to other parts of the same application. You can always use a relative path URI, just as you do in HTML elements, for instance to refer to another page in a `<jsp:include>` action:

```
<jsp:include page="navigation.jsp" />
```

This type of URI is called a *page-relative path* in the JSP specification. It's interpreted by the container as relative to the page where it's used. In other words, it's exactly the same type of path as the HTTP specification calls simply a relative path.

Sometimes it's nice to be able to refer to an internal application resource with a URI that is not interpreted relative to the containing page. An example is a reference to a customized error page that is used by all pages in the application independent of where in the path structure they are located:

```
<%@ page errorPage="/errorMsg.jsp" %>
```

When a URI in a JSP element attribute starts with a slash, the container interprets it as relative to the application's context path. The JSP specification calls this type of URI a *context-relative path*. This type of URI is useful for all sorts of common application resources, such as error pages and images, that have fixed URIs within the application path structure.

In summary, a URI used in an HTML element can be:

- An absolute URI (a scheme and server name, plus the resource path)
- An absolute-path URI (a path starting with a slash), interpreted as the absolute path to a resource on the server that sent the response containing the URI
- A relative-path URI (a path without a starting slash), interpreted as relative to the absolute path used to request the response that contains it

A URI used in a JSP element (or a servlet method) can be:

- A context-relative path (a path starting with a slash), interpreted as relative to the application's context path
- A page-relative path (a path without a starting slash), interpreted as relative to the path for the page where it's used.

As long as you remember that URIs used in HTML elements are interpreted by the browser, and URIs used in JSP elements are interpreted by the web container, it's not so hard to figure out which type of URI to use in a given situation.

PART III

JSP in J2EE and JSP Component Development

If you're a programmer, this is the part of the book where the real action is. Here you will learn how to develop your own custom actions and JavaBeans, and how to combine JSP with other Java server-side technologies, such as servlets and Enterprise JavaBeans (EJB):

CHAPTER 18

Web Application Models

Part II of this book describes how you can create many different types of applications using only JSP pages with generic components—JSTL actions, custom actions and beans—to access databases, present content in different languages, protect pages, and so forth—all without knowing much about Java programming. This approach works fine for many types of web applications, such as employee registers, product catalogs, and conference room reservation systems. But for applications with complicated schemas, intricate business rules, and tricky control flows, the generic components just don't cut it, and you suddenly find that you need a more powerful way to handle the request processing and the business logic.

As I mentioned in Chapter 3, JSP can be combined with other Java technologies such as servlets and EJB in more complex applications. In this chapter, we look at how JSP fits into this larger picture. After the brief description of the most common application models in this chapter, Chapter 19 describes the combination of servlets and JSP in detail.

The material presented in this part of the book is geared towards Java programmers. If you're not a programmer, you may still want to browse through this part to get a feel for the possibilities, but don't expect to understand everything. To really appreciate the techniques described in this part of the book, you should have experience with Java programming in general. Familiarity with Java servlets also helps, and a short introduction is included in Chapter 19 for those who are new to this technology.

The Java 2 Enterprise Edition Model

At the JavaOne conference in San Francisco in June 1999, Sun Microsystems announced a new architecture for Java, with separate editions for different types of applications: the Java 2 Standard Edition (J2SE) for desktop and workstation devices; the Java 2 Micro Edition (J2ME) for small devices such as cell phones, pagers, and PDAs; and the Java 2 Enterprise Edition (J2EE) for server-based applications.

J2EE is a compilation of various Java APIs that have previously been offered as separate packages; an Application Programming Model (APM) (also known as the J2EE Blueprints) that describes how they can all be combined; and a test suite J2EE vendors can use to test their products for compatibility. J2EE has gone through a number of revisions since 1999, and the latest version (J2EE 1.4) includes the following enterprise-specific APIs among others:

- JavaServer Pages (JSP)
- Java Servlet
- Enterprise JavaBeans (EJB)
- Java Database Connection (JDBC)
- Java Transaction API (JTA) and Java Transaction Service (JTS)
- Java Naming and Directory Interface (JNDI)
- Java Message Service (JMS)
- Java IDL and Remote Method Invocation (RMI)
- Java API for XML Parsing (JAXP), Java API for XML-based RPC (JAX-RPC), SOAP with Attachments API for Java (SAAJ), and Java API for XML Registries (JAXR)
- JavaMail and JavaBeans Activation Framework (JAF)
- J2EE Connector Architecture (JCX)
- Java Authentication and Authorization Service (JAAS)
- Java Management Extensions (JMX)

In addition, all the J2SE APIs can be used when developing a J2EE application. These APIs can be used in numerous combinations. The first three J2EE APIs—EJB, JSP, and servlets—represent different component technologies, managed by what the J2EE documents call *containers*. A web container provides the runtime environment for servlets and JSP components, translating requests and responses into standard Java objects. EJB components are similarly handled by an *EJB container*. Don't be fooled by the name similarity between JavaBeans and Enterprise JavaBeans (EJB); they are completely different animals. A JavaBeans component is a regular Java class, following a few simple naming conventions, which can be used by any other Java class. An Enterprise JavaBean component, on the other hand, must be developed in compliance with a whole set of strict rules and works only in the environment provided by an EJB container.

Components in the two types of containers can use the other J2EE APIs to access databases (JDBC and JTA/JTS) and other EIS tier applications (JCX), authenticate users and control access (JAAS), locate various resources (JNDI), and communicate with other server resources (JavaMail/JAF, JMS, Java IDL, RMI, JAXP, JAX-RPC, SAAJ and JAXR). Figure 18-1 shows a high-level view of the main pieces and their relationship.

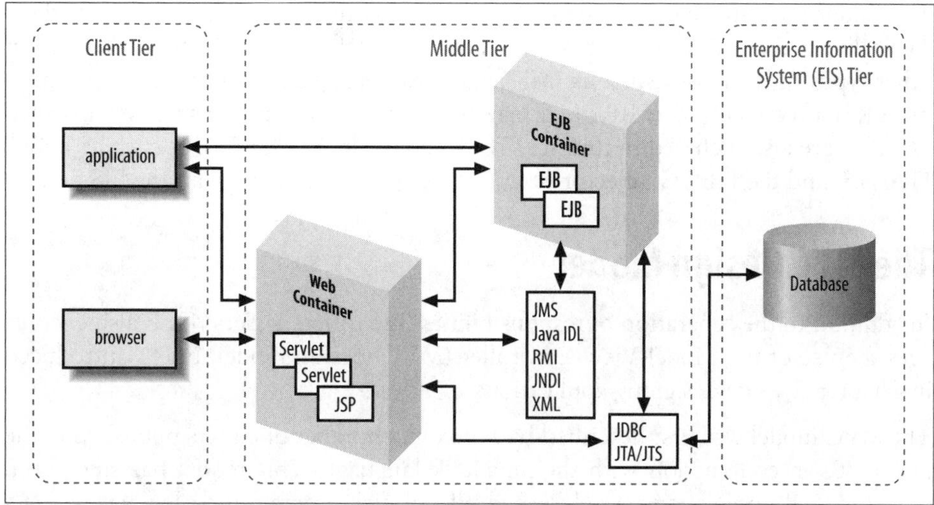

Figure 18-1. EE overview

Enterprise applications are often divided into a set of tiers, and J2EE identifies three: the client tier, the middle tier, and the Enterprise Information System (EIS) tier. The middle tier can be further divided into the web tier and the EJB tier. This logical separation, with well-defined interfaces, makes it possible to build scalable applications. Initially one or more tiers can be running on the same physical server. With increased demands, the tiers can be separated and distributed over multiple servers without modifying the code, just by changing the configuration.

The client tier contains browsers as well as regular GUI applications. A browser uses HTTP to communicate with the web container. A standalone application can also use HTTP or communicate directly with the EJB container using RMI or IIOP (a CORBA protocol). Another type of client that's becoming more and more popular is the extremely thin client, such as a cell phone or PDA. This type of client typically uses the Wireless Access Protocol (WAP), typically converted into HTTP via a gateway, to communicate with the web container.

The middle tier provides client services through the web container and the EJB container. A client that communicates with the server through HTTP uses components in the web container, such as servlets and JSP pages, as entry points to the application. Many applications can be implemented solely as web container components. In other applications, the web components just act as an interface to the application logic implemented by EJB components. A standalone application, written in Java or any other programming language, can also communicate directly with the EJB components. General guidelines for when to use the different approaches are discussed later in this chapter. Components in this tier can access databases and communicate with other server applications using all the other J2EE APIs.

The Enterprise Information System (EIS) tier holds the application's business data. Typically, it consists of one or more relational database management servers, but other types of databases such as IMS databases; legacy applications such as Enterprise Resource Planning (ERP); and mainframe transaction processing systems such as CICS, are also included in this tier. The middle tier uses J2EE APIs such as JDBC, JTA/JTS, and the J2EE Connector Architecture (JCX) to interact with the EIS tier.

The MVC Design Model

In addition to the separation of responsibilities into different tiers, J2EE also encourages the use of the Model-View-Controller (MVC) design model, briefly introduced in Chapter 3, when designing applications.

The MVC model was first described by Xerox in a number of papers published in the late 1980s in conjunction with the Smalltalk language. This model has since been used for GUI applications developed in all popular programming languages. Let's review: the basic idea is to separate the application data and business logic, the presentation of the data, and the interaction with the data into distinct entities labeled the Model, the View, and the Controller, respectively.

The Model represents pure business data and the rules for how to use this data; it knows nothing about how the data is displayed or the user interface for modifying the data. The View, on the other hand, knows all about the user interface details. It also knows about the public Model interface for reading its data, so that it can render it correctly, and it knows about the Controller interface, so it can ask the Controller to modify the Model.

Using an employee registry application as an example, an `Employee` class may represent a Model. It holds information about an employee: name, employment date, vacation days, salary, etc. It also holds rules for how this information can be changed; for instance, the number of vacation days may be limited based on the employment time. The user interface that shows the information is a View. It gets hold of an `Employee` object by asking the Controller for it and then renders the information by asking the `Employee` object for its property values. The View also renders controls that allow the user to modify the information. The Views sends the modification request to the Controller, which updates the `Employee` object and then tells the View that the Model has been modified. The View, finally, updates the user interface to display the updated values.

Using the MVC design model makes for a flexible application architecture, in which multiple presentations (Views) can be provided and easily modified, and changes in the business rules or physical representation of the data (the Model) can be made without touching any of the user interface code.

Even though the model was originally developed for standalone GUI applications, it translates fairly well into the multitier application domain of J2EE. The user interacts with the Controller to ask for things to be done, and the Controller relays these requests to the Model in a client-type independent way. Say, for instance, that you have two types of clients: an HTTP client such as a browser and a GUI client application using IIOP to talk to the server. In this scenario you can have one Controller for each protocol that receives the requests and extracts the request information in a protocol-dependent manner. Both Controllers then call the Model the same way; the Model doesn't need to know what kind of client it was called by. The result of the request is then presented to the two types of clients using different Views. The HTTP client typically gets an HTTP response message, possibly created by a JSP page, while the GUI application may include a View component that communicates directly with the Model to get its new state and render it on the screen.

The J2EE platform includes many APIs and component types, as I have just shown. However, there's no reason to use them all for a specific application. You can pick and choose the technology that makes most sense for your application's scope and functionality, the longevity of the application, the skills in your development team, and so on.

The assignment of MVC roles to the different types of J2EE components depends on the scenario, the types of clients supported, and whether or not EJB is used. The following sections describe possible role assignments for the three most common scenarios in which JSP pages play an important role.

Using Only JSP

As you saw in Part II, there are all sorts of applications that can be developed using just JSP pages with JSTL, a few JavaBeans components and custom actions. If you're primarily a page author working alone, with limited or no Java knowledge, you can still develop fairly sophisticated applications using JSTL and the custom actions in this book. And if that's not enough, many generic tag libraries are available from both commercial companies and open source projects, making it possible to do even more with just the JSP part of the J2EE platform.

A pure JSP approach can be a good approach even for a team if most of the team members are skilled in page design and layout, and only a few are Java programmers. The programmers can then develop application-specific beans and custom actions to complement the generic components and minimize the amount of SQL and Java code in the JSP pages.

A pure JSP approach is also a suitable model for testing new ideas and prototyping. Using generic components and a few application-specific beans and actions is often the fastest way to reach a visible result. Once the ideas have been proven, and the team has a better understanding of the problems, a decision can be made about the ultimate application architecture for the real thing. The danger here is that the last step—evaluating the prototype and deciding how it should be redesigned—never happens; I have seen prototypes being relabeled as production systems overnight too many times and also experienced the inevitable maintenance nightmares that follow.

The MVC model makes sense even for a pure JSP play. I recommend that you use separate JSP pages for presentation (the View) and request processing (the Controller), and place all business logic in beans (the Model), as shown in Figure 18-2. Let Controller pages initialize the beans, and let View pages generate the response by reading their properties. That's the model used in most examples in Part II. If you follow this model, it's easy to move to a combination of servlets and JSP the day you find that the pure JSP application is becoming hard to maintain.

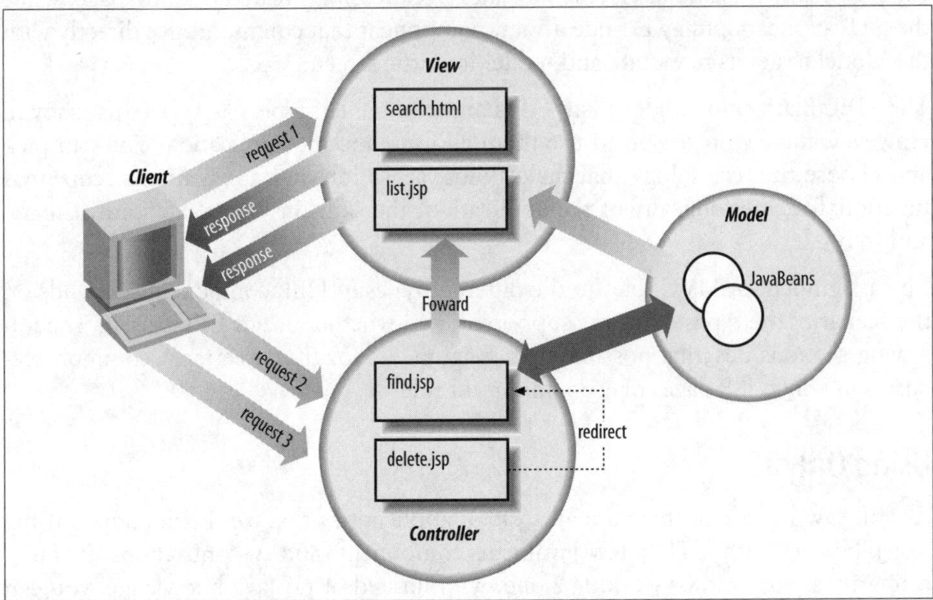

Figure 18-2. MVC roles in a pure JSP scenario

Using Servlets and JSP

The combination of servlets and JSP is a powerful tool for developing well-structured applications that are easy to maintain and extend as new requirements surface. Since a servlet is a regular Java class, you can use the full power of the Java language to implement the request processing, using standard Java development and debugging tools. JSP pages can then be used for what they are best at: rendering the response by including information collected or generated by the servlets.

A common combination of servlets and JSP is to use one servlet as the Controller (or front component, as it's called in the J2EE documents) for an application, with a number of JSP pages acting as Views. This approach lets you develop the application in a more modular fashion, with the servlet acting as a gateway, dispatching requests to specialized processing components and picking the appropriate JSP page for the response based on success or failure.

Prior to the 2.3 version of the servlet specification, servlets were often used to also make sure that application policies were applied for all requests. For instance, with application-controlled authentication and access control, centralizing the security controls in a servlet instead of counting on everyone remembering to put custom actions in all protected pages was less error-prone. Using a servlet as the single entry point to the application also made it easier to do application-specific logging (for instance collect statistics in a database), maintain a list of currently active users, and other things that apply to all requests. The Servlet 2.3 specification, however, introduced two new component types that are more appropriate for these tasks: *filters* and *listeners*. We take a closer look at how to use filters and listeners in Chapter 19. Moving concerns about application policies to the new component types leaves the servlet with the tasks that are purely in the Controller domain.

When servlets and JSP are combined, the MVC roles are assigned as shown in Figure 18-3. All requests are sent to the servlet acting as the Controller with an indication about what needs to be done. The indication can be in the form of a request parameter or as a part of the URI path. As in the pure JSP scenario, beans are used to represent the Model. The servlet either performs the requested action itself or delegates it to individual processing classes per action. Depending on the outcome of the processing, the Controller servlet picks an appropriate JSP page to generate a response to the user (the View). For instance, if a request to delete a document in a document archive is executed successfully, the servlet can pick a JSP page that shows the updated archive contents. If the request fails, it can pick a JSP page that describes exactly why it failed. We look at this approach in more detail in Chapter 19.

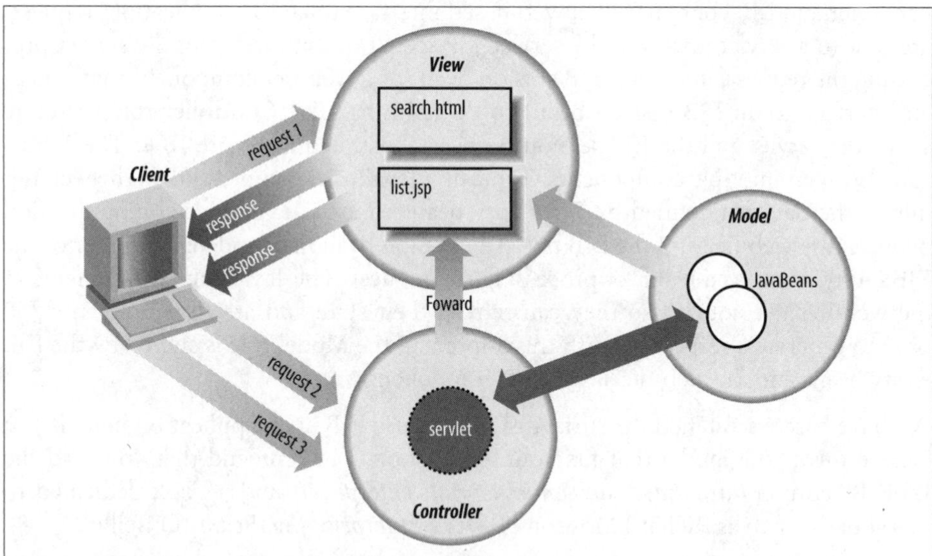

Figure 18-3. MVC roles in a servlet/JSP scenario

Using Servlets, JSP, and EJB

An application based on EJB is today commonly viewed as the Holy Grail. However, it's also the most complex model of the ones described in this chapter, and it therefore comes with overhead in the development, deployment, operation, and administration areas. While EJB may be the way to go for some types of applications, it's overkill for many others. Think long and hard about if you really need EJB, or if you're just influenced by all the hype around it, before you decide to go this route.

What EJB brings to the table is primarily transaction management and a client type-independent component model. Even though it's impossible to say with certainty that a specific type of application should definitely use EJB, if you develop an application with numerous database write-access operations accessed through different types of clients (such as browser, standalone application, PDA, or another server in a B2B application), EJB is probably the way to go. An EJB-based application also enforces the separation between the Model, View, and Controller aspects, leading to an application that's easy to extend and maintain.

There are two primary types of EJB components: entity beans and session beans. An entity bean represents a specific piece of business data, such as an employee or a customer. Each entity bean has a unique identity, and all clients that need access to the entity represented by the bean use the same bean instance. Session beans, on the other hand, are intended to handle business logic and are used only by the client that created them. Typically, a session bean operates on entity beans on behalf of its client.

With EJB in the picture, the MVC roles often span multiple components in the web container and EJB container. In a web-based interface to an EJB application, requests are sent to a servlet just as in the servlet/JSP scenario. But instead of the servlet processing the request, it asks an EJB session bean (or a web-tier component that acts as an interface to an EJB session bean) to do its thing. The Controller role therefore spans the servlet and the EJB session bean, as illustrated in Figure 18-4. The Model can also span multiple components. Typically, JavaBeans components in the web tier mirror the data maintained by EJB entity beans to avoid expensive communication between the web tier and the EJB tier. The session bean may update a number of the EJB entity beans as a result of processing the request. The JavaBeans components in the web tier get notified so they can refresh their state and are then used in a JSP page to generate a response. With this approach, the Model role is shared by the EJB entity beans and the web-tier JavaBeans components.

We have barely scratched the surface of how to use EJB in an application here. If you believe this is the model that fits your application, I recommend that you read the J2EE Blueprints (*http://java.sun.com/blueprints/enterprise/*) and a book dedicated to this subject, such as Richard Monson-Haefel's *Enterprise JavaBeans* (O'Reilly).

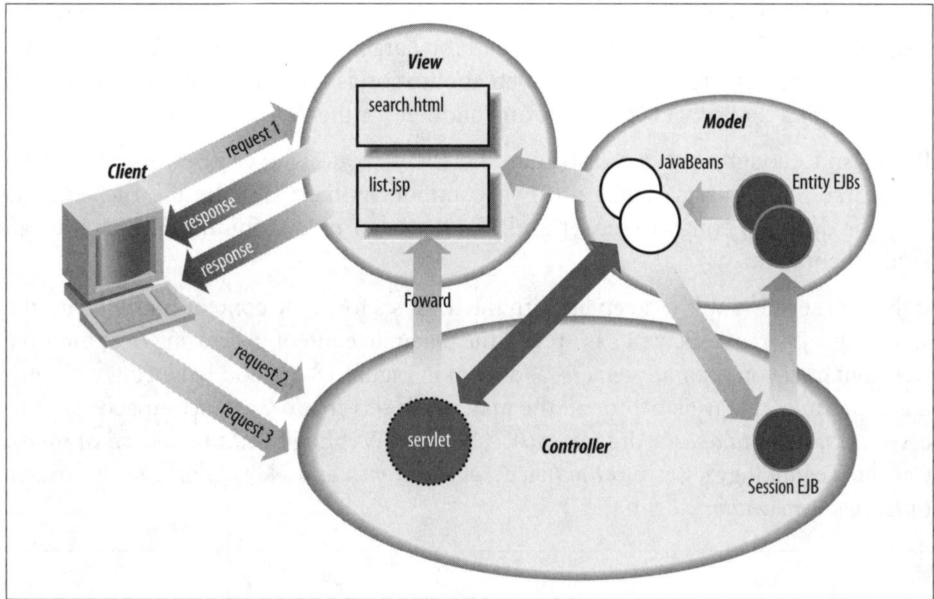

Figure 18-4. MVC roles in a servlet/JSP/EJB scenario

Scalability

For a large, complex application, there are many reasons to move to a model that includes Enterprise JavaBeans components. But, contrary to popular belief, scalability and great performance should not be the one deciding factor. There are many ways to develop scalable applications using just JSP or the servlet/JSP combination, often with better performance than an EJB-based application, because the communication overhead between the web tier and EJB tier is avoided.

Scalability means that an application can deal with more and more users by changing the hardware configuration rather than the application itself. Typically this means, among other things, that it's partitioned into pieces that can run on separate servers. Most servlet- and JSP-based applications use a database to handle persistent data, so the database is one independent piece. They also use a mixture of static and dynamically generated content. Static content, such as images and regular HTML pages, is handled by a web server, while dynamic content is generated by the servlets and JSP pages running within a web container. So without even trying, we have three different pieces that can be deployed separately.

Initially, you can run all three pieces on the same server. However, both the web container and the database use a lot of memory. The web container needs memory to load all servlet and JSP classes, session data, and shared application information. The database server needs memory to work efficiently with prepared statements, cached indexes, statistics used for query optimization, etc. The server requirements for these two pieces are also different; for instance, the web server must be able to cope with a large number of network connections, and the database server needs fast disk access. Therefore, the first step in scaling a web application is typically to use one server for the web server and servlet container, and another for the database.

If this isn't enough, you can distribute the client requests over a set of servers processing HTTP requests. There are two common models: distributing the requests only for dynamic content (servlet and JSP requests) or distributing requests for all kinds of content.

If the web server is able to keep up with the requests for static content but not with the servlet and JSP requests, you can spread the dynamic content processing over multiple web containers on separate servers, as shown in Figure 18-5. Load balancing web container modules are available for all the major web servers, for instance Apache's Tomcat (*http://jakarta.apache.org/tomcat/*), BEA's WebLogic (*http://www.bea.com/*), Caucho Technology's Resin (*http://www.caucho.com/*), and New Atlanta's ServletExec (*http://www.newatlanta.com/*).

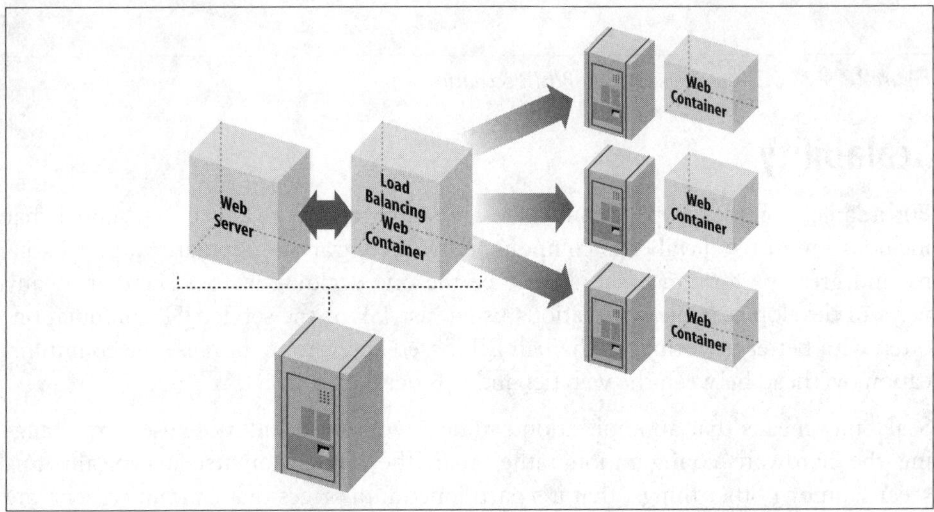

Figure 18-5. Web server distributing load over multiple web containers

The tricky part when distributing dynamic content requests over multiple servers is ensuring that session data is handled appropriately. Most containers keep session data only in memory. In this case, the load balance module picks the server with the lowest load to serve the first request from a client. If a session is created by this request, all subsequent requests within the same session are sent to the same server. Alternatively, a container can also save session data on disk or in a database. It can then freely distribute each request over all servers in the cluster and can also offer failure recovery in case a server crashes. A container is allowed to move a session from one server to another only for applications marked as *distributable*, as described in the next section. You can find which model a certain product uses by looking at the vendor's web site and documentation. Pick one that satisfies your requirements as well as your wallet.

For a high-traffic site, you may need to distribute requests for both static and dynamic content over multiple servers, as illustrated in Figure 18-6. You can then place a load-balancing server in front of a set of servers, each running a web server and a web container. The same as with the previous configuration, session data must be considered when selecting a server for the request. The easiest way to deal with it is to use a load-balancing product that sends all requests from the same client to the same server. This is not ideal though, since all clients behind the same proxy or firewall appear as the same host. Some load-balancing products try to solve this problem using cookies or SSL sessions to identify individual clients behind proxies and firewalls. In this configuration, you get the best performance from a web server that runs a web container in the same process, eliminating the process-to-process communication between the web server and the web container. Most of the web containers mentioned here can be used in-process with all the major web servers. Another alternative for this configuration is a pure Java server that acts like both a web server and a web container. Examples are Apache's Tomcat, Ironflare AB's Orion Application Server (*http://www.orionserver.com/*), and Gefion Software's LiteWebServer (*http://www.gefionsoftware.com/LiteWebServer/*). Compared to adding a web container to a standard web server, this all-in-one alternative is easier to configure and maintain. The traditional servers written in C or C++ may still be faster for serving static content, but with faster and faster Java runtimes, pure Java servers come very close.

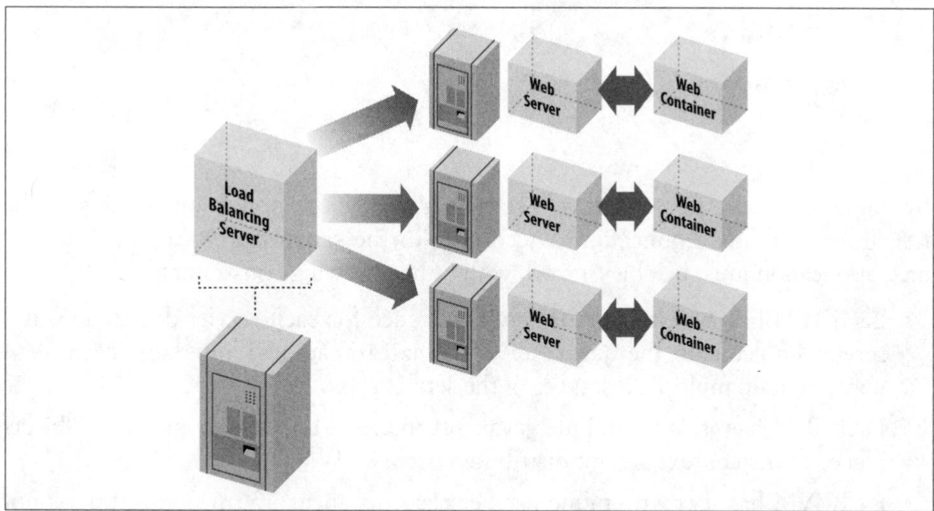

Figure 18-6. Load balancing server distributing requests over multiple servers with a web server and container

You shouldn't rely on configuration strategies alone to handle the scalability needs of your application. The application must also be designed for scalability, using all the traditional tricks of the trade. Finally, you must load-test your application with the configuration you will deploy it on to make sure it can handle the expected load. There are many pure Java performance testing tools to choose from, spanning from the simple but powerful Apache's JMeter (*http://jakarta.apache.org/jmeter/index.html*) to sophisticated tools such as Minq Software's PureLoad (*http://www.minq.se/products/pureload/*) that supports data-driven, session aware tests to be executed on a cluster of test machines.

Preparing for Distributed Deployment

As I described in the previous section, some web containers can distribute the requests for a web application's resources over multiple servers, each server running its own Java Virtual Machines (JVM). Of course, this has implications for how you develop your application. So, by default, a web container must use only one JVM for an application.

If you want to take advantage of web-container controlled load balancing, you must do two things: mark the application as distributable and follow the rules for a distributed application defined by the servlet specification.

To mark an application as *distributable* means adding a `<distributable/>` element in the deployment descriptor for the application:

```
<web-app>
  <description>A distributable application</description>

  <distributable/>

  <context-param>
    ...

</web-app>
```

By doing so, you're telling the web container that your application adheres to the rules for distributed applications. According to the servlet specification, a distributed application must be able to work within the following constraints:

- Each JVM has its own unique servlet instance for each servlet declaration. If a servlet implements the `javax.servlet.SingleThreadModel` interface, each JVM may maintain multiple instances of the servlet class.
- Each JVM has its own unique `javax.servlet.ServletContext` instance. Objects placed in the context are not distributed between JVMs.
- Each JVM has its own unique listener class instances. Event notification is not propagated to other JVMs.
- Each object stored in the session must be serializable (must implement the `java.io.Serializable` interface).

This means you cannot rely on instance variables to keep data shared by all requests for a certain servlet; each JVM has its own instance of the servlet class. For the same reason, be careful with how you use application scope objects (`ServletContext` attributes); each JVM has its own context, with its own set of objects. In most cases, this is not a problem. For instance, if you use the application scope to provide shared access to cached read-only data, it just means you may have copies of the cached data in each JVM. If you really need access to the *same instance* of some data between JVMs, you must share it through an external mechanism, such as a database, a file in a filesystem available to all servers, or an EJB component.

The most interesting part about distributed applications is how sessions are handled. The web container allows only one server at a time to handle a request that's part of a session, but since all objects put into the session must be serializable, the container can save them on disk or in a database as well as in memory. If the server that handles a session gets overloaded or crashes, the container can therefore move the responsibility for the session to another server. The new server simply loads all serialized session data and picks up where the previous server left off. This means that an object may be placed in the session in one JVM but actually used on another.

Listeners (described in Chapter 19) are also unique per JVM, and events are sent only to the local listeners. Since a session may migrate to another JVM, this means that a session lifecycle listener in one JVM may be notified about the start of the session, while a listener in another JVM gets the end-of-session notification.

CHAPTER 19
Combining JSP and Servlets

As I described in the previous chapter, combining JSP with servlets lets you clearly separate the application logic from the presentation of the application; in other words, it lets you use the most appropriate component types for the roles of Model, View, and Controller. To illustrate how a servlet can act as the Controller for an application—using beans as the Model and JSP pages as Views—we redesign the Project Billboard application from Chapter 13 in this chapter. Along the way, we look at how servlets and JSP pages can share data, how to deal with references between servlets and JSP pages in a flexible manner, how to use filters and listeners, and how to handle runtime errors consistently in an application that mixes these two technologies.

Java servlets offer a powerful API that provides access to all the information about the request, the session, and the application. If you're not familiar with the Servlet API, I give you a crash course in the first section of this chapter. It's just a brief introduction, but it should be enough to get you going and to understand the rest of this chapter. If you're an old servlet pro, you may still want to scan through the last part of the introduction to learn about the new component types available in recent versions of the specification (Servlet 2.3 or later): filters and listeners. If you plan to make heavy use of servlets in your application, I recommend that you also read up on the details. You should pick up a copy of *Java Servlet Programming* by Jason Hunter and William Crawford (O'Reilly).

Servlets, Filters, and Listeners

A *servlet* is a Java class that extends a server with functionality for processing a request and producing a response. It's implemented using the classes and interfaces defined by the Servlet API. The API consists of two packages: the `javax.servlet` package contains classes and interfaces that are protocol-independent, while the `javax.servlet.http` package provides HTTP-specific extensions and utility classes.

What makes a servlet a servlet is that the class implements an interface named `javax.servlet.Servlet`, either directly or by extending one of the support classes. This interface defines the methods used by the web container to manage and interact with the servlet. A servlet for processing HTTP requests typically extends the `javax.servlet.http.HttpServlet` class. This class implements the `Servlet` interface and provides additional methods suitable for HTTP processing.

Servlet Lifecycle

The web container manages all aspects of the servlet's lifecycle. It creates an instance of the servlet class when needed, passes requests to the instance for processing, and eventually removes the instance. For an `HttpServlet`, the container calls the following methods at the appropriate times in the servlet lifecycle:

`public void init( ) throws ServletExecption`
: Called once, before the first request is delivered. This method can be used to initialize the servlet's state, for instance by reading initialization parameters defined in the web application deployment descriptor and saving the values in instance variables to be used during request processing.

`public void doGet(HttpServletRequest request, HttpServletResponse response) throws ServletException, IOException`
: Called repeatedly to let the servlet process a `GET` request. The `request` parameter provides detailed information about the request, and the servlet uses the `response` parameter to generate the response.

`public void doPost(HttpServletRequest request, HttpServletResponse response) throws ServletException, IOException`
: Called repeatedly to let the servlet process a `POST` request.

`public void destroy( )`
: Called once, before the servlet is taken out of service. This method can be used to save to permanent storage data accumulated during the servlet's lifetime and to remove references to objects held by the servlet.

Besides the `doGet( )` and `doPost( )` methods, there are methods corresponding to the other HTTP methods: `doDelete( )`, `doHead( )`, `doOptions( )`, `doPut( )`, and `doTrace( )`. Typically you don't implement these methods; the `HttpServlet` class already takes care of `HEAD`, `OPTIONS`, and `TRACE` requests in a way that's suitable for most servlets, and the `DELETE` and `PUT` HTTP methods are rarely used in a web application.

Example 19-1 shows an example of a Hello World servlet.

Example 19-1. Lifecycle for a Hello World servlet

```
import java.io.*;
import javax.servlet.*;
import javax.servlet.http.*;

public class HelloWorld extends HttpServlet {
    private String greeting;

    public void init( ) {
        ServletConfig config = getServletConfig( );
        greeting = config.getInitParameter("greeting");
        if (greeting == null) {
          greeting = "Hello World!";
        }
    }

    public void doGet(HttpServletRequest request,
        HttpServletResponse response)
        throws ServletException, IOException {

        PrintWriter out = response.getWriter( );
        out.println(greeting);
    }

    public void destroy( ) {
      greeting = null;
    }
}
```

The `HelloWorld` class extends the `HttpServlet` class, which makes it a valid servlet. In the `init( )` method, it initializes an instance variable named `greeting` based on configuration information defined in the *WEB-INF/web.xml* file (I'll show you how to define initialization parameters in this file later). It gets the configured value from the `ServletConfig` object associated with the servlet by the container. If no initialization parameter is defined, it sets the instance variable to a default value: `Hello World!`

The servlet implements the `doGet( )` method to process `GET` requests. This method first gets a `PrintWriter` for the response body from the `response` object passed as an argument and then prints the greeting.

Finally, the implementation of the `destroy( )` method removes the reference to the greeting string.

It's important to realize that the container creates only *one* instance of each servlet. This means that the servlet must be thread safe—able to handle multiple requests at the same time, each executing as a separate thread through the servlet code. Without getting lost in details, you satisfy this requirement with regards to instance variables if you modify the referenced objects only in the `init( )` and `destroy( )` methods, and just read them in the request processing methods. Example 19-1 initializes the greeting instance variable in the `init( )` method, sets it to null in the `destroy( )` method, and reads it only in the `doGet( )` methods, so it complies with these rules.

You must, however, be careful with write access to external objects shared by threads, such as session and application scope objects.

Compiling and Installing a Servlet

To compile a servlet, you must first ensure that you have the JAR file containing all Servlet API classes in the CLASSPATH environment variable. The JAR file is distributed with all web containers. Tomcat includes it in a file called *servlet-api.jar*, located in the *common/lib* directory. On a Windows platform, you include the JAR file in the CLASSPATH like this (assuming Tomcat is installed in *C:\Jakarta\jakarta-tomcat-5*):

```
C:/> set CLASSPATH=C:\Jakarta\jakarta-tomcat-5\common\lib\servlet-api.jar;
%CLASSPATH%
```

You can then compile the HelloWorld servlet from Example 19-1 with the *javac* command, like this:

```
C:/> javac HelloWorld.java
```

To make the servlet visible to the container, you can place the resulting class file in the *WEB-INF/classes* directory for the example application:

```
C:/> copy HelloWorld.class C:\Jakarta\jakarta-tomcat-5\webapps\ora\
WEB-INF\classes
```

The container automatically looks for classes in the *WEB-INF/classes* directory structure, so you can use this directory for all application class files. The `HelloWorld` servlet is part of the default package, so it goes in the *WEB-INF/classes* directory itself. If you use another package, say `com.mycompany`, you must put the class file in a directory under *WEB-INF/classes* that mirrors the package structure. In other words, it should be placed in a directory named *WEB-INF/classes/com/mycompany*. Alternatively, you can package the class files in a JAR file (see the Java SDK documents for details) and place the JAR file in the *WEB-INF/lib* directory. The internal structure of the JAR file must also mirror the package structure for all your classes.

Next you must tell the container that it should invoke your servlet when it receives a request for a specific URL. You do this with `<servlet>` and `<servlet-mapping>` elements in the application deployment descriptor (*WEB-INF/web.xml*) file:

```
<web-app>
  ...
  <servlet>
    <servlet-name>helloWorld</servlet-name>
    <servlet-class>HelloWorld</servlet-class>
  </servlet>

  <servlet-mapping>
    <servlet-name>helloWorld</servlet-name>
    <url-pattern>/hello/*</url-pattern>
  </servlet-mapping>
  ...
</web-app>
```

The <servlet> element gives the servlet class a unique name, and the <servlet-mapping> element links a URL pattern to the named servlet. We'll look at this in more detail later.

With the class in the correct place and the servlet and a mapping declared, you're ready to test the servlet. Type this URL in the browser address field and see what happens:*

http://localhost:8080/ora/hello

If you followed all instructions, you'll see the text "Hello World!" in your browser.

Reading a Request

One of the arguments passed to the doGet( ) and doPost( ) methods is an object that implements the HttpServletRequest interface. This interface defines methods that provide access to a wealth of information about the request. Example 19-2 illustrates the use of the most common methods.

Example 19-2. Using HttpServletRequest methods

```
import java.io.*;
import java.util.*;
import javax.servlet.*;
import javax.servlet.http.*;

public class HelloYou extends HttpServlet {
    public void doGet(HttpServletRequest request,
        HttpServletResponse response)
        throws ServletException, IOException {

        String name = request.getParameter("name");
        if (name == null) {
            name = "you";
        }
        response.setContentType("text/html");
        PrintWriter out = response.getWriter( );
        out.println("<html><body>");
        out.println("<h1>Hello " + name + "</h1>");

        out.println("I see that:<ul>");
        String userAgent = request.getHeader("User-Agent");
        out.println("<li>your browser is: " + userAgent);
        String requestURI = request.getRequestURI( );
        out.println("<li>the URI for this page is: " +
            requestURI);
```

* Previous editions of this book used the *http://localhost:8080/ora/servlet/HelloWorld* URL, relying on the convention that the */servlet* prefix signals that a servlet should be invoked, with the rest of the path identifying the servlet (by the declared name or the class name). While this convention may still be supported by default in some containers, it comes with a number of security concerns. It's therefore disabled by default in recent versions of Tomcat, and you're encouraged to use explicit mappings instead.

Example 19-2. Using HttpServletRequest methods (continued)

```
        String contextPath = request.getContextPath( );
        out.println("<li>the context path for this app is" +
            contextPath);
        String servletPath = request.getServletPath( );
        out.println("<li>this servlet is mapped to: " +
            servletPath);
        String pathInfo = request.getPathInfo( );
        out.println("<li>the remaining path is: " + pathInfo);
        Map parameters = request.getParameterMap( );
        out.println("<li>you sent the following params:<ul>");
        Iterator i = parameters.keySet().iterator( );
        while (i.hasNext( )) {
            String paramName = (String) i.next( );
            out.println("<li><b>" + paramName + "</b>:");
            String[] paramValues =
                (String[]) parameters.get(paramName);
            for (int j = 0; j < paramValues.length; j++) {
                if (j != 0) {
                    out.print(", ");
                }
                out.print(paramValues[j]);
            }
        }
        out.println("</ul></ul></body></html>");
    }
}
```

After compiling and installing the HelloYou servlet, and mapping it to the */helloYou/** URL pattern as described earlier, you can test it with this URL:

http://localhost:8080/ora/helloYou/extra?name=Bob&a=1&a=2

The result should be similar to that shown in Figure 19-1.

In Example 19-2, the getParameter( ) method gets the value of a request parameter. This method returns a single value for the parameter. But a request may contain multiple parameters with the same name. For multivalue parameters, you can use a method called getParameterValues( ) instead. It returns a String array with all values. Further down in the example, note that you can also use the getParameterMap( ) to get a Map containing all parameters in the request. Each key is a String with the parameter name, and the values are String arrays with all values for the parameter. The getParameterMap( ) method was added in the Servlet 2.3 API. For previous versions, you can use a combination of getParameterNames( ) and getParameterValues( ) to accomplish the same thing. All these parameter access methods work the same for both GET and POST requests.

Example 19-2 also shows how you can use the getHeader( ) method to read request header values, getRequestURI( ) to get the complete URI, and various getXXXPath( ) methods to get different parts of the URI path. You can read more about these methods and all other HttpServletRequest methods in Appendix D.

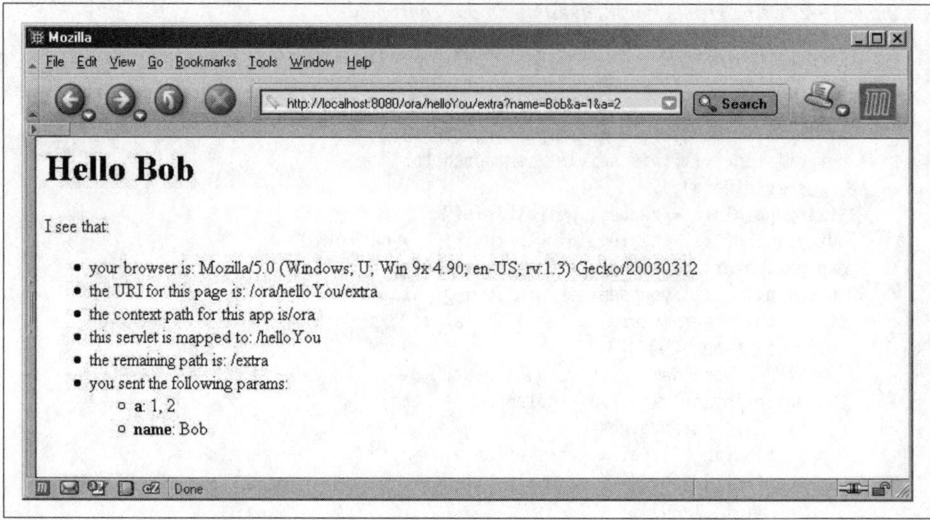

Figure 19-1. Response generated by the HelloYou servlet

Generating a Response

Besides the request object, the container passes an object that implements the `HttpServletResponse` interface as an argument to the `doGet( )` and `doPost( )` methods. This interface defines methods for getting a writer or stream for the response body. It also defines methods for setting the response status code and headers. Example 19-3 contains the code for a servlet that uses some of the methods.

Example 19-3. Using HttpServletResponse methods

```
import java.io.*;
import javax.servlet.*;
import javax.servlet.http.*;

public class HelloMIME extends HttpServlet {
    private static final int TEXT_TYPE = 0;
    private static final int IMAGE_TYPE = 1;

    public void doGet(HttpServletRequest request,
        HttpServletResponse response)
        throws ServletException, IOException {

        String greeting = "Hello World!";
        int majorType = TEXT_TYPE;
        String type = request.getParameter("type");
        if ("plain".equals(type)) {
            response.setContentType("text/plain");
        }
        else if ("html".equals(type)) {
            response.setContentType("text/html");
```

Example 19-3. Using HttpServletResponse methods (continued)

```
            greeting = "<html><body><h1>" + greeting +
                "</h1></body></html>";
        }
        else if ("image".equals(type)) {
            response.setContentType("image/gif");
            majorType = IMAGE_TYPE;
        }
        else {
            response.sendError(HttpServletResponse.SC_BAD_REQUEST,
                "Please specify a valid response type");
            return;
        }

        if (majorType == TEXT_TYPE) {
            PrintWriter out = response.getWriter( );
            out.println(greeting);
        }
        else {
            OutputStream os = response.getOutputStream( );
            ServletContext application = getServletContext( );
            InputStream is =
                application.getResourceAsStream("/ora.gif");
            copyStream(is, os);
        }
    }

    private void copyStream(InputStream in, OutputStream out)
            throws IOException {
        int bytes;
        byte[] b = new byte[4096];

        while ((bytes = in.read(b, 0, b.length)) != -1) {
            out.write(b, 0, bytes);
            out.flush( );
        }
    }
}
```

Example 19-3 shows how you can generate different types of responses for a request. Here a request parameter named type is used to choose between a plain text, an HTML, or a GIF response. You must tell the browser what type of content the response body contains using the `Content-Type` response header, which is set by the `setContentType( )` method. It takes the MIME type for the content as its single argument. The `HttpServletResponse` interface contains a number of methods like this for setting specific response headers. For headers not covered by specific methods, you can use the `setHeader( )` method.

If no type or an invalid type is specified, the servlet in Example 19-3 returns an error response using the `sendError( )` method. This method takes two arguments: the HTTP response status code and a short message to be used as part of the response body. If you prefer to use the default message for the status code, you can use another version of the sendError( ) method that omits the message argument.

With the content type setting out of the way, it's time to generate the response body. For a body containing either plain text or a markup language such as HTML or XML, you acquire a PrintWriter for the response by calling the getWriter( ) method and just write the text to it. For a binary body, such as an image, you need to use an OutputStream instead, which is exactly what the getOutputStream( ) method provides. When the type parameter has the value image, I use this method to grab the stream and write the content of a GIF file to it.

The recommended way to access external files, such as the GIF file, is also illustrated in Example 19-3:

```
ServletContext application = getServletContext( );
InputStream is = application.getResourceAsStream("/ora.gif");
```

The getServletContext( ) method returns a reference to the ServletContext instance for this servlet. A ServletContext represents a web application and provides access to various shared application resources. Servlet context attributes, for instance, hold references to the objects accessible as application scope data in JSP pages. The getResourceAsStream( ) method takes the context-relative path to a file resource as its argument and returns an InputStream. The Servlet API contains methods that let you open a file using the standard Java File class as well, but there's no guarantee that this will work in all containers. A container may serve the application files directly from a compressed WAR file, from a database, or any other way that it sees fit. Using a File object in such a container doesn't work, but using the getResourceAsStream( ) method does, because the container is responsible for providing the stream no matter how it stores the application data.

Using Filters and Listeners

The Servlet 2.3 specification introduced two component types beside servlets: *filters* and *listeners*.

Filters

A filter is a component that can intercept a request targeted for a servlet, JSP page, or static page, as well as the response before it's sent to the client. This makes it easy to centralize tasks that apply to all requests, such as access control, logging, and charging for the content or the services offered by the application. A filter has full access to the body and headers of the request and response, so it can also perform various transformations. One example is compressing the response body if the Accept-Encoding request header indicates that the client can handle a compressed response.

A filter can be applied to either a specific servlet or to all requests matching a URL pattern, such as URLs starting with the same path elements or having the same extension. We look at the implementation and configuration of an access-control filter later in this chapter. You may also want to read Jason Hunter's *JavaWorld* article about filters, *http://www.javaworld.com/javaworld/jw-06-2001/jw-0622-filters.html.*

In this article, he describes filters for measuring processing time, click and click-streams monitoring, response compression, and file uploading.

Listeners

Listeners allow your application to react to certain events. Prior to Servlet 2.3, you could handle only session attribute binding events (triggered when an object was added or removed from a session). You could do this by letting the object saved as a session attribute (using the `HttpSession.setAttribute( )` method) implement the `HttpSessionBindingListener` interface. With the new interfaces introduced in the 2.3 and 2.4. versions of the servlet specification, you can create listeners for servlet context, session and request lifecycle events as well as session activation and passivation events (used by a container that temporarily saves session state to disk or migrates a session to another server). A session attribute event listener also makes it possible to deal with attribute binding events for all sessions in one place, instead of placing individual listener objects in each session.

The new types of listeners follow the standard Java event model. In other words, a listener is a class that implements one or more of the listener interfaces. The interfaces define methods that correspond to events. The listener class is registered with the container when the application starts, and the container then calls the event methods at the appropriate times.

Example 19-4 is a session event listener that keeps track of the number of active sessions for an application.

Example 19-4. Session counter listener

```
package com.ora.jsp.servlets;

import javax.servlet.*;
import javax.servlet.http.*;

public class SessionCounterListener implements HttpSessionListener {
    private static final String COUNTER_ATTR = "session_counter";

    public void sessionCreated(HttpSessionEvent hse) {
        int[] counter = getCounter(hse);
        counter[0]++;
    }

    public void sessionDestroyed(HttpSessionEvent hse) {
        int[] counter = getCounter(hse);
        counter[0]--;
    }
```

Example 19-4. Session counter listener (continued)

```
    private int[] getCounter(HttpSessionEvent hse) {
        HttpSession session = hse.getSession( );
        ServletContext context = session.getServletContext( );
        int[] counter = (int[]) context.getAttribute(COUNTER_ATTR);
        if (counter == null) {
            counter = new int[1];
            context.setAttribute(COUNTER_ATTR, counter);
        }
        return counter;
    }
}
```

For every new session, the `sessionCreated( )` method increments a counter maintained as a servlet context attribute. When a session ends, the counter is decremented by the `sessionDestroyed( )` method. As part of the main example later in this chapter, we'll use this listener and display the counter value in a JSP page. You can also combine this listener with a filter that rejects new users if a maximum session threshold is reached (to ensure optimal performance), or whatever makes sense in your application.

The interfaces for the other types are named `ServletContextAttributeListener`, `ServletContextListener`, `ServletRequestAttributeListener`, `ServletRequestListener`, `HttpSessionActivationListener`, and `HttpSessionAttributeListener`. You can find out about their methods in Appendix D. Any number of listeners, of any type, can be registered for an application in the application deployment descriptor. Event listeners can also be registered as part of a tag library. You'll find more about this option in Chapter 22.

Sharing Data Between the Component Types

When an application uses servlets, filters, and listeners as well as JSP pages, all components need access to shared data. For instance, you may want a JSP page to show the counter maintained by the session listener in Example 19-4, and let the servlet create beans and pass them to a JSP page for display.

This turns out to be very easy. The JSP request, session, and application scopes, described in Chapter 11, are just abstractions for the set of attributes the other component types can associate with various servlet objects they have access to: `HttpServletRequest`, `HttpSession`, and `ServletContext`, respectively. All these classes provide a set of methods that can be used to set, get, and remove attributes:

```
public void setAttribute(String name, Object value)
public Object getAttribute(String name)
public void removeAttribute(String name)
```

The session listener maintains the active session counter as a ServletContext attribute, as shown in Example 19-4, so a JSP page can access it as an application scope variable:

```
Number of active sessions: ${session_counter[0]}
```

Note how the JSTL EL expression uses the same variable name as the session listener uses for its ServletContext attribute. The EL locates the variable by looking for an attribute with the same name in the request, session, and context objects, in this order.

The same data is available to servlets and filters in the application since they all share the same ServletContext instance:

```
ServletContext context = config.getServletContext( );
int[] counter = (int[]) context.getAttribute("session_counter");
if (counter[0] > 100) {
    // Do something
}
```

A servlet that creates a bean for a JSP page to display can save it as a request attribute and pass it on to the page like this:

```
public void doGet(HttpServletRequest request,
    HttpServletResponse response) throws ServletException,
    IOException {

    String userName = request.getParameter("userName");
    UserInfoBean userInfo = userReg.getUserInfo(userName);

    request.setAttribute("userInfo", userInfo);
    RequestDispatcher rd =
        request.getRequestDispatcher("welcome.jsp");
    rd.forward(request, response);
}
```

To the JSP page, the bean appears as a request scope variable. It can therefore obtain the bean using an EL expression similar to the previous example, or use the <jsp:useBean> action and then access the properties of the bean using the <jsp:getProperty> action:

```
<h1>Welcome
  <jsp:useBean id="userInfo" scope="request"
    class="com.ora.jsp.beans.userinfo.UserInfoBean" />
  <jsp:getProperty name="userInfo" property="userName" />
</h1>
```

The <jsp:useBean> action, with the id attribute value matching the request attribute name and the scope attribute set to request, makes the bean available to the <jsp:getProperty> action.

If the bean needs to be available throughout the session, the servlet uses an HttpSession attribute instead:

```
HttpSession session = request.getSession( );
session.setAttribute("userInfo", userInfo);
```

The JSP page then has access to the bean in the session scope through the EL or a `<jsp:useBean>` action with the `scope` attribute set to `session`.

Passing beans in the other direction, from a JSP page to a servlet, is not so common, but it can be done. Here's how. The JSP page creates the bean in the request scope using `<jsp:useBean>` and sets the properties using `<jsp:setProperty>`:

```
<jsp:useBean id="userInfo" scope="request"
  class="com.ora.jsp.beans.userinfo.UserInfoBean" >
  <jsp:setProperty name="userInfo" property="*" />
</jsp:useBean>

<jsp:forward page="/myServlet" />
```

It then forwards the request to the servlet (mapped to `/myServlet`) using `<jsp:forward>`. The servlet retrieves the bean using `getAttribute( )` method on the `HttpServletRequest` object passed to the `doGet( )` or `doPost( )` method:

```
UserInfoBean userInfo =
    (UserInfoBean) request.getAttribute("userInfo");
```

Picking the Right Component Type for Each Task

The Project Billboard application introduced in Chapter 13 is a fairly complex application. Half the pages are pure controller and business logic processing, it accesses a database to authenticate users, and most pages require access control. In real life, it would likely contain even more pages, for instance, pages for access to a shared document archive, time schedules, and a set of pages for administration. As the application evolves, it may become hard to maintain as a pure JSP application. It's easy to forget to include the access control code in new pages, for instance.

This is clearly an application that can benefit from using a combination of JSP pages and the component types defined by the servlet specification for the MVC roles. Let's look at the main requirements and see how we can map them to appropriate component types:

- Database access should be abstracted, to avoid knowledge of a specific data schema or database engine in more than one part of the application: beans in the role of Model can be used to accomplish this.
- The database access beans must be made available to all other parts of the application when it starts: an application lifecycle event listener is the perfect component type for this task.
- Only authenticated users must be allowed to use the application: a filter can perform access control to satisfy this requirement.

- Request processing is best done with Java code: a servlet, acting as the Controller, fits the bill.
- It must be easy to change the presentation: this is where JSP shines, acting as the View.

Adding servlets, listeners and filters to the mix minimizes the need for complex logic in the JSP pages. Placing all this code in Java classes instead makes it possible to use a regular Java compiler and debugger to fix potential problems. Figure 19-2 shows the components of the new design.

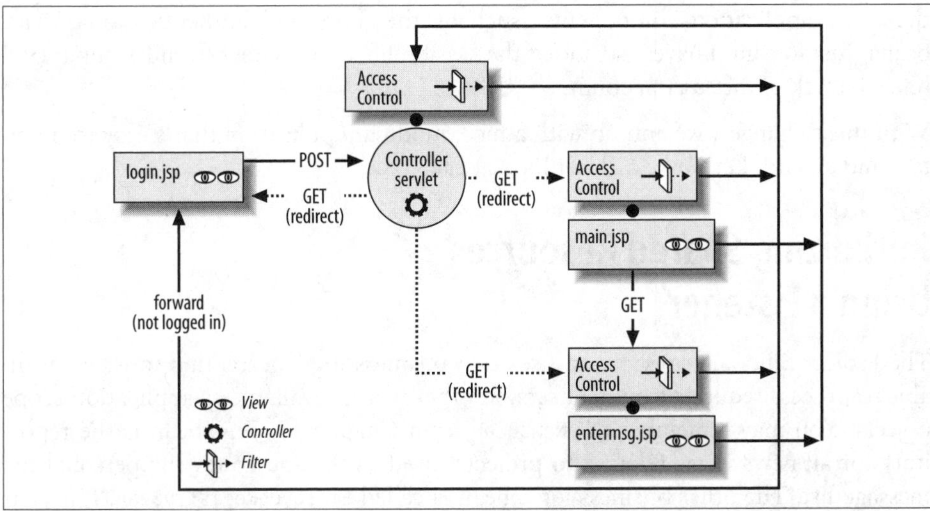

Figure 19-2. Project Billboard application combining servlet and JSP components

Compare this design with that described in Chapter 13. First, all request for the servlet and all JSP pages, except the login page and the authentication request, go through the access-control filter. The filter first verifies that the user is authenticated. If not, it forwards the request to the *login.jsp* page, where the URI for the requested page is saved as a hidden field in the same way as in Chapter 13. If the user is authenticated, the filter just passes the request on to the intended target. This allows you to remove the access control code from all JSP pages.

Next, note that the pure presentation JSP pages remain the same but the request processing pages are replaced by the servlet. So, as before, the user first requests the *login.jsp* page. This page still contains a form with fields for username and password, but with the new design, it invokes the servlet instead of a request-processing JSP page. The servlet is invoked with a URI that includes information about the action to perform. The servlet performs the authentication, and if successful, it creates an `EmployeeBean` object and saves it in the session scope as proof of authentication. It then redirects the browser to a JSP page. As before, the page selected depends on whether the user loaded the *login.jsp* page or tried to access an application page directly, without first logging in.

The *main.jsp* page contains a form for updating the project subscription list and a link for logging out. The difference from Chapter 13 is that both the form and the link now invoke the servlet instead of request-processing JSP pages. As it is for the authentication request, information encoded in URIs lets the servlet distinguish each type of request. The servlet performs the requested action and redirects to the main page after updating the subscription list, or to the login page after logging out. The *entermsg.jsp* page is changed in the same way; instead of submitting the message to a JSP page, it submits it to the servlet using a unique URI.

The application lifecycle event listener (not shown) initializes all resources needed by the other application components, such as the news and authentication service beans. Just for fun, I have also added the session lifecycle listener from Example 19-4 to keep track of the session count.

With these changes, we end up with a nice, modular application that's easy to maintain and extend. Let's take a closer look at each piece.

Initializing Shared Resources Using a Listener

The Project Billboard application uses two business logic beans that must be available to process requests from all users; in other words, available as application scope objects. You may remember the `NewsBean` from Chapter 13. This bean is the repository for all news items relating to projects, used as the source for the personalized message list. The other business logic bean is called `EmployeeRegistryBean`. It acts as an abstraction of the database with employee information, containing methods for user authentication and retrieving and saving employee information. The `EmployeeRegistryBean` class is described in more detail in Chapter 20.

Beans like this typically need to be initialized before they can be used. For instance, they may need a reference to a database or some other external data source and may create an initial information cache in memory to provide fast access even to the first request for data. You can include code for initialization of the shared resources in the servlet and JSP pages that need them, but a more modular approach is to place all this code in one place and let the other parts of the application work on the assumption that the resources are already initialized and available. An application lifecycle listener is a perfect tool for this type of resource initialization. Example 19-5 shows a listener suitable for the billboard application's needs. This type of listener implements the `javax.servlet.ServletContextListener` interface, with methods called by the container when the application starts and when it shuts down.

Example 19-5. Listener for application resource initialization

```
package com.ora.jsp.servlets;

import javax.servlet.*;
```

Example 19-5. Listener for application resource initialization (continued)

```
import javax.servlet.http.*;
import javax.sql.*;
import com.ora.jsp.beans.emp.*;
import com.ora.jsp.beans.news.*;
import com.ora.jsp.sql.*;

public class ResourceManagerListener implements ServletContextListener {

    public void contextInitialized(ServletContextEvent sce) {

        ServletContext application  = sce.getServletContext( );
        String driverClass = application.getInitParameter("driverClass");
        String jdbcURL = application.getInitParameter("jdbcURL");

        DataSourceWrapper ds = null;
        try {
            ds = new DataSourceWrapper( );
            ds.setDriverClassName(driverClass);
            ds.setUrl(jdbcURL);
        }
        catch (Exception e) {
            application.log("Error creating connection pool: ", e);
        }
        EmployeeRegistryBean empReg = new EmployeeRegistryBean( );
        empReg.setDataSource(ds);
        application.setAttribute("empReg", empReg);

        NewsBean news = new NewsBean( );
        application.setAttribute("news", news);
    }

    public void contextDestroyed(ServletContextEvent sce) {
        ServletContext application  = sce.getServletContext( );
        application.removeAttribute("empReg");
        application.removeAttribute("news");
    }
}
```

The `contextInitialized( )` method is called when the application starts, before any requests are delivered. The `ServletContextEvent` object passed as an argument has a method for getting a reference to the `ServletContext` instance for this application. The `ServletContext` provides a number of methods for accessing information about the web application as well as for sharing data between all application components, such as servlets, listeners, filters, and JSP pages.

The first context method used in Example 19-5 is the `getInitParameter( )` method. It returns the value of a context initialization parameter defined in the deployment descriptor. We look at the definition later. The listener gets the values of two initialization parameters containing information about the employee-information database: `driverClass` and `jdbcURL`.

A javax.sql.DataSource instance is then created using these values. A DataSource, an interface that was introduced by the JDBC 2.0 Optional Package and is now part of JDBC 3.0 (bundled with Java SDK 1.4), provides access to JDBC database connections for retrieving and modifying database data. It can represent a connection pool, letting you reuse a set of open connections instead of opening and closing a new connection for every request. Many JDBC driver vendors offer connection pool DataSource implementations, but here we use a simple wrapper class that implements its own connection pool based on standard JDBC 1.0 classes. The wrapper class is discussed in more detail in Chapter 24, where I also describe how to use a vendor-provided DataSource implementation.*

Finally, the business logic beans are created. The EmployeeRegistryBean is used by the Project Billboard application instead of accessing the database directly. It's always a good idea to encapsulate database access functions in a separate class, so that you have to make changes in only one place in case the database schema is changed at some point. The bean instance is initialized with the DataSource and saved as a context attribute named empReg. Next, the NewsBean instance is created and saved as a context attribute named news. The implementation used in this example keeps all messages in memory. If a database was used instead (a likely requirement for a real application), the NewsBean would also need to be initialized with the DataSource.

The listener saves references to the two beans as ServletContext attributes. This makes it easy for both servlets and JSP pages to get hold of them, as described earlier.

A listener that creates and initializes shared beans should also make sure that the beans are being removed and shut down gracefully, if needed. This is done in the listener's contextDestroyed( ) method, as shown in Example 19-5.

Let's look at the configuration needed to use the listener. As I mentioned earlier, the listener needs a couple of context-initialization parameters for the JDBC driver information. The listener itself must also be defined, so that the container knows which class to notify about the events. You use the following elements in the application deployment descriptor (the *WEB-INF/web.xml* file) for these definitions:

```
<web-app>
  <context-param>
    <param-name>driverClass</param-name>
    <param-value>
      sun.jdbc.odbc.JdbcOdbcDriver
    </param-value>
  </context-param>
  <context-param>
    <param-name>jdbcURL</param-name>
    <param-value>
```

* When you have a choice, I recommend using the database vendor's DataSource instead of a custom pool. I use the custom pool with a DataSource wrapper here because the examples are easy to run with pretty much any database and web container, without the need for vendor-dependent configuration.

```
      jdbc:odbc:example
    </param-value>
  </context-param>

  ...

  <listener>
    <listener-class>
      com.ora.jsp.servlets.ResourceManagerListener
    </listener-class>
  </listener>

  <listener>
    <listener-class>
      com.ora.jsp.servlets.SessionCounterListener
    </listener-class>
  </listener>

  ...
</web-app>
```

First the context initialization parameters are defined, using `<context-param>` elements with nested `<param-name>` and `<param-value>` elements. Next comes the listener definition, using the `<listener>` element with a nested `<listener-class>` element. Both the `ResourceManagerListener`, described in Example 19-5, and the `SessionCounterListener`, described in Example 19-4, are defined here because both are used in the Project Billboard application.

Access Control Using a Filter

The Project Billboard application uses application-controlled authentication and access control to ensure that only registered users can use the application. As discussed in Chapter 13, your first choice should be to use container-controlled authentication and access control, but let's assume that, in this case, there are valid reasons for going at it on our own.

Not all requests require a user to be logged in. For instance, if the login form and authentication request are protected, you're faced with a Catch 22; it's impossible to log in because you have to be logged in to load the login form. It's also reasonable to accept a log-out request from a user who isn't logged in; the session that contains the authentication information may have timed out before the user tries to log out.

You can use the URI path to distinguish between requests that need access control and those that don't. In this application, all requests that need access control include the */protected* path element, as shown in Table 19-1.

Table 19-1. Project Billboard context-relative URI paths

Context-relative path	Resource
/ch19/login.jsp	The login JSP page
/ch19/protected/main.jsp	The main JSP page
/ch19/protected/enterMsg.jsp	The message entry form JSP page
/ch19/authenticate.do	The authenticate action
/ch19/logout.do	The logout action
/ch19/protected/storeMsg.do	The action for storing a new message
/ch19/protected/updateProfile.do	The action for updating the subscription list

A few things of interest. All URIs start with */ch19*. This is just the convention I use in this book to identify which chapter the examples belongs to; in a real application, you would most likely not use this type of prefix. Also note that the application accepts URIs for JSP pages, as you're used to, but also URIs that end with *.do*. These are the URIs that invoke the servlet. I'll get back to why the URIs look like this in the next section. For now, just accept that this type of URI tells the servlet what to do.

A filter makes it easy to implement the access-control requirement. All URLs for protected resource are prefixed with */ch19/protected*, so we can configure the application to pass all requests matching this pattern through an access-control filter. Example 19-6 shows how the application deployment descriptor (the *WEB-INF/web.xml* file) should look like to accomplish this.

Example 19-6. Filter configuration

```
<web-app>
  ...
  <filter>
    <filter-name>accessControl</filter-name>
    <filter-class>
      com.ora.jsp.servlets.AccessControlFilter
    </filter-class>
    <init-param>
      <param-name>loginPage</param-name>
      <param-value>/ch19/login.jsp</param-value>
    </init-param>
  </filter>

  <filter-mapping>
    <filter-name>accessControl</filter-name>
    <url-pattern>/ch19/protected/*</url-pattern>
  </filter-mapping>
  ...
</web-app>
```

The `<filter>` element with its nested `<filter-name>` and `<filter-class>` defines a name and an implementation class for the filter. The nested `<init-param>` element defines an initialization parameter for the filter, containing the context-relative path to the login page for the application. I'll show how this value is accessed and used in the filter class in a moment.

The <filter-mapping> element with its nested <filter-name> and <url-pattern> elements tells the container that all requests matching the pattern should be passed through the access-control filter. Example 19-7 shows the filter implementation class.

Example 19-7. The access-control filter

```
package com.ora.jsp.servlets;

import java.io.*;
import java.net.*;
import javax.servlet.*;
import javax.servlet.http.*;

public class AccessControlFilter implements Filter {

    private FilterConfig config = null;
    private String loginPage;

    public void init(FilterConfig config) throws ServletException {
        this.config = config;
        loginPage = config.getInitParameter("loginPage");
        if (loginPage == null) {
            throw new ServletException("loginPage init param missing");
        }
    }

    public void destroy( ) {
        config = null;
    }

    public void doFilter(ServletRequest request,
        ServletResponse response, FilterChain chain)
        throws IOException, ServletException {

        HttpServletRequest httpReq = (HttpServletRequest) request;
        HttpServletResponse httpResp = (HttpServletResponse) response;

        if (!isAuthenticated(httpReq)) {
            String forwardURI = getForwardURI(httpReq);

            // Forward to the login page and stop further processing
            ServletContext context = config.getServletContext( );
            RequestDispatcher rd =
                context.getRequestDispatcher(forwardURI);
            if (rd == null) {
                httpResp.sendError(
                    HttpServletResponse.SC_INTERNAL_SERVER_ERROR,
                    "Login page doesn't exist");
```

Example 19-7. The access-control filter (continued)

```
            }
            rd.forward(request, response);
            return;
        }
        /*
         * Process the rest of the filter chain, if any, and ultimately
         * the requested servlet or JSP page.
         */
        chain.doFilter(request, response);
    }

    /**
     * Returns true if the session contains the authentication token.
     */
    private boolean isAuthenticated(HttpServletRequest request) {
        boolean isAuthenticated = false;
        HttpSession session = request.getSession( );
        if (session.getAttribute("validUser") != null) {
            isAuthenticated = true;
        }
        return isAuthenticated;
    }

    /**
     * Returns the context-relative path to the login page, with the
     * parameters used by the login page.
     */
    private String getForwardURI(HttpServletRequest request) {
        StringBuffer uri = new StringBuffer(loginPage);
        uri.append("?errorMsg=Please+log+in+first&origURL=").
            append(URLEncoder.encode(getContextRelativeURI(request)));
        return uri.toString( );
    }

    /**
     * Returns a context-relative path for the request, including
     * the query string, if any.
     */
    private String getContextRelativeURI(HttpServletRequest request) {
        int ctxPathLength = request.getContextPath().length( );
        String requestURI = request.getRequestURI( );
        StringBuffer uri =
            new StringBuffer(requestURI.substring(ctxPathLength));
        String query = request.getQueryString( );
        if (query != null) {
            uri.append("?").append(query);
        }
        return uri.toString( );
    }
}
```

A filter class must implement the javax.servlet.Filter interface, with lifecycle methods that are similar to the ones in the Servlet interface: init( ), doFilter( ), and destroy( ). The access-control filter in Example 19-7 saves a reference to the FilterConfig argument in the init( ) method so that it can later get access to the ServletContext object. It also gets the loginPage filter-initialization parameter. The destroy( ) method can be used just as in a servlet to release resources, and the access-control filter use it to remove the FilterConfig reference.

The container calls the doFilter( ) method when it receives a request matching the mapping for the filter. The request and response arguments are the same as for the doGet( ) and doPost( ) methods for a servlet. The third argument is an instance of the FilterChain interface. It contains references to an ordered list of all filters with pattern mappings matching the request. Its doFilter( ) method invokes the next filter in the chain, or the target resource (servlet or JSP page) when there are no more filters in the chain.

The doFilter( ) method for the access-control filter in Example 19-7 checks if the user is authenticated by looking for the EmployeeBean in the session. If it can't find it, it gets a RequestDispatcher for the login page URI with a query string with an error-message parameter and a parameter with the path for the currently requested page, and asks the RequestDispatcher to forward to the login page (the RequestDispatcher is discussed in more detail later).

The getContextRelativeURI( ) method creates the context-relative URI path to send as the origURL parameter. It does it by stripping off the context path from the absolute (server-relative) URI returned by the getRequestURI( ) method and then adding the query string, if any.

Centralized Request Processing Using a Servlet

With resource initialization and access control out of the way, delegated to appropriate component types, we can focus on the implementation of the main application logic.

We have already decided to use a servlet as a Controller. With a servlet as the common entry point for all application requests, you gain control over the page flow of the application. The servlet can decide which type of response to generate depending on the outcome of the requested action, such as returning a common error page for all requests that fail, or different responses depending on the type of client making the request. With the help from some utility classes, it can also provide services such as input validation, I18N preparations, and in general, encourage a more streamlined approach to request handling.

When you use a servlet as a Controller, you must deal with the following basic requirements:

- All processing requests must be passed to the single Controller servlet.
- The servlet must be able to distinguish requests for different types of processing.

Here are other features you may want to support, even though they may not be requirements for all applications:

- A strategy for extending the application to support new types of processing requests in a flexible manner
- A mechanism for changing the page flow of the application without modifying code

You can, of course, develop a servlet that fulfills these requirements yourself, but there are servlets available as open source that do all of this and more. In this chapter, I describe how to use the servlet from the Apache Struts project (*http://jakarta.apache.org/struts/*), Version 1.0.2.* It's probably the most popular framework for integration with JSP, and its servlet satisfies all our requirements. Using Struts gives you the following benefits:

- A highly configurable servlet
- Support for a modular design, making it easier to maintain and extend the application to handle new types of requests
- Support for mapping of symbolic page names to the real URIs, making it easier to change the site organization and control flow if needed
- A time-tested solution, actively supported by the Struts community, so you can focus on your application instead of framework development

If you decide to develop your own Controller servlet anyway, the description of how Struts deals with the requirements gives you some good ideas about how to do it.

Struts is a large framework. In addition to the Controller servlet and the associated classes, it also contains a number of custom tag libraries† that you can use in your JSP pages. I use only a fraction of the Struts servlet functionality in this example and none of the tag libraries. You may want to read the Struts documentation as well to see if your application can use the other features.

* As of this writing, a 1.1 version is about to be released. It adds a number of new features but is intended to be backward compatible with 1.0.2, so what I describe here should still be valid.

† Some of the Struts tag libraries are made obsolete by JSTL. If you use JSP 1.2 or later, you should use the JSTL libraries instead, but the Struts libraries will also be supported for some time. Over time, the Struts libraries that aren't made obsolete will likely be adjusted to integrate seamlessly with JSTL and JSP 2.0, for instance, to follow the JSTL design conventions and drop support for the "Struts EL" in favor of the JSP EL.

Struts Request Processing Overview

With power comes complexity, unfortunately. Before jumping into the details, here's a brief summary of the parts of Struts I use for the Project Billboard application.

The Struts servlet delegates the real processing of requests to classes that extends the Struts `Action` class. The main method in this class is the `perform()` method. For each type of request the application supports, you create a separate action class and provide the code for processing this request type in the `perform()` method. Figure 19-3 shows the action classes used by the Project Billboard application.

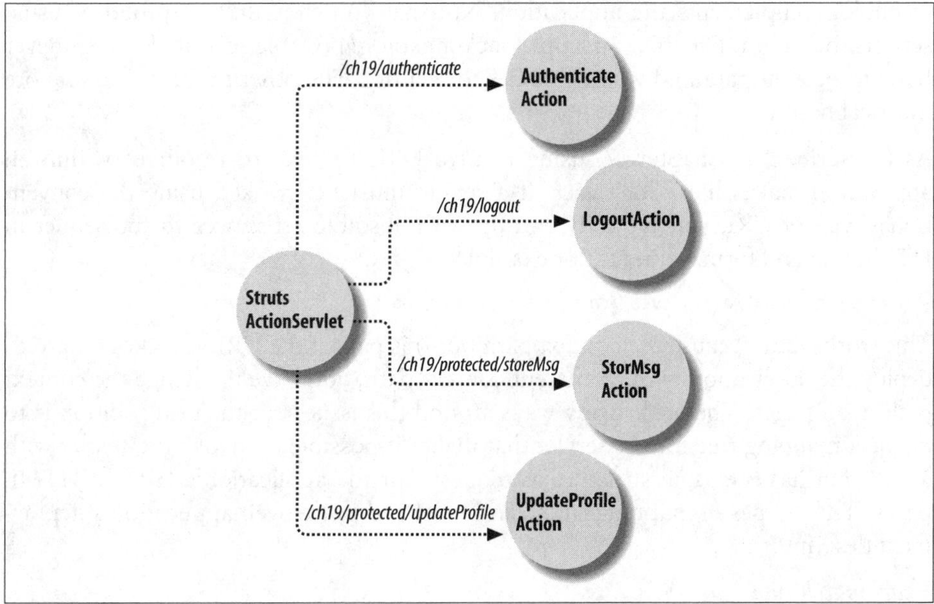

Figure 19-3. Controller split over dispatcher servlet and action classes

The Struts servlet uses parts of the request URI to figure out which type of request it is, locates the corresponding action class (using configuration information), and invokes the `perform()` method. Note that this method doesn't render a response; it takes care of business logic only, for instance, updating a database. The `perform()` method returns a Struts `ActionForward` instance, containing information about the JSP page that should be invoked to render the response. The page is identified by a logical name (`errorPage`, `mainPage`, etc.), mapped to the real page path in a configuration file. The page flow can therefore be controlled, at least to some extent, by reconfiguration instead of code changes.

Mapping Application Requests to the Servlet

The first requirement for using a Controller servlet is that all requests must pass through it. This can be satisfied in many ways. If you have played around a bit with servlets previously, you're probably used to invoking a servlet with a URI that starts with */myApp/servlet*. This is a convention introduced by Sun's Java Web Server (JWS), the first product to support servlets before the API was standardized. Some servlet containers still support this convention,* even though it's not formally defined in the servlet specification. But using this type of URI has a couple of problems. First, it makes it perfectly clear to a user (at least a user who knows about servlets) what technology implements the application. Not that you shouldn't be proud of using servlets, but a hint like this can help a hacker explore possible security holes; it never hurts to be a bit paranoid when it comes to security. The other problem is of a more practical nature.

As I described in Chapter 17, using relative URIs to refer to resources within an application makes life a lot easier. If a servlet must be invoked using the conventional type of URI, you typically end up with absolute references to the servlet in HTML link and form elements, for example:

```
<form action="/ora/servlet/controller/someAction">
```

This works, but because the context path (*/ora*) is part of the URI, it makes it hard to deploy the application with a different context path; you have to change the context path in all pages. There are many ways around this issue, but the best solution is to define a mapping rule for the servlet that makes it possible to invoke the servlet with a URI that has the same structure as requests for the application's JSP and HTML pages. Three types of mapping rules can be defined in the web application's deployment descriptor:

Exact match rule
: Matches a URI to a pattern path that is exactly the same as the URI, for instance the request */contextPath/exactMatch* matches the pattern */exactMatch*, but the request */contextPath/exactMatch/pathInfo* doesn't match this pattern.

Longest path prefix rule
: Matches a URI to the pattern path that has the most path elements in common with the URI, for instance the request */contextPath/pathPrefix* and */contextPath/pathPrefix/pathInfo* both match the pattern */pathPrefix/**, assuming no other pattern matches the full path for the second example.

Extension rule
: Matches a URI to the extension pattern that has the same extension as the URI. For instance, the requests */contextPath/name.extension* and */contextPath/aPath/name.extension* both match the pattern **.extension*.

* It's disabled by default in Tomcat, since Version 4.1.12.

The web container compares each request URI to the defined mapping rules, looking for matches in the order "exact-match," "longest path-prefix," and "extension" and invokes the servlet that's mapped to the first pattern that matches.

The exact match rule is rarely used, and the Struts servlet works only with the path-prefix and extension rules. The extension rule, using the extension *.do*, is the one that's recommended for mapping requests that should be processed by Struts. To define this mapping for the Struts servlet, we add these elements to the application's deployment descriptor (the *WEB-INF/web.xml* file):

```
<web-app>
  ...
  <servlet>
    <servlet-name>action</servlet-name>
    <servlet-class>
      org.apache.struts.action.ActionServlet
    </servlet-class>
  </servlet>

  <servlet-mapping>
    <servlet-name>action</servlet-name>
    <url-pattern>*.do</url-pattern>
  </servlet-mapping>
  ...
</web-app>
```

First we define a name for the Struts servlet class using the `<servlet>` element and the nested `<servlet-name>` and `<servlet-class>` elements. This definition associates the logical name `action` with the fully qualified class name `org.apache.struts.action.ActionServlet`. An extension mapping for this servlet is defined by the `<servlet-mapping>` element and the nested `<servlet-name>` and `<url-pattern>` elements. Note how the value of the `<servlet-name>` elements in the `<servlet>` and `<servlet-mapping>` elements match. With this mapping in place, the container invokes the Struts servlet for all requests that end with *.do*, making it possible to use a relative reference like this in HTML:

```
<form action="someAction.do">
```

If you prefer the path-prefix mapping, you need to change the `<servlet-mapping>` element like this for the Project Billboard application:

```
<servlet-mapping>
  <servlet-name>action</servlet-name>
  <url-pattern>/ch19/do/*</url-pattern>
</servlet-mapping>
<servlet-mapping>
  <servlet-name>action</servlet-name>
  <url-pattern>/ch19/protected/do/*</url-pattern>
</servlet-mapping>
```

Note that you need two mappings: one for requests that don't need access control and another for those that do. These mappings tell the container to invoke the Struts servlets for all requests that start with */ch19/do* or */ch19/protected/do*, allowing a relative reference like this in a page invoked with */ora/ch19/login.jsp*:

```
<form action="do/someAction">
```

It turns out, however, that even with a separate mapping for protected resources, it's easy to bypass the access control for a Struts action when you use the path prefix mapping. I'll show you why in a moment. To avoid security issues, I recommend you stick to the extension-mapping model.

Dispatching Requests to an Action Class

The second requirement for using a Controller servlet is that the servlet must be able to distinguish requests for different types of actions. The Struts servlet uses a configuration file with mappings from a part of the request path to the corresponding action class to handle this. The file is named *struts-config.xml* and is located in the *WEB-INF* directory for the application by default. Example 19-8 shows the configuration file used for the Project Billboard application.

Example 19-8. Struts configuration file

```
<?xml version="1.0" encoding="ISO-8859-1" ?>

<!DOCTYPE struts-config PUBLIC
  "-//Apache Software Foundation//DTD Struts Configuration 1.0//EN"
  "http://jakarta.apache.org/struts/dtds/struts-config_1_0.dtd">

<struts-config>
  <global-forwards>
    <forward name="login" path="/ch19/login.jsp" redirect="true" />
    <forward name="main" path="/ch19/protected/main.jsp"
        redirect="true" />
  </global-forwards>

  <action-mappings>
    <action path="/ch19/authenticate"
      type="com.ora.jsp.servlets.AuthenticateAction" />
    <action path="/ch19/logout"
      type="com.ora.jsp.servlets.LogoutAction" />
    <action path="/ch19/protected/storeMsg"
      type="com.ora.jsp.servlets.StoreMsgAction" />
    <action path="/ch19/protected/updateProfile"
      type="com.ora.jsp.servlets.UpdateProfileAction" />
  </action-mappings>
</struts-config>
```

It's an XML file, as are most configuration files nowadays. The first part of the file defines what Struts calls global forward mappings. I'll get back to them in the next section.

The second part contains an <action-mapping> element with nested <action> elements for each action class in the application. For each action, the element attributes specify the context-relative request path for the action and the class name for the corresponding action class.

If the Struts servlet is mapped to a path-prefix rule instead of an extension rule in the *web.xml* file, you must use different paths in the Struts configuration file as well:

```
<action-mappings>
  <action path="/authenticate"
    type="com.ora.jsp.servlets.AuthenticateAction" />
  <action path="/logout"
    type="com.ora.jsp.servlets.LogoutAction" />
  <action path="/storeMsg"
    type="com.ora.jsp.servlets.StoreMsgAction" />
  <action path="/updateProfile"
    type="com.ora.jsp.servlets.UpdateProfileAction" />
</action-mappings>
```

Note that only the last part of the URI path identifies the action in this case. To see why it's so, let's look at the method Struts uses to process the request path and figure out which action is requested. A slightly simplified version of the method used by Struts 1.0.2 is shown in Example 19-9.

Example 19-9. Extracting the action identifier

```
protected String processPath(HttpServletRequest request) {

    String path = null;

    path = request.getPathInfo( );
    if ((path != null) && (path.length( ) > 0))
        return (path);

    path = request.getServletPath( );
    int slash = path.lastIndexOf("/");
    int period = path.lastIndexOf(".");
    if ((period >= 0) && (period > slash))
        path = path.substring(0, period);
    return (path);

}
```

The processPath( ) method first calls getPathInfo( ) on the request object to get the part of the path that remains after removing the part the container uses to identify the servlet. For instance, with a path-prefix mapping such as */ch19/protected/do/** for the Struts servlet in the deployment descriptor and a request URI such as */ora/ch19/protected/do/storeMsg*, the getPathInfo( ) method returns */storeMsg*. If it returns null, it means that an extension mapping is used for the Struts servlet or that the URI is invalid. If so, the getServletPath( ) method is called to get the complete context-relative path for the request. With a mapping such as **.do* and a request URI such as */ora/ch19/protected/storeMsg.do*, it returns */ch19/protected/doStoreMsg.do*. The `processPath()` method strips off the extension part and returns the rest of the path, i.e., */ch19/protected/doStoreMsg*.

Hence, when you use path-prefix mapping, only the part of the request URI path that comes after the part that identifies the Struts servlet is returned and subsequently finds a matching action, while with an extension mapping, the whole context-relative path is returned and identifies the action. This is what causes the security problem I mentioned earlier. With the access-control filter mapped to */ch19/protected/**, and the Struts servlet mapped to */ch19/do/** and */ch19/protected/do/**, an adventurous user can access a protected action with a URI like */ch19/do/storeMsg* instead of */ch19/protected/do/storeMsg*, completely bypassing the access-control filter. This means the only secure way to provide access control for Struts actions when you use path-prefix mapping is to do the access control within the actions instead of with a filter. It's easier to just stick to extension mapping, as I recommended earlier.

Implementing the Action Classes

The servlet mapping rule in the deployment descriptor ensures that all requests reach the Struts servlet, and the action mappings in the *struts-config.xml* provides the information needed to distinguish different requests from each other. It's finally time to do some good old coding and implement the action classes.

Struts creates only a single instance of each action class and uses it for all requests, so you have to ensure that the class is thread-safe in the same way as for a servlet class. Thus, you should avoid using instance variables for anything except read-only access, and synchronize the access to shared data that must be modified.

Example 19-10 shows the main part of the action class that handles authentication requests in the Project Billboard application.

Example 19-10. Authenticate action class

```
package com.ora.jsp.servlets;

import java.io.*;
import java.net.*;
import java.sql.*;
import javax.servlet.*;
import javax.servlet.http.*;
import com.ora.jsp.beans.emp.*;
import org.apache.struts.action.*;

public class AuthenticateAction extends Action {

    public ActionForward perform(ActionMapping mapping,
        ActionForm form, HttpServletRequest request,
        HttpServletResponse response)
        throws IOException, ServletException {
```

Example 19-10. Authenticate action class (continued)

```
        String userName = request.getParameter("userName");
        String password = request.getParameter("password");

        ActionForward nextPage = mapping.findForward("main");

        EmployeeBean emp = null;
        try {
            EmployeeRegistryBean empReg = (EmployeeRegistryBean)
                getServlet().getServletContext( ).getAttribute("empReg");
            emp = empReg.authenticate(userName, password);
        }
        catch (SQLException e) {
            throw new ServletException("Database error", e);
        }
        if (emp != null) {
            // Valid login
            HttpSession session = request.getSession( );
            session.setAttribute("validUser", emp);
            setLoginCookies(request, response, userName, password);

            // Next page is the originally requested URL or main
            String next = request.getParameter("origURL");
            if (next != null && next.length( ) != 0) {
                nextPage = new ActionForward(next, true);
            }
        }
        else {
            // Invalid login. Redirect to the login page
            String loginPage = mapping.findForward("login").getPath( );
            String loginURL = loginPage +
                "?errorMsg=Invalid+User+Name+or+Password";
            nextPage = new ActionForward(loginURL, false);
        }
        return nextPage;
    }
    ...
}
```

The class extends the Struts `Action` class and overrides one method named `perform( )`. As the name implies, this is the method that performs the processing of the request. It returns an instance of another Struts class, named `ActionForward`. An `ActionForward` instance holds three pieces of information: a name, a path to a page (or a servlet), and information about how the specified path should be invoked (through a redirect or a forward). When the `perform( )` method returns, the Struts servlet invokes the specified resource, typically a JSP page that renders the response for the request.

The `perform( )` method has four arguments. The `request` and `response` arguments are the same as in a servlet, but the `form` and `mapping` arguments contain references to instances of Struts classes. The `form` argument is a reference to an `ActionForm`, a class that collects and validates form data. I don't use this feature, because it's tightly coupled to the Struts tag libraries. You can read about it in the Struts documentation to see if it makes sense for your application.

The `mapping` argument holds a reference to an `ActionMapping` instance. The `ActionMapping` class encapsulates all mapping information that can be defined in the Struts configuration file. I use only one of its features in this example, namely mappings between logical page names and the actual paths for the pages. This lets me change the page flow for the application without touching the action code. You set these mappings using the `<forward>` elements, as shown in Example 19-8. A mapping defined by a `<forward>` element nested within the body of a `<global-forwards>` element is available to all actions, while a `<forward>` element nested within an `<action>` element is available only to that action. All mappings used in the Project Billboard application are global, but local mappings can be handy for an action that uses different, action-specific JSP pages to render the response depending on the outcome of the request processing.

Let's look at how all these Struts classes are used in the `AuthenticateAction` class in Example 19-10. The `perform()` method first retrieves the values of the `userName` and `password` request parameters with the `getParameter()` method. It then gets a reference to the `ActionForward` instance representing the application main page, using the `findForward()` method on the `ActionMapping` instance. Within a try block, a reference to the `EmployeeRegistryBean` is retrieved from the servlet context attribute (where the initialization listener placed it when the application was started) and is then used to authenticate the user based on the username and password.

If the authentication is successful, the `EmployeeBean` returned by the `authenticate()` method is saved as a session attribute to serve as an authentication token. The call to `setLoginCookies()` adds the username and password cookies to the response. If the request includes a parameter named `origURL`, it means that the authentication was triggered by an attempt to load a protected page without being logged in. If so, a new `ActionForward()` instance is created for this page and eventually returned to the Struts servlet to send the user directly to the protected page she tried to load.

If the authentication fails, the `findForward()` method gets a reference to the `ActionForward` instance that represents the login page. But you can't use this instance as is, because you need to add a query string with an error message. The `getPath()` method extracts the page path, and then a new `ActionForward` instance is created from the combination of the path and the query string. This way, the global forward mapping serves its purpose of removing hardcoded paths in the action code even for a dynamically created URI. Also note that the second argument to the `ActionForward` constructor is set to `false`. This tells the Struts servlet it should use the forward method instead of the redirect method to invoke the page, giving the page access to both the original parameters (`userName` and `password`) and the new `errorMsg` parameter.

Example 19-11 shows the code for the `setLoginCookies()` method.

Example 19-11. Adding cookies to the response

```
private void setLoginCookies(HttpServletRequest request,
    HttpServletResponse response, String userName, String password) {

    Cookie userNameCookie = new Cookie("userName", userName);
    Cookie passwordCookie = new Cookie("password", password);
    // Cookie age in seconds: 30 days * 24 hours * 60 min * 60 seconds
    int maxAge = 30 * 24 * 60 * 60;
    if (request.getParameter("remember") == null) {
        // maxAge = 0 to delete the cookie
        maxAge = 0;
    }
    userNameCookie.setMaxAge(maxAge);
    passwordCookie.setMaxAge(maxAge);
    userNameCookie.setPath(request.getContextPath( ));
    passwordCookie.setPath(request.getContextPath( ));
    response.addCookie(userNameCookie);
    response.addCookie(passwordCookie);
}
```

The `javax.servlet.http.Cookie` class is defined by the servlet specification. The `setLoginCookies( )` method creates two instances, one each for the username and the password. How long a cookie should be kept by the browser is specified in seconds. In this example I calculate the number of seconds corresponding to 30 days and use it to set the age with the `setMaxAge( )` method, unless the user has requested no cookies (the `remember` parameter is not sent). In this case the maximum age is set to 0, which tells the browser to remove the cookie.

The `setPath( )` method sets the path attribute for both cookies to the context path for the application. This tells the browser to send only cookies with requests targeted for this application, instead of with all requests for this web server.

All the other action classes used by the Project Billboard are similar to the `AuthenticateAction` described in this section. They all override the `perform( )` method, do what they are supposed to do, and use the `findForward( )` method to get hold of the correct `ActionForward` instance to return. The source code for all classes is included in the book examples download. Instead of describing each class here, and boring you with a lot of tedious repetition, I suggest that you instead look at them at your leisure.

When you compile your action classes, you must ensure you have both the servlet classes and the Struts classes included in the classpath. You'll find the Struts classes in a JAR file named *struts.jar* in the Struts installation's *lib* directory. A copy of this JAR file for Struts 1.0.2 is bundled with the book examples in the *WEB-INF/lib* directory, but I suggest that you get the latest version directly from the Struts project web site (*http://jakarta.apache.org/struts/*) instead.

Processing Requests

When the Struts servlet receives a request, it first uses the `processPath()` method (Example 19-9) to extract the path part that is mapped to an action class. It then locates, or creates, the instance of the matching action class and calls its `perform()` method. The `ActionForward` instance returned by the `perform()` method is processed by the Struts servlet's `processActionForward()` method shown in Example 19-12.

Example 19-12. Forward processing

```
protected void processActionForward(ActionForward forward,
    ActionMapping mapping, ActionForm formInstance,
    HttpServletRequest request, HttpServletResponse response)
    throws IOException, ServletException {

    if (forward != null) {
        String path = forward.getPath( );
        if (forward.getRedirect( )) {
            if (path.startsWith("/"))
                path = request.getContextPath( ) + path;
            response.sendRedirect(response.encodeRedirectURL(path));
        } else {
            RequestDispatcher rd =
                getServletContext( ).getRequestDispatcher(path);
            if (rd == null) {
                response.sendError(response.SC_INTERNAL_SERVER_ERROR,
                    internal.getMessage("requestDispatcher", path));
                return;
            }
            rd.forward(request, response);
        }
    }
}
```

This method illustrates a number of interesting things about how to pass control to another part of the application—a servlet or a JSP page—that you need to be aware of if you decide to implement your own Controller servlet.

The `ActionForward` argument contains all the information Struts needs to pass control to the next component. Again, this is typically a JSP page that renders the response. The `getRedirect()` method returns `true` if a redirect response should be returned, ending this request and telling the browser to make a new request for the page that describes the result of the action. In versions of the Servlet API prior to 2.3, the `sendRedirect()` method officially accepted only an absolute URI (e.g., *http://localhost:8080/ora/mypage.jsp*). But in reality, a server-relative path (a URI without the scheme and server-name parts, e.g., */ora/mypage.jsp*) worked fine because all browsers handle such a path correctly in a redirect response, despite the fact that the HTTP specification doesn't allow it. In Version 2.3 of the specification, the absolute URI requirement was relaxed to also allow absolute and relative paths (e.g., */mypage.jsp* or *mypage.jsp*), relying on the container to convert the path to the absolute URI demanded by the HTTP specification. But there's a twist: an absolute path (starting with a slash) is interpreted as a *server-relative* path by the container instead of as a context-relative path, as is the case for all other methods in the API that use path arguments. This behavior was defined for backward-compatibility reasons since so many existing applications take advantage of the loophole in previous versions of the servlet specification. To shield developers from the path-interpretation issue, the `processActionForward()` method is designed to expect a context-relative path for an `ActionForward` instance even when the redirect method is used. If the path starts with a slash, the context path is added automatically, resulting in the server-relative absolute path the `sendRedirect()` method can handle.

The path passed to `sendRedirect()` method is also processed by the `encodeRedirectURL()`. This method inserts the session ID in the URL if the browser doesn't support cookies, as described in Chapter 10.

If `getRedirect()` returns `false`, it means that the forward method should be used to continue the request processing using the resource represented by the specified path. A `RequestDispatcher` for the path is retrieved from the `ServletContext`. A `RequestDispatcher` is a Servlet API class that programmatically invokes another servlet or a JSP page. It has two methods. The `include()` method temporarily passes control to the target, letting it generate a part of the response body but not set any response headers. It corresponds to the `<jsp:include>` action in a JSP page. The `forward()` method, used here, permanently passes control to the target in the same way as the `<jsp:forward>` action element in a JSP page. When a request is forwarded, the originating servlet delegates all processing to the target resource. The originating servlet is not allowed to modify the response in any way, neither before calling `forward()` nor when the method returns. In most cases, it should simply return after calling `forward()`, possibly after doing some clean up that doesn't involve modifying the response.

There are two ways to obtain a `RequestDispatcher` for a resource identified by a path. In Example 19-12, it is retrieved from the `ServletContext`. The path argument to its `getRequestDispatcher()` method must be a context-relative path, because the context has no knowledge about the path for the current request. If you want to use a path that's relative to the URI path for the current request, you can instead use the `getRequestDispatcher()` method on the request object. This method, defined in the `javax.servlet.ServletRequest` interface, accepts both types of paths.

Calling the Controller Servlet from JSP Pages

All that remains to complete the conversion of the Project Billboard application from a pure JSP application to an application that uses a mix of filters, listeners, servlets, and JSP pages is to modify the JSP pages to invoke the Controller servlet. To make the application a little bit more interesting, let's add information about the number of active sessions (loosely, the number of logged in users) to the main page.

By moving all request processing to other components, there are only three JSP pages left: *login.jsp*, *main.jsp*, and *entermsg.jsp*. The single change needed in the *login.jsp* page is the form element's `action` attribute:

```
<form action="<c:url value="/ch19/authenticate.do" />" method="post">
```

This application uses resources on different levels in the URI structure, and the login page can be invoked directly by the user as well as by a forwarded request for a resource in the *protected* directory if the user isn't logged in. The base URI differs depending on how it was invoked—*/ora/ch19/login.jsp* if it's invoked directly or */ora/ch19/protected/main.jsp* if it's invoked through a forward caused by an unauthenticated request for the main page. Thus, a relative path as the action value doesn't work; the browser converts a relative path in a page to an absolute path based in the URI that generated the response, as described in Chapter 17. The solution is to use an absolute path instead. To avoid hardcoding the context path in the page, I use the `<c:url>` action to convert the context-relative path to a server-relative path.

The *.do* extension tells the container to invoke the Struts servlet. When the Struts servlet processes the request, the `processPath( )` method (see Example 19-9) returns */ch19/authenticate*, which matches the path mapped to the `AuthenticateAction` class (see Example 19-10) in the *struts-config.xml* file (see Example 19-8). Everything is in order and works exactly as intended.

The *main.jsp* page is invoked by the Struts servlet if the authentication succeeds, as commanded by the `AuthenticateAction` class through the `ActionForward` instance its `perform( )` method returns. The context-relative path for the page is */ch19/protected/main.jsp*. The `AccessControlFilter` (Example 19-7) is mapped to this path, ensuring that only an authenticated user can access the page. The first change in the *main.jsp* page is therefore to remove the access-control code; it's not needed anymore. To display the number of active sessions, add an EL expression that displays the current value maintained by the `SessionCounterListener` (Example 19-4) at the beginning of the page:

```
<h1>Welcome ${fn:escapeXml(validUser.firstName)}</h1>
<h2>Number of active sessions: ${session_counter[0]}</h2>
```

The form and link elements also need attention:

```
Your profile currently shows you like information about the
following checked-off projects. If you like to update your
profile, make the appropriate changes below and click
Update Profile.
<form action="updateProfile.do" method="post">
  ...
</form>
<hr>
```

```
When you're done reading the news, please <a href="../logout.do">log out</a>.

<hr>
<a href="entermsg.jsp">Post a new message</a>
...
```

The *main.jsp* page is always invoked with the */ch19/protected/main.jsp* context-relative path, so here a relative URI for the form element's action attribute works fine. Compared to Chapter 13, the only difference is that it refers to the Struts action instead of a JSP page. The link element for the logout action must use a relative reference that moves up one level in the URI namespace: *../logout.do*. Remember, the main page was invoked with the */ch19/protected/main.jsp* path, but the logout action is unprotected, because it's mapped to the */ch19/logout.do* path in the *struts-config .xml* file.

Finally, the *entermsg.jsp* page; besides removing the access control code, the only change needed is the form element's action attribute:

```
<form action="storeMsg.do" method="post">
```

It follows the same pattern as the form-element changes in the *main.jsp* page.

Using a Common JSP Error Page

Before we end the exploration of the combination of JSP and servlets, I'd like to give you one more useful tip, namely how to use a JSP error page that displays a user-friendly error page for all runtime errors, no matter if they originate in a JSP page, a servlet, or a filter.

In Chapter 9, I showed you how to use the page directive's errorPage attribute to specify a JSP page that is invoked in case an exception is thrown while processing the page. I also mentioned that an alternative is to declare an error page in the deployment descriptor (the *WEB-INF/web.xml* file). It's then used for exceptions thrown by a servlet, a filter, or a JSP page that doesn't declare an error page:

```
<error-page>
  <exception-type>java.lang.Throwable</exception-type>
  <location>/errorpage.jsp</location>
</error-page>
```

To recap, the <exception-type> element contains the fully qualified name of the type of exception you want to handle with the servlet, JSP page, or static page specified by the <location> element. The <location> value must be a context-relative path (starting with a slash). You can use multiple <error-page> elements to use different pages for different exceptions, and the container picks the one with the <exception-type> element that most closely matches the type of the exception thrown.

You can also define a custom handler for response status codes other than 200 (i.e., status codes that signal some kind of problem):

```
<error-page>
```

```
    <error-code>404</error-code>
    <location>/notfound.jsp</location>
  </error-page>
```

If you use a JSP page as the handler, it has access to the all information about the request that failed and the reason (the exception or status code) through the properties of the pageContext.errorData variable, as described in Chapter 9. Prior to JSP 2.0, you had to work around a mismatch between the JSP and servlet specifications in order to access exception information in an error handling JSP page: the name of the request attributes used to pass on this information differed between the specifications. Fortunately, the JSP 2.0 specification is aligned with the servlet specification in this regard, so now you can use a JSP page like the one described in Chapter 9 even as a global error handler, without resorting to any tricks.

For a servlet error handler, the error information is available through the request attributes shown in Table 19-2.

Table 19-2. Error information request attributes

Attribute name	Java type	Description
javax.servlet.error.request_uri	String	The context-relative URI for the erroneous request
javax.servlet.error.servlet_name	String	The name of the servlet handling the erroneous request
javax.servlet.error.status_code	int	The status code for the erroneous request
javax.servlet.error.exception	Throwable	The exception thrown by the erroneous request, if any

You can use the error information to display informative messages to the user, or to log it along with information about request parameters, headers, etc., for analysis of the kind of problems your users experience when using the application.

CHAPTER 20

Developing JavaBeans Components for JSP

The JavaBeans specification* was developed with graphical components in mind. But JavaBeans represents a design pattern for components that also makes sense for faceless components in a server-side application. The JSP and JSTL specifications provide a number of ways to use JavaBeans components in web applications through standard actions and the JSP EL, as described in the previous chapters.

You can use JavaBeans components in a pure JSP application to structure the application and minimize the amount of logic needed in the JSP pages. In an application that uses both servlets and JSP pages, beans carry data between the two domains. By using beans with an eye towards the recommendations in the J2EE application programming model, you can also make it easier to migrate the business logic to Enterprise JavaBeans when warranted by new requirements.

In this chapter, we look at the JavaBeans model and how it applies to the type of faceless beans used for server-side applications; beans used in previous chapters will serve as examples.

Beans as JSP Components

JavaBeans components, or beans for short, are simply regular Java classes designed according to a set of guidelines. By following these guidelines, development tools can figure out how you intend the bean to be used and how it can be linked to other beans. The JavaBeans specification characterizes beans as classes that support:

- *Introspection* so that a builder tool can analyze how a bean works
- *Customization* so that, when using an application builder, a user can customize the appearance and behavior of a bean

* This specification is available at *http://java.sun.com/products/javabeans/docs/spec.html*.

- *Events* as a simple communication metaphor than notify beans of interesting things
- *Properties*, both for customization through a tool and for programmatic use
- *Persistence*, so that a bean can be customized in an application builder and then have its state saved away and reloaded later

Introspection means that information about a class, such as details about its methods and their parameters and return types, can be discovered by another class. By following certain naming conventions for the methods, the external class can figure out how the bean class is intended to be used. Specifically, the beans properties and the events it generates or observes can be found using the Java Introspection API. For GUI beans, a builder tool uses introspection to discover the bean's properties and present them to the user in a property window where they can be modified. In a JSP scenario, the JSP standard actions and the EL evaluator use introspection to find the methods for reading or writing property values and to declare variables of appropriate types.

A property is an attribute of a bean that can be read or written by the bean's client through regular methods named according to the JavaBeans guidelines. Typically, the property value is represented by an instance variable in the bean, but a read-only property can also represent a value that's calculated at runtime. The property methods are used to customize the bean; for instance, you can set the label text for a bean used as a button in a GUI application or set the name of the data source for a faceless server-side bean. Besides property access methods, a bean class can have regular methods that perform actions such as saving the bean's properties in a database or sending a mail composed from its properties.

A bean can generate or observe events. In a GUI bean, typical events are "button clicked" and "item selected." For a server-side bean, a typical event is "data source updated," allowing a bean that represents the data to refresh its copy.

Support for persistence means that a bean should implement the `java.io.Serializable` interface. This interface flags a class that can be saved in an external format, such as a file. When tools customize a bean, it's possible to save the customized state during application development and then let the customized bean be instantiated at runtime. The `<jsp:useBean>` action allows you to take advantage of this feature, but it's not commonly used today because no JSP authoring tools provide a customization interface. There's another reason for supporting persistence in JSP beans, however. A servlet container can support session persistence, by saving all session data when a servlet context is shut down and reloading it again when the context is restarted. This works only if the beans you save in the session scope implement `Serializable`. In addition, beans (or any other object) placed in the session scope of an application marked as being distributable must be serializable, so that the container can migrate the session from one server to another.

JavaBeans Naming Conventions

As I mentioned earlier, a Java bean is a class that has a no-argument constructor and conforms to the JavaBeans naming conventions. The bean properties are accessed through *getter* and *setter* methods, collectively known as a bean's *accessor* methods. Getter and setter method names are composed of the word *get* or *set*, respectively, plus the property name with the first character of each word capitalized. A regular getter method has no parameters but returns a value of the property's type, while a setter method has a single parameter of the property's type and has a `void` return type. Here's an example:

```
public class CustomerBean implements java.io.Serializable {

    String firstName;
    String lastName;
    int accountNumber;
    int[] categories;
    boolean preferred;

    public String getFirstName( ) {
      return firstName;
    }

    public void setFirstName(String firstName) {
      this.firstName = firstName;
    }
```

A readable property has a getter method; a writable property has a setter method. Depending on the combination of getter and setter methods, a property is read-only, write-only, or read/write. Note that it's the presence of the accessor methods that defines the property; how the property value is represented inside the class makes no difference at all.

A read-only property doesn't necessarily have to match an instance variable one-to-one. Instead, it can combine instance variable values, or any values, and return a computed value:

```
public String getFullName( ) {
  return (new StringBuffer(firstName).append(" ")
    .append(lastName).toString( ));
}
```

The type of a property can be a Java class, interface, or a primitive type such as `int`:

```
public int getAccountNumber( ) {
  return accountNumber;
}
```

Besides simple single-value properties, beans can also have multivalue properties represented by an array of any type. This is called an *indexed property* in the specification. Two types of access methods can be used for an indexed property: methods reading or writing the whole array or methods working with just one element, specified by an index:

```
public int[] getCategories( ) {
  return categories;
}

public void setCategories(int[] categories) {
  this.categories = categories;
}

public int getCategories(int i) {
  return categories[i];
}

public void setCategories(int i, int category) {
  this.categories[i] = category;
}
```

The naming convention for a Boolean property getter method is different from all other types. You *can* use the regular getter name pattern, but the recommendation is to use the word *is* combined with the property name, to form a question:

```
public boolean isPreferred( ) {
  return preferred;
}
```

This helps to make the source code more readable. The setter method for a Boolean property follows the regular pattern:

```
public void setPreferred(boolean preferred) {
  this.preferred = preferred;
}
```

Event handling is based on event observers implementing a listener interface, and event generators providing methods for observers to register their interest in the events. A listener interface defines the methods a listener needs to implement to be notified when the corresponding event is triggered. A bean identifies itself as a listener by declaring that it's implementing a listener interface, and an event source is identified by its listener registration methods.

Let's look at an example. A listener interface for observing events related to the customer data handled by the example bean can look like this:

```
import java.util.EventListener;

public interface CustomerUpdatedListener extends EventListener {
    void customerUpdated(CustomerUpdatedEvent e);
}
```

The interface shown here defines only one event notification method, but an interface may also group a number of methods for related events. The `CustomerBean` identifies itself as an observer of the event by implementing the interface:

```
public class CustomerBean implements CustomerUpdatedListener {
  ...
    public void customerUpdated(CustomerUpdatedEvent e) {
      if (e.getAccountNumber( ) == accountNumber) {
          // Refresh local copy
      }
    }
```

Another bean, perhaps one acting as the gatekeeper to the customer database, identifies itself as a source for the event by defining methods for registration of listeners:

```
import java.util.Vector;

public class CustomerRegister {
    private Vector listeners = new Vector( );

    public
    void addCustomerUpdatedListener(CustomerUpdatedListener cul) {
      listeners.addElement(cul);
    }

    public
    void removeCustomerUpdatedListener(CustomerUpdatedListener cul) {
      listeners.removeElement(cul);
    }

    public void updateCustomer(CustomerBean customer) {
      // Update persistent customer storage
      notifyUpdated(customer);
    }
```

It notifies all listeners when the customer data is modified, like this:

```
    protected void notifyUpdated(CustomerBean customer) {
        Vector l;
        CustomerUpdatedEvent e =
            new CustomerUpdatedEvent(this, customer.getAccountNumber( ));
        synchronized(listeners) {
            l = (Vector)listeners.clone( );
        }
        for (int i = 0; i < l.size( ); i++) {
            ((CustomerUpdatedListener)l.elementAt(i)).customerUpdated(e);
        }
    }
}
```

By following these simple naming conventions, the JSP standard actions `<jsp:getProperty>` and `<jsp:setProperty>`, as well as the EL evaluator and custom action classes, can discover how to use your beans correctly. At this time, no JSP features rely on the event-naming conventions, but future development tools may do so. So if your beans need to handle events, it's a good idea to follow the conventions. Besides, it's a well-known design pattern (you probably recognize it from the listener classes described in Chapter 19), so using it makes your code more readable to other developers familiar with this design.

Handling session events

A bean used in a JSP application can actually register itself to receive session-related events. The Servlet API includes an interface called `javax.servlet.http.HttpSessionBindingListener`; an object that implements this interface is notified when it's placed in or removed from a session, through these two methods:

```
public void valueBound(HttpSessionBindingEvent event);
public void valueUnbound(HttpSessionBindingEvent event);
```

The `valueBound( )` method is called when the object is added to a session, and the `valueUnbound( )` method is called when it's removed. The `HttpSessionBindingEvent` class contains these two methods:

```
public String getName( );
public HttpSession getSession( );
```

The `getName( )` method returns the name used for the object in the session, and the `getSession( )` method returns a reference to the session object itself.

This is different from the session attribute listener interface in the Servlet 2.3 specification—`javax.servlet.http.HttpSessionAttributeListener`, described briefly in Chapter 18. An object registered as an `HttpSessionAttributeListener` is notified when any session attribute is set, removed, or replaced, in all sessions; an object implementing the `HttpSessionBindingListener` interface is notified only when the object itself is added to or removed from the session it's placed in. The former is useful for application scope tasks, such as keeping track of the amount of memory used for session data; the latter can perform initialization and cleanup tasks for an individual object.

Using a package name for a bean class

Even though the bean specification doesn't require it, I recommend that you always declare a specific package name for all beans you intend to use in JSP pages, via the Java package statement:

```
package com.mycompany.beans;
public class MyBean {
    ...
}
```

If you don't, you can't use the bean in a JSP page in a portable manner. As you may recall from Chapter 16, the page implementation class may use a vendor-dependent package name. Because Java doesn't permit a class without a package qualifier to be used in a class that belongs to a package,* a JSP page containing beans that don't belong to a package cannot be compiled if the generated implementation class uses a package.

* Sun's Java SDK 1.4 enforces this rule; previous versions didn't, even though the Java language specification said it was not permitted.

Compiling and Installing a Bean

Compiling and installing a bean for a web application is done in the same way as for a servlet class, as described in Chapter 19. You need to include all classes the bean uses, if any, in the classpath and compile the bean, for instance using the *javac* command:

```
C:/> set CLASSPATH=C:\someDir\someClasses.jar;%CLASSPATH%
C:/> javac MyBean.java
```

To make the bean available to the web application, place the resulting class file in the *WEB-INF/classes* directory for the example application:

```
C:/> copy MyBean.class C:\Jakarta\jakarta-tomcat-5\webapps\ora\WEB-INF\classes
```

If you followed my advice and declared a package name for the bean class, say `com.mycompany.beans`, you should put the class file in a directory under *WEB-INF/classes* that mirrors the package structure, for instance *WEB-INF/classes/com/mycompany/beans*. Alternatively, you can package the bean class file in a JAR file (see the Java SDK documents for details) and place the JAR file in the *WEB-INF/lib* directory. The internal structure of the JAR file must also mirror the package structure for all your classes.

JSP Bean Examples

In a JSP-based application, two types of beans are primarily used: value beans and utility beans. A *value bean* encapsulates all information about some entity, such as a user or a product. A *utility bean* performs some action, such as saving information in a database or sending email. Utility beans can use value beans as input or produce value beans as a result of an action.

If you develop beans for your application, you're also preparing for migration to a full-blown J2EE application. The utility beans can be changed into proxies for one or more EJB session beans, acting as part of the Controller for the application.

Value beans may act as what are called Value Objects in the J2EE Blueprints. In an EJB-based application, the application's data is represented by EJB entity beans. Getting a property value from an EJB entity bean requires a remote call, consuming both system resources and bandwidth. Instead of making a remote call for each property value that is needed, the web component can make one remote call to an EJB session bean (possibly via a JSP utility bean) that returns all properties of interest packaged as a value bean. The web component can then get all the properties from the value bean with inexpensive local calls. The value bean can also act as cache in the web container to minimize remote calls even more, and it can combine information from multiple EJB entity beans that is meaningful to the web interface. If you plan to move to the EJB model eventually, I encourage you to read the J2EE Blueprint papers (*http://java.sun.com/blueprints/enterprise/index.html*) before you design your application to make the migration as smooth as possible.

Value Beans

Value beans are useful even without EJB. They are handy for capturing form input, because the <jsp:setProperty> JSP action automatically sets all properties with names corresponding to request parameter names, as described in Chapter 8. In addition, the <jsp:getProperty> action and the JSP EL let you include the property values in the response without using scripting elements.

Another benefit of value beans is that they can be used to minimize expensive database accesses for entities that rarely change their value. By placing a value bean in the application scope, all users of your application can use the cached value instead. Example 20-1 shows the source code for the ProductBean used in Chapter 10 to represent products in an online shopping application. This is a pure value bean, with only property accessor methods, that can represent data retrieved from a database.

Example 20-1. ProductBean

```
package com.ora.jsp.beans.shopping;

import java.io.*;

public class ProductBean implements Serializable {
    private String id;
    private String name;
    private String descr;
    private float price;

    public String getId( ) {
        return id;
    }

    public String getName( ) {
        return name;
    }

    public String getDescr( ) {
        return descr;
    }

    public float getPrice( ) {
        return price;
    }

    void setId(String id) {
        this.id = id;
    }

    void setName(String name) {
        this.name = name;
    }

    void setDescr(String descr) {
```

Example 20-1. ProductBean (continued)

```
        this.descr = descr;
    }

    void setPrice(float price) {
        this.price = price;
    }
}
```

This bean is created and initialized by the single instance of the `CatalogBean`. All setter methods have package accessibility, while the getter methods are public. Using package accessibility for the setter methods ensures that only the `CatalogBean` can set the property values. For instance, a JSP page can read the product information but not change the price.

Another example of a value bean is the `UserInfoBean` introduced in Chapter 8. Part of this bean is shown in Example 20-2. Besides encapsulating the property values of the entity it represents, it also provides methods for validation of the data.

Example 20-2. Part of the UserInfoBean

```
package com.ora.jsp.beans.userinfo;

import java.io.*;
import java.util.*;
import com.ora.jsp.util.*;

public class UserInfoBean implements Serializable {
    // Validation constants
    private static String DATE_FORMAT_PATTERN = "yyyy-MM-dd";
    private static String[] GENDER_LIST = {"m", "f"};
    private static String[] FOOD_LIST = {"z", "p", "c"};
    private static int MIN_LUCKY_NUMBER = 1;
    private static int MAX_LUCKY_NUMBER = 100;

    // Properties
    private String birthDate;
    private String emailAddr;
    private String[] food;
    private String luckyNumber;
    private String gender;
    private String userName;

    public String getBirthDate( ) {
        return (birthDate == null ? "" : birthDate);
    }

    public void setBirthDate(String birthDate) {
        this.birthDate = birthDate;
    }

    public boolean isBirthDateValid( ) {
```

Example 20-2. Part of the UserInfoBean (continued)

```
        boolean isValid = false;
        if (birthDate != null &&
            StringFormat.isValidDate(birthDate, DATE_FORMAT_PATTERN)) {
            isValid = true;
        }
        return isValid;
    }
    ...
```

In addition to the setter and getter methods for the `birthDate` property, the `UserInfoBean` includes a separate method for validation. It follows the naming conventions for a Boolean getter method, so it can be used in an EL expression to test if the value is valid. The getter method returns an empty string in case the property is not set. Without this code, a `<jsp:getProperty>` action adds the string `null` to the response. The JSTL `<c:out>` action and EL expressions, on the other hand, automatically convert a null value to the empty string, so this type of code is not needed in an application that always uses `<c:out>` or the EL for adding bean property values to the response.

This type of getter, setter, and validation method combo represents all `UserInfoBean` properties. In addition, the bean includes other validation and test methods, all of them posing as Boolean read-only getter methods. They are shown in Example 20-3.

Example 20-3. Validation and test methods

```
    public boolean isValid( ) {
        return isBirthDateValid() && isEmailAddrValid( ) &&
            isFoodValid() && isLuckyNumberValid( ) &&
            isGenderValid() && isUserNameValid( );
    }

    public boolean isPizzaSelected( ) {
        return isFoodTypeSelected("z");
    }

    public boolean isPastaSelected( ) {
        return isFoodTypeSelected("p");
    }

    public boolean isChineseSelected( ) {
        return isFoodTypeSelected("c");
    }

    private boolean isFoodTypeSelected(String foodType) {
        if (food == null) {
            return false;
        }
        boolean selected = false;
        for (int i = 0; i < food.length; i++) {
            if (food[i].equals(foodType)) {
```

Example 20-3. Validation and test methods (continued)

```
                selected = true;
                break;
            }
        }
        return selected;
    }
```

As you may remember from Chapter 8, these read-only properties dramatically simplify the process of validation and filling out a form with the current values.

Utility Beans

A utility bean performs some action, such as processing information, as opposed to simply acting as a container for information.

The `UserInfoBean` contains processing code in addition to the plain property setter and getter methods, namely the validation and test code. The way the bean is used in this book, it's perfectly okay to keep the validation code in the bean itself. However, let's say you would like to add a property that references another bean, a `friends` property for instance, that holds an array of other `UserInfoBean` objects. It may then be better to let a utility bean that knows about all users in the application perform the validation, including verifying that the friends exist.

A bean used for validation is one example of a utility bean you can use to make the application easy to maintain. The `CatalogBean` used in Chapter 10 is another example. The version developed for this book simply creates a set of `ProductBean` objects with hardcoded values and provides a method that returns all products in the catalog. In a real application, it would likely get the information from a database instead and have methods for updating catalog information, such as adding and removing products or changing the information about a product, as well as methods that return only the products matching various search criteria. If all catalog update requests go through the `CatalogBean`, it can create, delete, and update the `ProductBean` objects so that they always match the information stored in the database. The number of database accesses can be greatly reduced this way.

Chapter 19 offers another example of how you can use a utility bean. As opposed to the examples in Chapter 12 and Chapter 13, in which the generic JSTL actions are used to access a database, Chapter 19 uses a bean to encapsulate all database access code. This strategy gives you an application that's easier to maintain because modifications due to a possible database schema change need to be done only in one place. Example 20-4 shows part of the utility bean that handles all database interactions in Chapter 19.

Example 20-4. EmployeeRegistryBean

```
package com.ora.jsp.beans.emp;

import java.io.*;
import java.sql.*;
import java.text.*;
import java.util.*;
import javax.sql.*;
import javax.servlet.jsp.jstl.sql.*;
import com.ora.jsp.beans.sql.*;

public class EmployeeRegistryBean implements Serializable {
    private DataSource dataSource;

    /**
     * Sets the dataSource property value.
     */
    public void setDataSource(DataSource dataSource) {
        this.dataSource = dataSource;
    }

    /**
     * Returns an EmployeeBean if the specified user name and password
     * match an employee in the database, otherwise null.
     */
    public EmployeeBean authenticate(String userName, String password)
        throws SQLException {

        EmployeeBean empInfo = getEmployee(userName);
        if (empInfo != null && empInfo.getPassword( ).equals(password)) {
            return empInfo;
        }
        return null;
    }

    /**
     * Returns an EmployeeBean initialized with the information
     * found in the database for the specified employee, or null if
     * not found.
     */
    public EmployeeBean getEmployee(String userName) throws SQLException

        // Get the user info from the database
        Connection conn = dataSource.getConnection( );
        Map empRow = null;
        Map[] projects = null;
        try {
            empRow = getSingleValueProps(userName, conn);
            projects = getProjects(userName, conn);
        }
        finally {
            try {
                conn.close( );
```

Example 20-4. EmployeeRegistryBean (continued)

```
            }
            catch (SQLException e) {} // Ignore
        }

        // Create a EmployeeBean if the user was found
        if (empRow == null) {
            // Not found
            return null;
        }

        EmployeeBean empInfo = new EmployeeBean( );
        empInfo.setDept((String) empRow.get("Dept"));
        empInfo.setEmpDate((java.util.Date) empRow.get("EmpDate"));
        empInfo.setEmailAddr((String) empRow.get("EmailAddr"));
        empInfo.setFirstName((String) empRow.get("FirstName"));
        empInfo.setLastName((String) empRow.get("LastName"));
        empInfo.setPassword((String) empRow.get("Password"));
        empInfo.setUserName((String) empRow.get("UserName"));
        empInfo.setProjects(toProjectsArray(projects));
        return empInfo;
    }

    /**
     * Inserts the information about the specified employee, or
     * updates the information if it's already defined.
     */
    public void saveEmployee(EmployeeBean empInfo) throws SQLException {

        // Save the user info from the database
        Connection conn = dataSource.getConnection( );
        conn.setAutoCommit(false);
        try {
            saveSingleValueProps(empInfo, conn);
            saveProjects(empInfo, conn);
            conn.commit( );
        }
        catch (SQLException e) {
            conn.rollback( );
        }
        finally {
            try {
                conn.setAutoCommit(true);
                conn.close( );
            }
            catch (SQLException e) {} // Ignore
        }
    }

    /**
     * Returns a Map with all information about the specified
     * employee except the project list, or null if not found.
     */
```

Example 20-4. EmployeeRegistryBean (continued)

```
    private Map getSingleValueProps(String userName, Connection conn)
        throws SQLException {

        if (userName == null) {
            return null;
        }

        SQLCommandBean sqlCommandBean = new SQLCommandBean( );
        sqlCommandBean.setConnection(conn);
        StringBuffer sql = new StringBuffer( );
        sql.append("SELECT * FROM Employee ")
            .append("WHERE UserName = ?");
        sqlCommandBean.setSqlValue(sql.toString( ));
        List values = new ArrayList( );
        values.add(userName);
        sqlCommandBean.setValues(values);
        Result result = sqlCommandBean.executeQuery( );
        if (result == null || result.getRowCount( ) == 0) {
            // User not found
            return null;
        }
        return result.getRows( )[0];
    }
    ...
```

The `EmployeeRegistryBean` has one property, `dataSource`, that must be set when the bean is created. Chapter 19 describes how an application lifecycle listener can create the bean and initialize it with a `DataSource` when the application starts, and then save it in the application scope where the rest of the application can reach it. The other public methods in this bean perform the same function as the generic database actions in Chapters 12 and 13. The `getSingleValueProps( )` method, as well other private methods not shown in Example 20-4, uses an `SQLCommandBean` to execute the SQL statement. This bean is included in the source code package for this book, so you can use it in your own beans as well. We will look at the implementation in Chapter 24.

A database access utility bean such as the `EmployeeRegistryBean` can be used in an application that combines servlets and JSP. Custom actions developed to simplify a JSP-only application can also use it. For instance, the authentication code in the *authenticate.jsp* file used in the Chapter 13 example can be reduced with a couple of custom actions using the `EmployeeRegistryBean`:

```
...
<%--
  See if the user name and password combination is valid. If not,
  redirect back to the login page with a message.
--%>
<myLib:ifUserNotValid user="${param.userName}" pw="${param.password}">
  <c:redirect url="login.jsp" >
    <c:param name="errorMsg"
```

```
        value="The User Name or Password you entered is not valid." />
  </c:redirect>
</my:ifUserNotValid>

<%--
  Create an EmployeeBean and save it in the session scope
--%>
<myLib:createEmployeeBean var="validUser" scope="session"
  user="${param.username}" />
```

The <myLib:ifUserNotValid> action implementation can use the authenticate( ) method and process its body only if it returns null, and the <myLib:createEmployeeBean> action can call the getEmployee( ) method to get an initialized bean and save it in the session scope.

Multithreading Considerations

As you have seen, putting business logic in beans leads to a more structured and maintainable application. However, there's one thing you need to be aware of: beans shared between multiple pages must be thread safe.

Thread safety is an issue for beans only in the session and application scopes. Beans in the page and request scope are executed by only one thread at a time. A bean in the session scope can be executed by more than one thread initiated by requests from the same client. This may happen if the user brings up multiple browsers, repeatedly clicks a submit button in a form, or if the application uses frames to request multiple JSP pages at the same time. All application users share application scope beans, so it's very likely that more than one thread is using an application scope bean.

Java provides mechanisms for dealing with concurrent access to resources, such as synchronized blocks and thread notification methods. But there are other ways to avoid multithreading issues in the type of beans used in JSP pages.

Value beans are typically placed in the request or session scope as containers for information used in multiple pages. In most cases, they are created and initialized in one place only, such as by a Controller servlet or by a <jsp:useBean> and <jsp:setProperty> combination in the request processing page invoked by a form, or by a custom action or utility bean. In all other places, the bean is used only within EL expressions or by the <jsp:getProperty> action to read its property values. Because only one thread writes to the bean and all others just read it, you don't have to worry about different threads overwriting each other.

If you have a value bean that can be updated, such as the NewsBean used in Chapter 13, you have to be careful, though. The NewsBean contains an instance variable that holds a list of NewsItemBean objects and has methods for retrieving, adding, and removing news items. If one thread calls removeNewsItem( ) while another is executing getNewsItems( ), a runtime exception may occur unless you take the necessary precautions. Example 20-5 shows how to use synchronization to guard against this problem.

Example 20-5. Synchronized access to instance variable

```
package com.ora.jsp.beans.news;

import java.io.*;
import java.util.*;
import com.ora.jsp.util.*;

public class NewsBean implements Serializable {
    private ArrayList newsItems = new ArrayList( );
    private int[] idSequence = new int[1];
    ...
    public NewsItemBean[] getNewsItems( ) {
        NewsItemBean[] a = null;
        synchronized (newsItems) {
            a = (NewsItemBean[])
                newsItems.toArray(new NewsItemBean[newsItems.size( )]);
        }
        return a;
    }

    public void setNewsItem(NewsItemBean newsItem) {
        synchronized (idSequence) {
            newsItem.setId(idSequence[0]++);
        }
        synchronized (newsItems) {
            newsItems.add(newsItem);
        }
    }

    public void removeNewsItem(int id) {
        synchronized (newsItems) {
            for (int i = 0; i < newsItems.size( ); i++) {
                NewsItemBean item = (NewsItemBean) newsItems.get(i);
                if (id == item.getId( )) {
                    newsItems.remove(i);
                    break;
                }
            }
        }
    }
    ...
}
```

The `java.util.ArrayList` used to hold the news items is not thread-safe, meaning it does not provide any synchronization on its own. All public `NewsBean` methods that read or modify the list must therefore synchronize on the `newsItems` object. The effect is that while one thread is manipulating the list of news items through one of these methods, all other threads wait until the current thread leaves the synchronized block. I could have used a `java.util.Vector` instead of the `ArrayList` in this bean; it's a class that synchronizes all access to its elements, so the bean would not have had to. In many cases, you want to use unsynchronized access when you're sure only one thread has access to the list to gain performance, and then the ArrayList is a better choice. In the NewsBean, for instance, the list is filled with existing news items in the bean's constructor; only one thread can run the constructor, so it's safe to add the items without synchronization.

The setNewsItem( ) method also synchronizes on idSequence, a variable that generates a unique ID for each item. idSequence is an int array with one component. This is a neat trick for synchronized access to an integer value; Java doesn't support synchronization on primitive types, only on objects, but an array of a primitive type is an object. You can use an Integer object instead, but you can't change the value of an Integer. To increment the value, a new Integer must be created. Using an array avoids these repeated object creations (and creating an object is a fairly expensive operation in Java).

Another approach that avoids multithreading problems is used in the EmployeeRegistryBean described in the previous section. It defines setter methods only for customization that takes place when the bean is created and defines all data needed to perform a task as method parameters instead of properties. Each thread has its own copy of method parameter values and local variables, so with this approach, there's no risk that one thread will step on another.

Unexpected <jsp:setProperty> Behavior

The <jsp:setProperty> action can automatically set all properties in a bean with names matching the names of the parameters received with the request. This is a great feature that's used in many of the examples in this book, but unless you know how it works behind the scenes, you can be in for a surprise.

When the <jsp:setProperty> code is invoked, it gets a list of all request parameter names and uses bean introspection to find the corresponding property setter methods. It then calls all setter methods to set the properties to the values of the parameters. This means that if you have a property in your bean that doesn't match a parameter, the setter method for this property is not called. In most cases, this is not surprising. If the parameter is present in some requests but not in others, however, things may get a bit confusing. This is the case with parameters corresponding to checkbox, radio button, and selection list elements in an HTML form. If this type of element is selected, the browser sends a parameter with the element's name and the value of the selected item. If the element is not selected, it doesn't send a parameter at all.

For example, let's say you have a bean with an indexed property, such as the projects property in the com.ora.jsp.beans.emp.EmployeeBean used in Chapter 13. This bean is kept in the session scope. The user can change the value of the property through a group of checkboxes in a form. To unregister all projects, the user deselects all checkboxes and submits the form. You may think the following code would then clear the property (setting it to null):

```
<jsp:setProperty name="validUser" property="*" />
```

Yet it doesn't. Without any checkbox selections, the projects parameter is not sent, and the corresponding property setter method is not called. This is so even if you explicitly specify the property and request parameter names:

```
<jsp:setProperty name="validUser" property="projects" param="projects" />
```

The workaround (described in Chapter 13) is to use the JSTL <c:set> action instead, with an EL expression to explicitly set the property to either the array of parameter values representing selected checkboxes or null if none is selected:

```
<c:set target="validUser" property="projects" value="${paramValues.projects}" />
```

If you have been developing web applications for a while, you may not think the <jsp:setProperty> behavior is so surprising. It behaves the same way, however, even when a parameter matching a property is received, but its value is an empty string. It happens to text fields the user leaves empty.

If you have properties matching text fields, make sure the code that uses the values of the corresponding properties can deal with null values or initialize them to empty strings. If you keep a bean like this in a scope other than the page and request scopes (where a new instance is created for each request), also be aware that the user can't clear the property by erasing the field in a form. One possible workaround is to define a reset property with a setter method that clears all properties. You then call it explicitly like this in the JSP page before setting the other properties:

```
<jsp:setProperty name="validUser" property="reset" value="any value" />
<jsp:setProperty name="validUser" property="*" />
```

All properties are first reset by the first <jsp:setProperty> action and then all properties matching request parameters are set by the second action.

CHAPTER 21

Developing Custom Tag Libraries Using Java

Custom actions let you encapsulate logic and make it available to page authors in a familiar format. Throughout this book, JSTL actions and a number of other custom actions are used for such tasks as accessing a database, including localized content, encoding URLs, and much more. Using these actions, the amount of Java code in your JSP pages can be kept to a minimum, making your application easier to debug and maintain. However, for complex applications, these generic actions may not be enough. Perhaps you want to develop business-specific actions to access the database instead of putting SQL statements in the JSP pages. You may want to present complex data as a set of nested HTML tables with cells formatted differently depending on their values. Instead of using JSTL conditional and loop actions in the JSP page to generate this table, an application-specific custom action can be used.

In Chapter 11, I showed you how to use tag files to implement custom actions. Tag files allow nonprogrammers to develop custom actions and are also suitable for custom actions that generate a lot of markup, such as HTML tables. But custom actions can also be implemented as Java classes, and that's the focus of this chapter. A Java implementation is a good choice for very complex actions or when you need to squeeze out every ounce of performance.

To develop a custom action as a Java class, you use a set of classes and interfaces referred to in the JSP specification as the *tag extension mechanism*. The class that implements the behavior of a custom action is called a *tag handler* class. It is basically a bean, with property setter methods corresponding to the custom action element's attributes, that also implements one of four Java interfaces defined as part of the tag extension mechanism.

JSP 2.0 introduces a new type of tag handler, represented by a single interface. A tag handler of this type is referred to as a *simple tag handler*. Tag handlers based on the three interfaces defined by JSP 1.1 and 1.2 are still supported and are now referred to as *classic tag handlers*. A simple tag handler can do everything a classic tag handler can but is a lot easier to implement. The only caveat is that the body of a custom action implemented as a simple tag handler cannot contain Java code (scripting elements). We'll look at the most common and simple aspects of both types in this chapter, starting with the simple tag handler, and then work through more advanced features in Chapters 22 and 23.

Developing Simple Tag Handlers

The simple tag handler is new as of JSP 2.0. Don't be fooled by the name; a simple tag handler can implement complex behavior for a custom action, such as conditional evaluation of its body, iteration over its body any number of times, and processing of the body evaluation result. The name refers to the implementation task, which is indeed much simpler than it was for the type of tag handlers supported in previous versions of the JSP specification.

The simplifications are made possible by prohibiting the use of scripting elements (Java code) in the custom action's body. This would have been met with a great deal of resistance not too long ago, but with the introduction of the EL and JSTL, you rarely (if ever) need to use scripting elements. If this restriction is not acceptable for your application, you must implement the custom action using a classic tag handler instead.

A simple tag handler implements the `javax.servlet.jsp.tagext.SimpleTag` interface. This interface has five methods, but most tag handlers just extend a base class named `javax.servlet.jsp.tagext.SimpleTagSupport` and inherit implementations of all but one method: `doTag( )`. In addition, the tag handler must implement standard JavaBeans setter methods for all of its custom action attributes (if it has any, of course).

As you may recall, a *tag library* is a collection of custom actions. For instance, all custom actions used in this book are packaged as one tag library. Besides the tag-handler class files, a tag library contains a *Tag Library Descriptor* (TLD) file. This is an XML file that maps all custom action names to the corresponding tag handlers and describes all attributes supported by each custom action. The class files and the TLD can be packaged in a JAR file to make installation easier. We look at the TLD syntax and packaging details at the end of this chapter.

Before getting into all the intricate details, let's use a simple example to see what it takes to develop, deploy, and use a custom action using a simple tag handler. First, you implement the tag handler class:

```
package com.mycompany;

import java.io.*;
import javax.servlet.jsp.*;
import javax.servlet.jsp.tagext.*;

public class HelloTag extends SimpleTagSupport {
    private String name = "World";

    public void setName(String name) {
```

```
        this.name = name;
    }

    public void doTag( ) throws IOException{
        getJspContext().getOut( ).println("Hello " + name);
    }
}
```

The tag handler class extends the `SimpleTagSupport` class to get most of the `SimpleTag` interface methods implementations for free. It implements a setter method only for an attribute called `name` and the `doTag( )` method. The `doTag( )` method (defined by the `SimpleTag` interface) simply writes "Hello" plus the `name` attribute value to the response. Note that the tag handler class must be part of a package, for the same reason a bean must be part of a package, described in detail in Chapter 16: classes in the default, unnamed package cannot be used in a class that belongs to a package (such as the class generated for the JSP page).

To compile the class, include the servlet and JSP API classes in your classpath. The API classes are distributed with all compliant containers. For Tomcat, you find them in the *servlet-api.jar* and *jsp-api.jar* files located in the *common/lib* directory under the Tomcat installation directory. When you have compiled the tag handler, place the class file in the *WEB-INF/classes* directory structure for the application so the container can find it.

Next, you create the TLD file. The following is a minimal TLD file for a library with just one custom action element:

```
<?xml version="1.0" encoding="ISO-8859-1" ?>
<taglib xmlns="http://java.sun.com/xml/ns/j2ee"
  xmlns:xsi="http://www.w3.org/2001/XMLSchema-instance"
  xsi:schemaLocation="http://java.sun.com/xml/ns/j2ee
    http://java.sun.com/xml/ns/j2ee/web-jsptaglibrary_2_0.xsd"
  version="2.0">

  <tlib-version>1.0</tlib-version>
  <short-name>test</short-name>
  <uri>com.mycompany.mylib</uri>

  <tag>
    <name>hello</name>
    <tag-class>com.mycompany.HelloTag</tag-class>
    <body-content>empty</body-content>
    <attribute>
      <name>name</name>
    </attribute>
  </tag>
</taglib>
```

The TLD maps the custom action name `hello` to the tag handler class `com.mycompany.HelloTag` and defines the `name` attribute. Place the TLD file in the application's *WEB-INF/tlds* directory, for instance with the filename *mylib.tld*.

Now you're ready to use the custom action in a JSP page, like this:

```
<%@ taglib prefix="test" uri="com.mycompany.mylib" %>
<html>
  <body bgcolor="white">
    <test:hello name="Hans" />
  </body>
</html>
```

When the page is requested, the JSP container uses the `taglib` directive to find the TLD, and the TLD to figure out which class to execute for the custom action. It then calls all the appropriate methods, resulting in the text "Hello Hans" being added to the response. That's all there is to it for the most simple case. In the remainder of this chapter, we go through all of this in greater detail.

Accessing Context Information

As you have seen in the previous chapters, a custom action element in a JSP page consists of a start tag (possibly with attributes), optionally a body, and an end tag:

```
<prefix:actionName attr1="value1" attr2="value2">
  The body
</prefix:actionName>
```

If the action element doesn't have a body, the following shorthand notation can be used instead:

```
<prefix:actionName attr1="value1" attr2="value2" />
```

A tag handler implements the custom action's behavior. When the container encounters a custom action, it creates an instance of the corresponding tag handler class, based on the information declared in the TLD.

In order for the tag handler to do anything interesting, it needs access to context information, such as the request and scope information, as well as the action element's attribute values (if any). The container calls methods defined in the `SimpleTag` interface to provide this information. The container calls the `setJspContext()` method to provide the context information in the form of a `JspContext` instance. For the attribute values, the JSP container treats the tag handler as a bean and calls a setter method for each attribute. When the tag handler has been initialized, the container asks it to do its thing by calling the `doTag()` method, as shown in Figure 21-1.

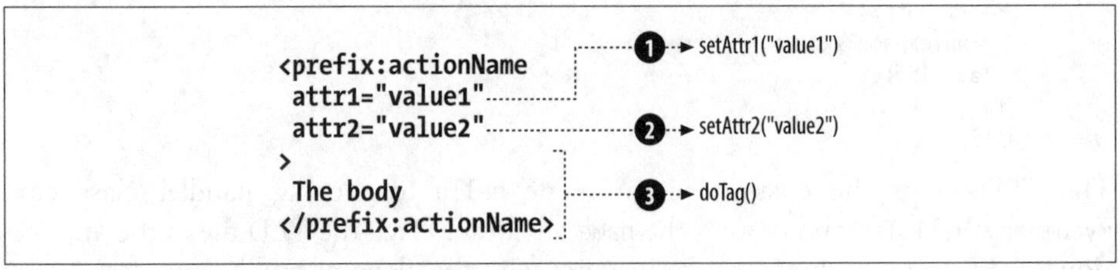

```
<prefix:actionName
 attr1="value1"               ❶ setAttr1("value1")
 attr2="value2"               ❷ setAttr2("value2")
>
 The body
</prefix:actionName>          ❸ doTag()
```

Figure 21-1. SimpleTag interface methods and property setter methods

Here are the SimpleTag interface methods of importance for all simple tag handlers:

```
public void setJspContext(JspContext jspContext);
public void doTag( ) throws JspException;
```

Most simple tag handlers extend the SimpleTagSupport class, and its implementation of the setJspContext( ) method simply saves a reference to the instance in a private instance variable named jspContext, where it can then be accessed by a subclass by calling the corresponding getter method implemented by the SimpleTagSupport class: getJspContext( ).

The JspContext provides access to all the JSP scope variables and the current output stream for the page, and it implements a number of utility methods the tag handler may use. We use most of these methods in the examples in this chapter. Appendix D includes a complete list of all JspContext methods.

The container calls the doTag( ) method when the tag handler has been initialized. The SimpleTagSupport implementation of this method does nothing, so you have to provide an implementation in the subclass.

Let's implement the tag handler for the <ora:addCookie> action, introduced in Chapter 13, to get a better idea of how all this works. The tag handler class is called com.ora.jsp.tags.AddCookieTag and extends the SimpleTagSupport class to inherit most of the SimpleTag interface method implementations:

```
package com.ora.jsp.tags;

import javax.servlet.http.*;
import javax.servlet.jsp.*;
import javax.servlet.jsp.tagext.*;
import com.ora.jsp.util.*;

public class AddCookieTag extends SimpleTagSupport {
```

The <ora:addCookie> action has two mandatory attributes, name and value, and one optional attribute, maxAge. Each attribute is represented by an instance variable and a standard property setter method:

```
    private String name;
    private String value;
    private String maxAgeString;

    public void setName(String name) {
        this.name = name;
    }

    public void setValue(String value) {
        this.value = value;
    }
```

```
    public void setMaxAge(String maxAgeString) {
        this.maxAgeString = maxAgeString;
    }
```

The purpose of the custom action is to create a new `javax.servlet.http.Cookie` object with the name, value, and maximum age values specified by the attributes, and to add the cookie to the response. The tag handler class overrides the `doTag( )` method to carry out this work:

```
    public void doTag( ) throws JspException {
        int maxAge = -1;
        if (maxAgeString != null) {
            try {
                maxAge = Integer.valueOf(maxAgeString).intValue( );
            }
            catch (NumberFormatException e) {
                throw new JspTagException("Invalid maxAge", e);
            }
        }
        PageContext pageContext = (PageContext) getJspContext( );
        HttpServletResponse response =
            (HttpServletResponse) pageContext.getResponse( );
        CookieUtils.sendCookie(name, value, maxAge, response);
    }
}
```

The `maxAge` attribute is optional, so before the corresponding `String` value is converted into an `int`, a test is performed to see if it's set or not. The `name` and `value` attributes are declared as mandatory in the TLD. The JSP container refuses to process the page if the mandatory attributes are not set, so you can always be sure that variables corresponding to mandatory attributes have values.

The `JspContext` class is an abstraction introduced in JSP 2.0 to allow the simple tag handler machinery to be used in nonservlet environment in the future. It provides access to scoped variables, but you don't find the specific scopes (page, request, session, and application) defined here. Nor do you find access methods for the request, the response, or other servlet specific objects. These things are instead defined in the `PageContext` class, which is a subclass of `JspContext`. In a servlet-based JSP container (the only type of container currently available), the context object passed to the tag handler through the `setJspContext( )` method is always an instance of `PageContext`. To get the response object needed as an argument to the `sendCookie( )` method, I call `getJspContext( )` and cast the returned context object to `PageContext` so I can call its `getResponse( )` method.

The code that actually creates the `Cookie` object and adds it to the response object is performed by the `sendCookie( )` method in the `com.ora.jsp.util.CookieUtils` class. This is a common practice. The utility class knows nothing about JSP, so it can be used in other environments such as servlets and applets. The tag handler acts as a simple adapter for the reusable environment agnostic class, getting all information it needs about the request, the response, and all the variables in the JSP scopes through the `PageContext`.

The sendCookie( ) method is implemented like this in the CookieUtils class:

```
public static void sendCookie(String name, String value, int maxAge,
    HttpServletResponse res) {

    Cookie cookie = new Cookie(name, value);
    cookie.setMaxAge(maxAge);
    res.addCookie(cookie);
}
```

The sendCookie( ) method and the <ora:addCookie> custom action could be improved to handle other cookie attributes, such as the domain and path. I leave that as an exercise that you may want to do if you use these classes in your applications.

Aborting the Page Processing

For some custom actions, the processing of the page must stop after the custom action has been processed. An example is a custom action that redirects or forwards to another page, such as the JSTL <c:redirect> action.

A simple tag handler can throw a javax.servlet.jsp.tagext.SkipPageException to signal to the container that the rest of the page must not be evaluated. The container respects this no matter how deeply the custom action is nested within bodies of other actions. To show how it's done, here's a simple tag handler with the sole purpose of aborting the page processing:

```
package com.ora.jsp.tags.xmp;

import javax.servlet.jsp.*;
import javax.servlet.jsp.tagext.*;

public class AbortPageTag extends SimpleTagSupport {
    public void doTag( ) throws JspException {
        throw new SkipPageException( );
    }
}
```

You could use this feature to, for instance, develop a smart forwarding action that decides which page to forward to based on runtime conditions, such as the time of the day, the current user, or the type of browser accessing the page. After the forwarding call, throwing the SkipPageException terminates the processing of the rest of the page that contains the forwarding action.

Processing the Action Body as an Executable Fragment

An action element's body can contain other actions, EL expressions, and template text. The body can be used for input values spanning multiple lines; the JSTL database actions described in Chapter 12 use the body this way. The SQL statement is often large, so it's cleaner to let the page author write it in the action body instead of as an attribute value. A similar example is an action that processes the body content in one way or another before it's added to the response. Chapter 15 shows how the JSTL `<x:transform>` action processes its XML body using the XSL stylesheet specified as an attribute.

Some actions do not really use the body as input but process it in other ways. One example is a conditional custom action, such as the JSTL `<c:if>` action, which only passes the body through if a runtime condition is met. A custom action that processes the dynamic elements in the body a number of times, like the JSTL `<c:forEach>` action, is another example.

You can use simple tag handlers to implement all these types of custom actions. The key to unlocking this magic lies in what's called a *JSP fragment* and a `SimpleTag` method I haven't told you about so far:

```
public void setJspBody(JspFragment body)
```

The container calls this method with a reference to a JSP fragment representing the custom action body before calling `doTag()`. If the custom action doesn't have a body, this method is not called at all.

A JSP fragment is an internal representation of dynamic JSP elements (actions and EL expressions), possibly mixed with template text. The container converts the body of a custom action implemented as a simple tag handler to this internal format and exposes it to the tag handler as an object of the type `javax.servlet.jsp.tagext.JspFragment`. This fragment is associated with the `JspContext` for the page where it's defined, so the dynamic elements in the fragment access the same scoped variables and request and response objects as the page. The tag handler invokes the fragment by calling the `invoke()` method on the `JspFragment` instance. Invoking the fragment means that all the dynamic elements in the fragment are executed, and the output they produce is combined with the template text, if any, to form a textual evaluation result. Since the elements in the fragment have access to the current values of all scoped variables, the result typically differs from invocation to invocation.

Conditional and iterating processing

A tag handler for a custom action that only processes the body based on some condition should call the `invoke()` method on the fragment representing the body only if the given condition is true. Example 21-1 shows how a somewhat simplified version of the JSTL `<c:if>` action could be implemented as a simple tag handler.

Example 21-1. Conditional tag handler (IfTag.java)

```
package com.ora.jsp.tags.xmp;

import java.io.*;
import javax.servlet.jsp.*;
import javax.servlet.jsp.tagext.*;

public class IfTag extends SimpleTagSupport {
```

Example 21-1. Conditional tag handler (IfTag.java) (continued)

```
    private boolean test;

    public void setTest(boolean test) {
        this.test = test;
    }

    public void doTag( ) throws JspException, IOException {
        if (test && getJspBody( ) != null) {
            getJspBody( ).invoke(null);
        }
    }
}
```

As I described earlier, the container calls the `setJspBody( )` method to give the tag handler a reference to the body fragment. This method is implemented by the `SimpleTagSupport` class and saves the reference in a private instance variable. The `getJspBody( )` method—used in the `doTag( )` method in this example—is also inherited from the `SimpleTagSupport` class, and it simply returns the reference.

In the tag handler subclass, implement a setter method for the `test` attribute, and in the `doTag( )` method, call the `invoke( )` method on the body fragment if the condition specified as the `test` attribute value is `true`. Note that you must also check that `getJspBody( )` returns a fragment to prevent a `NullPointerException` in case the custom action is used without a body. You can pass a `java.io.Writer` to the `invoke( )` method to capture the output, as I will show you later. When you pass it `null`, as I do here, the output is added to the response stream for the page that contains the custom action.

Implementing a tag handler for an iterating custom action, similar to `<c:forEach>`, is almost as easy: just call the body fragment's `invoke( )` method for each pass through the iteration until the end condition is reached. In most cases, an iterating tag handler also makes the current item available as a page scope variable, so the elements in the body can use it to produce different results for each iteration.

To illustrate how an iterating custom action works, let's implement a scaled-down version of the `<c:forEach>` action that supports only `Collection` data structures and call this action `<ora:simpleLoop>`. It can, for instance, be used like this with a `Collection` that contains beans with `firstName` and `lastName` properties:

```
<%@ page contentType="text/html" %>
<%@ taglib prefix="ora" uri="orataglib" %>

<ul>
  <ora:simpleLoop items="${myCollection}" var="current">
    <li>
      ${current.lastName}, ${current.firstName}
    </li>
  </ora:simpleLoop>
</ul>
```

The custom action iterates through the collection and exposes the current element as a page scoped variable named by the var attribute. The body contains two EL expressions and some template text. Since the EL expressions refer to properties of the variable containing the current element, each pass through it produces a different result.

The tag handler class for the <ora:simpleLoop> action is shown in Example 21-2.

Example 21-2. Iteration tag handler (SimpleLoopTag.java)

```
package com.ora.jsp.tags.xmp;

import java.io.*;
import java.util.*;
import javax.servlet.jsp.*;
import javax.servlet.jsp.tagext.*;

public class SimpleLoopTag extends SimpleTagSupport {
    private Collection items;
    private String var;

    public void setItems(Collection items) {
        this.items = items;
    }

    public void setVar(String var) {
        this.var = var;
    }

    public void doTag( ) throws JspException, IOException {
        JspFragment body = getJspBody( );
        if (body != null) {
            PageContext pageContext = (PageContext) getJspContext( );
            Iterator i = items.iterator( );
            while (i.hasNext( )) {
                Object currValue = i.next( );
                getJspContext( ).setAttribute(var, currValue);
                body.invoke(null);
            }
        }
    }
}
```

There's really nothing to this that you haven't seen before. The tag handler extends the SimpleTagSupport class, so it inherits the setJspBody( ) and getJspBody( ) methods, described earlier. It implements setter methods for the two mandatory attributes: items and var. The doTag( ) method first verifies that there's indeed a body to evaluate and, if so, gets an Iterator for the collection. For each element in the collection, it saves the current element as a page scope variable and calls invoke( ) on the body fragment.

Processing the action body

As you see, it's easy to implement a custom action as a simple tag handler, even one that conditionally evaluates the body 0 or any number of times. To develop a tag handler that reads and processes the result of the body evaluation, we just need one more thing: a way to capture the result of this evaluation.

Let's look at a tag handler class for the <ora:menuItem> custom action introduced in Chapter 17. As you may remember, this action reads its body and wraps it with an HTML link element if the specified page isn't the current page. Here's how the action can be used for a navigation bar, included in the main pages for an application:

```
<%@ page contentType="text/html" %>
<%@ taglib prefix="ora" uri="orataglib" %>
<table bgcolor="lightblue">
  <tr>
    <td>
      <ora:menuItem page="page1.jsp">
        <b>Page 1</b>
      </ora:menuItem>
    </td>
  </tr>
  <tr>
    <td>
      <ora:menuItem page="page2.jsp">
        <b>Page 2</b>
      </ora:menuItem>
    </td>
  </tr>
  <tr>
    <td>
      <ora:menuItem page="page3.jsp">
        <b>Page 3</b>
      </ora:menuItem>
    </td>
  </tr>
</table>
```

In this example, the contents of the custom action element is plain HTML template text, but as before, it could also contain other actions and EL expressions.

The tag handler class for the <ora:menuItem> action is shown in Example 21-3.

Example 21-3. Tag handler reading body evaluation (MenuItemTag.java)

```
package com.ora.jsp.tags;

import java.io.*;
import javax.servlet.http.*;
import javax.servlet.jsp.*;
import javax.servlet.jsp.tagext.*;
import com.ora.jsp.util.StringFormat;

public class MenuItemTag extends SimpleTagSupport {
```

Example 21-3. Tag handler reading body evaluation (MenuItemTag.java) (continued)

```
    private String page;

    public void setPage(String page) {
        this.page = page;
    }

    public void doTag( ) throws JspException, IOException {
        JspFragment body = getJspBody( );
        if (body == null) {
            throw new JspTagException("'menuItem' used without a body");
        }

        PageContext pageContext = (PageContext) getJspContext( );
        HttpServletRequest request =
            (HttpServletRequest) pageContext.getRequest( );
        String requestURI = request.getServletPath( );
        // Convert the specified page URI to a context-relative URI
        String pageURI = StringFormat.toContextRelativeURI(page, requestURI);

        if (requestURI.equals(pageURI)) {
            // Add the body as is
            body.invoke(null);
        }
        else {
            // Add the body as the text of an HTML link to page
            String uri = request.getContextPath( ) + pageURI;
            HttpServletResponse response =
                (HttpServletResponse) pageContext.getResponse( );

            StringWriter evalResult = new StringWriter( );
            StringBuffer buff = evalResult.getBuffer( );
            buff.append("<a href=\"").append(response.encodeURL(uri)).
                append("\">");
            body.invoke(evalResult);
            buff.append("</a>");
            getJspContext().getOut( ).print(buff);
        }
    }
}
```

The action has one attribute named page, implemented by the tag handler as a setter method that saves the value in a private instance variable.

In the doTag( ) method, I first check if there's a body. Because this custom action doesn't make sense without a body, I throw an exception if it doesn't have one. If it has a body, the page attribute value is converted to a context-relative URI and compared to the URI for the current request. If they match, the text to be written by the action is set to the body content as is; if not, the body content is wrapped in an HTML link element, using the page attribute value as the href attribute value and the body content as the link text.

The most interesting part of this tag handler is how it reads the body content and writes its output to the current response stream. To capture the result of the body evaluation, a `java.io.Writer` is passed to the `invoke()` method. Here I use an instance of the `StringWriter` subclass. This allows me to get hold of the evaluation result through its internal `StringBuffer` and add the HTML link element start and stop tags around it. The combination of the tags and the body evaluation result is then written to the `JspWriter` returned by the context's `getOut()` method. We'll discuss the `JspWriter` in more detail when we look at classic tag handlers, but it's really just a representation of the `Writer` for the response.

Processing Fragment Attributes

In all the examples so far, the custom action attribute types have been either regular Java classes or primitive types. The container evaluates attributes like these once and passes the resulting value to the tag handler through the attribute setter methods; however, it's perfectly legal to declare an attribute of type `JspFragment`. In this case, the container does not evaluate the value. Instead it passes a fragment representation of the value to the setter method that the tag handler can evaluate as many times as needed, in exactly the same manner as the body fragment.

Fragment attributes make a lot of sense for a custom action where the page author should be able to specify dynamic templates, or patterns, that are applied to elements of a collection. One example is a custom action that iterates over the days in a month. The page author should be able to describe different templates for rendering weekdays than for weekends, for instance. Let's develop a tag handler for a custom action that does just that and more. Here's how the custom action can be used in a JSP page:

```
<table border="1" cellspacing="0">
  <caption>
    <fmt:formatDate value="${now}" pattern="MMMM yyyy" />
  </caption>
  <ora:calendar date="${now}" var="c">
    <jsp:attribute name="beforePattern">
      <tr>
    </jsp:attribute>
    <jsp:attribute name="afterPattern">
      </tr>
    </jsp:attribute>
    <jsp:attribute name="dayNamePattern">
      <th><fmt:formatDate value="${c}" pattern="EE" /></th>
    </jsp:attribute>
    <jsp:attribute name="padPattern">
      <td bgcolor="lightgrey" width="30" height="30" valign="top">
        <fmt:formatDate value="${c}" pattern="d" />
      </td>
    </jsp:attribute>
    <jsp:attribute name="weekdayPattern">
```

```
      <td bgcolor="lightblue" width="30" height="30" valign="top">
        <fmt:formatDate value="${c}" pattern="d" />
      </td>
    </jsp:attribute>
    <jsp:attribute name="weekendPattern">
      <td bgcolor="yellow" width="30" height="30" valign="top">
        <fmt:formatDate value="${c}" pattern="d" />
      </td>
    </jsp:attribute>
  </ora:calendar>
</table>
```

The <ora:calendar> custom action has two regular attributes: date, which must be set to a java.util.Date representing the month to render, and var, which can optionally specify a variable to hold a reference to a java.util.Date instance for the current day of the month the fragments are asked to process.

Fragment attributes are used for the different patterns, such as weekday and weekend patterns. All fragment attributes must be set using the <jsp:attribute> action. The beforePattern and afterPattern fragments are evaluated before and after the first and last day of a week, respectively. In this example, the calendar is rendered as an HTML table, so these attributes are set to table row begin and end elements. The dayNamePattern fragment is evaluated once for each day in a week, and the weekdayPattern and weekendPattern fragments are evaluated for each workday and weekend day in the month. The padPattern attribute, finally, is evaluated for the days of the previous month and the following month needed to produce full weeks. All these fragment attributes define a table cell with different background colors, containing just the date. You could, of course, put any dynamic content in these fragments, such as custom actions that add information about events scheduled for each day, pulled from a database or some other type of data source.

Allowing the page author to specify the different patterns like this is very flexible. The same custom action can be used to produce a completely different type of calendar:

```
<code>
  <fmt:formatDate value="${now}" pattern="MMMM yyyy" />
  <br>
  <ora:calendar date="${now}" var="c">
    <jsp:attribute name="afterPattern">
      <br>
    </jsp:attribute>
    <jsp:attribute name="padPattern">
      | ------ |
    </jsp:attribute>
    <jsp:attribute name="weekdayPattern">
      | <fmt:formatDate value="${c}" pattern="EE dd" /> |
    </jsp:attribute>
  </ora:calendar>
</code>
```

Here I use only the `afterPattern`, `padPattern` and `weekDayPattern` (which is then also used for weekend days) fragments to generate a simple ASCII calendar. Figure 21-2 shows how both versions look in a browser.

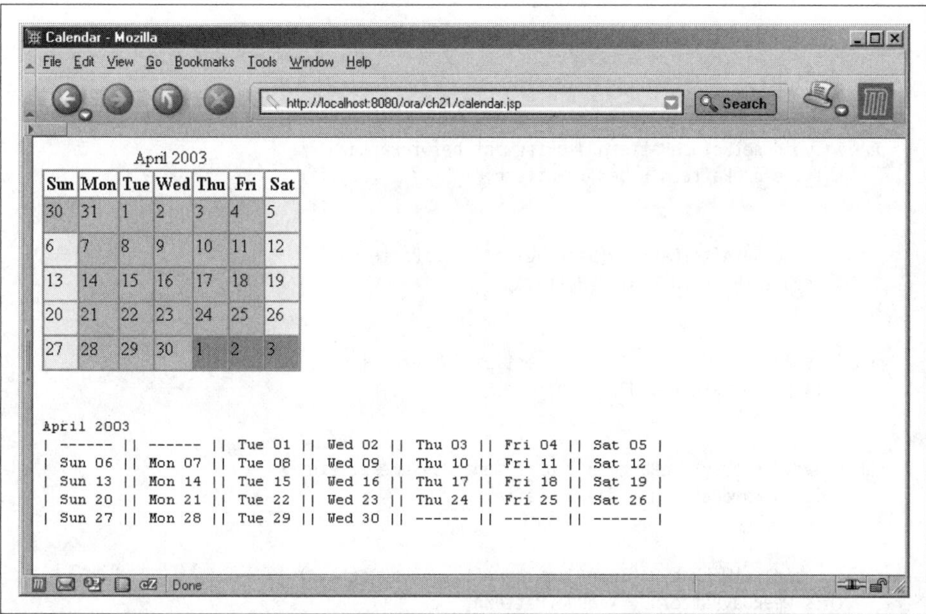

Figure 21-2. Different calendar layout produced by the same custom action using fragments for customization

Pretty cool, huh? Let's see the code. Example 21-4 shows the first part of the tag handler class for the `<ora:calendar>` custom action.

Example 21-4. Setter methods for fragment attributes (MonthCalendarTag.java)

```
package com.ora.jsp.tags;

import java.util.*;
import java.io.*;
import javax.servlet.jsp.*;
import javax.servlet.jsp.tagext.*;

public class MonthCalendarTag extends SimpleTagSupport {
    private Date date;
    private String var;
    private JspFragment padPattern;
    private JspFragment beforePattern;
    private JspFragment afterPattern;
    private JspFragment dayNamePattern;
    private JspFragment weekdayPattern;
    private JspFragment weekendPattern;
```

Example 21-4. Setter methods for fragment attributes (MonthCalendarTag.java) (continued)

```
    public void setDate(Date date) {
        this.date = date;
    }

    public void setVar(String  var) {
        this.var = var;
    }

    public void setBeforePattern(JspFragment beforePattern) {
        this.beforePattern = beforePattern;
    }

    public void setAfterPattern(JspFragment afterPattern) {
        this.afterPattern = afterPattern;
    }

    public void setPadPattern(JspFragment padPattern) {
        this.padPattern = padPattern;
    }

    public void setDayNamePattern(JspFragment dayNamePattern) {
        this.dayNamePattern = dayNamePattern;
    }

    public void setWeekdayPattern(JspFragment weekdayPattern) {
        this.weekdayPattern = weekdayPattern;
    }

    public void setWeekendPattern(JspFragment weekendPattern) {
        this.weekendPattern = weekendPattern;
    }
```

The type of all fragment attributes is `javax.servlet.jsp.tagext.JspFragment`. Fragment attributes must also be declared as such in the TLD for the tag library:

```
<tag>
  <name>calendar</name>
  <tag-class>com.ora.jsp.tags.MonthCalendarTag</tag-class>
  <body-content>empty</body-content>
  ...
  <attribute>
    <name>padPattern</name>
    <required>false</required>
    <fragment>true</fragment>
  </attribute>
  ...

</tag>
```

The default value for the `<fragment>` element is `false`, so if you leave it out, the attribute is handled as a standard attribute.

Example 21-5 shows the doTag( ) method, where the basic calendar processing control flow is implemented.

Example 21-5. Calendar processing control flow (MonthCalendarTag.java)

```
public void doTag( ) throws JspException, IOException {
    Calendar calendar = new GregorianCalendar( );
    int firstDayOfWeek = calendar.getFirstDayOfWeek( );

    if (dayNamePattern != null) {
        evalDayNamePattern(calendar, firstDayOfWeek);
    }

    calendar.setTime(date);
    calendar.set(Calendar.DAY_OF_MONTH, 1);

    if (padPattern != null) {
        evalPrePadPattern(calendar, firstDayOfWeek);
    }

    evalDayPatterns(calendar, firstDayOfWeek);

    if (padPattern != null) {
        evalPostPattern(calendar, firstDayOfWeek);
    }
}
```

A java.util.GregorianCalendar instance drives the processing. If a dayNamePattern fragment is provided, it's evaluated once for each day in a week (e.g., Sunday through Saturday). Next, the calendar is set to the first day of the month specified by the date attribute. If there's a padPattern fragment and the first day of this month is not the first day of the week, the fragment is evaluated once for each day in the last week of the previous month to get a full first week. The weekdayPattern and weekendPattern (if any) fragments are then evaluated for all days of the specified month, and finally, the padPattern fragment is processed again for all days in the following month if needed to fill the last week.

The actual fragment evaluation is implemented in a number of private methods. Example 21-6 shows the method that evaluates the dayNamePattern fragment.

Example 21-6. Day name fragment evaluation method (MonthCalendarTag.java)

```
private void evalDayNamePattern(Calendar calendar, int firstDayOfWeek)
    throws JspException, IOException {
    if (beforePattern != null) {
        beforePattern.invoke(null);
    }
    for (int i = 0, day = firstDayOfWeek; i < 7; i++, day++) {
        calendar.set(Calendar.DAY_OF_WEEK, day);
        if (var != null) {
            getJspContext().setAttribute(var, calendar.getTime( ));
        }
```

Example 21-6. Day name fragment evaluation method (MonthCalendarTag.java) (continued)

```
            dayNamePattern.invoke(null);
        }
        if (afterPattern != null) {
            afterPattern.invoke(null);
        }
    }
```

The method loops through the calendar seven times, from the first day of the week to the last. For each iteration, the method saves a `java.util.Date` instance representing the current calendar date as a page scope variable with the name specified by the var attribute. Dynamic elements in the day name pattern can use this variable to create a header with the day names, as shown in Figure 21-2. The fragment is evaluated just as the body fragment in the previous section, by calling the `invoke()` method. Because this tag handler doesn't need to process the result, `null` is passed as the argument value.

The rest of the fragment evaluation methods are very similar, as shown in Example 21-7.

Example 21-7. Remaining fragment evaluation methods (MonthCalendarTag.java)

```
    private void evalPrePadPattern(Calendar calendar, int firstDayOfWeek)
        throws JspException, IOException {
        // Reset to start of week, possibly in the previous month
        int firstDayOfMonth = calendar.get(Calendar.DAY_OF_WEEK);
        calendar.add(Calendar.DATE, firstDayOfWeek - firstDayOfMonth);

        if (beforePattern != null) {
            beforePattern.invoke(null);
        }

        int padDays = firstDayOfMonth - firstDayOfWeek;
        for (int i = 0; i < padDays; i++) {
            if (var != null) {
                getJspContext().setAttribute(var, calendar.getTime( ));
            }
            padPattern.invoke(null);
            calendar.add(Calendar.DAY_OF_WEEK, 1);
        }
    }

    private void evalDayPatterns(Calendar calendar, int firstDayOfWeek)
        throws JspException, IOException {

        int daysInMonth = calendar.getActualMaximum(Calendar.DAY_OF_MONTH);
        int lastDayOfWeek = firstDayOfWeek - 1 == 0 ? 7 : firstDayOfWeek - 1;
        for (int i = 0; i < daysInMonth; i++) {
            if (var != null) {
                getJspContext().setAttribute(var, calendar.getTime( ));
            }
            int day = calendar.get(Calendar.DAY_OF_WEEK);
```

Example 21-7. Remaining fragment evaluation methods (MonthCalendarTag.java) (continued)

```
            if (day == firstDayOfWeek && beforePattern != null) {
                beforePattern.invoke(null);
            }

            if ((day == Calendar.SATURDAY || day == Calendar.SUNDAY) &&
                weekendPattern != null) {
                weekendPattern.invoke(null);
            }
            else {
                weekdayPattern.invoke(null);
            }

            if (day == lastDayOfWeek && afterPattern != null) {
                afterPattern.invoke(null);
            }
            calendar.add(Calendar.DAY_OF_MONTH, 1);
        }
    }

    private void evalPostPattern(Calendar calendar, int firstDayOfWeek)
        throws JspException, IOException {
        while (calendar.get(Calendar.DAY_OF_WEEK) != firstDayOfWeek) {
            if (var != null) {
                getJspContext().setAttribute(var, calendar.getTime( ));
            }
            padPattern.invoke(null);
            calendar.add(Calendar.DAY_OF_MONTH, 1);
        }
        if (afterPattern != null) {
            afterPattern.invoke(null);
        }
    }
}
```

All methods save the current date as a page scope variable and invoke the fragment corresponding to the pattern the method handles.

Fragment attributes are very handy for some types of custom actions, as you can see, and are very easy to use. If you're developing a custom action with multiple aspects that can be customized and processed a variable number of times, you should consider using fragment attributes.

Handling Exceptions

Methods called by a tag handler may throw exceptions. Exception handling in a simple tag handler is very easy compared to how it's done for a classic tag handler, since all processing takes place in the single `doTag( )` method. You must catch exceptions and either deal with them, or rethrow them wrapped in a `JspException` or the `JspTagException` subclass. Both exception classes have the same types of constructors:

```
    public JspTagException( );
    public JspTagException(String msg);
    public JspTagException(String msg, Throwable rootCause);
    public JspTagException(Throwable rootCause);
```

When you rethrow an exception that you have caught, use one of the two latter constructors and pass on the exception, since the root cause is often needed to figure out what the problem is. Most containers unwrap the exception chain and write stack traces for all of the exceptions in the chain to the application log file. When throwing exceptions, you should avoid the no-argument constructor, since it doesn't let you say what's wrong, and use the second one for exceptions generated internally in the tag handler, for instance to report an invalid input type or insufficient privileges.

An exception thrown by a custom action can be caught and handled in the JSP page with the JSTL `<c:catch>` action, as I described in Chapter 9. If it's not caught, it's handled by the JSP container by forwarding to a custom error page, if specified, or to a container default page.

Calling the `invoke( )` method of a fragment may result in either a `JspException` or an `IOException`. Typically, the `doTag( )` method is declared to throw these same exceptions, so if it's okay to just let them propagate, you don't need to do anything. The only time you really need to worry about catching exceptions thrown by a fragment is in tag handlers that use resources that must be closed, such as a file, or returned to a pool, such as a database connection. If you fail to catch exceptions thrown by a fragment in this type of tag handler, the application will eventually run out of its limited resources. To illustrate how to handle fragment exceptions, Example 21-8 shows the tag handler for an action that writes the result of the evaluation of its body to a file, identified by an attribute named `fileName`.

Example 21-8. A tag handler that handles exceptions properly

```
package com.ora.jsp.tags;

import java.io.*;
import javax.servlet.*;
import javax.servlet.jsp.*;
import javax.servlet.jsp.tagext.*;

public class FileWriteTag extends SimpleTagSupport {
    private String fileName;

    public void setFileName(String fileName) {
        this.fileName = fileName;
    }

    public void doTag( ) throws JspException {
        JspFragment body = getJspBody( );
        if (body == null) {
            throw new JspTagException("'fileWrite' used without a body");
        }
```

Example 21-8. A tag handler that handles exceptions properly (continued)

```
        PrintWriter pw = null;
        if (fileName != null && !"log".equals(fileName)) {
            try{
                pw = new PrintWriter(new FileWriter(fileName, true));
            }
            catch (IOException e) {
                throw new JspTagException("Can not open file " + fileName +
                                          " for writing", e);
            }
        }

        ServletContext application =
            ((PageContext) getJspContext()).getServletContext( );
        StringWriter evalResult = new StringWriter( );
        try {
            body.invoke(evalResult);
            if (fileName == null) {
                System.out.println(evalResult);
            }
            else if ("log".equals(fileName)) {
                application.log(evalResult.toString( ));
            }
            else {
                pw.print(evalResult);
            }
        }
        catch (Throwable t) {
            String msg = "Exception in body of " +  this.getClass().getName( );
            application.log(msg, t);
            throw new JspTagException(msg, t);
        }
        finally {
            if (pw != null) {
                pw.close( );
            }
        }
    }
}
```

The doTag( ) method first verifies that there's a body and throws a JspTagException if not, just as in Example 21-3. It then tries to open the file for writing by creating a PrintWriter for it. If this fails, for instance because of an invalid filename or access permission problems, the IOException is caught, and a JspTagException is thrown with a message about what went wrong as well as the root cause exception.

The body fragment evaluation, plus any file manipulation operations that can go wrong, are protected by a try/catch/finally block. If an exception is thrown, a message is written to the application log file and the exception is rethrown, wrapped in a JspTagException, and the file is closed in the finally block. This way, no matter what happens, the file is always closed.

Developing Classic Tag Handlers

Classic tag handler is the designation used in the JSP 2.0 specification for the original version of the tag handler API, to distinguish it from the new, easier-to-use API. Given that a simple tag handler is so much easier to implement than a classic tag handler and can do exactly the same things, why bother with the classic tag handler at all? The answer is "you shouldn't," unless one of the following is true:

- The tag library must work with JSP 1.1 or 1.2 as well as 2.0
- The page author must be able to use Java code (scripting elements) in the custom action bodies
- The tag handler instance is very expensive to create or initialize

It is hard to do anything about the first reason; if the tag library must work with JSP versions prior to 2.0, you have no choice but to use classic tag handlers.

Scripting code is rarely needed nowadays, so the second reason should be looked at with suspicion. I suggest that you think long and hard about other solutions, such as using JSTL, more custom actions, and EL expressions instead.

The third reason is related to the fact that simple tag handlers cannot be reused; the container creates a new instance for every invocation. A container is, however, allowed to reuse classic tag handlers for multiple custom action invocations, as long as the strict rules (described later) are followed. While this may sound like a great performance boost, benchmarks have shown that it has very little effect in reality when using a modern Java version (J2SE 1.4 or later). In most cases, the cost of maintaining the pool eats up most of the gain from reduced object creation, since modern Java versions are pretty good at dealing with short-lived objects. Reuse can make a difference with an efficient pool for tag handlers that use resources that are very expensive to create but can be retained between multiple invocations, but these are very rare. A workaround is to maintain the resources as scoped variables instead, created by the first tag handler instance and reused by all others.

That said, the classic tag handler is still supported in JSP 2.0, so I describe it in detail in this section. The main reasons for its complexity are due to the support for scripting elements in the custom action body and potentially reusable tag handler instances.

The classic tag handler API contains three primary interfaces, all part of the `javax.servlet.jsp.tagext` package: `Tag`, `IterationTag`, and `BodyTag`. The `Tag` interface defines the methods you need to implement for any tag handler. The `IterationTag` interface extends the `Tag` interface and adds methods needed for iteration over the action element's body. The `BodyTag` interface extends the `IterationTag` interface and adds methods that provide access to the action element's body evaluation result.

There's also a fourth interface named `TryCatchFinally`; it's a so-called *mix-in interface*, meaning it can be implemented in addition to any of the three main interfaces. It defines methods that let the tag handler deal with exceptions, for instance, exceptions thrown by JSP elements nested in the action element's body.

To make it easier to develop a classic tag handler, two support classes are defined by the API: `TagSupport` and `BodyTagSupport`, as shown in Figure 21-3. The `TagSupport` class provides default implementations for the methods in both the `Tag` and the `IterationTag` interfaces, and `BodyTagSupport` adds defaults for the `BodyTag` interface methods.

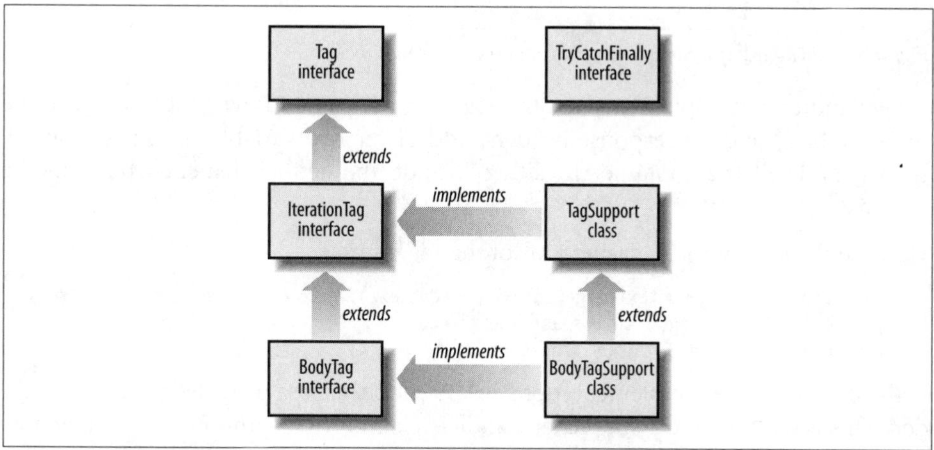

Figure 21-3. The primary classic tag handler interfaces and support classes

Declaration and deployment of classic tag handlers follow the same process as for simple tag handlers: declare the tag handlers in a TLD and make the TLD and class files available to the web application, either as files directly in the filesystem or packaged as a JAR file. The TLD elements are identical for both types, and you can mix simple and classic tag handlers in the same tag library.

Developing a Basic Action

The main difference between the simple and classic tag handler APIs is that while the `SimpleTag` interface has only one method for asking the tag handler to complete its processing, the `Tag` interface has two: `doStartTag( )` and `doEndTag( )` (the `Tag` subinterfaces for more specialized classic tag handlers add even more methods). The container calls these methods when the start tag and end tag are encountered, as shown in Figure 21-4.

Attribute values are set using bean setter methods, just as for the simple tag handler. The `doStartTag( )` and `doEndTag( )` method return values that controls what happens next, for instance how to deal with the custom action body. This is another significant difference compared to the simple tag handler; a classic tag handler needs to ask the container (through the return value) to evaluate the body rather than doing it itself.

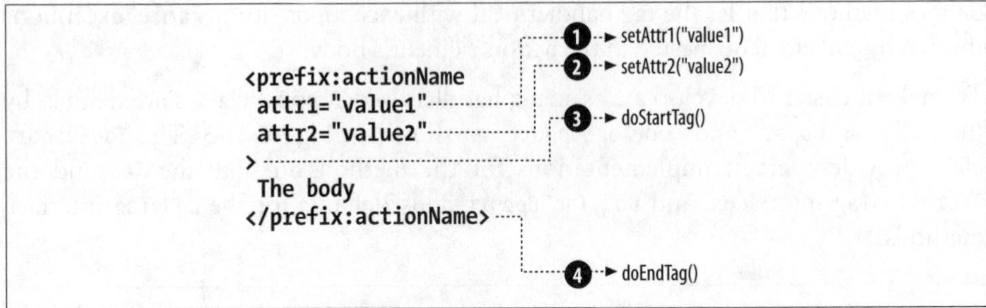

Figure 21-4. Tag interface methods and property setter methods

A tag handler that implements just the Tag interface can add dynamic content to the response body and set response headers, add or remove variables in one of the JSP scopes, and tell the container to either include the action element's body in the response or ignore it.

Here are the most important methods of the Tag interface:

```
public void setPageContext(PageContext pageContext);
public int doStartTag( ) throws JspException;
public int doEndTag( ) throws JspException;
```

Let's first look at the implementations the TagSupport class provides for these methods. This is the class most simple tag handlers extend, so it's important to know how TagSupport implements the methods the tag handler inherits.

The first method of interest is the setPageContext( ) method:

```
public class TagSupport implements IterationTag, Serializable {
    ...
    protected PageContext pageContext;
    ...
    public void setPageContext(PageContext pageContext) {
        this.pageContext = pageContext;
    }
```

The JSP container calls this method before the tag handler is used. The TagSupport implementation simply sets an instance variable to the current PageContext object. As you may recall, the PageContext provides access to the request and response object and all the JSP scope variables, and it implements a number of utility methods the tag handler may use.

When the start tag is encountered, the JSP container calls the doStartTag( ) method, implemented like this in the TagSupport class:

```
public int doStartTag( ) throws JspException {
    return SKIP_BODY;
}
```

This method gives the tag handler a chance to initialize itself, perhaps verifying that all attributes have valid values. Another use for this method is to decide what to do with the element's body content, if a body exists. The method returns an `int` that must be one of two values defined by the `Tag` interface: `SKIP_BODY` or `EVAL_BODY_INCLUDE`. The default implementation returns `SKIP_BODY`. As the name implies, this tells the JSP container to ignore the body completely. If `EVAL_BODY_INCLUDE` is returned, the JSP container evaluates the body (for instance, executes scripting elements and other actions in the body) and includes the result in the response. You can create a simple conditional tag—similar to the JSTL `<c:if>` action—by testing some condition (set by action attributes) in the `doStartTag( )`, and return either `SKIP_BODY` or `EVAL_BODY_INCLUDE`, depending on whether the condition is `true` or `false`.

No matter which value the `doStartTag( )` method returns, the JSP container calls `doEndTag( )` when it encounters the end tag for the corresponding action element:

```
public int doEndTag( ) throws JspException {
    return EVAL_PAGE;
}
```

This is the method that most classic tag handlers override to do the real work. It can also return one of two `int` values defined by the `Tag` interface. The `TagSupport` class returns `EVAL_PAGE`, to tell the JSP container to continue processing the rest of the page. A tag handler can also return `SKIP_PAGE`, which aborts the processing of the rest of the page. This is appropriate for an action that forwards the processing to another page or sends a redirect response to the browser; the JSTL `<c:redirect>` action is one example.

To get a better idea of how it all fits together, let's look at a classic tag implementation for the `<ora:addCookie>` action. You can compare it to the simple tag handler implementation for the same custom action described earlier to see how the two tag handler APIs differ. The tag handler class is called `com.ora.jsp.tags.xmp.ClassicAddCookieTag` and extends the `TagSupport` class to inherit most of the `Tag` interface method implementations:

```
package com.ora.jsp.tags.xmp;

import javax.servlet.http.*;
import javax.servlet.jsp.*;
import javax.servlet.jsp.tagext.*;
import com.ora.jsp.util.*;

public class ClassicAddCookieTag extends TagSupport {

    private String name;
    private String value;
    private String maxAgeString;

    public void setName(String name) {
        this.name = name;
    }

    public void setValue(String value) {
```

```
        this.value = value;
    }

    public void setMaxAge(String maxAgeString) {
        this.maxAgeString = maxAgeString;
    }
```

So far, the implementation is identical to the simple tag implementation, with setter methods for each attribute.

The doEndTag( ) method looks like this:

```
    public int doEndTag( ) throws JspException {
        int maxAge = -1;
        if (maxAgeString != null) {
            try {
                maxAge = Integer.valueOf(maxAgeString).intValue( );
            }
            catch (NumberFormatException e) {
                throw new JspException("Invalid maxAge: " +
                    e.getMessage( ));
            }
        }
        CookieUtils.sendCookie(name, value, maxAge,
            (HttpServletResponse) pageContext.getResponse( ));
        return EVAL_PAGE;
    }
```

Compared to the simple tag handler implementation there are two differences. First, the classic tag handler gets initialized with a PageContext instance instead of the more generic JspContext used for simple tag handlers; this happens in the setPageContext( ) method, as shown earlier. Hence, the response object can be retrieved directly from the context object without having to first cast it to the correct type. Second, the doEndTag( ) method has an int return type and must return one of EVAL_PAGE or SKIP_PAGE, as opposed to the void return type declared for the simple tag handler's doTag( ) method.

The rest is the same as for the simple tag handler. The optional maxAge attribute is converted to an int, and the cookie is created and added to the response object by the sendCookie( ) method in the com.ora.jsp.util.CookieUtils class.

A classic tag handler class should also implement the release( ) method, to release all references to objects that it has acquired:

```
    public void release( ) {
        name = null;
        value = null;
        maxAgeString = null;
        super.release( );
    }
```

The container calls the release( ) method when the tag handler is no longer needed. The ClassicAddCookieTag class sets all its properties to null and calls super.release( )

to let the TagSupport class do the same. This makes all objects used by the tag handler available for garbage collection.

Developing an Iterating Action

For a simple tag handler, iterative evaluation of the body is simply done within the doTag( ) method, as described earlier. A classic tag handler doesn't have this luxury. Instead, it must ask the container to evaluate the action element's body repeatedly until some condition is true. To do so, it implements the IterationTag interface, which contains only one method: public int doAfterBody( ) throws JspException, which is called by the container after it has processed the action element's body.

A tag handler that implements the IterationTag interface is at first handled the same way as a tag handler implementing the Tag interface: the container calls all property setter methods and the doStartTag( ) method. Then things divert slightly, as illustrated in Figure 21-5.

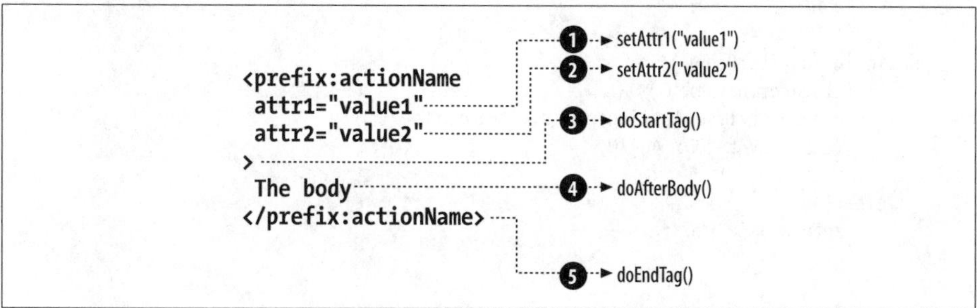

Figure 21-5. IterationTag interface methods

After the call to doStartTag( ), the doAfterBody( ) method may be called any number of times before the doEndTag( ) method is called.

Let's implement the same scaled-down version of the <c:forEach> action that I used to illustrate iteration with a simple tag handler again but this time as a classic tag handler. As before, the scaled down version supports only Collection data structures. The class tag handler class is shown in Example 21-9.

Example 21-9. A tag handler implementing the IterationTag interface

```
package com.ora.jsp.tags.xmp;

import java.util.*;
import javax.servlet.jsp.*;
import javax.servlet.jsp.tagext.*;

public class ClassicSimpleLoopTag extends TagSupport {
    private Iterator iterator;
    private String items;
    private String var;
```

Example 21-9. A tag handler implementing the IterationTag interface (continued)

```
    public void setItems(String items) {
        this.items = items;
    }

    public void setVar(String var) {
        this.var = var;
    }

    public int doStartTag( ) throws JspException {
        iterator = items.iterator( );
        if (iterator.hasNext( )) {
            pageContext.setAttribute(var, iterator.next( ));
            return EVAL_BODY_INCLUDE;
        }
        else {
            return SKIP_BODY;
        }
    }

    public int doAfterBody( ) {
        if (iterator.hasNext( )) {
            pageContext.setAttribute(var, iterator.next( ));
            return EVAL_BODY_AGAIN;
        }
        else {
            return SKIP_BODY;
        }
    }
}
```

The `ClassicSimpleLoopTag` class extends `TagSupport`. The `TagSupport` class implements the `IteratorTag` interface and provides a default implementation for the method in this interface in addition to the methods in the `Tag` interface.

The custom action has two mandatory attributes, each represented by a setter method in the tag handler class. The `items` attribute specifies an object that implements the `Collection` interface. The tag handler iterates over all collection elements and makes the current element available as a page-scope variable in the element's body. The `var` attribute specifies the name of the page-scope variable.

The `doStartTag( )` method first creates an `Iterator` for the collection. Note that the `Iterator` must be declared as an instance variable, since it's also used in the `doAfterBody( )` method. If the `Iterator` contains at least one element, the `doStartTag( )` method makes the first element in the `Collection` available as a page-scope object with the name specified by the `var` attribute and returns `EVAL_BODY_INCLUDE`. This tells the container to add the contents of the action element's body to the response and then call `doAfterBody( )`.

The `doAfterBody( )` method must return either `EVAL_BODY_AGAIN` (to iterate over the body) or `SKIP_BODY` (to stop the iteration). The `TagSupport` default implementation just returns `SKIP_BODY`. Except for not initializing the `Iterator`, the `doAfterBody( )` method in the `ClassicSimpleLoopTag` class does exactly the same as the `doStartTag( )` method. As long as the `Iterator` contains at least one more element, `doAfterBody( )` returns `EVAL_BODY_AGAIN`. When all elements have been processed, it returns `SKIP_BODY` to stop the iteration.

When the `doAfterBody( )` method returns `SKIP_BODY`, the container calls the `doEndTag( )` method. In this example, the default implementation provided by the `TagSupport` class is sufficient so there's no need to override it. It simply returns `EVAL_PAGE` to tell the container to process the rest of the page.

Processing the Action Body

It's fairly easy to develop the most basic type of tag handlers even with the classic tag handler API. For a tag handler that needs to read and process the element body, the difference between the simple and the classic API is more apparent.

A classic tag handler that needs access to the action element's body must implement the `BodyTag` interface and tell the container to capture the body evaluation result in an instance of the `BodyContent` class.

The `BodyTag` interface extends the `IterationTag` interface and adds two new methods:

`public void setBodyContent(BodyContent bodyContent)`
: Provides a reference to the `BodyContent` instance that buffers the body evaluation result for this tag handler

`public void doInitBody( ) throws JspException`
: Can be implemented by a tag handler to prepare for the first evaluation of the body

Figure 21-6 illustrates the container calling these new methods, which are relative to the methods inherited from the `IterationTag` interface.

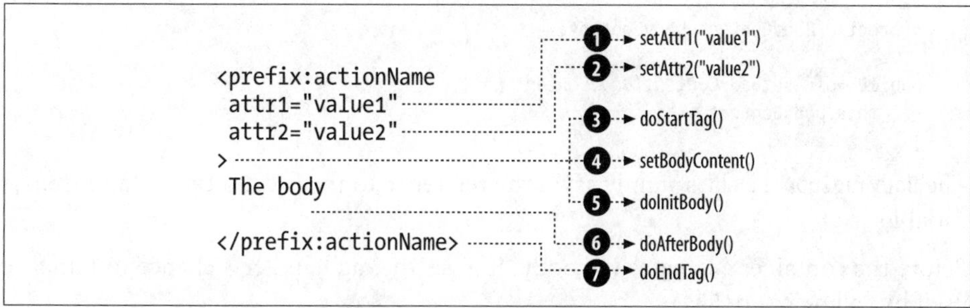

Figure 21-6. BodyTag interface methods

As with the Tag and IterationTag interfaces, there's a support class that implements all the methods of the BodyTag interface, plus a few utility methods:

```
public class BodyTagSupport extends TagSupport implements BodyTag
```

The BodyTagSupport class overrides the doStartTag( ) method inherited from the TagSupport class:

```
public int doStartTag( ) throws JspException {
    return EVAL_BODY_BUFFERED;
}
```

Instead of returning SKIP_BODY as the TagSupport class does, it returns EVAL_BODY_BUFFERED. The EVAL_BODY_BUFFERED value is only valid for a tag handler that implements the BodyTag interface. It means that not only should the action's body be evaluated, but the container must also buffer the result and make it available to the tag handler.

The container uses a BodyContent object to buffer the body evaluation result—static text as well as dynamic content created by nested action and scripting elements. This is a subclass of the JspWriter, the class used to write text to the response body. In addition to the inherited methods for writing text, the BodyContent class has methods the tag handler can use to read the body evaluation result.

This is how it works. To buffer the response body, as described in Chapter 17, the container creates an instance of the JspWriter class before processing the page and directs all output to this instance. Everything that's added to the response body—explicitly by JSP elements or implicitly by the JSP container (template text)—therefore ends up in the JspWriter first before it's sent to the browser. When the JSP container encounters a custom action with a tag handler that implements the BodyTag interface, it temporarily redirects all output to a BodyContent instance until it reaches the action's end tag. The content produced when the element body is processed is therefore buffered in the BodyContent instance where the tag handler can then read it.

The container gives the tag handler a reference to the BodyContent instance by calling the setBodyContent( ) method:

```
...
protected BodyContent bodyContent;
...
public void setBodyContent(BodyContent b) {
    this.bodyContent = b;
}
```

The BodyTagSupport class simply saves the reference to the BodyContent in an instance variable.

Before the container evaluates the body, it gives the tag handler a chance to initialize itself by calling doInitBody( ):

```
public void doInitBody( ) throws JspException {
}
```

The implementation in BodyTagSupport does nothing. A tag handler can override this method to prepare for the first pass through the action body, perhaps writing initial content to the BodyContent that should precede any content added by the evaluation of the nested elements. This method is, however, rarely used.

When the body has been processed, the doAfterBody( ) method is invoked:

```
public int doAfterBody( ) throws JspException {
    return SKIP_BODY;
}
```

The same as with the IterationTag interface, this method gives the tag handler a chance to decide whether the body should be processed again. If so, it returns the EVAL_BODY_AGAIN value, otherwise SKIP_BODY. As opposed to a tag handler that implements only the IterationTag interface, a BodyTag implementation can also use this method to read the buffered body content and process it in some way. We'll look at an example of this shortly. The BodyTagSupport implementation returns SKIP_BODY to let the processing continue to the doEndTag( ) method. As with a tag handler implementing the Tag interface, this method must return either EVAL_PAGE or SKIP_PAGE.

To see how it all comes together we implement the <ora:menuItem> custom action from Chapter 17 again, but as a classic tag handler this time. Example 21-10 shows the code for the tag handler class.

Example 21-10. The ClassicMenuItemTag class

```
package com.ora.jsp.tags.xmp;

import java.io.*;
import java.util.*;
import javax.servlet.http.*;
import javax.servlet.jsp.*;
import javax.servlet.jsp.tagext.*;
import com.ora.jsp.util.StringFormat;

public class ClassicMenuItemTag extends BodyTagSupport {
    private String page;

    public void setPage(String page) {
        this.page = page;
    }

    public int doEndTag( ) throws JspException {
        HttpServletRequest request =
            (HttpServletRequest) pageContext.getRequest( );
        String requestURI = request.getServletPath( );
        String pageURI = StringFormat.toContextRelativeURI(page,
            requestURI);

        StringBuffer text = null;
        String body = getBodyContent().getString( );
        if (requestURI.equals(pageURI)) {
```

Example 21-10. The ClassicMenuItemTag class (continued)

```
            text = new StringBuffer(body);
        }
        else {
            String contextPath = request.getContextPath( );
            String uri = contextPath + pageURI;
            HttpServletResponse res =
                (HttpServletResponse) pageContext.getResponse( );
            text = new StringBuffer("<a href=\"");
            text.append(res.encodeURL(uri)).append("\">").
                append(body).append("</a>");
        }
        try {
            JspWriter out = getPreviousOut( );
            out.print(text);
        }
        catch (IOException e) {}
        return EVAL_PAGE;
    }

    public void release( ) {
        page = null;
        super.release( );
    }
}
```

The tag handler extends the `BodyTagSupport` class and overrides only the `doEndTag( )` method. It also implements a setter method for the page attribute.

Except for how the body evaluation result is captured and how text is added to the current response stream, the `doEndTag( )` method looks identical to the `doTag( )` method in the simple tag handler we developed earlier. The classic tag handler in Example 21-10 uses `BodyTagSupport` utility methods to handle both tasks.

The `getBodyContent( )` method returns a reference to the `BodyContent` object and its content is read by the `getString( )` method. The `BodyContent` class also provides a `getReader( )` method to get the content as a `Reader`, which can be handy if you need to process the content as a stream, perhaps with an XML parser.

To get hold of an appropriate writer for the generated content, the tag handler calls the `getPreviousOut( )` method. It returns the `BodyContent` of the enclosing action, if any, or the main `JspWriter` for the page if the action is at the top level. You may be wondering why the method is called `getPreviousOut( )` as opposed to `getOut( )`. The name is intended to emphasize the fact that you want to use the object assigned as the output for the enclosing element in a hierarchy of nested action elements. Say you have the following action elements in a page:

```
<xmp:foo>
    <xmp:bar>
        Some template text
    </xmp:bar>
</xmp:foo>
```

Let's recap how buffering works. The JSP container first creates a JspWriter and directs all output to it. When it encounters the <xmp:foo> action, it creates a BodyContent object and temporarily redirects the output. It creates another BodyContent for the <xmp:bar> action and, again, redirects the output. The container keeps track of this hierarchy of output objects. Template text and output produced by JSP elements end up in the current output object. Each element can get access to its own BodyContent object by calling the getBodyContent( ) method and then reading the content. For the <xmp:bar> element, the content is the template text. After processing the content, it can write it to the <xmp:foo> body by getting the BodyContent for this element through the getPreviousOut( ) method. Finally, the <xmp:foo> element can process the content provided by the <xmp:bar> element and add it to the top-level output object; it gets the JspWriter object by calling the getPreviousOut( ) method. This method is implemented by the BodyTagSupport class like this:

```
public JspWriter getPreviousOut( ) {
    return bodyContent.getEnclosingWriter( );
}
```

By calling getPreviousOut( ), the tag handler in Example 21-10 gets the proper writer: either a parent action's BodyContent or the top-level JspWriter. It then writes either the plain body content or the dynamically generated HTML link to it.

Dealing with empty elements

One thing to note about tag handlers: when they're implementing the BodyTag interface, the container doesn't call all methods if the action element doesn't have a body in the JSP page—in other words, when the action is represented by an empty element in the page. An action element is considered empty if it's:

- Represented by the XML shorthand notation for an empty element:

  ```
  <xmp:myTag/>
  ```

- Represented by an opening and closing tag with an empty body:

  ```
  <xmp:myTag></xmp:myTag>
  ```

Note that the element isn't considered empty if the body contains anything—even so-called whitespace characters (blank, tab, linefeed) or scripting elements.

For an empty custom action element with a tag handler that implements the BodyTag interface, the container doesn't call the following methods: setBodyContent( ), doInitBody( ), or doAfterBody( ). This allows the container to generate more efficient code for an empty BodyTag element, since it avoids creating a BodyContent instance that will never be used.*

* At least that was the intention with a number of clarifications in JSP 1.2. Unfortunately it turns out that JSP 1.2 is still not perfectly clear about this, so some JSP 1.2 containers call all the methods even for an empty element. Even more clarifications were added to JSP 2.0, so eventually all containers should deal with this consistently.

If you're not careful, this can cause a problem for an action that can be used both with and without a body. An example is an action that lets the page author specify input either as an attribute value or as the element body. A typical mistake in this case is to assume that the tag handler always has access to a BodyContent instance and thus use code like this (directly or indirectly by calling the getPreviousOut( ) method) to get hold of the writer in the doEndTag( ) method:

```
JspWriter out = bodyContent.getEnlosingWriter( );
```

This code throws a NullPointerException if the custom action is used without a body, because the setBodyContent( ) method is never called, and the bodyContent variable is therefore null. To avoid this problem, you should always check for null with code like this instead:

```
JspWriter out = null;
if (bodyContent != null) {
    out = bodyContent.getEnclosingWriter( );
}
else {
    out = pageContext.getOut( );
}
```

An alternative is to access the bodyContent variable only in methods that are called exclusively for an element with a body, in other words, the doInitBody( ) and doAfterBody( ) methods.

Another thing to think about for an action that is supposed to work with or without a body is this: do not put any logic that should be executed even for an empty tag in the doInitBody( ) and doAfterBody( ) methods. Logic that's needed even for an empty tag must be implemented by the doStartTag( ) and doEndTag( ) methods.

Handling Exceptions

In most cases, the default handling for an exception thrown by JSP elements is sufficient; the container forwards control to an error page where you can display a nice, user-friendly message. But for some types of tag handlers—for instance a tag handler that uses a pooled resource (such as a connection from a connection pool)—there must be a fail-safe way to handle exceptions thrown by nested elements, for instance to return the shared resource to the pool. If exceptions aren't handled correctly, the resource pool "leaks," and eventually the application runs out of resources and comes to an embarrassing halt. None of the three main classic tag handler interfaces include methods that are called in case of an exception in the element's body, but a separate interface lets you deal with possible exceptions.

The TryCatchFinally interface is a so-called *mix-in interface*, which means that a tag handler can only implement it in addition to one of the three main tag handler interfaces. It has two methods:

```
public void doCatch(Throwable t) throws Trowable
public void doFinally( )
```

Example 21-11 shows the classic tag handler version for the action that writes the result of the evaluation of its body to a file.

Example 21-11. A tag handler implementing TryCatchFinally

```
package com.ora.jsp.tags.xmp;

import java.io.*;
import javax.servlet.*;
import javax.servlet.jsp.*;
import javax.servlet.jsp.tagext.*;

public class ClassicFileWriteTag extends BodyTagSupport
    implements TryCatchFinally {

    private String fileName;
    private PrintWriter pw;

    public void setFileName(String fileName) {
        this.fileName = fileName;
    }

    public int doStartTag( ) throws JspException {
        if (fileName != null && !"log".equals(fileName)) {
            try{
                pw = new PrintWriter(new FileWriter(fileName, true));
            }
            catch (IOException e) {
                throw new JspException("Can not open file " + fileName +
                                       " for writing", e);
            }
        }
        return EVAL_BODY_BUFFERED;
    }

    public int doAfterBody( ) throws JspException {
        String content = bodyContent.getString( );
        if (fileName == null) {
            System.out.println(content);
        }
        else if ("log".equals(fileName)) {
            ServletContext application = pageContext.getServletContext( );
            application.log(content);
        }
        else {
            pw.print(bodyContent.getString( ));
        }
        return SKIP_BODY;
    }

    public void doCatch(Throwable t) throws Throwable {
        ServletContext application = pageContext.getServletContext( );
        application.log("Exception in body of " +
```

Example 21-11. A tag handler implementing TryCatchFinally (continued)

```
            this.getClass().getName( ), t);
        throw t;
    }

    public void doFinally( ) {
        if (pw != null) {
            pw.close( );
        }
    }
}
```

If a filename is specified, the `doStartTag( )` method tries to open the file for writing by creating a `PrintWriter` for it. If this fails, for instance because of an invalid filename or access permission problems, the `IOException` is caught, and a `JspException` is thrown with a message about what went wrong. In the `doAfterBody( )` method, the content of the `BodyContent` instance for the tag handler is written to the file.

The most interesting parts of this example are the `doCatch( )` and the `doFinally( )` methods. The container calls the `doCatch( )` method if elements nested in the body or any of the `doStartTag( )`, `doEndTag( )`, `doInitBody( )`, or `doAfterBody( )` methods throw a `Throwable`—the mother of all exceptions. In this example, it's called if the file can't be opened in the `doStartTag( )` method or if a nested element throws an exception. All this method does in this example is to log the problem and rethrow the `Throwable` to let the container deal with it in the standard way. You don't have to rethrow the `Throwable` passed as an argument; in some cases it makes sense to throw another type of exception or no exception at all (to allow the processing of the rest of the page to continue).

The `doFinally( )` method is always called by the container—after `doEndTag( )` in case of normal execution or after `doCatch( )` in the exception case. In this example, the method simply closes the `PrintWriter`. By doing this in the `doFinally( )` method, you're guaranteed that the file is always closed, ensuring that the application doesn't run out of file descriptors. One other thing to note here: I test if the `pw` variable is null before I close it. That's because this method is called even in the case where the `doStartTag( )` method throws an exception because it can't create the `PrintWriter`. If I didn't check for `null`, the `doFinally( )` method would throw a `NullPointerException`, hiding the real problem.

The Classic Tag Handler Lifecycle and What It Means to You

Creating a new object is considered a relatively expensive operation in Java, even though it's less of an issue with the latest Java runtime environments. For high-performance applications, it's therefore common to try to minimize the number of objects created and reuse existing objects instead. The lifecycle defined for classic tag handlers in JSP 1.2 allowed a tag handler instance to be reused within the code generated for JSP pages under certain circumstances. This feature has caused a lot of pain and misunderstanding, which is why the simple tag handlers introduced in JSP 2.0 cannot be reused at all; the potential small loss of performance is a huge gain in simplicity, leading to less error prone code. For backward compatibility and for the scenarios where reuse still makes a difference, classic tag handlers are still reusable in JSP 2.0.

The classic tag handler lifecycle details are pretty complex and are mostly of interest to container developers. But if you develop classic tag handlers, you need to know at least how the lifecycle relates to instance reuse to ensure that your tag handlers work correctly in a container that takes advantage of this feature. Figure 21-7 shows a state diagram for a tag handler that implements just the `Tag` interface.

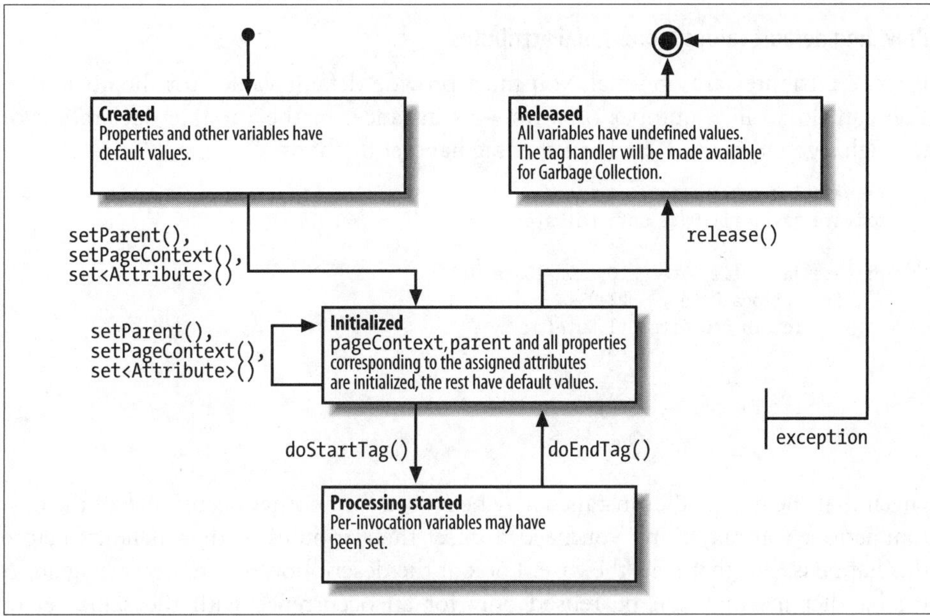

Figure 21-7. Lifecycle for a tag handler implementing the Tag interface

When the tag handler instance is created, all instance variables have default values; then all setter methods (`setPageContext( )`, `setParent( )`, and all setters for attributes) are called. This brings the instance to a state where it's initialized for use. The `doStartTag( )` method is then called. This method may set instance variables to values that are valid only for the current invocation. The `doEndTag( )` method is called if no exception is thrown by `doStartTag( )` or while processing the element's body. The tag handler instance may then be reused for another occurrence of the custom action that uses the same set of attributes, with the same or different values, in the same or a different page. If an attribute for the other occurrence has a different value, the corresponding setter method is called, followed by the `doStartTag( )`/`doEndTag( )` called as before. Eventually, the container is ready to get rid of the tag handler instance. At this point, it calls the release( ) method to let the tag handler release internal resources it may have used.

Let's look at what this means from a tag handler developer's perspective. There are a number of things you may need to do in your tag handler, for instance:

- Provide default values for optional attributes
- Reset per-invocation state
- Keep expensive resources for the lifetime of the tag handler object

The following sections describe the requirements the tag handler lifecycle places on you to get this right.

Providing default values for optional attributes

If some attributes are optional, you must provide default values for the attributes. You can do so in a number of ways—for instance, in the variable declaration or through a getter method used by other tag handler methods:

```
private int optionalInt = 5;
private java.util.Date optionalDate;

private java.util.Date getOptionalDate( ) {
    if (optionalDate == null) {
        return new java.utl.Date( );
    }
    else {
        return optionalDate;
    }
}
```

Given that the tag handler instance may be reused for another occurrence of the custom action, you may think you need to reset the attributes to their defaults before this happens. But that isn't the case. Look at the description of the lifecycle again. A tag handler instance can be reused only for an occurrence with the same set of attributes. Put another way, if a tag handler instance is used for an occurrence that doesn't use an optional attribute, it can be reused only for other occurrences that also omit this attribute. The default value will never need to be reset; it's never set for any of the occurrences that use the instance in the first place.

Let's look at an example:

```
<xmp:myAction attr1="one" />
<xmp:myAction attr1="one" attr2="two" />
<xmp:myAction attr1="one" attr2="new" />
```

Here the container creates one tag handler instance for the first action element and calls the setter method for attr1. This tag handler uses its default value for the optional attr2 attribute.

The container isn't allowed to use the same tag handler instance for the other two action elements because they don't use the same set of attributes as the first element. Instead, it must create a new tag handler instance and call the setter methods for both attributes with the values specified by the second element. After using the tag handler for the second element, the container can reuse it for the third element. Only the setter method for `attr2` must be called, because the value for `attr1` is the same in the second and third elements.

Resetting per-invocation state

A tag handler may create or collect data that is only valid for one invocation. One example is a list of values set by custom actions nested in the body of the main action, for instance JSTL `<c:param>` actions adding values used by the `<c:redirect>` actions:

```
<c:redirect url="mypage.jsp">
  <c:param name="foo" value="bar" />
  <c:param name="fee" value="baz" />
</c:forward>
```

In this example, the nested parameter actions call a method in the tag handler for the parent action to add the parameter to a list that is then used in the forward URI:

```
private Map params;
 ...
public void addParameter(String name, String value) {
    if (params == null) {
        params = new HashMap( );
    }
    params.put(name, value);
}
```

If the container decides to reuse this tag handler, the list grows for each invocation unless you reset it at some point. There's no guarantee that the `doEndTag( )` method is called (in case of an exception in the body), so the best place to reset the list is in the `doStartTag( )` method:

```
public int doStartTag( ) throws JspException {
  // Reset per-invocation state
  params = null;
  ...
}
```

This approach works fine for objects that can hang around until the tag handler is used again. But what if you need to use an expensive resource, such as a database connection, that must be released (or returned to a pool) as soon as possible? That's when the `TryCatchFinally` interface comes in handy. As I described earlier and showed in Example 21-11, the `doFinally( )` method is always called, no matter if an exception is thrown or not. Expensive resources that are used only on a per-invocation basis can be released in this method.

Keeping expensive resources for the lifetime of the tag handler instance

Some objects used by a tag handler can be expensive to create, such as a `java.text.SimpleDateFormat` instance or an XML parser. Instead of creating objects like this every time the tag handler is invoked, it's better to create them once when the tag handler itself is created or the first time they are used. The place to get rid of objects like this is in the `release( )` method:

```
private java.text.SimpleDateFormat dateFormat =
    new java.text.SimpleDateFormat( );

  ...
public void release( ) {
    dateFormat = null;
}
```

The `release( )` method is called just before the container gets rid of the tag handler to let it do this kind of cleanup. It's never called between invocations.

Developing Tag Library Functions

Besides tag handlers, a tag library can also contain EL functions. An EL function is implemented as a static method in a regular Java class. There are no special interfaces to implement or any special conventions to follow; any static method will do.

Example 21-12 shows a class with static methods for converting between degrees in Celsius and Fahrenheit.

Example 21-12. A class with static methods that can be used as EL functions

```
package com.ora.jsp.util;

public class TempConverter {
    public static double toCelsius(double fahrenheit) {
        return (fahrenheit - 32) * 5 / 9;
    }

    public static double toFahrenheit(double celsius) {
        return celsius * 9 / 5 + 32;
    }
}
```

The `toCelsius( )` method takes a degree in Fahrenheit as its single argument and returns the corresponding Celsius value, and `toFahrenheit( )` does the reverse.

To make these methods accessible as EL functions, they must be declared in the TLD for the tag library. We'll look at the details in the next section, but here's the bare minimum you need to add:

```
...
  <function>
    <name>toCelsius</name>
```

```
    <function-class>com.ora.jsp.util.TempConverter</function-class>
    <function-signature>double toCelsius(double)</function-signature>
  </function>

  <function>
    <name>toFahrenheit</name>
    <function-class>com.ora.jsp.util.TempConverter</function-class>
    <function-signature>double toFahrenheit(double)</function-signature>
  </function>
...
```

Each function is declared by three mandatory elements. The `<name>` element declares the function name to use in an EL expression. It doesn't have to match the method name, but it often does. The `<function-class>` element contains the fully qualified class name for the class containing the static method, and the `<function-signature>` element contains the method signature. It's declared as a return type (a primitive type or a fully qualified class name), the method name, and a comma-separated list of the argument types.

The container takes care of type conversion for the arguments according to the EL coercion rules. For instance, you can use the `toCelsius` function like this in a JSP page:

```
<%@ taglib prefix="ora" uri="orataglib" %>

The temperature ${param.celsius} degrees Celsius
corresponds to ${ora:toFahrenheit(celsius)} degrees Fahrenheit
```

Here the argument is a `String` (the `celsius` request parameter value), so the container converts it to a `double` before invoking the method mapped to the `toFahrenheit( )` function in the TLD.

Creating the Tag Library Descriptor

Now you have a good idea about what the Java classes for tag library functions and both simple and classic tag handlers looks like. When the JSP container processes a page, it converts EL functions and custom action elements into code that creates and calls the correct classes. To do this, it needs information about which tag handler implements which custom action element, and which Java method corresponds to an EL function. It gets this information from the Tag Library Descriptor (TLD). As you will see in Chapter 22, the JSP container also uses the TLD information to verify that the attribute list for an action element is correct.

The TLD is an XML file with information about all custom actions and functions in a library. A JSP page that uses a custom tag library must identify the corresponding TLD and the namespace prefix used for the actions and functions in the page with the `taglib` directive:

```
<%@ taglib prefix="ora" uri="orataglib" %>
...
<ora:addCookie name="userName" value="${param.userName}" />
```

```
...
${ora:toCelsius(param.f)}
```

The uri attribute identifies the TLD, in one of several ways that I describe later in this section. The prefix attribute assigns a prefix to use for the action elements and functions included in the library.

The JSP container then uses the TLD to find the information it needs to generate code for invoking the correct class when it encounters action elements and functions with a matching prefix.

Example 21-13 shows a part of the JSP 2.0 version of the TLD for the custom actions in this book. Some changes were made to the format of the TLD between JSP 2.0 and JSP 1.2, as well as between JSP 1.1 and 1.2; I describe the differences at the end of this section. A JSP 2.0 container is required to accept a TLD in the JSP 1.1 and 1.2 formats as well.

Example 21-13. Tag Library Descriptor (TLD)

```
<?xml version="1.0" encoding="ISO-8859-1" ?>
<taglib xmlns="http://java.sun.com/xml/ns/j2ee"
  xmlns:xsi="http://www.w3.org/2001/XMLSchema-instance"
  xsi:schemaLocation="http://java.sun.com/xml/ns/j2ee
    http://java.sun.com/xml/ns/j2ee/web-jsptaglibrary_2_0.xsd"
  version="2.0">

  <description>
    A tag library for the examples in the O'Reilly JSP book
  </description>
  <tlib-version>3.0</tlib-version>
  <short-name>ora</short-name>
  <uri>orataglib</uri>

  <tag>
    <description>
       Processes the patterns specified as attributes to render a
       calendar for the specified month.
    </description>
    <name>calendar</name>
    <tag-class>com.ora.jsp.tags.MonthCalendarTag</tag-class>
    <body-content>empty</body-content>

    <attribute>
      <name>date</name>
      <required>true</required>
      <rtexprvalue>true</rtexprvalue>
    </attribute>
    ...
    <attribute>
      <description>
        A fragment used as a pattern for days in the previuous and following
        months, evaluated to get full weeks.
      </description>
```

Example 21-13. Tag Library Descriptor (TLD) (continued)

```
      <name>padPattern</name>
      <required>false</required>
      <fragment>true</fragment>
    </attribute>
    ...
  </tag>
  ...
  <function>
    <description>
      Converts from Fahrenheit to Celsius
    </description>
    <name>toCelsius</name>
    <function-class>com.ora.jsp.util.TempConverter</function-class>
    <function-signature>double toCelsius(double)</function-signature>
  </function>
  ...
</taglib>
```

At the top of the TLD file, you find a standard XML declaration. Next follows the `<taglib>` root element with namespace and XML Schema declarations and the version of the JSP specification the tag library is compliant with. An XML Schema defines the rules for how elements in an XML file must be used, such as the order of the elements, which elements are mandatory and which are optional, if an element can be included multiple times, etc. If you're not familiar with XML, don't worry about this. Just accept the fact that you need to copy the first two elements in Example 21-13 faithfully into your own TLD files. With regards to the order of the elements, just define them in the order in which they are described here. Whether an element is mandatory or optional is also spelled out in the description of each element that follows. If you're curious about the formal XML Schemas, it's available online at *http://java.sun.com/xml/ns/j2ee/web-jsptaglibrary_2_0.xsd*.*

The root element of the TLD file must be the `<taglib>` element. This element encloses more specific elements that describe the library as such, as well as the individual tag handlers and functions.

General Library Elements

The first set of top-level elements, in this order, describes the library itself:

- The optional `<description>` element can provide a short description of the library, perhaps something a tool may display to help users decide if the library is what they are looking for.

* The XML Schema allows additional extension elements to be used that are not described here, because they are intended for use by tool vendors and their content is proprietary. See the JSP specification and the XML Schema for details about these elements.

- The `<display-name>` element is an optional element, containing a name of the library suitable for display by an authoring tool.
- An `<icon>` element with nested `<small-icon>` and `<large-icon>` elements can optionally be used to name image files containing icons for the library, again something a page-authoring tool may use. The values are file paths for files containing either GIF or JPEG images, interpreted as relative to the TLD file. The small icon should be 16x16 pixels, and the large 32x32 pixels.
- The `<tlib-version>` element is mandatory and specifies the tag library version. The version should be specified as a series of numbers separated by dots. In other words, the normal conventions for software version numbers, such as 1.1 or 2.0.3, should be used.
- The `<short-name>` element is intended for use by page-authoring tools. It's a mandatory element that should contain the default prefix for the action elements. In Example 21-13, the value is `ora`, meaning that an authoring tool by default generates custom action elements using the `ora` prefix, for instance `<ora:menuItem page="page1.jsp">`. A tool may also use the element value as the value of the `prefix` attribute if it generates the `taglib` directive in the JSP page. The element value must not include whitespace characters or other special characters, or start with a digit or underscore.
- The `<uri>` element value can be used as the default for the `uri` attribute in a `taglib` directive generated by an authoring tool. It's an optional element, following the same character rules as the `<short-name>` element. While the element is optional according to the Schema, it's required for the tag library auto-discovery feature introduced in JSP 1.2. More about this feature later, but because of this, I recommend you always include this element.

Validator and Listener Elements

Next comes an optional `<validator>` element, with nested `<description>`, `<validator-class>`, and `<init-param>` elements. I describe how to use these elements in Chapter 22.

Another optional element is the `<listener>` element, with a mandatory `<listener-class>` element. These elements are also described in detail in Chapter 22.

Tag Elements

Following the general tag library elements, any number of `<tag>` elements can be used to describe tag handlers implemented as Java classes. The `<tag>` element contains other elements that describe different aspects of the custom action. In order, they are `<description>`, `<display-name>`, `<icon>`, `<name>`, `<tag-class>`, `<tei-class>`, `<body-content>`, `<variable>`, `<attribute>`, `<dynamic-attributes>`, and `<example>`.

General tag elements

The <description>, <display-name>, and <icon> elements are all optional and can be used to describe each tag handler in the same way as for the tag library itself.

The <name> element is mandatory and contains the name for the corresponding custom action element in the JSP pages. It must be a name that is unique among all Java tag handlers and tag files in the tag library.

The <tag-class> element, also mandatory, contains the fully qualified class name for the tag handler class.

Actions that introduce variables or do special syntax validation, as described in Chapter 22, may need a TagExtraInfo subclass in addition to the tag handler class. The optional <tei-class> element specifies the fully qualified class name for the TagExtraInfo subclass. This class is rarely needed.

The <body-content> is mandatory for JSP 2.0. It can contain one of four values: empty, JSP, scriptless, or tagdependent.

The empty value means that the action body must be empty. If a custom action backed by this tag handler is included in a page with a body, an error message is displayed.

If the body can contain JSP elements, such as EL expressions, standard and custom actions as well as scripting elements, the JSP value must be used. If it can contain EL expressions and actions but not scripting elements, use the scriptless value. Note that if the value is set to JSP, the tag handler must be implemented using the classic tag handler API. All JSP elements in a JSP or scriptless body are processed and the result is handled as specified by the tag handler (processed by the tag handler or sent through to the response body). JSP is the default value in case you omit the <body-content> element.

The fourth alternative is tagdependent; this value means that the body can contain content that looks like JSP elements but the container shouldn't evaluate them. Typically, this value is used when the tag handler processes the body and the content may contain characters that could be confused with JSP elements, such as:

```
SELECT * FROM MyTable WHERE Name LIKE '<%>'.
```

If a tag that expects this kind of body content is declared as JSP, the <%> is likely to confuse the JSP container. The tagdependent value can avoid this risk for confusion, but note that it also disables the processing of valid JSP elements. Hence, this value is rarely used. Special characters can be escaped instead, as described in Appendix A, to avoid potential confusion.

Variable elements

The <variable> element, with its nested <description>, <name-given>, or <name-from-attribute>, <variable-class>, <declare>, and <scope> elements, can provide information about variables a custom action exposes as scripting variables. I describe this in detail in Chapter 22.

Attribute elements

The `<tag>` element must also contain an `<attribute>` element for each action attribute it supports. Each `<attribute>` element in turn contains nested elements that describe the attribute: `<description>`, `<name>`, `<required>`, `<rtexprvalue>`, and `<type>` or `<fragment>`.

- The optional `<description>` element can describe the purpose and use of the attribute, the same as for all other places where this element may appear in the TLD.
- The mandatory `<name>` element specifies the attribute name, which must be unique among all attributes for the tag handler.
- The optional `<required>` element tells whether the attribute is required. The values `true`, `false`, `yes`, and `no` are valid, with `false` being the default.
- The `<rtexprvalue>` element is an optional element that can have the same values as the `<required>` element. If it's `true` or `yes`, a request-time expression (an EL or Java expression) can specify the attribute value, for instance:

  ```
  attr="${param.par}"
  attr='<%= request.getParameter("par") %>'
  ```

  The default value is `false`.
- The optional `<type>` element can specify the attribute's Java type for attributes that allow a request-time expression as its value. The value must be the fully qualified name of the Java class or interface for the corresponding setter method in the tag handler class. This element is intended to be used only by authoring tools and documentation generating tools in JSP 2.0; the container doesn't have to use it, but it may report an error if the specified type doesn't match the type of the attribute in the tag handler class.
- If the attribute value should be handled as a fragment (as described earlier in this chapter), you must include the `<fragment>` element with the value `true` or `yes`. The default value is `false`.

Dynamic attributes element

After (or instead of) the `<attribute>` elements, you can use the `<dynamic-attributes>` element with the value `true` or `yes` to specify that the tag handler accepts undeclared attributes, as described earlier in this chapter. If you omit this element it defaults to `false`.

Example element

The final subelement for the `<tag>` element is the optional `<example>` element. As the name implies, it can provide an example of how the custom action can be used. Tools can use this information, for instance display it as part of a tool tip for the action or include it in automatically generated documentation.

Tag File Elements

A TLD can also include declarations of tag files, described in Chapter 11, with any number of `<tag-file>` elements following the `<tag>` elements, if any. The `<tag-file>` element contains other elements that describe different aspects of the custom action. In order, they are `<description>`, `<display-name>`, `<icon>`, `<name>`, `<path>`, and `<example>`.

The `<description>`, `<display-name>`, and `<icon>` elements are all optional and can be used to describe each tag file in the same way as for other tag library artifacts.

The `<name>` element is mandatory and contains the name for the corresponding custom action element in the JSP pages. It must be a name that is unique among tags and tag files in the tag library.

The mandatory `<path>` element contains the path to the tag file. If the tag file is packaged together with the TLD in a JAR file, it must start with `/META-INF/tags`, and consequently, the tag file must be located somewhere in this structure in the JAR file. If the tag file and the TLD reside directly in the web application structure (e.g., during development), the path must start with `/WEB-INF/tags`.

An optional `<example>` element can be used to include an example of how the custom action implemented by the tag file should be used, just as for the `<tag>` element.

Function Elements

Functions used in EL expressions are mapped to static methods in a Java class using any number of `<function>` elements after the `<tag-file>` elements, if any. As with the other main elements, a number of nested elements define the details: `<description>`, `<display-name>`, `<icon>`, `<name>`, `<function-class>`, `<function-signature>`, and `<example>`.

The optional `<description>`, `<display-name>`, and `<icon>` elements can be used to describe the function in the same way as for all other items.

The mandatory `<name>` element contains the function name. Each function must have a unique name within the tag library.

The name of the class that contains the implementation of the function is specified by the mandatory `<function-class>` element as a fully qualified class name (i.e., including the package name).

The mandatory <function-signature> element specifies the function parameters and return type in the format *returnType functionName(parameterType, ...)*, e.g.:

```
java.lang.String truncate(java.lang.String, int)
```

The optional nested <example> element is used the same as in all other elements.

Differences Between a JSP 1.2 and a JSP 2.0 TLD

A JSP 2.0 container is required to accept a TLD in the JSP 1.1 or 1.2 format, but you must use the new JSP 2.0 format in order to take advantage of the new features, such as tag files and functions.

Some of the differences between the JSP 1.2 and JSP 2.0 TLD file format are due to the fact that JSP 2.0 uses XML Schema for declaration (and validation) of the elements while JSP 1.2 used a Document Type Definition (DTD) for the same purpose. The switch to XML Schema applies to all descriptor files in the specifications grouped under the J2EE 1.4 umbrella, allowing for shared type definitions and grouping rules for the elements they have in common. The following differences can be attributed to the switch to XML Schema:

- The namespace and schema declarations in the <taglib> root element replace the DTD DOCTYPE declaration, for consistency with all other J2EE 1.4 configuration files.
- The <jsp-version> element is replaced by the version attribute in the <taglib> root element.
- The order and grouping of the description elements are changed: the <description> and <display-name> elements have switched places and an <icon> element has been added to contain the <small-icon> and <large-icon> elements. This group of elements now also always appear as the first nested elements where they are supported; in the JSP 1.2 spec they were sometimes included in the middle of more specific elements.
- The <body-content> element is mandatory, because the default used in previous versions of the specification is invalid for the new simple tag handler type.

The other differences are due to new features:

- The scriptless value for the <body-content> element is added to support the new simple tag handler API.
- The <fragment> element is added to support the new fragment attribute feature.
- The <tag-file> top-level element is added to support the new tag file feature.
- The <function> top-level element is added to declare EL functions.

Differences Between a JSP 1.1 and a JSP 1.2 TLD

If you're jumping from JSP 1.1 directly to JSP 2.0, you may feel that the list above is incomplete. That's because a number of things changed between JSP 1.1 and 1.2 as well.

Most of the differences were name changes for some elements for consistency with the naming conventions used in other J2EE descriptor files. More precisely, hyphens were added to separate words in element names, and the `<info>` element was replaced with the `<description>` element that is used for the same purpose in other descriptors. The following table summarizes these name changes:

JSP 1.1	JSP 1.2
`<tlibversion>`	`<tlib-version>`
`<jspversion>`	`<jsp-version>`
`<shortname>`	`<short-name>`
`<info>`	`<description>`
`<tagclass>`	`<tag-class>`
`<teiclass>`	`<tei-class>`
`<bodycontent>`	`<body-content>`

A number of new elements were also added to allow more descriptive information in the TLD. This information may be used by page-authoring tools and also by tools that generate user documentation from the TLD: `<display-name>`, `<small-icon>`, `<large-icon>`, `<example>`, `<type>`, and `<variable>`. How to use these new elements is described earlier in this section.

Packaging and Installing a Tag Library

There are basically two ways the files that make up a tag library (the TLD and all the class files) can be made available to a container: packaged in a JAR file or kept as regular files directly in the web application structure in a WAR file (or the filesystem for most containers). On top of this, there are three ways to identify the tag library you use in a JSP page. Let's look at the topics one at a time.

Making the Tag Library Files Available to the Container

During development, you may want to let the tag library classes and the TLD file reside as is in the filesystem, since it makes it easy to change the TLD and modify and recompile the classes. Just make sure the class files are stored in a directory that's part of the classpath for the JSP container, such as the *WEB-INF/classes* directory for the web application. The TLD must also be available as a file with a *.tld* extension in a directory where the JSP container can find it. The recommended location is the *WEB-INF/tlds* directory.

When you're done with the development, you may want to package all class files and the TLD in a JAR file. This makes it easier to install the library in an application. In this case, the TLD must be placed as a file with a *.tld* extension in the *META-INF* directory in the JAR file, for instance as *META-INF/taglib.tld*. Tag files, if any, must be stored under *META-INF/tags*, and the TLD must point to the exact location.

To create the JAR file, first arrange the files in a directory with a structure like this:

```
META-INF/
  taglib.tld
  tags/
    mytags/
      copyright.tag
      forEvenAndOdd.tag
com/
  ora/
    jsp/
      tags/
        AddCookieTag.class
        ...
      util/
        StringFormat.class
        ...
```

The structure for the class files must match the package names for your classes. I've shown a few of the classes in the tag library for this book as an example.

With the file structure in place, use the *jar* command to create the JAR file:

```
jar cvf orataglib_3_0.jar META-INF com
```

This command creates a JAR file named *orataglib_3_0.jar* containing the files in the *META-INF* and *com* directories. Use any JAR filename that makes sense for your own tag library. Including the version number for the library is also a good idea, because it makes it easy for the users to see which version of the library they are using. The JAR file should be placed in the *WEB-INF/lib* directory for the application.

Identifying the Tag Library in a JSP Page

To identify the library in JSP pages, you use a `taglib` directive like this:

```
<%@ taglib prefix="ora" uri="orataglib" %>
```

The container uses the `uri` attribute value to locate the TLD file for the tag library. The value must be either a symbolic name or a file path. A symbolic name is any string that is unique in the application. An HTTP URL is often used to be reasonably sure that it's unique in any application. Even when an HTTP URL is used, the container uses it only as a symbolic name; it does not try to get the resource specified by the URL.

If the `uri` value is a symbolic name, it must be mapped to the actual location of the TLD file somehow. In JSP 1.2, a new auto-discovery mechanism was introduced to make this very easy. Here's how it works. The TLD includes a `<uri>` element to define the default URI for the library:

```
<taglib>
  ...
  <uri>orataglib</uri>
  ...
</taglib>
```

When the web application is started, the container scans through the *WEB-INF* directory structure for files with *.tld* extensions and all JAR files containing files with *.tld* extensions in their *META-INF* directory. In other words, locating all TLD files. For each TLD, the container looks for the `<uri>` element and creates a map from the URI to the TLD that contains it. In your JSP page, you just have to place a `taglib` directive with a `uri` attribute value matching the URI in the TLD.

Prior to JSP 1.2, you had to define the mapping manually in the deployment descriptor for the application (*WEB-INF/web.xml*):

```
<web-app>
  ...
  <taglib>
    <taglib-uri>
      orataglib
    </taglib-uri>
    <taglib-location>
      /WEB-INF/lib/orataglib_1_0.jar
    </taglib-location>
  </taglib>
  ...
</web-app>
```

The `<taglib-uri>` element contains the symbolic name, and the `<taglib-location>` element contains the path to either the JAR file or the extracted TLD file.

If the `uri` attribute value doesn't match a known symbolic name, the container assumes that it's a file path:

```
<%@ taglib prefix="ora" uri="/WEB-INF/lib/orataglib_3_0.jar" %>
```

If the path starts with a slash, it's interpreted as a context-relative path, otherwise as a path relative to the JSP page. The file can be either the TLD file itself or a JAR file that includes the TLD file as *META-INF/taglib.tld*.

With the introduction of the auto-discovery feature in JSP 1.2, there's rarely a reason to use any of the other mechanisms for identifying the tag library. The only reason I can think of is if you're unfortunate enough to be faced with two third-party libraries that have the same default URI specified in their TLD files. To avoid the conflict, you can use one of the explicit mapping types to identify one of the libraries.

Packaging Multiple Libraries in One JAR File

A beneficial side effect of the auto-discovery feature is that you can bundle more than one tag library in the same JAR file. In JSP 1.1, a TLD contained in a JAR file had to be named exactly *META-INF/taglib.tld*, which meant that a JAR file could contain only one TLD.

The auto-discovery feature, however, treats any file with a *.tld* extension in a JAR file's *META-INF* directory as a TLD. You can therefore put multiple TLDs (along with the class files for the libraries) in one JAR file. This makes it easier for your users to deploy related tag libraries. Note that you must use the auto-discovery mechanism to deploy multilibrary JAR files, because there's no way to specify the path to an individual TLD in such a JAR file.*

* You can deliver the TLDs separate from the JAR file and require that they be mapped with `<taglib>` elements in the application deployment descriptor as well, but that defeats the purpose of making deployment easy.

CHAPTER 22

Advanced Custom Tag Library Features

In the previous chapter, you learned how to develop basic tag handlers, such as conditional and iteration actions, with and without access to the element body. But there's a lot more that you can do. In this chapter we look at some more advanced features: how actions can cooperate, how to work with undeclared action element attributes, how to verify that actions are used correctly, how to bundle listener classes with a tag library, and how to convert text attribute values into types more appropriate for the tag handler. Most of these features work the same for both simple and classic tag handlers.

Developing Cooperating Actions

It's often necessary to develop custom actions so that they can be combined with other actions, letting them cooperate in some fashion. You have seen examples of this throughout this book. For instance, in Chapter 12, `<sql:param>` action elements are nested within the body of a `<sql:query>` action to set the values of placeholders in the SQL statement. Another example of cooperation is how the `<c:forEach>` action can use the query result produced by the `<sql:query>` action. In this section, we take a look at the cooperation techniques demonstrated by these two examples: explicit cooperation between a parent element and elements nested in its body and implicit cooperation through objects exposed as scoped variables.

Using Explicit Parent-Child Cooperation

Let's look at a possible implementation of the `<sql:param>` tag handler as one example of explicit parent-child cooperation. As you may recall from Chapter 12, this action can be nested within the body of either an `<sql:query>` or an `<sql:update>` action:

```
<sql:update sql="UPDATE Employee SET Salary = ? WHERE EmpId = ?">
  <sql:param value="${param.newSalary}" />
  <sql:param value="${param.empId}" />
</sql:update>
```

How does the <sql:param> action tell the enclosing <sql:update> action about the parameter it defines? The answer to this question lies in a couple of SimpleTag and Tag interface methods that I didn't cover in Chapter 21, plus a utility method implemented by both the SimpleTagSupport class and the TagSupport class.

The interface methods are setParent( ) and getParent( ), implemented like this by the TagSupport class:

```
...
private Tag parent;
...
public void setParent(Tag t) {
    parent = t;
}

public Tag getParent( ) {
    return parent;
}
```

These two methods are standard accessor methods for the parent instance variable. The SimpleTagSupport implementation differs only in that the parent's type is JspTag—the common superclass for Tag and SimpleTag—instead of Tag.

For a nested action element, the setParent( ) method is always called on the tag handler with a reference to the enclosing tag handler as its value. This way a nested tag handler always knows its parent. So a tag handler at any nesting level can ask for its parent, using getParent( ), and then ask for the parent's parent, and so on until it reaches a tag handler that doesn't have a parent (getParent( ) returns null). This means it has reached the top level.

This is part of the puzzle. However, a tag handler is usually interested only in finding a parent it's been designed to work with. It would be nice to have a method that works its way up the hierarchy until it finds the parent of interest. That's exactly what the findAncestorWithClass( ) method does. Here's the TagSupport implementation:

```
public static final Tag findAncestorWithClass(Tag from, Class klass) {
    boolean isInterface = false;

    if (from == null ||
        klass == null ||
        (!Tag.class.isAssignableFrom(klass) &&
            !(isInterface = klass.isInterface( )))) {
        return null;
    }

    for (;;) {
        Tag tag = from.getParent( );
        if (tag == null) {
            return null;
        }
        if ((isInterface && klass.isInstance(tag)) ||
            klass.isAssignableFrom(tag.getClass( )))
```

```
                return tag;
            else
                from = tag;
        }
    }
```

The SimpleTagHandler implementation is similar but also deals with details needed in order to allow simple tag handlers to be nested within the body of a classic tag handler. It's used exactly the same in both classic and simple tag handlers, though, so don't worry about these details.

First of all, note that the findAncestorWithClass( ) method is a static method. Consequently, even tag handlers that implement the SimpleTag or Tag interface explicitly, instead of extending the support classes, can use it. The method takes two arguments: the tag handler instance to start searching from and the class or interface of the parent. After making sure all parameters are valid, it starts working its way up the hierarchy of nested tag handlers. It stops when it finds a tag handler of the specified class or interface and returns it. If the specified parent type isn't found, the method returns null.

This is all that's needed to let a nested action communicate with its parent—the parent accessor methods and the method that walks the action hierarchy to find the parent of interest. Example 22-1 shows how a <sql:param> tag handler class (loosely based on the JSTL reference implementation) can use this mechanism to find the enclosing tag handler instance.

Example 22-1. An <sql:param> tag handler class

```
...
import javax.servlet.jsp.*;
import javax.servlet.jsp.tagext.*;

public class SQLParamTag extends SimpleTagSupport {
    private Object value;

    public void setValue(String value) {
        this.value = value;
    }

    public void doTag( ) throws JspException {
        SQLExecutionTag parent = (SQLExecutionTag)
            findAncestorWithClass(this, SQLExecutionTag.class);
        if (parent == null) {
            throw new JspTagException("The param action is not " +
                "enclosed by a supported action type");
        }
        parent.addSQLParameter(value);
    }
}
```

The class has one instance variable, value, and the corresponding setter method. The most interesting method is the doTag() method. This method first uses the findAncestorWithClass() method to try to locate the enclosing <sql:query> or <sql:update> tag handler instance. Note that an interface, SQLExecutionTag, is used as the method argument instead of a specific class. This makes it possible to let the <sql:param> action find both types of actions it cooperates with; all that's required is that the parent tag handlers implement the SQLExecutionTag interface:

```
package javax.servlet.jsp.jstl.sql;

public interface SQLExecutionTag {
    void addSQLParameter(Object value);
}
```

The interface defines one method: addSQLParameter(). This is the method the nested SQLParamTag tag handler uses to communicate with its parent. For each nested <sql:param> action, the addSQLParameter() method gets called when the parent's body is processed. The value for each <sql:param> action is accumulated in the parent tag handler, ready to be used when the parent's doTag() method is called. Example 22-2 shows how the addSQLParameter() method can be implemented by the <sql:query> and <sql:update> tag handler classes.

Example 22-2. An <sql:param> parent tag handler class

```
...
public class SQLQueryTag extends SimpleTagSupport,
    implements SQLExecutionTag {
    private List params;
    ...
    public void addSQLParameter(Object value) {
        if (params == null) {
            params = new ArrayList();
        }
        params.add(value);
    }
...
```

In addSQLParameter(), the parameter value is saved in an ArrayList. Since I choose a simple tag handler implementation here, I don't have to worry about tag handler reuse issues. If I instead had implemented it as a classic tag handler, I would also need to reset the parameter list, e.g., in the doStartTag() method.

Using Implicit Cooperation Through Variables

Many JSTL actions cooperate implicitly through JSP scoped variables; one action exposes the result of its processing as a variable in one of the JSP scopes and another action uses the variable as its input. This type of cooperation is simple yet powerful.

All that is required is that the tag handler that exposes the data saves it in one of the JSP scopes, for instance using the PageContext.setAttribute( ) method:

```
public class VariableProducerTag extends SimpleTagSupport {
    private String var;
    private int scope = PageContext.PAGE_SCOPE;

    public void setVar(String var) {
        this.var = var;
    }

    public void setScope(String scope) {
        if ("page".equals(scopeName)) {
            scope = PageContext.PAGE_SCOPE;
        }
        else if ("request".equals(scopeName)) {
            scope = PageContext.REQUEST_SCOPE;
        }
        else if ("session".equals(scopeName)) {
            scope = PageContext.SESSION_SCOPE;
        }
        else if ("application".equals(scopeName)) {
            scope = PageContext.APPLICATION_SCOPE;
        }
    }

    public void doTag( ) {
        // Perform the main task for the action
        ...
        getJspContext( ).setAttribute(var, result, scope);
        JspFragment body = getJspBody( );
        if (body != null) {
            body.invoke(null);
        }
    }
}
```

Here an attribute named var lets the page author specify the name of the variable. Even though this isn't strictly a requirement (cooperating tags could be designed to use a predefined, hardcoded variable name), it's the most flexible approach. The attribute name can be anything, but var is the name used by all JSTL actions. I suggest that you follow the same convention to help page authors understand how to use your custom actions. Another convention is to support a scope attribute, so the page author can decide how widely the variable should be made available.

You must also decide where in the page you want the variable to be available to other actions. If it should be available to actions nested in the body of your custom action, you need to save the variable before invoking the body fragment in a simple tag handler, or in the doStartTag( ) or doInitBody( ) method for a classic tag handler.

For a classic tag handler, you may also need to replace the variable with a new one in the doAfterBody( ) method. This is the typical behavior of an iteration action, in which the doStartTag( ) or doInitBody( ) method saves the initial value, and the doAfterBody( ) method replaces it with a new value for each iteration, for instance the current element of a collection the action iterates over. If you implement the tag handler as a simple tag handler, just replace the value before invoking the body fragment again, as described in Chapter 21.

If it's important that the variable is available for nested actions only and not available outside the body of your action, you can remove it before exiting the doTag( ) method in a simple tag handler, or remove it in the doEndTag( ) method for a classic tag handler:

```
pageContext.removeAttribute(var);
```

This is what all JSTL actions do for nested availability variables. Another JSTL convention for this type of nested variable is to always make it available in the page scope, without giving the page author the option to set another scope.

In some cases, the variable should not be available until after the end tag, perhaps because the value depends on the evaluation of the body, or the custom action doesn't support a body. For a classic tag handler, you can then save the variable in the doEndTag( ) method. With a simple tag handler, you simply set it after invoking the body fragment in the doTag( ) method.

In the examples in this section, the tag handlers expose only one variable, but there's no limitation on the number of variables that can be exposed. If more than one variable is exposed, the recommendation is to use the var and scope attribute names for the primary variable and names starting with var and scope for the others.

Other tag handlers can find the scoped variable using the JspContext.findAttribute( ) method:

```
public class VariableConsumerTag extends SimpleTagSupport {
    private String items;

    public void setItems(String items) {
        this.items = items;
    }

    public void doTag( ) throws JspException {
        Collection c = getJspContext( ).findAttribute(items);
        if (c == null) {
            throw new JspTagException("Collection named " + items +
                " could not be found");
        }
        // Perform the main task for the action
        ...
    }
}
```

The findAttribute( ) method looks for the specified attribute (variable) in all scopes, in the order page, request, session, and application, and returns the first one it finds, or null if it can't find one.

A better approach, starting with JSP 2.0, is to delegate the variable lookup to the EL. In other words, declare the attribute to be of the type you support instead of a variable name represented by a String:

```
public class VariableConsumerTag extends SimpleTagSupport {
    private Collection items;

    public void setItems(Collection items) {
        this.items = items;
    }

    public void doTag( ) throws JspException {
        if (items == null) {
            throw new JspTagException("The 'items' attribute is null");
        }
        // Perform the main task for the action
        ...
    }
}
```

When an EL expression is used as the attribute value, the EL machinery looks up the variable saved by the variable producer tag handler:

```
<xmp:varProducer var="someList" />
<xmp:varConsumer items="${someList}" />
```

Creating a scripting variable

Besides making a variable available through the standard JSP scopes, a custom action can additionally make it available as a scripting variable in the same way as the standard <jsp:useBean> action.

Note that creating a scripting variable isn't a requirement; actions can cooperate nicely through variables in the JSP scopes. As I described in Chapter 16, there are almost no reasons for using scripting elements any longer, since the JSTL actions and the EL provide convenient solutions for the type of problems that typically required scripting elements in previous versions of JSP. In the rare event that the data exposed by a custom action needs to be accessed through a scripting variable, the page author can use the <jsp:useBean> to declare a scripting variable and assign it a reference to the object:

```
<xmp:varProducer var="someList" scope="session" />
<jsp:useBean id="someList" class="java.util.Collection" scope="session" />
<%= foo.size( ) %>
```

You may therefore want to think twice about if you really need to expose the data through a scripting variable, and if so, why the <jsp:useBean> action isn't good enough for your needs. Not that it's extremely hard to let a custom action create a scripting variable, but it does create overhead in terms of extra code generation and potential problems due to the complex interaction with other code generated by the container when it converts the JSP page to a servlet.

That said, the basic requirements for a custom action that creates a scripting variable are the same as for an action exposing a variable through the JSP scopes: the tag handler needs to save the variable using the `JspContext.setAttribute()` method in the `doTag()` method for a simple tag handler, or the `doStartTag()`, `doInitBody()`, `doAfterBody()`, or `doEndTag()` method for a classic tag handler, depending on where it needs to be available to other actions.

On top of this, you must also tell the container about the variable, so it can generate the code for declaring the scripting variable and assign it the value that your tag handler saves.

The id Versus the var Attribute

The JSP 1.1 specification suggested that an attribute named `id` should be used to name a variable created by an action; the value of the `id` attribute had to be unique within the page, and because it was used as a scripting variable name, it had to follow the variable naming rules for the scripting language. In JSP 1.2, this rule was downplayed and now applies only to the `<jsp:useBean>` action, but if your tag handler creates a scripting variable, it's still nice to use the same convention and name the attribute `id`.

For JSTL, the attribute name `var` was selected instead of `id` to clarify that the JSTL actions expose data only as variables in a JSP scope, not through scripting variables. Using a name that is a valid Java identifier is still a good idea to avoid having to quote the name when used in an EL expression. For variables that are visible outside the body of an action element, the name should be unique, unless you want to overwrite an existing variable with the same name.

The easiest way to tell the container what it needs to know is by declaring the variable in the TLD. As you may remember from Chapter 21, a `<variable>` element can be nested in the body of a `<tag>` element in the TLD, as shown in Example 22-3.

Example 22-3. Variable declaration using the TLD

```
<tag>
  <name>varProducer</name>
  <tag-class>com.xmp.VariableProducerTag</tag-class>

  <variable>
    <name-from-attribute>id</name-from-attribute>
    <variable-class>java.util.Collection</variable-class>
    <declare>true</declare>
    <scope>AT_END</scope>
```

Example 22-3. Variable declaration using the TLD (continued)

```
    <description>This variable contains ...</description>
  </variable>
  ...
</tag>
```

In this example, the varProducer custom action introduces a scripting variable with the name specified by the page author in the id attribute (defined by the <name-from-attribute> element) of type java.util.Collection (defined by the <variable-class> element). The variable name specified by the page author through the id attribute must be unique within the page. Because it's used as a scripting variable name, it must also follow the variable name rules for the scripting language. For Java, this means it must start with a letter, followed by a combination of letters and digits and must not contain special characters, such as a dot or a plus sign.

In most cases, letting the page author decide the variable name is the preferred design, but a hardcoded variable name can be specified if it's more appropriate for a specific action. To do so, replace the <name-from-attribute> element with the <name-given> element:

```
<variable>
    <name-given>foo</name-given>
    ...
</variable>
```

With this declaration in place, the container uses the hardcoded name foo as the variable name. Note that same rules apply to the hardcoded name as for a name picked by the page author: it must be unique and a valid Java variable name.

The <declare> element can be true or false. If it's true, the container creates a scripting variable declaration for this variable. If you specify false instead, the container assumes that the variable has already been declared by another action or a scripting element and just reassigns it the value saved in a JSP scope by the tag handler for this action.

The <scope> element tells the container where the variable should be available; it has nothing to do with the JSP scopes we have seen so far (page, request, session, and application). Instead, it defines where the new scripting variable is available to JSP scripting elements. A value of AT_BEGIN means that the variable is available from the action's start tag and stays available after the action's end tag. AT_END means it isn't available until after the action's end tag. A variable with scope NESTED is available only in the action's body, between the start and the end tag. The AT_BEGIN and NESTED values don't make sense for a simple tag handler, since the body of an action element implemented by a simple tag handler cannot contain scripting elements.

To understand how all this works, let's look at the code the container generates from a JSP page that contains the varProducer action, declared as in Example 22-3:

```
<%@ taglib prefix="xmp" uri="xmptaglib" %>
```

```
<xmp:varProducer id="someList" />

<%= someList.size( ) %>
```

The <xmp:varProducer> action creates a Collection object and saves it in the page scope with the name specified by the var attribute, someList in this case. Because of the <variable> declaration for this action in the TLD, the container declares a scripting variable with the same name and assigns it the value saved by the tag handler. The JSP scripting expression calls the size( ) method of the Collection referenced by the scripting variable and writes the value to the response. This JSP page fragment results in code similar to that shown in Example 22-4 in the generated servlet, assuming the custom action is implemented as a classic tag handler.

Example 22-4. Code generated for JSP actions

```
// Code for <xmp:varProducer>
com.xmp.VariableProducerTag _jspx_th_xmp_varProducer_1 =
  new com.xmp.VariableProducerTag ( );
_jspx_th_xmp_varProducer_1.setPageContext(pageContext);
_jspx_th_xmp_varProducer_1.setParent(null);
_jspx_th_xmp_varProducer_1.setId("myVariable");
try {
  _jspx_th_xmp_varProducer_1.doStartTag( );
  if (_jspx_th_xmp_varProducer_1.doEndTag( ) == Tag.SKIP_PAGE)
    return;
} finally {
  _jspx_th_xmp_varProducer_1.release( );
}
java.util.Collection someList = null;
someList = (String) pageContext.findAttribute("someList");
...
// Code for <%= someList.size( ) %>
out.print( someList.size( ) );
```

First, a tag handler instance is created and initialized with the standard properties (pageContext and parent) plus the property corresponding to the id attribute. Next, the doStartTag( ) and doEndTag( ) methods are called. Then comes the code that makes the object created by the action available as a scripting variable. Note how a variable with the name specified by the id attribute (someList) is declared, using the type specified by the <variable-class> element in the TLD.

Also note that the variable is declared after the call to the doEndTag( ) method. This is because the <scope> element in the TLD is set to AT_END. If the scope is specified as AT_BEGIN instead, the declaration is added before the doStartTag() call, and the assignment code is added right after the call. In this case, the tag handler must save the variable in a JSP scope in the doStartTag( ) method. If the tag handler implements IterationTag, assignment code is also added so that the variable gets reassigned for every evaluation of the body and after the call to doAfterBody( ). This allows the tag handler to modify the variable value in the doAfterBody( ) method, so each evaluation of the body has a new value. Finally, if the scope is set to NESTED, both the declaration and the value assignment code is inserted in the code block representing the action body. The tag handler must therefore make the variable available in either the `doStartTag( )` method or the `doInitBody( )` method, and can also modify the value in the `doAfterBody( )` method. For a simple tag handler, there's only on method: `doTag( )`. Hence, there's only one place where the variable can be created, so the `AT_BEGIN` and `NESTED` values are not useful for a simple tag handler, as I mentioned earlier.

The variable is assigned the value of the object saved by the tag handler in one of the standard JSP scopes, using the `findAttribute( )` method. As you may recall, this method searches through the scopes in the order page, request, session, and application, until it finds the specified object. With the value assigned to the Java variable, it's available to the JSP expression.

Using a TagExtraInfo subclass to declare a variable

In most cases, the TLD can declare all information about a variable created by a custom action. Here are the exceptions:

- The type of the variable depends on attribute values
- Whether to declare the variable or not depends on attribute values

To deal with these cases, you have to implement a `TagExtraInfo` subclass instead of declaring the variables in the TLD. The `TagExtraInfo` class contains two methods a subclass can override to inform the container about scripting variables and to perform validation. I describe the variable information method here and the validation method later in this chapter. The `TagExtraInfo` class also provides a number of property access methods that can be used by the subclass to get information about the custom action attributes specified by the page author.

Let's assume that the `<xmp:varProducer>` action lets the page author specify whether the variable should be declared using an attribute named `declare`, which accepts `true` and `false` values. Let's also assume that the variable type can be specified by a `type` attribute. Example 22-5 shows a `TagExtraInfo` subclass that handles these requirements.

Example 22-5. TagExtraInfo subclass for <xmp:varProducer>

```
package com.xmp;

import javax.servlet.jsp.tagext.*;

public class VariableProducerTEI extends TagExtraInfo {
    public VariableInfo[] getVariableInfo(TagData data) {
        String name = data.getAttributeString("id");
        String declare = data.getAttributeString("declare");
        String type = data.getAttributeString("type");
        VariableInfo[] vi = new VariableInfo[1];
        vi[0] =
            new VariableInfo(name, type,
```

Example 22-5. TagExtraInfo subclass for <xmp:varProducer> (continued)

```
            ("true".equals(declare) ? true : false),
            VariableInfo.AT_END)
        }
        return vi;
    }
}
```

When the JSP container converts the JSP page to a servlet it calls the getVariableInfo( ) method. The method returns an array of VariableInfo objects, one per scripting variable exposed by the tag handler.

The VariableInfo class is a simple bean with four properties, all of them initialized to the values passed as arguments to the constructor: varName, className, declare, and scope. These values have the same meaning as the corresponding <variable> subelements in the TLD: the variable name, the variable class name, whether to declare the variable or not (true or false), and where the variable should be visible (AT_BEGIN, AT_END, or NESTED).

The VariableProducerTEI class sets the varName and className properties of the VariableInfo bean to the values of the var and type attributes specified by the page author in the JSP page. The declare property is set to true or false depending on the value of the declare attribute.

To get the attribute value specified by the page author, another simple class named TagData is used. An instance of this class is passed as the argument to the getVariableInfo( ) method as shown in Example 22-5. The TagData instance is created by the JSP container and contains information about all action attributes specified by the page author in the JSP page. It has two methods of interest. First, the getAttributeString( ) method simply returns the specified attribute as a String. Some attributes values, however, may be specified by a JSP expression instead of a string literal, a so-called request-time attribute value. Since such a value isn't known during the translation phase, the TagData class also provides the getAttribute( ) method to indicate if an attribute value is a literal string, a request-time attribute value, or not set at all. The getAttribute( ) method returns an Object. If the attribute is specified as a request-time attribute value, the special REQUEST_TIME_VALUE object is returned. Otherwise a String is returned or null if the attribute isn't set.

The final piece of the puzzle is to tell the container to actually use the TagExtraInfo subclass for your custom action. You do so with the <tei-class> element in the TLD:

```
<tag>
  <name>varProducer</name>
  <tag-class>com.xmp.VariableProducerTag</tag-class>
  <tei-class>com.xmp.VariableProducerTEI</tei-class>
  ...
</tag>
```

Note that you can't use both a <tei-class> element and a <variable> element for the same tag handler.

Supporting Undeclared Attributes

Say you need to generate an HTML table with product information in a number of pages. The information to be shown for each product is subject to change, so you decide to create a custom action that does all the dirty work, allowing you to make the changes in one place when needed. However, the HTML `<table>` element supports a number of attributes affecting the table's look; there are 23 different attributes in HTML 4.0.1, to be exact.

You *could* define all 23 attributes for the custom action, in addition to the specific ones needed for the custom action's core functionality, but then you would constantly have to add new attributes as they are added to new versions of the HTML specification. A better approach is to tell the container that the custom action supports *dynamic attributes* (a more accurate name would have been "undeclared attributes"). The dynamic attributes support is a new feature added in JSP 2.0. When a custom action is marked as supporting dynamic attributes, the page author can use attributes that are not explicitly declared for the tag handler in the custom action element, without the container flagging them as errors.

You tell the container that the tag handler can handle dynamic attributes by adding a declaration in the TLD:

```
.. ...
  <tag>
    <name>prodTable</name>
    <tag-class>com.ora.jsp.tags.xmp.ProdTableTag</tag-class>
    <body-content>empty</body-content>
    <attribute>
      <name>prods</name>
      <required>true</required>
      <rtexprvalue>true</rtexprvalue>
    </attribute>
    <dynamic-attributes>true</dynamic-attributes>
  </tag>
  ...
```

We'll look at the TLD in more detail later, but notice the `<dynamic-attributes>` element here. This element, with the value `true`, is what tells the container that the tag handler is ready to deal with dynamic attributes.

For regular attributes, the tag handler implements setter methods that the container calls, but that would defeat the purpose for dynamic attributes. Hence, we need another way for the container to provide the dynamic attribute names and values to the tag handler, and a way for the tag handler to read them. That's accomplished by the `javax.servlet.jsp.tagext.DynamicAttributes` interface that can be implemented by both classic and simple tag handlers. This interface declares a single method:

```
setDynamicAttribute(String uri, String localName, Object value);
```

The container calls this method for each undeclared attribute, in the order the attributes are encountered in the page. The uri argument holds the XML namespace URI for the attribute if specified, or null otherwise, the localName argument holds the attribute name minus the namespace prefix, and the value argument provides the value. Dynamic attributes implicitly support request-time attribute values (i.e., Java and EL expressions), so the real type of the value depends on the expression used to set it. In most cases, though, dynamic attributes are used for static string values, such as optional HTML element attributes to be pushed through to the elements generated by the tag handler.

Example 22-6 shows the interesting part of the tag handler for the fictitious table-generating custom action.

Example 22-6. Tag handler that accesses context information (ProdTableTag.java)

```
package com.ora.jsp.tags.xmp;

import java.io.*;
import java.util.*;
import javax.servlet.jsp.*;
import javax.servlet.jsp.tagext.*;

public class ProdTableTag extends SimpleTagSupport
    implements DynamicAttributes {

    private List prods;
    private Map dynamicAttrs;

    public void setProds(List prods) {
        this.prods = prods;
    }

    public void setDynamicAttribute(String uri, String localName, Object value) {
        if (dynamicAttrs == null) {
            dynamicAttrs = new HashMap( );
        }
        dynamicAttrs.put(localName, value);
    }

    public void doTag( ) throws JspException, IOException {
        StringBuffer html = new StringBuffer("<table");
        if (dynamicAttrs != null) {
            Iterator i = dynamicAttrs.keySet().iterator( );
            while (i.hasNext( )) {
                String name = (String) i.next( );
                String value = dynamicAttrs.get(name).toString( );
                html.append(" ").append(name).append("=\"").append(value).
                    append("\"");
            }
        }
        JspWriter out = getJspContext().getOut( );
        out.println(html.toString( ));
```

Example 22-6. Tag handler that accesses context information (ProdTableTag.java) (continued)

```
        // Generate rows from product list
        ...
        out.println("</table>");
    }
}
```

Every time the `setDynamicAttribute( )` method is called, the attribute name and value are saved in a `Map`. Later, in the `doTag( )` method, all attributes accumulated in the `Map` are added as attributes of the generated HTML `<table>` element.

I ignore the namespace argument in this example. It is rarely, if ever, used. It could potentially be used for a custom action in a JSP Document (i.e., JSP pages in XML format), where an action element attribute can contain a namespace prefix declared in the document. JSP 2.0, however, doesn't provide a way to get the prefix declared for the namespace URI; hence, it's hard to do much with it. I advise you to consider the namespace argument as preparation for XML support enhancements in a future version of the specification, where additional support features can be fleshed out.

Validating Syntax

It's easy to make mistakes when using custom actions in a JSP page. Everyone types the wrong attribute name now and then or forgets to specify a mandatory attribute. When custom actions depend on each other, using the cooperation techniques described earlier in this chapter, they typically need to be used in a specific order or nesting structure, and this isn't always obvious from the documentation. As a custom action developer, you have a number of tools at your disposal to help the page author find and correct errors like these.

The first tool is the TLD. The TLD contains information about the attributes each action element supports and whether a body is supported or not. The JSP container uses this information to verify that the page author uses the custom action correctly, at least in the most basic sense.

For more advanced validation, I'm afraid you have to do a bit of coding yourself. The most powerful validation tool defined by the JSP specification is the `TagLibraryValidator` class. You can extend this class and bundle the subclass with your tag library to validate all aspects of JSP pages that use your library. A less powerful option, but still useful in some cases, is the `TagExtraInfo` class. Extensions of this class can validate the use of a single custom action, for instance that optional attributes are used correctly.

The next three sections describe these validation alternatives in detail.

Validation Based on the TLD

When the JSP container converts a JSP page to a servlet, it compares each custom action element to the specification of the action element in the TLD. First, it makes sure that the action name matches the name of an action specified in the TLD corresponding to the action element's prefix. It then looks at the attribute list in the page and compares it to the attribute specification in the TLD. If a required attribute is missing or an attribute is used in the page but not specified in the TLD, it reports it as an error so the page author can correct the mistake. It also reports an error if a body is used for a custom action that is declared to be empty.

Using a TagLibraryValidator

A feature introduced in JSP 1.2 is the tag library validator, represented by the `javax.servlet.jsp.tagext.TagLibraryValidator` class. The container gives a validator access to an XML representation of the complete page. A validator can therefore verify interactions between custom actions, for instance that a custom action that must be used as a subelement of another action element isn't used anywhere else, or that action elements are used in the appropriate order. It can also analyze the use of custom action attributes, perhaps making sure that mutually exclusive optional attributes aren't used for an action element.

The container uses the validator defined for a tag library when it converts a JSP page to a servlet, after performing validation of the page based on the information available in the TLD (attributes and empty bodies).

Example 22-7 shows the top part of a validator that verifies that a `<xmp:child>` custom action element is used only within the body of an `<xmp:parent>` action element.

Example 22-7. Validator class declaration

```
package com.ora.jsp.tlv;

import java.util.*;
import javax.servlet.jsp.tagext.*;
import org.jdom.*;
import org.jdom.input.*;
public class OraTLV extends TagLibraryValidator {
    private SAXBuilder builder = new SAXBuilder( );
    private Namespace jspNamespace =
        Namespace.getNamespace("http://java.sun.com/JSP/Page");
```

The validator class extends the `TagLibraryValidator` class that is part of the JSP API. In this particular validator, I use JDOM to work with the XML representation of the page. JDOM is a great open source product that lets you work with XML data in a way that's more suitable for Java than the standard DOM format defined by W3C. You can find out more about JDOM at the project web site: *http://www.jdom.org/*. To use JDOM, you must import the JDOM packages containing classes for parsing and the JDOM tree. If you don't want to use JDOM for some reason, you can, of course, use any XML parser and validation tools you want.

For the validator in Example 22-7, I create an instance of the JDOM SAXBuilder class and save it as an instance variable. If the container caches instances of validators, this saves me from having to create this object for every page that's validated. I also create a JDOM Namespace instance for the JSP namespace as an instance variable. More about this later.

The validator must override the validate( ) method:

```
public ValidationMessage[] validate(String prefix, String uri,
    PageData pd) {

    ValidationMessage[] vms = null;
    ArrayList msgs = new ArrayList( );
    Namespace taglibNamespace = Namespace.getNamespace(uri);
    try {
        Document doc = builder.build(pd.getInputStream( ));
        Element root = doc.getRootElement( );
        validateElement(root, taglibNamespace, msgs);
    }
    catch (Exception e) {
        vms = new ValidationMessage[1];
        vms[0] = new ValidationMessage(null, e.getMessage( ));
    }

    if (msgs.size( ) != 0) {
        vms = new ValidationMessage[msgs.size( )];
        msgs.toArray(vms);
    }
    return vms;
}
```

The container invokes the validate( ) method with an instance of the PageData class Through the PageData instance, the validator can get the XML representation of the page by calling the getInputStream( ) method. The XML representation is formally called the page's *XML View*. It's is almost the same as a JSP Document (a JSP page written from scratch with the JSP XML syntax, described in Chapter 17). What's different is that all include directives have been processed, and all template text is wrapped with <jsp:text> elements if the page being validated is written using the classic JSP syntax. The JSP elements in the XML View also have a special jsp:id attribute that I'll get back to later. The prefix argument is the tag library prefix declared for this library, for instance xmp in this example, and the uri argument is the URI for the library, as it appear in the XML View.

In a JSP Document, different prefixes can be declared for different parts of a page (using standard XML namespace declarations). In this case, the container calls the validator with the first prefix declared for the tag library. Since the prefix is not accurate in all cases, I create a Namespace from the uri attribute value and use it to identify elements from the tag library, as you will soon see.

In this example, the validator( ) method gets the XML View for the page and uses JDOM to parse it. It then calls the validateElement( ) method with the document's root element, the namespace for this tag library, and an ArrayList used to collect error messages. If the validateElement( ) method finds any errors, the message list is converted to an array of ValidationMessage instances, used as the return value.

As you will see later, a ValidationMessage instance contains the error message itself and information about where the error was found in the JSP source file. The fact that the validate( ) method returns an array of ValidationMessage instances means that all errors found in the page can be presented in one shot, allowing the page author to fix them all at once instead of one by one.

The validateElement( ) method is a dispatcher to methods that validate specific elements:

```
private void validateElement(Element e, Namespace ns, ArrayList msgs) {

    if (ns.equals(e.getNamespace())) {
        if (e.getName( ).equals("child")) {
            validateChild(e, ns, msgs);
        }
    }
    if (e.hasChildren( )) {
        List kids = e.getChildren( );
        Iterator i = kids.iterator( );
        while(i.hasNext( )) {
            validateElement((Element) i.next( ), ns, msgs);
        }
    }
}
```

It's a recursive method that is called for all elements in the document tree. First, it checks if the namespace for the current element matches the namespace for this tag library, i.e., if it's a custom action defined in this tag library. It then checks if it's an element that needs to be validated, and if so, calls the appropriate method. In this example, I validate only elements of type child, but this method can easily be extended to validate other elements as well.

For all types of elements that have child nodes, the validateElement( ) method calls itself with each child node. That's how the method recursively scans the whole tree.

The real validation code in this example is found in the validateChild( ) method:

```
private void validateChild(Element e, Namespace ns, ArrayList msgs) {
    Element parent = findParent(e, ns, "parent");
    if (parent == null) {
        String id = e.getAttributeValue("id", jspNamespace);
        ValidationMessage vm = new ValidationMessage(id,
            e.getQualifiedName( ) +
            " must only be used with 'parent'");
        msgs.add(vm);
    }
}
```

The validateChild( ) method uses the private findParent( ) method to see if the current child element has a parent element of type parent. If it doesn't, it means that the child element is used incorrectly. In this case, a ValidationMessage instance is created to report the error and added to the list of error messages.

A ValidationMessage contains two pieces of information: the error message itself and a unique ID for the element that the message refers to. The unique ID is assigned by the container and is passed to the validator as an element attribute named id in the JSP namespace, in other words, typically an attribute named jsp:id. Therefore, the first thing the validateParam( ) method does if it finds an error is to try to get this attribute so it can include it in the ValidationMessage. This is where the Namespace instance variable mentioned earlier is used. The container maintains a map between the ID and the location (line and column) of the element in the JSP source file. With this information, it can generate user-friendly error messages that include the location of the error. Figure 22-1 shows how Tomcat reports the errors reported by the sample validator when faces with the page in Example 22-8.

Example 22-8. A page using the <xmp:child> action incorrectly (validation.jsp)

```
<%@ page contentType="text/plain" %>
<%@ taglib prefix="xmp" uri="xmplib" %>
<%@ taglib prefix="c" uri="http://java.sun.com/jsp/jstl/core" %>

<%-- Correct usage. --%>
<xmp:parent>
  <xmp:child/>
</xmp:parent>

<%-- Incorrect usage. The validator finds and reports these errors. --%>
<xmp:child/>
<c:if test="true">
  <xmp:child/>
</c:if>
```

Finally, the findParent( ) method that locates parent elements of a certain type looks like this:

```
    private Element findParent(Element e, Namespace ns, String name) {
        if (e.getName( ).equals(name) &&
            ns.equals(e.getNamespace( ))) {
            return e;
        }
        Element parent = e.getParent( );
        if (parent != null) {
            return findParent(parent, ns, name);
        }
        return null;
    }
```

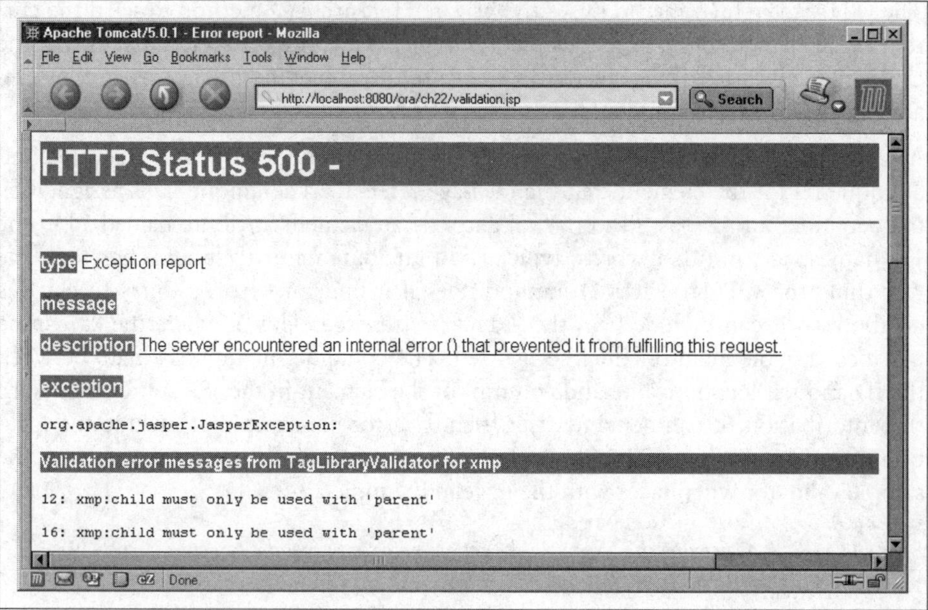

Figure 22-1. Validator error messages

It simply calls itself recursively until it either finds an element of the specified type or reaches the top of the document tree. If it finds a matching element, it returns it. Otherwise it returns null.

A validator is associated with a tag library through the <validator> element in the TLD:

```
<?xml version="1.0" encoding="ISO-8859-1" ?>
<taglib xmlns="http://java.sun.com/xml/ns/j2ee"
  xmlns:xsi="http://www.w3.org/2001/XMLSchema-instance"
  xsi:schemaLocation="http://java.sun.com/xml/ns/j2ee
    http://java.sun.com/xml/ns/j2ee/web-jsptaglibrary_2_0.xsd"
  version="2.0">

  <description>
    A tag library that illustrates the use of a TagLibraryValidator,
    containing two dummy custom actions and a validator. The "child"
    action must be nested within the body of a "parent" action element.
  </description>
  <tlib-version>1.0</tlib-version>
  <short-name>xmp</short-name>
  <uri>xmplib</uri>

  <validator>
    <validator-class>com.ora.jsp.tlv.OraTLV</validator-class>
  </validator>

  <tag>
```

```
    <name>child</name>
    <tag-class>com.ora.jsp.tags.xmp.ChildTag</tag-class>
    <body-content>empty</body-content>
  </tag>

  <tag>
    <name>parent</name>
    <tag-class>com.ora.jsp.tags.xmp.ParentTag</tag-class>
    <body-content>scriptless</body-content>
  </tag>
</taglib>
```

The <validator-class> element specifies the validator class name. Optional <init-param> elements can be nested within the <validator> element to configure a generic validator for a specific tag library:

```
<validator>
  <validator-class>com.ora.jsp.tlv.OraTLV</validator-class>
  <init-param>
    <param-name>logErrors</param-name>
    <param-value>true</param-name>
  </init-param>
  <init-param>
    <param-name>logFormat</param-name>
    <param-value>detailed</param-name>
  </init-param>
</validator>
```

The validator can read its parameters with the getParameters( ) method inherited from the TagLibraryValidator base class:

```
Map params = getInitParameters( );
String myInitParam = (String) params.get("myInitParam");
```

Using a TagExtraInfo Class for Validation

The TagLibraryValidator is the most powerful validation mechanism, but it comes at the price of complexity. You need to be pretty well versed in XML to validate the use of your tag library. I recommend that you give it a shot and make it your first choice, but it may be overkill for a small library with modest validation needs. If that's the case, you can develop TagExtraInfo subclasses for the individual custom actions that need validation. A TagExtraInfo subclass can validate the use of the action element attributes. Optional attributes may be mutually exclusive—if one is used, the other must not be used—or using one optional attribute may require another optional attribute be used as well. A TagExtraInfo subclass can verify rules like this, but it can't verify that a custom action is used correctly in the JSP page relative to other actions.

After the JSP container has checked everything it can on its own and has used the TagLibraryValidator classes for all libraries used in the page, it looks for TagExtraInfo declarations for each custom action element used in the page:

```
<tag>
  <name>myOptionalAttributesAction</name>
  <tag-class>com.foo.MyOptionalAttributesTag</tag-class>
  <tei-class>com.foo.MyOptionalAttributesTEI</tei-class>
  ...
</tag>
```

If it finds a <tei-class> element for an action, the container creates a TagData instance with the attribute values specified in the action element and calls the TagExtraInfo validate( ) method:

```
public ValidationMessage[] validate(TagData data) {
    ValidationMessage[] vms = null;
    List errors = new ArrayList( );
    // Mutually exclusive attributes: can't mix attr1 and attr2
    if (data.getAttribute("attr1") != null &&
        data.getAttribute("attr2" != null) {
        errors.add(new ValidationMessage(null,
            "'attr1' and 'attr2' are mutually exclusive"));
    }

    // Dependent optional attributes: attr3 requires attr4
    if (data.getAttribute("attr3") != null &&
        data.getAttribute("attr4" == null) {
        errors.add(new ValidationMessage(null, "'attr3' requires 'attr4'"));
    }

    if (errors.size( ) != 0) {
        vms = new ValidationMessage[errors.size( )];
        errors.toArray(vms);
    }
    return vms;
}
```

A TagExtraInfo subclass uses the TagData argument to verify that all attribute dependencies are okay, as in this example, and returns a ValidationMessage[] to report the errors, just as a TagLibraryValidator. The TagExtraInfo instance doesn't have access to the jsp:id attribute, though. A smart container can still produce a friendly error message including the element location, since it knows for which action element it called the validate( ) method.

Using a Listener in a Tag Library

In Chapter 19, I described how to implement various types of listener components, as specified by the Servlet API: servlet context, session and request lifecycle event listeners, session attribute modification listeners, and session activation and passivation event listeners.

If you develop custom actions that interact with a listener in some way (for instance, an action that shows the current number of active sessions maintained by the session lifecycle event listener described in Chapter 19), you can bundle the event listener with your tag library. To get the listeners registered, you just define the listener implementation classes in the TLD for your library using the `<listener>` element (placed after the `<validator>` element):

```
<taglib ...>
  ...
  <listener>
    <listener-class>
      com.ora.jsp.servlets.SessionCounterListener
    </listener-class>
  </listener>
  ...
</taglib>
```

When the container loads the web application, it looks through all TLDs for listener definitions and registers all listeners it finds.

You can use listeners for a number of tasks. For instance, a servlet context lifecycle event listener can initialize resources used by the custom actions in the library (such as a connection pool) when the application starts and shut them down gracefully when it stops. A session lifecycle listener can initialize new sessions or keep track of the number of active sessions.

Dynamic Attribute Values and Types

Throughout this book, you've seen how action element attributes can be given dynamic values, evaluated at runtime. A dynamic attribute value can be assigned by an EL expression, a Java expression (as shown in Chapter 16), or by a `<jsp:attribute>` element.

Not all attributes accept dynamic values, though. To tell the container that a custom action attribute accepts a dynamic value, or a *request-time attribute value* as it's also called, you have to declare this fact in the TLD:

```
<tag>
  <name>geekContestEntry</name>
  <tag-class>com.xmp.GeekContextEntry</tag-class>
  <description>
    Saves the submitted data in the Geek Contest database.
  </description>
  .
  <attribute>
    <name>yearsSinceLastVacation</name>
    <rtexprvalue>true</rtexprvalue>
  </attribute>
  <attribute>
    <name>hoursWithoutSleep</name>
```

```
      <rtexprvalue>true</rtexprvalue>
    </attribute>
    <attribute>
      <name>employersInAMonth</name>
      <rtexprvalue>true</rtexprvalue>
    </attribute>
  </tag>
```

An <rtexprexprvalue> element with the value true enables this feature. You can then assign dynamic values to the attributes in a page like this:

```
<xmp:geekContestEntry
  yearsSinceLastVacation="${param.noVacation}"
  hoursWithoutSleep='<%= request.getParameter("noSleep") %>'>
  <jsp:attribute name="employersInAMonth">
    <xmp:getAvgEmployers id="${param.geekId}" />
  </jsp:attribute>
</xmp:geekContestEntry>
```

An EL expression assigns the value of the noVacation request parameter to the first attribute, a Java expression assigns the noSleep parameter value to the second attribute, and a <jsp:attribute> element assigns the value produced by another custom action to the third attribute.

In the tag handler, each action attribute is implemented as a property setter method that takes one argument (the value), in accordance with the JavaBeans conventions. As with regular beans, the property type for a tag handler attribute can be of any Java type, for instance an int:

```
public setYearsSinceLastVacation(int value) {
    yearsSinceLastVacation = value;
}
```

When a Java expression is used to set the value of the attribute, the return type of the expression must match the Java type declared for the property; otherwise an exception is thrown. For an EL expression, the value is converted to the attribute's type according to the rules described in Table 22-1.

Table 22-1. EL type conversion rules

Attribute Java type	Value conversion rule
String	null: to empty string ("")
	All other types: to the corresponding String value
char or Character	null or empty string: to 0
	String: to the first character
	Numeric types: to the Short value of the number
Primitive number or Number	null: 0
	Character or char: to the value represented by the character code
	String: parse as an Integer or Floating point literal
	Numeric types: to the requested precision

Table 22-1. EL type conversion rules (continued)

Attribute Java type	Value conversion rule
boolean or Boolean	null: to false
	String: to `true` if the value is "true," ignoring case, otherwise `false`
Other type	`null`: keep as `null`
	String: use the `PropertyEditor` for the requested type, if any, otherwise `null` if the string is empty
	Other: type cast, if possible

When the value is set by a `<jsp:attribute>` element, the body is evaluated and the result is converted to a `String`. This value is then converted to the attribute's type according to the rules described next.

Even an attribute that accepts a dynamic value must sometimes be set to a fixed value. Let's look at an example. For an attribute of type `int`, you can assign a fixed value with an EL expression like this:

```
<xmp:geekContestEntry
  yearsSinceLastVacation="${5}"
  ...
/>
```

It would be much nicer, however, if the value could be entered as a regular text value and still be converted to the correct type:

```
<xmp:geekContestEntry
  yearsSinceLastVacation="5"
  ...
/>
```

That's exactly what the container does, with some help from the tag handler developer for types other than the most basic ones. This lets a page author set an action attribute declared to accept a request-time attribute value to either a static text value or a dynamic value. The next two sections describe this mechanism in detail.

Conversions Performed by the Container

The container automatically takes care of the conversion from text values to the most commonly used Java types. A JSP 2.0-compliant container supports the type conversions shown in Table 22-2.

Table 22-2. Conversion of text value to property type

Property type	Conversion method
`boolean` or `Boolean`	`Boolean.valueOf(String), false for an empty string`
`byte` or `Byte`	`Byte.valueOf(String), 0 for an empty string`
`char` or `Character`	`String.charAt(0), 0 for an empty string`

Table 22-2. Conversion of text value to property type (continued)

Property type	Conversion method
`double` or `Double`	`Double.valueOf(String), 0 for an empty string`
`int` or `Integer`	`Integer.valueOf(String), 0 for an empty string`
`float` or `Float`	`Float.valueOf(String), 0 for an empty string`
`long` or `Long`	`Long.valueOf(String), 0 for an empty string`
`short` or `Short`	`Short.valueOf(String), 0 for an empty string`
`Object`	`new String(String)`

These rules apply to attributes for standard actions and custom actions alike.

Using a PropertyEditor for Conversion

If the standard conversion rules are not enough for your needs, you can use a bean `PropertyEditor` to convert a literal string value to any Java data type you like. If an action attribute value is specified as a literal string for an attribute of a type other than `String`, the container looks for a property editor that can convert the string to the attribute's data type. The property editor is also used for EL expressions that evaluate to a `String`, and for `<jsp:attribute>` element values.

Say you have an attribute of type `java.util.Date`. To let the page author specify it as a text value, you need a `PropertyEditor` that converts a `String` to a `Date`. Here's how it's done.

First you implement the `PropertyEditor`:

```
package com.foo;

import java.beans.*;
import java.text.*;
import java.util.*;
public class MyDatePE extends PropertyEditorSupport
    implements PropertyEditor {

    private SimpleDateFormat sdf = new SimpleDateFormat("yyyy-MM-dd");
    private Date value;

    public Object getValue( ) {
        return value;
    }

    public void setAsText(String text)
        throws IllegalArgumentException {

        try {
            value = sdf.parse(text);
        }
        catch (ParseException e) {
```

```
                throw new IllegalArgumentException(e.getMessage( ));
            }
        }
    }
```

The container calls the `setAsText( )` method with the attribute's `String` value. This method creates a `Date` object from the string and saves it in the instance variable named `value`. The container then calls the `getValue( )` method—which returns the new `Date` object—and uses the value to set the action's attribute value.

Simple enough, but you must also tell the container to use your `PropertyEditor` for this action. You can do so by creating a `BeanInfo` class for the action's tag handler:

```
package com.foo;

import java.beans.*;
import java.util.*;
public class MyTagBeanInfo extends SimpleBeanInfo {

    public PropertyDescriptor[] getPropertyDescriptors( ) {
        PropertyDescriptor[] pds = new PropertyDescriptor[4];
        try {
            pds[0] = new PropertyDescriptor("anInt", MyTag.class,
                null, "setAnInt");
            pds[1] = new PropertyDescriptor("aString", MyTag.class,
                null, "setAString");
            pds[2] = new PropertyDescriptor("firstDate", MyTag.class,
                null, "setFirstDate");
            pds[3] = new PropertyDescriptor("secondDate", MyTag.class,
                null, "setSecondDate");
        }
        catch (Exception e) {}

        pds[2].setPropertyEditorClass(MyDatePE.class);
        pds[3].setPropertyEditorClass(MyDatePE.class);
        return pds;
    }
}
```

This `BeanInfo` class is for a tag handler with four attributes, named `anInt`, `aString`, `firstDate`, and `secondDate`. The `getPropertyDescriptors( )` method first creates an array with one `PropertyDescriptor` for each attribute and then sets the property editors for the two `Date` attributes to the `PropertyEditor` class described earlier.

A `BeanInfo` class is automatically bound to its bean class (in this case, the tag handler class is considered to be a bean) through a class-naming convention: the name of the `BeanInfo` class for a bean simply has the same name as the bean class plus "BeanInfo." So in this example, `MyTagBeanInfo` is the `BeanInfo` class for the `MyTag` class. The `MyTag` class is a regular tag handler class. You don't need to do anything special in the tag-handler class itself to use a `PropertyEditor` to convert string values to other types.

CHAPTER 23

Integrating Custom Code with JSTL

In addition to providing a powerful set of JSP actions, the JSTL specification also contains a number of classes and interfaces for setting defaults for the JSTL actions and for developing custom actions that integrate nicely with JSTL actions. Another component of the JSTL specification is a couple of generic tag library validators you can use to enforce policies in your application, such as preventing scripting elements and restricting the set of tag libraries that can be used.

Setting and Using Configuration Variables

Some of the JSTL tag libraries use default values for attributes that are not specified explicitly in the action elements, e.g., the data source to be used by the database actions and the locale used by the I18N actions. As I described in Part II, you can set these default values using context parameters in the deployment descriptor, but you can also set them dynamically using a servlet, filter, or listener. A typical example is a filter or a servlet that sets the locale based on user profile information. The term used for the dynamic settings in the JSTL spec is *configuration variables*, and when combined with a context parameter, it's called a *configuration setting*.

Each configuration setting is identified by a unique name, such as `javax.servlet.jsp.jstl.fmt.locale` for the default locale. This is the name you use when you set a default value through a context parameter:

```
<web-app ...>
  ...
  <context-param>
    <param-name>
      javax.servlet.jsp.jstl.fmt.locale
    </param-name>
    <param-value>
      en-US
    </param-value>
  </context-param>
  ...
</web-app>
```

The same names are used to set, read, and remove the configuration variables programmatically, using a JSTL class called javax.servlet.jsp.jstl.core.Config. It has the following fields:

```
public static final String FMT_LOCALE =
    "javax.servlet.jsp.jstl.fmt.locale";
public static final String FMT_FALLBACK_LOCALE =
    "javax.servlet.jsp.jstl.fmt.fallbackLocale";
public static final String FMT_LOCALIZATION_CONTEXT =
    "javax.servlet.jsp.jstl.fmt.localizationContext";
public static final String FMT_TIME_ZONE =
    "javax.servlet.jsp.jstl.fmt.timeZone";

public static final String SQL_DATA_SOURCE =
    "javax.servlet.jsp.jstl.sql.dataSource";
public static final String SQL_MAX_ROWS =
    "javax.servlet.jsp.jstl.sql.maxRows";
```

The fields are simply constants for all variables names, to make it a bit easier to use the class.

The following get( ) methods read the value of a configuration variable:

```
public static Object get(javax.servlet.jsp.tagext.PageContext page,
    String name, int scope)
public static Object get(javax.servlet.ServletRequest request,
    String name)
public static Object get(javax.servlet.http.HttpSession session,
    String name)
public static Object get(javax.servlet.ServletContext application,
    String name)
```

These methods get a variable value from any scope, the request scope, the session scope, and the application scope, respectively. The method that takes a PageContext instance and a scope identifier as arguments is intended for custom actions, while the others are primarily intended for other component types, such as a servlet, that do not have access to a PageContext. The name argument is the configuration variable name, typically specified using the corresponding constant.

To set a configuration value, use one of the following methods:

```
public static void set(javax.servlet.jsp.tagext.PageContext page,
    String name, Object var, int scope)
public static void set(javax.servlet.ServletRequest request,
    String name, Object var)
public static void set(javax.servlet.http.HttpSession session,
    String name, Object var)
public static void set(javax.servlet.ServletContext application,
    String name, Object var)
```

The set( ) methods set a variable value in any scope, the request scope, the session scope and the application scope, respectively, following the same pattern as the get( ) methods.

The find( ) method scans all scopes in the order page, request, session, and application and returns the first occurrence, or null if it can't find it:

```
public static Object find(javax.servlet.jsp.tagext.PageContext page,
    String name)
```

The remaining methods remove configuration variables:

```
public static void remove(javax.servlet.jsp.tagext.PageContext page,
    String name, int scope)
public static void remove(javax.servlet.ServletRequest request,
    String name)
public static void remove(javax.servlet.http.HttpSession session,
    String name)
public static void remove(javax.servlet.ServletContext application,
    String name)
```

Even though the configuration variables are simply attributes of the objects that represent the different JSP scopes, it's important that you use the Config class methods to manipulate them, instead of calling the setAttribute( ), getAttribute( ), and removeAttribute( ) methods directly on the scope objects. The reason is that the JSP specification states that all scopes should behave as a single namespace,* which means, for instance, that if you set a variable in the page scope, it should replace a variable with the same name in any other scope. The configuration variables, on the other hand, are intended to just temporarily override a value for the same variable in another scope, for instance temporarily override an application scope value with a page or request scope value. To accomplish this in a portable way, the Config class uses implementation-depended attribute names for the configuration variables in each scope (typically, it appends the scope name to the configuration variable name).

To set the locale for the JSTL I18N actions based on a clever combination of the preferences sent with the request headers and the client's IP address, for instance, a controller servlet or a filter can use the Config class like this before asking a JSP page to render the result:

```
import javax.servlet.jsp.jstl.core.Config;
import java.util.Locale;
import javax.servlet.*;
...
Locale prefLocale = getPrefLocale(request);
Config.set(request, Config.FMT_LOCALE, prefLocale);
```

The details about each configuration setting are described in the sections that follow.

* This rule is not enforced by many containers, but breaking it can lead to portability problems between containers that do and those that don't.

Integrating Custom Conditional Actions

The JSTL core library contains one, generic conditional action: <c:if>. This action handles all conditions that can be expressed as Boolean EL expressions, but you often need more than that. Examples from Part II of this book include: testing if a mail address has valid syntax and if the current user belongs to a specific group.

To help developing this type of conditional custom action, JSTL includes a base class called `javax.servlet.jsp.jstl.core.ConditionalTagSupport`:

```
public abstract class ConditionalTagSupport
  extends javax.servlet.jsp.tagext.TagSupport
```

It contains the following public methods:

```
protected abstract boolean condition( ) throws JspTagException
public void setVar(String var)
public void setScope(String scope)
public int doStartTag( ) throws JspException
public void release( )
```

The `doStartTag( )` implementation calls the `condition( )` method and takes care of saving the result if the `var` and `scope` attributes are set.

By extending this class and providing an implementation of the `condition( )` and setter methods for all attributes you need, you get a conditional action that is consistent with the semantics of the JSTL version.

Example 23-1 shows the tag handler class for `<ora:ifUserInRole>`, which takes advantage of this JSTL support class.

Example 23-1. Tag handler for a conditional action

```
package com.ora.jsp.tags;

import javax.servlet.http.*;
import javax.servlet.jsp.*;
import javax.servlet.jsp.jstl.core.*;
import org.apache.taglibs.standard.lang.support.*;

public class IfUserInRoleTag extends ConditionalTagSupport {
    private String value;

    public void setValue(String value) {
        this.value = value;
    }

    public boolean condition( ) throws JspTagException {
        HttpServletRequest request =
            (HttpServletRequest) pageContext.getRequest( );
        return request.isUserInRole(value);
    }
}
```

The only method of interest is `condition( )`. All it does is calling the `isUserInRole( )` method provided by the `HttpServletRequest` class. It's that simple.

You may wonder if there's a similar support class for custom actions to be used within a `<c:choose>` block. The answer is no. Allowing custom actions as alternatives to `<c:when>` can cause strange side-effects, so instead, the recommended model is to use a conditional action, save the result as a variable, and test the variable value with a `<c:when>` action:

```
<ora:ifUserInRole value="admin" var="isAdmin" />
<c:choose>
  <c:when test="${isAdmin}">
    ...
  </c:when>
  <c:otherwise>
    ...
  </c:otherwise>
</c:choose>
```

It's a little bit more work, but it's a clean solution.

Integrating Custom Iteration Actions

JSTL offers two utilities for customized iterations: a support class that can be extended for application-specific iteration actions and interfaces that actions nested in the body of an iteration action can use to get information about the iteration status.

Implementing a Custom Iteration Action

The JSTL `<c:forEach>` action is so flexible that it probably covers most cases, but to help develop application-specific iteration actions when needed, JSTL provides a base class for this as well. It's named `javax.servlet.jsp.jstl.core.LoopTagSupport`:

```
public abstract class LoopTagSupport
  extends javax.servlet.jsp.tagext.TagSupport
  implements javax.servlet.jsp.jstl.core.LoopTag,
    javax.servlet.jsp.tagext.IterationTag,
    javax.servlet.jsp.tagext.TryCatchFinally
```

The class has the following fields a subclass can access:

```
protected int begin
protected int end
protected int step
protected String itemId
protected String statusId
protected boolean beginSpecified
protected boolean endSpecified
protected boolean stepSpecified
```

These variables hold the value of the corresponding attributes. The variable names for the var and varStatus attributes (itemId and statusId) are, unfortunately, not in sync with the attribute names, due to an oversight when the attribute naming conventions where changed. Nobody's perfect. For the int variables, there are also boolean variables that tell whether the corresponding attributes were set.

Here are the main methods a subclass must implement:

```
protected abstract void prepare( )
  throws javax.servlet.jsp.JspTagException
protected abstract Object next( ) throws javax.servlet.jsp.JspTagException
protected abstract boolean hasNext( )
  throws javax.servlet.jsp.JspTagException
```

The prepare( ) method prepares for the iteration, for instance by creating an Iterator for the collection to iterate over. The next( ) method returns the next item from the collection, and the hasNext( ) method tells whether there are more items.

The LoopTagSupport class provides implementations for the standard Tag and TryCatchFinally methods, plus setter methods for the var and varStatus attributes:

```
public void setVar(String varName)
public void setVarStatus(String statusName)
public void doStartTag( ) throws JspException
public void doAfterBody( ) throws JspException
public void doCatch(Throwable t) throws Throwable
public void doFinally( )
public void release( )
```

Setter methods for begin, end, and step must be implemented by the subclass. They are not included in the support class because some subclasses may not want to support these attributes.*

The doStartTag( ) method calls the prepare( ) method. It then calls the hasNext( ) and next( ) methods begin number of times to throw away the items up to the start index (if it's not 0). Next, it calls hasNext( ), and if that returns true, it calls next( ) to advance to the first item to process and saves a reference to this item.

If step is set to a value other than 1, it calls next( ) as many times as needed to advance to the next valid item. Finally it exposes the current item and the status object through the variables defined by var and varStatus, if any, and returns EVAL_BODY_INCLUDE.

The doAfterBody( ) method is similar to doStartTag( ). It calls hasNext( ) to see if there are more items, and if it returns true and the end index has not been reached, it calls next( ), exposes the returned item through var, calls next( ) again to advance according to step, and returns EVAL_BODY_AGAIN.

* Another reason is that before the EL got integrated in the JSP spec, how to deal with dynamic values was best left to each tag handler subclass. This class was introduced in JSTL 1.0, based on JSP 1.2, and the EL processing was then a part of the JSTL specification so it required special processing in the tag handler.

The doCatch( ) method simply rethrows the exception, and doFinally( ) removes the var and varStatus variables, since they are available only to nested actions.

The LoopTagSupport class also provides implementations for the methods defined by the LoopTag interface:

```
public Object getCurrent( ) throws javax.servlet.jsp.JspTagException
public LoopTagStatus getLoopStatus( )
```

This interface can be used by custom actions that depend on the loop status. The getCurrent( ) method returns the current item, and the getLoopStatus( ) method returns a LoopTagStatus instance. I show an example of a custom action that uses this information at the end of this section.

Finally, there are three utility methods for validating the values of the begin, end, and step attribute values:

```
protected void validateBegin( )throws javax.servlet.jsp.JspTagException
protected void validateEnd( )throws javax.servlet.jsp.JspTagException
protected void validateStep( ) throws javax.servlet.jsp.JspTagException
```

A custom action should use these to make sure the basic requirements for these values are satisfied: begin and end must be greater than or equal to 0, and step must be greater than or equal to 1.

To see how you can use all of this in a custom iteration action, let's develop an action that helps generate HTML form elements for selecting predefined values, such as a selection list or a group of checkboxes or radio buttons. The custom action can be used as shown in Example 23-2.

Example 23-2. Using a custom iteration action

```
<form action="validate.jsp">
  <xmp:forEachOption options="${options}"
    selections="${paramValues.choice}" var="current">
    <input type="checkbox" name="choice"
      value="${current.value}" ${current.selected ? 'checked' : ''}>
      ${current.text}
    <br>
  </xmp:forEachOption>
  <input type="submit">
</form>
```

The <xmp:forEachOption> action takes a Map as the value of the options attribute. The Map contains keys representing the text and value for each option. The selections attribute takes an array of String objects, each representing the value for an option that should be marked as selected. The action uses this information to expose a bean with three properties to the actions in its body: text, value, and selected. The first two are the key and value of the current Map entry, while the third is a boolean with the value true if the value for the current entry is present in the selections list. As shown in Example 23-2, EL expressions use the bean properties to set the checkbox value and text and test if the checked attribute should be set.

Extending the LoopTagSupport class makes it easy to implement this action. The complete class is shown in Example 23-3.

Example 23-3. The ForEachOptionTag class

```
package com.ora.jsp.tags.xmp;

import java.util.*;
import java.lang.reflect.Array;
import javax.servlet.jsp.*;
import javax.servlet.jsp.jstl.core.*;
import org.apache.taglibs.standard.lang.support.*;
import com.ora.jsp.util.StringFormat;

public class ForEachOptionTag extends LoopTagSupport {
    private Map options;
    private String[] selections;
    private Iterator iterator;

    public void setOptions(Map options) {
        this.options = options;
    }

    public void setSelections(String[] selections) {
        this.selections = selections;
    }

    protected void prepare( ) {
        if (options != null) {
            iterator = options.entrySet().iterator( );
        }
    }

    protected boolean hasNext( ) {
        if (iterator == null) {
            return false;
        }
        else {
            return iterator.hasNext( );
        }
    }

    protected Object next( ) {
        Map.Entry me = (Map.Entry) iterator.next( );
        String text = (String) me.getKey( );
        String value = (String) me.getValue( );
        boolean selected = isSelected(value);
        return new OptionBean(text, value, selected);
    }

    private boolean isSelected(String value) {
        return StringFormat.isValidString(value, selections, false);
    }
```

Example 23-3. The ForEachOptionTag class (continued)

```
    public class OptionBean {
        private String text;
        private String value;
        private boolean selected;

        public OptionBean(String text, String value, boolean selected) {
            this.text = text;
            this.value = value;
            this.selected = selected;
        }

        public String getText( ) {
            return text;
        }

        public String getValue( ) {
            return value;
        }

        public boolean isSelected( ) {
            return selected;
        }
    }
}
```

The only things you need to implement are setter methods for the two unique attributes and the three iteration methods: `prepare( )`, `hasNext( )`, and `next( )`. The `LoopTagSupport` class takes care of the rest.

The `prepare( )` method saves a reference to the `Iterator` for the `Map` entries in an instance variable, unless the `options` attribute value is `null`. In this case, the action should simply do nothing, just as the `<c:forEach>` action.

The `hasNext( )` method returns `false` if the `options` attribute is `null` and calls `hasNext( )` on the `Iterator` created by `prepare( )` if not.

The real magic happens in the `next( )` method. This method can be called only if `hasNext( )` returns `true`, so we don't have to worry about the `Iterator` being `null`. First, the next entry is retrieved from the `Iterator`, and the `text` and `value` values are extracted. Then the private `isSelected( )` method sets the `selected` value, and a bean with the text, value, and selected flag is returned. The `LoopTagSupport` class exposes this bean as the current item through the variable specified by the `var` attribute.

The rest is just plain old Java code. The bean class is defined as an inner class, with a constructor for all property values and getter methods for each property. The `isSelected( )` method uses a utility class that's bundled with the source code for this book to see if the specified value is included in the list of selected values.

Interacting with an Iteration Action

The JSTL specification also defines two interfaces for iteration actions. The `javax.servlet.jsp.jstl.core.LoopTag` interface must be implemented by iteration actions that want to cooperate with actions nested in their bodies:

```
public interface LoopTag extends javax.servlet.jsp.tagext.Tag
```

It defines two methods nested actions can call:

```
public java.lang.Object getCurrent( )
public LoopTagStatus getLoopStatus( )
```

The `getCurrent( )` method returns the current object in the collection the action iterates over. The `getLoopStatus( )` returns an object that implements the other JSTL iteration interface: `javax.servlet.jsp.jstl.core.LoopTagStatus`.

Before we look at the `LoopTagStatus` interface, let's see how a custom action can use the `LoopTag` interface. Example 23-4 shows how such a custom action can be used for the same purpose as the custom iteration action described earlier, namely to generate an HTML checkbox element with the `checked` attribute set depending on a dynamic list of selections.

Example 23-4. Using a custom action that gets the iteration status from its parent

```
<form action="foreachoption.jsp">
  <c:forEach items="${options}">
    <xmp:buildCheckbox name="choice"
      selections="${paramValues.choice}" />
    <br>
  </c:forEach>
  <input type="submit">
</form>
```

Here the JSTL `<c:forEach>` action loops through a `Map` with option texts and values, the same way as in the previous example. The `<xmp:buildCheckbox>` action generates a checkbox element using the specified name as the `name` attribute value, the current `Map` entry value as the `value` attribute, and the current `Map` entry key as the text. To decide whether to set the `checked` attribute or not, it checks if the current `Map` entry value is included in the list specified by the `selections` attribute.

Example 23-5 shows the code for the custom action.

Example 23-5. The BuildCheckboxTag class

```
package com.ora.jsp.tags.xmp;

import java.io.*;
import java.util.*;
import java.lang.reflect.Array;
import javax.servlet.jsp.*;
import javax.servlet.jsp.tagext.*;
```

Example 23-5. The BuildCheckboxTag class (continued)

```
import javax.servlet.jsp.jstl.core.*;
import org.apache.taglibs.standard.lang.support.*;
import com.ora.jsp.util.StringFormat;

public class BuildCheckboxTag extends TagSupport {
    private String name;
    private String[] selections;

    public void setName(String name) {
        this.name = name;
    }

    public void setSelections(String[] selections) {
        this.selections = selections;
    }

    public int doEndTag( ) throws JspException {
        LoopTag parent =
            (LoopTag) findAncestorWithClass(this, LoopTag.class);
        if (parent == null) {
            throw new JspTagException("buildCheckbox: invalid parent");
        }

        Map.Entry current = (Map.Entry) parent.getCurrent( );
        String text = (String) current.getKey( );
        String value = (String) current.getValue( );
        JspWriter out = pageContext.getOut( );
        StringBuffer checkbox =
            new StringBuffer("<input type=\"checkbox\"");
        checkbox.append(" name=\"").append(name).append("\"").
            append(" value=\"").append(value).append("\"");
        if (isSelected(value, selections)) {
            checkbox.append(" checked");
        }
        checkbox.append(">").append(text);
        try {
            out.write(checkbox.toString( ));
        }
        catch (IOException e) {}
        return EVAL_PAGE;
    }

    private boolean isSelected(String value, String[] selections) {
        return StringFormat.isValidString(value, selections, false);
    }
}
```

The `doEndTag( )` method is where all the action takes place. The parent tag is located using the `findAncestorWithClass( )` method from Chapter 22. Note how the `LoopTag` interface is specified as the type of parent to look for. With a reference to a `LoopTag` parent in hand, the current iteration object is retrieved simply by calling the getCurrent( ) method. The key and the value is extracted and used as the text and value for the generated <input> element, and the checked attribute is set if the current value matches one in the selections list.

This custom action doesn't need the detailed status information provided by the LoopTagStatus interface, but it's as easy to get as the current iteration object; just call the parent's getLoopStatus( ) method. The LoopTagStatus interface provide a wealth of information through the following methods:

```
public java.lang.Object getCurrent( )
public int getIndex( )
public int getCount( )
public boolean isFirst( )
public boolean isLast( )
public Integer getBegin( )
public Integer getEnd( )
public Integer getStep( )
```

The getIndex( ) method returns the actual 0-based index of the current element in the collection, while getCount( ) returns the 1-based number for the current iteration. For example, for the second pass through the body of a <c:forEach> action with begin set to 10, getIndex( ) returns 11, and getCount( ) returns 2. The isFirst( ) and isLast( ) methods returns true for the first and last iteration, respectively, taking the values of begin, end, and step into consideration. The other methods are self-explanatory.

You can use the methods in this interface for custom actions that should do something only at certain points in the iteration, for instance for every second pass or only for the first or last pass.

Integrating Custom I18N Actions

The default locale, resource bundle, and time zone for the JSTL I18N actions can be specified through four configuration settings, described in Tables 23-1 through 23-4.

Table 23-1. Locale configuration setting

Variable name:	Javax.servlet.jsp.jstl.fmt.locale
Java constant:	Config.FMT_LOCALE
Java type:	String or java.util.Locale
Set by:	<fmt:setLocale>, context parameter, or custom code
Used by:	<fmt:bundle>, <fmt:setBundle>, <fmt:message>, <fmt:formatNumber>, <fmt:parseNumber>, <fmt:formatDate>, and <fmt:parseDate>

Table 23-2. Fallback locale configuration setting

Variable name:	javax.servlet.jsp.jstl.fmt.fallbackLocale
Java constant:	Config.FMT_FALLBACK_LOCALE
Java type:	String or java.util.Locale

Table 23-2. Fallback locale configuration setting (continued)

Setby:	Context parameter or custom code
Used by:	`<fmt:bundle>`, `<fmt:setBundle>`, `<fmt:message>`, `<fmt:formatNumber>`, `<fmt:parseNumber>`, `<fmt:formatDate>`, and `<fmt:parseDate>`

Table 23-3. Localization context configuration setting

Variable name:	`javax.servlet.jsp.jstl.fmt.localizationContext`
Java constant:	`Config.FMT_LOCALIZATION_CONTEXT`
Java type:	`String` or `javax.servlet.jsp.jstl.fmt.LocalizationContext`
Set by:	`<fmt:setBundle>`, context parameter, or custom code
Used by:	`<fmt:message>`, `<fmt:formatNumber>`, `<fmt:parseNumber>`, `<fmt:formatDate>`, and `<fmt:parseDate>`

Table 23-4. Time zone configuration setting

Variable name:	`javax.servlet.jsp.jstl.fmt.timeZone`
Java constant:	`Config.FMT_TIME_ZONE`
Java type:	`String` or `java.util.TimeZone`
Set by:	`<fmt:setTimeZone>`, context parameter, or custom code
Used by:	`<fmt:formatDate>` and `<fmt:parseDate>`

Setting the locale variable disables the lookup of a locale based on user preferences (passed through the `Accept-Language` header value), while setting the fallback locale variable preserves this feature and provides a default value that is used only if none of the preferred locales are available. When `String` values are used to set these two variables, they must be specified as a two-letter lowercase ISO-639 language code, optionally followed by a two-letter uppercase ISO-3166 country code, separated by a hyphen or an underscore character.

The localization context variable can be set to a `String` value containing the name of the default resource bundle base name. The formatting actions then locate the locale-specific version of this bundle. The `<fmt:setBundle>` sets the variable to an instance of the `LocalizationContext` class, which contains references to both a locale and a resource bundle for a locale.

`String` values for the time-zone setting must be of the type defined for the `java.util.TimeZone` class: an abbreviation, a full name, or a GMT offset.

The configuration variables can be set by the calling the `Config.set( )` methods, as described earlier in this chapter. It can be used to simplify the JSP pages in an application with a Controller implemented in Java and JSP only for the View part. For instance, the Controller may pick up the preferred locale and time zone from a database when a user logs in and sets the corresponding configuration settings.

If you develop custom actions that need to produce localized text, you can piggyback on the locale-lookup logic provided by JSTL by using the `javax.servlet.jsp.jstl.fmt.LocaleSupport` class. It provides the following methods:

```
public static String getLocalizedMessage(PageContext pc, String key)
public static String getLocalizedMessage(PageContext pc, String key,
    String basename)

public static String getLocalizedMessage(PageContext pc, String key,
    Object[] args)
public static String getLocalizedMessage(PageContext pc, String key,
    Object[] args, String basename)
```

There are two sets of methods. The first is for simple messages and the second for parameterized messages. In each set, one method has a `basename` parameter and one doesn't. The versions without the `basename` parameter rely on the localization context configuration setting to find the resource bundle to get the message from, and the others locate the locale-specific resource bundle for the specified base name. Both sets return the localized message for the specified key.

Integrating Custom Database Actions

The JSTL database access actions look for the default values set by the configuration settings described in Tables 23-5 and 23-6.

Table 23-5. Data-source configuration setting

Variable name:	`javax.servlet.jsp.jstl.sql.dataSource`
Java constant:	`Config.SQL_DATA_SOURCE`
Java type:	`String` or `javax.sql.DataSource`
Set by:	`<sql:setDataSource>`, context parameter or custom code
Used by:	`<sql:query>`, `<sql:update>`, and `<sql:transaction>`

Table 23-6. Maximum rows configuration setting

Variable name:	`javax.servlet.jsp.jstl.sql.maxRows`
Java constant:	`Config.SQL_MAX_ROWS`
Java type:	`String` or `Integer`
Set by:	Context parameter or custom code
Used by:	`<sql:query>`

The data-source setting can be set as a `String` in this format, in which optional parts are shown between brackets:

```
url [, [driver] [, [user] [, [password]]]
```

Commas separate the parts, so if the value for any part contains a comma, it must be escaped with a backslash. This type of value creates a simple `DataSource` without any pooling capabilities, and is intended only for prototype and low-end applications, as described in Chapter 12. It can also be set to a JNDI path for a DataSource made available by the container or to a DataSource created by custom code, such as a servlet or listener. These options are described in detail in Chapter 24.

The maximum rows setting can be set as a String value for a context parameter or as an Integer by custom code. It can be used to prevent runaway queries, because it sets a limit for how many rows are retrieved for a query result.

There are also two support classes related to the JSTL database actions. The javax.servlet.jsp.jstl.sql.SQLExcecutionTag interface is implemented by the tag handlers for both <sql:query> and <sql:update>. It provides one method that allows a nested custom action to add a value for a parameter placeholder in the SQL statement:

```
public void addSQLParameter(Object value)
```

The value must be of a type that is accepted for the corresponding column when set by calling java.sql.PreparedStatement.setObject(int index, Object value).

The ResultSupport class provides methods for converting a JDBC ResultSet into a JSTL Result object, described in Chapter 12:

```
public static Result toResult(java.sql.ResultSet rs)
public static Result toResult(java.sql.ResultSet rs, int maxRows)
```

I'll show you an example of how to use it in Chapter 24.

Using JSTL Tag Library Validators

JSP 1.2 introduced a powerful mechanism for validation of the elements used in a page: the tag library validator described in Chapter 22. JSTL includes two generic validators you can configure and use in your application to control how scripting elements and custom tag libraries are used.

The ScriptFreeTLV class is a validator that can be configured to reject pages with scripting elements. To use it, you can include it in the TLD for your custom library or create a TLD file that defines it as the validator for a dummy library, used only for validation:

```
<?xml version="1.0" encoding="ISO-8859-1" ?>
<taglib xmlns="http://java.sun.com/xml/ns/j2ee"
  xmlns:xsi="http://www.w3.org/2001/XMLSchema-instance"
  xsi:schemaLocation="http://java.sun.com/xml/ns/j2ee
    http://java.sun.com/xml/ns/j2ee/web-jsptaglibrary_2_0.xsd"
  version="2.0">

  <description>
    Validates JSP pages to prohibit use of scripting elements.
  </description>
  <tlib-version>1.1</tlib-version>
  <short-name>scriptfree</scriptfree>
```

```
  <uri>http://mycompany.org/taglibs/scriptfree</uri>

  <validator>
    <validator-class>
      javax.servlet.jsp.jstl.tlv.ScriptFreeTLV
    </validator-class>
    <init-param>
      <param-name>allowDeclarations</param-name>
      <param-value>false</param-value>
    </init-param>
    <init-param>
      <param-name>allowScriptlets</param-name>
      <param-value>false</param-value>
    </init-param>
    <init-param>
      <param-name>allowExpressions</param-name>
      <param-value>true</param-value>
    </init-param>
    <init-param>
      <param-name>allowRTExpressions</param-name>
      <param-value>true</param-value>
    </init-param>
  </validator>
</taglib>
```

The initialization parameters define which type of scripting elements to accept and reject. By default, all are rejected. Starting with JSP 2.0, you can disable all types of scripting elements with a configuration setting in the *web.xml* file. I recommend that option, but this validator is still available and can be used if you need more fine-grained control.

The `PermittedTaglibsTLV` can limit the set of tag libraries that are used in a page:

```
<?xml version="1.0" encoding="ISO-8859-1" ?>
<taglib xmlns="http://java.sun.com/xml/ns/j2ee"
  xmlns:xsi="http://www.w3.org/2001/XMLSchema-instance"
  xsi:schemaLocation="http://java.sun.com/xml/ns/j2ee
    http://java.sun.com/xml/ns/j2ee/web-jsptaglibrary_2_0.xsd"
  version="2.0">

  <description>
    Validates JSP pages to only allow a defined set of tag libraries.
  </description>
  <tlib-version>1.1</tlib-version>
  <short-name>onlyJSTL</scriptfree>
  <uri>http://mycompany.org/taglibs/onlyJSTL</uri>

  <validator>
    <validator-class>
      javax.servlet.jsp.jstl.tlv.PermittedTaglibsTLV
    </validator-class>
    <init-param>
      <param-name>permittedTaglibs</param-name>
      <param-value>
```

```
        http://java.sun.com/jsp/jstl/core
        http://java.sun.com/jsp/jstl/xml
        http://java.sun.com/jsp/jstl/fmt
        http://java.sun.com/jsp/jstl/sql
        http://java.sun.com/jsp/jstl/functions
      </param-value>
    </init-param>
  </validator>
</taglib>
```

Here it's configured to allow only the JSTL 1.1 libraries to be used. You can, of course, add other custom tag libraries that should be permitted to the list.

Including `taglib` directives that should be checked activates the validators:

```
<%@ taglib prefix="scriptfree" uri="http://mycompany.org/taglibs/scriptfree" %>
<%@ taglib prefix="onlyJSTL" uri="http://mycompany.org/taglibs/onlyJSTL" %>
```

To make sure all pages include these directives, you may want to create a file that contains these `taglib` directives plus the `taglib` directives for all real tag libraries that you use for the application. You can then include this file in all JSP pages using the *web.xml* prelude configuration element described in Chapter 17, instead of including the `taglib` directives in every page.

CHAPTER 24

Database Access Strategies

In this final chapter, we take a closer look at the strategies for using a database in a web application that I've mentioned in the previous chapters.

In case you're new to Java database access, we start with a brief overview of the most important JDBC classes and interfaces. Next, we focus in on the JDBC `Connection` class and how pooling `Connection` objects helps to solve a number of common problems. We look at two ways to implement connection-pooling capabilities: the JDBC 2.0 way and using a JDBC 1.0 connection pool that simulates a JDBC 2.0 pool.

A connection pool can be made available to the rest of the application—servlets as well as the JSTL database access actions—in a number of ways. In this chapter we discuss the approach used in Chapter 19 (using an application event listener) in more detail, as well as an approach that's more flexible but that only works in web containers that support the Java Naming and Directory Interface (JNDI).

No matter if you use a servlet or a custom action to access the database, there are a number of JDBC details that must be handled. To help with this grunt work, we look at a generic database access bean that simplifies life and makes the result of a query easy to use. The last section contains an example of an application-specific custom action using this bean.

If you need to learn more about JDBC programming than what's covered here, I recommend that you look at the JDBC documentation online at *http://java.sun.com/products/jdbc/* or read a book about JDBC, such as George Reese's *Database Programming with JDBC and Java* (O'Reilly) or *Java Database Best Practices* (O'Reilly)—which also covers how to use Java Database Objects (JDO) and Enterprise JavaBeans (EJB) for database access.

JDBC Basics

The JDBC API is a set of classes and interfaces that allows a Java application to send SQL statements to a database in a vendor-independent way. The API consists mostly of interfaces that define the methods you use in your program. Database engine vendors and third parties provide implementations of these interfaces for a specific database engine; such an implementation is called a *JDBC driver*. This allows you to develop your program in a database-independent way and connect to a specific database engine by plugging in the appropriate JDBC driver at deployment time. There are JDBC drivers for most database engines on the market, both commercial and open source. If you can't get one from your vendor, check out Sun's list of third-party drivers at *http://industry.java.sun.com/products/jdbc/drivers*.

Figure 24-1 shows how the main interfaces and classes are related.

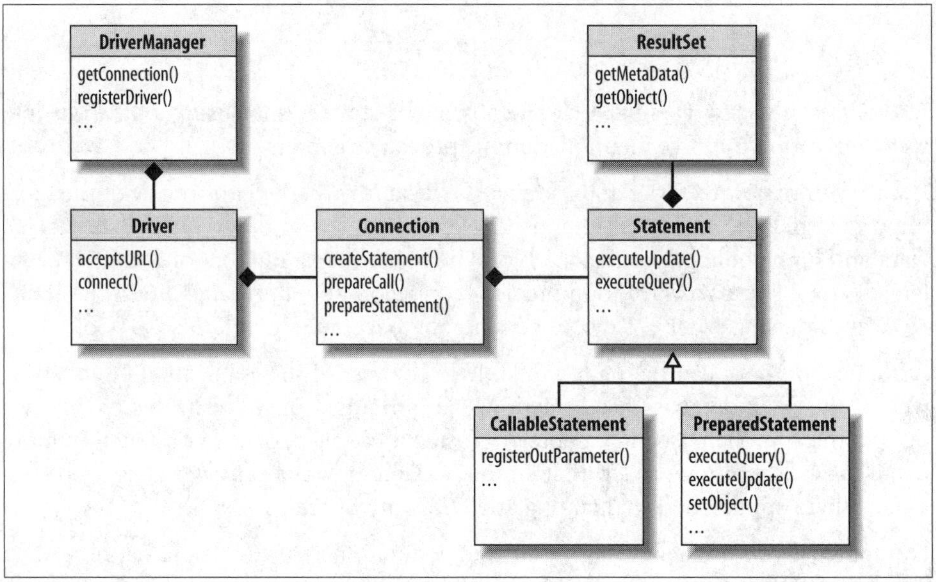

Figure 24-1. Main JDBC interfaces and classes

All JDBC core classes and interfaces belong to the `java.sql` package. Of the types shown in Figure 24-1, only the `DriverManager` is a class (part of the standard J2SE package); the rest are interfaces implemented by each unique JDBC driver.

The `Driver` implementation is the entry point to all the other interface implementations. When the `Driver` is loaded, it register itself with the `DriverManager`. When the JDBC application needs a connection to a database, it asks the `DriverManager` for one, and the `DriverManager` asks each registered `Driver` if it knows how to create connections for the requested database. When a `Driver` replies "yes," the `DriverManager` asks it for a `Connection` on the application's behalf; the `Driver` attempts to create one and return it to the application.

The `Connection` is another core JDBC type. Through the `Connection` instance, the JDBC application can create `Statement` instances of different types. The main `Statement` type can execute a plain SQL statement, such as SELECT, UPDATE, or

DELETE. When a SELECT statement is executed, the result is returned as an instance of ResultSet. The ResultSet has methods for navigating the result rows and asking for the column values in the current row.

There are two specialized Statement types: PreparedStatement and CallableStatement. For a PreparedStatement, you can specify an SQL statement where, instead of literal column values, the statement contains parameter placeholders, symbolized by question marks:

```
SELECT * FROM Enployee WHERE UserName = ?
```

Special setter methods assign values to the placeholders before the SQL statement is executed. The same PreparedStatement can then be assigned new placeholder values and executed again. This allows a database to parse the statement once, typically caching a strategy for how to execute it in the most efficient way, and then execute it over and over again with new values. This can result in dramatically improved performance over using a regular Statement. The PreparedStatement is also useful in other ways, as we will discuss later.

The CallableStatement is for stored procedures. The same as for a PreparedStatement, you can assign values to input arguments, but in addition, there are methods for declaring the types of output arguments.

Other interfaces in the JDBC API provide access to metadata about the database and the JDBC driver itself (DatabaseMetaData, available from the Connection, containing information about supported features) as well as about a ResultSet (ResultSetMetaData, available from the ResultSet, containing information about column data types, null values, etc.).

To see how it all fits together, here's a simple program that uses most of these classes:

```
import java.sql.*;
public class DBTest {
    public static void main(String[] args) throws Exception {
        // Load the JDBC Driver
        Class.forName("oracle.jdbc.OracleDriver");

        // Get a Connection
        String url = "jdbc:oracle:thin:@myhost:1521:ORASID";
        Connection conn = DriverManager.getConnection(url, "scott",
            "tiger");

        ResultSet rs = null;
        PreparedStatement pstmt = null;
        String sql = "SELECT * From Employee WHERE UserName = ?";
        try {
            pstmt = conn.prepareStatement(sql);
            pstmt.setString(1, "hans");
            rs = pstmt.executeQuery( );
```

```
                while (rs.next( )) {
                    System.out.println(rs.getString("FirstName"));
                    System.out.println(rs.getString("LastName"));
                }
            }
            finally {
                if (rs != null) {
                    try {rs.close( );} catch (SQLException e) {}
                }
                if (pstmt != null) {
                    try {pstmt.close( );} catch (SQLException e) {}
                }
                if (conn != null) {
                    try {conn.close( );} catch (SQLException e) {}
                }
            }
        }
    }
```

It first loads a `Driver` (an Oracle JDBC driver in this example) and then gets a `Connection`. The `getConnection( )` argument is a JDBC URL that identifies a specific database. Different JDBC drivers use different URL syntax. All JDBC URLs starts with `jdbc:` followed by a JDBC driver identifier, such as `oracle:` for Oracle's drivers. The rest of the URL is used to identify other details for the driver and database instance. For the Oracle driver used here, it's the type of driver, the host and port where the database runs, and the database instance system identifier. Consult the documentation for your JDBC driver to see how the URL should look like if you use a different driver.

The program then creates a `PreparedStatement` for an SQL statement with a placeholder symbol, assigns a value to the placeholder, executes the query, and loops through all result rows represented by the `ResultSet`.

To run a program that uses JDBC, you need to include the JDBC driver classes for your database in the class path. They are typically delivered as a JAR file, so for a web application you just place the JAR file in the *WEB-INF/lib* directory. If they are delivered as a ZIP file (as some of Oracle's JDBC drivers are, for instance), you can still place it in the *WEB-INF/lib* directory if you change the file extension from *.zip* to *.jar*.

Using Connections and Connection Pools

In a JDBC-based application, a lot revolves around the `java.sql.Connection` interface. Before any database operations can take place, the application must create a `Connection` to the database. It then acts as the communication channel between the application and the database, carrying the SQL statements sent by the application and the results returned by the database. A `Connection` is associated with a database user account to allow the database to enforce access control rules for the SQL statements submitted through the `Connection`. Finally, the `Connection` is also the boundary for database transactions. Only SQL statements executed through the same `Connection` can make up a transaction. A transaction consists of a number of SQL statements that must either all succeed or all fail as one atomic operation. A transaction can be committed (the changes resulting from the statements are permanently saved) or rolled back (all changes are ignored) by calling `Connection` methods.

In a standalone application, a `Connection` is typically created once and kept open until the application is shut down. This isn't surprising, since a standalone application serves only one user at a time, and all database operations initiated by a single user are typically related to each other. In a server application that deals with unrelated requests from many different users, it's not so obvious how to deal with connections. There are three things to consider: a `Connection` is time-consuming to create, it must be used for only one user at a time to avoid transaction clashes, and it's expensive to keep open.

Creating a `Connection` is an operation that can actually take a second or two to perform. Besides establishing a network connection to the database, the database engine must authenticate the user and create a context with various data structures to keep track of transactions, cached statements, results, and so forth. Creating a new `Connection` for each request received by the server, while simple to implement, is far too time-consuming in a high-traffic server application.

One way to minimize the number of times a connection needs to be created is to keep one `Connection` per servlet or JSP page that need access to the database. A `Connection` can be created when the web resource is initialized and be kept in an instance variable until the application is shut down. As you will discover when you deploy an application based on this approach, this route leads to numerous multithreading issues. Each request executes as a separate thread through the same servlet or JSP page. Some JDBC drivers don't support multiple threads accessing the same `Connection` at all, causing all kinds of runtime errors. Others support it by serializing all calls, leading to poor scalability. Another serious problem with this approach is that requests from multiple users, all using the same `Connection`, operate within the same transaction. If one request leads to a rollback, all other database operations using the same `Connection` are also rolled back.

A connection is expensive to keep open in terms of server resources such as memory. Many commercial database products use licenses that are priced based on the number of simultaneously open connections, so a connection can also be expensive in terms of real money. Therefore, it's wise to try to minimize the number of connections the application needs. An alternative to the "one `Connection` per resource" approach is to create a `Connection` for each user when the first request is received and keep it as a session scope object. However, a drawback with this approach is that the `Connection` will be inactive most of the time, because the user needs time to look at the result of one request before making the next.

The best alternative is to use a connection pool. A *connection pool* contains a number of `Connection` objects shared by all servlets and JSP pages. For each request, one `Connection` is checked out from the pool, used, and checked back in. Using a pool solves the problems described for the other alternatives:

It's time consuming to create a Connection
: A pooled `Connection` is created only once and then reused. Most pool implementations let you specify an initial number of `Connection` objects to create at start up, as well as a maximum number. New `Connection` objects are created as needed up to the maximum number. Once the maximum number has been reached, the pool clients wait until an existing `Connection` object becomes available instead of creating a new one.

There are multithreading problems with a shared Connection
: With a pool, each request gets its own `Connection` so it's used by only one thread at a time, eliminating any potential multithreading issues.

A Connection is a limited resource
: With a pool, each `Connection` is used efficiently. It never sits idle if there are requests pending. If the pool allows you to specify a maximum number of `Connection` objects, you can also balance a license limit for the number of simultaneous connections against acceptable response times.

A connection pool doesn't solve all problems, however. Because all users are using the same `Connection` objects, you can't rely on the database engine to limit access to protected data on a per-user basis. Instead, you have to define data-access rules in terms of roles (groups of users with the same access rights). You can then use separate pools for different roles, each pool creating `Connection` objects with a database account that represents the role.

Using a JDBC 2.0 Optional Package Connection Pool

Connection pools exist in many forms. You find them in books, articles, and on the Web. Yet prior to JDBC 2.0, there was no standard defined for how a Java application would interact with a connection pool. The JDBC 2.0 Optional Package (formerly known as a Standard Extension), now part of JDBC 3.0 and included in the Java SDK 1.4, changed this by introducing a set of interfaces that connection pools should implement:

`javax.sql.DataSource`
: A `DataSource` represents a database. This is the interface the application always uses to get a `Connection`. The class that implements the interface can provide connection-pooling capabilities or hand out regular, unpooled `Connection` objects; the application code is identical for both cases, as described later.

`javax.sql.ConnectionPoolDataSource`

A `DataSource` implementation that provides pooling capabilities uses a class that implements the `ConnectionPoolDataSource` interface. A `ConnectionPoolDataSource` is a factory for `PooledConnection` objects. The application code never calls methods in this interface directly.

`javax.sql.PooledConnection`

The objects a `DataSource` with pooling capabilities keeps in its pool implement the `PooledConnection` interface. When the application asks the `DataSource` for a `Connection`, it locates an available `PooledConnection` object or gets a new one from its `ConnectionPoolDataSource` if the pool is empty.

The `PooledConnection` provides a `getConnection( )` method that returns a `Connection` object. The `DataSource` calls this method and returns the `Connection` to the application. This `Connection` object behaves like a regular `Connection` with one exception: when the application calls the `close( )` method, instead of closing the connection to the database, it informs the `PooledConnection` it belongs to that it's no longer used. The `PooledConnection` relays this information to the `DataSource`, which returns the `PooledConnection` to the pool.

Figure 24-2 outlines how an application uses implementations of these interfaces to obtain a pooled connection and how to return it to the pool.

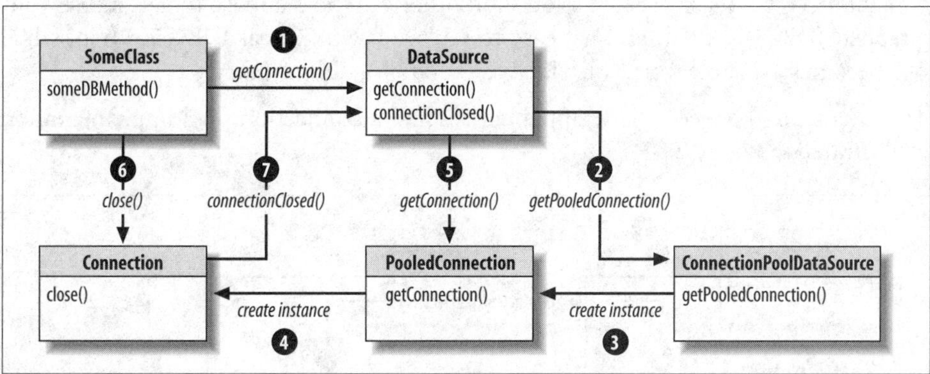

Figure 24-2. Application using a JDBC connection pool

The application calls the `DataSource` `getConnection( )` method. The `DataSource` looks for an available `PooledConnection` object in its pool. If it doesn't find one, it uses its `ConnectionPoolDataSource` object to create a new one. It then calls the `getConnection( )` method on the `PooledConnection` object and returns the `Connection` object associated with the `PooledConnection`. The application uses the `Connection` and calls its `close( )` method when it's done. This results in a notification event being sent to the `DataSource`, which puts the corresponding `PooledConnection` object back in the pool. If you would like to learn more about the JDBC 2.0 connection pool model, you can download the JDBC 2.0 Optional Package specification or the JDBC 3.0 specification from *http://java.sun.com/products/jdbc/*.

By implementing these JDBC 2.0 interfaces, JDBC driver vendors and middleware vendors can offer portable connection pooling implementations. The latest version of the JDBC specification, JDBC 3.0, adds *statement pooling* to the list of features a `DataSource` can provide. What this means is that in addition to pooling connections, an implementation can pool prepared statements associated with each pooled connection. The result can be dramatically improved performance, while leaving the application untouched; it doesn't need to do anything different compared to using a JDBC 2.0 `DataSource`. When I write this, very few (if any) vendors offer statement pooling, but you should ask your vendor if they support it.

Making a JDBC 1.0 Connection Pool Behave as a JDBC 2.0 Connection Pool

If you can't find a JDBC 2.0 connection pool implementation for your database, there are plenty of implementations based on JDBC 1.0 available. A popular one is the `DBConnectionBroker`, available at *http://www.javaexchange.com/*. Another one, DBCP, is developed by the Jakarta Commons project: *http://jakarta.apache.org/commons/index.html* and is bundled with Tomcat. In this section I describe a couple of wrapper classes you can use with minimal changes for implementations like these so they can be used in place of a JDBC 2.0 connection pool implementation. This way the JSTL database access actions and other generic database tools can use your wrapped JDBC 1.0 pool, and it's easy to replace it with a real JDBC 2.0 pool when one becomes available from your database vendor or a third party.

The interaction between the wrapper classes and a connection pool implementation is illustrated in Figure 24-3.

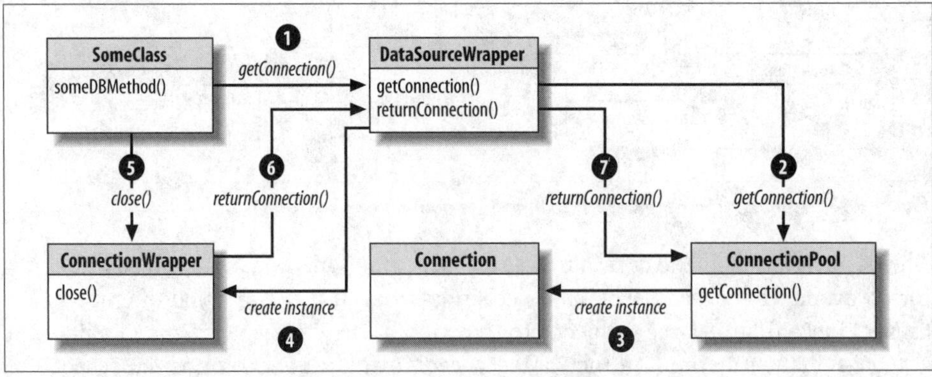

Figure 24-3. A connection pool wrapped with JDBC 2.0 interface classes

The application calls the `DataSourceWrapper` `getConnection()` method. The `DataSourceWrapper` obtains a `Connection` object from its `ConnectionPool` object (which represents the JDBC 1.0 pool implementation). The `ConnectionPool` either finds an available `Connection` in its pool or creates a new one. The `DataSourceWrapper` creates a new ConnectionWrapper object for the Connection it obtained or created and returns the ConnectionWrapper to the application. The application uses the ConnectionWrapper object as a regular Connection. The ConnectionWrapper relays all calls to the corresponding method in the Connection it wraps except for the close( ) method. When the application calls the close( ) method, the ConnectionWrapper returns its Connection to the DataSourceWrapper, which in turn returns it to its ConnectionPool.

The wrapper classes included with the book examples wrap the connection pool described in *Java Servlet Programming* by Jason Hunter and William Crawford (O'Reilly). It's a simple connection pool implementation, intended only to illustrate the principles of connection pooling. The source code for the connection pool is included with the code for this book, but I will not discuss the implementation of the pool itself, only how to make it look like a JDBC 2.0 connection pool using the wrapper classes. For production use, I recommend that you use a pool intended for real use instead of this code, such as one of the implementations mentioned earlier. The first wrapper class is called com.ora.jsp.sql.ConnectionWrapper, shown in Example 24-1.

Example 24-1. The ConnectionWrapper class

```
package com.ora.jsp.sql;

import java.sql.*;
import java.util.*;

class ConnectionWrapper implements Connection {
    private Connection realConn;
    private DataSourceWrapper dsw;
    private boolean isClosed = false;

    public ConnectionWrapper(Connection realConn,
        DataSourceWrapper dsw) {
        this.realConn = realConn;
        this.dsw = dsw;
    }

    /**
     * Inform the DataSourceWrapper that the ConnectionWrapper
     * is closed.
     */
    public void close( ) throws SQLException {
        isClosed = true;
        dsw.returnConnection(realConn);
    }

    /**
     * Returns true if the ConnectionWrapper is closed, false
     * otherwise.
     */
    public boolean isClosed( ) throws SQLException {
```

Example 24-1. The ConnectionWrapper class (continued)

```
        return isClosed;
    }

    /*
     * Wrapped methods.
     */
    public void clearWarnings( ) throws SQLException {
        if (isClosed) {
            throw new SQLException("Pooled connection is closed");
        }
        realConn.clearWarnings( );
    }
    ...
}
```

An instance of this class is associated with a real `Connection` object, retrieved from a connection pool, in the constructor. The constructor parameter list also includes a reference to the `DataSourceWrapper` instance that creates it.

The `ConnectionWrapper` class implements the `Connection` interface. The implementations of all the methods except two simply relay the call to the real `Connection` object, so it can perform the requested database operation. The implementation of the `close( )` method, however, doesn't call the real `Connect` object's method. Instead, it calls the `DataSourceWrapper` object's `returnConnection( )` method, to return the `Connection` to the pool. The `isClosed( )` method, finally, returns the state of the `ConnectionWrapper` object as opposed to the real `Connection` object.

Example 24-2 shows how the `com.ora.jsp.sql.DataSourceWrapper` gets a connection from a pool and returns it when the pool client is done with it.

Example 24-2. The DataSourceWrapper class

```
package com.ora.jsp.sql;

import java.io.*;
import java.sql.*;
import javax.sql.*;

public class DataSourceWrapper implements DataSource {
    private ConnectionPool pool;
    private String driverClassName;
    private String url;
    private String user;
    private String password;
    private int initialConnections;

    public void setDriverClassName(String driverClassName) {
        this.driverClassName = driverClassName;
    }

    public void setUrl(String url) {
```

Example 24-2. The DataSourceWrapper class (continued)

```
        this.url = url;
    }

    public void setUser(String user) {
        this.user = user;
    }

    public void setPassword(String password) {
        this.password = password;
    }

    private void setInitialConnections(int initialConnections) {
        this.initialConnections = initialConnections;
    }

    /**
     * Gets a connection from the pool and returns it wrapped in
     * a ConnectionWrapper.
     */
    public Connection getConnection( ) throws SQLException {
        if (pool == null) {
            createConnectionPool( );
        }
        return new ConnectionWrapper(pool.getConnection( ), this);
    }

    /**
     * Returns a Connection to the pool. This method is called by
     * the ConnectionWrapper's close( ) method.
     */
    public void returnConnection(Connection conn) {
        pool.returnConnection(conn);
    }

    /**
     * Always throws an SQLException. Username and password are set
     * with the setter methods and can not be changed.
     */
    public Connection getConnection(String username, String password)
            throws SQLException {
        throw new SQLException("Not supported");
    }

    public int getLoginTimeout( ) throws SQLException {
        throw new SQLException("Not supported");
    }
    ...
    /**
     * Create a Connection pool based on the configuration properties.
     */
    private void createConnectionPool( ) throws SQLException {
```

Example 24-2. The DataSourceWrapper class (continued)

```
        try {
            pool = new ConnectionPool(driverClassName, url, user,
                password, initialConnections);
        }
        catch (SQLException e) {
            throw e;
        }
        catch (Exception e) {
            SQLException sqle =
                new SQLException("Error creating pool: " +
                    e.getClass().getName() + " : " + e.getMessage( ));
            throw sqle;
        }
    }
}
```

The DataSourceWrapper class implements the DataSource interface, so it can be used as a JDBC 2.0 connection pool implementation:

```
DataSource ds = null;
try {
    ds = new DataSourceWrapper( );
    ds.setDriverClassName("org.gjt.mm.mysql.Driver");
    ds.setUrl("jdbc:mysql:///test");
    ds.setUser("scott");
    ds.setPassword("tiger");
}
catch (Exception e) {
    // Deal with it
}

Connection conn = ds.getConnection( );
```

The getConnection( ) method creates an instance of the real connection pool class the first time it's called, using the JDBC driver, URL, user, and password information provided through the corresponding setter methods. The two most interesting methods are getConnection( ) and returnConnection( ).

The pool client application calls the getConnection( ) method, and the DataSourceWrapper relays the call to the connection pool class. It then wraps the Connection object it receives in a ConnectionWrapper object and returns it to the client application.

As described earlier, the ConnectionWrapper object calls the returnConnection( ) method when the pool client calls close( ) on the ConnectionWrapper object. The returnConnection( ) method hands over the Connection to the real connection pool so it can be recycled.

All other DataSource interface methods throw an SQLException in this implementation. If you modify the wrapper classes presented here to wrap a more sophisticated connection pool, you may be able to relay some of these method calls to the real connection pool instead.

The real beauty of the JDBC 2.0 connection pool interfaces is that the application doesn't have to be aware it's using a connection pool. All configuration data, such as which driver class and JDBC URL to use, the number of initial and maximum number of pooled connections, and the database account name and password, are set by a server administrator. The completely configured DataSource object is made available to the application, as described in the next section, and then any component can get, use, and return a Connection with code like this:

```
Connection conn = null;
try {
  conn = ds.getConnection( );
  // Use the Connection
}
catch (SQLException e) {
  // Deal with it
}
finally {
  // Return the Connection to the pool
  if (conn != null)
    try {
      conn.close( );
    }
    catch (SQLException e) {}
}
```

If the DataSource provides connection-pooling capabilities, the close( ) call returns the Connection to the pool; otherwise it's really closed. The application doesn't care; these details are in the hands of the server administrator, as they should be. As shown here, you should always use a try/catch/finally statement for all code that uses the Connection, and close it in the finally block to make sure it's closed no matter what happens.

Making a Connection Pool Available to Application Components

The next part of the puzzle is how to make the DataSource available to the application components that need it. In principle, there are two ways to do this. The first one—using an application scope variable—works in any type of web container, while the second one—using JNDI—is more flexible but only works in a container that supports J2EE style resource access.

Using an Application Scope Variable

One place for resources that all components in an application need access to is the application scope, corresponding to ServletContext attributes in the servlet world. As I described in Chapter 19, the most appropriate component for initialization and release of this type of shared resources is the application lifecycle listener.

The container informs an application lifecycle listener when the application is started and stopped. It can create the resource objects and make them available to other application components in its `contextInitialized( )` method before any user requests are received, and release them when the application is shut down in its `contextDestroyed( )` method. Finally, a listener can use configuration data (defined as context parameters in the deployment descriptor) to work in different settings. To recap, here's an application lifecycle listener similar to the one used in Chapter 19:

```
package com.ora.jsp.servlets;

import javax.servlet.*;
import javax.servlet.http.*;
import oracle.jdbc.pool.*;

public class ResourceManagerListener2 implements
    ServletContextListener {
    private OracleConnectionCacheImpl ds = null;

    public void contextInitialized(ServletContextEvent sce) {

        ServletContext application  = sce.getServletContext( );
        String jdbcURL = application.getInitParameter("jdbcURL");
        String user = application.getInitParameter("user");
        String password = application.getInitParameter("password");
        String maxLimit = application.getInitParameter("maxLimit");

        try {
            ds = new OracleConnectionCacheImpl( );
            ds.setURL(jdbcURL);
            ds.setMaxLimit(Integer.parseInt(maxLimit));
            ds.setUser("scott");
            ds.setPassword("tiger");
        }
        catch (Exception e) {
            application.log("Failed to create data source: " +
                e.getMessage( ));
        }
        application.setAttribute("appDataSource", ds);
    }

    public void contextDestroyed(ServletContextEvent sce) {
        ServletContext application  = sce.getServletContext( );
        application.removeAttribute("appDataSource");
        // Close the connections in the DataSource
        try {
            ds.close( );
        }
        catch (java.sql.SQLException e) {}
        ds = null;
    }
}
```

In the contextInitialized( ) method, the JDBC URL, database user, and password, and the maximal number of connections to keep in the pool are read from the deployment descriptor and used to create and configure an instance of Oracle's DataSource implementation that provides pooling capabilities: oracle.jdbc.pool.OracleConnectionCacheImpl. I'm using only some of its features here, so you should also read Oracle's documentation if you plan to use it in your application. When the data source has been configured, it's saved as a servlet context attribute named appDataSource. To refresh your memory on the implementation and configuration details, you may want to take a look at Chapter 19 again.

An application component, such as a servlet, can pick up the DataSource registered by the listener like this:

```
ServletContext application = getServletContext( );
DataSource ds = (DataSource) application.getAttribute("appDataSource");
```

Servlet context attributes appear to JSP as application scope variables, so you can also tell the JSTL database actions to use this DataSource by specifying it with an EL expression for the dataSource attribute:

```
<sql:query dataSource="${appDataSource}" ... />
```

If you want to make the DataSource the default used by the JSTL database actions, you must use the application scope variable name they expect, controlled by the javax.servlet.jsp.jstl.core.Config class described in Chapter 23:

```
public void contextInitialized(ServletContextEvent sce) {

        ServletContext application  = sce.getServletContext( );
        String jdbcURL = application.getInitParameter("jdbcURL");
        String user = application.getInitParameter("user");
        String password = application.getInitParameter("password");
        String maxLimit = application.getInitParameter("maxLimit");

        try {
            ds = new OracleConnectionCacheImpl( );
            ds.setURL(jdbcURL);
            ds.setMaxLimit(Integer.parseInt(maxLimit));
            ds.setUser("scott");
            ds.setPassword("tiger");
        }
        catch (Exception e) {
            application.log("Failed to create data source: " +
                e.getMessage( ));
        }
        Config.set(application, Config.SQL_DATA_SOURCE, ds);
    }
```

Using the Config class set( ) method guarantees that the implementation-dependent variable is set so that the JSTL actions find and use this DataSource by default. Other components in the application can access it through the Config class get( ) method:

```
import javax.servlet.jsp.jstl.core.Config;
```

```
...
ServletContext application = getServletContext( );
DataSource ds =
  (DataSource) Config.get(application, Config.SQL_DATASOURCE);
```

The listener also implements the contextDestroyed( ) method, called by the container before the application is shut down. In this method, the context attribute is removed, and all connections in the data source are closed. How to gracefully shut down a DataSource isn't defined by the JDBC specification, but for Oracle, you do it by calling the close( ) method on the OracleConnectionCacheImpl instance.

Using JNDI

J2EE defines an even more flexible way to make a DataSource, or any other shared resource, available through a Java Naming and Directory Interface (JNDI) service. Through JNDI, the connection pool is available to all parts of the application, even to components that don't have access to the servlet context. This should therefore be your first choice for resource sharing, unless you need to target containers that don't support JNDI. All J2EE-compliant application servers support JNDI, and many pure web containers (containers without EJB support), such as Tomcat, JRun, Resin, and ServletExec, provide resource access through JNDI even though the servlet and JSP specifications don't require it.

To use JNDI, you first define the resource in the web application deployment descriptor, using the <resource-ref> element:

```
<web-app ...>
  ...
  <resource-ref>
    <description>
      JNDI DataSource for example database
    </description>
    <res-ref-name>jdbc/Example</res-ref-name>
    <res-type>javax.sql.DataSource</res-type>
    <res-auth>Container</res-auth>
    <res-sharing-scope>Sharable</res-sharing-scope>
  </resource-ref>
```

The optional <description> element describes the resource and may be used to help the person that deploys the application.

The <res-ref-name> element is mandatory and must contain the unique name that the application components use to retrieve the resource, as you will see shortly. For a data-source resource, the J2EE specification recommends that you use the naming convention shown here, i.e., a name in the JNDI jdbc subcontext.

The type of the resource must be defined by the <res-type> element. It must be the fully qualified class name for the resource, and for a data source, it's always javax.sql.DataSource.

Next comes the <res-auth> element. It accepts one of two values: Container or Application. Container means that database account information needed to get connections from the data source must be provided to the container when the data source is registered as a JNDI resource, so the container can take care of authentication. Application means that the application will provide this information every time it gets a connection. This boils down to whether the application will call getConnection( ) (in the container-controlled authentication case) or getConnection(String username, String password) (in the application-controlled case). In most cases you want the container to take care of it.

The <res-sharing-scope> element is optional and accepts one of Sharable or Unsharable. This element tells the data source if it should return the same connection when being asked for one multiple times within the same transaction (if the transaction is controlled by the container or the Java Transaction API, JTA) or if it should return a unique connection each time. If you use only the JDBC transaction control methods, commit( ) and rollback( ), this element doesn't matter because the connections can never be shared. The default is Sharable, and that's fine for almost all cases.

Application components—servlets, custom actions, beans, or any other type of class used by the application—use the JNDI API to grab the DataSource and a Connection like this:

```
import javax.naming.Context;
import javax.naming.InitialContext;
import javax.sql.DataSource;
import java.sql.Connection;
...

    Context ctx = new InitialContext( );
    DataSource ds =
        (DataSource) ctx.lookup("java:comp/env/jdbc/Example");
    Connection conn = ds.getConnection( );
```

The InitialContext represents the entry point to the container's JNDI resource naming service. The lookup( ) method argument is the path for the DataSource. The first part, java:comp/env/ is the base for all J2EE resources, followed by the value declared by the <res-ref-name> element in the deployment descriptor. With the DataSource retrieved through JNDI, the application gets a Connection by calling getConnection( ) as usual.

When you use the JSTL database actions, you can specify a JNDI path as the data source, either as the corresponding configuration setting as described in Chapter 23 or as the dataSource attribute value:

```
<sql:query dataSource="jdbc/Example" ... />
```

The path must be the path relative to the J2EE base; in other words, the same value as you define with the <res-ref-name> element.

All I've said about how to declare the resource in the deployment descriptor and get access to it through JNDI is defined by the J2EE and servlet specifications. How to register a DataSource with a container's naming service, however, is a process that differs between containers. I'll show you how it's done for Tomcat, but you need to read the documentation to see how to do it for other containers.

For Tomcat, resource registration is done in the *conf/server.xml* file. This is the main configuration file for Tomcat. To register the JNDI resource, you must use a <Context> element to declare your web application explicitly in the *conf/server.xml* file (just placing it in Tomcat's *webapps* directory isn't enough in this case) and add a nested <ResourceParams> element to register and configure the JNDI DataSource factory for your application:

```
<Server port="8005" shutdown="SHUTDOWN" debug="0">
  ...
  <Service name="Tomcat-Standalone">
    ...
    <Engine name="Standalone" defaultHost="localhost" debug="0">
      ...
      <Host name="localhost" debug="0" appBase="webapps"
        unpackWARs="true">
        ...
        <!-- Book examples context -->
        <Context path="/ora" docBase="ora">
          <ResourceParams name="jdbc/Example">
            <parameter>
              <name>factory</name>
              <value>com.ora.jsp.sql.DataSourceFactory</value>
            </parameter>
            <parameter>
              <name>dataSourceClassName</name>
              <value>oracle.jdbc.pool.OracleConnectionCacheImpl</value>
            </parameter>
            <parameter>
              <name>maxLimit</name>
              <value>2</value>
            </parameter>
            <parameter>
              <name>URL</name>
              <value>jdbc:oracle:thin:@voyager2:1521:Oracle9i</value>
            </parameter>
            <parameter>
              <name>user</name>
              <value>scott</value>
            </parameter>
            <parameter>
              <name>password</name>
              <value>tiger</value>
            </parameter>
          </ResourceParams>
        </Context>
        ...
```

The Tomcat server can be configured in many different ways, with or without some of the higher-level elements shown here. I'm using the default configuration, so the <Context> element is nested within a <Host> element that defines the base directory for all applications, and the <Context> element defines its base directory (*ora* in this example) relative to the host's base (*webapps* in this example) and its context path (*/ora* in this example). To learn more about the *conf/server.xml* file and all its elements, I suggest you read the Tomcat *Server Configuration Reference*, available at *http://jakarta.apache.org/tomcat/tomcat-5.0-doc/config/index.html.*

The <ResourceParams> element's name attribute must be set to the same name as you defined for the resource with the <res-ref-name> element in the deployment descriptor. With exception for factory and dataSourceClassName, the nested <parameter> elements set the parameter values supported by the specific DataSource you use. In this example I use some of the parameters supported by the Oracle OracleConnectionCacheImpl data source.

The factory parameter identifies the JNDI object factory Tomcat uses to create the data source object. A JNDI object factory is a class that implements the single method defined by the javax.naming.spi.ObjectFactory interface. Some JDBC drivers may bundle an object factory that produces data-source objects for the implementations included with the driver, but here I use a generic data source factory that I implemented for this book. It uses introspection to set the parameters for any DataSource implementation, for instance the Oracle connection pool data source in this example.

The object factory source code is shown in Example 24-3.

Example 24-3. A generic DataSource factory class

```
package com.ora.jsp.sql;

import java.beans.*;
import java.lang.reflect.*;
import java.util.*;
import javax.naming.*;
import javax.naming.spi.ObjectFactory;

public class DataSourceFactory implements ObjectFactory {
    public Object getObjectInstance(Object obj, Name name,
        Context nameCtx, Hashtable environment)
        throws NamingException {

        System.out.println("Generic factory called");
        Reference ref = (Reference) obj;
        RefAddr ra = ref.get("dataSourceClassName");
        if (ra == null) {
            throw new NamingException("No class name specified");
        }

        String className = (String) ra.getContent( );
```

Example 24-3. A generic DataSource factory class (continued)

```
        Object ds = null;
        try {
            ds = Class.forName(className).newInstance( );
        }
        catch (Exception e) {
            throw new NamingException("Can't create DataSource: "
                + e.getMessage( ));
        }

        Enumeration addrs = ref.getAll( );
        while (addrs.hasMoreElements( )) {
            RefAddr addr = (RefAddr) addrs.nextElement( );
            String prop = addr.getType( );
            String value = (String) addr.getContent( );
            if (!(prop.equals("dataSourceClassName") ||
                prop.equals("scope") ||
                prop.equals("auth") || prop.equals("factory"))) {
                setProperty(prop, value, ds);
            }
        }
        return ds;
    }
    ...
}
```

Tomcat calls the `getObjectInstance( )` method the first time the application asks for the JNDI resource with the name the factory is registered for. The method creates an instance of the `DataSource` class specified by the `dataSourceClassName` parameter in the *config/server.xml* file, calls all setter methods matching the parameters specified within the `<ResourceParams>` element, and returns the configured instance. A number of private methods, not shown here, use the Introspection API to find and call the setter methods for the parameters. The source code is bundled with the book examples, so you can look at these details at your leisure.

When you use JNDI, you must also place the JDBC driver classes in a directory that Tomcat itself can use: namely in the *common/lib* directory if they are packaged in a JAR file, otherwise in *common/classes*. Classes in the *WEB-INF/lib* and *WEB-INF/classes* directories are available only to the application, not the container, so they are no good in this case. The same goes for the factory class. The factory class shown in Example 24-3 is part of the *oraclasses_2_0.jar* file, located in the *WEB-INF/lib* directory for the book examples application. To use this factory, you must move the JAR file to the *common/lib* directory.

Using a Generic Database Bean

Some consider using the JSTL database access actions in JSP pages a bad idea because so much business logic ends up in the presentation layer (the View). For a very simple application, it's no big deal, but for a more complex application it's better to move the SQL statements to some other component type. You have basically two options: move it to a Controller servlet (or an action class that the servlet delegates to), as in the Chapter 19 example, or encapsulate it in a custom action. In both cases it makes sense to add yet another abstraction layer in the form of a bean that encapsulates the SQL statements and let the servlet or tag handler access the data in a purer form. One example of such a bean is the `EmployeeRegistryBean` used in Chapter 19 for authentication as well as for retrieving and saving information about an employee.

When you develop this type of database access components, you can of course use the JDBC API directly. I find it handy to use a generic JDBC bean, such as the `com.ora.jsp.beans.sql.SQLCommandBean` described in this section. Besides taking care of a lot of the grunt work, it also converts a query result into an instance of the same class that the JSTL `<sql:query>` action uses to expose the result. This makes it easy to use in a JSP page that renders the result.

The `SQLCommandBean` has three write-only properties. Example 24-4 shows the beginning of the class file with the setter methods.

Example 24-4. SQLCommandBean property setter methods

```
package com.ora.jsp.beans.sql;

import java.util.*;
import java.sql.*;
import javax.servlet.jsp.jstl.sql.*;

public class SQLCommandBean {
    private Connection conn;
    private String sqlValue;
    private List values;

    public void setConnection(Connection conn) {
        this.conn = conn;
    }

    public void setSqlValue(String sqlValue) {
        this.sqlValue = sqlValue;
    }

    public void setValues(List values) {
        this.values = values;
    }
    ...
```

The `connection` property holds the `Connection` to use, and the `sqlValue` property is set to the SQL statement to execute, with question marks as placeholders for variable values, if any. The application provides the values for the placeholders through the `values` property, a `List` with one object per placeholder.

Two methods in the SQLCommandBean execute the SQL statement: the executeQuery( ) method for a SELECT statement and the executeUpdate( ) method for all other types of statements. Example 24-5 shows the executeQuery( ) method.

Example 24-5. The SQLCommandBean's executeQuery() method

```
public Result executeQuery( ) throws SQLException {
    Result result = null;
    ResultSet rs = null;
    PreparedStatement pstmt = null;
    Statement stmt = null;
    try {
        if (values != null && values.size( ) > 0) {
            // Use a PreparedStatement and set all values
            pstmt = conn.prepareStatement(sqlValue);
            setValues(pstmt, values);
            rs = pstmt.executeQuery( );
        }
        else {
            // Use a regular Statement
            stmt = conn.createStatement( );
            rs = stmt.executeQuery(sqlValue);
        }
        result = ResultSupport.toResult(rs);
    }
    finally {
        if (rs != null) {
            try {rs.close( );} catch (SQLException e) {}
        }
        if (stmt != null) {
            try {stmt.close( );} catch (SQLException e) {}
        }
        if (pstmt != null) {
            try {pstmt.close( );} catch (SQLException e) {}
        }
    }
    return result;
}
```

If the values property is set, a JDBC PreparedStatement is needed to associate the values with the placeholders in the SQL statement. A private method named setValues( ) takes care of setting all values using the PreparedStatement setObject( ) method. If the values property isn't set, a regular JDBC Statement is created instead. In both cases, the JDBC driver is asked to execute the statement, and the resulting ResultSet is turned into a javax.servlet.jsp.jstl.sql.Result, which is returned to the caller. The conversion is performed by a static method in the javax.servlet.jsp.jstl.sql.ResultSupport support class defined by the JSTL specification. Besides the toResult( ) method used in Example 24-5, this class also provides a toResult( ) method that takes the maximum number of rows to include in the Result object as an argument.

You may wonder why a Result object is created and returned instead of returning the ResultSet directly. The reason is that a ResultSet is tied to the Connection that was used to generate it. When the Connection is closed or executes a new SQL statement, all open ResultSet objects for the Connection are released. You must therefore make sure you save the information from the ResultSet in a new data structure before reusing the Connection or return it to the pool.

The code for the creation of the PreparedStatement or Statement object and the execution of the statement is enclosed in a try/finally block. This is important, because if something fails (due to an invalid SQL statement, for instance), the JDBC methods throw an SQLException. The exception should be handled by the application using the SQLCommandBean, but first, all JDBC resources must be released, and the Connection object returned to the pool. Using a try block with a finally clause but no catch clause provides this behavior. If an exception is thrown, the finally clause is executed, and the exception is automatically thrown to the object that called the executeQuery( ) method. In the finally clause, the ResultSet object and either the PreparedStatement or Statement object are closed. It should be enough to close the statement object according to the JDBC specification (closing the statement should also close the ResultSet associated with the statement) but closing all resources used by the statement explicitly doesn't hurt and makes the code work even with a buggy JDBC driver. Each resource is closed within its own try/catch block, since the close( ) method can also throw an exception.

Example 24-6 shows the private setValues( ) method.

Example 24-6. The SQLCommandBean's setValues() method

```
private void setValues(PreparedStatement pstmt, List values)
    throws SQLException {
    for (int i = 0; i < values.size( ); i++) {
        Object v = values.get(i);
        // Set the value using the method corresponding to the type.
        // Note! Set methods are indexed from 1, so we add 1 to i
        pstmt.setObject(i + 1, v);
    }
}
```

The setValues( ) method loops through all elements in the List with values. For each element, it uses the setObject( ) method to set the value of the corresponding placeholders in the PreparedStatement. You may wonder why a PreparedStatement is used here, since it's used only once. It's true that a PreparedStatement is intended to be reused over and over again to execute the same SQL statement with new values. However, it offers a convenient solution to the problem with different literal value syntax for date/time and number column values. When a PreparedStatement is used, the placeholders in the SQL statement can be set using the appropriate Java types instead, without worrying about what literal representation a certain JDBC driver supports. So even though it's only used once here, a PreparedStatement still has an advantage over a regular Statement.

The executeUpdate( ) method, shown in Example 24-7, is very similar to the executeQuery( ) method.

Example 24-7. The SQLCommandBean's executeUpdate() method

```
public int executeUpdate( ) throws SQLException {
    int noOfRows = 0;
    ResultSet rs = null;
    PreparedStatement pstmt = null;
    Statement stmt = null;
    try {
        if (values != null && values.size( ) > 0) {
            // Use a PreparedStatement and set all values
            pstmt = conn.prepareStatement(sqlValue);
            setValues(pstmt, values);
            noOfRows = pstmt.executeUpdate( );
        }
        else {
            // Use a regular Statement
            stmt = conn.createStatement( );
            noOfRows = stmt.executeUpdate(sqlValue);
        }
    }
    finally {
        if (rs != null) {
            try {rs.close( );} catch (SQLException e) {}
        }
        if (stmt != null) {
            try {stmt.close( );} catch (SQLException e) {}
        }
        if (pstmt != null) {
            try {pstmt.close( );} catch (SQLException e) {}
        }
    }
    return noOfRows;
}
```

The main difference is that the executeUpdate( ) method executes SQL statements that don't return rows, only the number of rows affected by the statement. Examples of such statements are UPDATE, INSERT, and DELETE. As for the executeQuery( ) method, a PreparedStatement is created and initialized with the values defined by the values property, if set. Otherwise a regular Statement is used. The statement is executed, and the number of affected rows is returned to the caller.

Developing Application-Specific Database Components

The SQLCommandBean class described in this chapter can be used for application-specific components that access a database. The bean is used like this:

```
SQLCommandBean sqlCommandBean = new SQLCommandBean( );
sqlCommandBean.setConnection(dataSource.getConnection( ));
String sql = "SELECT * FROM Employee WHERE UserName = ?");
sqlCommandBean.setSqlValue(sql);
List values = new ArrayList( );
values.add(userName);
sqlCommandBean.setValues(values);
Result result = sqlCommandBean.executeQuery( );
```

Chapter 19 includes a more advanced example of an application-specific bean (the EmployeeRegisterBean) that uses the SQLCommandBean.

You can also use these classes in your application-specific custom actions. One example is the custom action that's mentioned in Chapter 12 as an alternative to the generic database actions for inserting or updating employee information:

```
<%@ taglib prefix="c" uri="http://java.sun.com/jsp/jstl/core" %>
<%@ taglib prefix="sql" uri="http://java.sun.com/jsp/jstl/sql" %>
<%@ taglib prefix="myLib" uri="mytaglib" %>

<myLib:saveEmployeeInfo dataSource="${appDataSource}" />

<%-- Get the new or updated data from the database --%>
<sql:query var="newEmpDbInfo"="${example}" scope="session">
  SELECT * FROM Employee
    WHERE UserName = ?
  <sql:param value="${param.userName}" />
</sql:query>

<%-- Redirect to the confirmation page --%>
<c:redirect url="confirmation.jsp" />
```

Example 24-8 shows one way to implement this custom action.

Example 24-8. SaveEmployeeInfoTag class

```
package com.mycompany.tags;

import java.sql.*;
import java.text.*;
import java.util.*;
import javax.sql.*;
import javax.servlet.*;
import javax.servlet.jsp.*;
import javax.servlet.jsp.tagext.*;
import javax.servlet.jsp.jstl.sql.Result;
import com.ora.jsp.beans.sql.SQLCommandBean;
import com.ora.jsp.util.*;

public class SaveEmployeeInfoTag extends SimpleTagSupport {
    private DataSource dataSource;

    public void setDataSource(DataSource dataSource) {
        this.dataSource = dataSource;
```

Example 24-8. SaveEmployeeInfoTag class (continued)

```
    }

    public void doTag( ) throws JspException {
        // Get all request parameters
        PageContext pageContext = (PageContext) jspContext;
        ServletRequest request = pageContext.getRequest( );
        String userName = request.getParameter("userName");
        String password = request.getParameter("password");
        String firstName = request.getParameter("firstName");
        String lastName = request.getParameter("lastName");
        String dept = request.getParameter("dept");
        String empDateString = request.getParameter("empDate");
        String emailAddr = request.getParameter("emailAddr");
        if (userName == null || password == null ||
            firstName == null || lastName == null ||
            dept == null || empDateString == null ||
            emailAddr == null) {
            throw new JspException("Missing a mandatory parameter");
        }

        SQLCommandBean sqlCommandBean = new SQLCommandBean( );
        if (dataSource == null) {
            throw new JspException("The data source cannot be found");
        }

        Connection conn = null;
        try {
            conn = dataSource.getConnection( );
            sqlCommandBean.setConnection(conn);

            // Get the current info, if any
            String sqlValue =
                "SELECT * FROM Employee WHERE UserName = ?";
            List values = new ArrayList( );
            values.add(userName);
            sqlCommandBean.setSqlValue(sqlValue);
            sqlCommandBean.setValues(values);
            Result result = sqlCommandBean.executeQuery( );

            // Create values for insert/update
            values.clear( );
            values.add(password);
            values.add(firstName);
            values.add(lastName);
            values.add(dept);
            // Must convert the String value to java.sql.Date
            java.util.Date empDate =
                StringFormat.toDate(empDateString, "yyyy-MM-dd")
            java.sql.Date empSQLDate =
                new java.sql.Date(empDate.getTime( ));
            values.add(empSQLDate);
            values.add(emailAddr);
```

Example 24-8. SaveEmployeeInfoTag class (continued)

```
            values.add(new Timestamp(System.currentTimeMillis( )));
            values.add(userName);

            if (result.getRowCount( ) == 0) {
                // New user. Insert
                StringBuffer sb = new StringBuffer( );
                sb.append("INSERT INTO Employee ").
                    append("(Password, FirstName, LastName, Dept, ").
                    append("EmpDate, EmailAddr, ModDate, UserName) ").
                    append("VALUES(?, ?, ?, ?, ?, ?, ?, ?)");
                sqlCommandBean.setSqlValue(sb.toString( ));
            }
            else {
                // Existing user. Update
                StringBuffer sb = new StringBuffer( );
                sb.append("UPDATE Employee ").
                    append("SET Password = ?, FirstName = ?, ").
                    append("LastName = ?, Dept = ?, EmpDate = ?, ").
                    append("EmailAddr = ?, ModDate = ? ").
                    append("WHERE UserName = ?");
                sqlCommandBean.setSqlValue(sb.toString( ));
            }
            sqlCommandBean.executeUpdate( );
        }
        catch (SQLException e) {
            throw new JspException("SQL error: " + e.getMessage( ));
        }
        catch (ParseException e) {
            throw new JspException("Invalid empDate format: " +
                e.getMessage( ));
        }
        finally {
            try {
                if (conn != null) {
                    conn.close( );
                }
            }
            catch (SQLException e) {
                // Ignore
            }
        }
    }
}
```

This tag handler has one property, named dataSource. It's marked as required in the TLD for the tag so it must always be set. It's also declared to accept a request-time attribute value, so an EL expression can be used to assign it a reference to the data source:

```
...
<tag>
  <name>saveEmployeeInfo</name>
```

```
    <tag-class>com.mycompany.tags.SaveEmployeeInfoTag</tag-class>
    <body-content>empty</body-content>

    <attribute>
      <name>dataSource</name>
      <required>true</required>
      <rtexprvalue>true</rtexprvalue>
    </attribute>
  </tag>
  ...
```

In the doTag( ) method, all request parameters with information about the employee are first retrieved. If a parameter is missing, an exception is thrown. An SQLCommandBean instance is then created and provided a Connection, retrieved from the DataSource.

The tag handler uses the bean to execute a SELECT statement to find out if the specified employee is already defined in the database. If not, the tag handler sets the bean's SQL statement to an INSERT statement and executes it with all the information provided through the request parameters; otherwise the tag handler uses the bean to execute an UPDATE statement.

The tag handler class described here is intended to show you how to use the database access classes to implement your own custom actions. The tag handler class can be improved in several ways. For instance, it can use the JSTL Config class (see Chapter 23) to get hold of a default DataSource if the dataSource attribute is omitted, and provide default values for missing parameters, such as the current date for a missing employment date and an email address based on the employee's first and last name if the email address is missing. You can also use a bean as input to the action instead of reading request parameters directly. This allows the bean to be used as described in Chapter 8 to capture and validate user input until all information is valid, and then pass it on to the custom action for permanent storage of the information in a database. Finally, it's a good idea to encapsulate all database access in a bean, such as the EmloyeeRegistryBean, and use this bean in the tag handler class instead of using the SQLCommandBean directly.

PART IV

Appendixes

In this part of the book, you'll find reference material, such as descriptions of JSP and JSTL elements and classes, the JSTL Expression Language, all book example components, and the web application deployment descriptor:

APPENDIX A

JSP Elements Reference

JSP defines three types of elements: directives, scripting elements, and action elements. In addition, you can define your own custom actions. This appendix contains descriptions of all standard JSP elements, as well as the general syntax rules for custom actions.

Each element is described with an overview, a syntax reference, an attribute table, and an example. The syntax reference shows all supported attributes, with optional attributes embedded in square brackets ([ ]). Mutually exclusive attributes are separated with vertical bars (|). For attributes that accept predefined values, all values are listed separated with vertical bars; the default value (if any) is in boldface. Italics are used for attribute values that don't have a fixed set of accepted values.

Directive Elements

Directive elements are used to specify information about the page itself, especially information that doesn't differ between requests for the page. The classic general directive syntax is:

```
<%@ directiveName attr1="value1" attr2="value2" %>
```

The following XML equivalent syntax must be used in a JSP Document (a JSP page written in XML syntax) and can optionally be used as an alternative to the classic syntax in a regular JSP page:

```
<jsp:directive.directiveName attr1="value1" attr2="value2" />
```

Only the classic syntax is shown in the detailed sections that follow.

The attribute values can be enclosed with single quotes instead of double quotes. The directive name and all attribute names are case-sensitive.

Attribute Directive

This directive can only be used in tag files. It declares the attributes the tag file supports.

Syntax

```
<%@ attribute name="attrName"
  [description="description"] [required="true|false"]
  [fragment="true|false" | [type="attrDataType"] [rtexprvalue="true|false"]]
%>
```

Attributes

Attribute name	Default	Description
`description`	No default	A description of the attribute that can be presented to a page author by an authoring tool.
`fragment`	`false`	Set to `true` if the attribute represents a fragment, set by a `<jsp:attribute>` element. If `false`, the attribute is converted to the type specified by the `type` attribute.
`name`	No default	The attribute name.
`required`	`false`	Set to `true` if the page author must provide an attribute value.
`rtexprvalue`	`true`	Set to `false` if the attribute value must be provided as a static text value. If `true`, the attribute can be set by an EL or Java expression or a `<jsp:attribute>` element, evaluated at runtime.
`type`	`String`	The attribute data type. Primitive types are not supported, only Java classes and interfaces.

When the `fragment` attribute is used, the `rtexprvalue` and `type` attributes must not be used. For a fragment, a runtime expression value is always accepted and the type is fixed to `javax.servlet.jsp.tagext.JspFragment`.

Example

```
<%@ attribute name="date" type="java.util.Date" %>
<%@ attribute name="pattern" fragment="true" %>
```

Include Directive

Includes a static file, merging its content with the including page before the combined result is converted to a JSP page implementation class.

Syntax

```
<%@ include file="pageOrContextRelativePath" %>
```

Attributes

Attribute name	Default	Description
`file`	No default	A page-relative or context-relative URI path for the file to include.

A page can contain multiple `include` directives. The including page and all included pages taken together forms what is called a *JSP translation unit*.

Example

```
<%@ include file="header.html" %>
```

Page Directive

This directive can only be used in JSP pages, not in tag files. It defines page-dependent attributes, such as scripting language, error page, and buffering requirements.

Syntax

```
<%@ page [autoFlush="true|false"] [buffer="8kb|NNkb|none"]
  [contentType="mimeType"] [errorPage="pageOrContextRelativePath"]
  [extends="className"] [import="packageList"] [info="info"]
  [isELIgnored="true|false] [isErrorPage="true|false"]
  [isThreadSafe="true|false"] [language="java|language"]
  [pageEncoding="encoding"] [session="true|false"]
%>
```

Attributes

Attribute name	Default	Description
`autoFlush`	`true`	Set to `true` if the page buffer should be flushed automatically when it's full, or to `false` if an exception should be thrown when it's full.
`buffer`	`8kb`	Specifies the buffer size for the page. The value must be expressed as the size in kilobytes followed by `kb`, or be the keyword `none` to disable buffering.
`contentType`	`text/html` or `text/xml`	The MIME type for the response generated by the page and optionally the response charset, e.g., `text/html;charset=Shift_JIS`. The charset applies to the JSP page file as well, if `pageEncoding` isn't specified. The default MIME type is `text/html` for a regular JSP page and `text/xml` for a JSP Document. If no charset is specified, ISO-8859-1 is used for a regular JSP page and UTF-8 for a JSP Document.
`errorPage`	No default	A page- or context-relative URI path for the JSP page, servlet, or static page to forward to in case an exception is thrown by code in the page.

Attribute name	Default	Description
extends	No default	The fully qualified name of a Java class that the generated JSP page implementation class shall extend. The class must implement the JspPage or HttpJspPage interface in the javax.servlet.jsp.package. Note that the recommendation is to *not* use this attribute. Specifying your own superclass restricts the JSP container's ability to provide a specialized, high-performance superclass.
import	No default	A Java import declaration, i.e., a comma-separated list of fully qualified class names or package names followed by .* (for all public classes in the package).
info	No default	Text that a web container may use as a description of the page in its administration user interface.
isELIgnored	false[a]	Set to true to treat ${...} character sequences as template text instead of EL expressions, false otherwise.
isErrorPage	false	Set to true for a page that is used as an error page, to make the implicit exception variable available to scripting elements. Use false for regular JSP pages.
isThreadSafe	true	Set to true if the container is allowed to run multiple threads through the page (i.e., let the page serve parallel requests). If set to false, the container serializes all requests for the page. It may also use a pool of page implementation class instances to serve more than one request at a time. The recommendation is to always use true and handle multithread issues by avoiding JSP declarations, and to ensure that all objects used by the page are thread-safe.
language	java	Defines the scripting language used in the page.
pageEncoding	See Description	The encoding used for the JSP page file, as well as the response charset if no charset is specified by contentType. If this attribute is omitted, but a charset is specified for contentType, that charset is also used of the page; if contentType doesn't specify a charset, ISO-8859-1 is used for a regular JSP page, and UTF-8 is used for a JSP Document.
session	true	Set to true if the page should participate in a user session. If set to false, neither the session scope nor the implicit session variable is available to JSP elements in the page.

[a] The default is false for a JSP 2.0 application (i.e., an application deployed with a Servlet 2.4 deployment descriptor), but it's true for an application deployed with a deployment descriptor for any prior version of the JSP/Servlet specification to ensure backward compatibility.

A translation unit (the JSP source file and any files included via the include directive) can contain more than one page directive, as long as duplicated attributes all have the same value, with the exception for the import and pageEncoding attributes. If multiple import attribute values are used, they are combined into one list of import definitions. The pageEncoding attribute must only be used once in each file in the translation unit and applies only to the file in which it appears.

Example

```
<%@ page language="java" contentType="text/html;charset=Shift_JIS"%>
<%@ page import="java.util.*, java.text.*" %>
<%@ page import="java.sql.Date" %>
```

Taglib Directive

Declares a tag library, containing custom actions, that is used in the page.

Syntax

```
<%@ taglib prefix="prefix" [uri="taglibURI" | tagdir="contextRelativePath"]%>
```

Attributes

Attribute name	Default	Description
prefix	No default	The prefix to use in the action element names for all actions in the library.
uri	No default	Either a symbolic name for the tag library that is defined in the TLD for the library or in the *web.xml* file for the application, or a page-relative or context-relative URI path for the library's TLD file or JAR file.
tagdir	No default	The context-relative path to a directory containing tag files, starting with */WEB-INF/tags*.

Example

```
<%@ taglib prefix="ora" uri="orataglib" %>
<%@ taglib prefix="c" uri="http://java.sun.com/jstl/core" %>
<%@ taglib prefix="mylib" tagdir="/WEB-INF/tags/mylib" %>
```

Tag Directive

This directive can only be used in tag files. It defines properties of the file itself, such as encoding and how to treat EL expressions, as well as properties of the custom action the tag file implements the behavior for, such as developer information an authoring tool can display.

Syntax

```
<%@ tag [body-content="empty|scriptless|tagdependent"]
  [description="description"] [display-name="displayName"]
  [dynamic-attributes="attrCollVar"] [example="example"]
  [import="packageList"] [isELIgnored="true|false"] [language="java|language"]
  [large-icon="largeIconPath"] [pageEncoding="encoding"]
  [small-icon="smallIconPath"]
%>
```

Attributes

Attribute name	Default	Description
body-content	scriptless	The custom action body content type, one of empty, scriptless, or tagdependent.
description	No default	A description of the custom action that can be displayed by a page-authoring tool.

Attribute name	Default	Description
display-name	No default	A descriptive name for the custom action that can be displayed by a page-authoring tool.
dynamic-attributes	No default	The name of a variable to hold undeclared attributes. The variable is made available in the tag file's page scope as a java.util.Map with the attribute names as keys and the attribute values as the values.
example	No default	An example of how to use the custom action that can be displayed by a page-authoring tool.
import	No default	A Java import declaration, i.e., a comma-separated list of fully qualified class names or package names followed by .* (for all public classes in the package).
isElIgnored	false[a]	Set to true to treat ${...} character sequences as template text instead of EL expressions, false otherwise.
language	java	Defines the scripting language used in the page.
large-icon	No default	A context- or file-relative path to a 32x32 pixel GIF or JPEG image file that can be displayed by a page-authoring tool.
pageEncoding	ISO-8859-1	The encoding used for the tag file.
small-icon	No default	A context- or file-relative path to a 16x16 pixel GIF or JPEG image file that can be displayed by a page-authoring tool.

[a] The default is false for a JSP 2.0 application (i.e., an application deployed with a Servlet 2.4 deployment descriptor), but it's true for an application deployed with a deployment descriptor for any prior version of the JSP/Servlet specification to ensure backward compatibility.

Example

```
<%@ tag body-content="empty" dynamic-attributes="dynAttrs" %>
```

Variable Directive

This directive can be used only in tag files. It declares variables exposed by the tag file to the page where the corresponding custom action is used.

Syntax

```
<%@ variable name-given="attrAndVarName" |
  name-from-attribute="attrName" alias="varName"
  [declare="true|false"] [description="description"]
  [scope="AT_BEGIN|AT_END|NESTED"] [variable-class="varType"]
%>
```

Attributes

Attribute Name	Default	Description
alias	No default	The name of the local page scope variable the tag file uses to hold the value it creates. The container copies the value of the local variable to the variable in the invoking page's page scope named by the attribute specified by the name-from-attribute attribute.

Attribute Name	Default	Description
declare	true	Set to false if no scripting variable declaration should be created in the page implementation class.
description	No default	A description of the variable that can be displayed by a page-authoring tool.
name-from-attribute	No default	The name of the attribute that specifies the variable to hold the value created by the tag file. This attribute must be used in combination with the alias attribute, and must not be used with the name-given attribute.
name-given	No default	The name of the variable in the invoking page's page scope the tag file uses to expose the value it creates. This attribute must not be used with the name-from-attribute attribute.
scope	NESTED	The visibility of the variable, one of AT_BEGIN, AT_END, or NESTED.
variable-class	String	The variable type; a fully qualified class or interface name.

Example

```
<%@ variable name-from-attribute="var" alias="current"
  variable-class="java.util.Date" scope="AT_END" %>
<%@ attribute name="var" required="true" rtexprvalue="false" %>
```

Scripting Elements

The scripting elements let you add small pieces of code in a JSP page, such as an `if` statement to generate different HTML depending on some condition. The scripting code must be written in the language defined by the page directive.

Declaration

Declarations are used to declare scripting language variables or methods. The content must be a complete valid declaration in the language defined by the page directive. The JSP implicit scripting variables aren't visible in a declaration element.

When the language is Java, a variable declared by a declaration element ends up as an instance variable in the JSP page implementation class. It's therefore visible to parallel threads (requests) processing the page and needs to be handled in a thread-safe manner. A thread-safe alternative is to declare variables within a scriptlet element instead. It then becomes a local variable of the method in the page implementation class used to process each request, and isn't shared by parallel threads.

Syntax 1: In a regular JSP page

```
<%! declaration %>
```

Syntax 2: In a JSP Document (a JSP page written in XML syntax)

```
<jsp:declaration>declaration</jsp:declaration>
```

Attributes

None.

Example

```
<%! int globalCounter = 0; %>
```

Expression

An expression is used to add the result of executing a scripting expression to the response. The content between the start and the end characters must be a complete valid expression in the language defined by the page directive that results in a string or can be converted to a string. All JSP implicit scripting variables are visible in an expression element.

Syntax 1: In a regular JSP page

```
<%= expression %>
```

Syntax 2: In a JSP Document (a JSP page written in XML syntax)

```
<jsp:expression>expression</jsp:expression>
```

Attributes

None.

Example

```
<%= globalCounter++ %>
```

Scriptlet

Scriptlets are used to embed scripting code fragments in a page. The content must be a code fragment in the language defined by the page directive. Scriptlet code fragments are combined with code for sending the template data between them to the browser. The combination of all scriptlets in a page must form valid scripting language statements. All JSP implicit scripting variables are visible in a scripting element.

Syntax 1: In a regular JSP page

```
<% scripting code fragment %>
```

Syntax 2: In a JSP Document (a JSP page written in XML syntax)

```
<jsp:scriptlet> scripting code fragment </jsp:scriptlet>
```

Attributes

None.

Example

```
<% java.util Date clock = new java.util.Date( ) %>

<% if (clock.getHours( ) < 12) { %>
  Good morning!
<% } else if (clock.getHours( ) < 17) { %>
  Good day!
<% } else { %>
  Good evening!
<% } %>
```

Action Elements

Action elements use XML element syntax and represent components that are invoked when a client requests the JSP page. They may encapsulate functionality such as input validation using beans, database access, or passing control to another page. The JSP specification defines a few standard action elements, described in this section, and also includes a framework for developing custom action elements.

An action element consists of a start tag (optionally with attributes), a body, and an end tag. Template text and other JSP elements can be nested in the body. Here's an example:

```
<jsp:forward page="nextPage.jsp">
  <jsp:param name="aParam" value="aValue" />
</jsp:forward>
```

If the action element doesn't have a body, a shorthand notation can be used where the start tag ends with "/>" instead of ">", as shown by the `<jsp:param>` action in this example. The action element name and attribute names are case-sensitive.

Some standard action attributes accept a request-time attribute value (marked with "Yes" in the "Dynamic value accepted" column in the Attributes table for each action that follows). For such an attribute, the value can be specified as an EL or Java expression, or by a `<jsp:attribute>` element:

```
<% String headerPage = currentTemplateDir + "/header.jsp"; %>
<%-- Using a Java expression --%>
<jsp:include page="<%= headerPage %>" />

<% pageContext.setAttribute("scopedVar", headerPage);

<%-- Using an EL expression --%>
<jsp:include page="${scopedVar}" />

<%-- Using a <jsp:attribute> element --%>
<jsp:include>
  <jsp:attribute name="page">
    ${scopedVar}
  </jsp:attribute>
</jsp:include>
```

The attribute descriptions for each action in this section define whether a request-time attribute value is accepted or not.

<jsp:attribute>

The `<jsp:attribute>` element defines an attribute value for another JSP action element, as an alternative to entering the attribute value as a regular XML attribute value in the opening tag or to define fragment input. It can also be used in conjunction with the `<jsp:element>` action to dynamically build a template text markup element.

Syntax

```
<jsp:attribute name="attrName" [trim="true|false"]>
  Attribute value, typically created by nested JSP elements
</jsp:attribute>
```

Attributes

Attribute name	Java type	Dynamic value accepted	Description
name	String	No	The name of the attribute to assign a value. When the action is used with an action other than `<jsp:element>`, the named attribute must accept a dynamic value.
trim	boolean	No	Set to `false` to disable removal of leading and trailing whitespace from the body evaluation result.

Example

```
<%-- Setting a JSP action attribute value --%>
<jsp:include>
  <jsp:attribute name="page">
    ${someValue}
  </jsp:attribute>
</jsp:include>

<%-- Defining an attribute for a generated markup element --%>
<jsp:element name="a">
  <jsp:attribute name="href">
    <c:url value="${someURL}" />
  </jsp:attribute>
</jsp:element>
```

<jsp:body>

The `<jsp:body>` action defines a body for an action element. It's required only when the action attributes are defined by `<jsp:attribute>` elements.

Syntax

```
<jsp:body>
  Body content
</jsp:body>
```

Attributes

None.

Example

```
<jsp:plugin type="applet" code="Clock2.class"
  codebase="applet" jreversion="1.2">
  <jsp:attribute name="width">160</jsp:attribute>
  <jsp:attribute name="height">150</jsp:attribute>
  <jsp:body>
    <jsp:params>
      <jsp:param name="bgcolor" value="ccddff" />
    </jsp:params>
    <jsp:fallback>
      Plugin tag OBJECT or EMBED not supported by browser.
    </jsp:fallback>
  </jsp:body>
</jsp:plugin>
```

<jsp:doBody>

The `<jsp:doBody>` action must only be used in a tag file. It evaluates the corresponding custom action body, adding the output to the calling page's output stream or capturing it in a variable.

Syntax

```
<jsp:doBody [var="var" | varReader="varReader"]
  [scope="page|request|session|application"] />
```

Attributes

Attribute name	Java type	Dynamic value accepted	Description
scope	String	No	The scope for the variable.
var	String	No	The name of the variable to hold the evaluation result as a String.
varReader	String	No	The name of the variable to capture and expose the evaluation result as a java.io.Reader.

Example

```
<%-- Adding the evaluation result to the response --%>
<jsp:doBody/>
```

```
<%-- Capturing the evaluation result for further processing --%>
<jsp:doBody var="result" />
```

<jsp:element>

The `<jsp:element>` dynamically creates an XML element and adds it to the response. It's useful primarily in JSP Documents (JSP pages in XML syntax), where other approaches can't be used because of the well-formedness requirement.

Syntax 1: Without a body

```
<jsp:element name="elementName" />
```

Syntax 2: With a body

```
<jsp:element name="elementName">
  <jsp:attribute> and/or <jsp:body> actions
</jsp:element>
```

Attributes

Attribute name	Java type	Dynamic value accepted	Description
name	String	Yes	The name of the generated element.

Example

```
<%-- Generates <a href="somepage.jsp">Some text</a>
<jsp:element name="a">
  <jsp:attribute name="href">somepage.jsp</jsp:attribute>
  <jsp:body>Some text</jsp:body>
</jsp:element>
```

<jsp:fallback>

The `<jsp:fallback>` action can only be used in the body of a `<jsp:plugin>` action. Its body specifies the template text to use for browsers that don't support the HTML `<embed>` or `<object>` elements.

Syntax

```
<jsp:fallback>
  Fallback body
</jsp:fallback>
```

Attributes

None.

Example

```
<jsp:plugin type="applet" code="Clock2.class"
  codebase="applet"
  jreversion="1.2" width="160" height="150" >
  <jsp:fallback>
    Plugin tag OBJECT or EMBED not supported by browser.
  </jsp:fallback>
</jsp:plugin>
```

<jsp:forward>

The `<jsp:forward>` action passes the request processing control to another JSP page or servlet in the same web application. The execution of the current page is terminated, giving the target resource full control over the request.

If any response content has been buffered when the `<jsp:forward>` action is executed, the buffer is cleared first. If the response has already been committed (i.e., partly sent to the browser), the forwarding fails with an `IllegalStateException`.

The URI path information available through the request object is adjusted to reflect the URI path information for the target resource. All other request information is left untouched, so the target resource has access to all the original parameters and headers passed with the request. Additional parameters can be passed to the target resource through `<jsp:param>` elements in the `<jsp:forward>` element's body.

Syntax 1: Without parameters

```
<jsp:forward page="pageOrContextRelativePath" />
```

Syntax 2: With nested <jsp:param> actions

```
<jsp:forward page="pageOrContextRelativePath" />
  One or more <jsp:param> actions
</jsp:forward>
```

Attributes

Attribute name	Java type	Dynamic value accepted	Description
page	String	Yes	Page- or context-relative URI path for the resource to forward to.

Example

```
<jsp:forward page="list.jsp" />
```

<jsp:getProperty>

The `<jsp:getProperty>` action adds the value of a bean property, converted to a string, to the response generated by the page.

Syntax

```
<jsp:getProperty name="beanVariableName" property="propertyName" />
```

Attributes

Attribute name	Java type	Dynamic value accepted	Description
name	String	No	The name assigned to a bean in one of the JSP scopes.
property	String	No	The name of the bean's property to include in the page.

Example

```
<jsp:getProperty name="clock" property="hours" />
```

<jsp:include>

The `<jsp:include>` action includes the response from another JSP page, servlet, or static file in the same web application. The execution of the current page continues after including the response generated by the target resource.

If any response content has been buffered when the `<jsp:include>` action is executed, the `flush` attribute controls whether or not to flush the buffer.

The URI path information available through the request object reflects the URI path information for the source JSP page even in the target resource. All other request information is also left untouched, so the target resource has access to all the original parameters and headers passed with the request. Additional parameters can be passed to the target resource through `<jsp:param>` elements in the `<jsp:include>` element's body.

Syntax

```
<jsp:include page="pageOrContextRelativePath" [flush="true|false"] />
```

Attributes

Attribute name	Java type	Dynamic value accepted	Description
page	String	Yes	A page- or context-relative URI path for the resource to include.
flush	boolean	No	Set to `true` to flush the buffer before including the target.

Example

```
<jsp:include page="navigation.jsp" />
```

<jsp:invoke>

The `<jsp:invoke>` action must only be used in a tag file. It evaluates the named fragment, adding the output to the calling page's output stream or capturing it in a variable.

Syntax

```
<jsp:invoke fragment="fragmentName" [var="var" | varReader="varReader"]
  [scope="page|request|session|application"] />
```

Attributes

Attribute name	Java type	Dynamic value accepted	Description
`fragment`	`String`	No	The name of an attribute that defines a fragment.
`scope`	`String`	No	The scope for the variable.
`var`	`String`	No	The name of the variable to hold the evaluation result as a `String`.
`varReader`	`String`	No	The name of the variable to capture and expose the evaluation result as a `java.io.Reader`.

Example

```
<%@ attribute name="pattern" fragment="true" %>

<%-- Adding the evaluation result to the response --%>
<jsp:invoke fragment="pattern"/>

<%-- Capturing the evaluation result for further processing --%>
<jsp:invoke fragment="pattern" var="result" />
```

<jsp:output>

The `<jsp:output>` element can only be used in JSP Documents (JSP pages in XML syntax) and tag files in XML syntax. It modifies properties of the generated response.

Syntax

```
<jsp:output [omit-xml-declaration="true|yes|false|no"]
  [doctype-root-element="elementName"
    [doctype-public="publicID"] doctype-system="systemID"]
/>
```

Attributes

Attribute name	Java type	Dynamic value accepted	Description
omit-xml-declaration	boolean	No	Set to true or yes to prevent an XML declaration to be added to the response, or to false or no to force an XML declaration to be added. The default is yes for a JSP Document with a <jsp:root> element and for tag files in XML syntax, no for all other cases.
doctype-root-element	String	No	The root element name to use in the generated DOCTYPE declaration.
doctype-public	String	No	The Public ID to use in the generated DOCTYPE declaration.
doctype-system	String	No	The System ID to use in the generated DOCTYPE declaration.

Example

```
<!-- Add an XML declaration to the response -->
<jsp:output omit-xml-declaration="true" />

<!-- Add a DOCTYPE declaration to the response -->
  <jsp:output doctype-root-element="html"
    doctype-public="-//W3C//DTD XHTML 1.0 Transitional//EN"
    doctype-system='http://www.w3c.org/TR/xhtml1/DTD/xhtml1-transitional.dtd'/>
```

<jsp:param>

The <jsp:param> action can be used in the body of a <jsp:forward> or <jsp:include> action to specify additional request parameters for the target resource, as well as in the body of a <jsp:params> action to specify applet parameters.

Syntax

```
<jsp:param name="parameterName" value="parameterValue" />
```

Attributes

Attribute name	Java type	Dynamic value accepted	Description
name	String	No	The parameter name.
value	String	Yes	The parameter value.

Example

```
<jsp:include page="navigation.jsp">
  <jsp:param name="bgColor" value="<%= currentBGColor %>" />
</jsp:include>
```

<jsp:params>

The <jsp:params> action can only be used in the body of a <jsp:plugin> action to enclose a set of <jsp:param> actions that specify applet parameters.

Syntax

```
<jsp:params>
  One or more <jsp:param> actions
</jsp:params>
```

Attributes

None.

Example

```
<jsp:plugin type="applet" code="Clock2.class"
  codebase="applet"
  jreversion="1.2" width="160" height="150" >
  <jsp:params>
    <jsp:param name="bgcolor" value="ccddff" />
  </jsp:params>
</jsp:plugin>
```

<jsp:plugin>

The <jsp:plugin> action generates HTML <embed> or <object> elements (depending on the browser type) that result in the download of the Java Plugin software (if required) and subsequent execution of the specified Java applet or JavaBeans component. The body of the action can contain a <jsp:params> element to specify applet parameters and a <jsp:fallback> element to specify the text shown in browsers that don't support the <embed> or <object> HTML elements. For more information about the Java Plugin, see *http://java.sun.com/products/plugin/*.

Syntax

```
<jsp:plugin [align="bottom|middle|top"] [archive="archiveList"]
  code="className" codeBase="relativePath" [height="height"]
  [hspace="horizontalSpace"] [iepluginurl="pluginURL"]
  [jreversion="jreVersion"] [name="appletName"]
  [nspluginurl="pluginURL"] [title="title"] type="applet|bean"
  [vspace="verticalSpace"] [width="width"] >
  Optionally one <jsp:param> and one <jsp:fallback> action
</jsp:plugin>
```

Attributes

Attribute name	Java type	Dynamic value accepted	Description
align	String	No	Alignment of the applet area. One of bottom, middle, or top.
archive	String	No	A comma-separated list of URIs for archives containing classes and other resources that will be preloaded. The classes are loaded using an instance of an AppletClassLoader with the given codebase. Relative URIs for archives are interpreted with respect to the applet's codebase.
code	String	No	The fully qualified class name for the applet.
codebase	String	No	The relative URL for the directory that contains the class file. The directory must be a subdirectory to the directory holding the page according to the HTML 4.0 spec.
height	String	Yes	The height of the applet area, in pixels or percentage.
hspace	String	No	The amount of whitespace to be inserted to the left and right of the applet area, in pixels.
iepluginurl	String	No	The URL for the location of the Internet Explorer Java Plugin. The default is implementation dependent.
jreversion	String	No	Identifies the spec version number of the JRE the component requires in order to operate. The default is 1.1.
name	String	No	Applet name, used by other applets on the same page that need to communicate with it.
nspluginurl	String	No	The URL for the location of the Netscape Java Plugin. The default is implementation dependent.
title	String	No	Text to be rendered by the browser for the applet in some way, for instance as a tool tip.
type	String	No	The type of object to embed, one of applet or bean.
vspace	String	No	The amount of whitespace to be inserted above and below the applet area, in pixels.
width	String	Yes	The width of the applet area, in pixels or percentage.

Example

```
<jsp:plugin type="applet" code="Clock2.class"
  codebase="applet"
  jreversion="1.2" width="160" height="150" >
  <jsp:params>
    <jsp:param name="bgcolor" value="ccddff" />
  </jsp:params>
  <jsp:fallback>
    Plugin tag OBJECT or EMBED not supported by browser.
  </jsp:fallback>
</jsp:plugin>
```

<jsp:root>

The <jsp:root> action element can only be used as the root element in a JSP Document (a JSP page in XML syntax). In specification versions prior JSP 2.0, using a <jsp:root> element was the only way to identify a JSP page as a JSP Document, but there are now other means (see Chapter 16) to do so. Hence, the <jsp:root> element is optional and should rarely be used.

Syntax

```
<jsp:root version="jspVersion">
  Well-formed XML content
</jsp:root>
```

Attributes

Attribute name	Java type	Dynamic value accepted	Description
version	String	No	The JSP specification with which the JSP Document is compliant.

Example

```
<jsp:root version="2.0">
  <employee>
    <name>${param.empName}</name>
    <dept>${param.empDept}</dept>
  <employee>
</jsp:root>
```

<jsp:setProperty>

The <jsp:setProperty> action sets the value of one or more bean properties.

Syntax

```
<jsp:setProperty name="beanVariableName" property="propertyName"
  [param="parameterName" | value="value"] />
```

Attributes

Attribute name	Java type	Dynamic value accepted	Description
name	String	No	The name assigned to a bean in one of the JSP scopes.
property	String	No	The name of the bean's property to set or an asterisk (*) to set all properties with name matching request parameters.
param	String	No	The name of a request parameter that holds the value to use for the specified property. If omitted, the parameter name and the property name must be the same.

Attribute name	Java type	Dynamic value accepted	Description
value	See below	Yes	An explicit value to assign to the property. This attribute can't be combined with the param attribute.

The property type can be any valid Java type, including primitive types and arrays (i.e., an indexed property). If a runtime attribute value is specified by the value attribute as a Java expression, the type of the expression must match the property's type.

If the value is a String, either in the form of a request parameter value or explicitly specified by the value attribute, it's converted to the property's type as follows:

Property type	Conversion method
boolean or Boolean	Boolean.valueOf(String), false for an empty string
byte or Byte	Byte.valueOf(String), 0 for an empty string
char or Character	String.charAt(0), 0 for an empty string
double or Double	Double.valueOf(String), 0 for an empty string
int or Integer	Integer.valueOf(String), 0 for an empty string
float or Float	Float.valueOf(String), 0 for an empty string
long or Long	Long.valueOf(String), 0 for an empty string
short or Short	Short.valueOf(String), 0 for an empty string
Object	new String(String)

For other types, such as a java.util.Date, the JSP container use a java.beans.PropertyEditor registered for the type and calls its setAsText(String) method. A property editor associated with a bean can, for instance, convert a string like 2001-11-22 to a Date object that represents this date. How to do so is described in Chapter 22.

Example

```
<jsp:setProperty name="user" property="*" />
<jsp:setProperty name="user" property="modDate"
  value="<%= new java.util.Date( ) %>" />
```

<jsp:text>

The <jsp:text> action is primarily intended for JSP Documents (JSP pages in XML syntax). Its body must only contain template text and EL expressions; neither JSP action elements nor scripting elements are allowed. When used in an XML document, the body content must be well-formed. The action's body content is evaluated and the result is added to the response with whitespace preserved.

Syntax

```
<jsp:text>
  Template text and EL expressions only
</jsp:text>
```

Attributes

None.

Example

```
<jsp:text>
  Some text and ${anELexpression}
</jsp:text>

<jsp:text>
  <![CDATA[<unknownelement/>]]>
</jsp:text>
```

<jsp:useBean>

The <jsp:useBean> action associates a Java bean with a name in one of the JSP scopes and also makes it available as a scripting variable. An attempt is first made to find a bean with the specified name in the specified scope. If it's not found, a new instance of the specified class is created.

Syntax 1: Using a concrete class, no body

```
<jsp:useBean id="beanVariableName" class="className"
  [scope="page|request|session|application"] />
```

Syntax 2: Using a concrete class, with a body

```
<jsp:useBean id="beanVariableName" class="className"
  [scope="page|request|session|application"]>
  Evaluated if a new instance is created
</jsp:useBean>
```

Syntax 3: Using a type and optionally a class or a serialized bean, no body

```
<jsp:useBean id="beanVariableName" type="className"
  [class="className" | beanName="className"]
  [scope="page|request|session|application"] />
```

Syntax 4: Using a type and optionally a class or a serialized bean, with a body

```
<jsp:useBean id="beanVariableName" type="className"
  [class="className" | beanName="className"]
  [scope="page|request|session|application"]>
  Evaluated if a new instance is created
</jsp:useBean>
```

Attributes

Attribute name	Java type	Dynamic value accepted	Description
beanName	String	Yes	The name of the bean, as expected by the instantiate( ) method of the Beans. class in the java.beans package.
class	String	No	The fully qualified class name for the bean.
id	String	No	The name to assign to the bean in the specified scope, as well as the name of the scripting variable.
scope	String	No	The scope for the bean, one of page, request, session, or application. The default is page.
type	String	No	The fully qualified type name for the bean (i.e., a superclass or an interface implemented by the bean's class).

Of the optional attributes, at least one of class or type must be specified. If both are specified, class must be assignable to type. The beanName attribute must be combined with the type attribute, and isn't valid with the class attribute.

The action is processed in these steps:

1. Attempt to locate an object based on the id and scope attribute values.
2. Define a scripting language variable with the given id of the specified type or class.
3. If the object is found, the variable's value is initialized with a reference to the located object, cast to the type specified by type or class. This completes the processing of the action. If the action element has a nonempty body, it's ignored.
4. If the object isn't found in the specified scope and neither class nor beanName is specified, an InstantiationException is thrown. This completes the processing of the action.
5. If the object isn't found in the specified scope, and the class attribute specifies a non-abstract class with a public no-args constructor, a new instance of the class is created and associated with the scripting variable and with the specified name in the specified scope. After this, step 7 is performed.

   If the object isn't found, and the specified class doesn't fulfill the requirements, an InstantiationException is thrown. This completes the processing of the action.
6. If the object isn't found in the specified scope, and the beanName attribute is specified, the instantiate( ) method of the java.beans.Beans class is invoked with the ClassLoader of the JSP implementation class instance and the beanName as arguments. If the method succeeds, the new object reference is associated with the scripting variable and with the specified name in the specified scope. After this, step 7 is performed.

7. If the action element has a nonempty body, the body is processed. The scripting variable is initialized and available within the scope of the body. The text of the body is treated as elsewhere; if there is template text, it's passed through to the response; scriptlets and action tags are evaluated.

   A common use of a nonempty body is to complete initializing the created instance; in that case, the body typically contains `<jsp:setProperty>` actions and scriptlets.

Example

```
<jsp:useBean id="clock" class="java.util.Date" />
```

Custom actions

A custom action can be developed by a programmer to extend the JSP language. The JSP Standard Tag Library (JSTL) actions are developed using the API defined by the JSP specification. Application-specific custom actions can also be developed using this API, such as the custom actions for adding cookies to a response and setting headers for no caching used in this book. The JSTL actions are described in Appendix B and all custom actions of a generic nature used in this book are described in Appendix E.

The general syntax for custom actions is the same as for the JSP standard actions: a start tag (optionally with attributes), a body, and an end tag. Other elements and template text can be nested in the body. Here's an example:

```
<ora:ifUserInRole value="admin">
  Greetings Master, I hope your day has been pleasant.
</ora:ifUserInRole>
```

The tag library containing the custom actions must be declared by the `taglib` directive, assigning a prefix for the custom action elements (`ora` in this example), before a custom action can be used in a JSP page.

Comments

You can use JSP comments in JSP pages to describe what a scripting element or action is doing:

```
<%-- This is a comment --%>
```

All text between the start and stop tag is ignored by the JSP container and isn't included in the response. The comment text can be anything except the character sequence representing the closing tag: `--%>`.

Besides describing what's going on in the JSP page, comments can also be used to "comment out" portions of the JSP page, for instance during testing:

```
<jsp:useBean id="user" class="com.mycompany.UserBean" />
<%--
<jsp:setProperty name="user" property="*" />
<jsp:setProperty name="user" property="modDate"
  value="<%= new java.util.Date( ) %>" />
<% boolean isValid = user.isValid( ); %>
--%>
```

The action and scripting elements within the comment aren't executed.

Escape Characters

Because certain character sequences are used to represent start and stop tags, you sometimes need to escape a character so the container doesn't interpret it as part of a special character sequence.

In a scripting element, if you need to use the characters %> literally, you must escape the greater-than character with a backslash:

```
<% String msg = "Literal %\> must be escaped"; %>
```

To avoid the character sequence <% in template text to be interpreted as the start of a scripting element, you must escape the percent sign:

```
This is template text and <\% is not a start of a scriptlet.
```

Similarly, the dollar sign that start an EL expression must be escaped in a page where EL evaluation is enabled:

```
This is template text and \${this is not an EL expression}.
```

In an attribute value, you must use the following escapes:

```
attr='a value with an escaped \' single quote'
attr="a value with an escaped \" double quote"
attr="a value with an escaped \\ backslash"
attr="a value with an escaped %\> scripting end tag"
attr="a value with an escaped <\% scripting start tag"
attr="a value with an escaped \$ dollar sign"
```

As an alternative to escaping quote characters, you can use the ' and " character entities.

APPENDIX B

JSTL Actions and API Reference

This appendix contains reference material for all JSTL actions, functions, support and utility classes, and configuration settings.

The actions are described using the same conventions as for the JSP standard actions in Appendix A.

JSTL Library URIs and Default Prefixes

The URIs and default prefixes for the JSTL libraries are listed in Table B-1.

Table B-1. URIs and prefixes for the JSTL libraries

Library	URI	Prefix
Core	`http://java.sun.com/jsp/jstl/core`	`c`
XML Processing	`http://java.sun.com/jsp/jstl/xml`	`x`
I18N Formatting	`http://java.sun.com/jsp/jstl/fmt`	`fmt`
Database Access	`http://java.sun.com/jsp/jstl/sql`	`sql`
Functions	`http://java.sun.com/jsp/jstl/functions`	`fn`

Core Library Actions

The core library contains actions for control-flow, URL manipulation, importing resources, and other general-purpose tasks.

<c:catch>

The `<c:catch>` action catches an exception thrown by JSP elements in its body, providing fine-grained error control. The exception can optionally be saved as a page scope variable.

Syntax

```
<c:catch [var="var"]>
  JSP elements
</c:catch>
```

Attributes

Attribute name	Java type	Dynamic value accepted	Description
var	String	No	The variable name.

Example

```
<c:catch var="importException">
  <fmt:parseDate value="${param.empDate}" dateStyle="short" />
</c:catch>
<c:if test="${importException != null}">
  <jsp:forward page="input.jsp">
    <jsp:param name="msg" value="Invalid date format" />
  </jsp:forward>
</c:if>
```

<c:choose>

The <c:choose> action controls the processing of nested <c:when> and <c:otherwise> actions. It allows only the first <c:when> action with a test expression that evaluates to true to be processed; it gives the go-ahead to the single <c:otherwise> action if none do.

Syntax

```
<c:choose>
  <c:when> actions and optionally one <c:otherwise> action
</c:choose>
```

Attributes

None.

Example

```
<c:choose>
  <c:when test="${product.onSale}">
    ${product.salesPrice} On sale!
  </c:when>
  <c:otherwise>
    ${product.price}
  </c:otherwise>
</c:choose>
```

<c:forEach>

The `<c:forEach>` action evaluates its body a fixed number of times or once for each element in a collection. The current element (or the current index if no collection is specified) and the iteration status can be exposed to action elements in the body through nested variables.

The action accepts collections of the types listed in the Attributes table. The type of the current element is the type of the underlying collection, with two exceptions. For an array of a primitive type, the current element is exposed as an instance of the corresponding wrapper class (`Integer`, `Float`, etc.) For a `java.util.Map`, the current element is exposed as a `java.util.Map.Entry`.

Syntax 1: Iteration over collection elements

```
<c:forEach items="collection" [var="var"] [varStatus="varStatus"]
  [begin="startIndex"] [end="stopIndex"] [step="increment"]>
  JSP elements
</c:forEach>
```

Syntax 2: Fixed number of iterations

```
<c:forEach [var="var"] [varStatus="varStatus"]
  begin="startIndex" end="stopIndex" [step="increment"]>
  JSP elements
</c:forEach>
```

Attributes

Attribute name	Java type	Dynamic value accepted	Description
`begin`	`int`	Yes	The start index, 0-based when used with a collection. Default is 0 for a collection.
`end`	`int`	Yes	The stop index (inclusive), 0-based when used with a collection. The default is the last element for a collection. If end is less than `begin`, the body is not evaluated at all.
`items`	`java.util.Collection`, `java.util.Iterator`, `java.util.Enumeration`, `java.util.Map`, array of objects or primitive types.	Yes	The collection to iterate over.
`step`	`int`	Yes	The index-increment value for each iteration. Default is 1.
`var`	`String`	No	The name of the nested variable holding the current element.

Attribute name	Java type	Dynamic value accepted	Description
varStatus	String	No	The name of the nested variable holding the LoopTagStatus object.

Example

```
<%-- Iterate five times, writing 1, 2, 3, 4, 5 --%>
<c:forEach begin="1" end="5" var="current">
  ${current}
</c:forEach>

<%-- Iterate over all request parameters --%>
<c:forEach items="${param}" var="current">
  Name: <c:out value="${current.key}" />
  Value: <c:out value="${current.value}" />
</c:forEach>
```

<c:forTokens>

The <c:forTokens> action evaluates its body once for each token in a String, delimited by one of the specified delimiter characters. The current token and the iteration status can be exposed to action elements in the body through nested variables.

Syntax

```
<c:forTokens items="stringOfTokens" delims="delimiters"
  [var="var"] [varStatus="varStatus"]
  [begin="startIndex"] [end="stopIndex"] [step="increment"]>
  JSP elements
</c:forTokens>
```

Attributes

Attribute name	Java type	Dynamic value accepted	Description
items	String	Yes	The tokens to iterate over.
delims	String	Yes	The list of delimiter characters.
var	String	No	The name of the nested variable holding the current element.
varStatus	String	No	The name of the nested variable holding the LoopTagStatus object.
begin	int	Yes	The 0-based start index. Default is 0.
end	int	Yes	The 0-based stop index (inclusive). The default is the last token. If end is less than begin, the body is not evaluated at all.
step	int	Yes	The index-increment value for each iteration. Default is 1.

Example

```
<%-- Iterate over tokens separated by vertical bars --%>
<c:forTokens items="${tokens}" delims="|" var="current">
  <c:out value="${current }" />
</c:forTokens>
```

<c:if>

The `<c:if>` action evaluates its body only if the specified expression evaluates to `true`. Alternatively, the evaluation result can be saved as a scoped `Boolean` variable.

Syntax 1: Without a body

```
<c:if test="booleanExpression"
  var="var" [scope="page|request|session|application"]/>
```

Syntax 1: With a body

```
<c:if test="booleanExpression">
  JSP elements
</c:if>
```

Attributes

Attribute name	Java type	Dynamic value accepted	Description
`test`	`boolean`	Yes	The test expression.
`var`	`String`	No	The variable name.
`scope`	`String`	No	The variable scope.

Example

```
<c:if test="${empty param.empDate}">
  <jsp:forward page="input.jsp">
    <jsp:param name="msg" value="Missing the Employment Date" />
  </jsp:forward>
</c:if>
```

<c:import>

The `<c:import>` action imports the content of an external or internal (same web application) resource. An external resource can be either a resource owned by a different application in the same web container or a resource on a different server that can be accessed through one of the protocols supported by the web container (e.g., HTTP or FTP).

When importing an internal resource, the behavior is the same as for the `<jsp:include>` standard action; the target resource has access to the same request parameters and the same request, session, and application scope variables as the originating page. A target resource owned by a different application in the same web container has access only to the same request parameters and request scope data, and a resource owned by a different server has access only to the request parameters specified as a query string or nested `<c:param>` actions.

An internal resource can be identified by a context- or page-relative path. An external resource owned by another application in the same container must be identified by a context-relative path plus the context-path for the application. For resources owned by an external server, an absolute URL with a scheme (protocol), server name and resource identifier must be used.

The character encoding for the imported content can be specified for the cases where it can't be determined through other means (e.g., HTTP headers). This is typically needed only for resources imported using a protocol other than HTTP with a character encoding other than ISO-8859-1, which is the default.

This action throws an exception if the underlying import mechanism throws an exception or if the target resource responds with an HTTP status code other than 200 through 299. In the latter case, the exception message includes the resource path and the status code.

The imported content can be added to the current response buffer (`JspWriter`), saved as a `String` in a scoped variable, or exposed through a `java.io.Reader` to nested actions.

Syntax 1: Content saved in a String variable or added to the response

```
<c:import url="url" [context="externalContextPath"]
  [var="var"] scope="page|request|session|application"]]
  [charEncoding="charEncoding"]>
  Optional <c:param> actions
</c:import>
```

Syntax 2: Content exposed as a Reader to nested actions

```
<c:import url="url" [context="externalContextPath"]
  varReader="varReader"
  [charEncoding="charEncoding"]>
  Actions using the Reader
</c:import>
```

Attributes

Attribute name	Java type	Dynamic value accepted	Description
`url`	`String`	Yes	The URL for the resource to import.
`context`	`String`	Yes	The context-path for an external application in the same container, starting with a slash.
`var`	`String`	No	The name of the variable to hold the content as a `String`.

Attribute name	Java type	Dynamic value accepted	Description
scope	String	No	The scope for the variable.
varReader	String	No	The name of the nested variable to expose the content as a java.io.Reader.
charEncoding	String	Yes	Character encoding for the content. Default is the encoding reported by the import mechanism or ISO-8859-1 if none is reported.

Example

```
<%--
  Add the response produced by an internal resource to the response.
-->
<c:import url="navigation.jsp" />

<%-- Process the imported content -->
<c:import url="http://meerkat.oreillynet.com/?&p=4999&_fl=xml&t=ALL"
  varReader="xmlSource">
  <x:parse var="doc" xml="${xmlSource}" scope="application" />
</c:import>
```

<c:otherwise>

The <c:otherwise> action represents the default alternative within a <c:choose> block. It evaluates its body only if none of the <c:when> actions in the block has a test expression that evaluates to true.

Syntax

```
<c:otherwise>
  JSP elements
</c:otherwise>
```

Attributes

None.

Example

```
<c:choose>
  <c:when test="${product.onSale}">
    ${product.salesPrice} On sale!
  </c:when>
  <c:otherwise>
    ${product.price}
  </c:otherwise>
</c:choose>
```

<c:out>

The <c:out> action adds the evaluation result of an expression to the current response buffer (JspWriter), or a default value if the main expression evaluates to null. The evaluation result is always converted to a Stringfollowing the coercing rules described in Appendix C unless the evaluation result is of type java.io.Reader. For a Reader, the characters it contains are used instead of the value returned by the toString( ) method.

Syntax 1: Without a body

```
<c:out value="expression" [escapeXml="[true|false]"]
  [default="defaultExpression"] />
```

Syntax 2: With a body

```
<c:out value="expression" [escapeXml="[true|false]"]>
  defaultExpression
</c:out>
```

Attributes

Attribute name	Java type	Dynamic value accepted	Description
value	Object	Yes	The expression to evaluate.
escapeXml	boolean	Yes	If true, the characters < > & ' " are converted to the corresponding XML character entity codes.
default	Object	Yes	The default expression to use if the expression defined by value evaluates to null. If no default is specified, the empty string is used as the ultimate default.

Example

```
<c:out value="${param.phone}" default="No phone" />

<c:out value="${user.imageURL}">
  <c:url value="/defaultUserImage.jpg" />
</c:out>
```

<c:param>

The <c:param> action is used as a nested action for <c:import>, <c:redirect>, and <c:url> to add a request parameter to a URL.

Syntax 1: Without a body

```
<c:param name="parameterName" value="parameterValue" />
```

Syntax 2: With a body

```
<c:param name="parameterName">
  parameterValue
</c:param>
```

Attributes

Attribute name	Java type	Dynamic value accepted	Description
name	String	Yes	Parameter name
value	String	Yes	Parameter value

Example

```
<c:import value="stock.jsp">
  <c:param name="id" value="${param.stockSymbol}" />
</c:import>
```

<c:redirect>

The `<c:redirect>` action sends a redirect response to the client, telling it to make a new request for the specified resource. Internal and external resources can be specified in the same ways as for `<c:url>`, and the URL and parameters specified by nested `<c:param>` actions are also converted in the same way, if needed.

Syntax 1: Without a body

```
<c:redirect url="url" [context="externalContextPath"] />
```

Syntax 1: With a body

```
<c:redirect url="url" [context="externalContextPath"]>
  <c:param> actions
</c:redirect>
```

Attributes

Attribute name	Java type	Dynamic value accepted	Description
value	String	Yes	A page- or context-relative path, or an absolute URL.
context	String	Yes	The context-path for an external application in the same container, starting with a slash.

Example

```
<c:redirect url="result.jsp" />
```

<c:remove>

The <c:remove> action removes a scoped variable. If no scope is specified, the variable is removed from the first scope where it's found; it scans the scopes in the order page, request, session, and application, otherwise from the specified scope. If the variable is not found, this action does nothing.

Syntax

```
<c:remove var="var" [scope="page|request|session|application"] />
```

Attributes

Attribute name	Java type	Dynamic value accepted	Description
var	String	No	The name of the variable to remove.
scope	String	No	The variable scope.

Example

```
<c:remove var="authenticationToken" scope="session" />
```

<c:set>

The <c:set> action sets a scoped variable or a property of a target object to the value of an expression evaluation result. The target object must be a java.util.Map or a bean with a matching property setter method.

If the evaluation result is null, the variable is removed or the property is reset (removed or set to null, depending on the type of target). Otherwise, when setting a variable or a Map entry, the type of the value is the type of the expression evaluation value. When setting a bean property, the expression evaluation value is coerced to the property type according to the rules described in Appendix C.

Syntax 1: Setting a variable, without a body

```
<c:set value="expression" var="var"
  [scope="page|request|session|application"] />
```

Syntax 2: Setting a variable, with a body

```
<c:set var="var" [scope="page|request|session|application"]>
  JSP elements
</c:set>
```

Syntax 3: Setting a property, without a body

```
<c:set value="expression" target="beanOrMap" property="propertyName" />
```

Syntax 4: Setting a property, with a body

```
<c:set target="beanOrMap" property="propertyName">
  JSP elements
</c:set>
```

Attributes

Attribute name	Java type	Dynamic value accepted	Description
value	Object	Yes	The expression to use as the value.
var	String	No	The name of the variable.
scope	String	No	Scope for the variable.
target	Object	Yes	The target object, either a `java.util.Map` or a bean with a setter method for `property`.
property	String	Yes	The target object's property name.

Example

```
<c:set var="selectedLocale" value="${bundle.locale}" />

<c:set target="${msgMap}" property="empDateError">
  The Employment Date format is invalid
</c:set>
```

<c:url>

The `<c:url>` action applies the appropriate encoding and conversion rules for a relative or absolute URL. Specifically, it handles three types of rules: URL encoding of parameters specified by nested `<c:param>` actions (converting special characters to hexadecimal codes); converting a context-relative path into a server-relative path; and adding a session ID path parameter for a context- or page-relative path ("URL rewriting"), if needed to enable session tracking. The result is either saved in a scoped variable or added to the current response buffer (`JspWriter`).

Syntax 1: Without a body

```
<c:url value="url" [context="externalContextPath"]
  [var="var"] scope="page|request|session|application"]] />
```

Syntax 2: With a body

```
<c:url value="url" [context="externalContextPath"]
  [var="var"] scope="page|request|session|application"]]>
  <c:param> actions
</c:url>
```

Attributes

Attribute name	Java type	Dynamic value accepted	Description
value	String	Yes	A page- or context-relative path, or an absolute URL.
context	String	Yes	The context-path for an external application in the same container, starting with a slash.
var	String	No	The variable name. The type is String.
scope	String	No	The variable scope.

Example

```
<a href="<c:url value="/privacypolicy.jsp" />">Our privacy policy</a>
```

<c:when>

The <c:when> action represents one of the mutually exclusive alternatives within a <c:choose> block. It evaluates its body only if it's the first <c:when> action in the block with a test expression that evaluates to true.

Syntax

```
<c:when test="booleanExpression">
  JSP elements
</c:when>
```

Attributes

Attribute name	Java type	Dynamic value accepted	Description
test	Boolean	Yes	The test expression.

Example

```
<c:choose>
  <c:when test="${product.onSale}">
    ${product.salesPrice} On sale!
  </c:when>
  <c:otherwise>
    ${product.price}
  </c:otherwise>
</c:choose>
```

Internationalization and Formatting Actions

<fmt:bundle>

The `<fmt:bundle>` action establishes a localization context for actions in its body. The localization context contains a locale and the best match for the specified resource bundle. The locale is either the locale defined by the locale configuration setting or the best match for the user preferences specified by the `Accept-Language` HTTP request header.

Syntax

```
<fmt:bundle basename="resourceBundleBasename" [prefix="keyPrefix"]>
  JSP elements
</fmt:bundle>
```

Attributes

Attribute name	Java type	Dynamic value accepted	Description
`basename`	`String`	Yes	The basename for a resource bundle, see `java.util.ResourceBundle` for details.
`prefix`	`String`	Yes	Prefix to be prepended to keys specified for nested `<fmt:message>` actions.

Example

```
<fmt:bundle basename="labels">
  <h1><fmt:message key="title" /></h1>
</fmt:bundle>
```

<fmt:formatDate>

The `<fmt:formatDate>` action formats a date and time value according to locale specific rules. A custom pattern can be specified or locale-dependent default patterns for one or both of the date and the time portion can be selected.

The locale is taken from the locale configuration setting or the locale from the localization context setting, or if none of these are set, determined as the best match for the user preferences (`Accept-Language` request header).

If the value to format is `null` or an empty string, no output is generated, and if a variable to hold the output is specified, it's removed.

Syntax

```
<fmt:formatDate value="dateAndTime"
```

```
[pattern="pattern" |
  [type="time|date|both"]
  [dateStyle="default|short|medium|long|full"]
  [timeStyle="default|short|medium|long|full"]]
[timeZone="timeZone"]
[var="var" [scope="page|request|session|application"]] />
```

Attributes

Attribute name	Java type	Dynamic value accepted	Description
`value`	`java.util.Date`	Yes	The date and time to format.
`pattern`	`String`	Yes	A custom pattern in the form accepted by `java.text.SimpleDateFormat` (see the next table).
`type`	`String`	Yes	Which portions to format.
`dateStyle`	`String`	Yes	One of the predefined locale-dependent date patterns.
`timeStyle`	`String`	Yes	One of the predefined locale-dependent time patterns.
`timeZone`	`String` or `java.util.TimeZone`	Yes	The time zone to use instead of the default.
`var`	`String`	No	The variable name. The type is `String`.
`scope`	`String`	No	The variable scope.

The symbols that can be used in a custom pattern, set by the `pattern` attribute, are the same as those supported by the `java.text.SimpleDateFormat`:

Symbol	Description	Presentation format	Example
`G`	Era designator	Text	AD
`y`	Year	Number	2002
`M`	Month in year	Text or Number	May or 05
`d`	Day in month	Number	16
`h`	Hour in AM/PM (1–12)	Number	4
`H`	Hour in day (0–23)	Number	16
`m`	Minute in hour	Number	18
`s`	Second in minute	Number	23
`S`	Millisecond	Number	678
`E`	Day in week	Text	Thursday
`D`	Day in year	Number	144
`F`	Day of week in month	Number	3
`w`	Week in year	Number	20

Symbol	Description	Presentation format	Example
W	Week in month	Number	3
a	AM/PM marker	Text	PM
k	Hour in day (1–24)	Number	17
K	Hour in AM/PM (0–11)	Number	3
z	Time zone	Text	GMT
'	Escape for text	Delimiter	
''	Single quote in text	Literal	'

The number of symbols in the pattern determines the presentation format. For Text, four or more symbols means that the full form is used (e.g., "Thursday"), while less than four means that an abbreviation is used (e.g., "Thu"). For Number, the number of symbols sets the minimum number of digits. For Text or Number values, three or more symbols mean that the text format is used, otherwise the number format is used.

Example

```
<fmt:formatDate value="${now}" type="both" dateStyle="full" />
```

<fmt:formatNumber>

The `<fmt:formatNumber>` action formats a numeric value according to locale specific rules. A custom pattern can be specified, or the locale-dependent default pattern for a certain number type (currency, percentage, or a regular number) can be used as a starting point and optionally adjusted (currency code, max and min number of digits and fractional digits, grouping character or not).

The locale is taken from the locale configuration setting or the locale from the localization context setting. If neither is set, the locale is determined as the best match for the user preferences (`Accept-Language` request header).

If the value to format is `null` or an empty string, no output is generated, and if a variable to hold the output is specified, it's removed.

Syntax 1: Without a body

```
<fmt:formatNumber value="number"
  [pattern="pattern" |
    [type="number|currency|percent"]
    [currencyCode="currencyCode" | currencySymbol="currencySymbol"]
    [groupingUsed="true|false"]
    [minIntegerDigits="min"] [maxIntegerDigits="max"]
    [minFractionDigits="min"] [maxFractionDigits="max"]]
  [var="var" [scope="page|request|session|application"]] />
```

Syntax 1: With a body

```
<fmt:formatNumber
  [pattern="pattern" |
    [type="number|currency|percent"]
    [currencyCode="currencyCode" | currencySymbol="currencySymbol"]
    [groupingUsed="true|false"]
    [minIntegerDigits="min"] [maxIntegerDigits="max"]
    [minFractionDigits="min"] [maxFractionDigits="max"]]
  [var="var" [scope="page|request|session|application"]]>
  number
</fmt:formatNumber>
```

Attributes

Attribute name	Java type	Dynamic value accepted	Description
value	String or Number	Yes	The value to format. If specified as a String it must be in the format of a Java numeric literal.
pattern	String	Yes	A custom pattern in the form accepted by java.text.DecimalFormat (see the next table).
type	String	Yes	The name of one of the predefined locale-dependent patterns.
currencyCode	String	Yes	An ISO-4217 currency code.
currencySymbol	String	Yes	A Java string to use as the currency symbol.
groupingUsed	boolean	Yes	Set to true to include grouping separators in the result.
minIntegerDigits	int	Yes	The minimum number of digits in the integer portion.
maxIntegerDigits	int	Yes	The maximum number of digits in the integer portion.
minFractionDigits	int	Yes	The minimum number of digits in the fractional portion.
maxFractionDigits	int	Yes	The maximum number of digits in the fractional portion.
var	String	No	The variable name. The type is String.
scope	String	No	The variable scope.

The symbols that can be used in a custom pattern, set by the pattern attribute, are the same as those supported by the java.text.DecimalFormat:

Symbol	Description	Location
0	Required digit	Number
#	Digit, zero is not displayed	Number
.	Decimal separator	Number
-	Minus sign	Number
,	Grouping separator	Number

Symbol	Description	Location
E	Separates mantissa and exponent in scientific notation	Number
%	Multiply by 100 and show as percentage	Prefix or suffix
\u2030	Multiply by 1000 and shows as mille	Prefix or suffix
¤ or \u00A4	Currency sign	Prefix or suffix
'	Escape for text	Prefix or suffix
''	Single quote in text	Prefix or suffix

Example

```
<fmt:formatNumber value="1000.00" type="currency" />
<fmt:formatNumber value="${aNumber}" minFractionDigits="2" />
```

<fmt:message>

The `<fmt:message>` action adds the localized message for the specified key to the current response buffer (`JspWriter`) or saves it in a scoped variable. For a parameterized message, the parameter values are specified by nested `<fmt:param>` actions.

Syntax 1: Without a body

```
<fmt:message key="messageKey" [bundle="resourceBundle"]
  [var="var" [scope="page|request|session|application"]] />
```

Syntax 2: With a body for parameters

```
<fmt:message key="messageKey" [bundle="resourceBundle"]
  [var="var" [scope="page|request|session|application"]]>
  <fmt:param> actions
</fmt:message>
```

Syntax 3: With a body for the key and parameters

```
<fmt:message [bundle="resourceBundle"]
  [var="var" [scope="page|request|session|application"]]>
  messageKey
  <fmt:param> actions
</fmt:message>
```

Attributes

Attribute name	Java type	Dynamic value accepted	Description
key	String	Yes	Message key.
bundle	javax.servlet.jsp.jstl.fmt.LocalizationContext	Yes	Localization context with the resource bundle to use.
var	String	No	The variable name. The type is `String`.
scope	String	No	The variable scope.

Example

```
<fmt:message key="simpleMessage" />

<fmt:message key="result">
  <fmt:param value="${result.total}" />
  <fmt:param value="${result.percentage}" />
</fmt:message>
```

<fmt:param>

The `<fmt:param>` action is used as a nested action for `<fmt:message>` to supply a parameter value for a parameterized message.

The parameter syntax that can be used in the parameterized message is the syntax accepted by the `java.text.MessageFormat` class, i.e., a 0-based order number optionally followed by a data type name and a format specification, within curly braces:

```
{orderNumber [, dataType [, format ]]}
```

The data type must be one of `time`, `date`, `number`, or `choice`.

For a `time` or `date` type, the format specification can be one of `short`, `medium`, `long`, `full`, or the type of customized pattern described for `<fmt:formatDate>`.

For a `number` type, the format specification can be `currency`, `percent`, `integer`, or the type of customized pattern described for `<fmt:formatNumber>`.

See the `java.text.MessageFormat` documentation for details about the `choice` type.

Syntax 1: Without a body

```
<fmt:param value="parameterValue" />
```

Syntax 2: With a body

```
<fmt:param>
  parameterValue
</fmt:param>
```

Attributes

Attribute name	Java type	Dynamic value accepted	Description
`value`	`Object`	Yes	The parameter value.

Example

```
<fmt:message key="result">
  <fmt:param value="${result.total}" />
  <fmt:param value="${result.percentage}" />
</fmt:message>
```

<fmt:parseDate>

The <fmt:parseDate> action parses a date and time value formatted according to locale specific rules. A custom pattern can be specified or locale-dependent default patterns for one or both of the date and the time portion can be selected.

The locale used is the one explicitly specified or is taken from the locale configuration setting or the locale from the localization context setting. If none of these are set, the locale is determined as the best match for the user preferences (Accept-Language request header).

Syntax 1: Without a body

```
<fmt:parseDate value="dateAndTime"
  [pattern="pattern" |
    [type="time|date|both"]
    [dateStyle="default|short|medium|long|full"]
    [timeStyle="default|short|medium|long|full"]]
  [timeZone="timeZone"]
  [parseLocale="locale"]
  [var="var" [scope="page|request|session|application"]] />
```

Syntax 2: With a body

```
<fmt:parseDate
  [pattern="pattern" |
    [type="time|date|both"]
    [dateStyle="default|short|medium|long|full"]
    [timeStyle="default|short|medium|long|full"]]
  [timeZone="timeZone"]
  [parseLocale="locale"]
  [var="var" [scope="page|request|session|application"]]>
  dateAndTime
</fmt:parseDate>
```

Attributes

Attribute name	Java type	Dynamic value accepted	Description
value	String	Yes	The date and time to parse.
pattern	String	Yes	A custom pattern in the form accepted by java.text.SimpleDateFormat; see <fmt:formatDate>.
type	String	Yes	Which portions the value contains.
dateStyle	String	Yes	One of the predefined locale-dependent date patterns.
timeStyle	String	Yes	One of the predefined locale-dependent time patterns.
timeZone	String or java.util.TimeZone	Yes	The time zone to use instead of the default.

Attribute name	Java type	Dynamic value accepted	Description
parseLocale	String or java.util. Locale	Yes	A locale to be used instead of the default.
var	String	No	The variable name. The type is java.util.Date.
scope	String	No	The variable scope.

Example

```
<fmt:parseDate value="${param.emDate}" pattern="yyyy-MM-dd" />
```

<fmt:parseNumber>

The <fmt:parseNumber> action parses a number formatted according to locale specific rules. A custom pattern can be specified or a locale specific default pattern for a certain number type (currency, percentage, or a regular number) can be used.

The locale used is the one explicitly specified or is taken from the locale configuration setting or the locale from the localization context setting. If none of these are set, the locale is determined as the best match for the user preferences (Accept-Language request header).

Syntax 1: Without a body

```
<fmt:parseNumber value="number"
  [pattern="pattern" | type="number|currency|percent"]
  [parseLocale="locale"]
  [integerOnly="true|false"]
  [var="var" [scope="page|request|session|application"]] />
```

Syntax 1: With a body

```
<fmt:formatNumber
  [pattern="pattern" | type="number|currency|percent"]
  [parseLocale="locale"]
  [integerOnly="true|false"]
  [var="var" [scope="page|request|session|application"]]>
  number
</fmt:parseNumber>
```

Attributes

Attribute name	Java type	Dynamic value accepted	Description
value	String	Yes	The value to parse.
pattern	String	Yes	A custom pattern in the form accepted by java.text. DecimalFormat, see <fmt:formatNumber>.
type	String	Yes	The name of one of the predefined locale-dependent patterns.

Attribute name	Java type	Dynamic value accepted	Description
parseLocale	String or java. util. Locale	Yes	A locale to be used instead of the default.
integerOnly	boolean	Yes	Set to true to only parse the integer portion.
var	String	No	The variable name. The type is Number.
scope	String	No	The variable scope.

Example

```
<fmt:parseNumber value="${param.annualSalary}" type="currency" />
```

<fmt:requestEncoding>

The <fmt:requestEncoding> action sets the character encoding for the request to facilitate correct interpretation of request parameter values when the encoding is different from ISO-8859-1. The encoding can be specified explicitly. It can also be determined based on the request Content-Type header, if any, or the encoding session variable set by all JSTL actions that set the locale for a response (javax.servlet.jsp.jstl.fmt.request.charset).

Syntax

```
<fmt:requestEncoding [value="encodingName"] />
```

Attributes

Attribute name	Java type	Dynamic value accepted	Description
Value	String	Yes	The encoding name.

Example

```
<%--
  Sets the request encoding to the same encoding as was used for
  the previous response in the current session.
-->
<fmt:requestEncoding />
```

<fmt:setBundle>

The <fmt:setBundle> action sets the localization context configuration variable, which establishes the localization context for all other JSTL actions that rely on one and disables the locale lookup based on user preferences. Alternatively, the localization context may be saved as a scoped variable and provided as explicit input to other actions.

The localization context contains a locale and the best match for the specified resource bundle. The locale for the localization context is either the locale defined by the locale configuration setting or the best match for the user preferences specified by the `Accept-Language` HTTP request header.

Syntax

```
<fmt:setBundle basename="resourceBundleBasename"
  [var="var"] [scope="page|request|session|application"] />
```

Attributes

Attribute name	Java type	Dynamic value accepted	Description
`basename`	`String`	Yes	The basename for a resource bundle, see `java.util.ResourceBundle` for details.
`var`	`String`	No	The variable name. If omitted, the actions sets the localization context configuration variable. The type is `javax.servlet.jsp.jstl.fmt.Localization.Context`.
`scope`	`String`	No	The scope for the variable or the configuration variable.

Example

```
<fmt:setBundle basename="labels" scope="session" />
```

<fmt:setLocale>

The `<fmt:setLocale>` action sets the locale configuration variable, establishing the locale for all other JSTL actions that rely on a locale and disabling the locale lookup based on user preferences.

Syntax

```
<fmt:setLocale value="locale" [variant="variant"]
  [scope="page|request|session|application"] />
```

Attributes

Attribute name	Java type	Dynamic value accepted	Description
`value`	`String` or `java.util.Locale`	Yes	The locale. If set as a `String`, it must be an ISO-639 language code, optionally followed by an ISO-3166 country code, separated by a hyphen or an underscore character.
`variant`	`String`	Yes	A locale variant, see `java.util.Locale` for details.
`scope`	`String`	No	The configuration variable scope.

Example

```
<fmt:setLocale value="en-US" />
```

<fmt:setTimeZone>

The <fmt:setTimeZone> action sets the time zone configuration variable, establishing the time zone for all other JSTL actions that rely on one. Alternatively, the time zone may be saved as a scoped variable and provided as explicit input to other actions.

Syntax

```
<fmt:setTimeZone value="timeZone"
  [var="var"] [scope="page|request|session|application"] />
```

Attributes

Attribute name	Java type	Dynamic value accepted	Description
value	String or java.util.TimeZone	Yes	The time zone. If specified as a String, it's an abbreviation, a name, or a GMT offset; see java.util.TimeZone for details.
var	String	No	The variable name. If omitted, the actions sets the time-zone context configuration variable. The type is java.util.TimeZone.
scope	String	No	The scope for the variable or the configuration variable.

Example

```
<fmt:setTimeZone value="GMT-8" />
```

<fmt:timeZone>

The <fmt:timeZone> action establishes the time zone for actions in its body.

Syntax

```
<fmt:TimeZone value="timeZone">
  JSP elements
</fmt:timeZone>
```

Attributes

Attribute name	Java type	Dynamic value accepted	Description
value	String or java.util.TimeZone	Yes	The time zone. If specified as a String, it's an abbreviation, a name, or a GMT offset; see java.util.TimeZone for details.

Example

```
<fmt:timeZone value="America/Los Angeles">
  <fmt:formatDate value="${now}" type="both" />
</fmt:timeZone>
```

Database Access Actions

<sql:dateParam>

The <sql:dateParam> action is used as a nested action for <sql:query> and <sql:update> to supply a date and time value for a value placeholder. If a null value is provided, the value is set to SQL NULL for the placeholder. To ensure portability between different database engines, this action must be used when setting values for DATE, TIME, and TIMESTAMP columns.

The value must be of type java.util.Date or one of the SQL specific subclasses: java.sql.Date, java.sql.Time or java.sql.Timestamp. If it's a java.util.Date, the action converts it to the specified subclass.

Syntax

```
<sql:dateParam value="parameterValue"
  [type="timestamp|time|date"] />
```

Attributes

Attribute name	Java type	Dynamic value accepted	Description
value	java.util.Date	Yes	The parameter value.
type	String	Yes	The SQL type the value should be converted to, if needed.

Example

```
<sql:update>
  UPDATE Employee SET EmpDate = ? WHERE EmpId = ?
  <sql:dateParam value="${empDate}" />
  <sql:param value="${empId}" />
</sql:update>
```

<sql:param>

The <sql:param> action is used as a nested action for <sql:query> and <sql:update> to supply a value for a value placeholder. If a null value is provided, the value is set to SQL NULL for the placeholder. To ensure portability between different database engines, the value type must be a supported type for the target column, for instance a numeric value for an INT or FLOAT column and a String value for a CHAR or VARCHAR column. See <sql:dateParam> for setting values for DATE, TIME, and TIMESTAMP columns.

Syntax 1: Without a body

```
<sql:param value="parameterValue" />
```

Syntax 2: With a body

```
<sql:param>
  parameterValue
</sql:param>
```

Attributes

Attribute name	Java type	Dynamic value accepted	Description
value	Object	Yes	The parameter value.

Example

```
<sql:update>
  DELETE * FROM Employee WHERE Id = ?
  <sql:param value="${empId}" />
</sql:update>
```

<sql:query>

The <sql:query> action executes an SQL SELECT statement and saves the result in a scoped variable. The statement may contain question marks as placeholders for values assigned by nested <sql:param> and <sql:dateParam> actions.

The action uses a connection provided by an <sql:transaction> action, or—if not part of a transaction—from the explicitly specified data source or the data-source configuration setting. The number of rows to retrieve can be limited explicitly or by the maximum rows configuration setting.

Syntax 1: Without a body

```
<sql:query sql="sqlSelectStatement"
  [dataSource="dataSource"]
  [maxRows="maxRows"]
  [startRow="index"]
  var="var" [scope="page|request|session|application"] />
```

Syntax 2: With a body for parameters

```
<sql:query sql="sqlSelectStatement"
  [dataSource="dataSource"]
  [maxRows="maxRows"]
  [startRow="index"]
  var="var" [scope="page|request|session|application"]>
  <sql:param> actions
</sql:query>
```

Syntax 3: With a body for the statement and parameters

```
<sql:query
  [dataSource="dataSource"]
  [maxRows="maxRows"]
```

```
  [startRow="index"]
  var="var" [scope="page|request|session|application"]>
  sqlSelectStatement
  <sql:param> actions
</sql:query>
```

Attributes

Attribute name	Java type	Dynamic value accepted	Description
sql	String	Yes	The SQL statement.
dataSource	String or javax.sql.DataSource	Yes	The data source to use. If specified as a String, it can be either a JNDI path or a list of JDBC parameters as described for the data-source configuration setting.
maxRows	int	Yes	The maximum number of rows to include in the result. If omitted or -1, all rows are included.
startRow	int	Yes	The 0-based index for the first row to include in the result.
var	String	No	The variable name. The type is javax.servlet.jsp.jstl.sql.Result.
scope	String	No	The variable scope.

Example

```
<sql:query var="result">
  SELECT * FROM Employee WHERE Name = ?
  <sql:param value="${param:empName}" />
</sql:query>
```

<sql:setDataSource>

The <sql:setDataSource> action sets the data source configuration variable, or saves the data source information in a scoped variable that can be used as input to the other JSTL database actions.

This action is primarily intended for prototyping and small, simple applications. See Chapter 12 and Chapter 24 for alternative ways to make a data source available.

Syntax

```
<sql:setDataSource
  [dataSource="dataSource" |
    url="url"
    [driver="driverClassName"]
    [user="username"]
    [password="password"]]
  [var="var"] [scope="page|request|session|application"] />
```

Attributes

Attribute name	Java type	Dynamic value accepted	Description
dataSource	String or javax.sql.DataSource	Yes	The data source to expose. If specified as a String, it can be either a JNDI path or a list of JDBC parameters as described for the data-source configuration setting.
url	String	Yes	The JDBC URL.
driver	String	Yes	The JDBC driver class name.
user	String	Yes	The database username.
password	String	Yes	The database user password.
var	String	No	The variable name. If omitted, the data source configuration variable is set. The type is either javax.sql.DataSource or String.
scope	String	No	The variable or configuration variable scope.

Example

```
<sql:setDataSource var="snapshot"
  url="jdbc:odbc:snapshot"
  driver="sun.jdbc.odbc.JdbcOdbcDriver" />
<sql:query dataSource="${snapshot}" sql="..." var="result" />
```

<sql:transaction>

The <sql:transaction> action establishes a transaction context for a set of <sql:query> and <sql:update> actions. It ensures that the database modifications performed by the nested actions are either committed or rolled back if an exception is thrown by any nested action.

The action provides a connection to the nested database actions, either from the explicitly specified data source or from the data-source configuration setting.

Syntax

```
<sql:transaction [dataSource="dataSource"]
  [isolation="read_committed|read_uncommitted|repeatable_read|
    serializable"]>
  <sql:query> and <sql:update> actions, and optionally other JSP elements
</sql:transaction>
```

Attributes

Attribute name	Java type	Dynamic value accepted	Description
dataSource	String or javax.sql.DataSource	Yes	The data source to use. If specified as a String, it can be either a JNDI path or a list of JDBC parameters as described for the data-source configuration setting.
isolation	String	Yes	The transaction isolation level. If omitted, the isolation level the data source has been configured with is used.

Example

```
<sql:transaction>
  <sql:update>
    UPDATE Account
      SET Balance = Balance - ?
      WHERE AccountNo = ?
    <sql:param value="${amount}" />
    <sql:param value="${fromAccount}" />
  </sql:update>
  <sql:update>
    UPDATE Account
      SET Balance = Balance + ?
      WHERE AccountNo = ?
    <sql:param value="${amount}" />
    <sql:param value="${toAccount}" />
  </sql:update>
</sql:transaction>
```

<sql:update>

The <sql:update> action executes an SQL statement that updates the database, such as an INSERT, UPDATE, or DELETE statement, and optionally saves the number of affected rows in a scoped variable. SQL DDL statements, such as CREATE TABLE, can also be executed with this action. The statement may contain question marks as placeholders for values assigned by nested <sql:param> and <sql:dateParam> actions.

The action uses a connection provided by an <sql:transaction> action, or—if not part of a transaction—from the explicitly specified data source or the data-source configuration setting.

Syntax 1: Without a body

```
<sql:update sql="sqlStatement"
  [dataSource="dataSource"]
  [var="var" [scope="page|request|session|application"]] />
```

Syntax 2: With a body for parameters

```
<sql:update sql="sqlStatement"
  [dataSource="dataSource"]
  [var="var" [scope="page|request|session|application"]]>
  <sql:param> actions
</sql:update>
```

Syntax 3: With a body for the statement and parameters

```
<sql:update
  [dataSource="dataSource"]
  [var="var" [scope="page|request|session|application"]]>
  sqlStatement
  <sql:param> actions
</sql:update>
```

Attributes

Attribute name	Java type	Dynamic value accepted	Description
sql	String	Yes	The SQL statement.
dataSource	String or javax.sql.DataSource	Yes	The data source to use. If specified as a String, it can be either a JNDI path or a list of JDBC parameters as described for the data-source configuration setting.
var	String	No	The variable name. The type is Integer.
scope	String	No	The variable scope.

Example

```
<sql:update>
  DELETE * FROM Employee WHERE Id = ?
  <sql:param value="${empId}" />
</sql:update>
```

XML Processing Actions

<x:choose>

The <x:choose> action controls the processing of nested <x:when> and <x:otherwise> actions. It allows only the first <x:when> action with a test expression that evaluates to true to be processed, or gives the go-ahead to the single <x:otherwise> action if none do.

Syntax

```
<x:choose>
  <x:when> actions and optionally one <x:otherwise> action
</x:choose>
```

Attributes

None.

Example

```
<x:choose>
  <x:when select="category[. = 'General']">
    <td bgcolor="lightgreen">
  </x:when>
  <x:otherwise>
    <td>
  </x:otherwise>
</x:choose>
```

<x:forEach>

The <x:forEach> action evaluates its body once for each node in an XPath expression evaluation result and sets the context node used by XPath expressions in nested actions to the current node. The current node can also be exposed to action elements in the body through a nested variable.

Syntax

```
<x:forEach select="XPathExpression" [var="var"] [varStatus="varStatus"]
  [begin="startIndex"] [end="stopIndex"] [step="increment"]>
  JSP elements
</x:forEach>
```

Attributes

Attribute name	Java type	Dynamic value accepted	Description
begin	int	Yes	The first index, 0-based.
end	int	Yes	The last index, 0-based. If end is less than begin, the body is not evaluated at all.
select	String	No	The XPath expression.
step	int	Yes	Optional. Index increment per iteration.
var	String	No	The name of the nested variable holding the current element.
varStatus	String	No	The name of the variable to hold a LoopTagStatus object.

Example

```
<x:forEach select="$doc//story">
  <x:out select="title/text()" />
</x:forEach>
```

<x:if>

The `<x:if>` action evaluates its body only if the specified XPath expression evaluates to `true`. Alternatively, the evaluation result can be saved as a scoped `Boolean` variable.

Syntax 1: Without a body

```
<x:if select="booleanXPathExpression"
  var="var" [scope="page|request|session|application"]/>
```

Syntax 1: With a body

```
<x:if select="booleanXPathExpression">
  JSP elements
</x:if>
```

Attributes

Attribute name	Java type	Dynamic value accepted	Description
`select`	`String`	No	The XPath expression to evaluate.
`var`	`String`	No	The variable name. The type is `Boolean`.
`scope`	`String`	No	The variable scope.

Example

```
<x:if select="category[. = 'General']">
  <b>General</b>
</x:if>
```

<x:otherwise>

The `<x:otherwise>` action represents the default alternative within an `<x:choose>` block. It evaluates its body only if none of the `<x:when>` action in the block has a test expression that evaluates to `true`.

Syntax

```
<x:otherwise>
  JSP elements
</x:otherwise>
```

Attributes

None.

Example

```
<x:choose>
  <x:when select="category[. = 'General']">
    <td bgcolor="lightgreen">
```

```
  </x:when>
  <x:otherwise>
    <td>
  </x:otherwise>
</x:choose>
```

<x:out>

The <x:out> action adds the evaluation result of an XPath expression to the current response buffer (JspWriter). The evaluation result is always converted to a String, following the coercing rules for the XPath string( ) function.

Syntax

```
<x:out select="XPathExpression" [escapeXml="true|false"] />
```

Attributes

Attribute name	Java type	Dynamic value accepted	Description
select	String	No	The XPath expression to evaluate.
escapeXml	boolean	Yes	If true, the characters < > & ' " are converted to the corresponding XML character entity codes.

Example

```
<x:out select="$doc/meerkat/image/url/text( )" />
```

<x:param>

The <x:param> action supplies a value to a parameter used in an XSLT stylesheet. It can only be used within the body of an <x:transform> action.

Syntax

```
<x:param name="parameterName" value="parameterValue" />
```

Attributes

Attribute name	Java type	Dynamic value accepted	Description
name	String	Yes	The parameter name.
value	Object	Yes	The parameter value.

Example

```
<x:transform xml="${doc}" xslt="${stylesheet}">
  <x:param name="custId" value="${param.id}" />
</x:transform>
```

<x:parse>

The `<x:parse>` action parses an XML document and saves the result either as a standard `org.w3c.dom.Document` object or as an implementation-dependent object.

Syntax 1: Without a body

```
<x:parse doc="xmlDocument"
  [var="var" [scope="page|request|session|application"] |
   varDom="var" [scopeDom="page|request|session|application"]]
  [systemId="systemId"]
  [filter="filter"] />
```

Syntax 2: With a body

```
<x:parse
  [var="var" [scope="page|request|session|application"] |
   varDom="var" [scopeDom="page|request|session|application"]]
  [systemId="systemId"]
  [filter="filter"]>
  xmlDocument
</x:parse>
```

Attributes

Attribute name	Java type	Dynamic value accepted	Description
`doc`	`String` or `Reader`	Yes	The XML document.
`systemId`	`String`	Yes	A URI to use as a base for relative references in the document, as an absolute URL, or as a page- or context-relative path.
`filter`	`org.xml.sax.XMLFilter`	Yes	A filter that can remove elements that aren't of interest.
`var`	`String`	No	The variable name. The type is implementation-dependent.
`scope`	`String`	No	The variable scope.
`varDom`	`String`	No	The DOM variable name. The type is `org.w3c.dom.Document`.
`scopeDom`	`String`	No	The DOM variable scope.

Example

```
<c:import url="http://meerkat.oreillynet.com/?&p=4999&_fl=xml&t=ALL"
  varReader="xmlSource">
  <x:parse var="doc" xml="${xmlSource}" scope="application" />
</c:import>
```

<x:set>

The <x:set> action sets a scoped variable to the value of an XPath expression evaluation result.

Syntax

```
<x:set select="XPathExpression"
  var="var" [scope="page|request|session|application"] />
```

Attributes

Attribute name	Java type	Dynamic value accepted	Description
select	String	No	The XPath expression to evaluate.
var	String	No	The variable name. The type is the type of the expression evaluation, converted to the corresponding Java type.
scope	String	No	The variable scope.

Example

```
<x:set var="nodes"
  select="$doc//story/category[. = $param:selCat]/.." />
```

<x:transform>

The <x:transform> action transforms an XML document using an XSLT stylesheet. The result is added to the current response buffer (`JspWriter`), saved in a scoped variable, or captured or processed further by a `javax.xml.transform.Result` object. Nested <x:param> actions can supply values for parameters used in the stylesheet.

Syntax 1: Without a body

```
<x:transform doc="XMLDocument" xslt="XSLTStylesheet"
  [docSystemId="systemId"] [xsltSystemId="systemId"]
  [var="var" [scope="page|request|session|application"] |
    result="resultObject"] />
```

Syntax 2: With a body for parameter values

```
<x:transform doc="XMLDocument" xslt="XSLTStylesheet"
  [docSystemId="systemId"] [xsltSystemId="systemId"]
  [var="var" [scope="page|request|session|application"] |
    result="resultObject"]>
  <x:param> actions
</x:transform>
```

Syntax 2: With a body for the XML document and parameter values

```
<x:transform xslt="XSLTStylesheet"
```

```
    [docSystemId="systemId"] [xsltSystemId="systemId"]
    [var="var" [scope="page|request|session|application"] |
      result="resultObject"]>
    XMLDocument
    <x:param> actions
  </x:transform>
```

Attributes

Attribute name	Java type	Dynamic value accepted	Description
doc	String, Reader, javax.transformation.Source, org.w3c.dom.Document, or object exposed by <x:parse> or <x:set>	Yes	The XML document.
xslt	String, Reader, javax.transformation.Source	Yes	The XSLT stylesheet.
docSystemId	String	Yes	A URI to use as a base for relative references in the document, as an absolute URL or as a page- or context-relative path.
xsltSystemId	String	Yes	A URI to use as a base for relative references in the stylesheet, as an absolute URL or as a page- or context-relative path.
result	javax.xml.transform.Result	Yes	Object that captures or processes the result.
var	String	No	The variable name. The type is org.w3c.dom.Document.
scope	String	No	The variable scope.

Example

```
<x:transform xml="${doc}" xslt="${stylesheet}" />
```

<x:when>

The <x:when> action represents one of the mutually exclusive alternatives within an <x:choose> block. It evaluates its body only if it's the first <x:when> action in the block with a test expression that evaluates to true.

Syntax

```
<x:when select="booleanXPathExpression">
  JSP elements
</x:when>
```

Attributes

Attribute name	Java type	Dynamic value accepted	Description
select	String	No	The test XPath expression.

Example

```
<x:choose>
  <x:when select="category[. = 'General']">
    <td bgcolor="lightgreen">
  </x:when>
  <x:otherwise>
    <td>
  </x:otherwise>
</x:choose>
```

EL Functions

Starting with JSTL 1.1, one tag library contains a set of functions for use in EL expressions. The description of each function follows a similar pattern as the action descriptions: an overview, a syntax reference, a parameter table, and an example. The syntax reference section shows the return type, followed by the function name and the parameters in italics within parentheses.

Unless otherwise stated, a parameter value of `null` is treated as an empty string.

fn:contains

This function tests if a string contains a substring and returns `true` if it does, otherwise `false`.

Syntax

```
boolean: fn:contains(string, substring)
```

Parameters

Parameter name	Java type	Description
string	String	The string to test.
substring	String	The substring to look for.

Example

```
<c:if test="${fn:contains(header['User-Agent'], 'MSIE')}">
  Your browser claims to be Internet Explorer
</c:if>
```

fn:containsIgnoreCase

This function tests if a string contains a substring regardless of the character case, and returns `true` if it does, otherwise `false`.

Syntax

```
boolean: fn:containsIgnoreCase(string, substring)
```

Parameters

Parameter name	Java type	Description
`string`	`String`	The string to test.
`substring`	`String`	The substring to look for.

Example

```
<c:if test="${fn:containsIgnoreCase(param:answer, 'YES')}">
  You answered Yes (or YES, or yes, or YEs, or ...)
</c:if>
```

fn:endsWith

This function tests if a string ends with a specific suffix and returns `true` if it does, otherwise `false`.

Syntax

```
boolean: fn:endsWith(string, suffix)
```

Parameters

Parameter name	Java type	Description
`string`	`String`	The string to test.
`suffix`	`String`	The suffix to look for.

Example

```
<c:if test="${fn:endsWith(pageContext.request.requestURI, '.asp')}">
  You must be kidding!
</c:if>
```

fn:escapeXml

This function replaces all characters with a special meaning in XML and HTML (i.e., `< > & ' "`) to their corresponding character entity code (i.e., `< > & ' "`) and returns the resulting string.

Syntax

```
String: fn:escapeXml(string)
```

Parameters

Parameter name	Java type	Description
string	String	The string to convert.

Example

```
<input name="firstName" value="${fn:escapeXml(param.firstName)}">
```

fn:indexOf

This function looks for a substring in a string and returns the 0-based index of the first occurrence or -1 if the substring is not found.

Syntax

```
int: fn:indexOf(string, substring)
```

Parameters

Parameter name	Java type	Description
string	String	The string to test.
substring	String	The substring to look for.

Example

```
<%-- Pick the first word from a text --%>
  fn:substring(descr, 0, $fn:indexOf(descr, ' '))}
```

fn:join

This function creates and returns a string constructed by concatenating array elements, separated by a separator string. If the array is null an empty string is returned.

Syntax

```
String: fn:join(array, separator)
```

Parameters

Parameter name	Java type	Description
array	String[]	The array to process.
separator	String	The string used to separate the elements in the returned value.

Example

```
All 'foo' parameter values: ${fn:join(paramValues.foo, ', ')}
```

fn:length

This function returns the number of characters in a string or the number of elements in a collection. It returns 0 if the value is null.

Syntax

```
int: fn:length(value)
```

Parameters

Parameter name	Java type	Description
value	Any type that can be used as a <c:forEach> items attribute value, or String.	The string or collection to measure.

Example

```
There are ${fn:length(collection)} items in this collection.
```

fn:replace

This function replaces all occurrences of one substring in a string with another substring and returns the resulting string.

Syntax

```
String: fn:replace(string, before, after)
```

Parameters

Parameter name	Java type	Description
string	String	The string to convert.
before	String	The substring to replace.
after	String	The substring to replace with.

Example

```
${fn:replace(descr, 'ASP', 'JSP')}
```

fn:split

This function creates and returns an array where the elements are the parts of a string that are separated by a separator. The separators are not included in the result.

Syntax

```
String[]: fn:split(string, separator)
```

Parameters

Parameter name	Java type	Description
string	String	The string to split.
separator	String	The string that separates the parts of the source string.

Example

```
<c:forEach items="${fn:split(csvString, ',')}">
  ...
</c:forEach>
```

fn:startsWith

This function tests if a string starts with a specific prefix and returns true if it does, otherwise false.

Syntax

```
boolean: fn:startsWith(string, prefix)
```

Parameters

Parameter name	Java type	Description
string	String	The string to test.
prefix	String	The prefix to look for.

Example

```
<c:if test="${fn:startsWith(fn:toUpperCase(param:day), 'THU')}">
  It must be Thursday!
</c:if>
```

fn:substring

This function extracts the part of a string between two indexes and returns it. If the "begin" index is less than 0 it's treated as 0, and if it's greater than the length of the string, an empty string is returned. If the "end" index is less than 0 or greater than the length of the string, it's treated as if it had the length of the string as its value. If the "end" index is less than the "begin" index, an empty string is returned.

Syntax

```
String: fn:substring(string, begin, end)
```

Parameters

Parameter name	Java type	Description
string	String	The string to extract from.
begin	int	The index of the first character to include, inclusive.
end	Int	The index of the last character to include, exclusive.

Example

```
You can't spell Evil without ${fn:substring('Evil', 1, 3)}
```

fn:substringAfter

This function extracts the part of a string that follows a substring and returns it.

Syntax

```
String: fn:substringAfter(string, substring)
```

Parameters

Parameter name	Java type	Description
string	String	The string to extract from.
substring	String	The substring to look for.

Example

```
${fn:substringAfter('Writing appendixes is no fun', 'no')}
```

fn:substringBefore

This function extracts the part of a string that precedes a substring and returns it.

Syntax

```
String: fn:substringBefore(string, substring)
```

Parameters

Parameter name	Java type	Description
string	String	The string to extract from.
substring	String	The substring to look for.

Example

```
${fn:substringBefore('Writing appendixes is fun, not!', ', not')}
```

fn:toLowerCase

This function converts all characters in a string to lowercase and returns the resulting string.

Syntax

```
String: fn:toLowerCase(string)
```

Parameters

Parameter name	Java type	Description
string	String	The string to convert.

Example

```
<c:if test="${fn:startsWith(fn:toLowerCase(param:day), 'fri')}">
  It must be Friday!
</c:if>
```

fn:toUpperCase

This function converts all characters in a string to uppercase and returns the resulting string.

Syntax

```
String: fn:toUpperCase(string)
```

Parameters

Parameter name	Java type	Description
string	String	The string to convert.

Example

```
<c:if test="${fn:startsWith(fn:toUpperCase(param:day), 'SAT')}">
  It must be Saturday!
</c:if>
```

fn:trim

This function removes leading and trailing whitespace (blanks, tabs, and linefeed characters) from a string and returns the resulting string.

Syntax

```
String: fn:trim(string)
```

Parameters

Parameter name	Java type	Description
`string`	`String`	The string to convert.

Example

```
${fn:trim(param:descr)}
```

Support and Utility Types

ConditionalTagSupport

The `ConditionalTagSupport` class can be extended by a tag handler for a custom conditional action.

Synopsis

Class Name:	`javax.servlet.jsp.jstl.core.ConditionalTagSupport`
Extends:	`javax.servlet.jsp.tagext.TagSupport`
Implements:	None

Methods

`protected abstract boolean condition( )throws javax.servlet.jsp.tagext.JspTagException`

Returns the value of test condition. This method must be implemented by the subclass.

`public void setScope(String scope)`

Sets the scope attribute value.

`public void setVar(String var)`

Sets the var attribute value.

LocaleSupport

The `LocaleSupport` class can be used by a tag handler to get a localized message from a resource bundle.

Synopsis

Class name:	`javax.servlet.jsp.jstl.core.LocaleSupport`
Extends:	None
Implements:	None

Methods

`public static String getLocalizedMessage(javax.servlet.jsp.PageContext p, String key)`

Returns the message matching the key from the resource bundle and locale specified by the localization context setting, or ???*key*??? if the key isn't found.

`public static String getLocalizedMessage(javax.servlet.jsp.PageContext p, String key, String basename)`

Returns the message matching the key from the specified resource bundle and the locale specified by the locale context setting or the localization context setting, or ???*key*??? if the key isn't found.

`public static String getLocalizedMessage(javax.servlet.jsp.PageContext p, String key, Object[] params)`

Returns the parameterized message matching the key from the resource bundle and locale specified by the localization context setting, or ???*key*??? if the key isn't found.

`public static String getLocalizedMessage(javax.servlet.jsp.PageContext p, String key, Object[] params, String basename)`

Returns the parameterized message matching the key from the specified resource bundle and the locale specified by the locale context setting or the localization context setting, or ???*key*??? if the key isn't found.

LocalizationContext

The `LocalizationContext` class represents a localization context.

Synopsis

Class name:	`javax.servlet.jsp.jstl.core.LocaleSupport`
Extends:	None
Implements:	None

Constructors

`public LocalizationContext()`

Creates an empty context.

`public LocalizationContext(java.util.ResourceBundle bundle)`

Creates a context with the specified resource bundle but no locale.

`public LocalizationContext(java.util.ResourceBundle bundle, java.util.Locale locale)`

Creates a context with the specified resource bundle and locale.

Methods

`public java.util.ResourceBundle getResourceBundle()`

Returns the resource bundle.

`public java.util.Locale getLocale()`

Returns the locale.

LoopTag

The `LoopTag` interface is implemented by tag handlers for iteration actions, such as the `<c:forEach>` action. Its methods provide access to the current iteration element and the iteration status.

Synopsis

Interface name:	`javax.servlet.jsp.jstl.core.LoopTag`
Extends:	`javax.servlet.jsp.tagext.Tag`
Implemented by:	JSTL and custom action tag handler classes

Methods

`public Object getCurrent()`

Returns the current iteration element.

`public javax.servlet.jsp.jstl.core.LoopTagStatus getLoopStatus()`

Returns the iteration status.

LoopTagStatus

The `LoopTagStatus` interface methods provides access to the iteration status and the current iteration element. Instances of this interface can be accessed through the `LoopTag` interface, implemented by iteration actions such as the `<c:forEach>` action.

Synopsis

Interface name:	`javax.servlet.jsp.jstl.core.LoopTagStatus`
Extends:	None
Implemented by:	JSTL and custom action tag handler classes

Methods

`public Integer getBegin()`
: Returns the `begin` attribute value for the associated action element, or `null` if not specified.

`public int getCount()`
: Returns the current 1-based iteration count.

`public Object getCurrent()`
: Returns the current iteration element.

`public int getIndex()`
: Returns the current 0-based iteration index.

`public Integer getStart()`
: Returns the `start` attribute value for the associated action element, or `null` if not specified.

`public Integer getStep()`
: Returns the `step` attribute value for the associated action element, or `null` if not specified.

`public boolean isFirst()`
: Returns `true` for the first iteration round.

`public boolean isLast()`
: Returns `true` for the last iteration round.

LoopTagSupport

The `LoopTagSupport` class can be extended by a tag handler for a custom iteration action.

Synopsis

Class name:	`javax.servlet.jsp.jstl.core.LoopTagSupport`
Extends:	`javax.servlet.jsp.tagext.TagSupport`

Implements:	`javax.servlet.jsp.jstl.core.LoopTag,`
	`javax.servlet.jsp.tagext.IterationTag,`
	`javax.servlet.jsp.tagext.TryCatchFinallyTag`

Fields

```
protected int begin
protected boolean beginSpecified
```

```
protected int end
protected boolean endSpecified
protected int itemId
protected int statusId
protected int step
protected boolean stepSpecified
```

Methods

`public void doAfterBody( ) throws javax.servlet.jsp.tagext.JspTagException`
Prepares for the next iteration until `hasNext( )` returns `false`.

`public void doCatch(Throwable t) throws Throwable`
Rethrows the exception.

`public void doFinally( ) throws javax.servlet.jsp.tagext.JspTagException`
Removes the nested variables.

`public void doStartTag( ) throws javax.servlet.jsp.tagext.JspTagException`
Prepares for the iteration.

`protected abstract Object getCurrent( )`
Returns the current iteration element.

`public javax.servlet.jsp.jstl.core.LoopTagStatus getLoopStatus( )`
Returns the iteration status.

`protected abstract boolean hasNext( ) throws javax.servlet.jsp.tagext.JspTagException`
Returns true if there are more iteration elements.

`protected abstract Object next( ) throws javax.servlet.jsp.tagext.JspTagException`
Returns the next iteration element.

`protected abstract void prepare( ) throws javax.servlet.jsp.tagext.JspTagException`
Prepares for the iteration.

`public void setScope(String scope)`
Sets the scope attribute value.

`public void setVar(String var)`
Sets the `var` attribute value.

`protected void validateBegin( ) throws javax.servlet.jsp.tagext.JspTagException`
Throws an exception if the `begin` attribute has an invalid value.

`protected void validateEnd( ) throws javax.servlet.jsp.tagext.JspTagException`
Throws an exception if the `end` attribute has an invalid value.

`protected void validateStep( ) throws javax.servlet.jsp.tagext.JspTagException`
Throws an exception if the `step` attribute has an invalid value.

Result

The Result interface is implemented by the object returned as the result from the <sql:query> action. Its methods provide access to the query result.

Synopsis

Interface name:	javax.servlet.jsp.jstl.sql.Result
Extends:	None
Implemented by:	The JSTL <sql:query> tag handler class

Methods

`public String[] getColumnNames()`
: Returns an array of String objects, representing the column values in the same order as in the arrays returned by getRowsByIndex().

`public int getRowCount()`
: Returns the number of rows in the result.

`public java.util.SortedMap[] getRows()`
: Returns an array of SortedMap objects. Each array element represents a row, and the map contains the column values, with the column name as a case-insensitive key.

`public Object[][] getRowsByIndex()`
: Returns an array of arrays. The first array dimension represents rows and the second the column values.

`public boolean isLimitedByMaxRows()`
: Returns true if the result was limited by the maximum rows configuration setting or action element attribute.

ResultSupport

The ResultSupport class can be used by custom code to create a Result object from a java.sql.ResultSet.

Synopsis

Class name:	javax.servlet.jsp.jstl.sql.ResultSupport
Extends:	None
Implements:	None

Methods

`public static javax.servlet.jsp.jstl.sql.Result toResult (java.sql.ResultSet rs)`
: Returns a Result object with the data from the specified ResultSet.

```
public static javax.servlet.jsp.jstl.sql.Result toResult
(java.sql.ResultSet rs, int maxRows)
```

Returns a `Result` object with the data from the specified `ResultSet`, up to the specified number of maximum rows

SQLExecutionTag

The `SQLExecutionTag` interface is implemented by the `<sql:query>` and `<sql:update>` tag handlers so that they can receive placeholder parameter values from nested actions.

Synopsis

Interface name:	`javax.servlet.jsp.jstl.sql.SQLExecutionTag`
Extends:	None
Implemented by:	The JSTL `<sql:query>` and `<sql:update>` tag handler classes

Methods

```
public void addSQLParameter(Object value)
```

Adds a parameter value suitable for use with `java.sql.PreparedStatement.setObject()`.

Configuration Settings

Data Source

The data-source configuration setting can be set as a `String` in this format, in which optional parts are embedded in brackets:

```
url [, [driver] [, [user] [, [password]]]
```

This type of value creates a simple `DataSource` without any pooling capabilities, and is intended only for prototype and low-end applications, as described in Chapter 12. It can also be set to a JNDI path for a `DataSource` made available by the container, or to a `DataSource` created by custom code, such as a servlet or listener. These options are described in detail in Chapter 24.

Details

Variable name:	`javax.servlet.jsp.jstl.sql.dataSource`
Java constant:	`Config.SQL_DATA_SOURCE`
Java type:	`String` or `javax.sql.DataSource`
Set by:	`<sql:setDataSource>`, context parameter or custom code
Used by:	`<sql:query>`, `<sql:update>`, and `<sql:transaction>`

Fallback Locale

Setting the fallback locale configuration setting provides a default locale to be used when the lookup of a locale based on user preferences (passed through the Accept-Language header value) fails to match an available locale. When a String value is used to set this variable, it must be specified as a two-letter lowercase ISO-639 language code, optionally followed by a two-letter uppercase ISO-3166 country code, separated by a hyphen or an underscore character.

Details

Variable name:	`javax.servlet.jsp.jstl.fmt.fallbackLocale`
Java constant:	`Config.FMT_FALLBACK_LOCALE`
Java type:	`String` or `java.util.Locale`
Set by:	Context parameter or custom code
Used by:	`<fmt:bundle>`, `<fmt:setBundle>`, `<fmt:message>`, `<fmt:formatNumber>`, `<fmt:parseNumber>`, `<fmt:formatDate>` and `<fmt:parseDate>`

Locale

Setting the locale configuration setting disables the lookup of a locale based on user preferences (passed through the Accept-Language header value). When a String value is used to set this variable, it must be specified as a two-letter lowercase ISO-639 language code, optionally followed by a two-letter uppercase ISO-3166 country code, separated by a hyphen or an underscore character.

Details

Variable name:	`javax.servlet.jsp.jstl.fmt.locale`
Java constant:	`Config.FMT_LOCALE`
Java type:	`String` or `java.util.Locale`
Set by:	`<fmt:setLocale>`, context parameter or custom code
Used by:	`<fmt:bundle>`, `<fmt:setBundle>`, `<fmt:message>`, `<fmt:formatNumber>`, `<fmt:parseNumber>`, `<fmt:formatDate>`, and `<fmt:parseDate>`

Localization Context

The localization context setting can be set to a String value containing the name of the default resource bundle base name. The formatting actions then locate the locale-specific version of this bundle. The <fmt:setBundle> sets the variable to an instance of the LocalizationContext class, which contains references to both a locale and a resource bundle for a locale.

Details

Variable name:	`javax.servlet.jsp.jstl.fmt.localizationContext`
Java constant:	`Config.FMT_LOCALIZATION_CONTEXT`
Java type:	`String` or `javax.servlet.jsp.jstl.fmt.LocalizationContext`
Set by:	`<fmt:setBundle>`, context parameter or custom code
Used by:	`<fmt:message>`, `<fmt:formatNumber>`, `<fmt:parseNumber>`, `<fmt:formatDate>`, and `<fmt:parseDate>`

Max Rows

The maximum rows configuration setting can be set as a `String` value for a context parameter or as an `Integer` by custom code. It can be used to prevent run-away queries, because it sets a limit as to how many rows are retrieved for a query result.

Details

Variable name:	`javax.servlet.jsp.jstl.sql.maxRows`
Java constant:	`Config.SQL_MAX_ROWS`
Java type:	`String` or `Integer`
Set by:	Context parameter or custom code
Used by:	`<sql:query>`

Time Zone

The time zone configuration setting provides a default time zone for the JSTL actions formatting and parsing dates. `String` values for the time zone setting must be of the type defined for the `java.util.TimeZone` class: an abbreviation, a full name, or a GMT offset.

Details

Variable name:	`javax.servlet.jsp.jstl.fmt.timeZone`
Java constant:	`Config.FMT_TIME_ZONE`
Java type:	`String` or `java.util.TimeZone`
Set by:	`<fmt:setTimeZone>`, context parameter or custom code
Used by:	`<fmt:formatDate>` and `<fmt:parseDate>`

APPENDIX C

JSP Expression Language Reference

This appendix contains a reference to the JSP Expression Language (EL). EL expressions can be used directly in template text and in attribute values for action attributes declared to accept request-time attribute values, for both standard and custom actions.

Syntax

An EL expression starts with the ${ delimiter (a dollar sign plus a left curly brace) and ends with } (a right curly brace):

```
${anExpression}
```

When used in an attribute value, any number of EL expressions and static text parts can be combined. The attribute is set to the evaluation result of each expression converted to a `String` concatenated with the text parts:

```
<c:out value="The result of 1 + 2 + 3 is ${1 + 2 + 3}" />
```

If the type for the attribute is not `String`, the result is converted to the attribute's Java type as described later.

The language is case-sensitive. All keywords are in lowercase, and identifiers must be written with correct capitalization.

Literals

Literals represent strings, numbers, Boolean values, and the null value.

String	Enclosed with single or double quotes. A quote of the same type within the string must be escaped with backslash: \' in a string enclosed with single quotes, \" in a string enclosed with double quotes. The backslash character must be escaped as \\ in both cases.
Integer	An optional sign (+ or -) followed by digits between 0 and 9.
Floating point	The same as an Integer literal, except that a dot is used as the separator for the fractional part and that an exponent can be specified as e or E followed by an Integer literal.

Boolean	`true` or `false`.
Null	`null`.

Keywords and Reserved Words

The following words are keywords or reserved for potential use in a future version:

```
and or not eq ne lt gt le ge true false null instanceof empty div mod
```

They can't be used as property names or variable names, unless they are quoted.

Variables

Variables are named references to data (objects), created by the application or made available implicitly by the EL. Application-specific variables can be created in many ways, for instance using the `<jsp:useBean>` action. They can also be created by custom actions or be passed to the JSP page by a servlet. Every object that is available in one of the JSP scopes can be used as an EL variable:

```
${aScopedVariable}
```

Implicit Variables

All information about a request and other data can be accessed through the EL implicit variables:

Variable name	Description
`pageScope`	A collection (a `java.util.Map`) of all page scope variables.
`requestScope`	A collection (a `java.util.Map`) of all request scope variables.
`sessionScope`	A collection (a `java.util.Map`) of all session scope variables.
`applicationScope`	A collection (a `java.util.Map`) of all application scope variables.
`param`	A collection (a `java.util.Map`) of all request parameter values as a single `String` value per parameter.
`paramValues`	A collection (a `java.util.Map`) of all request parameter values as a `String` array per parameter.
`header`	A collection (a `java.util.Map`) of all request header values as a single `String` value per header.
`headerValues`	A collection (a `java.util.Map`) of all request header values as a `String` array per header.
`cookie`	A collection (a `java.util.Map`) of all request cookie values as a single `javax.servlet.http.Cookie` value per cookie. See Appendix D for a list of properties for the `Cookie` class.
`initParam`	A collection (a `java.util.Map`) of all application initialization parameter values as a single `String` value per parameter.
`pageContext`	An instance of the `javax.servlet.jsp.PageContext` class, providing access to various request data. See Appendix D for a list of its properties.

Data Types

A variable is always of a specific Java type. Besides the standard Java types for numeric, Boolean, and text values, the EL provides special support for custom classes developed according to the JavaBeans guidelines, `java.util.Map` objects, `java.util.List` objects, and arrays.

Bean properties can be accessed using the special property accessor operator (a dot), and be nested to any length:

```
${aBean.aProperty.aPropertyOfTheProperty.andSoOn}
```

`Map` entries can be accessed the same way:

```
${aMap.aKey}
```

`List` and array elements can be accessed using the array accessor operator (square brackets):

```
${aList[0]}
${anArray[0]}
${anArrayOrList[anExressionWithANumbericValue]}
```

The array accessor operator can also access bean properties and `Map` entries. It *must* be used when the property name is determined by a subexpression, the property name is a reserved word or contains characters used for operators, such as a dot:

```
${aMap[param.customerName]}
${aBean['empty']}
${aMap['com.mycomp.logo']}
```

Coercion Rules

The EL automatically converts, or *coerces*, variable values and the result of an expression to the type required by an attribute or an operator:

To Java type	Conversion rule
`String`	`null`: to empty string (`""`). All other types: to the corresponding `String` value.
`Primitive number or Number`	`null` or empty string: 0. `Character` or `char`: to the value represented by the character code. `String`: parse as an Integer or Floating point literal. Numeric types: coerce to the requested precision.
`boolean or Boolean`	`null`: to `false`. `String`: to `true` if the value is "true", ignoring case, otherwise `false`.
Other type	`null`: keep as `null`. String: use the `PropertyEditor` for the requested type, if any, otherwise `null` if the string is empty. Other: type cast, if possible.

In all cases, the EL evaluator throws an exception for attempts to convert between types not defined in the table or if the defined conversion rule fails.

Expressions and Operators

The combination of literal values, variables, and the following operators form an EL expression:

Operator	Precedence	Operation performed
.	1	Access a bean property or Map entry.
[]	1	Access an array or List element.
()	2	Group a subexpression to change the evaluation order.
? :	10	Conditional test: *condition* ? *ifTrue* : *ifFalse*.
+	5	Addition.
-	5	Subtraction.
-	3	Negation of a value.
*	4	Multiplication.
/ or div	4	Division.
% or mod	4	Modulo (remainder).
== or eq	7	Test for equality.
!= or ne	7	Test for inequality.
< or lt	6	Test for less than.
> or gt	6	Test for greater than.
<= or le	6	Test for less than or equal.
>= or ge	6	Test for greater than or equal.
&& or and	8	Test for logical AND.
|| or or	9	Test for logical OR.
! or not	3	Unary Boolean complement.
empty	3	Test for empty variable values (null or an empty String, array, Map, or Collection).
func(args)	N/A	A function call, where func is the function name and args is a comma-separated list of arguments.

Expressions are evaluated in the order defined by the operator precedence and left to right for operators of the same precedence.

Operand Coercing Rules

Before the operator is applied, the EL evaluator coerces the types of the operand values. An exception is thrown if no rule matches, the coercing fails, or applying the operator leads to an exception.

Property and array accessor operators

An expression of the form `${exprA.identifierB}` is evaluated the same way as `${exprA['identifierB']}`.

To evaluate an expression of the form `${exprA[exprB]}`, the following rules are used:

- If `exprA` is `null`, return `null`.
- If `exprB` is `null`, return `null`.
- If `exprA` is a `Map` with a key matching `exprB`, return the value.
- If `exprA` is a `List` or array with an index matching `exprB` coerced to an `int`, return the value.
- If `exprA` is a bean with a property matching `exprB` coerced to a `String`, return the value.

Arithmetic operators

For addition, subtraction, and multiplication, if any operand is `null`, the result is 0. Otherwise both operands are coerced to numbers (to `BigDecimal` if one of them is `BigDecimal` or if one is `BigInteger` and the other is `Float`, `Double`, or a `String` with floating-point syntax, to `double` if one of them is `Float`, `Double`, or a `String` with floating-point syntax, to `BigInteger` if one of them is `BigInteger`, to `long` otherwise), and the result of applying the operator is returned.

For division, if any operand is `null`, the result is 0. Otherwise both operands are coerced to numbers (to `BigDecimal` if one of them is `BigInteger` or `BigDecimal`, to `double` otherwise), and the result of applying the operator is returned.

For modulo, if any operand is `null`, the result is 0. Otherwise both operands are coerced to numbers (to `double` if one of them is `BigDecimal`, `Float`, `Double`, or a `String` with floating-point syntax, to `BigInteger` if one of them is `BigInteger`, to `long` otherwise), and the result of applying the operator is returned.

For negation, if the operand is `null`, the result is 0. Otherwise if the operand is a `String`, it's coerced to a number (to `double` if it represents a floating-point value, to `long` otherwise), and the result of applying the operator is returned. For numeric types, the operator is applied without coercing the value and the result is returned.

Relational operators

For "less than," "greater than," "less than or equal," and "greater than or equal," if the operands are equal, `true` is returned for "less than or equal" and "greater than or equal"; `false` otherwise. If the operands are not equal and one of them is `null`, `false` is returned. If one of the operands is a `BigDecimal`, the other is coerced to `BigDecimal` and the result of `compareTo()` is returned. If one of the operands is a `Float` or a `Double`, both are coerced to `double`, and the result of applying the operator is returned. If one of the operands is a `BigInteger`, the other is coerced to `BigInteger` and the result of compareTo( ) is returned. If one of the operands is a Byte, Short, Character, Integer, or Long, both are coerced to long, and the result of applying the operator is returned. If one operand is a String, the other is coerced to a String, and the result of compareTo( ) is returned. Otherwise, if one of the operands is a Comparable, the result of comparing it to the other with the compareTo( ) method is returned.

For "equal" and "not equal," if the operands are equal, the operator is applied and the result is returned. If one of the operands is null, false is returned for "equal" and true for "not equal." If one of the operands is a BigDecimal, the other is coerced to BigDecimal and the result of equals( ) is used, negated for "not equal." If one of the operands is a Float or a Double, both are coerced to double, and the result of applying the operator is returned. If one of the operands is a BigInteger, the other is coerced to BigInteger and the result of equals( ) is used, negated for "not equal." If one of the operands is a Byte, Short, Character, Integer, or Long, both are coerced to long, and the result of applying the operator is returned. If one of the operands is a Boolean, both are coerced to boolean, and the result of applying the operator is returned. Otherwise, the result of comparing the values with the equals( ) method is returned, negated for "not equal."

Logical operators

For "and" and "or," both operands are coerced to boolean, and the result of applying the operator is returned. The evaluation stops as soon as the result can be determined, i.e., for the expression ${a && b && c && d}, only ${a && b} is evaluated if b is false.

For "not," the operand is coerced to boolean and the result of applying the operator is returned.

Empty operator

The "empty" operator returns true if the operand is null or an empty string, an empty array, an empty Map, or an empty Collection; otherwise it returns false.

APPENDIX D

JSP API Reference

Besides the JSP elements described in Appendix A, the JSP specification also defines a number of Java classes and interfaces. Instances of some of these classes are assigned to the implicit variables available to scripting elements and Expression Language (EL) expressions in a JSP page. Others are used to develop custom actions and to allow JSP container vendors to encapsulate internal implementations. This appendix describes the classes and interfaces in all these categories in the JSP 2.0 specification, as well as the classes and interfaces exposed through the JSP types defined by the Servlet 2.4 specification.

Implicit Variables

The JSP specification defines a number of implicit scripting variables. Most of the implicit variables have types defined by classes and interfaces in the Servlet specification's `javax.servlet.http` package, but two are part of the JSP `javax.servlet.jsp` package and one is part of the Java core API. Scripting elements in a JSP page can use these objects to access request and response information as well as objects saved in one of the JSP scopes: page, request, session, and application.

Most of these objects are also available to EL expressions through the EL implicit variables. The detailed sections include the EL expression in the Synopsis sections where applicable.

application

The `application` variable contains a reference to a `ServletContext` instance. The `ServletContext` provides resources shared within a web application. It holds attribute values representing the JSP application scope. An attribute value can be an instance of any Java class. It also defines a set of methods that a JSP page or a servlet use to communicate with its container, for example, to get the MIME type of a file, dispatch requests, or write to a log file. The web container is responsible for providing an implementation of the `ServletContext` interface.

A `ServletContext` is assigned a specific URI path prefix within a web server. For example a context could be responsible for all resources under *http://www.mycorp.com/catalog*. All requests that start with the */catalog* request path, which is known as the *context path*, are routed to this servlet context.

A single instance of a `ServletContext` is available to the all servlets and JSP pages in a web application, unless the web application indicates that it is distributable. For a distributed application, there's a single instance of the `ServletContext` class per application per Java Virtual Machine (JVM).

Synopsis

Variable name:	`application`
EL expression	`${pageContext.servletContext}`
Interface name:	`javax.servlet.ServletContext`
Extends:	None
Implemented by:	Internal container-dependent class
JSP page type:	Available in both regular JSP pages and error pages

Methods

`public Object getAttribute(String name)`

Returns the servlet context attribute with the specified name, or `null` if there is no attribute by that name. Context attributes, representing the JSP application scope, can be set by a servlet or a JSP page. A container can also use attributes to provide information that is not already available through methods in this interface.

`public java.util.Enumeration getAttributeNames( )`

Returns an `Enumeration` of `String` objects containing the attribute names available within this servlet context.

`public ServletContext getContext(String uripath)`

Returns a `ServletContext` object that corresponds to the specified URI in the web container. This method allows servlets and JSP pages to gain access to other contexts than its own. The URI path must be absolute (beginning with "/") and is interpreted based on the containers' document root. In a security-conscious environment, the container may return `null` for a given URI.

`public String getInitParameter(String name)`

Returns a `String` containing the value of the named context-wide initialization parameter or `null` if the parameter does not exist. Context initialization parameters can be defined in a web application deployment descriptor.

`public java.util.Enumeration getInitParameterNames()`
: Returns the names of the context's initialization parameters as an `Enumeration` of `String` objects or an empty `Enumeration` if the context has no initialization parameters.

`public int getMajorVersion()`
: Returns the major version of the Java Servlet API that this web container supports. A container that complies with the Servlet 2.3 API returns 2.

`public String getMimeType(String filename)`
: Returns the MIME type of the specified file or `null` if the MIME type is not known. The MIME type is determined by the configuration of the web container and may be specified in a web application deployment descriptor.

`public int getMinorVersion()`
: Returns the minor version of the Java Servlet API that this web container supports. A container that complies with the Servlet 2.3 API returns 3.

`public RequestDispatcher getNamedDispatcher(String name)`
: Returns a `RequestDispatcher` object that acts as a wrapper for the named servlet or JSP page. Names can be defined for servlets and JSP pages in the web application deployment descriptor.

`public String getRealPath(String path)`
: Returns a `String` containing the filesystem path for specified context-relative path. This method returns `null` if the web container can't translate the path to a filesystem path for any reason (such as when the content is being made available directly from a WAR archive).

`public RequestDispatcher getRequestDispatcher(String path)`
: Returns a `RequestDispatcher` object that acts as a wrapper for the resource located at the specified context-relative path. The resource can be dynamic (servlet or JSP) or static (for instance, a regular HTML file).

`public java.net.URL getResource(String path) throws MalformedURLException`
: Returns a `URL` to the resource that is mapped to the specified context-relative path. This method allows the web container to make a resource available to servlets and JSP pages from sources other than a local filesystem, such as a database or a WAR file.

  The `URL` provides access to the resource content directly, so be aware that requesting a JSP page returns a `URL` for the JSP source page as opposed to the processed result. Use a `RequestDispatcher` instead to include results of an execution.

  This method returns `null` if no resource is mapped to the pathname.

`public java.io.InputStream getResourceAsStream(String path)`
: Returns the resource mapped to the specified context-relative path as an `InputStream` object. See `getResource()` for details.

`public java.util.Set getResourcePaths(String path)`

Returns a list of `String` instances with all valid resource paths under the specified path in the resource namespace hierarchy. Values ending with a slash represent a directory in the hierarchy. All paths are returned as context-relative paths, so they can be used directly as the argument to `getResource( )` or `getResourceAsStream( )`.

`public String getServerInfo( )`

Returns the name and version of the servlet container on which the servlet or JSP page is running as a `String` with the format "*servername/versionnumber*" (for example, "Tomcat/3.2"). Optionally, a container may include other information, such as the Java version and operating system information, within parentheses.

`public String getServletContextName( )`

Returns the servlet context (application) name defined by the `<display-name>` element in the deployment descriptor.

`public void log(String message)`

Writes the specified message to a container log file. The name and type of the log file is container dependent.

`public void log(String message, Throwable cause)`

Writes the specified message and a stack trace for the specified `Throwable` to the servlet log file. The name and type of the log file is container dependent.

`public void removeAttribute(String name)`

Removes the attribute with the specified name from the servlet context.

`public void setAttribute(String name, Object attribute)`

Binds an object to the specified attribute name in this servlet context. If the specified name is already used for an attribute, this method removes the old attribute and binds the name to the new attribute.

The following methods are deprecated:

`public Servlet getServlet(String name) throws ServletException`

This method was originally defined to retrieve a servlet from a `ServletContext`. As of the Servlet 2.1 API, this method always returns `null` and remains only to preserve binary compatibility. This method will be removed permanently in a future version of the Java Servlet API.

`public Enumeration getServlets( )`

This method was originally defined to return an `Enumeration` of all the servlets known to this servlet context. As of the Servlet 2.1 API, this method always returns an empty `Enumeration` and remains only to preserve binary compatibility. This method will be removed permanently in a future version of the Java Servlet API.

`public Enumeration getServletNames()`

This method was originally defined to return an `Enumeration` of all the servlet names known to this context. As of Servlet 2.1, this method always returns an empty `Enumeration` and remains only to preserve binary compatibility. This method will be permanently removed in a future version of the Java Servlet API.

`public void log(Exception exception, String message)`

This method was originally defined to write an exception's stack trace and an explanatory error message to the web container log file. As of the Servlet 2.1 API, the recommendation is to use `log(String, Throwable)` instead.

config

The `config` variable contains a reference to a `ServletConfig` instance. A web container uses a `ServletConfig` instance to pass information to a servlet or JSP page during initialization. The configuration information contains initialization parameters (defined in the web application deployment descriptor) and the `ServletContext` object representing the web application the servlet or JSP page belongs to.

Synopsis

Variable name:	`config`
EL expression	`${pageContext.servletConfig}`
Interface name:	`javax.servlet.ServletConfig`
Extends:	None
Implemented by:	Internal container-dependent class
JSP page type:	Available in both regular JSP pages and error pages

Methods

`public String getInitParameter(String name)`

Returns a `String` containing the value of the specified servlet or JSP page initialization parameter or `null` if the parameter does not exist.

`public java.util.Enumeration getInitParameterNames()`

Returns the names of the servlet's or JSP page's initialization parameters as an Enumeration of `String` objects or an empty `Enumeration` if the servlet has no initialization parameters.

`public ServletContext getServletContext()`

Returns a reference to the `ServletContext` the servlet or JSP page belongs to.

`public String getServletName()`

Returns the name of this servlet instance or JSP page. The name may be assigned in the web application deployment descriptor. For an unregistered (and thus unnamed) servlet instance or JSP page, the servlet's class name is returned.

exception

The `exception` variable is assigned a reference to the subclass of `Throwable` that caused an error page to be invoked. The `Throwable` class is the superclass of all error and exception classes in the Java language. Only instances of this class (or of one of its subclasses) are thrown by the Java Virtual Machine (JVM) or can be thrown by an application using the Java `throw` statement.

Synopsis

Variable name:	`exception`
EL expression	`${pageContext.exception}`
Class name:	`java.lang.Throwable`
Extends:	None
Implements:	`java.io.Serializable`
Implemented by:	Part of the standard Java library
JSP page type:	Available only in a page marked as an error page using the page directive `isErrorPage` attribute

Methods

See the Java documentation at *http://java.sun.com/docs/index.html* for a description of the `Throwable` class.

out

The out variable is assigned to a concrete subclass of the `JspWriter` abstract class by the web container. `JspWriter` emulates some of the functionality found in the `java.io.BufferedWriter` and `java.io.PrintWriter` classes. It differs, however, in that it throws a `java.io.IOException` from the print methods, which the `PrintWriter` does not.

If the page directive attribute `autoflush` is set to `true`, all the I/O operations on this class automatically flush the contents of the buffer when it's full. If `autoflush` is set to `false`, all the I/O operations on this class throws an `IOException` when the buffer is full.

Synopsis

Variable name:	`out`
EL expression	N/A
Class name:	`javax.servlet.jsp.JspWriter`
Extends:	`java.io.Writer`
Implements:	None
Implemented by:	A concrete subclass of this abstract class is provided as an internal container-dependent class
JSP page type:	Available in both regular JSP pages and error pages

Constructor

`protected JspWriter(int bufferSize, boolean autoFlush)`
: Creates an instance with at least the specified buffer size and the specified auto-flush behavior.

Methods

`public abstract void clear() throws java.io.IOException`
: Clears the contents of the buffer. If the buffer has already been flushed, throws an `IOException` to signal the fact that some data has already been irrevocably written to the client response stream.

`public abstract void clearBuffer() throws java.io.IOException`
: Clears the current contents of the buffer. Unlike `clear()`, this method does not throw an `IOException` if the buffer has already been flushed. It just clears the current content of the buffer and returns.

`public abstract void close() throws java.io.IOException`
: Closes the `JspWriter` after flushing it. Calls to `flush()` or `write()` after a call to `close()` cause an `IOException` to be thrown. If `close()` is called on a previously closed `JspWriter`, it is ignored.

`public abstract void flush() throws java.io.IOException`
: Flushes the current contents of the buffer to the underlying writer and flushes the underlying writer as well. This means that the buffered content is delivered to the client immediately.

`public int getBufferSize()`
: Returns the size of the buffer in bytes, or 0 if it is not buffered.

`public abstract int getRemaining()`
: Returns the number of unused bytes in the buffer.

`public boolean isAutoFlush()`
: Returns `true` if this `JspWriter` is set to auto-flush the buffer, `false` otherwise.

`public void newLine()`
: Writes a line separator, as defined by the `line.separator` system property, to the buffer.

It also overrides all print methods inherited from `java.io.Writer` to handle buffering.

page

The `page` variable is assigned to the instance of the JSP implementation class, declared as an `Object`. This variable is rarely, if ever, used.

Synopsis

Variable name:	`page`
EL expression	N/A
Class name:	`Object`
Extends:	None
Implements:	None
Implemented by:	Part of the standard Java library
JSP page type:	Available in both regular JSP pages and error pages

Methods

See the Java documentation at *http://java.sun.com/docs/index.html* for a description of the `Object` class.

pageContext

A `PageContext` instance provides access to all the JSP scopes and several page attributes. It offers a layer above the container-implementation details that enables a container to generate portable JSP implementation classes. The JSP page scope is represented by `PageContext` attributes. The web container assigns a unique instance of this class to the `pageContext` variable for each request.

The `PageContext` is provided to tag handler classes to give them access to the runtime context data. The class was refactored in JSP 2.0 to extend a generic context class: `JspContext`. All nonservlet specific methods were moved to the `JspContext` class, described in the Tag Handler Types section. Classic tag handlers are given an instance of `PageContext` but the new simple tag handler API uses the new `JspContext` type instead. In a servlet-based JSP container, the instance provided to a simple tag handler is always a `PageContext`, so tag handlers can safely cast the `JspContext` instance to a `PageContext`. These changes were made to allow the simple tag handler mechanism to be used in nonservlet based environments in the future.

Synopsis

Variable name:	`pageContext`
EL expression	`${pageContext}`
Class name:	`javax.servlet.jsp.PageContext`
Extends:	`javax.servlet.jsp.JspContext`
Implements:	None
Implemented by:	A concrete subclass of this abstract class is provided as an internal container-dependent class
JSP page type:	Available in both regular JSP pages and error pages

Fields

```
public static final String APPLICATION
public static final int APPLICATION_SCOPE
public static final String CONFIG
public static final String EXCEPTION
public static final String OUT
public static final String PAGE
public static final int PAGE_SCOPE
public static final String PAGECONTEXT
public static final String REQUEST
public static final int REQUEST_SCOPE
public static final String RESPONSE
public static final String SESSION
public static final int SESSION_SCOPE
```

Constructor

`public PageContext( )`

Creates an instance of the `PageContext` class. Typically, an instance is created and initialized by the `JspFactory` class.

Methods

`public abstract void forward(String relativeUrlPath) throws ServletException, java.io.IOException`

Forwards the current request to another active component, such as a servlet or JSP page, in the application. If the specified URI starts with a slash, it's interpreted as a context-relative path, otherwise as a page-relative path.

The response must not be modified after calling this method, because the response is committed before this method returns.

`public abstract ErrorData getErrorData( )`

Returns an instance of `ErrorData` containing information about the error that caused an error JSP page (declared by the `isErrorPage` attribute of the page directive) to be invoked. If this method is called while processing a page that isn't an error page, the information it contains is meaningless.

`public abstract Exception getException( )`

Returns the `Exception` that caused the current page to be invoked if its page directive `isErrorPage` attribute is set to `true`.

`public abstract Object getPage( )`

Returns the object that represents the JSP page implementation class instance this `PageContext` is associated with.

`public abstract ServletRequest getRequest( )`

Returns the current `ServletRequest`.

`public abstract ServletResponse getResponse( )`

Returns the current `ServletResponse`.

`public abstract ServletConfig getServletConfig( )`

Returns the `ServletConfig` for this JSP page implementation class instance.

`public abstract ServletContext getServletContext( )`

Returns the `ServletContext` for this JSP page implementation class instance.

`public abstract HttpSession getSession( )`

Returns the current `HttpSession` or `null` if the page directive `session` attribute is set to `false`.

`public abstract void handlePageException(Exception e) throws ServletException, java.io.IOException`

This method is only kept for backward compatibility. New implementations should use the version that takes a `Throwable` argument instead.

`public abstract void handlePageException(Throwable e) throws ServletException, java.io.IOException`

This method is intended to be called only by the JSP page implementation class to process unhandled exceptions by forwarding the request exception to either the error page specified by the page directive `errorPage` attribute or perform an implementation dependent action if no error page is specified.

`public abstract void include(String relativeUrlPath) throws ServletException, java.io.IOException`

Causes the specified resource to be processed as part of the current request. The current `JspWriter` is flushed before invoking the target resource, and the output of the target resource's processing of the request is written directly to the current `ServletResponse` object's writer. If the specified URI starts with a slash, it's interpreted as a context-relative path, otherwise as a page-relative path.

`public abstract void include(String relativeUrlPath, boolean flush) throws ServletException, java.io.IOException`

Causes the specified resource to be processed as part of the current request. If `flush` is `true`, the current `JspWriter` is flushed before invoking the target resource. The output of the target resource's processing of the request is written to the current `JspWriter` object's writer. If the specified URI starts with a slash, it's interpreted as a context-relative path, otherwise as a page-relative path.

`public abstract void initialize(Servlet servlet, ServletRequest request, ServletResponse response, String errorPageURL, boolean needsSession, int bufferSize, boolean autoFlush) throws java.io.IOException, IllegalStateException,IllegalArgumentException`

This method is called to initialize a `PageContext` object so that it may be used by a JSP implementation class to service an incoming request. This method is typically called from the `JspFactory.getPageContext( )` method.

`public BodyContent pushBody()`
: This method is intended to be called only by the JSP page implementation class to get a new `BodyContent` object and save the current `JspWriter` on the `PageContext` object's internal stack.

`public abstract void release()`
: Resets the internal state of a `PageContext`, releasing all internal references and preparing the `PageContext` for potential reuse by a later invocation of `initialize()`. This method is typically called from the `JspFactory.releasePageContext()` method.

request

The `request` variable is assigned a reference to an internal container-dependent class that implements a protocol-dependent interface that extends the `javax.servlet.ServletRequest`. Since HTTP is the only protocol support by JSP 2.0, the class always implements the `javax.servlet.http.HttpServletRequest` interface. The method descriptions in this section include all methods from both interfaces.

Information stored as `ServletRequest` attributes corresponds to objects in the JSP request scope.

Synopsis

Variable name:	`request`
EL expression	`${pageContext.request}`
Interface name:	`javax.servlet.http.HttpServletRequest`
Extends:	`javax.servlet.ServletRequest`
Implemented by:	Internal container-dependent class
JSP page type:	Available in both regular JSP pages and error pages

Fields

```
public static final String BASIC_AUTH
public static final String CLIENT_CERT_AUTH
public static final String DIGEST_AUTH
public static final String FORM_AUTH
```

Methods

`public Object getAttribute(String name)`
: Returns the value of the named attribute as an `Object` or `null` if no attribute of the given name exists.

`public java.util.Enumeration getAttributeNames()`
: Returns an `Enumeration` containing the names of the attributes available to this request. The `Enumeration` is empty if the request doesn't have any attributes.

`public String getAuthType()`

Returns the name of the authentication scheme used to protect the servlet, one of `BASIC_AUTH`, `CLIENT_CERT_AUTH`, `DIGEST_AUTH`, `FORM_AUTH`, or a container-dependent string or `null` if the servlet isn't protected.

`public String getCharacterEncoding()`

Returns the name of the character encoding used in the body of this request or `null` if the request doesn't specify a character encoding.

`public int getContentLength()`

Returns the length, in bytes, of the request body and made available by the input stream or -1 if the length is not known.

`public String getContentType()`

Returns the MIME type of the body of the request or `null` if the type is not known.

`public String getContextPath()`

Returns the portion of the request URI that indicates the context of the request.

`public javax.servlet.http.Cookie[] getCookies()`

Returns an array containing all of the `Cookie` objects the client sent with this request, or `null` if the request contains no cookies.

`public long getDateHeader(String name)`

Returns the value of the specified request header as a `long` value that represents a date value or -1 if the header isn't included in the request.

`public String getHeader(String name)`

Returns the value of the specified request header as a `String` or `null` if the header isn't included with the request.

`public java.util.Enumeration getHeaderNames()`

Returns all the header names this request contains as an `Enumeration` of `String` objects. The `Enumeration` is empty if the request doesn't have any headers.

`public java.util.Enumeration getHeaders(String name)`

Returns all the values of the specified request header as an `Enumeration` of `String` objects. The `Enumeration` is empty if the request doesn't contain the specified header.

`public ServletInputStream getInputStream() throws java.io.IOException`

Retrieves the body of the request as binary data using a `ServletInputStream`.

`public int getIntHeader(String name)`

Returns the value of the specified request header as an `int` or -1 if the header isn't included in the request.

`public String getLocalAddr()`

Returns the IP address of the interface on which the request was received.

`public java.util.Locale getLocale()`
: Returns the preferred `Locale` that the client will accept content in, based on the `Accept-Language` header.

`public java.util.Enumeration getLocales()`
: Returns an `Enumeration` of `Locale` objects indicating, in decreasing order and starting with the preferred locale, the locales that are acceptable to the client based on the `Accept-Language` header.

`public String getLocalName()`
: Returns the host name associated with the IP address of the interface on which the request was received.

`public String getLocalPort()`
: Returns the IP port number of the interface on which the request was received.

`public String getMethod()`
: Returns the name of the HTTP method with which this request was made, for example GET, POST, or PUT.

`public String getParameter(String name)`
: Returns the value of a request parameter as a `String` or `null` if the parameter does not exist.

`public java.util.Map getParameterMap()`
: Returns a `Map` of all parameters for the request with the parameter names as keys and `String` arrays as values.

`public java.util.Enumeration getParameterNames()`
: Returns an `Enumeration` of `String` objects containing the names of the parameters contained in this request.

`public String[] getParameterValues(String name)`
: Returns an array of `String` objects containing all of the values the given request parameter has or `null` if the parameter does not exist.

`public String getPathInfo()`
: Returns any extra path information associated with the URI the client sent when it made this request or `null` if there is no extra path information. For a JSP page, this method always returns `null`.

`public String getPathTranslated()`
: Returns the result of `getPathInfo()` translated into the corresponding file system path. Returns `null` if `getPathInfo()` returns `null`.

`public String getProtocol()`
: Returns the name and version of the protocol the request uses in the form *protocol/majorVersion.minorVersion*, for example, `HTTP/1.1`.

`public String getQueryString()`
: Returns the query string that is contained in the request URI after the path.

`public java.io.BufferedReader getReader() throws java.io.IOException`
: Retrieves the body of the request as character data using a `BufferedReader`.

`public String getRemoteAddr()`
: Returns the Internet Protocol (IP) address of the client that sent the request.

`public String getRemoteHost()`
: Returns the fully qualified name of the client host or last proxy that sent the request or the IP address if the hostname can't be determined.

`public String getRemotePort()`
: Returns the IP source port of the client or last proxy that sent the request.

`public String getRemoteUser()`
: Returns the login name of the user making this request if the user has been authenticated or `null` if the user has not been authenticated.

`public RequestDispatcher getRequestDispatcher(String path)`
: Returns a `RequestDispatcher` object that acts as a wrapper for the resource located at the given path.

`public String getRequestedSessionId()`
: Returns the session ID specified by the client.

`public String getRequestURI()`
: Returns the part of this request's URL from the protocol name up to the query string in the first line of the HTTP request.

`public StringBuffer getRequestURL()`
: Returns a reconstructed request URL, including the protocol, server name, port number, and the URI path, but not the query string.

`public String getScheme()`
: Returns the name of the scheme (protocol) used to make this request, for example, `http`, `https`, or `ftp`.

`public String getServerName()`
: Returns the hostname of the server that received the request.

`public int getServerPort()`
: Returns the port number on which this request was received.

`public String getServletPath()`
: Returns the part of this request's URI that identifies the servlet. For a JSP page, this is the complete context-relative path for the JSP page.

`public HttpSession getSession()`
: Returns the current `HttpSession` associated with this request. If the request doesn't have a session, a new `HttpSession` object is created, associated with the request, and returned.

`public HttpSession getSession(boolean create)`
: Returns the current `HttpSession` associated with this request. If there is no current session, and `create` is `true`, a new `HttpSession` object is created, associated

with the request, and returned. If create is `false`, and the request isn't associated with a session, this method returns `null`.

`public java.security.Principal getUserPrincipal( )`
: Returns a `Principal` object containing the name of the current authenticated user.

`public boolean isRequestedSessionIdFromCookie( )`
: Checks whether the requested session ID came in as a cookie.

`public boolean isRequestedSessionIdFromURL( )`
: Checks whether the requested session ID came in as part of the request URL.

`public boolean isRequestedSessionIdValid( )`
: Checks whether the requested session ID is still valid.

`public boolean isSecure( )`
: Returns a `boolean` indicating whether this request was made using a secure channel, such as HTTPS.

`public boolean isUserInRole(String role)`
: Returns a `boolean` indicating whether the authenticated user is included in the specified logical "role."

`public void removeAttribute(String name)`
: Removes the specified attribute from this request.

`public Object setAttribute(String name, Object attribute)`
: Stores the specified attribute in this request.

`public void setCharacterEncoding(String encoding)`
: Sets the character encoding name used when reading the request. This method must be called before reading request parameters or reading the body through a `Reader` returned by `getReader( )`.

The following methods are deprecated:

`public String getRealPath( )`
: As of the Servlet 2.1 API, use `ServletContext.getRealPath(String)` instead.

`public boolean isRequestSessionIdFromUrl( )`
: As of the Servlet 2.1 API, use `isRequestedSessionIdFromURL( )` instead.

response

The `response` variable is assigned a reference to an internal container-dependent class that implements a protocol-dependent interface that extends the `javax.servlet.ServletResponse`. Since HTTP is the only protocol supported by JSP 2.0, the class always implements the `javax.servlet.http.HttpServletResponse` interface. The method descriptions in this section include all methods from both interfaces.

Synopsis

Variable name:	`response`
EL expression	`${pageContext.response}`
Interface name:	`javax.servlet.http.HttpServletResponse`
Extends:	`javax.servlet.ServletResponse`
Implemented by:	Internal container-dependent class
JSP page type:	Available in both regular JSP pages and error pages

Methods

`public void addCookie(Cookie cookie)`
: Adds the specified cookie to the response.

`public void addDateHeader(String headername, long date)`
: Adds a response header with the given name and date value. The date is specified in terms of milliseconds since the epoch (January 1, 1970, 00:00:00 GMT).

`public void addHeader(String headername, String value)`
: Adds a response header with the specified name and value.

`public void addIntHeader(String headername, int value)`
: Adds a response header with the given name and integer value.

`public boolean containsHeader(String name)`
: Returns a `boolean` indicating whether the named response header has already been set.

`public String encodeRedirectURL(String url)`
: Encodes the specified URL for use in the `sendRedirect()` method by including the session ID in it. If encoding (URL rewriting) isn't needed, it returns the URL unchanged.

`public String encodeURL(String url)`
: Encodes the specified URL for use in a reference element (e.g., <a>) by including the session ID in it. If encoding (URL rewriting) isn't needed, it returns the URL unchanged.

`public void flushBuffer() throws IOException`
: Forces any content in the response body buffer to be written to the client.

`public int getBufferSize()`
: Returns the actual buffer size (in bytes) used for the response. If no buffering is used, this method returns 0.

`public String getCharacterEncoding()`
: Returns the name of the charset used for the MIME body sent in this response.

`public String getContentType()`
: Returns the content type for the MIME body sent in this response.

`public Locale getLocale()`
: Returns the locale assigned to the response. This is either a `Locale` object for the server's default locale or the `Locale` set with `setLocale()`.

`public ServletOutputStream getOutputStream() throws IOException`
: Returns a `ServletOutputStream` suitable for writing binary data in the response. It's recommended that this method is not used in a JSP page, since JSP pages are intended for text data.

`public PrintWriter getWriter throws IOException`
: Returns a `PrintWriter` object that can send character text to the client. It's recommended that this method not be used in a JSP page, because it may interfere with the container's writer mechanism. Use the `PageContext` methods instead to get the current `JspWriter`.

`public boolean isCommitted()`
: Returns a `boolean` indicating if the response has been committed.

`public void reset()`
: Clears any data that exists in the buffer as well as the status code and headers. If the response has been committed, this method throws an `IllegalStateException`.

`public void resetBuffer()`
: Clears any data that exists in the buffer without clearing the status code and headers. If the response has been committed, this method throws an `IllegalStateException`.

`public void sendError(int status) throws IOException`
: Sends an error response to the client using the specified status. If the response has already been committed, this method throws an `IllegalStateException`. After using this method, the response should be considered to be committed and should not be written to.

`public void sendError(int status, String message) throws IOException`
: Sends an error response to the client using the specified status code and descriptive message. If the response has already been committed, this method throws an `IllegalStateException`. After using this method, the response should be considered to be committed and should not be written to.

`public void sendRedirect(String location) throws IOException`
: Sends a temporary redirect response to the client using the specified redirect location URL. This method can accept relative URLs; the servlet container converts the relative URL to an absolute URL before sending the response to the client. If the response is already committed, this method throws an `IllegalStateException`. After using this method, the response should be considered to be committed and should not be written to.

`public void setBufferSize(int size)`
: Sets the preferred buffer size (in bytes) for the body of the response. The servlet container uses a buffer at least as large as the size requested. The actual buffer size used can be found using `getBufferSize( )`.

`public void setCharacterEncoding(String encoding)`
: Sets the character encoding for the response body, communicated through `charset` attribute of the `Content-Type` response header. If a character encoding has already been set, this method overrides it. It must be called before the `getWriter( )` method is called.

`public void setContentLength(int length)`
: Sets the length (in bytes) of the content body in the response. In HTTP servlets, this method sets the HTTP `Content-Length` header. It's recommended that this method not be used in a JSP page, because it may interfere with the container's writer mechanism.

`public void setContentType(String type)`
: Sets the content type of the response being sent to the client, communicated through the `Content-Type` response header. If the type includes a `charset` attribute, it's used to set the character encoding for the response body. If a content type and character encoding have already been set, this method overrides them. It must be called before the `getWriter( )` method is called.

`public void setDateHeader(String headername, long date)`
: Sets a response header with the given name and date value. The date is specified in terms of milliseconds since the epoch (January 1, 1970, 00:00:00 GMT). If the header is already set, the new value overwrites the previous one.

`public void setHeader(String headername, String value)`
: Sets a response header with the given name and value. If the header is already set, the new value overwrites the previous one.

`public void setIntHeader(String headername, int value)`
: Sets a response header with the given name and integer value. If the header is already set, the new value overwrites the previous one.

`public void setLocale(Locale locale)`
: Sets the locale of the response, communicated to an HTTP client through the `Content-Language` response header. If a character encoding for the response has not been set with calls to `setCharacterEncoding()` or `setContentType( )`, this method implicitly sets the character encoding based on mappings in the web application deployment descriptor or container-dependent mappings if no mapping is found.

`public void setStatus(int statuscode)`
: Sets the status code for this response. As opposed to the `sendError( )` method, this method only sets the status code; it doesn't add a body, and it doesn't commit the response.

The following methods are deprecated:

`public String encodeRedirectUrl(String url)`
: As of the Servlet 2.1 API, use `encodeRedirectURL(String url)` instead.

`public String encodeUrl(String url)`
: As of the Servlet 2.1 API, use `encodeURL(String url)` instead.

`public void setStatus(int statuscode, String message)`
: As of the Servlet 2.1 API, due to ambiguous meaning of the message parameter. To set a status code, use `setStatus(int)`; to send an error with a description, use `sendError(int, String)`.

session

The `session` variable is assigned a reference to the `HttpSession` object that represents the current client's session. Information stored as `HttpSession` attributes corresponds to objects in the JSP session scope.

By default, the session persists for a time period, specified in the web application deployment descriptor, across more than one page request from the user. The container can maintain a session in many ways such as using cookies or rewriting URLs.

Synopsis

Variable name:	`session`
EL expression	`${pageContext.session}`
Interface name:	`javax.servlet.http.HttpSession`
Extends:	None
Implemented by:	Internal container-dependent class
JSP page type:	Available in both regular JSP pages and error pages, unless the page directive session attribute is set to `false`

Methods

`public Object getAttribute(String name)`
: Returns the object associated with the specified name in this session or `null` if the object isn't found.

`public java.util.Enumeration getAttributeNames()`
: Returns an `Enumeration` of `String` objects containing the names of all the objects in this session.

`public long getCreationTime()`
: Returns the time when this session was created, measured in milliseconds since midnight January 1, 1970 GMT.

`public String getId()`
: Returns a string containing the unique identifier assigned to this session.

`public long getLastAccessedTime( )`
: Returns the time for the previous request associated with this session as the number of milliseconds since midnight January 1, 1970 GMT.

`public int getMaxInactiveInterval( )`
: Returns the maximum time interval, in seconds, that the servlet container will keep this session active between client accesses.

`public javax.servlet.ServletContext getServletContext( )`
: Returns the `ServletContext` the session belongs to.

`public void invalidate( )`
: Invalidates this session and unbinds any objects bound to it.

`public boolean isNew( )`
: Returns `true` if a request for this session has not yet been received from the client.

`public void removeAttribute(String name)`
: Removes the object bound with the specified name from this session.

`public void setAttribute(String name, Object attribute)`
: Associates the specified object with this session using the name specified.

`public void setMaxInactiveInterval(int interval)`
: Specifies the time, in seconds, between client requests before the servlet container invalidates this session.

The following methods are deprecated:

`public HttpSessionContext getSessionContext( )`
: As of the Servlet 2.1 API, this method is deprecated and has no replacement.

`public Object getValue(String name)`
: As of the Servlet 2.2 API, this method is replaced by `getAttribute(String)`.

`public String[] getValueNames( )`
: As of the Servlet 2.2 API, this method is replaced by `getAttributeNames( )`.

`public void putValue(String name, Object value)`
: As of the Servlet 2.2 API, this method is replaced by `setAttribute(String, Object)`.

`public void removeValue(String name)`
: As of the Servlet 2.2 API, this method is replaced by `setAttribute(String, Object)`.

Other Servlet Types Accessible Through Implicit Variables

This section contains descriptions of the servlet API classes that methods on the objects assigned to the implicit variables can return instances of.

Cookie

A `Cookie` object represents an HTTP cookie—a small amount of information sent by a server to a web browser, saved by the browser, and later sent back to the server with new requests. A cookie's value can uniquely identify a client, so cookies are commonly used for session management. A cookie has a name, a single value, and optional attributes such as a comment, path and domain qualifiers, a maximum age, and a version number.

This class supports both the Version 0 (the informal specification first introduced by Netscape) and the Version 1 (formally defined by RFC 2109) cookie specifications. By default, cookies are created using Version 0 to ensure the best interoperability.

Synopsis

Class name:	`javax.servlet.http.Cookie`
Extends:	None
Implements:	`Clonable`
Implemented by:	Internal container-dependent class. Most containers use the reference implementation of the class (developed in the Apache Jakarta project)

Constructor

`public Cookie(String name, String value)`

Creates a new instance with the specified name and value. The name must conform to RFC 2109, meaning it can't contain commas, semicolons, whitespace, or start with a dollar sign.

Methods

`public Object clone()`

Overrides the standard `Object.clone()` method to return a copy of this cookie.

`public String getComment()`

Returns the comment describing the purpose of this cookie or `null` if the cookie has no comment. For a cookie received from the browser, this method always returns `null`.

`public String getDomain()`
: Returns the domain name set for this cookie or `null` if the cookie has no domain. For a Version 0 cookie received from the browser, this method always returns `null`.

`public int getMaxAge()`
: Returns the maximum age of the cookie, specified in seconds, or -1 if not set, indicating that the cookie will persist until browser shutdown. For a cookie received from the browser, this method always returns -1.

`public String getName()`
: Returns the name of the cookie.

`public String getPath()`
: Returns the server path to which the browser returns this cookie. For a Version 0 cookie received from the browser, this method always returns `null`.

`public boolean getSecure()`
: Returns `true` if the browser should be required to send the cookie only over a secure protocol or `false` if the browser is allowed to send it using any protocol. For a cookie received from the browser, this method always returns -1.

`public String getValue()`
: Returns the value of the cookie.

`public int getVersion()`
: Returns the version of the protocol this cookie complies with. A value of 0 means that the cookie complies with the original Netscape specification; a value of 1 means that the cookie complies with RFC 2109.

`public void setComment(String comment)`
: Specifies a comment that describes a cookie's purpose.

`public void setDomain(String domain)`
: Specifies the domain within which this cookie should be presented, as defined by RFC 2109. By default, the cookie is returned only to the server that sets it.

`public void setMaxAge(int expiry)`
: Sets the maximum age of the cookie in seconds. 0 means that the cookie shall be deleted from the browser, and -1 that it should only be kept until the browser is shut down.

`public void setPath(String uriPath)`
: Specifies a server path to which the client should return the cookie, as defined by RFC 2109. By default, the cookie is returned with all requests for any resource on the server.

`public void setSecure()`
: Indicates to the browser whether the cookie should only be sent using a secure protocol, such as HTTPS.

`public void setValue(String value)`

Assigns a new value to a cookie after the cookie is created. With Version 0 cookies, values should not contain whitespace, brackets, parentheses, equal signs, commas, double quotes, slashes, question marks, at signs, colons, and semicolons. Empty values may not behave the same way on all browsers.

`public void setVersion(int version)`

Sets the version of the cookie protocol this cookie complies with. A value of 0 means that the cookie must be sent to the browser as described by the original Netscape specification; 1 that the cookie must be sent as defined by RFC 2109.

RequestDispatcher

The `RequestDispatcher` class defines an object that receives requests from the client and sends them to any resource (such as a servlet, HTML file, or JSP file) in the same web container. The container creates the `RequestDispatcher` object, which is used as a wrapper around a resource located at a particular URI path or identified by a particular name.

Synopsis

Interface name:	`javax.servlet.RequestDispatcher`
Extends:	None
Implemented by:	Internal container-dependent class

Methods

`public void forward(ServletRequest req, ServletResponse res)`

Forwards a request from a servlet to another resource (servlet, JSP file, or HTML file) on the server. For a `RequestDispatcher` obtained via `getRequestDispatcher( )`, the `ServletRequest` object has its path elements and parameters adjusted to match the path of the target resource.

This method must be called before the response has been committed to the client (before response body output has been flushed). If the response has already been committed, this method throws an `IllegalStateException`. Uncommitted output in the response buffer is automatically cleared before the forward.

The request and response parameters must be the same objects as were passed to the calling servlet's service method or be subclasses of the `ServletRequestWrapper` or `ServletResponseWrapper` classes that wrap them.

`public void include(ServletRequest req, ServletResponse res)`

Includes the response generated by a resource (servlet, JSP page, HTML file) in the response.

The `ServletResponse` object's path elements and parameters remain unchanged from the caller's. The included servlet cannot change the response status code or set headers; any attempt to make a change is ignored.

The request and response parameters must be the same objects that were passed to the calling servlet's service method or be subclasses of the `ServletRequestWrapper` or `ServletResponseWrapper` classes that wrap them.

Tag Handler Types

The JSP specification defines a number of classes and interfaces in the `javax.servlet.jsp.tagext` package. These classes are used to develop tag handler classes for JSP custom actions. This section contains descriptions of each class and interface. Chapter 21 and Chapter 22 show examples of how you can use these classes and interfaces to develop custom actions.

BodyContent

The container creates an instance of the `BodyContent` class to encapsulate the element body of a custom action element if the corresponding tag handler implements the `BodyTag` interface. The container makes the `BodyContent` instance available to the tag handler by calling the `setBodyContent( )` method, so the tag handler can process the body content.

Synopsis

Class name:	`javax.servlet.jsp.tagext.BodyContent`
Extends:	`javax.servlet.jsp.JspWriter`
Implements:	None
Implemented by:	Internal container-dependent class

Constructor

`protected BodyContent(JspWriter e)`
: Creates a new instance with the specified `JspWriter` as the enclosing writer.

Methods

`public void clearBody( )`
: Removes all buffered content for this instance.

`public void flush( ) throws java.io.IOException`
: Overwrites the behavior inherited from `JspWriter` to always throw an `IOException`, because it's invalid to flush a `BodyContent` instance.

public JspWriter getEnclosingWriter( )
: Returns the enclosing JspWriter, i.e., either the top level JspWriter or the JspWriter (BodyContent subclass) of the parent tag handler.

public abstract java.io.Reader getReader( )
: Returns the value of this BodyContent as a Reader with the content produced by evaluating the element's body.

public abstract String getString( )
: Returns the value of this BodyContent as a String with the content produced by evaluating the element's body.

public abstract void writeOut(java.io.Writer out)throws java.io.IOException
: Writes the content of this BodyContent into a Writer.

BodyTag

The BodyTag interface extends the IterationTag interface. It must be implemented by classic tag handler classes that need access to the body contents of the corresponding custom action element, for instance in order to perform a transformation of the contents before it's included in the response. A tag handler that implements this interface must return EVAL_BODY_BUFFERED from doStartTag( ) to tell the container to capture the result of evaluating the body. It can also return EVAL_BODY_AGAIN from doAfterBody( ) to tell the container to evaluate the body again and capture the result.

Unless you need to allow scripting elements in the corresponding custom action element body, I recommend that you use the SimpleTag interface instead.

Synopsis

Interface name:	javax.servlet.jsp.tagext.BodyTag
Extends:	javax.servlet.jsp.tagext.IterationTag
Implemented by:	Custom action tag handler classes and javax.servlet.jsp.tagext.BodyTagSupport

Fields

public static final int EVAL_BODY_BUFFERED

Methods

public void doInitBody( ) throws JspException
: Prepares for evaluation of the body. This method is invoked once per action invocation by the page implementation after a new BodyContent has been obtained and set on the tag handler via the setBodyContent( ) method and before the evaluation of the element's body.

  This method isn't invoked if the element body is empty or if doStartTag( ) returns SKIP_BODY.

```
public void setBodyContent(BodyContent b)
```
Sets the `BodyContent` created for this tag handler. This method isn't invoked if the element body is empty or if `doStartTag( )` returns `SKIP_BODY`.

BodyTagSupport

`BodyTagSupport` is a support class that provides default implementations of all `BodyTag` interface methods. It's intended to be used as a superclass for classic tag handlers that need access to the body contents of the corresponding custom action element.

Unless you need to allow scripting elements in the corresponding custom action element body, I recommend that you use the `SimpleTagSupport` class instead.

Synopsis

Class name:	`javax.servlet.jsp.tagext.BodyTagSupport`
Extends:	`javax.servlet.jsp.tagext.TagSupport`
Implements:	`javax.servlet.jsp.tagext.BodyTag`
Implemented by:	Internal container-dependent class. Most containers use the reference implementation of the class (developed in the Apache Jakarta project)

Fields

```
protected javax.servlet.jsp.tagext.BodyContent bodyContent
```

Constructor

```
public BodyTagSupport( )
```
Creates a new `BodyTagSupport` instance.

Methods

```
public int doAfterBody( )
```
Returns SKIP_BODY.

```
public int doEndTag( )
```
Returns EVAL_PAGE.

```
public void doInitBody( )
```
This method does nothing in the `BodyTagSupport` class.

```
public int doStartTag( )
```
Returns EVAL_BODY_BUFFERED.

```
public BodyContent getBodyContent( )
```
Returns the `BodyContent` object assigned to this instance.

```
public JspWriter getPreviousOut( )
```
Returns the enclosing writer of the `BodyContent` object assigned to this instance.

public void release( )

Removes the references to all objects held by this instance.

public void setBodyContent(BodyContent b)

Saves a reference to the BodyContent in the bodyContent instance variable.

DynamicAttributes

The DynamicAttributes interface can be implemented by a tag handler in addition to one of the main tag handler interfaces to support attributes not declared in the TLD.

Synopsis

Interface name:	javax.servlet.jsp.tagext.DynamicAttributes
Extends:	None
Implemented by:	Custom action tag handler classes

Methods

public void setDynamicAttribute(String uri, String localName, Object value) throws JspException

Called by the container to pass the tag handler an undeclared attribute. The URI is the attribute's XML namespace identifier or null if it's in the default namespace.

IterationTag

The IterationTag interface extends the Tag interface. Classic tag handler classes that need their corresponding action element body evaluated more than once but that don't need to access the result of the body evaluation must implement this interface.

Unless you need to allow scripting elements in the corresponding custom action element body, I recommend that you use the SimpleTag interface instead.

Synopsis

Interface name:	javax.servlet.jsp.tagext.IterationTag
Extends:	javax.servlet.jsp.tagext.Tag
Implemented by:	Custom action tag handler classes and javax.servlet.jsp.tagext.TagSupport.

Fields

public static final int EVAL_BODY_AGAIN

Methods

`public int doAfterBody( ) throws JspException`

Performs actions after the body has been evaluated. This method is invoked after every body evaluation. If this method returns `EVAL_BODY_AGAIN`, the body is evaluated again, typically after changing the value of variables used in the body. If it returns `SKIP_BODY`, the processing continues with a call to `doEndTag( )`.

This method is not invoked if the element body is empty or if `doStartTag( )` returns `SKIP_BODY`.

JspContext

The `JspContext` class represents an interface to the generic runtime environment available to a simple tag handler, even in a nonservlet environment. In a servlet-based JSP container, an instance of the `PageContext` subclass, described in the Implicit Variables section, is always used.

Synopsis

Class name:	`javax.servlet.jsp.JspContext`
Extends:	None
Implements:	None
Implemented by:	Internal container-dependent class; most containers use the reference implementation of the class (developed in the Apache Jakarta project)

Constructor

`public JspContext( )`

Creates a new `JspContext` instance.

Methods

`public abstract Object findAttribute(String name)`

Searches for the named attribute in the page, request, session (if valid), and application scope in order and returns the first value it finds or `null` if the attribute is not found.

`public abstract Object getAttribute(String name)`

Returns the object associated with the specified attribute name in the page scope or `null` if the attribute is not found.

`public abstract Object getAttribute(String name, int scope)`

Returns the object associated with the specified attribute name in the specified scope or `null` if the attribute is not found. The `scope` argument must be one of the `int` values specified by the `PageContext` static scope variables.

`public abstract java.util.Enumeration getAttributeNamesInScope(int scope)`
: Returns an enumeration of `String` objects containing all attribute names for the specified scope. The `scope` argument must be one of the `int` values specified by the `PageContext` static scope variables.

`public abstract int getAttributesScope(String name)`
: Returns one of the `int` values specified by the `PageContext` static scope variables for the scope of the object associated with the specified attribute name or 0 if the attribute is not found.

`public abstract ExpressionEvaluator getExpressionEvaluator()`
: Returns an `ExpressionEvaluator` that can be used for programmatic EL expression evaluation.

`public abstract JspWriter getOut()`
: Returns the current `JspWriter` for the page. When a tag handler that implements `BodyTag` (or is nested in the body of another action element) calls this method, the returned object may be an instance of the `BodyContent` subclass.

`public abstract VariableEvaluator getVariableEvaluator()`
: Returns a `VariableEvaluator` that can be used with an `ExpressionEvaluator` for programmatic EL expression evaluation.

`public JspWriter popBody()`
: This method is intended to be called only by the JSP page implementation class. It reassigns the previous `JspWriter`, saved by the matching `pushBody()` method, as the current `JspWriter` and returns the same instance.

`public JspWriter pushBody(java.io.Writer writer)`
: This method is intended to be called only by the JSP page implementation class. It returns a new `JspWriter` that ultimately writes to the provided `Writer` and updates the out variable to point to the new instance. A reference to the old `JspWriter`, if any, is also kept so it can be reassigned when `popBody()` is called.

`public abstract void removeAttribute(String name)`
: Removes the object reference associated with the specified attribute name in the page scope.

`public abstract void removeAttribute(String name, int scope)`
: Removes the object reference associated with the specified attribute name in the specified scope. The `scope` argument must be one of the `int` values specified by the `PageContext` static scope variables.

`public abstract void setAttribute(String name, Object attribute)`
: Saves the specified attribute name and object in the page scope.

`public abstract void setAttribute(String name, Object o, int scope)`
: Saves the specified attribute name and object in the specified scope. The `scope` argument must be one of the `int` values specified by the `PageContext` static scope variables.

JspFragment

The JspFragment class represents an object that encapsulates a set of JSP actions and/or EL expressions, possibly mixed with template text, that a tag handler can invoke as many times as needed. The container creates an instance of this class for the body of a custom action implemented by a simple tag handler, as well as for the body of the <jsp:attribute> for an attribute of type JspFragment.

Synopsis

Class name:	javax.servlet.jsp.tagext.JspFragment
Extends:	None
Implements:	None
Implemented by:	Internal container-dependent class; most containers use the reference implementation of the class (developed in the Apache Jakarta project)

Methods

`public abstract JspContext getJspContext()`

Returns the JspContext that is bound to this fragment.

`public abstract void invoke(java.io.Writer out) throws JspException`

Executes the fragment and directs all output to the provided Writer or to the JspWriter returned by the getOut() method of the JspContext associated with the fragment if no Writer is provided.

JspTag

The JspTag interface is an empty interface, serving as the common parent interface for the Tag and SimpleTag interfaces to allow nesting of custom actions implemented by both classic and simple tag handlers.

SimpleTag

The SimpleTag interface defines the new, easier to use, tag handler API introduced in JSP 2.0. Tag handlers implementing this interface are referred to as *simple tag handler* (tag handlers based on the older API are referred to as *classic tag handlers*). The container creates a new instance of the class that implements this interface for each invocation.

A tag handler implementing this interface can do everything a classic tag handler can do, except that the corresponding custom action element must not contain scripting elements (i.e., the tag handler must be declared to have a body content of empty, scriptless, or tagdependent).

Synopsis

Interface name:	`javax.servlet.jsp.tagext.SimpleTag`
Extends:	`javax.servlet.jsp.tagext.JspTag`
Implemented by:	Custom action tag handler classes

Methods

`public void doTag( ) throws JspException, SkipPageException, java.io.IOException`

Performs all processing for the tag handler using the properties and attributes previously set by the setter methods. If the page processing must be terminated after processing of this tag handler (e.g., if the tag handler forwards or redirects to another resource), this method must throw a `SkipPageException`.

`public JspTag getParent( )`

Returns the parent tag handler or `null` if there's no parent.

`public void setJspBody(JspFragment jspBody)`

Sets the fragment that represents the custom action element's body. The container doesn't call this method if the custom action element body is empty.

`public void setJspContext(JspContext context)`

Sets the context for the JSP page. In a JSP environment, this is always an instance of the `PageContext` subclass. The tag handler can access all JSP scopes, request and response information, and more through the context object.

`public void setParent(JspTag parent)`

Sets the parent tag handler. The container doesn't call this method if the tag handler doesn't have a parent.

SimpleTagSupport

The `SimpleTagSupport` class provides default implementations of all `SimpleTag` interface methods, plus a method for finding a parent of a specific type. It's intended to be used as a superclass for simple tag handlers.

Synopsis

Class name:	`javax.servlet.jsp.tagext.SimpleTagSupport`
Extends:	None
Implements:	`javax.servlet.jsp.tagext.SimpleTag`
Implemented by:	Internal container-dependent class; most containers use the reference implementation of the class (developed in the Apache Jakarta project)

Constructor

`public SimpleTagSupport( )`

Creates a new instance.

Methods

`public void doTag() throws JspException, SkipPageException, java.io.IOException`

Performs all processing for the tag handler using the properties and attributes previously set by the setter methods. If the page processing must be terminated after processing of this tag handler (e.g., if the tag handler forwards or redirects to another resource), this method must throw a `SkipPageException`. The default implementation in this class doesn't do anything, so this method must be implemented by the subclass.

`public static final JspTag findAncestorWithClass(JspTag from, Class klass)`

Locates the closest parent tag handler of the specified class for the specified tag handler. It uses the `getParent()` method of the `Tag` and `SimpleTag` interfaces to look for the parent. For every instance of `TagAdapter` returned by a `getParent()` call, the object returned by `TagAdapter getAdaptee()` is compared to the specified class. If a match is found this way, the `getAdaptee()` value is returned by this method.

`public JspFragment getJspBody()`

Returns the fragment passed to the `setJspBody()` method or `null` if there's nobody.

`public JspContext getJspContext()`

Returns the context passed to the `setJspContext()` method.

`public JspTag getParent()`

Returns the parent tag handler passed to the `setParent()` method or `null` if there's no parent.

`public void setJspBody(JspFragment jspBody)`

Sets the fragment that represents the custom action element's body. The container doesn't call this method if the custom action element body is empty.

`public void setJspContext(JspContext context)`

Sets the context for the JSP page. In a JSP environment, this is always an instance of the `PageContext` subclass. The tag handler can access all JSP scopes, request and response information, and more through the context object.

`public void setParent(JspTag parent)`

Sets the parent tag handler. The container doesn't call this method if the tag handler doesn't have a parent.

Tag

The `Tag` interface is the main classic tag handler interface. It should be implemented by classic tag handler classes that do not need the body of the corresponding action element evaluated more than once and that do not need access to the result of the body evaluation.

Unless you need to allow scripting elements in the corresponding custom action element body, I recommend that you use the SimpleTag interface instead.

Synopsis

Interface name:	javax.servlet.jsp.tagext.Tag
Extends:	javax.servlet.jsp.tagext.JspTag
Implemented by:	Custom action tag handler classes

Fields

```
public static final int EVAL_BODY_INCLUDE
public static final int EVAL_PAGE
public static final int SKIP_BODY
public static final int SKIP_PAGE
```

Methods

`public int doEndTag( ) throws JspException`
: Performs actions when the end tag is encountered. If this method returns SKIP_PAGE, execution of the rest of the page is aborted, and the _jspService( ) method of JSP page implementation class returns. If EVAL_PAGE is returned, the code following the custom action in the _jspService( ) method is executed.

`public int doStartTag( ) throws JspException`
: Performs actions when the start tag is encountered. This method is called after all property setter methods have been called. The return value from this method controls how the action's body, if any, is handled. If it returns EVAL_BODY_INCLUDE, the JSP container evaluates the body and processed possible JSP elements. The result of the evaluation is added to the response. If SKIP_BODY is returned, the body is ignored.

  A tag handler class that implements the BodyTag interface (extending the IterationTag interface, which extends the Tag interface) can return EVAL_BODY_BUFFERED instead of EVAL_BODY_INCLUDE. The JSP container then creates a BodyContent instance and makes it available to the tag handler for special processing.

`public Tag getParent( )`
: Returns the tag handler's parent (the Tag instance for the enclosing action element, if any) or null if the tag handler doesn't have a parent.

`public void release( )`
: Removes the references to all objects held by this instance.

`public void setPageContext(PageContext pc)`
: Saves a reference to the current PageContext.

public void setParent(Tag t)

Saves a reference to the tag handler's parent (the Tag instance for the enclosing action element).

TagAdapter

The TagAdapter class makes it possible to nest classic and simple tag handlers by working around a type mismatch between the old and new tag handler APIs, namely the fact that the setParent( ) method in the Tag interface takes an instance of Tag while the SimpleTag interface doesn't extend Tag.

The container creates an instance of TagAdapter to wrap a SimpleTag implementation when a simple tag handler is the parent of a classic tag handler and uses the TagAdapter as the setParent( ) argument. The findAncestorWithClass( ) method in SimpleTagSupport knows how to deal with TagAdapter instances it may find in the parent chain.

Synopsis

Class name:	javax.servlet.jsp.tagext.TagAdapter
Extends:	None
Implements:	javax.servlet.jsp.tagext.Tag
Implemented by:	Internal container-dependent class; most containers use the reference implementation of the class (developed in the Apache Jakarta project)

Constructor

public TagAdapter(SimpleTag adaptee)

Creates a new instance that wraps the given SimpleTag.

Methods

public int doEndTag( ) throws JspException

Never called by the container. Throws UnsupportedOperationException.

public int doStartTag( ) throws JspException

Never called by the container. Throws UnsupportedOperationException.

public JspTag getAdaptee( )

Returns the wrapped tag handler.

public Tag getParent( )

Returns the wrapped tag handler's parent tag handler.

public void release( )

Never called by the container. Throws UnsupportedOperationException.

public void setPageContext( )

Never called by the container. Throws UnsupportedOperationException.

`public void setParent()`
: Never called by the container. Throws `UnsupportedOperationException`.

TagSupport

`TagSupport` is a support class that provides default implementations of all `IterationTag` interface methods. It's intended to be used as a superclass for classic tag handlers that do not need to evaluate the corresponding action element body or need access to the evaluation result.

Unless you need to allow scripting elements in the corresponding custom action element body, I recommend that you use the `SimpleTagSupport` class instead.

Synopsis

Class name:	`javax.servlet.jsp.tagext.TagSupport`
Extends:	None
Implements:	`java.io.Serializable, javax.servlet.jsp.tagext.IterationTag`
Implemented by:	Internal container-dependent class; most containers use the reference implementation of the class (developed in the Apache Jakarta project)

Fields

```
protected String id
protected PageContext pageContext
```

Constructor

`public TagSupport()`
: Creates a new instance.

Methods

`public int doAfterBody()`
: Returns SKIP_BODY.

`public int doEndTag()`
: Returns EVAL_PAGE.

`public int doStartTag()`
: Returns SKIP_BODY.

`public static final Tag findAncestorWithClass(Tag from, Class klass)`
: Returns the instance of the specified class, found by testing for a match of each parent in a tag handler nesting structure (corresponding to nested action elements) starting with the specified `Tag` instance or `null` if not found.

`public String getId()`
: Returns the `id` attribute value or `null` if not set.

`public Tag getParent( )`

Returns the parent of this Tag instance (representing the action element that contains the action element corresponding to this Tag instance) or null if the instance has no parent (at the top level in the JSP page).

`public Object getValue(String k)`

Returns the value for the specified attribute that has been set with the setValue( ) method or null if not found.

`public java.util.Enumeration getValues( )`

Returns an Enumeration of all attribute names for values set with the setValue( ) method.

`public void release( )`

Removes the references to all objects held by this instance.

`public void removeValue(String k)`

Removes a value set with the setValue( ) method.

`public void setId(String id)`

Sets the id attribute value.

`public void setPageContext(PageContext pageContext)`

Saves a reference to the current PageContext.

`public void setParent(Tag t)`

Saves a reference to the parent for this instance.

`public void setValue(String k, Object o)`

Saves the specified attribute with the specified value. Subclasses can use this method to save attribute values as an alternative to instance variables.

TryCatchFinally

The TryCatchFinally interface provides methods for handling exceptions thrown while evaluating the body of an action element and can be implemented by a tag handler in addition to one of the main tag handler interfaces: Tag, IterationTag, and BodyTag.

Synopsis

Interface name:	javax.servlet.jsp.tagext.TryCatchFinally
Extends:	None
Implemented by:	Custom action tag handler classes

Methods

`public void doCatch(Throwable exception) throws Throwable`

Handles the specified exception and may optionally rethrow the same exception or a new exception. This method is invoked by the container if an exception is thrown when evaluating the body or by calling `doStartTag( )`, `doEndTag( )`, `doInitBody( )`, or `doAfterBody( )`.

`public void doFinally( )`
Typically clears per-invocation state, such as closing expensive resources used only for one invocation. This method is invoked after `doEndTag( )` or after `doCatch( )` if an exception is thrown when evaluating the body or by calling `doStartTag( )`, `doEndTag( )`, `doInitBody( )`, or `doAfterBody( )`.

Translation Time Types

This section describes the classes and interfaces used when a JSP page is translated into an implementation class, such as the types used for the tag library validation and the types for holding information about the JSP pages, tag files, and the TLD used by the container.

FunctionInfo

The container uses the `FunctionInfo` class to hold information about an EL function declaration from the TLD. It's primarily intended to be used by the JSP container itself during the translation phase.

Synopsis

Class name:	`javax.servlet.jsp.tagext.FunctionInfo`
Extends:	None
Implements:	None
Implemented by:	Internal container-dependent class; most containers use the reference implementation of the class (developed in the Apache Jakarta project)

Constructor

`public FunctionInfo(String name, String klass, String signature)`
Creates a new instance.

Methods

`public String getFunctionClass( )`
Returns the function class name.

`public String getFunctionSignature( )`
Returns the function signature.

`public String getName( )`
Returns the function name.

PageData

The PageData class provides access to the JSP page in the form of its *XML View*, essentially an XML version of the page with all include directives expanded (see Chapter 17 for details).

Synopsis

Class name:	javax.servlet.jsp.tagext.PageData
Extends:	None
Implements:	None
Implemented by:	Internal container-dependent class; most containers use the reference implementation of the class (developed in the Apache Jakarta project)

Constructor

public PageData( )
Creates a new instance.

Methods

public abstract java.io.InputStream getInputStream( )
Returns an input stream for the XML View of the JSP page, in which all include directives have been expanded.

TagAttributeInfo

TagAttributeInfo instances are created by the JSP container to provide information found in the Tag Library Descriptor (TLD) about each attribute supported by a custom action. It's primarily intended to be used by the JSP container itself during the translation phase.

Synopsis

Class name:	javax.servlet.jsp.tagext.TagAttributeInfo
Extends:	None
Implements:	None
Implemented by:	Internal container-dependent class; most containers use the reference implementation of the class (developed in the Apache Jakarta project)

Fields

```
public static final String ID
```

Constructor

`public TagAttributeInfo(String name, boolean required, String type, boolean reqTime)`

Pre-JSP 2.0 constructor. Creates a new instance with the specified information from the TLD. Instances of this class should only be created by the JSP container.

`public TagAttributeInfo(String name, boolean required, String type, boolean reqTime, boolean fragment)`

Creates a new instance with the specified information from the TLD, including information about whether the attribute is a fragment. Instances of this class should only be created by the JSP container.

Methods

`public boolean canBeRequestTime()`

Returns `true` if a request time attribute value can be used for this attribute.

`public static TagAttributeInfo getIdAttribute(TagAttributeInfo[] a)`

Convenience method that returns the `TagAttributeInfo` instance in the specified array that represents an attribute named `id` or `null` if not found.

`public String getName()`

Returns the attribute name.

`public String getTypeName()`

Returns the attribute's Java type (a fully qualified class or interface name).

`public boolean isFragment()`

Returns `true` if this attribute is a fragment attribute, `false` otherwise.

`public boolean isRequired()`

Returns `true` if this attribute is required, `false` otherwise.

`public String toString()`

Returns a `String` representation of the attribute info.

TagData

`TagData` instances are created by the JSP container during the translation phase to provide information about the attribute values specified for a custom action to the `TagExtraInfo` subclass for the corresponding tag handler, if any.

Synopsis

Class name:	`javax.servlet.jsp.tagext.TagData`
Extends:	None
Implements:	`Clonable`
Implemented by:	Internal container-dependent class; most containers use the reference implementation of the class (developed in the Apache Jakarta project)

Fields

`public static final Object REQUEST_TIME_VALUE`

Constructors

`public TagData(Object[][] attrs)`
: Creates a new instance with the attribute name/value pairs specified by the `Object[][]`. Element 0 of each `Object[]` contains the name and element 1 the value or `REQUEST_TIME_VALUE` if the attribute value is defined as a request time value (a JSP expression).

`public TagData(java.util.Hashtable attrs)`
: Creates a new instance with the attribute name/value pairs specified by the `Hashtable`.

Methods

`public Object getAttribute(String attName)`
: Returns the specified attribute value as a `String` or as the `REQUEST_TIME_VALUE` `Object` if the attribute value is defined as a request-time value (a Java expression, an EL expression or set by `<jsp:attribute>`).

`public java.util.Enumeration getAttributes()`
: Returns an `Enumeration` of all attributes names.

`public String getAttributeString(String attName)`
: Returns the specified attribute value as a `String`. A `ClassCastException` is thrown if the attribute value is defined as a request time value (a JSP expression).

`public String getId()`
: Returns the attribute named `id` as a `String` or `null` if not found.

`public void setAttribute(String attName, Object value)`
: Sets the specified attribute to the specified value.

TagExtraInfo

For custom actions that expose scripting variables or require additional translation time validation of the tag attributes, a subclass of the `TagExtraInfo` class can be developed for the custom action and declared in the Tag Library Descriptor. The JSP container creates an instance of the `TagExtraInfo` subclass during the translation phase.

Note that for most cases, the variable information can instead be declared in the TLD, and a `TagLibraryValidator` class can perform validation in a more flexible manner than a `TagExtraInfo` class.

Synopsis

Class name:	`javax.servlet.jsp.tagext.TagExtraInfo`
Extends:	None
Implements:	None
Implemented by:	Internal container-dependent class; most containers use the reference implementation of the class (developed in the Apache Jakarta project)

Constructor

`public TagExtraInfo( )`

Creates a new `TagExtraInfo` instance.

Methods

`public TagInfo getTagInfo( )`

Returns the `TagInfo` instance for the custom action associated with this `TagExtraInfo` instance. The `TagInfo` instance is set by the `setTagInfo( )` method (called by the container).

`public VariableInfo[] getVariableInfo(TagData data)`

Returns a `VariableInfo[]` with information about scripting variables created by the tag handler class associated with this `TagExtraInfo` instance. The default implementation returns an empty array. A subclass must override this method if the corresponding tag handler creates scripting variables, unless the variable declarations can be made in the TLD instead.

`public boolean isValid(TagData data)`

Returns `true` if the set of attribute values specified for the custom action associated with this `TagExtraInfo` instance is valid, `false` otherwise. The default implementation returns `true`. A subclass can override this method if the validation performed by the JSP container based on the TLD information is not enough, but starting with JSP 2.0, the preferred method for validation is `validate( )`. In a JSP 2.0 container, the `isValid( )` method is only called indirectly by the default `validate( )` implementation.

`public void setTagInfo(TagInfo tagInfo)`

Sets the `TagInfo` for this instance. This method is called by the JSP container before any of the other methods are called.

`public ValidationMessage[] validate(TagData data)`

Returns an array with one `ValidationMessage` instance per error or null or an empty array if no errors are found. This method is preferred over `isValid( )` because it allows the subclass implementation to return meaningful error messages instead of just a Boolean value. For backward compatibility, the default implementation in this class calls `isValid( )` and returns a generic error message if it returns `false`.

TagFileInfo

The container creates instances of the `TagFileInfo` class to hold information found in the TLD about a custom action implemented as a tag file. It's primarily intended to be used by the JSP container itself during the translation phase.

Synopsis

Class name:	`javax.servlet.jsp.tagext.TagFileInfo`
Extends:	None
Implements:	None
Implemented by:	Internal container-dependent class; most containers use the reference implementation of the class (developed in the Apache Jakarta project)

Constructor

`public TagFileInfo(String name, String path, TagInfo tagInfo)`
: Creates a new instance with the specified values, based on the information available in the TLD.

Methods

`public String getName( )`
: Returns the custom action name.

`public String getPath( )`
: Returns the path for the tag file.

`public String getTagInfo( )`
: Returns tag file information based on the directives in the tag file.

TagInfo

`TagInfo` instances are created by the JSP container to provide information about a custom action found in the TLD or in a tag file, as well as information about the attribute values used in a JSP page for an instance of the custom action. It's primarily intended to be used by the JSP container itself during the translation phase.

Synopsis

Class name:	`javax.servlet.jsp.tagext.TagInfo`
Extends:	None
Implements:	None
Implemented by:	Internal container-dependent class; most containers use the reference implementation of the class (developed in the Apache Jakarta project)

Fields

```
public static final String BODY_CONTENT_EMPTY
public static final String BODY_CONTENT_JSP
public static final String BODY_CONTENT_SCRIPTLESS
public static final String BODY_CONTENT_TAG_DEPENDENT
```

Constructor

`public TagInfo(String tagName, String tagClassName, String bodycontent, String infoString, TagLibraryInfo taglib, TagExtraInfo tagExtraInfo, TagAttributeInfo[] attributeInfo)`

Creates a new instance with the specified values, based on the information available in a JSP 1.1 TLD.

`public TagInfo(String tagName, String tagClassName, String bodycontent, String infoString, TagLibraryInfo taglib, TagExtraInfo tagExtraInfo, TagAttributeInfo[] attributeInfo, String displayName, String smallIcon, String largeIcon, TagVariableInfo[] tvi)`

Creates a new instance with the specified values, based on the information available in a JSP 1.2 TLD.

`public TagInfo(String tagName, String tagClassName, String bodycontent, String infoString, TagLibraryInfo taglib, TagExtraInfo tagExtraInfo, TagAttributeInfo[] attributeInfo, String displayName, String smallIcon, String largeIcon, TagVariableInfo[] tvi, boolean dynamicAttributes)`

Creates a new instance with the specified values, based on the information available in a JSP 2.0 TLD.

Methods

`public TagAttributeInfo[] getAttributes()`

Returns information from the TLD about all attribute values or `null` if no attributes are declared.

`public String getBodyContent()`

Returns one of `BODY_CONTENT_EMPTY`, `BODY_CONTENT_JSP`, or `BODY_CONTENT_TAG_DEPENDENT` based on the value in the TLD.

`public String getDisplayName()`

Returns the display name value from the TLD or `null` if no value is specified.

`public String getInfoString()`

Returns the tag information value from the TLD or `null` if no value is specified.

`public String getLargeIcon()`

Returns the large icon path from the TLD or `null` if no value is specified.

`public String getSmallIcon()`

Returns the small icon path from the TLD or `null` if no value is specified.

`public String getTagClassName( )`
: Returns the tag handler class name declared in the TLD.

`public TagExtraInfo getTagExtraInfo( )`
: Returns an instance of the `TagExtraInfo` subclass for the tag or `null` if no class is declared in the TLD.

`public TagLibraryInfo getTagLibrary( )`
: Returns a `TagLibraryInfo` instance for the library the tag is part of.

`public String getTagName( )`
: Returns the name for the tag declared in the TLD.

`public TagVariableInfo[] getTagVariableInfos( )`
: Returns an array with a `TagVariableInfo` instance for each variable declaration in the TLD.

`public VariableInfo[] getVariableInfo(TagData data)`
: Returns information about scripting variables created by the tag handler or `null` if no variables are created. This information is obtained from the `TagExtraInfo` for the tag, if any.

`public boolean hasDynamicAttributes( )`
: Returns `true` if the tag handler is declared to accept dynamic (undeclared) attributes.

`public boolean isValid(TagData data)`
: Returns `true` if the set of attributes specified for the custom action associated with this `TagExtraInfo` instance is valid, `false` otherwise. This information is obtained from the `TagExtraInfo` for the tag, if any.

`public void setTagExtraInfo(TagExtraInfo tei)`
: Sets the `TagExraInfo` value held by the instance.

`public void setTagLibrary(TagLibrary tl)`
: Sets the `TagLibrary` value held by the instance.

`public ValidationMessage[] validate(TagData data)`
: Calls the `validate( )` method on the `TagExtraInfo` class held by an instance of this class, if any.

TagLibraryInfo

`TagLibraryInfo` instances are created by the JSP container to provide information found in the TLD about a tag library as well as information from the `taglib` directive used in a JSP page. It's primarily intended to be used by the JSP container itself during the translation phase.

Synopsis

Class name:	`javax.servlet.jsp.tagext.TagLibraryInfo`
Extends:	None
Implements:	None
Implemented by:	Internal container-dependent class; most containers use the reference implementation of the class (developed in the Apache Jakarta project)

Fields

```
Protected FunctionInfo[] functions
protected String info
protected String jspversion
protected String prefix
protected String shortname
protected TagFileInfo[] tagFiles
protected TagInfo[] tags
protected String tlibversion
protected String uri
protected String urn
```

Constructor

`protected TagLibraryInfo(String prefix, String uri)`
: Creates a new instance with the specified prefix and URI (from the `taglib` directive in the JSP page).

Methods

`public FunctionInfo getFunction(String name)`
: Returns the information about the specified function or `null` if the function is not declared in this library.

`public FunctionInfo[] getFunctions()`
: Returns the information about all functions declared in this library or an empty array if no functions are declared.

`public String getInfoString()`
: Returns the information string from the TLD for the library.

`public String getPrefixString()`
: Returns the prefix assigned by the `taglib` directive for the library.

`public String getReliableURN()`
: Returns URI value from the TLD for the library.

`public String getRequiredVersion()`
: Returns the required JSP version from the TLD for the library.

`public String getShortName()`
: Returns the short name (prefix) from the TLD for the library.

public TagInfo getTag(String shortname)
: Returns a TagInfo instance for the specified tag in the library or null if the tag is not declared.

public TagFileInfo getTagFile(String shortname)
: Returns a TagFileInfo instance for the specified tag file in the library or null if the tag file is not declared.

public TagFileInfo[] getTagFiles()
: Returns a TagFileInfo[] for all tag files in the library or an empty array if no tag files are declared.

public TagInfo[] getTags()
: Returns a TagInfo[] for all tags in the library or an empty array if no tags are declared.

public String getURI()
: Returns the URI assigned by the taglib directive for the library.

TagLibraryValidator

A subclass of the TagLibraryValidator class can be declared as the validator for a tag library. The container invokes it at translation time, providing it with the XML View of the page through a PageData instance.

Synopsis

Class name:	javax.servlet.jsp.tagext.TagLibraryValidator
Extends:	None
Implements:	None
Implemented by:	Internal container-dependent class; most containers use the reference implementation of the class (developed in the Apache Jakarta project)

Constructor

public TagLibraryValidator()
: Creates a new instance.

Methods

public java.util.Map getInitParameters()
: Returns a Map containing all initialization parameters declared in the TLD for the validator, with the parameter names as keys.

public void release()
: Releases any resources kept as instance data.

public void setInitParameters(java.util.Map)
: Sets the Map containing all initialization parameters declared in the TLD for the validator, with the parameter names as keys.

`public ValidationMessage[] validate(String prefix, String uri, PageData page)`
Validates the specified page data, and returns `null` or an empty array if the page is valid. If errors are found, descriptions of the errors are returned as an array of `ValidationMessage` instances. The `prefix` and `uri` arguments have the values of the corresponding `taglib` directive attributes or the first corresponding namespace declaration in a JSP Document. Note that in a JSP Document, the tag library can be bound to more than one prefix in the same document, so the namespace URI should always be used when determining if a tag belongs to the library the validator is associated with.

TagVariableInfo

The `TagVariableInfo` instance represents a variable declaration in the TLD. The container creates instances of this class during the translation phase and it's used to generate variable declarations in the JSP page implementation class.

Synopsis

Class name:	`javax.servlet.jsp.tagext.TagVariableInfo`
Extends:	None
Implements:	None
Implemented by:	Internal container-dependent class; most containers use the reference implementation of the class (developed in the Apache Jakarta project)

Constructor

`public TagVariableInfo(String nameGiven, String nameFromAttribute, String className, boolean declare, int scope)`
Creates a new instance with the specified values.

Methods

`public String getClassName()`
Returns the declared class name.

`public boolen getDeclare()`
Returns true if the variable is defined as one to be declared.

`public String getNameFromAttribute()`
Returns the name of the attribute declared to hold the name of the variable at translation time.

`public String getNameGiven()`
Returns the declared variable name.

`public int getScope()`
Returns the declared scope, as one of `VariableInfo.AT_BEGIN`, `VariableInfo.AT_END`, or `VariableInfo.NESTED`.

ValidationMessage

A `ValidationMessage` instance holds information about an error found by a tag library validator.

Synopsis

Class name:	`javax.servlet.jsp.tagext.ValidationMessage`
Extends:	None
Implements:	None
Implemented by:	Internal container-dependent class; most containers use the reference implementation of the class (developed in the Apache Jakarta project)

Constructor

`public ValidationMessage(String id, String message)`
Creates a new instance with the specified values.

Methods

`public String getId( )`
Returns the value of the `jsp:id` attribute for the element associated with this validation message or `null` if no `jsp:id` attribute is available.

`public String getMessage( )`
Returns the validation message text, describing the problem.

VariableInfo

`VariableInfo` instances are created by `TagExtraInfo` subclasses to describe each scripting variable that the corresponding tag handler class creates.

Synopsis

Class name:	`javax.servlet.jsp.tagext.VariableInfo`
Extends:	None
Implements:	None
Implemented by:	Internal container-dependent class; most containers use the reference implementation of the class (developed in the Apache Jakarta project)

Fields

```
public static final int AT_BEGIN
public static final int AT_END
public static final int NESTED
```

Constructor

`public VariableInfo(String varName, String className, boolean declare, int scope)`

Creates a new instance with the specified values.

Methods

`public String getClassName( )`

Returns the scripting variable Java type.

`public boolean getDeclare( )`

Returns `true` if the JSP container should create a declaration statement for the scripting variable. It returns `false` if the variable has already been declared by another tag handler and is only updated by the tag handler corresponding to the `TagExtraInfo` subclass creating this `VariableInfo` instance. If so, the JSP container assigns the new value to the existing variable.

`public int getScope( )`

Returns one of `AT_BEGIN` (make the scripting variable available from the start tag to the end of the JSP page), `AT_END` (make the variable available after the end tag to the end of the JSP page), or `NESTED` (make the variable available only between the start and the stop tag.

`public String getVarName( )`

Returns the variable name.

Other JSP Types

The JSP specification defines a number of other classes and interfaces that don't fit into the categories above. The exception classes, the interface for JSP page implementation classes, and the classes that let a JSP container vendor hide implementation details are described in this section.

ErrorData

The container makes an instance of `ErrorData` available to JSP error pages through the `PageContext` for the page.

Synopsis

Class name:	`javax.servlet.jsp.ErrorData`
Extends:	None
Implements:	None
Implemented by:	Internal container-dependent class; most containers use the reference implementation of the class (developed in the Apache Jakarta project)

Constructor

`public ErrorData(Throwable throwable, int statusCode, String uri, String name)`
Creates a new instance.

Methods

`public String getRequestURI( )`
Returns the URI for the failed request.

`public String getServletName( )`
Returns the name of the servlet that handled the failed request.

`public int getStatusCode( )`
Returns the status code that caused the error page to be invoked.

`public Throwable getThrowable( )`
Returns the exception that caused the error page to be invoked.

HttpJspPage

The `HttpJspPage` interface must be implemented by the generated JSP page implementation classes when HTTP is used.

The `jspInit( )` and `jspDestroy( )` methods (inherited from the `JspPage` interface) can be defined by a JSP page author, but the `_jspService( )` method is automatically defined by the JSP container based on the contents of the JSP page.

Synopsis

Interface name:	`javax.servlet.jsp.HttpJspPage`
Extends:	`javax.servlet.jsp.JspPage`
Implemented by:	JSP page implementation classes serving HTTP requests

Methods

```
public void _jspService(javax.servlet.http.HttpServletRequest request,
javax.servlet.http.HttpServletResponse response) throws
javax.servlet.ServletException, java.io.IOException
```
This method corresponds to the body of the JSP page. This method is defined automatically by the JSP processor and should never be defined by the JSP page author.

JspEngineInfo

`JspEngineInfo` is an abstract class that provides information about the JSP container. Each specific JSP container provides a concrete subclass.

Synopsis

Class name:	`javax.servlet.jsp.JspEngineInfo`
Extends:	None
Implements:	None
Implemented by:	Internal container-dependent class; most containers use the reference implementation of the class (developed in the Apache Jakarta project)

Constructor

`public JspEngineInfo()`

Creates a new `JspEngineInfo` instance.

Methods

`public abstract String getSpecificationVersion()`

Returns the version of the JSP specification implemented by the container, for instance "2.0" for a JSP 2.0 compliant container.

JspException

The `JspException` class is the superclass for all JSP-related exceptions.

Synopsis

Class name:	`javax.servlet.jsp.JspException`
Extends:	`Exception`
Implements:	None
Implemented by:	Internal container-dependent class; most containers use the reference implementation of the class (developed in the Apache Jakarta project)

Constructors

`public JspException()`

Creates a new `JspException` instance.

`public JspException(String msg)`

Creates a new `JspException` instance with the specified message.

`public JspException(String msg, Throwable rootCause)`

Creates a new `JspException` instance with the specified message and root cause.

`public JspException(Throwable rootCause)`

Creates a new `JspException` instance with the specified root cause.

Methods

`public Throwable getRootCause()`

Returns the root cause for this exception.

JspFactory

The JspFactory is an abstract class that defines a number of factory methods available to a JSP page at runtime for the purposes of creating instances of various interfaces and classes used to support the JSP implementation.

A JSP container creates an instance of a concrete subclass during its initialization phase and makes it globally available for use by JSP implementation classes by registering the instance via the static setDefaultFactory( ) method.

Synopsis

Class name:	javax.servlet.jsp.JspFactory
Extends:	None
Implements:	None
Implemented by:	Internal container-dependent class; most containers use the reference implementation of the class (developed in the Apache Jakarta project)

Constructor

public JspFactory( )

Creates a new JspFactory instance.

Methods

public static synchronized JspFactory getDefaultFactory( )

Returns the default JspFactory for the container.

public abstract JspEngineInfo getEngineInfo( )

Returns the JspEngineInfo for the container.

public abstract getPageContext getPageContext(javax.servlet.Servlet servlet, javax.servlet.ServletRequest request, javax.servlet.ServletResponse response, String errorPageURL, boolean needsSession, int buffer, boolean autoflush)

Returns a properly initialized instance of an implementation dependent PageContext subclass. This method is typically called early in the processing of the _jspService( ) method of a JSP implementation class to get a PageContext object for the request being processed. Calling this method results in the PageContext.initialize( ) method being invoked.

public abstract void releasePageContext(PageContext pc)

Releases a previously allocated PageContext object. Calling this method results in PageContext.release( ) being invoked. This method should be invoked prior to returning from the _jspService( ) method of a JSP implementation class.

public static synchronized void setDefaultFactory(JspFactory deflt)

Sets the default factory for this implementation. It is illegal for any other than the JSP container to call this method.

JspPage

The `JspPage` interface must be implemented by the generated JSP page implementation classes. The interface defines a protocol with three methods; only two of them, `jspInit()` and `jspDestroy()`, are part of this interface as the signature of the third method, `_jspService()`, depends on the specific protocol used and cannot be expressed in a generic way in Java. See also `HttpJspPage`.

The `JspPage` interface represents the basic, protocol-independent contract between the container and a JSP page implementation object. A protocol-dependent subinterface, such as `HttpJspPage`, must be implemented by the class generated from a JSP page.

The `jspInit()` and `jspDestroy()` methods can be defined by a JSP page author.

Synopsis

Interface name:	`javax.servlet.jsp.JspPage`
Extends:	`javax.servlet.Servlet`
Implemented by:	JSP page implementation classes

Methods

`public void jspDestroy()`

This method is invoked when the JSP page implementation instance is about to be destroyed. It can be used to perform clean-up, such as saving the state kept in instance variables to permanent storage.

`public void jspInit()`

This method is invoked when the JSP page implementation instance is initialized. It can be used to perform tasks such as restoring the state kept in instance variables from permanent storage.

JspTagException

The `JspTagException` is intended to be used by a tag handler to indicate an unrecoverable error.

Synopsis

Class name:	`javax.servlet.jsp.JspTagException`
Extends:	`javax.servlet.jsp.JspException`
Implements:	None
Implemented by:	Internal container-dependent class. Most containers use the reference implementation of the class (developed in the Apache Jakarta project)

Constructors

`public JspTagException( )`
: Creates a new `JspTagException` instance.

`public JspTagException(String msg)`
: Creates a new `JspTagException` instance with the specified message.

`public JspTagException(String msg, Throwable throwable)`
: Creates a new `JspTagException` instance with the specified message and root cause.

`public JspTagException(Throwable throwable)`
: Creates a new `JspTagException` instance with the specified root cause.

SkipPageException

A simple tag handler throws a `SkipPageException` to tell the container to stop processing the page, e.g., because the tag handler forwards or redirects the request to another resource.

Synopsis

Class name:	`javax.servlet.jsp.SkipPageException`
Extends:	`javax.servlet.jsp.JspException`
Implements:	None
Implemented by:	Internal container-dependent class; most containers use the reference implementation of the class (developed in the Apache Jakarta project)

Constructors

`public SkipPageException( )`
: Creates a new `SkipTagException` instance.

`public SkipPageException(String msg)`
: Creates a new `SkipTagException` instance with the specified message.

`public SkipPageException(String msg, Throwable throwable)`
: Creates a new `SkipPageException` instance with the specified message and root cause.

`public SkipPageException(Throwable throwable)`
: Creates a new `SkipPageException` instance with the specified root cause.

Expression Language Types

The API for EL evaluation is defined in the `javax.servlet.jsp.el` package. The types in this package are designed without dependencies on the rest of the JSP API, to allow the EL machinery to be used in other environments besides JSP. In a JSP environment, application code should rarely use these types directly—the container takes care of all EL evaluation—but they can be used for special cases, such as code getting text that contains EL expressions from an external source.

ELException

The EL evaluator signals parsing and evaluation errors by throwing an `ELException`.

Synopsis

Class name:	`javax.servlet.jsp.el.ELException`
Extends:	`Exception`
Implements:	None
Implemented by:	Internal container-dependent class; most containers use the reference implementation of the class (developed in the Apache Jakarta project)

Constructors

`public ELException()`

Creates a new `ELException` instance.

`public ELException(String msg)`

Creates a new `ELException` instance with the specified message.

`public ELException(String msg, Throwable throwable)`

Creates a new `ELException` instance with the specified message and root cause.

`public ELException(Throwable throwable)`

Creates a new `ELException` instance with the specified root cause.

Methods

`public Throwable getRootCause()`

Returns the root cause for this exception.

ELParseException

The EL evaluator signals parsing errors by throwing an `ELParseException`.

Synopsis

Class name:	`javax.servlet.jsp.el.ELParseException`
Extends:	`javax.servlet.jsp.el.ELException`
Implements:	None
Implemented by:	Internal container-dependent class; most containers use the reference implementation of the class (developed in the Apache Jakarta project)

Constructors

`public ELParseException( )`

Creates a new `ELParseException` instance.

`public ELParseException(String msg)`

Creates a new `ELParseException` instance with the specified message.

Expression

The `Expression` class represents an EL expression, which may or may not be syntactically valid.

Synopsis

Class name:	`javax.servlet.jsp.el.Expression`
Extends:	None
Implements:	None
Implemented by:	Internal container-dependent class; most containers use the reference implementation of the class (developed in the Apache Jakarta project)

Constructors

`public Expression( )`

Creates a new `Expression` instance.

Methods

`public abstract Object evaluate(VariableResolver variableResolver) throws ELException`

Evaluates the expression using the variables provided by the `VariableResolver`. Some implementations may need to parse the expression when this method is called, so the caller should be prepared to handle parse exceptions as well as runtime exceptions.

ExpressionEvaluator

The `ExpressionEvaluator` is the main class for the EL machinery, providing methods for preparation and evaluation of a single EL expression. In a JSP environment, an instance of this class can be obtained from the `JspContext`.

Synopsis

Class name:	`javax.servlet.jsp.el.ExpressionEvaluator`
Extends:	None
Implements:	None
Implemented by:	Internal container-dependent class; most containers use the reference implementation of the class (developed in the Apache Jakarta project)

Constructors

```
public ExpressionEvaluator( )
```

Creates a new `ExpressionEvaluator` instance.

Methods

```
public abstract Object evaluate(String expression, Class expectedType,
VariableResolver variableResolver, FunctionMapper functionMapper) throws
ELException
```

Evaluates the expression (a String starting with ${ and ending with }) using the variables provided by the `VariableResolver` and the functions provided by the `FunctionMapper`. The evaluation result is coerced to the specified expected type according to the rules described in Appendix C and returned.

```
public abstract Object parseExpression(String expression, Class expectedType,
FunctionMapper functionMapper) throws ELException
```

Prepares the expression (a String starting with ${ and ending with }) for later evaluation. The method typically performs syntactic validation and throws an `ELParseException` if an error is found.

FunctionMapper

The `FunctionMapper` interface is implemented by a container-dependent class that provides mappings between function names and the static methods implementing the functions.

Synopsis

Interface name:	`javax.servlet.jsp.el.FunctionMapper`
Extends:	None
Implemented by:	Internal container-dependent class

Methods

```
public java.lang.reflect.Method resolveFunction(String prefix, String
localName)
```

Returns the `Method` matching the prefix and name, or `null` if no match is found.

VariableResolver

The `VariableResolver` interface is implemented by a container-dependent class that resolves variable names to objects representing implicit variables or scoped variables.

Synopsis

Interface name:	`javax.servlet.jsp.el.VariableResolver`
Extends:	None
Implemented by:	Internal container-dependent class

Methods

`public Object resolveVariable(String name) throws ELException`

Returns the object matching the variable name or `null` if no match is found.

APPENDIX E

Book Example Custom Actions and API Reference

This appendix contains reference material for all custom actions, utility classes, and beans described in this book that can be used as is in other applications.

Example code used in the book that isn't intended for reuse isn't included in this appendix. All source code for the book can, however, be downloaded either from the O'Reilly web site at *http://www.oreilly.com/catalog/jserverpages3/* or from the web site dedicated to this book at *http://www.TheJSPBook.com/*.

The actions are described using the same conventions as for the JSP standard actions in Appendix A and the JSTL actions in Appendix B. Most of the custom actions accept request-time attribute values (EL or Java expressions), indicated by "Yes" in the "Dynamic value accepted" column in the Attribute tables.

Generic Custom Actions

<ora:addCookie>

The `<ora:addCookie>` action sets response headers for creating or deleting a cookie. It must be used before the response is committed, for instance before a `<jsp:include>` action with the `flush` attribute set to `true`.

Syntax

```
<ora:addCookie name="cookieName" value="cookieValue"
  [maxAge="ageInSeconds"] />
```

Attributes

Attribute name	Java type	Dynamic value accepted	Description
name	String	Yes	The cookie name.

Attribute name	Java type	Dynamic value accepted	Description
value	String	Yes	The cookie value.
maxAge	String	Yes	The number of seconds before the cookie expires. Default is -1, meaning that the cookie expires when the browser is closed. Use 0 to delete the cookie from the browser.

Example

```
<%--
  Add a cookie named "userName", using the value from a
  request parameter with the same name, that expires in
  30 days
--%>
<ora:addCookie name="userName"
  value="${param:username}"
  maxAge="${30 * 24 * 60 * 60}"
/>

<%--
  Delete a cookie named "userName"
--%>
<ora:addCookie name="userName"
  value="ignored"
  maxAge="0"
/>
```

<ora:calendar>

The <ora:calendar> action renders a calendar for the specified month using the patterns defined by the attributes representing weekdays, weekend days, etc. when rendering the individual days.

Syntax

```
<ora:calendar date="aDate" [var="var"]
  [beforePattern="beforePattern"] [afterPattern="afterPattern"]
  [padPattern="padPattern"] [dayNamePattern="dayNamePattern"]
  [weekdayPattern="weekdayPattern"] [weekendPattern="weekendPattern"]
/>
```

Attributes

Attribute name	Java type	Dynamic value accepted	Description
date	java.util.Date	Yes	A date in the month to render.
var	String	No	The name of the variable to hold the current Date while evaluating the patterns.

Attribute name	Java type	Dynamic value accepted	Description
beforePattern	javax.servlet.jsp.tagext.JspFragment	Yes	The pattern to use before rendering the first day in a week.
afterPattern	javax.servlet.jsp.tagext.JspFragment	Yes	The pattern to use after rendering the last day in a week.
padPattern	javax.servlet.jsp.tagext.JspFragment	Yes	The pattern to use for days in the previous and following months, to pad the current month to full weeks.
dayNamePattern	javax.servlet.jsp.tagext.JspFragment	Yes	The pattern to use for the day names, rendered once before rendering the days.
weekdayPattern	javax.servlet.jsp.tagext.JspFragment	Yes	The pattern to use for weekdays.
weekendPattern	javax.servlet.jsp.tagext.JspFragment	Yes	The pattern to use for weekends. If this pattern is omitted, the `weekdayPattern` is used for weekends as well.

Example

```
<code>
  <fmt:formatDate value="${now}" pattern="MMMM yyyy" />
  <br>
  <ora:calendar date="${now}" var="c">
    <jsp:attribute name="afterPattern">
      <br>
    </jsp:attribute>
    <jsp:attribute name="padPattern">
      | ------ |
    </jsp:attribute>
    <jsp:attribute name="weekdayPattern">
      | <fmt:formatDate value="${c}" pattern="EE dd" /> |
    </jsp:attribute>
  </ora:calendar>
</code>
```

<ora:debug>

The `<ora:debug>` action writes debug information to the response, the console or the application log, depending on the value of the debug request parameter: `resp`, `stdout`, or `log`, or a combination of these values.

Syntax

```
<ora:debug type="debugInfoType" />
```

Attributes

Attribute name	Java type	Dynamic value accepted	Description
type	String	Yes	The type of debug info to write, one of requestInfo, headers, cookies, params, pageScope, requestScope, sessionScope, or applicationScope.

Example

```
<%--
  Write all request information and parameters and page scope
  Variables.
--%>
<ora:debug type="requestInfo" />
<ora:debug type="params" />
<ora:debug type="pageScope" />
```

<ora:fileWrite>

The <ora:fileWrite> action writes its body content to the console, the application log, or a specific file.

Syntax

```
<ora:fileWrite [fileName="fileName"] />
```

Attributes

Attribute name	Java type	Dynamic value accepted	Description
fileName	String	Yes	Either an absolute file path or log to write to the application log file. If omitted, writes to System.out.

Example

```
<%--
  Write and error message to the application log file.
--%>
<ora:fileWrite filename="log">
  Error message: <c:out value="${pageContext.exception.message}" />
</ora:fileWrite>
```

<ora:ifUserInRole>

The <ora:ifUserInRole> action tests if the user authenticated for the request belongs to the specified role. If so, its body is evaluated or the Boolean test result is saved in the specified variable. Note that this action only works with container-provided authentication, using the security roles declared in the application deployment descriptor.

Syntax 1: Conditionally evaluate the body

```
<ora:ifUserInRole value="roleName">
  Evaluated if the current user belongs to roleName
</ora:ifUserInRole>
```

Syntax 2: Saving the test result

```
<ora:ifUserInRole value="roleName" var="var"
  [scope="page|request|session|application"] />
```

Attributes

Attribute name	Java type	Dynamic value accepted	Description
value	String	Yes	The role name.
var	String	No	The name of the variable.
scope	String	No	Scope for the variable.

Example

```
<%--
  Evaluate the body if the current user belongs to the "admin" role
--%>
<ora:ifUserInRole value="admin">
  You're an admin
</ora:ifUserInRole>

<%--
  Save true in the isAdmin variable if the current user belongs to
  the "admin" role
--%>
<ora:ifUserInRole value="admin" var="isAdmin" />
```

<ora:ifValidEmailAddr>

The `<ora:ifValidEmailAddr>` action tests if the specified value matches the syntax for a valid email address: only one at-sign (@), except as the first or last character, no whitespace and at least one dot after the at-sign, except as the first or last character. If so, its body is evaluated, or the Boolean test result is saved in the specified variable. Note that the validation rule isn't always correct; for example, on an intranet, it may be okay with just a name. It doesn't guarantee a valid Internet email address, but it takes care of the most obvious SMTP mail address format errors.

Syntax 1: Conditionally evaluate the body

```
<ora:ifValidEmailAddrs value="emailAddr">
  Evaluated if the emailAddr has valid syntax
</ora:ifValidEmailAddr>
```

Syntax 2: Saving the test result

```
<ora:ifValidEmailAddr value="emailAddr" var="var"
  [scope="page|request|session|application"] />
```

Attributes

Attribute name	Java type	Dynamic value accepted	Description
value	String	Yes	The email address to syntax validate.
var	String	No	The name of the variable.
scope	String	No	Scope for the variable.

Example

```
<%--
  Evaluate the body if the specified email address has valid syntax
--%>
<ora:ifValidEmailAddr value="${param.email}">
  You specified a valid email address
</ora:ifValidEmailAddr>

<%--
  Save true in the isValid variable if the specified email address
  has valid syntax
--%>
<ora:ifValidEmailAddr value="${param.email}" var="isValid" />
```

<ora:invalidateSession>

The <ora:invalidateSession> action invalidates the current session, telling the container to remove all session variables and mark the session as expired.

Syntax

```
<ora:invalidateSession />
```

Attributes

None.

Example

```
<%--
  Invalidate the current session
--%>
<ora:invalidateSession/>
```

<ora:menuItem>

The <ora:menuItem> action writes its body contents to the response. If the specified page is the currently requested page, the content is used as is; otherwise it's embedded in an HTML link element (<a>), using the specified page as the link target and the body contents as the link text. The page value is converted to a server-relative path and URL rewritten, if needed. The intended use for this action is in navigation bars to generate links for all page menu items except for the current page.

Syntax

```
<ora:menuItem page="pageOrContextRelativePath">
  Menu text for the page
</ora:menuItem>
```

Attributes

Attribute name	Java type	Dynamic value accepted	Description
page	String	Yes	The page path for the menu item.

Example

```
<%--
  Generate a navigation menu table with two page menu items.
--%>
<table bgcolor="lightblue">
  <tr>
    <td>
      <ora:menuItem page="page1.jsp">
        <b>Page 1</b>
      </ora:menuItem>
    </td>
  </tr>
  <tr>
    <td>
      <ora:menuItem page="page2.jsp">
        <b>Page 2</b>
      </ora:menuItem>
    </td>
  </tr>
</table>
```

<ora:noCache>

The <ora:noCache> action sets response headers that prevent the page from being cached by a browser or proxy server. It must be used before the response is committed, for instance before a <jsp:include> action with the flush attribute set to true.

Attributes

None.

Example

```
<%--
  Set headers to prevent caching.
--%>
<ora:noCache />
```

<ora:setHeader>

The `<ora:setHeader>` action sets the specified response headers to the specified value. It must be used before the response is committed, for instance before a `<jsp:include>` action with the `flush` attribute set to `true`.

Syntax

```
<ora:setHeader name="headerName" value="headerValue" />
```

Attributes

Attribute name	Java type	Dynamic value accepted	Description
name	String	Yes	The header name.
value	String	Yes	The header value.

Example

```
<%--
  Set the Content-Type header to "text/plain"
--%>
<ora:setHeader name="Content-Type" value="text/plain" />
```

Generic Utility Classes

ConnectionPool

This class implements a connection pool. It's the same class as the `ConnectionPool` class described in O'Reilly's *Java Servlet Programming*, copied with permission from Jason Hunter. It's used by the `DataSourceWrapper` class to provide a JDBC 2.0 `DataSource` interface to the pool. It's intended only as an example; there are many implementations with more features available on the Net.

Synopsis

Class name:	`com.ora.jsp.sql.ConnectionPool`
Extends:	None
Implements:	None

Constructors

`public ConnectionPool(String driverClassName, String dbURL, String user, String password, int initialConnections) throws java.sql.SQLException, ClassNotFoundException`

Creates a connection pool for the specified JDBC URL using the specified JDBC driver class and database user and password. The specified number of connections are created before service requests.

`public ConnectionPool(java.util.Properties props, int initialConnections) throws java.sql.SQLException, ClassNotFoundException`

Creates a connection pool for the JDBC URL, JDBC driver class, database user, and password specified by the properties: `connection.url`, `connection.driver`, `user`, `password`. The specified number of connections are created before service requests.

Methods

`public java.sql.Connection getConnection( ) throws java.sql.SQLException`

Returns a `Connection` from the pool.

`public void returnConnection(java.sql.Connection returned)`

Used by the connection pool client to return a `Connection` to the pool.

ConnectionWrapper

This class is a wrapper around a `Connection`, with a `close( )` method that just informs its `DataSourceWrapper` it's available for reuse again, and an `isClosed( )` method to return the state of the wrapper instead of the wrapped `Connection`. All other methods just relay the call to the wrapped `Connection`.

Synopsis

Class name:	`com.ora.jsp.sql.ConnectionWrapper`
Extends:	None
Implements:	`java.sql.Connection`

Constructor

`public ConnectionWrapper(Connection realConn, DataSourceWrapper dsw);`

Creates a new `ConnectionWrapper` around the specified `Connection`, owned by the specified `DataSourceWrapper`.

Methods

`public void close( ) throws SQLException;`

Informs the `DataSourceWrapper` that this `ConnectionWrapper` is closed by calling its `returnConnection( )` method.

`public boolean isClosed( ) throws SQLException;`

Returns `true` if the `close( )` method has been called, `false` otherwise.

All wrapped methods simply call the corresponding method on the wrapped `Connection`. See the Java documentation at *http://java.sun.com/docs/index.html* for details about these methods.

CookieUtils

The `CookieUtils` class contains a number of static methods that can be used to work with `javax.servlet.Cookie` objects.

Synopsis

Class name:	`com.ora.jsp.util.CookieUtils`
Extends:	None
Implements:	None

Methods

`public static String getCookieValue(String name, javax.servlet.http.HttpServletRequest req)`

Returns the value of the Cookie with the specified name, or `null` if not found.

`public static boolean isCookieSet(String name, javax.servlet.http.HttpServletRequest req)`

Returns true if a cookie with the specified name is present in the request.

`public static void sendCookie(String name, String value, int maxAge, javax.servlet.http.HttpServletResponse res)`

Creates a `Cookie` with the specified name, value and max age, and adds it to the response.

DataSourceFactory

This class is a generic JNDI object factory intended for producing `DataSource` instances using custom `DataSource` implementations, such as those often bundled with a JDBC driver. It can be used with Tomcat, and likely with other web containers that supports JNDI, such as Resin and JRun.

Synopsis

Class name:	com.ora.jsp.sql.DataSourceFactory
Extends:	None
Implements:	javax.naming.spi.ObjectFactory

Methods

`public Object getObjectInstance(Object obj, javax.naming.Name name, javax.naming.Context, java.util.Hashtable environment) throws javax.naming.NamingException`

Returns a `DataSource`, created as an instance of the class specified by the `dataSourceClassName` parameter accessible through the `javax.naming.Reference` instance passed as the `obj` argument, configured by calling all setter methods matching other parameters passed through the `Reference` instance.

DataSourceWrapper

This class is a wrapper implementing the JDBC 2.0 SE `DataSource` interface, used to make the `ConnectionPool` class look like a JDBC 2.0 `DataSource`. It can easily be modified to be used as a wrapper for any JDBC 1.0 connection pool implementation.

Synopsis

Class name:	com.ora.jsp.sql.DataSourceWrapper
Extends:	None
Implements:	javax.sql.DataSource

Methods

`public java.sql.Connection getConnection( ) throws java.sql.SQLException`

Returns a `ConnectionWrapper` from the pool.

`public void returnConnection(java.sql.Connection conn)`

Used by the `ConnectionWrapper` to return a `Connection` to the pool when the client calls `close( )`.

`public void setDriverClassName(String driverClassName)`

Sets the driver class to be used for the data source.

`public void setInitialConnections(int initialConnections)`

Sets the initial connections to be created by the data source.

`public void setPassword(String password)`

Sets the database user password to be used for the data source.

`public void setUrl(String url)`

Sets the JDBC URL to be used for the data source.

public void setUser(String user)
: Sets the database user to be used for the data source.

StringFormat

The StringFormat class contains a number of static methods that can be used to validate the format of strings, typically received as input from a user, and to format values as strings that can be used in HTML output without causing browser interpretation problems.

Synopsis

Class name:	com.ora.jsp.util.StringFormat
Extends:	None
Implements:	None

Methods

public static boolean isValidDate(String dateString, String dateFormatPattern)
: Returns true if the specified date string represents a valid date in the specified format. The dateFormatPattern is a String specifying the format to be used when parsing the dateString. The pattern is expressed with the pattern letters defined for the java.text.SimpleDateFormat class.

public static boolean isValidEmailAddr(String emailAddrString)
: Returns true if the email string contains only one at-sign, except as the first or last character, no whitespace and at least one dot after the at-sign, except as the first or last character. Note! This rule is not always correct (e.g., on an intranet it may be okay with just a name) and it does not guarantee a valid Internet email address, but it takes care of the most obvious Internet mail address format errors.

public static boolean isValidInteger(String numberString, int min, int max)
: Returns true if the specified number string represents a valid integer in the specified range.

public static boolean isValidString(String value, String[] validStrings, boolean ignoreCase)
: Returns true if the specified string matches a string in the set of provided valid strings, ignoring case if specified.

public static boolean isValidString(String[] values, String[] validStrings, boolean ignoreCase)
: Returns true if all the specified strings match as string in the set of provided valid strings, ignoring case if specified.

public static String replaceInString(String in, String from, String to)
: Replaces one String with another throughout a source String.

`public static String toContextRelativeURI(String relURI, String currURI) throws IllegalArgumentException`
: Returns the page-relative or context-relative `relURI` as a context-relative URI based on the `currURI`.

`public static java.util.Date toDate(String dateString, String dateFormatPattern) throws java.text.ParseException`
: Converts a `String` to a `Date`, using the specified pattern. (See `java.text.SimpleDateFormat` for pattern description.)

`public static String toHTMLString(String in)`
: Returns the specified string converted to a format suitable for HTML. All single-quote, double-quote, greater-than, less-than, and ampersand characters are replaces with their corresponding HTML Character Entity code.

`public static Number toNumber(String numString, String numFormatPattern) throws java.text.ParseException`
: Converts a `String` to a `Number`, using the specified pattern. (ee `java.text.NumberFormat` for pattern description.)

SQLCommandBean

The `SQLCommandBean` class is a bean for executing SQL statements, intended to encapsulate database access and to be used by database custom actions and other classes. The bean has three properties that can be set: `connection`, `sqlValue` and `values`. The `connection` and `sqlValue` properties must always be set before calling one of the execute methods. If the `values` property is set, the `sqlValue` property must be a SQL statement with question marks as placeholders for the value objects in the `values` property.

Synopsis

Class name:	`com.ora.jsp.beans.sql.SQLCommandBean`
Extends:	None
Implements:	None

Description

Property name	Java type	Access	Description
`connection`	`java.sql.Connection`	write	The database `Connection` to use.
`sqlValue`	`String`	write	The SQL statement to execute, optionally with question marks as placeholders for values.
`values`	`java.util.List`	write	A `Vector` with values for all placeholders in the SQL statement.

The `SQLCommandBean` class also provides the following regular methods for executing the SQL statement:

`public javax.servlet.jsp.jstl.sql.Result executeQuery( ) throws java.sql.SQLException`

Returns a JSTL Result object with the result of executing a `SELECT` statement.

`public int executeUpdate( ) throws java.sql.SQLException`

Returns the number of rows affected by a `DELETE`, `INSERT`, or `UPDATE` statement.

APPENDIX F

Web Application Structure and Deployment Descriptor Reference

A complete web application may consist of several different resources: JSP pages, servlets, applets, static HTML pages, custom tag libraries, and other Java class files. Starting with Version 2.2, the servlet specification defines a portable way to package all these resources together with a deployment descriptor that contains configuration information, such as how all the resources fit together, security requirements, etc. This appendix describes the standard file structure for a web application and how to use the deployment descriptor elements defined by the Servlet 2.4 and JSP 2.0 specifications to configure the application.

Web Application File Structure

The portable distribution and deployment format for a web application defined by the servlet specification is the Web Application Archive (WAR). All Servlet 2.2-compliant servers (or later) provide tools for installing a WAR file and associate the application with a servlet context.

A WAR file has a *.war* file extension and can be created with the Java *jar* command or a ZIP utility program, such as *WinZip*, as described at the end of this appendix. The internal structure of the WAR file is defined by the servlet specification:

```
/index.html
/company/index.html
/company/contact.html
/company/phonelist.jsp
/products/searchform.html
/products/list.jsp
/images/banner.gif
/WEB-INF/web.xml
/WEB-INF/lib/bean.jar
/WEB-INF/lib/actions.jar
/WEB-INF/classes/com/mycorp/servlets/PurchaseServlet.class
/WEB-INF/classes/com/mycorp/util/MyUtils.class
...
```

The top level in this structure is the document root for all application web page files. This is where you place all your HTML pages, JSP pages, and image files. A browser can access all these files, using a URI starting with the context-path. For instance, if the application has been assigned the context path */sales*, the URI */sales/products/list.jsp* is used to access the JSP page named *list.jsp* in the *products* directory in this example.

Placing Java Class Files in the Right Directory

The *WEB-INF* directory contains files and subdirectories for other types of resources used by the application. Files under this directory aren't directly accessible to a browser. Two *WEB-INF* subdirectories have special meaning: *lib* and *classes*. The *lib* directory contains JAR files with Java class files, for instance JavaBeans classes, custom action handler classes, and utility classes. The *classes* directory contains class files that are not packaged in JAR files. The web application has access automatically to all class files in the *lib* and *classes* directories (in other words, you do *not* have to add them to the `CLASSPATH` environment variable).

If you store class files in the *classes* directory, they must be stored in subdirectories mirroring the package structure. For instance, if you have a class named `com.mycorp.util.MyUtils`, you must store the class file in *WEB-INF/classes/com/mycorp/util/MyUtils.class*. Another type of file that can be stored in the classes directory is the type of a resource properties file used by the `PropertyResourceBundle` class, as described in Chapter 14.

The *WEB-INF* directory can also contain other directories. For instance, a directory named *tlds* is by convention used for tag library Tag Library Descriptor (TLD) files when they are not packaged in JAR files.

During development it's more convenient to work with the web application files in a regular filesystem structure instead creating a new WAR file every time something changes. Most containers therefore support the WAR structure in an open filesystem as well. The book example application is distributed as an open filesystem structure to make it easier for you to see all the files.

Web Application Deployment Descriptor

A very important file is the *WEB-INF/web.xml* file. It is the application deployment descriptor that contains all configuration information for the application. If your application consists only of JSP and HTML files, you typically don't need to worry about this file at all. But if the application also contains servlets or uses the container provided security mechanisms, you often need to define some configuration information in the *web.xml* file.

The deployment descriptor is an XML file. Starting with Servlet 2.3 and JSP 2.0, the elements it can contain and how they must be arranged are controlled by a number of XML Schema documents.* The main XML Schema document, which includes the others, is available online at *http://java.sun.com/xml/ns/j2ee/web-app_2_4.xsd*. This XML Schema document must be referenced in the root element of the deployment description, as shown in Example F-1.

Example F-1. Java Web Application Descriptor root element

```
<web-app xmlns="http://java.sun.com/xml/ns/j2ee"
  xmlns:xsi="http://www.w3c.org/2001/XMLSchema-instance"
  xsi:schemaLocation="http://java.sun.com/xml/ns/j2ee
    http://java.sun.com/xml/ns/j2ee/web-app_2_4.xsd"
  version="2.4>
  ...
</web-app>
```

If you're not familiar with the intricate details of XML Schema and namespace declarations, just accept the fact that you need to enclose all other elements in the deployment descriptor within a `<web-app>` element exactly as shown in Example F-1.

Within the `<web-app>` element body, top-level elements can be included in any order. Each top-level element is described in a separate section in this appendix. The top-level elements are all optional and can be included more than once, unless otherwise stated. Most top-level elements contain other elements.

I use syntax descriptions similar to those in the other appendixes to show the rules for the elements nested within top-level elements. The nested elements must be included in the order they are listed in the syntax description. Mutually exclusive elements are separated by vertical bars (|). Optional nested elements are embedded in square brackets ([ ]), followed by an asterisk (*) if more than one element of this type may be used. An element name followed by a plus sign (+) means the element is required, but it can be used more than once. For elements that accept predefined values, all values are listed separated by vertical bars; the default value (if any) is bold. Italics are used for element values that don't have a fixed set of accepted values. Element attribute values are described using the same syntax as element values.

<description>, <display>, and <icon>

These three elements provide information a web container deployment tool can use to describe the application. As an exception to the rule that top-level elements can be included in any order, these three must be in the order shown here.

* Prior versions used a Document Type Definition (DTD) to define the deployment descriptor content, with the rules being more strict in some areas (e.g., fixed ordering of top-level elements) but less strict in other areas (e.g., no formal uniqueness rules were defined).

Syntax

```
<description [xml:lang="lang"]>description</description>

<display-name [xml:lang="lang"]>displayName</display-name>

<icon [xml:lang="lang"]>
  [<small-icon>iconPath</small-icon>]
  [<large-icon>iconPath</large-icon>]
</icon>
```

The <icon> element can contain a <small-icon> and a <large-icon> element, each with a context-relative path to an image file (GIF and JPEG formats are supported). The small icon must be 16x16 pixels, and the large 32x32. The <display-name> element can specify a name for the application, and the <description> element a longer description.

You can use different versions of all these top-level elements for multiple languages, each with a unique `xml:lang` attribute value ("en", for English, is the default value):

```
<icon>
  <small-icon>/images/small.gif</small-icon>
  <large-icon>/images/large.gif</large-icon>
</icon>
<display-name>The application name</display-name>
<description>
  A longer description of
  the application.
</description>
```

<distributable>

The <distributable> element is used to tell the web container that the application is designed to run in a distributed web container.

Syntax

```
<distributable/>
```

This element does not contain a body. A distributable application does not rely on servlet instance variables, static classes or variables, servlet context attributes, or any other mechanism for shared information that is restricted to one Java Virtual Machine (JVM). It also means that all objects placed in the session scope are serializable, so that the container can move the session data from one JVM to another. For more information about distributed applications, see Chapter 18.

<context-param>

Using the <context-param> element, you can define context parameters that are available to all components of the application (both servlets and JSP pages).

Syntax

```
<context-param>
  [<description [xml:lang="lang"]>description</description>]*
  <param-name>paramName</param-name>
  <param-value>paramValue</param-value>
</context-param>
```

The <param-name> subelement specifies the name and the <param-value> element the value. Optionally, the <description> element can be used for a description that can be displayed by a deployment tool:

```
<context-param>
  <param-name>jdbcURL</param-name>
  <param-value>jdbc:idb:/usr/local/db/mydb.prp</param-value>
</context-param>
```

<filter>

The <filter> element registers a filter component, described in Chapter 20.

Syntax

```
<filter>
  [<description [xml:lang="lang"]>description</description>]*
  [<display-name [xml:lang="lang"]>displayName</display-name>]*
  [<icon [xml:lang="lang"]>
     [<small-icon>iconPath</small-icon>]
     [<large-icon>iconPath</large-icon>]
   </icon>]*
  <filter-name>filterName</filter-name>
  <filter-class>className</filter-class>
  [<init-param>
     [<description [xml:lang="lang"]>description</description>]*
     <param-name>paramName</param-name>
     <param-value>paramValue</param-value>
   </init-param>]*
</filter>
```

Nested <icon>, <display-name>, and <description> elements can optionally define icons and descriptions that can be used by a tool. The nested <filter-name> element defines a unique logical name for the filter, and the <filter-class> element the class name. A set of initialization parameters can optionally be defined by <init-param> elements.

```
<filter>
  <filter-name>accessControl</filter-name>
  <filter-class>com.mycomp.AccessControlFilter</filter-class>
  <init-param>
    <param-name>loginPage</param-name>
    <param-value>/login.jsp</param-value>
  </init-param>
</filter>
```

<filter-mapping>

A filter is mapped to either to a URI pattern or a servlet using the <filter-mapping> element.

Syntax

```
<filter-mapping>
  <filter-name>filterName</filter-name>
  <url-pattern>urlPattern</url-pattern> |
    <servlet-name>servletName</servlet-name>
  [<dispatcher>FORWARD|INCLUDE|REQUEST|ERROR</dispatcher>]*
</filter-mapping>
```

The <filter-name> subelement identifies the filter using a name defined by a <filter> element. A <url-pattern> or a <servlet-name> defines when the filter shall be invoked. If a URL mapping is used, the same values as for a <servlet-mapping> element can be used. More than one filter may match a specific request. If so, the container chains them in the order the matching <filter-mapping> elements appear in the deployment descriptor.

Up to four <dispatcher> elements may be used to define for what circumstances the filter should be applied: FORWARD and INCLUDE mean it's applied for internal request made through the javax.servlet.RequestDispatcher forward( ) and include( ) methods, respectively; ERROR means it's applied when dispatching to an error page as part of the error mechanism; REQUEST means it's applied for regular, external client requests. If no <dispatcher> element is used, the default behavior is as if an element with the REQUEST value had been specified:

```
<filter-mapping>
  <filter-name>accessControl</filter-name>
  <url-pattern>/protected</url-pattern>
</filter-mapping>
```

<listener>

All the listener types described in Chapter 20 must be registered with a <listener> element.

Syntax

```
<listener>
  [<description [xml:lang="lang"]>description</description>]*
  [<display-name [xml:lang="lang"]>displayName</display-name>]*
  [<icon [xml:lang="lang"]>
     [<small-icon>iconPath</small-icon>]
     [<large-icon>iconPath</large-icon>]
   </icon>]*
  <listener-class>className</listener-class>
</listener>
```

The <description>, <display-name>, and <icon>, elements can optionally be used, the same as for many other top-level elements. The nested <listener-class> element contains the listener class name:

```
<listener>
  <listener-class>com.mycomp.AppInitListener</listener-class>
</listener>
```

<servlet>

The <servlet> element defines servlet class or JSP page details.

Syntax

```
<servlet>
  [<description [xml:lang="lang"]>description</description>]*
  [<display-name [xml:lang="lang"]>displayName</display-name>]*
  [<icon [xml:lang="lang"]>
     [<small-icon>iconPath</small-icon>]
     [<large-icon>iconPath</large-icon>]
   </icon>]*
  <servlet-name>servletName</servlet-name>
  <servlet-class>className</servlet-class> |
    <jsp-file>jspPath</jsp-file>
  [<init-param>
     [<description [xml:lang="lang"]>description</description>]*
     <param-name>paramName</param-name>
     <param-value>paramValue</param-value>
   </init-param>]*
  [<load-on-startup>startupValue</load-on-startup>]
  [<run-as>roleName</run-as>]
  [<security-role-ref>
    [<description [xml:lang="lang">description</description>]*
    <role-name>internalRoleName</role-name>
    [<role-link>roleName</role-link>]
   </security-role-ref>]*
</servlet>
```

Most commonly, this element just associates a servlet or JSP page with a short name and specifies initialization parameters:

```
<servlet>
  <servlet-name>
    purchase
  </servlet-name>
  <servlet-class>
    com.mycorp.servlets.PurchaseServlet
  </servlet-class>
  <init-param>
    <param-name>maxAmount</param-name>
    <param-value>500.00</param-value>
  </init-param>
</servlet>
```

```
<servlet>
  <servlet-name>
    order-form
  </servlet-name>
  <jsp-file>
    /po/orderform.jsp
  </jsp-file>
  <init-param>
    <param-name>bgColor</param-name>
    <param-value>blue</param-value>
  </init-param>
</servlet>
```

The same servlet class (or JSP page) can be defined with multiple names, typically with different initialization parameters. The container creates one instance of the class for each name.

The <load-on-startup> subelement can tell the container to load the servlet when the application is started. The value is a positive integer, indicating when the servlet is to be loaded relative to other servlets. A servlet with a low value is loaded before a servlet with a higher value:

```
<servlet>
  <servlet-name>
    controller
  </servlet-name>
  <servlet-class>
    com.mycorp.servlets.ControllerServlet
  </servlet-class>
  <load-on-startup>1</load-on-startup>
</servlet>
```

The <icon>, <display-name>, and <description> elements describe the servlet or JSP page, the same way as for other top-level elements.

<security-role-ref> elements, combined with <security-role> elements, can link a security role name used in a servlet as the argument to the HttpServletRequest.isUserInRole( ) method to a role name known by the web container:

```
<servlet>
  <servlet-name>
    controller
  </servlet-name>
  <servlet-class>
    com.mycorp.servlets.ControllerServlet
  </servlet-class>
  <security-role-ref>
    <role-name>administrator</role-name>
    <role-link>admin</role-link>
  </security-role-ref>
</servlet>
...
<security-role>
  <role-name>admin</role-name>
</security-role>
```

All role names defined by <security-role> elements must be mapped to users and/or groups known by the web container. How this is done is container-dependent. The <security-role-ref> element allows you to use a servlet that uses a role name in the isUserInRole() method that is not defined by a <security-role> element. A typical scenario where this can be useful is when you combine servlets from different sources into one application, and the servlets use different role names for the same logical role.

Finally, the <run-as> element can define the security role that the servlet should be presented as if it makes calls into an EJB container. The nested <role-name> value must be defined by a <security-role> element:

```
<servlet>
  <servlet-name>
    controller
  </servlet-name>
  <servlet-class>
    com.mycorp.servlets.ControllerServlet
  </servlet-class>
  <run-as>
    <role-name>admin</role-name>
  </run-as>
</servlet>
...
<security-role>
  <role-name>admin</role-name>
</security-role>
```

See the J2EE documentation for details about how to use this element.

<servlet-mapping>

The <servlet-mapping> element maps a servlet or JSP page to a URL pattern.

Syntax

```
<servlet-mapping>
  <servlet-name>servletName</servlet-name>
  <url-pattern>urlPattern</url-pattern>
</servlet-mapping>
```

Most containers support a special URI prefix (*/servlet*) that can invoke any servlet class that the container has access to, for instance the URI */servlet/com.mycompany.MyServlet* can invoke the servlet class com.mycomapany.MyServlet. This isn't mandated by the specification, however, so to make sure the application is portable, it's better to map a unique path to a servlet instead. Explicit mapping also simplifies references between servlets and JSP pages, as described in Chapter 19. The <servlet-mapping> element is used for this purpose. The <servlet-name> subelement contains a name defined by a <servlet> element, and the <url-pattern> contains the pattern that should be mapped to the servlet (or JSP page):

```
<servlet-mapping>
  <servlet-name>purchase</servlet-name>
  <url-pattern>/po/*</url-pattern>
</servlet-mapping>

<servlet-mapping>
  <servlet-name>sales-report</servlet-name>
  <url-pattern>/report</url-pattern>
</servlet-mapping>

<servlet-mapping>
  <servlet-name>XMLProcessor</servlet-name>
  <url-pattern>*.xml</url-pattern>
</servlet-mapping>
```

A pattern can take one of four forms:

- A *path prefix pattern* starts with a slash (/) and ends with `/*`, for instance `/po/*`.
- An *extension mapping pattern* starts with `*.`, for instance `*.xml`.
- A *default servlet pattern* consists of just the / character.
- All other patterns are *exact match patterns*.

When the container receives a request, it strips off the context path and then tries to find a pattern that matches a servlet mapping. Exact match patterns are analyzed first, then the path prefix patterns starting with the longest one, and then the extension mapping patterns. If none of these patterns match, the default servlet pattern is used, if specified. As a last resort, the containers default request processor handles the request.

With the mappings defined here, a URI like */po/supplies* invokes the `purchase` servlet, */report* invokes the sales-report servlet (but note that */report/spring* doesn't, because an exact match pattern is used), and */eastcoast/forecast.xml* invokes the `XMLProcessor` servlet.

<session-config>

The `<session-config>` element can customize session handling attributes. You must only use one element of this type in a deployment descriptor.

Syntax

```
<session-config>
  [<session-timeout>minutes</session-timeout>]
</session-config>
```

It contains just one subelement: the `<session-timeout>` element used to specify the default session timeout value in minutes. A value of 0 or less means that sessions never time out. Omitting the nested element means the container uses its own default:

```
<session-config>
  <session-timeout>30</session-timeout>
</session-config>
```

<mime-mapping>

The <mime-mapping> element can define the mappings an application requires.

Syntax

```
<mime-mapping>
  <extension>fileExtension</extension>
  <mime-type>mimeType</mime-type>
</mime-mapping>
```

A servlet may need to know which MIME type a file extension corresponds to, and such a mapping can be defined with this element:

```
<mime-mapping>
  <extension>wml</extension>
  <mime-type>text/vnd.wap.wml</mime-type>
</mime-mapping>
```

Most containers provide default mappings for the most commonly used extensions, such as *.html*, *.htm*, *.gif*, *.jpg*, and so on, but if you need to be absolutely sure that a mapping is defined for your application, put it in the *web.xml* file.

<welcome-file-list>

The <welcome-file-list> element can define an ordered list of files to look for in the directory and serve if present. If you use more than one element of this type, the container merges them.

Syntax

```
<welcome-file-list>
  <welcome-file>fileName</welcome-file>+
</welcome-file-list>
```

A welcome file is a file (or a URL mapped to a servlet) that the container serves when it receives a request URI that identifies a directory as opposed to a web page or a servlet:

```
<welcome-file-list>
  <welcome-file>index.html</welcome-file>
  <welcome-file>index.htm</welcome-file>
  <welcome-file>default.html</welcome-file>
  <welcome-file>default.htm</welcome-file>
</welcome-file-list>
```

When a directory entry request (a request for a URI ending with a slash) is received that does not match a servlet mapping, the container appends each welcome file name in the order specified in the deployment descriptor to the request URI and checks whether a resource in the WAR is mapped to the new URI. If it is, the request is sent to the resource. If no matching resource is found, the behavior is container dependent. The container may, for instance, return a directory listing an HTTP 404 status code (Not Found).

<error-page>

The <error-page> element can define pages that inform the user about various errors.

Syntax

```
<error-page>
  <error-code>errorCode</error-code> |
    <exception-type>className</exception-type>
  <location>pagePath</location>
</error-page>
```

A page can be specified for an HTTP error status code, such as 404 (Not Found), using the <error-code> subelement. As an alternative, the <exception-type> subelement can be used to specify a Java exception class name, to use a special page to handle exceptions thrown by servlets and JSP pages. The <location> subelement contains the context-relative path for the error page:

```
<error-page>
  <error-code>404</error-code>
  <location>/errors/404.html</location>
</error-page>
<error-page>
  <exception-type>javax.servlet.ServletException</exception-type>
  <location>/errors/exception.jsp</location>
</error-page>
```

<jsp-config>

The <jsp-config> element embeds most elements dealing JSP configuration. You must only use one element of this type in a deployment descriptor.

Syntax

```
<jsp-config>
  [<taglib>
    <taglib-uri>taglibURI</taglib-uri>
    <taglib-location>filePath</taglib-location>
   </taglib>]*
  [<jsp-property-group>
     [<description [xml:lang="lang"]>description</description>]*
```

```
      [<display-name [xml:lang="lang"]>displayName</display-name>]*
      [<icon [xml:lang="lang"]>
        [<small-icon>iconPath</small-icon>]
        [<large-icon>iconPath</large-icon>]
       </icon>]*
      <url-pattern>urlPattern</url-pattern>+
      [<el-ignored>true|false</el-ignored>]
      [<page-encoding>encoding</page-encoding>]
      [<scripting-invalid>true|false</scripting-invalid>]
      [<is-xml>true|false</is-xml>]
      [<include-prelude>filePath</include-prelude>]*
      [<include-coda>filePath</include-coda]*
    </jsp-property-group>]*
  </jsp-config>
```

Nested <taglib> elements map the symbolic name for a tag library specified by the taglib directive in a JSP page to the location of the Tag Library Descriptor (TLD) file or JAR file that contains the TLD file. The <taglib-uri> element value must match the uri attribute value used in the JSP page and the <taglib-location> subelement contains the context-relative path to the library file:

```
<jsp-config>
  <taglib>
    <taglib-uri>orataglib</taglib-uri>
    <taglib-location>/WEB-INF/lib/orataglib_1_0.jar</taglib-location>
  </taglib>
</jsp-config>
```

With the introduction of the auto-discovery feature in JSP 1.2, this element is rarely needed. For more details, see Chapter 21.

Nested <jsp-property-group> elements define a number of attributes for a set of JSP pages. The set of pages is defined by one or more <url-pattern> elements, with the same pattern types as are valid for the <servlet-mapping> element. The other elements define the attributes shared by these pages.

```
<jsp-config>
  <jsp-property-group>
    <url-pattern>*.xml</url-pattern>
    <el-ignored>true</el-ignored>
    <page-encoding>Shift_JIS</page-encoding>
    <scripting-invalid>true</scripting-invalid>
    <is-xml>true</is-xml>
    <include-prelude>/copyright.txt</include-prelude>
  </jsp-property-grop>
</jsp-config>
```

An <el-ignored> value of true means that character sequences that look like EL expressions, i.e., starts with ${, are treated as template text instead of EL expressions. This can be useful when pre-JSP 2.0 pages must be used in a JSP 2.0 application. The default is true for an application deployed with a pre-JSP 2.0 deployment descriptor and it's false for an application with a JSP 2.0 deployment descriptor.

The `<page-encoding>` element defines the file encoding for all matching JSP files.

The `<scripting-invalid>` element can be used to define an application-wide policy for use of the JSP scripting elements (i.e., Java code). With a value of `true`, a page that contains scripting elements is rejected at translation time.

A `<is-xml>` element with a value of true tells the container that matching pages are written as JSP Documents, i.e., as XML documents instead of regular JSP pages.

The `<include-prelude>` and `<include-coda>` elements provide for automatic inclusion of files during the translation phase. Files defined by `<include-prelude>` elements are included at the top of each matching page; files defined by `<include-coda>` are included at the end. The file location is specified as a context-relative path.

For more on all the `<jsp-property-group>` elements, see Chapter 17.

<resource-env-ref>

The `<resource-env-ref>` element declares an application resource accessible through JNDI.

Syntax

```
<resource-env-ref>
  [<description [xml:lang="lang"]>description</description>]*
  <resource-env-ref-name>envRefName</resource-env-ref-name>
  <resource-env-ref-type>envRefType</resource-env-ref-type>
</resource-env-ref>
```

In a complete J2EE-compliant container (i.e., one that supports other J2EE technologies besides servlets and JSP), the container can provide access to so-called administered objects through JNDI. Examples of this type of object are the ones used by the Java Messaging System (JMS) API. The `<resource-env-ref>` elements declares the JNDI path used to access the object in the application and its type, using nested `<resource-env-ref-name>` and `<resource-end-ref-type>` elements:

```
<resource-env-ref>
  <resource-env-ref-name>/jms/StockQueue</resource-env-ref-name>
  <resource-env-ref-type>/javax.jms.Queue</resource-env-ref-type>
</resource-env-ref>
```

Optionally, descriptions can be provided by the `<description>` element.

<resource-ref>

The `<resource-ref>` element defines JNDI accessible object factories for application objects.

Syntax

```
<resource-ref>
  [<description [xml:lang="lang"]>description</description>]*
  <res-ref-name>refName</res-ref-name>
  <res-ref-type>refType</res-ref-type>
  <res-auth>Application|Container</res-auth>
  [<res-sharing-scope>Shareable|Unshareable</res-sharing-scope>]
</resource-ref>
```

A J2EE-compliant container (and some web containers that support JNDI in addition to servlets and JSP) can also provide access to resource factories that produce the objects used in an application, such as a `DataSource` that produces `Connection` objects for database access, as described in Chapter 24. The `<resource-ref>` element defines these factories using the `<res-ref-name>` to specify the JNDI path used in the application, the `<res-type>` for the factory type, and `<res-auth>` to define whether the authentication is performed by the application (with the `Application` value) or the container (with the `Container` value). An optional `<res-sharing-scope>` element can be used to define if the objects produced by the factory may be shared or not (with `Shareable` and `Unshareable`, respectively, the prior being the default):

```
<resource-ref>
  <res-ref-name>/jms/Production</res-ref-name>
  <res-ref-type>/javax.sql.DataSource</res-ref-type>
  <res-auth>Container</res-auth>
</resource-ref>
```

As for most elements, `<description>` elements can provide descriptions in multiple languages to help the deployer.

<security-constraint>

The `<security-constraint>` element defines how and by whom resources can be accessed.

Syntax

```
<security-constraint>
  [<display-name [xml:lang="lang"]>displayName</display-name>]*
  <web-resource-collection>
    <web-resource-name>resName</web-resource-name>
    [<description [xml:lang="lang"]>description</description>]*
    <url-pattern>urlPattern</url-pattern>+
    [<http-method>GET|POST|PUT|DELETE|HEAD|OPTIONS|TRACE</http-method>]
  </web-resource-collection>+
  [<auth-constraint>
     [<description [xml:lang="lang"]>description</description>]*
     [<role-name>roleName</role-name>]*
   </auth-constraint>]
  [<user-data-constraint>
     <transport-guarantee>
```

```
      NONE|INTEGRAL|CONFIDENTIAL
    </ transport-guarantee>
  </user-data-constraint>]
</security-constraint>
```

<security-constraint> contains a <web-resource-collection> subelement that defines the resources to be protected and an <auth-constraint> subelement that defines who has access to the protected resources. It can also contain a <user-data-constraint> subelement that describes security requirements for the connection used to access the resource:

```
<security-constraint>
  <web-resource-collection>
    <web-resource-name>admin</web-resource-name>
    <url-pattern>/admin/*</url-pattern>
    <http-method>GET</http-method>
  </web-resource-collection>
  <auth-constraint>
    <role-name>admin</role-name>
  </auth-constraint>
  <user-data-constraint>
    <transport-guarantee>CONFIDENTIAL</ transport-guarantee>
  </user-data-constraint>
</security-constraint>
```

Within the <web-resource-collection> element, the resource is given a name with the <web-resource-name> subelement and the URI patterns for the protected resources are specified with <url-pattern> elements. <http-method> subelements can also be used to restrict the types of accepted requests. This example protects all resources accessed with URIs that starts with */admin* and says that only the `GET` method can access these resources.

The <role-name> subelements within the <auth-constraint> element specify the roles that the current user must have to get access to the resource. The value must be a role name defined by a <security-role> element. In this example, the user must belong to the `admin` role in order to access resources under */admin*. How the role names are mapped to user and/or group names in the container's security system is container dependent.

A <transport-guarantee> element can contain one of three values:

- `NONE`. No special requirements. This is the default.
- `INTEGRAL`. Data must be sent between the client and server in such a way that it can't be changed in transit. Typically this means that an SSL connection is required.
- `CONFIDENTIAL`. Data must be sent in such a way that it can't be observed by others. This is also typically satisfied by an SSL connection.

<login-config>

The <login-config> element declares which authentication method to use for protected resources. You must only use one element of this type in a deployment descriptor.

Syntax

```
<login-config>
  [<auth-method>BASIC|DIGEST|FORM|CLIENT-CERT</auth-method>]
  [<realm-name>realmName</realm-name>]
  [<form-login-config>
     <form-login-page>loginPagePath</form-login-page>
     <form-error-page>errorPagePath</form-error-page>
   </form-login-config>]
</login-config>
```

For an application that uses the <security-constraint> element to protect resources, you must also define how to authenticate users with a <login-config> element. It can contain three subelements: <auth-method>, <realm-name>, and <form-login-config>:

```
<login-config>
  <auth-method>BASIC</auth-method>
  <realm-name>Protected pages</realm-name>
</login-config>
```

The <auth-method> element can have one of the values BASIC, DIGEST, FORM, and CLIENT-CERT, corresponding to the four container-provided authentication methods described in Chapter 13. The <realm-name> element can specify the name shown by the browser when it prompts for a password when the BASIC authentication is used.

If FORM authentication is used, the <form-login-config> element defines the login page and an error pages (used for invalid login attempts):

```
<login-config>
  <auth-method>FORM</auth-method>
  <form-login-config>
    <form-login-page>/login/login.html</form-login-page>
    <form-error-page>/login/error.html</form-error-page>
  </form-login-config>
</login-config>
```

For more about the FORM authentication method, see Chapter 13.

<security-role>

<security-role> elements are used to define the role names that the application uses.

Syntax

```
<security-role>
  [<description [xml:lang="lang"]>description</description>]*
```

```
    <role-name>roleName</role-name>
  </security-role>
```

All names used in isUserInRole( ) calls, in <security-role-ref> elements and <auth-constraint> elements must be declared by a separate <security-role> element:

```
<security-role>
  <role-name>admin</role-name>
</security-role>
<security-role>
  <role-name>user</role-name>
</security-role>
```

Each role must be mapped to a user and/or group in the container's security domain in a container dependent way.

<locale-encoding-mapping-list>

The <locale-encoding-mapping-list> element defines mappings between locales and response encodings. If you use more than one element of this type, the container merges them.

Syntax

```
<locale-encoding-mapping-list>
  <locale-encoding-mapping>
    <locale>locale</locale>
    <encoding>encoding</encoding>
  </locale-encoding-mapping>+
</locale-encoding-mapping-list>
```

Unless a specific response encoding is been specified explicitly, setting the locale for a response also sets its encoding. The <locale-encoding-mapping-list> element allows you to define how locales map to response encodings, overriding the container's default mappings. The <locale> element contains the locale value as an ISO-639 language code, optionally combined with an ISO-3166 country code, separated by an underscore or a dash. The <encoding> element contains an encoding (charset) value recognized by Java:

```
<locale-encoding-mapping-list>
  <locale-encoding-mapping>
    <locale>en-US</locale>
    <encoding>UTF-8</encoding>
  </locale-encoding-mapping>
  <locale-encoding-mapping>
    <locale>ja</locale>
    <encoding>Shift_JIS</encoding>
  </locale-encoding-mapping>
</locale-encoding-mapping-list>
```

<env-entry>

The <env-entry> element is used to define simple objects, such as a String or Boolean, accessed by the application through JNDI.

Syntax

```
<env-entry>
  [<description [xml:lang="lang"]>description</description>]*
  <env-entry-name>entryName</env-entry-name>
  <env-entry-type>entryType</env-entry-type>
  [<env-entry-value>entryValue</env-entry-value>]
</env-entry>
```

The <env-entry-name> defines the JNDI name relative to the java:comp/env context and <env-entry-type> the type, which must be one of java.lang.Boolean, java.lang.Byte, java.lang.Character, java.lang.String, java.lang.Short, java.lang.Integer, java.lang.Long, java.lang.Float, or java.lang.Double. The value can optionally be defined statically, using the <env-entry-value> element or be provided at deployment. An optional <description> element is also supported:

```
<env-entry>
  <env-entry-name>maxConnections</env-entry-name>
  <env-entry-type>java.lang.Integer</env-entry-type>
  <env-entry-value>100</env-entry-value>
</env-entry>
```

<ejb-ref>

The <ejb-ref> element is often used to declare a remote EJB reference used by the application.

Syntax

```
<ejb-ref>
  [<description [xml:lang="lang"]>description</description>]*
  <ejb-ref-name>ejbRefName</ejb-ref-name>
  <ejb-ref-type>Entity|Session</ejb-ref-type>
  <home>homeInterfaceName</home>
  <remote>remoteInterfaceName</remote>
  [<ejb-link>linkedEJBName</ejb-link>]
</ejb-ref>
```

In a J2EE-compliant container, the <ejb-ref> element is used to declare EJB objects. The name (JNDI path), type (Entity or Session), home and remote interface class names must be specified with the <ejb-ref-name>, <ejb-ref-type>, <home>, and <remote> elements:

```
<ejb-ref>
  <ejb-ref-name>ejb/Payroll</ejb-ref-name>
  <ejb-ref-type>Session</ejb-ref-type>
```

```
    <home>com.mycomp.PayrollHome</home>
    <remote>com.mycomp.Payroll</remote>
  </ejb-ref>
```

An optional <ejb-link> element can be used to uniquely identify a specific bean if more than one EJB has the same name. In addition, an optional <description> element can be used to add a description of the EJB.

<ejb-local-ref>

The <ejb-local-ref> element is often used to declare a local EJB reference used by the application.

Syntax

```
<ejb-local-ref>
  [<description [xml:lang="lang"]>description</description>]*
  <ejb-ref-name>ejbRefName</ejb-ref-name>
  <ejb-ref-type>Entity|Session</ejb-ref-type>
  <local-home>homeInterfaceName</local-home>
  <local>localInterfaceName</local>
  [<ejb-link>linkedEJBName</ejb-link>]
</ejb-local-ref>
```

The <ejb-local-ref> element serves the same purpose as the <ejb-ref> element but for local beans. It supports all the same nested elements, except that <home> is replaced by <local-home> and <remote> is replaced by <local>:

```
<ejb-local-ref>
  <ejb-ref-name>ejb/Payroll</ejb-ref-name>
  <ejb-ref-type>Session</ejb-ref-type>
  <local-home>com.mycomp.PayrollHome</local-home>
  <local>com.mycomp.Payroll</local>
</ejb-local-ref>
```

<service-ref>

The <service-ref> element is used to declare a reference to a web service used by the application.

Syntax

```
<service-ref>
  [<description [xml:lang="lang"]>description</description>]*
  [<display-name [xml:lang="lang"]>displayName</display-name>]*
  [<icon [xml:lang="lang"]>
    [<small-icon>iconPath</small-icon>]
    [<large-icon>iconPath</large-icon>]
   </icon>]*
  <service-ref-name>serviceRefName</service-ref-name>
  <service-interface>jaxrpcInterfaceName</service-interface>
```

```
    [<wsdl-file>wsdlFilePath</wsdl-file>]
    [<jaxrpc-mapping-file>mappingFilePath</jaxrpc-mapping-file>]
    [<service-qname>wdslQName</service-qname>]
    [<port-component-ref>portComponentRef</port-component-ref>]*
    [<handler>portComponentHandler</handler>]*
  </service-ref>
```

See the Servlet 2.4 and J2EE 1.4 web services specifications for details on how to use this element.

<message-destination-ref>

The <message-destination-ref> element declares a JMS message destination reference used by the application.

Syntax

```
<message-destination-ref>
  [<description [xml:lang="lang"]>description</description>]*
  <message-destination-ref-name>refName</message-destination-ref-name>
  <message-destination-type>typeName</message-destination-type>
  <message-destination-usage>
    Consumes|Produces|ConsumesProduces
  </message-destination-usage>
  [<message-destination-link>linkedDestName</message-destination-link>]
</message-destination-ref>
```

See the Servlet 2.4 and J2EE 1.4 messaging specifications for details on how to use this element.

<message-destination>

The <message-destination> element declares a logical name for a JMS message destination used by the application.

Syntax

```
<message-destination>
  [<description [xml:lang="lang"]>description</description>]*
  [<display-name [xml:lang="lang"]>displayName</display-name>]*
  [<icon [xml:lang="lang"]>
    [<small-icon>iconPath</small-icon>]
    [<large-icon>iconPath</large-icon>]
   </icon>]*
  <message-destination-name>destName</message-destination-name>
</message-destination>
```

See the Servlet 2.4 and J2EE 1.4 messaging specifications for details on how to use this element.

Example Application Deployment Descriptor

Example F-2 shows an example of a deployment descriptor (*web.xml*) file.

Example F-2. Example deployment descriptor file

```
<?xml version="1.0" encoding="ISO-8859-1"?>
<web-app xmlns="http://java.sun.com/xml/ns/j2ee"
  xmlns:xsi="http://www.w3c.org/2001/XMLSchema-instance"
  xsi:schemaLocation="http://java.sun.com/xml/ns/j2ee
    http://java.sun.com/xml/ns/j2ee/web-app_2_4.xsd"
  version="2.4>
  <servlet>
    <servlet-name>
      purchase
    </servlet-name>
    <servlet-class>
      com.mycomp.servlets.PurchaseServlet
    </servlet-class>
  </servlet>

  <servlet-mapping>
    <servlet-name>
      purchase
    </servlet-name>
    <url-pattern>
      /po/*
    </url-pattern>
  </servlet-mapping>
</web-app>
```

At the top of the file, you find a standard XML declaration and the `<web-app>` element, with the reference to the deployment descriptor schema. Then follows a `<servlet>` element that defines a servlet named `purchase`, and a `<servlet-mapping>` element that maps the servlet to the */po/** path prefix pattern.

Creating a WAR File

A WAR file is an archive file, used to group all application files into a convenient package. A WAR file can be created with the *jar* command, included in the Java runtime environment, or a ZIP utility program such as *WinZip*. To create a WAR file, you first need to create the file structure as directories in the filesystem and place all files in the correct location as described earlier.

With the file structure in place, *cd* to the top-level directory for the application in the filesystem. You can then use the *jar* command to create the WAR file:

```
C:\> cd myapp
C:\myapp> jar cvf myapp_1_0.war *
```

This command creates a WAR file named *myapp_1_0.war* containing all files in the *myapp* directory. You can use any filename that makes sense for your application, but avoid spaces in the filename, because they are known to cause problems on many platforms. Including the version number for the application in the filename is a good idea, because it is helpful for the users to know which version of the application the file contains.

Index

Symbols

A

We'd like to hear your suggestions for improving our indexes. Send email to *index@oreilly.com*.

B

C

D

E

F

I

J

K

L

M

N

O

P

T

U

V

W

X

About the Author

Hans Bergsten is the founder of Gefion Software, a company focused on server-side Java services and products based on the J2EE technologies. Hans has been an active participant in the working groups for both the servlet and JSP specifications from the time they were formed. He also contributes to other related JCP specifications, such as JSP Standard Tag Libraries (JSTL). As one of the initial members of the Apache Jakarta Project Management Committee, he helped initiate the development of the Apache Tomcat reference implementation for servlet and JSP.

Colophon

Our look is the result of reader comments, our own experimentation, and feedback from distribution channels. Distinctive covers complement our distinctive approach to technical topics, breathing personality and life into potentially dry subjects.

The animal on the cover of *JavaServer Pages*, Third Edition, is a grey wolf (*Canis lupus*), also known as a timberwolf. Once common all over North America, grey wolves wander the open tundra and forests of Alaska, Canada, and parts of the United States—just half their former range. These social animals mate for life and live in packs of two to fifteen animals; the strongest male is the leader of the group. Only the dominant pair in a pack breeds, the female giving birth to an average of seven pups sometime in April, May, or June, and all members of the group care for the young.

Sarah Sherman was the production editor and copyeditor, and Marlowe Shaeffer was the proofreader for *JavaServer Pages*, Third Edition. Mary Anne Weeks Mayo and Claire Cloutier provided quality control. John Bickelhaupt wrote the index.

Pam Spremulli designed the cover of this book, based on a series design by Edie Freedman. The cover image is an original engraving from the Dover Pictorial Archive. Emma Colby produced the cover layout with QuarkXPress 4.1 using Adobe's ITC Garamond font.

David Futato designed the interior layout. This book was converted by Julie Hawks to FrameMaker 5.5.6 with a format conversion tool created by Erik Ray, Jason McIntosh, Neil Walls, and Mike Sierra that uses Perl and XML technologies. The text font is Linotype Birka; the heading font is Adobe Myriad Condensed; and the code font is LucasFont's TheSans Mono Condensed. The illustrations that appear in the book were produced by Robert Romano and Jessamyn Read using Macromedia FreeHand 9 and Adobe Photoshop 6. The tip and warning icons were drawn by Christopher Bing. This colophon was written by Leanne Soylemez.

Need in-depth answers fast?

Access over 2,000 of the newest and best technology books online

Safari Bookshelf is the premier electronic reference library for IT professionals and programmers—a must-have when you need to pinpoint exact answers in an instant.

Access over 2,000 of the top technical reference books by twelve leading publishers including O'Reilly, Addison-Wesley, Peachpit Press, Prentice Hall, and Microsoft Press. Safari provides the technical references and code samples you need to develop quality, timely solutions.

Try it today with a FREE TRIAL
Visit *www.oreilly.com/safari/max/*

For groups of five or more, set up a free, 30-day corporate trial
Contact: *corporate@oreilly.com*

What Safari Subscribers Say:

"The online books make quick research a snap. I usually keep Safari up all day and refer to it whenever I need it."

—Joe Bennett, Sr. Internet Developer

"I love how Safari allows me to access new books each month depending on my needs. The search facility is excellent and the presentation is top notch. It is one heck of an online technical library."

—Eric Winslow, Economist-System,
Administrator-Web Master-Programmer

Related Titles Available from O'Reilly

Java

Ant: The Definitive Guide
Eclipse: A Java Developer's Guide
Enterprise JavaBeans, *3rd Edition*
Hardcore Java
Head First Java
Head First Servlets & JSP
Head First EJB
J2EE Design Patterns
Java and SOAP
Java & XML Data Binding
Java & XML
Java Cookbook
Java Data Objects
Java Database Best Practices
Java Enterprise Best Practices
Java Enterprise in a Nutshell, *2nd Edition*
Java Examples in a Nutshell, *3rd Edition*
Java Extreme Programming Cookbook
Java in a Nutshell, *4th Edition*
Java Management Extensions
Java Message Service
Java Network Programming, *2nd Edition*
Java NIO
Java Performance Tuning, *2nd Edition*
Java RMI
Java Security, *2nd Edition*
Java Serlet & JSP Cookbook
Java Servlet Programming, *2nd Edition*
Java Swing, *2nd Edition*
Java Web Services in a Nutshell
Learning Java, *2nd Edition*
Mac OS X for Java Geeks
NetBeans: The Definitive Guide
Programming Jakarta Struts
Tomcat: The Definitive Guide
WebLogic: The Definitive Guide

O'REILLY®

Our books are available at most retail and online bookstores.
To order direct: 1-800-998-9938 • *order@oreilly.com* • *www.oreilly.com*
Online editions of most O'Reilly titles are available by subscription at *safari.oreilly.com*